Impacts of Geoeconomics and Geopolitics on International Business

Bryan Christiansen
https://orcid.org/0000-0001-7282-8497
Southern New Hampshire University, USA

John D. Branch
https://orcid.org/0000-0002-5201-125X
University of Michigan, USA

IGI Global
Scientific Publishing
Publishing Tomorrow's Research Today

Vice President of Editorial Melissa Wagner
Director of Acquisitions Mikaela Felty
Director of Book Development Jocelynn Hessler
Production Manager Mike Brehm
Cover Design Jose Rosado

Published in the United States of America by
IGI Global Scientific Publishing
701 East Chocolate Avenue
Hershey, PA, 17033, USA
Tel: 717-533-8845 | Fax: 717-533-7115
Website: https://www.igi-global.com E-mail: cust@igi-global.com

Library of Congress Cataloging-in-Publication Data

LCCN: (CIP Data Pending)
ISBN13: 9798337312651
Isbn13Softcover: 9798337312668
EISBN13: 9798337312675
British Cataloguing in Publication Data
A Cataloguing in Publication record for this book is available from the British Library.

Table of Contents

Detailed Table of Contents

This study examines multinational corporations' (MNCs) role as political actors in a fragmented global order shaped by deglobalization and geopolitical rivalry. It argues that certain firms have acquired quasi-sovereign corporate power (QSCP), a form of influence rooted in their control over critical technologies and infrastructure, enabling them to exert state-like authority. The cases of Starlink's intervention in the Russia-Ukraine conflict and TSMC's strategic role in the U.S.-China-Taiwan triangle show how MNCs leverage technological assets and nonmarket strategies to shape regional security and global governance and demonstrate MNCs' influence on national security, diplomacy, and trade. We introduce QSCP as a novel conceptual lens to capture this emerging power and highlight ethical, legal, and governance challenges, particularly regarding accountability, sovereignty, and corporate responsibility. The findings suggest that QSCP calls for enhanced regulation, multinational coordination, and fundamentally rethinking the evolving relationship between states and corporate actors.

When addressing international trade, the most commonly referenced concepts include imports, exports, exchange rates, customs tariffs, and, naturally, supply and demand. This chapter examines geopolitical risk (GPR) as a critical factor that significantly influences financial markets and, by extension, each of these trade-related indicators. It reviews the historical development of this concept within academic literature and analyzes its spillover effects across economies. Through an in-depth examination of the implications of geopolitical risk in international trade —supported by a comprehensive bibliometric analysis and literature review—this study identifies thematic and emerging trends, as well as research gaps that may inform future lines of inquiry.

Sibel Elif Özdilek, Ufuk University, Turkey

Finally, it is clear that there is a parallel relationship between economic globalization and economic growth, which shows that the process of economic globalization positively affects growth. Although there are many studies on the relationship between political stability and economic growth, the fact that the relationship between political stability and economic growth and economic globalization; the limited number of literature review studies investigating the effect of political stability (political instability) on economic growth in the BRICS countries (Brazil, Russia, India, China and South Africa), which constitute 43% of the world population and approximately 30% of the world economy, made this study necessary. In this context, it is important for the study to explain the literature review of the BRICS countries that is covered in the study.

The Council of Europe, established in 1949, promotes human rights, democracy, and the rule of law across its 46 member states. Inspired by Winston Churchill's vision, it fosters collaboration among European nations. The European Court of Human Rights ensures justice, while various treaties and expert bodies protect individuals and provide essential recommendations. The Council remains a cornerstone of European integration, promoting peace and cooperation across the continent. Through its comprehensive approach, the Council of Europe continues to be a vital institution in upholding shared values and standards across Europe.

This chapter explores the complex regional conflicts in Northeast India through the lens of historical statehood movements, ethnic assertions, and cross-border cultural continuities. Focusing on the Koch-Rajbongshi community, the proposed Kamatapur state, and tribalhood, it analyzes the geo-ethno-political landscape involving Assam, North Bengal, and the bordering areas of Bangladesh, Bhutan, and Nepal. Drawing from the Kamata and Koch kingdom's historical legacies, the chapter situates the demand for Kamatapur within broader frameworks of linguistic rights, tribal autonomy, and national security concerns. Koch Rajbongshi, an Indigenous tribe tracing their lineage to the ancient Koch civilization and rightfully meets the criteria for Scheduled Tribe status, has long been denied their rightful recognition due to regional political intricacies. Through interdisciplinary insights, this study argues for a more nuanced understanding of regional self-determination, identity politics, and governance reforms in Eastern South Asia.

Geopolitical risk, the strength and direction of association with uncertainty factors, and new foreign direct investment (FDI) investments by country of origin as a measure of nearshoring in Mexico led to the objective of this chapter: to analyze the relationship between new FDI investments in Mexico by country of origin and Mexico's geopolitical risk, the United States' trade policy uncertainty, and Mexico's economic policy uncertainty, during the period from the first quarter of 2006 to the second quarter of 2024. The methodology was based on an analysis of Pearson and Spearman correlation coefficients, selected using the Shapiro-Wilk normality test. The main results establish that changes in Mexico´s new FDI investments by country of origin are associated with changes in Mexico's geopolitical risk index, the United States' trade policy uncertainty index, and Mexico´s economic policy uncertainty index. Consequently, by reducing risk and uncertainty, it is possible to establish public policies that increase new FDI investments and, therefore, nearshoring in Mexico.

Recent years have witnessed a surge in national security concerns associated with foreign direct investments (FDI). However, International Business research has hitherto paid limited attention to this phenomenon. While scholars in International Relations and International Law have examined the institutional and policy-level dimensions of FDI securitization, existing research remains predominantly macro-level and fails to explain how and why specific multinational enterprises' (MNEs) investments become national security threats. To address this gap, I draw on organizational field theory and develop the Dual-Field Framework (DFF) to introduce a field-level approach to demonstrate that the securitization of FDI is a field-driven process. This study highlights the central role of domestic politics and geopolitics in shaping how FDI translate into a national security threat. This chapter further outlines key directions for future research on FDI-related national security concerns, and offers managerial implications for MNEs from a field perspective.

In recent years consumer boycotts have gained renewed attention as a form of political and ethical expression, particularly in response to international conflicts and humanitarian crises.The objective of this study is to explore consumers' attitudes and behavioral responses to boycott calls against Israeli products as well as certain multinational brands perceived to support Israel in the context of the recent humanitarian crisis in Gaza.Specifically the research aims to identify the levels of participation in the boycott, the motivations and perceived barriers to compliance with boycott, generational differences in boycott engagement, perceived effectiveness of the boycott, the influence of social pressure and public visibility and the social and psychological factors influencing consumer behavior in this context. The research seeks to examine the extent and patterns of boycott participation by segmenting consumers into three groups: non-boycotters, strict boycott compliers and partial boycott compliers.It further aims to investigate the generational differences in boycott behavior.

The emerging space economy is being reshaped by and reshaping the current geopolitical and geoeconomic landscape, with significant implications for international business. As governments and commercial actors compete for strategic dominance in outer space, shifts in space governance, technological advancements, and the rise of private space ventures are influencing global trade and investment. The dual-use (military and commercial) nature of many space technologies

transparency and accountability. It offers a timely reflection on how multilateral action might finally close the gap between global ambition and implementation.

Preface

INTRODUCTION

In an era marked by increasing interdependence yet deepening fragmentation, understanding the interplay between geoeconomics, geopolitics, and international business has become indispensable. The forces shaping global markets are no longer confined to supply and demand, capital flows, or trade policies alone—they are increasingly influenced by political rivalries, security dilemmas, and strategic competition over technology, energy, and critical infrastructure. The international business environment, once driven primarily by efficiency and liberalization, now operates under the shadow of geopolitical recalibration and geoeconomic statecraft.

This edited volume, *Impacts of Geoeconomics and Geopolitics on International Business*, seeks to illuminate how businesses, governments, and institutions navigate this new reality. The chapters collectively examine how corporate strategies, financial systems, trade dynamics, and even consumer behavior are being reshaped by political tensions and shifting power configurations. Through a combination of theoretical insight, empirical analysis, and case-based exploration, the book provides a panoramic yet detailed view of the global economic order's evolving foundations.

The contributions assembled here bring together a distinguished group of scholars and practitioners from diverse disciplines and regions, reflecting the multifaceted nature of these transformations. Their research not only enriches our understanding of current developments but also offers forward-looking perspectives on how global business practices might adapt to sustain growth, mitigate risks, and uphold ethical and strategic responsibility amid profound geopolitical uncertainty.

CHAPTER OVERVIEW

Chapter 1, *From Corporate Diplomacy to Quasi-Sovereign Corporate Power*, by Ziqiao Wang and Marc Oberhauser, introduces the concept of Quasi-Sovereign Corporate Power (QSCP)—a novel framework to explain how multinational corporations (MNCs) have begun to exercise state-like influence through control over technology and infrastructure. Using Starlink and TSMC as case studies, the authors reveal how corporations shape national security and international governance in a fragmented world order.

Chapter 2, authored by Valeria Caro and Juan Espinosa, explores geopolitical risk (GPR) as a key determinant of financial market behavior and international trade. Through a bibliometric and thematic analysis, it identifies emerging trends and gaps in GPR research, offering a roadmap for future studies that bridge finance, trade, and political risk.

Chapter 3, by Sibel Elif Özdilek, provides a comprehensive literature review on the BRICS nations, investigating the interplay between economic growth, political stability, and globalization. The chapter underscores how the global South's experience, particularly within BRICS, challenges traditional narratives about growth and governance in a globalized world.

Chapter 4, by Sureyya Yigit, examines the Council of Europe's soft power and its enduring geopolitical role. By tracing the institution's evolution since 1949, this chapter highlights how the Council has promoted democracy and human rights, shaping the moral and political architecture of Europe amid shifting alliances and crises.

Chapter 5, by Surjit Singha and Ranjit Singha, turns attention to regional conflicts in Northeast India and the Koch-Rajbongshi community's struggle for recognition and autonomy. This study contextualizes local ethnic movements within broader geoeconomic and geopolitical frameworks, illustrating how identity politics intersect with regional and cross-border governance.

Chapter 6, authored by Minerva Ramos and colleagues, analyzes geopolitical risk and uncertainty in Mexico's foreign direct investment (FDI). Their empirical study connects geopolitical volatility, U.S. trade policy uncertainty, and Mexico's economic policies, offering evidence-based insights on how nearshoring trends can be optimized through strategic risk management.

Chapter 7, by Keyan Lai, develops an organizational field perspective on how foreign investments can become perceived as national security threats. By introducing the Dual-Field Framework (DFF), this chapter bridges gaps between International Business and International Relations, illuminating the processes behind FDI securitization.

Chapter 8, by Merve Kir and Süphan Nasir, investigates consumer boycotts as a tool of geopolitical expression, focusing on boycotts of Israeli products and brands during the humanitarian crisis in Gaza. The authors reveal generational differences and psychological drivers behind consumer activism in politically charged markets.

Chapter 9, by Gianni De Bruyn and Jingning Ao, explores the emerging space economy as a geopolitical and geoeconomic frontier. Their chapter provides a theoretical framework for understanding how competition in outer space impacts international business, governance, and security policy, highlighting the blurring boundaries between state and corporate actors in space exploration.

Chapter 10, by Abdullah Açik and Nergis Özispa, examines the interplay of geopolitical risk and container throughput using panel data from 39 countries. The findings offer critical insights for policymakers, showing how trade infrastructure and stability strategies should differ between advanced and emerging economies to sustain global trade resilience.

Chapter 11, by Isidore E. Agbokou, analyzes the global pursuit of sustainable development through international summits, emphasizing the need for coherence between policy, finance, and technology. The author argues for actionable diplomacy, digital monitoring, and inclusive collaboration to balance economic growth with environmental stewardship.

CONCLUSION

This volume underscores that the nexus of geopolitics and geoeconomics is not a peripheral concern but a defining feature of international business in the twenty-first century. The contributors collectively demonstrate how corporations, consumers, and states are recalibrating their roles in an increasingly contested and multipolar world. The rise of non-state actors wielding unprecedented power, the volatility of global financial systems, and the weaponization of trade and technology all signal a new paradigm that demands multidisciplinary analysis and responsive strategies.

Through its diverse range of cases—from corporate diplomacy and FDI securitization to consumer activism and space competition—this book illustrates how global business is not merely adapting to geopolitical forces but is actively reshaping them. The insights contained herein challenge readers to view international business as an arena of strategic interaction where power, influence, and values converge.

Ultimately, *Impacts of Geoeconomics and Geopolitics on International Business* offers both scholars and practitioners a timely framework for navigating complexity. In doing so, it contributes to a broader understanding of how nations and enterprises alike can forge pathways toward cooperation, innovation, and sustainable progress, even amid persistent rivalry and uncertainty. As the boundaries between economics and politics continue to blur, the future of international business will depend not only on market intelligence but also on geopolitical literacy and ethical foresight.

Chapter 1
From Corporate Diplomacy to Quasi-Sovereign Corporate Power:
Geopolitical Competition and the Reshaping of the Global Order

Ziqiao Wang
https://orcid.org/0009-0000-5154-6108
ESCP Business School, France

Marc Oberhauser
https://orcid.org/0000-0001-5736-7098
ESCP Business School, Spain

ABSTRACT

This study examines multinational corporations' (MNCs) role as political actors in a fragmented global order shaped by deglobalization and geopolitical rivalry. It argues that certain firms have acquired quasi-sovereign corporate power (QSCP), a form of influence rooted in their control over critical technologies and infrastructure, enabling them to exert state-like authority. The cases of Starlink's intervention in the Russia-Ukraine conflict and TSMC's strategic role in the U.S.-China-Taiwan triangle show how MNCs leverage technological assets and nonmarket strategies to shape regional security and global governance and demonstrate MNCs' influence on national security, diplomacy, and trade. We introduce QSCP as a novel conceptual lens to capture this emerging power and highlight ethical, legal, and governance challenges, particularly regarding accountability, sovereignty, and cor-

DOI: 10.4018/979-8-3373-1265-1.ch001

porate responsibility. The findings suggest that QSCP calls for enhanced regulation, multinational coordination, and fundamentally rethinking the evolving relationship between states and corporate actors.

1.0 INTRODUCTION

The global economy is entering a period of increasing disorder, shifting away from the stable foundations of globalization towards "deglobalization" (Luo, 2024; National Intelligence Council, 2021). While the multilateral system once provided a stable environment for multinational corporations (MNCs), geopolitical rivalries and rising protectionism are disrupting global value chains (GVCs) and redistributing power within international institutions (Luo, 2024; Witt *et al.*, 2023). This volatile geopolitical landscape demands that MNCs integrate geopolitics into their corporate strategies, as stressed by scholars like Teece (2020) and Buckley (2023), who emphasize the growing importance of corporate diplomacy.

Corporate diplomacy, as defined by Li *et al.* (2022), refers to the strategic use of nonmarket capabilities by MNCs to influence the geopolitical and regulatory environment. Employing such nonmarket strategies is increasingly essential for companies navigating an increasingly complex and unstable world (Li *et al.*, 2022). Consequently, MNCs are evolving beyond their traditional roles as purely economic agents. Particularly, those controlling critical technologies or extensive GVCs are emerging as powerful political actors. These firms increasingly appear to wield "quasi-sovereign" powers, shaping policy, influencing conflict dynamics, and engaging in interstate confrontations (Henisz, 2017; Li *et al.*, 2022; Timmers, 2024).

As traditional diplomatic institutions falter and technological interdependence hardens into geostrategic rivalry, control over critical infrastructures has become the new currency of power, particularly in areas that are non-substitutable and strategically indispensable. Companies like SpaceX's Starlink and Taiwan Semiconductor Manufacturing Company (TSMC) exemplify how MNCs are embedded in global defense and deterrence frameworks. Starlink's role in Ukraine during the Russia-Ukraine war and TSMC's "Silicon Shield" in Taiwan demonstrate how corporations influence both the micro-level distribution of information and the macro-level security of regional arrangements (Bryant, 2023; James, 2021). These cases highlight the expanding role of MNCs in geopolitics, starkly complicating traditional diplomatic and international relations theories. Realist theories, which typically place economic actors in subordinate roles, fail to capture the rising political autonomy and technologically derived power of MNCs (Morgenthau, 1948; Gilpin, 2016). Liberal theories, while emphasizing interdependence, often overlook the potential for corporate actions to generate conflict or vulnerability alongside interdependence, creating analytical tensions (Keohane & Nye, 2011; Kerr & Wiseman, 2017). Constructivism offers insights into the normative forces shaping corporate behavior but lacks robust analytical tools for assessing how MNCs leverage material power, especially derived from technology, during security crises (Henisz, 2016; Kobrin, 2009). While corporate diplomacy has gained attention, scholars have yet to fully explore the implications of firms becoming active political actors rather than passive responders to state policies (Autio *et al.*, 2021; Scherer & Palazzo, 2011).

The growing influence of MNCs reshapes international relations. Private companies are now deploying sophisticated strategies such as big-data analytics, algorithmic surveillance, and influence campaigns alongside their traditional lobbying efforts to align with states' strategic goals (Deibert, 2019; Marschlich, 2022). As these firms navigate complex geopolitical landscapes, their role as either enablers or disruptors of global order becomes increasingly important. This confluence of technologically empowered corporate actors, their exercise of apparently quasi-sovereign influence, and the noted limitations of existing theoretical frameworks to fully grasp this phenomenon create a critical research puzzle. Consequently, this study is guided by the research question: How do MNCs leverage their technological resources and nonmarket power to influence geopolitics during periods of deglobalization and disorder?

By addressing this question, we contribute to the emerging field of corporate diplomacy by offering insights into the nature and implications of quasi-sovereign corporate power (QSCP). We provide insights into how MNCs can be both enablers and disruptors within the international system. In contrast to traditional views of firms as mostly market-driven entities, this study frames MNCs as "active political actors" that influence diplomatic strategies and the distribution of power internationally by shaping public opinion, building alliances, and even intervening in armed conflicts (Meyer *et al.*, 2020; Scherer & Palazzo, 2011). Corporate diplomacy, therefore, in these evolving contexts, is no longer confined to public relations or corporate social responsibility (CSR) but is now deeply integrated with defense, international law, cross-border negotiations, and global media discourse (Henisz, 2017; Timmers, 2024). The ethical implications of this evolving role are central to understanding the potential risks of MNCs acquiring QSCP, which could further complicate global governance and security (Atlantic Council, 2021; James, 2021). As such, this paper underscores the need for scholars and practitioners to rethink the boundaries between state and corporate sovereignty, especially in the context of global geopolitical realignments.

2.0 BACKGROUND: DIPLOMATIC THEORY PERSPECTIVES AND THE RISE OF CORPORATE DIPLOMACY

2.1 Diplomatic Theory Perspectives: Realism, Liberalism, and Constructivism

Diplomacy, traditionally understood as the management of international relations via negotiation and dispute resolution among states, has long been a central concern in the study of IR. Over time, distinct theoretical paradigms have shaped the discourse on diplomacy, each offering different interpretations of the motivations, actions, and strategic behavior of international actors. Among the most influential schools of thought are Realism, Liberalism, and Constructivism, each with unique implications for understanding the role of non-state actors such as MNCs.

Realism, grounded in the works of Morgenthau (1948) and Waltz (1979), views international politics as a competition for power in an anarchic system without central authority. States, the primary actors in this model, are assumed to pursue self-interest, prioritizing survival, security, and economic strength. Within this tradition, MNCs are typically perceived as subordinate to state authority, constrained by national regulations and geopolitical agendas (Morgenthau, 1948; Gilpin, 2016). However, the continuous expansion of MNCs in terms of their global reach and economic power has gradually challenged this conventional viewpoint. As MNCs increasingly engage in international affairs, blurring the lines between state and corporate power, they can no longer be simply viewed as passive entities subservient to state dictates (Mende, 2023; Scherer & Palazzo, 2011). While Realism provides a useful framework for understanding power asymmetries, it struggles to account for the non-territorial forms of influence exercised by private actors in today's technologically driven global order (Berridge, 2022).

Liberalism, in contrast, underscores the potential for cooperation and mutual benefit in international relations. It emphasizes the role of institutions, norms, and interdependence in fostering peace and prosperity (Keohane & Nye, 2011). MNCs, from a liberal perspective, are often seen as facilitators of globalization, as drivers of trade, innovation, and economic integration who contribute to stability by embedding themselves in rules-based international systems (Berridge, 2022; Ruggie, 1982). However, liberal assumptions have come under pressure in the context of deglobalization and strategic decoupling. MNCs now operate in a world increasingly marked by geoeconomic competition, where interdependence is sometimes weaponized rather than harmonized (Farrell & Newman, 2019). While Liberalism remains essential for understanding institutional dynamics and global economic flows, it often underestimates the capacity of firms to act independently, or even disruptively, within and beyond the frameworks established by states (Aiyar et al., 2023; Luo, 2024).

Constructivism offers a distinct perspective, emphasizing the social construction of international relations. It focuses on how ideas, identities, and norms shape the behavior of states and non-state actors alike (Adler, 2013; Wendt, 1992). Applied to MNCs, Constructivism draws attention to the growing importance of norm-driven behavior, such as CSR or adherence to environmental, social, and governance (ESG) standards (Deitelhoff & Wolf, 2010; Haufler, 2013; Scherer & Palazzo, 2011). It views firms not merely as economic actors but as embedded social agents capable of reproducing or contesting international norms. However, Constructivism tends to emphasize ideational influence at the expense of material capabilities, such as control over infrastructure or technology. In contexts where MNCs exert power through their control of critical resources, especially in high-stakes geopolitical settings, constructivist frameworks offer limited tools for analyzing their strategic behavior (Henisz, 2016; Kobrin, 2009).

2.2 The Evolving Nature of Corporate Diplomacy: Towards Quasi-Sovereign Corporate Power

Corporate diplomacy, as defined by Li *et al.* (2022), refers to the strategic use of nonmarket capabilities by MNCs to manage external relationships, shape regulatory environments, and engage with governments and civil society through tools such as lobbying, advocacy, and public relations (Henisz, 2017; Saner *et al.*, 2000). In this view, corporate diplomacy is a mechanism by which firms navigate political risks and align their business strategies with stakeholder expectations across borders. As MNCs increasingly operate in volatile environments, these nonmarket strategies have become central to managing legitimacy and protecting value (Aiyar *et al.*, 2023; Doh *et al.*, 2012; Li *et al.*, 2022; Sun *et al.*, 2021).

Traditionally, corporate diplomacy has been conceptualized as reactive, shaped by firms' need to adapt to external pressures imposed by host governments, regulatory institutions, or social actors (Frynas & Stephens, 2015). This aligns with earlier assumptions that MNCs are economic actors embedded in a political system governed mainly by sovereign states (Aiyar *et al.*, 2023). In such a model, corporate diplomacy complements market strategies, minimizing conflict, lobbying for policy, or securing favorable conditions within a state-dominated international order (Frynas & Stephens, 2015).

However, recent developments suggest a qualitative shift in the role of certain MNCs. In industries such as satellite communications, advanced manufacturing, and cybersecurity, a few firms have acquired a degree of influence rivaling those of mid-sized nations (Flint, 2021; Witt *et al.*, 2023). These corporations now control non-substitutable and strategically indispensable resources, often technologies and infrastructures, that are integral to economic systems, national defense, and international diplomacy. Their embeddedness in global networks, combined with their control over Single Points of Failure (SPOFs), gives them significant leverage over states, allowing them to influence geopolitical outcomes directly. A SPOF is a critical component, such as a technology, process, or actor, whose malfunction or disruption can cause the entire system to fail or become inoperable.

The evolution of corporate diplomacy from reactive adaptation to proactive geopolitical agency marks a turning point. Rather than merely responding to state interests, some firms now shape the international environment through decisions with systemic implications. Starlink's continuous provision of satellite communication to Ukraine after the Russian invasion exemplifies this shift. Its intervention was not just of a technological nature but highly political, directly supporting Ukraine's military capacity while provoking tensions with Russia (Bryant, 2023). Similarly, TSMC's dominant position in global semiconductor manufacturing allows it to influence strategic calculations in the Taiwan Strait and to shape GVC strategies of both the U.S. and China (James, 2021; Morales, 2024). These cases illustrate that corporate diplomacy can become a source of geopolitical power, enabling firms to act as informal or even de facto diplomatic agents. In the absence of elected mandates or international legal responsibilities, such actions raise serious questions of accountability, transparency, and legitimacy. TSMC's chairman, for instance, has at times assumed a quasi-diplomatic role in cross-strait relations, a position necessitated by Taiwan's limited diplomatic recognition but made possible by the firm's strategic indispensability (Miller, 2022).

What emerges is a form of QSCP in which select firms do not merely influence political environments but are constitutive of them. This conceptualization must be distinguished from earlier forms of corporate geopolitical involvement. While business historians have documented how MNEs, such as United Fruit or Standard Oil, or the East India Company wielded significant political influence, their power was often contingent, derived from access to physical resources, colonial-era concessions, or the ability to lobby home governments for state-backed intervention (Bucheli & DeBerge, 2024). Crucially, these firms were largely substitutable, their functions could be replicated or absorbed by other companies or the state with relative ease. In contrast, QSCP is marked by control over non-substitutable, systemically embedded assets, most visibly, critical technological infrastructures such as satellite constellations and advanced manufacturing networks. QSCP actors set standards, arbitrate access to strategic systems, and shape deterrence frameworks through their entrenchment in the global order. Their decisions on where and how to deploy such assets confer direct leverage over geopolitical outcomes. Analytically, this challenges existing definitions of corporate diplomacy by blurring the line between economic influence and geopolitical intervention. Normatively, it raises concerns about the concentration of power in unelected, profit-driven actors operating in spaces once reserved for sovereign decision-making (Scherer & Palazzo, 2011; Luo & Van Assche, 2023).

3.0 METHODOLOGY

3.1 Case Study Approach

This study employs a multiple-case study design to analyze the role of MNCs in geopolitics, particularly focusing on their use of corporate diplomacy to influence national security. The inherent complexity of MNCs' interactions with governments, coupled with their substantial technological monopolies and nonmarket strategies, necessitates a methodological approach capable of capturing these multifaceted dynamics. By comparing two emblematic cases, SpaceX's Starlink and TSMC, the research benefits from insights into how these MNCs navigate and shape geopolitical and security issues (Eisenhardt & Graebner, 2007).

The cases were chosen using Seawright and Gerring's (2008, p.306) "most different systems but with key similarities" approach, which ensures that contrasting organizational characteristics (e.g., corporate scale, ownership structure, and diplomatic engagement) are examined considering their shared roles as influential global actors. This comparative design allows for more robust cross-case comparisons regarding the application of corporate diplomacy under varying political contexts (Seawright & Gerring, 2008).

Data collection incorporated multiple sources to enhance validity, including corporate documents such as corporate reports and white papers (Burnett *et al.*, 2024; TSMC, 2025), along with governmental publications (U.S. Department of Defense, 2022; Chang, 2021) and reports from international bodies such as the UN and WTO. Industry media and academic literature provided additional context, allowing for a comprehensive view of corporate behavior in relation to national and international security (Gibbert *et al.*, 2008; Yin, 2009). Given the highly sensitive nature of corporate involvement in geopolitical conflicts and national security matters, primary data collection through direct stakeholder engagement (e.g., interviews with corporate or government officials) was constrained by access and confidentiality limitations. Accordingly, this study primarily relies on a systematic analysis of publicly available secondary sources (Gibbert *et al.*, 2008; Yin, 2009). To ensure the accuracy and reliability of our findings, we cross-referenced potentially biased sources such as corporate or governmental reports with independent industry media, academic analyses, and publications from international organizations. This triangulation aimed to identify discrepancies and provide a balanced, evidence-based interpretation of the strategic behavior of the selected MNCs (Yin, 2009).

This study adopts a critical-realist epistemology, recognizing that while geopolitical phenomena are materially grounded (e.g., technological chokepoints), their meanings and consequences are socially constructed through institutional and strategic interaction. The aim is not only to describe QSCP as an empirical phenomenon, but to interrogate the normative and structural implications of corporate actors acquiring state-like agency. This dual emphasis on empirical rigor and ontological disruption reflects the study's commitment to both explanatory and emancipatory knowledge production.

3.2 Analysis Framework

Analyzing how MNCs, particularly those wielding QSCP, navigate and shape geopolitical contexts requires a structured multi-level approach. While recent literature has recognized the role of MNCs in geopolitical affairs, technological chokepoints, and nonmarket strategies (Farrell & Newman, 2019; Henisz, 2017; Luo & Van Assche, 2023), a comparative framework is needed to assess how these firms translate asset dominance into political agency. Accordingly, this study adapts the multi-level framework proposed by De Villa (2023), originally designed for assessing geopolitical risk from a corporate management perspective. Although focused on risk rather than diplomacy, the framework's attention to firm-, national-, and international-level interactions offers a valuable starting point for evaluating corporate geopolitical agency. Crucially, for the technologically pivotal MNCs central to this research, understanding exposure and interdependence across these levels is essential to interpreting their strategic positioning and diplomatic behavior.

Table 1. Five-Dimension Analysis

Dimensions	Focus	Assessment Criteria	Nonmarket Strategy Choices
Nature and Strategic Importance of SPOF Technology	Does the firm control a technology that is irreplaceable and foundational to economic or security systems?	• Is the technology foundational? • Does the technology have dual-use characteristics • Difficulty of substitution or replication • How does the technology facilitate or restrict the exercise of power by various parties, including its owner.	• Technology Lock-in (Farrell & Newman, 2019). • Standard Setting (Gawer, 2014). • Dual-Use Technology Development (Mazal, 2024).
Alignment and Tension with State Strategic Objectives	To what extent does the firm's technology align with national security and foreign policy goals?	• Are there areas where corporate interests converge with national interests? • Are there areas where corporate interests conflict with national interests? • How does the company manage these potential conflicts? • Does the company support a country's strategic goals through technology export, or influence a country to adjust its foreign policy stance through technology control?	• Coalition Building (Henisz, 2017; Li et al., 2022). • Strategic Information Disclosure (Keohane & Nye, 2011). • Multi-Stakeholder Engagement (Scherer & Palazzo, 2011).
Architecture of Cross-border Technological Dependencies	How are global dependencies structured and managed?	• How are these dependencies constructed? • Are they centralized or distributed? • Which countries or actors are most vulnerable to disruptions in technology supply? • How does the company manage these dependencies to maximize its own interests while mitigating risks? • How do these dependencies alter the power dynamics between states and between states and other non-state actors?	• GVC Diversification (Buckley, 2021). • Building Mutual Dependencies (Keohane & Nye, 2011). • Critical Node Control (Farrell & Newman, 2019).

continued on following page

Table 1. Continued

Dimensions	Focus	Assessment Criteria	Nonmarket Strategy Choices
Geopolitical Risk Management and Strategic Foresight	How well does the firm anticipate and mitigate geopolitical risks?	• Does the company have robust mechanisms to monitor changes in the global geopolitical environment? • Does it engage in scenario planning to anticipate potential risks and challenges? • How does the company adjust its strategy based on the evolving geopolitical landscape? • Does it take measures to prevent its technology resources from being used to exacerbate conflicts or promote diplomatic cooperation, and does it actively mediate risks or defuse tensions? • Does the company have sufficient organizational agility to respond to sudden crises?	• Scenario Planning: Developing contingency plans for different geopolitical risks (De Villa, 2023). • Stress Testing: Conducting stress tests on key technologies and GVCs to assess their resilience under extreme conditions (Ivanov & Dolgui, 2022). • Building Redundancy: Establishing backup systems and alternative solutions to reduce dependence on a single technology or supplier (Dohale et al., 2022).
Ethical, Legal, and Regulatory Considerations	How does the firm navigate normative obligations and related complexity?	• How does the company address the ethical, legal, and regulatory implications of its actions? • How does it navigate the complex and often conflicting legal and regulatory regimes across different jurisdictions? • How does it engage in the ongoing debates about the governance of emerging technologies? • Does it make ethical compromises or sacrifices for the security interests of specific countries? • Does the company play a leading role in developing and implementing responsible technology development and application standards?	• Lobbying (Frynas & Stephens, 2015) • Self-Regulation (Haufler, 2013) • Rule-Making Participation (Scherer & Palazzo, 2011) • Transparency and Accountability (Scherer & Palazzo, 2007)

All five dimensions are assessed using a 1–5 scale. A score of **1–2 (Low)** indicates that the firm's technology or behavior is not strategically significant, is easily replaceable, or has minimal impact on broader geopolitical dynamics. A score of **3 (Moderate)** suggests some strategic importance, limited substitutability, or alignment with specific national interests or risks, but without broader structural implications. A score of **4 (High)** reflects a strong degree of strategic relevance, e.g., difficult-to-replace technologies, significant geopolitical alignment, or sophisticated risk mitigation, typically across multiple jurisdictions. A score of **5 (Very High)** is reserved for cases where the firm's technology or positioning is foundational to national or international security, nearly irreplaceable, and deeply embedded in geopolitical strategies or security architectures (e.g., dual-use technologies, global chokepoints, or critical conflict-related infrastructure).

Sources: Framework adapted and modified by this study from De Villa (2023), incorporating concepts and criteria informed by Farrell & Newman (2019) on technological dependencies, Henisz (2017) and Li *et al.* (2022) on nonmarket strategies and state alignment, and Scherer & Palazzo (2007, 2011) and Haufler (2013) on ethical, considerations, among other sources cited within the table.

To better capture the distinctive power exercised by firms controlling critical technologies, we introduce two key modifications to De Villa's model. First, recognizing that the unique power of firms like Starlink and TSMC stems directly from their firm-level control over specific, hard-to-replicate technologies, the national-level dimension concerning 'Development by countries of technology' was reconfigured as a dedicated key technology dimension: 'Nature and Strategic Importance of SPOF Technology' developed by the MNC. This places analytical focus on the corporate locus of control rather than diffuse national capabilities. Second, given that the exercise of such significant, state-like power inherently raises profound normative questions that extend beyond risk mitigation, we added the dimension 'Ethical, Legal, and Regulatory Considerations'. This dimension is critical for evaluating the broader societal implications of QSCP, ensuring the analysis incorporates the crucial ethical responsibilities and governance challenges highlighted throughout this research and central to the concerns of business ethics.

The final framework comprises five dimensions, (1) the nature and strategic importance of SPOF technology, (2) alignment or tension between corporate technology and national strategic objectives, (3) the architecture of cross-border technological dependencies, (4) geopolitical risk management and strategic foresight, and (5) ethical, legal, and regulatory considerations. Detailed operational criteria for each dimension are provided in Table 1, which also illustrates how this framework can be applied to a specific case. Thematic analysis was conducted by systematically mapping data to the corresponding dimensions using predefined analytical criteria. This process culminates in the construction of a comprehensive five-dimension analysis table that delineates nuanced differences and similarities in strategic approaches, ensuring a robust, objective foundation for interpreting corporate diplomacy outcomes in geopolitically charged environments.

The framework serves both as an analytical lens and a comparative tool. It enables the identification of firm-specific strategies, the evaluation of technological leverage, and the contextualization of corporate behavior within broader geopolitical dynamics. For instance, TSMC's position as a potential SPOF in the global semiconductor industry exemplifies dimension one. TSMC's strategic significance in high-end chip manufacturing, the dual-use (civilian/military) applications of its technology, and the difficulty or impossibility of technological substitution justify a "5 (Very High)" rating. This status confers considerable geopolitical leverage. TSMC's nonmarket strategies, such as technology lock-in, standard setting in collaboration with international stakeholders, and dual-use technology development, are evaluated across the framework's dimensions.

4.0 CASE STUDIES: STARLINK AND TSMC'S GEOPOLITICAL IMPACT

4.1 SpaceX's Starlink

Starlink is a satellite-based internet constellation developed by SpaceX, designed to deliver global low-latency, high-speed internet connectivity, emphasizing rural and underserved regions (Pultarova, 2025). Its network of thousands of low-Earth orbit satellites (62% of all operational satellites) achieves significantly lower latency than traditional geostationary systems (Cuthbertson, 2024; Raswant et al., 2025). As of early 2025, Starlink had launched nearly 7,000 satellites and surpassed four million users (Johnson, 2025; Pultarova, 2025). While facing challenges such as elevated costs and weather-related signal disruptions, Starlink is reshaping digital infrastructure globally. Its deployment in the Russia-Ukraine war, providing critical battlefield and civilian communications, has propelled the firm into the geopolitical spotlight. This episode underscores how Starlink, beyond being a commercial venture, is becoming a strategic actor in modern warfare, state connectivity, and international diplomacy (Bryant, 2023; Cuthbertson, 2024).

4.1.1 Starlink's Diplomatic and Geopolitical Engagement in the Russia-Ukraine Conflict

After the Russian invasion of Ukraine on February 24, 2022, Russia swiftly destroyed Ukraine's communication infrastructure, creating enormous challenges for its military, government, and citizens (The Economic Times, 2024). Facing information isolation, the Ukrainian government sought assistance from global enterprises, specifically requesting satellite internet services from SpaceX (Bryant, 2023). Mykhailo Fedorov, Ukraine's Minister of Digital Transformation, publicly appealed to Elon Musk via X (formerly Twitter) for Starlink's support (Abels, 2024). In response, Starlink acted remarkably quickly, delivering the first batch of satellite terminal equipment to Ukraine within roughly 48 hours, ensuring uninterrupted wartime communication, and offering critical technological backing to Ukrainian military coordination (Bryant, 2023; Mizrak, 2024). This exemplifies how a private company can play a leading and even decisive role in modern conflict (Fitzgerald & Thompson, 2022; Lumineau & Keller, 2025). Starlink's prompt action stands out compared to traditional state-centric diplomacy, underscoring the potential of corporate diplomacy as a form of non-traditional diplomatic envoy. Starlink's expanding role in national security contexts also reflects a broader trend: its low-Earth orbit satellite network has become increasingly embedded in military communications and global defense infrastructure, blurring the lines between commercial service provision and strategic geopolitical influence (Du & Zhang, 2023).

Starlink's corporate diplomacy strategy went beyond merely reacting to Ukraine's requests; it reflected an intentional approach and strategic positioning in geopolitics. Initially, Starlink's service was a direct response to Ukraine's demands. However, Starlink expanded its service scope as the conflict evolved, becoming a crucial communication tool for the Ukrainian government and its military (Bryant, 2023). Through its low-latency, high-bandwidth satellite communications, Starlink enabled Ukraine's armed forces to maintain battlefield command-and-control systems, thereby enhancing Ukraine's operational capabilities. In March 2022, Starlink's technical support substantially boosted the Ukrainian military's efficiency, particularly in counteracting Russia's electronic warfare tactics (Abels, 2024). Starlink began adjusting its strategy as the conflict continued while still providing services. The decision-making process behind Starlink's engagement and its operational adjustments has often appeared centralized under its founder, Elon Musk. This concentration of control within a privately held entity introduced a form of personalized agency, a type of techno-exceptionalism where geopolitical decisions hinge on the will of a single actor rather than any institutional mandate (Isaacson, 2023). Notably, in October 2022, Elon Musk publicly mentioned the possibility of withdrawing some of Starlink's services and suggested Ukraine consider territorial concessions, indicating that while supporting Ukraine, the company also had to navigate geopolitical tensions with Russia (Gurantz, 2024). These public pronouncements, often made directly by Musk, highlighted the risks associated with relying on a single individual's discretion for critical wartime infrastructure and the potential for corporate decisions to become entangled with personal geopolitical views or business calculations (Bryant, 2023). This episode underscores the dual role of Starlink and SpaceX: they had to navigate their commercial objectives while also managing pressure from various governments and global public opinion, thus preserving the independence of their corporate identities (Frynas & Stephens, 2015).

Starlink's involvement sparked widespread international debate, particularly considering Russia's accusation that Starlink was acting as a 'Western proxy'. This criticism highlights how Starlink was framed as a "quasi-state" actor, actively influencing diplomatic and military conflicts between nation-states (Gurantz, 2024). Beyond shaping battlefield communications, Starlink's global infrastructure and operational control altered the diplomatic interactions among countries. Russia's allegations that Starlink's actions escalated the conflict and risked pulling private companies into international confrontations illustrate MNCs' potential risks and challenges when participating in war (Bryant, 2023; Lumineau & Keller, 2025).

Nevertheless, Starlink's role also strengthened its strategic relationship with the U.S. government, which offered financial and policy support to facilitate Starlink's operations in Ukraine (Abels, 2024). This government-MNC collaboration not only positioned Starlink as an integral part of U.S. aid to Ukraine but also amplified its global influence. This underscores how Starlink served the USA as a "strategic resource" while revealing its dual role and ethical responsibilities in national security and global governance (Fitzgerald & Thompson, 2022).

4.1.2 A Five-Dimensional Analysis of Starlink's Corporate Diplomacy

Starlink scores 20 out of 25 across the five adapted assessed dimensions, highlighting its technological capabilities, alignment with state actors, and capacity for geopolitical risk navigation. At the same time, the score also reveals ongoing challenges, particularly balancing commercial imperatives with ethical responsibilities and operating without coherent global regulatory frameworks for private-sector engagement in military or geopolitical crises.

Starlink scores 5 in "Nature and Strategic Importance of SPOF Technology," recognizing its indispensable role in providing satellite internet critical to military and humanitarian operations (Bryant, 2023). In Ukraine, Starlink enabled continuity of communications amid destroyed infrastructure, serving as a key component in battlefield coordination (Abels, 2024; U.S. Department of State, 2023). Its dual-use nature, as a civilian network and a wartime C4ISR system (Command, Control, Communications, Computers, Intelligence, Surveillance and Reconnaissance), further underscores its geopolitical salience (Burnett *et al.*, 2024; Fitzgerald and Thompson, 2022). Similarly, in the "Architecture of Cross-border Technological Dependencies," Starlink receives a 5. The company's infrastructure, deployed across borders, has become integral to maintaining critical communication channels, particularly in geopolitical flashpoints like Ukraine, which Fitzgerald and Thompson (2022) describe as central technology nodes in global information or intelligence communication networks. This strategic positioning gives Starlink considerable geopolitical leverage, with its technology embedded in national security strategies worldwide (U.S. Department of Defense, 2022). Starlink scores a 4 in both "Alignment with State Strategic Objectives" and "Geopolitical Risk Management and Strategic Foresight," indicating its ability to align with U.S. geopolitical goals, as seen in its support for Ukraine, which aligns with U.S. interests in countering Russian control over communication infrastructure (U.S. Government Accountability Office, 2020).

Nevertheless, its involvement in politically charged scenarios highlights the difficulties in navigating the interests of other global powers, particularly where Russian and Chinese geopolitical strategies conflict with U.S. priorities (U.S. Department of State, 2023). The company has demonstrated notable geopolitical foresight by swiftly responding to the needs of military and humanitarian organizations, particularly during the Russia-Ukraine war (U.S. Department of Defense,

2022). However, it must refine its risk management strategies to address concerns regarding state sovereignty, international law, and the ethical implications of its operations in high-stakes environments. Starlink scores a 2 in "Ethical, Legal, and Regulatory Considerations," due to significant concerns about accountability, transparency, and legal clarity. As Abels (2024) argues, private companies operating in conflict zones must be subject to more robust international regulations. Burnett *et al.* (2024) and Lumineau and Keller (2025) highlight the ethical dilemmas arising from the lack of binding rules for private-sector participation in war zones. While Starlink has been praised for bolstering Ukraine's resilience, its actions also raise questions about unilateral decision-making power in international security matters (United Nations, 2022). As Bryant (2023) notes, the firm's expanding influence necessitates more explicit guidance on whether it acts in pursuit of commercial profit, national security objectives, or global stability.

Starlink's role in the Russia-Ukraine war has far-reaching geopolitical implications, positioning the company as an essential actor in Ukraine's defense infrastructure. The case of Starlink highlights the intersection of corporate power and national security (Westermann-Behaylo *et al.*, 2015). However, Starlink's involvement also underscores the challenges of corporate diplomacy, as private companies like SpaceX become deeply embedded in state conflicts, often influencing diplomatic and military outcomes. From a legal perspective, the increasing reliance on private companies for strategic infrastructure raises questions about sovereignty and accountability. If Starlink were to withdraw its services or alter its level of involvement, it could significantly impact Ukraine's military capabilities and international alliances. This reflects Starlink's immense power, due to the control over critical resources traditionally falling under state authority (Berridge, 2022). This also raises ethical questions, such as whether a private company like Starlink should be allowed to accumulate such extensive power, eventually putting it in the hands of its CEO, or by which compass Starlink is guided in its decisions, profit, national security, or international peace (Gurantz, 2024; Lumineau & Keller, 2025)?

4.2 TSMC-Taiwan Semiconductor Manufacturing Company

TSMC is the world's leading semiconductor manufacturer, controlling more than 50% of the global foundry market share. The company's dominance is particularly evident in advanced process nodes such as 5nm, which commands a share exceeding 70%, and in 3nm, where its market share is forecasted to surpass 90% (Chang, 2024; Zhang, 2025). This technological supremacy not only solidifies TSMC's central role in global technology GVCs but also underscores its critical importance to Taiwan's economy and the global economic landscape (Wu, 2024b). Within this context, TSMC has become an influential geopolitical actor, especially in light of increasing Cross-Strait tensions and the ongoing technological rivalry between the United States and China (Xiong *et al.*, 2024). The strategic value of Taiwan, and by extension TSMC, has been amplified as geopolitical stakes rise, particularly regarding the "Silicon Shield" strategy that the company employs to deter military threats.

4.2.1 TSMC's Diplomatic and Geopolitical Engagement, and the "Silicon Shield" in Action

TSMC's technological leadership in semiconductor manufacturing situates it as a critical player within GVCs, particularly in producing high-end chips essential for smartphones, computers, and autonomous vehicles (Atlantic Council, 2021; James, 2021). With an advanced manufacturing market share hovering around 50%, TSMC's role transcends its economic contributions to become integral to Taiwan's security, particularly as part of its "Silicon Shield" strategy to deter military threats from mainland China (James, 2021). This strategy operates through TSMC's leadership in semiconductor innovation, which provides Taiwan with a technological and economic edge, bolstering the island's position in international geopolitics (Mark & Roberts, 2023; Wu, 2024a). The risk of disrupting TSMC's operations, whether by military action or other means, would send shockwaves through the global semiconductor GVC, triggering significant repercussions for the worldwide economy (Morales, 2024; Saxenian, 2006). As such, TSMC's status as a cornerstone of Taiwan's economy also embeds it within the broader geopolitical equation, where its economic dominance translates into strategic deterrence.

Amidst the growing rivalry between the United States and China, TSMC's position as a technology leader places it at the heart of this great power competition (Morales, 2024; Wu, 2024b). The U.S. government recognizes TSMC's advanced capabilities as a strategic asset, fostering collaboration with the company to mitigate China's technological rise (U.S. Department of Commerce, 2024). TSMC's decision to establish manufacturing plants in the United States reflects both market-driven motives and a recognition of Taiwan's precarious geopolitical position, with such initiatives further reinforcing Taiwan's alignment with U.S. interests in countering China (Gigliuto, 2023; Xiong *et al.*, 2024). Conversely, Beijing views TSMC's technological dominance as an obstacle to its ambition of becoming self-sufficient in semiconductor production, prompting increased investments in domestic Chinese semiconductor firms and initiatives aimed at reducing reliance on Taiwanese manufacturers (Neill, 2023). As a result, TSMC faces immense pressure from both superpowers, striving to preserve its leadership in the global market while navigating the geopolitical complexities of U.S.-China competition (Shattuck, 2021; Wu, 2024a).

The core of TSMC's "Silicon Shield" strategy is its ability to leverage its dominant position in the semiconductor sector to create an economic and technological barrier that deters potential military aggression from China. TSMC's ongoing innovation, in conjunction with its strategic collaborations with global governments and firms, has fortified its role as a key player in international security frameworks (Mark & Roberts, 2023). These initiatives, particularly those undertaken with the United States and Japan, exemplify how TSMC uses its technological dominance not only to strengthen its market position but also to exert influence on global security matters (Mark & Roberts, 2023; Wu, 2024a). By expanding its production facilities in the U.S., TSMC ensures that its strategic alignment with Washington remains firm, cementing its pivotal role in the ever-evolving semiconductor ecosystem. Moreover, given Taiwan's ambiguous international status, which often limits its political leaders' participation in international diplomacy, TSMC's chairman has, by leveraging the firm's pivotal position in the global semiconductor industry, increasingly assumed a de facto diplomatic role, particularly amid escalating U.S.-China tensions (Miller, 2022; Office of the President Republic of China, 2020).

The international strategic decisions made by TSMC's leadership further illustrate the company's transition from being a mere producer of semiconductors to a geopolitical influencer. For example, the 2019 announcement of the company's new plant in Arizona not only addressed market needs but also reflected Taiwan's security concerns, strategically positioning TSMC to secure further its global and regional standing (Morales, 2024; Wu, 2024b). TSMC's multifaceted approach integrates national security imperatives, global governance issues, and economic interests, demonstrating how corporate diplomacy has evolved into a critical tool for navigating complex geopolitical landscapes (Miller, 2022). By effectively managing its relationships with state actors and leveraging its technological capabilities, TSMC exemplifies how high-tech companies can preserve their commercial interests while contributing to the broader strategic objectives of their home territories (Mark & Roberts, 2023).

4.2.2 A Five-Dimensional Analysis of TSMC's Corporate Diplomacy

In an evaluation across the adapted five critical dimensions, TSMC scores 22 out of 25 (Appendix 3), reflecting its skillful management of technological and geopolitical challenges (Mark & Roberts, 2023; U.S. Department of Commerce, 2024). This score highlights TSMC's dominant position in the global semiconductor industry, its alignment with key state actors, and its proactive efforts to mitigate geopolitical risks. It also underscores the challenges TSMC faces in balancing competing national interests, particularly amid escalating U.S.-China tensions and increasing regulatory scrutiny (Gigliuto, 2023; Xiong *et al.*, 2024).

TSMC scores a 5 in the "Nature and Strategic Importance of SPOF Technology" and "Architecture of Cross-border Technological Dependencies", underscoring its centrality in global economic and political systems. As Shattuck (2021) notes, TSMC's manufacturing capabilities are indispensable to next-generation technologies, including 5G, AI, and advanced defense applications. Its ability to manage complex, multi-jurisdictional supply chains, spanning the U.S., EU, Japan, and China, is vital for maintaining GVC stability (Saxenian, 2006). This interdependence also makes TSMC a geopolitical asset: TSMC is an essential element of Taiwan's economic security (Republic of China Ministry of National Defense, 2023) and is considered a geopolitical instrument in the U.S.-China contest over technological supremacy (Mark & Roberts, 2023). In the "Geopolitical Risk Management and Strategic Foresight" dimension, TSMC scores a 4, reflecting the company's ability to foresee and mitigate risks associated with its operations. The Taiwan Ministry of Foreign Affairs (2025) notes TSMC's commitment to neutrality while aligning with global partners, with the company's efforts to expand production capabilities outside Taiwan, including new fabs in the U.S. and Japan, as a clear risk mitigation strategy (Martin *et al.*, 2023; Xiong *et al.*, 2024). This diversification of its production footprint is viewed as a hedge against geopolitical tensions (Shattuck, 2021). TSMC also receives a strong score of 4 in "Ethical, Legal, and Regulatory Considerations," a dimension incorporated explicitly into our framework to address the profound normative questions arising from QSCP, reflecting its commitment to ethical practices within a complex regulatory environment. Wu (2024a) notes that TSMC's growing scrutiny from the U.S. and Chinese governments influences its business decisions. However, the company's efforts to comply with regulatory demands from various jurisdictions have led to legal challenges, especially regarding its operations in China and its relationships with Chinese tech firms (U.S. Department of Commerce, 2024). Despite these challenges, TSMC has been relatively successful in aligning with state strategic objectives, earning a score of 4 in the "Alignment with State Strategic Objectives" dimension. Its strategic position as a critical supplier to the U.S. and China places it at the intersection of competing national interests. TSMC's alignment with Taiwan's government objectives, particularly ensuring national security and economic stability, further complicates its ability to navigate the strategic interests of other state actors (TSMC, 2025).

TSMC's role in Taiwan's "Silicon Shield" strategy highlights the growing intersection of technology and geopolitical security. By leveraging the firm's indispensability, Taiwan has embedded TSMC into its deterrence posture, banking on the assumption that a disruption in chip supply would trigger global economic shockwaves. This dependency creates a form of strategic leverage: TSMC becomes a valuable player in international diplomacy due to its indispensable role in the technological ecosystem (Mark & Roberts, 2023). As a linchpin of Taiwan's 'Silicon Shield,' TSMC's indispensability gives it diplomatic leverage, particularly with the United States, which is vested in preserving Taiwan's autonomy and global chip supply continuity.

As such, TSMC becomes a pivotal actor in this ongoing geopolitical struggle, where its operations not only shape the global economy but also influence the trajectory of international relations (Atlantic Council, 2021).

Despite these advantages, TSMC faces significant ethical and strategic vulnerabilities. As Cross-Strait tensions intensify, its operations become increasingly entangled with high-stakes security concerns. Any disruption to TSMC's operations, whether through direct military action, cyberattacks, or trade restrictions, could trigger severe economic repercussions far beyond Taiwan (Mark & Roberts, 2023). TSMC's actions now carry ethical weight: should it prioritize profitability and technological leadership, or actively consider the stability of regional peace? As its decisions increasingly affect the balance of power in East Asia, the company must navigate a fraught landscape in which economic efficiency and geopolitical responsibility may sharply diverge (Atlantic Council, 2021; Morales, 2024).

5.0 CROSS-CASE ANALYSIS

5.1 Contrasting Starlink and TSMC

A primary distinction emerges between the two cases regarding the modalities of power projection and geopolitical embeddedness. Starlink's influence manifested primarily through direct, operational intervention within an active conflict zone. By providing critical satellite communication infrastructure to Ukraine following the Russian invasion, SpaceX assumed a role traditionally reserved for states or international organizations, directly impacting battlefield dynamics and information flows (Bryant, 2023). Its power, therefore, was immediate, tangible, and overtly aligned with specific geopolitical objectives, positioning it as a significant, albeit non-state, actor within the immediate conflict calculus, arguably serving, at least initially, as a functional extension of Western support for Ukraine (Fitzgerald & Thompson, 2022). Conversely, TSMC wields power derived from structural indispensability within the global technological ecosystem, achieved largely through technological gatekeeping and its central position in global semiconductor GVC. Its near monopoly over advanced semiconductor manufacturing constitutes a critical node, or potential SPOF, upon which vast swathes of the global economy and numerous national security apparatuses depend (Mark & Roberts, 2023; Wu, 2024b). This confers upon TSMC a profound, albeit less direct, form of influence, a deterrent power encapsulated in Taiwan's "Silicon Shield" strategy, designed to make any disruption of its operations catastrophically costly for all parties, including potential aggressors (James, 2021; Mark & Roberts, 2023). While Starlink became operationally embedded in a hot war, TSMC is structurally embedded at the volatile nexus of

US-China strategic competition and the Cross-Strait security dilemma (Xiong *et al.*, 2024). Both cases exemplify different facets of what Farrell and Newman (2019, p. 42) term "weaponized interdependence," yet challenge state-centric assumptions by demonstrating corporate actors as central players, not mere instruments, in leveraging these dependencies.

This divergence in power modality is intimately linked to the paradoxical relationship between corporate autonomy and state dependency. Starlink, operating under the umbrella of the privately held SpaceX and subject to the pronounced influence of its founder, exhibited significant corporate latitude in its decisions regarding service provision, scope, and potential withdrawal in Ukraine (Bryant, 2023; Gurantz, 2024). This operational flexibility, characteristic of founder-led private firms, helps explain the speed and unilateral nature of Starlink's engagement, but also highlights the governance risks tied to centralized decision-making, particularly in cases where critical infrastructure decisions rest with a single individual. In contrast, TSMC, as a publicly listed company with a more dispersed ownership and a tradition of consensus-oriented leadership, navigates geopolitical pressures through carefully calibrated long-term investments and discreet diplomacy, reflecting the complex stakeholder management inherent in its governance structure (Wong *et al.*, 2024). This agility in Starlink's case, however, simultaneously highlighted the precarious reliance of a sovereign state's critical wartime functions on the potentially volatile decisions of a non-elected corporate entity, raising immediate concerns about accountability and reliability (Abels, 2024). TSMC, despite being a publicly listed company theoretically accountable to diverse shareholders and navigating complex regulatory environments, commands extraordinary negotiating leverage precisely because of its technological dominance. It must perform a delicate balancing act, managing intense pressure and inducements from major global powers like the United States and China, while aligning with Taiwan's security and economic imperatives (Shattuck, 2021; Xiong *et al.*, 2024). Its strategic decisions regarding global investments, such as establishing fabs in the US and Japan, reflect this complex calculus (Gigliuto, 2023; Martin *et al.*, 2023). This intricate dance between wielding near-monopolistic power and navigating multi-jurisdictional demands underscores a fundamental tension: states are increasingly dependent on the unique capabilities of these firms, yet struggle to reconcile this dependence with traditional notions of sovereignty and regulatory control. It is precisely this tension, the exercise of significant geopolitical agency by actors lacking traditional democratic legitimacy or formal political authority, that fuels the critical governance, legal, and ethical questions explored in the subsequent section.

Finally, the comparison illuminates distinct practices of corporate diplomacy and nonmarket strategy. Starlink's engagement was characterized by high-profile, reactive diplomacy, often conducted via public pronouncements and direct responses to governmental requests, blurring the lines between corporate communication and geopolitical signaling (Bryant, 2023). Its nonmarket strategy appeared intertwined with crisis management and maintaining operational viability amidst conflict. In stark contrast, TSMC's corporate diplomacy is more structural, longitudinal, and discreet. It relies on cultivating deep relationships with key governmental and industry stakeholders, strategic diversification of its manufacturing footprint to mitigate risk and build mutual dependencies, active participation in shaping industry standards, and leveraging its chairman's unique standing in high-level international forums (Miller, 2022; Office of the President Republic of China, 2020; Mark & Roberts, 2023). While Starlink's diplomacy was thrust into the crucible of war, TSMC's is a carefully constructed element of its long-term strategy for survival and prosperity amidst great power competition. Both cases demonstrate corporate diplomacy extending far beyond conventional corporate political activities (Sun *et al.*, 2021), representing proactive agency that deeply integrates into the realms of national security, defense policy, and international power politics (Henisz, 2017; Li *et al.*, 2022), demanding a reconceptualization of the firm's role in global affairs.

In synthesis, the comparative lens reveals that QSCP is not a monolithic concept but a multifaceted phenomenon, its expression shaped by the specific technological domain, the firm's structure and strategic posture, and the geopolitical context. Starlink's direct interventionism and TSMC's structural deterrence represent two powerful, yet distinct, manifestations of this trend. However, both underscore a fundamental shift: the ascent of technologically advanced MNCs as pivotal actors capable of shaping international security landscapes and challenging established global governance norms. This profound transformation, highlighted by the contrasts and convergences between these two critical firms, underscores the urgency of grappling with the complex regulatory, governance, and ethical challenges.

5.2 Regulatory and Governance Challenges

The growing involvement of MNCs in geopolitical matters engenders fundamental tensions within regulatory and governance structures, as international legal frameworks remain state-centric and largely unprepared to regulate corporate influence over geopolitical affairs. The absence of clear international regulations creates an acute accountability gap, allowing MNCs like Starlink and TSMC to influence security policy with limited oversight, despite their growing role in national defense infrastructures.

This evolving landscape, where MNCs wield significant influence, resonates with, yet distinctively extends, the broader scholarly discourse on the rise of 'private authority' in international relations (Avant *et al.*, 2010; Cutler *et al.*, 1999; Hall & Biersteker, 2002). While existing scholarship has extensively documented how non-state actors, including corporations, exert governance functions and influence through market mechanisms, expert knowledge, or delegated authority from states (e.g., Büthe & Mattli, 2011, on private standard-setting; Green, 2013, on private climate governance), the QSCP phenomenon we identify points to a more direct, and at times autonomous, exercise of strategic, state-like agency. This agency is primarily rooted in the control of critical, often contested, technological infrastructures and GVCs within an international system characterized by heightened geopolitical rivalry, rather than solely through institutionalized delegation or market-based regulation. QSCP thus represents a specific, technologically empowered facet of private authority that directly engages with and shapes core aspects of national and international security.

First, an acute accountability gap emerges. Historically, international law has been designed to regulate the conduct of sovereign states, leaving private corporations largely outside its jurisdiction unless specific treaties or national laws impose direct obligations. Existing legal instruments such as the United Nations Charter and Geneva Conventions focus primarily on state responsibilities in conflict and diplomacy but offer little guidance on the obligations of MNCs engaged in military and security affairs (Simma *et al.*, 2024). The involvement of Starlink in Ukraine underscores the legal ambiguity surrounding corporate engagement in warfare. By providing critical satellite communication services to Ukrainian forces, Starlink influences battlefield operations, raising questions about whether its actions should be subject to laws governing military engagement and neutrality (Bryant, 2023). Similarly, TSMC's strategic importance in the U.S.-China rivalry illustrates another legal complexity: its semiconductor manufacturing capabilities have become a geopolitical asset, affecting global security and military preparedness. Despite this, there is no international legal framework regulating the responsibilities of corporations in controlling such critical infrastructure (Mende, 2023). This legal ambiguity is amplified by the diverse modalities of corporate power projection observed in Section 5.1, ranging from Starlink's direct operational intervention to TSMC's structural indispensability, neither of which fits neatly into existing state-centric legal paradigms. The absence of a unified international legal framework for corporate involvement in conflict zones creates a gap in accountability, allowing MNCs to operate with minimal legal oversight despite their growing influence on security and foreign policy (Bilchitz, 2021). Should MNCs be legally obligated to maintain neutrality in geopolitical conflicts? Should they be subject to the same war and peace regulations as states? What legal consequences should exist if corporate actions exacerbate conflicts? The growing reliance on corporations in national security matters further complicates these questions, as MNCs increasingly function as indispensable actors in state defense strategies.

Second, a profound legitimacy deficit appears. Unlike states, MNCs are not democratically accountable to citizens, yet their decisions affect war, peace, and economic stability on a global scale (Gurantz, 2024). Their influence often extends beyond traditional corporate lobbying, making them key actors in diplomatic, security, and conflict-related negotiations. For instance, a recent report suggested that U.S. negotiators allegedly leveraged Ukraine's reliance on Starlink's satellite internet service as a bargaining chip in separate negotiations concerning access to Ukraine's critical minerals (Shalal & Roulette, 2025). This exemplifies how control over, or the perceived ability to influence, essential infrastructure provided by an MNC could become a potent tool in high-stakes state-to-state diplomacy, placing the corporation and its services at the heart of geopolitical bargaining far removed from conventional lobbying activities. Governments may rely on or be coerced by MNCs due to their monopoly over critical technologies. Ukraine's military dependence on Starlink's communication networks illustrates the risk of governments becoming overly reliant on private actors for national security. At the same time, the challenge of holding corporations accountable for their geopolitical interventions is rooted in the paradox of corporate autonomy and state dependency, and presents different complexities depending on their varying ownership structures (e.g., Starlink's private flexibility versus TSMC's public constraints). The absence of formal oversight allows MNCs to leverage their technological assets for political or commercial gain, sometimes in ways that are inconsistent with national security priorities. The fact that Starlink retains the ability to withdraw or modify services at its discretion affects military operations and leaves nation-states vulnerable to private corporate decision-making. The question of who holds corporations accountable for their geopolitical interventions remains largely unanswered.

The issue of democratic legitimacy in corporate diplomacy suggests that MNCs exert power comparable to states but lack equivalent oversight mechanisms (Scherer & Palazzo, 2007). As firms like Starlink and TSMC become embedded in state defense strategies, the lack of institutional mechanisms to ensure transparency, legal accountability, and strategic coordination becomes increasingly untenable. Yet addressing this regulatory vacuum is fraught with complexity: attempts to define binding obligations for firms operating in geopolitically sensitive sectors must grapple with tensions between state sovereignty, corporate autonomy, innovation incentives, and fragmented international legal traditions. These challenges raise difficult questions about how, and by whom, corporate geopolitical interventions should be governed, questions that remain largely unanswered in current legal and policy frameworks.

5.3 Ethical Considerations

These profound regulatory and governance deficits inevitably create fertile ground for complex ethical dilemmas, demanding scrutiny not only of what is legally permissible but what is morally justifiable in the exercise of such corporate power. The ethical implications of MNCs' involvement in geopolitics are multifaceted, encompassing issues of corporate responsibility, neutrality, and the unintended consequences of private-sector influence over international security. Unlike states, corporations do not have public mandates, yet their decisions influence the security and economic well-being of millions. The ability of MNCs to act as sovereign-like entities further complicates ethical assessments, as they operate at the intersection of profit-making and global governance.

A central ethical concern is whether MNCs should have the authority to make decisions with profound national security consequences. The involvement of Starlink in Ukraine raises the question of whether a private company should have the authority to decide the fate of a nation's military communications. From a deontological standpoint (Fort, 2000), one could argue that Starlink has a moral obligation to sustain access for humanitarian and security purposes, regardless of cost. From a consequentialist perspective (Frynas & Stephens, 2015), the company's actions, whether to provide, restrict, or threaten withdrawal of service, must be evaluated by their tangible impacts on conflict outcomes and civilian well-being. This dilemma became especially acute when Elon Musk repeatedly suggested that SpaceX could discontinue Starlink services due to financial and strategic concerns (Porter *et al.*, 2025). Musk acknowledged that shutting down Starlink would severely impact Ukraine's frontline operations, reinforcing the country's dependence on the service. His previous warnings about the financial burden of maintaining Starlink and discussions with the Pentagon about funding highlight the precarious nature of relying on a private entity for critical wartime infrastructure. His statements underscored both the ethical fragility of centralized corporate governance and the precarity of wartime infrastructure being contingent on the discretion of a single unelected actor. A deontological view would stress the duty to sustain critical services in the name of justice and human dignity. A consequentialist view would focus on the broader risks of escalation, political coercion, and battlefield disadvantage if services are withdrawn.

TSMC faces a different but equally complex set of ethical dilemmas. As the world's most advanced semiconductor producer, it sits at the center of U.S.-China technological rivalry, while simultaneously serving as a strategic pillar of Taiwan's national security. From a deontological lens, one might ask: does TSMC have a moral duty to prioritize Taiwan's defense, to protect its global customers, or to uphold shareholder value? These obligations often conflict. For example, the decision to expand fabrication facilities in the U.S. under the CHIPS Act supports long-term global resilience, but also aligns the company more closely with American strategic interests, raising ethical concerns in Beijing about alignment and autonomy (U.S. Department of Commerce, 2024). From a consequentialist standpoint, the relocation of TSMC's high-end fabs abroad may gradually dilute the "Silicon Shield". As more manufacturing shifts to the U.S. and Japan, the strategic calculus of potential aggressors may change, weakening the geopolitical leverage that once protected Taiwan (Mark & Roberts, 2023). At the same time, these moves improve global supply chain resilience, diversify risk, and reduce the concentration of technological capacity. These trade-offs illustrate how QSCP firms face conflicting ethical imperatives that transcend profit motives and require careful balancing of global security, regional stability, and commercial survival. Moreover, U.S. export controls and pressure to deny advanced chips to Chinese firms put TSMC in a morally compromised position. Complying with U.S. mandates may serve national security goals of one state, but it risks undermining the company's credibility as a neutral commercial actor. Ethical risk becomes not only a question of compliance but of legitimacy, especially for firms navigating tensions between global governance expectations and geopolitical alignment.

To navigate these ethical dilemmas, MNCs must develop ethical risk assessment frameworks that explicitly integrate considerations of human rights, security, and diplomatic consequences of their actions. Transparency in decision-making, particularly regarding service provision or production location in conflict-prone areas, is essential. Firms must engage proactively with international organizations and multistakeholder forums to co-create normative guidelines for conduct in geopolitically sensitive domains. QSCP calls for a fundamental rethink of corporate ethics, moving beyond CSR into the realm of strategic responsibility.

In sum, QSCP raises both immediate moral dilemmas and long-term normative concerns. It exposes the growing mismatch between firms' global power and the ethical frameworks available to guide their conduct. As Starlink and TSMC demonstrate in different ways, MNCs now shape warfighting capabilities, diplomatic alignments, and the resilience of global supply chains. Whether their power contributes to stability or destabilization will depend not only on governance mechanisms but on the ethical standards firms are willing and able to internalize. In this regard, the rise of QSCP demands not just better oversight but also new forms of corporate moral imagination.

Table 2 illustrates the key points and draws implications from them.

Table 2. Integrated Comparison of Starlink and TSMC

Dimensions	Starlink	TSMC	Implications
Modality of Power	Operational and event-driven: direct provision of critical infrastructure in an active conflict zone (Ukraine).	Structural and systemic: indispensable role in global semiconductor GVC and deterrence logic.	Different governance tools needed: service-based wartime rules vs. chokepoint infrastructure regulation.
Strategic Positioning	Embedded in wartime C4ISR systems; framed as a quasi-state actor aligned with U.S. geopolitical goals.	Embedded in GVCs; balances U.S., China, and Taiwan's national interests through site strategy.	Raises questions about how firms' alignment with state strategies affects neutrality and strategic leverage.
Geopolitical Leverage	Derived from exclusive control over low-Earth orbit satellite network and real-time service provision.	Derived from near-monopoly over advanced chip production and centrality to defense/innovation ecosystems.	Suggests a need for safeguards to prevent weaponization of essential technologies and infrastructures.
Form of Corporate Diplomacy	Reactive, public-facing, and crisis-driven; diplomacy via direct engagement (e.g., Musk's responses).	Strategic, long-term, and discreet; diplomacy via ecosystem building, standards shaping, and elite networks.	Highlights variation in diplomatic style and raises questions about transparency and legitimacy.
Governance Challenges	Highlights accountability gaps and risks of unilateral decision-making in wartime infrastructure.	Raises questions of corporate neutrality, regulatory capture, and erosion of strategic deterrence via offshoring.	Illustrates the need for differentiated regulatory regimes based on power type and exposure.

Sources: Own illustration and analysis based on Abels, 2024; Bryant, 2023; Burnett, *et al.*, 2024; Chang, 2021; Fitzgerald & Thompson, 2022; Gigliuto, 2023; Mark & Roberts, 2023; Martin, *et al.*, 2023; International Chamber of Commerce, 2016; Republic of China Ministry of National Defense, 2023; Saxenian, 2006; Shattuck, 2021; Taiwan Ministry of Foreign Affairs, 2025; TSMC, 2025; United Nation, 2022; U.S. Department of Commerce, 2024; U.S. Department of Defense, 2022; U.S. Department of State, 2023; U.S. Government Accountability Office, 2020; Wu, 2024a; WTO, 2023; Xiong *et al.*, 2024

6.0 CONCLUSION

6.1 Theoretical Contributions

The growing geopolitical influence of MNCs challenges traditional international relations theories, which have historically positioned states as the primary architects of global power dynamics (Autio *et al.*, 2021; Morgenthau, 1948). The cases of Starlink and TSMC illustrate the heterogeneous ways in which MNCs have evolved beyond passive market players to active agents in foreign policy, security, and deterrence strategies. This shift, brought into sharp relief by our comparative analysis, necessitates a reassessment of core assumptions within major international relations frameworks, including Realism, Liberalism, and Constructivism (Keohane & Nye, 2011; Kobrin, 2009). Our main contributions are twofold, offering both empirical insights and a significant conceptual refinement for understanding corporate geopolitical agency.

First, building on the concept of corporate diplomacy, we introduce and develop the notion of "quasi-sovereign corporate power" (see Figure 1), defined here as the capacity of certain MNCs, primarily through control over critical technologies and infrastructure, to exercise strategic functions and exert influence traditionally associated with state sovereignty, albeit without formal political authority or territorial control. This concept captures the reality that MNCs increasingly exercise influence once reserved for sovereign states. By controlling technologies, infrastructure, and essential GVCs, these firms shape military strategies and national security doctrines, posing a direct challenge to conventional concepts of sovereignty and political authority. Our concept of QSCP moves beyond traditional understandings of corporate influence, corporate political activity (Hillman & Hitt, 1999; Lux *et al.*, 2011), or nonmarket strategy (as discussed by Li *et al.*, 2022) by emphasizing the specific (a) foundational source of power – direct control over critical technologies and infrastructures; (b) its scale and scope of impact – influencing national/international security; and (c) the nature of its agency – exhibiting strategic, often autonomous, functions traditionally associated with state sovereignty. This reconceptualization advances the theory of corporate diplomacy by integrating the dimension of QSCP, thereby refining our understanding of how MNCs influence international security and reshape the boundaries between markets, states, and governance.

Figure 1. Conceptual Dynamics of Quasi-Sovereign Corporate Power (QSCP)

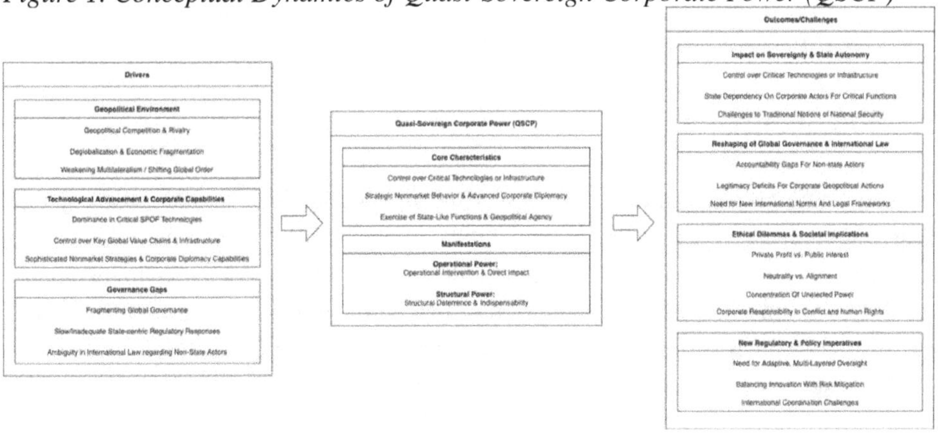

Second, we expand Realist perspectives by demonstrating that MNCs, far from being subordinate to state power (Morgenthau, 1948; Gilpin, 2016), actively shape security policies and military operations, potentially reconfiguring core realist assumptions about the sources and instruments of power. Starlink's provision of satellite communications to Ukraine and TSMC's role in Taiwan's defense infrastructure show that firms can influence conflict outcomes and geopolitical alignments, challenging traditional state-centric notions of power, especially when derived from control over critical global infrastructure (Bryant, 2023; James, 2021). Liberal theories, which emphasize economic interdependence and multilateralism, must now account for MNCs' ability to reshape trade, technology, and security landscapes outside formal institutional frameworks, thereby complicating liberal narratives of interdependence by demonstrating the potential for fragmentation and weaponized interdependence (Mende, 2023; Timmers, 2024; Farrell & Newman, 2019). Meanwhile, Constructivist theories offer valuable insights into how ideas, norms, and identities shape international behavior. However, they require refinement to account for the ways in which material capabilities, particularly technological control, enable firms not just to participate in normative discourse but to set de facto global standards. QSCP firms like Starlink and TSMC exert influence not merely through ideational alignment but through their ability to embed their technologies within the operational infrastructures of states, militaries, and economies. This positions them as *norm-setters* rather than traditional *norm-shapers*. For instance, the unilateral imposition of communication protocols by Starlink during wartime operations, or TSMC's centrality in shaping the semiconductor ecosystem, exemplifies how corporate technological dominance can outpace formal intergovernmental norm-making (Avant *et al.*, 2010; Cutler, 2001). These dynamics challenge the conventional constructivist assumption that norms emerge from collective deliberation and suggest a need to reconceptualize norm formation when infrastructure and influence are concentrated in private hands (Scherer & Palazzo, 2011; Marschlich, 2022).

6.2 Policy Implications

The rising geopolitical influence of MNCs presents significant regulatory and strategic challenges for governments. Traditionally, public policy has focused on market regulation, with limited attention to the implications of corporate involvement in matters of national security and international conflict. However, as demonstrated by Starlink's wartime role and TSMC's centrality in U.S.-China technological rivalry, the absence of targeted governance mechanisms leaves states vulnerable to the strategic discretion of corporate actors operating outside the bounds of democratic accountability.

To address these concerns, states should enhance export-controls guardrails and investment-screening mechanisms, particularly for technologies underpinning QSCP, to prevent MNCs from engaging in joint research or technology licensing that could facilitate "the improper use of CHIPS Act Funding" (National Institute of Standards and Technology, 2023, p. 65600; U.S. Department of Commerce, 2024). Clearer legal frameworks are needed to define corporate rights and responsibilities in military and security contexts, ensuring that private entities cannot unilaterally control critical service provision in ways that could undermine state sovereignty or strategic stability. These national efforts should be complemented by international action. Organizations like the United Nations, the WTO, and the OECD should develop governance instruments tailored to firms operating in security-sensitive domains, including guidelines for transparency, risk disclosure, and ethical engagement in geopolitical hotspots (Teece, 2020; WTO, 2023).

Yet implementing such measures is not without obstacles. Achieving global regulatory coherence in a fragmented geopolitical environment is difficult. Policymakers must carefully balance oversight with the need for innovation and design flexible mechanisms that accommodate diverse regulatory traditions while maintaining normative consistency. Moreover, regulation should not seek to sideline MNCs but rather integrate them more constructively into international security governance. Governments must recognize these firms as strategic partners, capable not only of projecting geopolitical influence but also of contributing to global public goods such as emergency communication, infrastructure resilience, and disaster relief coordination, while ensuring appropriate limits, responsibilities, and public accountability mechanisms are in place. To build resilient governance frameworks, firms like Starlink and TSMC must also engage actively with governments, civil society actors, and international institutions to co-develop norms of transparency, accountability, and compliance with evolving international standards.

6.3 Managerial Implications

The rise of QSCP introduces new responsibilities for managers leading firms with control over critical technologies and infrastructures. As geopolitical dynamics increasingly shape markets, managers must move beyond traditional risk assessments and incorporate geostrategic foresight into core decision-making processes. This includes mapping political fault lines, assessing dependency structures, and modeling scenario-based exposure to interstate conflict.

First, firms must invest in geopolitical foresight and scenario planning. TSMC's long-term diversification into the U.S. and Japan illustrates how strategic decisions can be based on sophisticated geopolitical risk assessments, not short-term cost-benefit calculations. Starlink's rapid deployment in Ukraine similarly shows the importance of anticipating geopolitical inflection points and preparing infrastructure in ways that allow flexible, high-stakes response. This means that executive teams need not just global market insight but dedicated geopolitical intelligence capacity to track dependencies, anticipate regulatory shifts, and understand how their technological assets might become entangled in conflict or diplomacy.

Second, corporate diplomacy must be professionalized and integrated into core business functions. This means managers in QSCP firms must cultivate diplomatic competencies, which go beyond lobbying or CSR. As seen in both cases, diplomacy can range from public crisis response (as in Musk's direct engagement in the Ukraine conflict) to quiet, long-term coalition building and government coordination (as practiced by TSMC). Senior leadership must be prepared to engage with multiple stakeholders, national governments, international organizations, civil society, and peer firms, not just to protect access and reputation, but to influence rulemaking in domains like export controls, infrastructure governance, or technology standards.

Third, internal governance structures must adapt to the ethical complexity of geopolitical influence. As MNCs become embedded in conflict zones, defense architectures, and strategic alliances, their actions increasingly carry not just legal ramifications but deep normative consequences. Decisions over whether to maintain services in wartime, to comply with export restrictions targeting rival states, or to locate key facilities in politically sensitive regions are not simply commercial; they are geopolitical acts. These choices raise fundamental questions of legitimacy: who authorizes such decisions, on what grounds, and with what safeguards? Boards of directors and executive leadership teams must go beyond conventional compliance models and embed ethical deliberation into high-level strategic processes. This includes establishing decision protocols for engagement in militarized settings, conducting ethical impact assessments alongside legal reviews, and setting clear red lines that delineate the firm's role vis-à-vis state interests. Without such structures, the risk grows that firms will act in ways that are strategically consequential but procedurally unaccountable, undermining both public trust and long-term organizational resilience.

Beyond strategic alignment, firms must also take seriously the physical and reputational risks faced by executives and employees operating in these environments. A recent case involving a foiled Russian plot to assassinate the CEO of a major arms manufacturer supplying Ukraine underscores the material risks that now accompany corporate geopolitical engagement (Bo Lillis et al., 2024). As corporate diplomacy becomes more central to security policy, risk management must expand to include the protection of personnel and organizational integrity.

6.4 Future Outlook

Future research should explore the less visible but equally impactful forms of corporate diplomacy, particularly the role of firms in cybersecurity, financial markets, and resource security, by employing interdisciplinary methodologies that bridge IR, international law, business ethics, and technology studies, to meticulously map the complex and often opaque networks of corporate-state interaction in these critical domains. While Starlink and TSMC provide high-profile examples of corporate geopolitical influence, less well-known and less visible firms exercise significant diplomatic and security-related functions, engaging in state-level negotiations and shaping strategic policymaking. Investigating these less visible corporate actors will be crucial for understanding the full spectrum of corporate power in international relations. As corporate diplomacy continues to blur the lines between business strategy and foreign policy, ethical concerns surrounding accountability, neutrality, and corporate responsibility in conflict zones must remain at the forefront of analysis. Ensuring that MNCs act in ways that align with international law, human rights, and global stability will be one of the defining challenges of 21st-century governance. Specifically concerning regulatory systems, a critical avenue for future inquiry involves designing adaptive and multi-layered governance frameworks (Djeffal *et al.*, 2022), as briefly outlined in our policy implications. This requires deeper investigation into co-regulatory models, accountability mechanisms for QSCP firms performing public interest functions, and international coordination for technology governance.

While the objective of this chapter was to introduce and illustrate the concept of QSCP based on a dual case study approach, it also lays the groundwork for a range of future research trajectories. On an inter-firm level of analysis, scholars should investigate the emergence of *techno-diplomatic ecosystems* in which QSCP firms not only interact with states but also strategically engage with one another. These interactions may include cooperation (e.g., standard-setting alliances), competition (e.g., infrastructure rivalry in critical regions), or even indirect geopolitical alignment through shared supply chains or cloud infrastructure. As more firms acquire QSCP capabilities, their relationships may begin to mirror or even rival traditional interstate dynamics, forming new spheres of influence that shape not just markets but regional and global security architectures (Moore & Tambini, 2018). Mapping these horizontal corporate relations will be essential to understanding whether QSCP leads to a multipolar, clustered, or fragmented distribution of geopolitical power among firms. On a within-firm level of analysis, future research could systematically unpack the internal governance dynamics that shape QSCP, examining how corporate structures, ownership models (private vs. public), leadership characteristics, and organizational cultures influence geopolitical positioning. Understanding these microfoundations is essential to developing a comprehensive theory of QSCP.

In conclusion, the rise of QSCP, exemplified by the diverse yet potent geopolitical agency of firms like Starlink and TSMC, marks a fundamental shift in the landscape of international relations. It challenges long-held theoretical assumptions and presents formidable governance dilemmas. As elaborated in our analysis, existing international legal and ethical frameworks are ill-equipped to manage the complex interplay between these powerful non-state actors and traditional state sovereignty. Addressing this gap necessitates more than incremental adjustments; it calls for a potential re-architecture of global governance frameworks. Forging a new compact that delineates the rights, responsibilities, and limits of both states and quasi-sovereign corporations is not merely an academic exercise but a historical imperative for inaugurating a new epoch where sovereignty is neither exclusive to states nor morally immune in corporate hands, a world where power without accountability is no longer acceptable, and where the frontier of diplomacy may well be drawn by satellites, semiconductors and the control of critical assets. The future trajectory of global governance, indeed, hinges on the urgent attention and concerted action of scholars, policymakers, and business leaders alike in confronting this new reality.

REFERENCES

Abels, J. (2024). Private infrastructure in geopolitical conflicts: The case of Starlink and the war in Ukraine. *European Journal of International Relations*, *30*(4), 842–866. DOI: 10.1177/13540661241260653

Adler, E. (2013). Constructivism in international relations: Sources, contributions, and debates. *Handbook of International Relations, 2*, 112–144.

Aiyar, M. S., Chen, M. J., Ebeke, C., Ebeke, M. C. H., Garcia-Saltos, M. R., Gudmundsson, T., Ilyina, M. A., Kangur, M. A., Kunaratskul, T., & Rodriguez, M. S. L. (2023). *Geo-economic fragmentation and the future of multilateralism*. International Monetary Fund.

Atlantic Council. (2021). The Longer Telegram: Toward A New American China Strategy. Atlantic Council. https://www.atlanticcouncil.org/wp-content/uploads/2021/01/The-Longer-Telegram-Toward-A-New-American-China-Strategy.pdf

Autio, E., Mudambi, R., & Yoo, Y. (2021). Digitalization and globalization in a turbulent world: Centrifugal and centripetal forces. *Global Strategy Journal*, *11*(1), 3–16. DOI: 10.1002/gsj.1396

Avant, D. D., Finnemore, M., & Sell, S. K. (Eds.). (2010). *Who governs the globe?* (Vol. 114). Cambridge University Press.

Berridge, G. R. (2022). *Diplomacy: Theory and practice*. Springer Nature.

Bilchitz, D. (2021). *Fundamental rights and the legal obligations of business*. Cambridge University Press.

Bo Lillis, K., Bertrand, N., & Pleitgen, F. (2024). *Exclusive: US and Germany foiled Russian plot to assassinate CEO of arms manufacturer sending weapons to Ukraine*. CNN. https://edition.cnn.com/2024/07/11/politics/us-germany-foiled-russian-assassination-plot/index.html

Bryant, W. J. (2023). *When a CEO plays president: Musk, Starlink, and the war in Ukraine*. Irregular Warfare Initiative. https://irregularwarfare.org/articles/when-a-ceo-plays-president-musk-starlink-and-the-war-in-ukraine/

Bucheli, M., & DeBerge, T. (2024). Multinational enterprises' nonmarket strategies: Insights from History. *International Business Review*, *33*(2), 102198.

Buckley, P. J. (2021). Exogenous and endogenous change in global value chains. *Journal of International Business Policy*, *4*(2), 221.

Buckley, P. J. (2023). Corporate reactions to the fracturing of the global economy. *International Business Review*, *32*(6), 102014.

Burnett, A., Arseneau, J. B., Darvishian, A., & Saigau, V. (2024). SpaceX: The independent investment guide Q1'24 update (Mach33 Capital Markets). https://spacedventure-marketing.s3.amazonaws.com/SpaceX+Public+Investment+Guide+M33+(Q1'24+Update).pptx+(4).pdf#page=46.25

Büthe, T., & Mattli, W. (2011). *The new global rulers: The privatization of regulation in the world economy*. Princeton University Press.

Chang, J. (2024). TSMC's advanced process remains strong and difficult to shake. *Yahoo Finance*. https://tw.stock.yahoo.com/news/%E5%8F%B0%E7%A9%8D%E9%9B%BB%E5%85%88%E9%80%B2%E8%A3%BD%E7%A8%8B%E5%A0%85%E6%8C%BA-%E9%9B%A3%E6%92%BC%E5%8B%95-201000970.html

Chang, J.-M. (2021). The future is small and fast: Assessing Taiwan's 2021 Quadrennial Defense Review and U.S. defense posture in the Indo-Pacific. *Institute for National Defense and Security Research*. https://indsr.org.tw/en/respublicationcon?uid=15&resid=44&pid=1501

Cuthbertson, A. (2024). Elon Musk now controls two thirds of all active satellites. *The Independent*. https://www.independent.co.uk/tech/elon-musk-satellites-starlink-spacex-b2606262.html

Cutler, A. C. (2001). Critical reflections on the Westphalian assumptions of international law and organization: A crisis of legitimacy. *Review of International Studies*, *27*(2), 133–150.

Cutler, A. C., Haufler, V., & Porter, T. (Eds.). (1999). *Private authority and international affairs*. Suny Press.

De Villa, M. A. (2023). Assessing geopolitical risk: A multi-level approach for top managers of multinationals. *AIB Insights*, *23*(1), 1–7.

Deibert, R. J. (2019). The road to digital unfreedom: Three painful truths about social media. *Journal of Democracy*, *30*(1), 25–39.

Deitelhoff, N., & Wolf, K. D. (2010). Corporate Security Responsibility: Corporate Governance Contributions to Peace and Security in Zones of Conflict. In Deitelhoff, N., & Wolf, K. D. (Eds.), *Corporate Security Responsibility?* (pp. 1–25)., DOI: 10.1057/9780230277052_1

Djeffal, C., Siewert, M. B., & Wurster, S. (2022). Role of the state and responsibility in governing artificial intelligence: A comparative analysis of AI strategies. *Journal of European Public Policy, 29*(11), 1799–1821.

Doh, J. P., Lawton, T. C., & Rajwani, T. (2012). Advancing nonmarket strategy research: Institutional perspectives in a changing world. *The Academy of Management Perspectives, 26*(3), 22–39.

Dohale, V., Ambilkar, P., Gunasekaran, A., & Verma, P. (2022). Supply chain risk mitigation strategies during COVID-19: Exploratory cases of "make-to-order" handloom saree apparel industries. *International Journal of Physical Distribution & Logistics Management, 52*(2), 109–129.

Du, Y., & Zhang, H. (2023). *Starlink militarization and its impact on global strategic stability*. Interpret: China, Center for Strategic and International Studies. https://interpret.csis.org/translations/starlink-militarization-and-its-impact-on-global-strategic-stability/

Eisenhardt, K. M., & Graebner, M. E. (2007). Theory Building From Cases: Opportunities And Challenges. *Academy of Management Journal, 50*(1), 25–32. DOI: 10.5465/amj.2007.24160888

Farrell, H., & Newman, A. L. (2019). Weaponized interdependence: How global economic networks shape state coercion. *International Security, 44*(1), 42–79.

Fitzgerald, M., & Thompson, C. (2022). What does Starlink's participation in Ukrainian defense reveal about U.S. space policy? *Lawfare*. https://www.lawfaremedia.org/article/what-does-starlinks-participation-ukrainian-defense-reveal-about-us-space-policy

Flint, C. (2021). *Introduction to geopolitics*. Routledge.

Fort, T. L. (2000). A Review of Donaldson and Dunfee's "Ties That Bind: A Social Contracts Approach to Business Ethics.". *Journal of Business Ethics, 28*(4), 383–387. https://www.jstor.org/stable/25074428

Frynas, J. G., & Stephens, S. (2015). Political Corporate Social Responsibility: Reviewing Theories and Setting New Agendas. *International Journal of Management Reviews, 17*(4), 483–509. DOI: 10.1111/ijmr.12049

Gawer, A. (2014). Bridging differing perspectives on technological platforms: Toward an integrative framework. *Research Policy, 43*(7), 1239–1249.

Gibbert, M., Ruigrok, W., & Wicki, B. (2008). What passes as a rigorous case study? *Strategic Management Journal, 29*(13), 1465–1474. DOI: 10.1002/smj.722

Gigliuto, G. (2023). The relevance of semiconductors manufacturing in Taiwan's foreign policy. https://unive.unitesi.cineca.it/handle/20.500.14247/12680

Gilpin, R. (2016). *The political economy of international relations*. Princeton University Press.

Green, J. F. (2013). Order out of chaos: Public and private rules for managing carbon. *Global Environmental Politics*, *13*(2), 1–25.

Gurantz, R. (2024). *Satellites in the Russia-Ukraine War*. https://press.armywarcollege.edu/monographs/971/

Hall, R. B., & Biersteker, T. J. (Eds.). (2002). *The emergence of private authority in global governance* (Vol. 85). Cambridge University Press.

Haufler, V. (2013). *A public role for the private sector: Industry self-regulation in a global economy*. Carnegie Endowment.

Henisz, W. J. (2016). The Dynamic Capability of Corporate Diplomacy. *Global Strategy Journal*, *6*(3), 183–196. DOI: 10.1002/gsj.1121

Henisz, W. J. (2017). *Corporate diplomacy: Building reputations and relationships with external stakeholders*. Routledge.

Hillman, A. J., & Hitt, M. A. (1999). Corporate political strategy formulation: A model of approach, participation, and strategy decisions. *Academy of Management Review*, *24*(4), 825–842.

International Chamber of Commerce. (2016). *ICC Business Charter for Sustainable Development 2015*. ICC - International Chamber of Commerce. https://iccwbo.org/news-publications/policies-reports/icc-business-charter-for-sustainable-development-2015/

Isaacson, W. (2023). *Elon Musk*. Simon and Schuster.

Ivanov, D., & Dolgui, A. (2022). Stress testing supply chains and creating viable ecosystems. *Operations Management Research*, *15*(1–2), 475–486. DOI: 10.1007/s12063-021-00194-z

James, L. (2021). Supply chains critical to Taiwan's security. *East Asia Forum*. https://eastasiaforum.org/2021/03/10/geoeconomics-and-the-security-of-taiwan/

Johnson, J. (2025). Why Elon Musk is a headache for broadband bosses. *Thomson Reuters*. https://www.reuters.com/breakingviews/why-elon-musk-is-headache-broadband-bosses-2025-02-11/

Keohane, R. O., & Nye, J. S. (2011). *Power and interdependence* (4th ed.). Longman.

Kerr, P., & Wiseman, G. (2017). *Diplomacy in a globalizing world*. Oxford University Press.

Kobrin, S. J. (2009). Private political authority and public responsibility: Transnational politics, transnational firms, and human rights. *Business Ethics Quarterly*, *19*(3), 349–374.

Li, J., Shapiro, D., Peng, M. W., & Ufimtseva, A. (2022). Corporate diplomacy in the age of US–China rivalry. *The Academy of Management Perspectives*, *36*(4), 1007–1032. DOI: 10.5465/amp.2021.0076

Lumineau, F., & Keller, A. (2025). War as a phenomenon of inquiry in management studies. *Journal of Management Studies*. Advance online publication. DOI: 10.1111/joms.13213

Luo, Y. (2024). Paradigm shift and theoretical implications for the era of global disorder. *Journal of International Business Studies*, *55*(2), 127–135.

Luo, Y., & Van Assche, A. (2023). The rise of techno-geopolitical uncertainty: Implications of the United States CHIPS and Science Act. *Journal of International Business Studies*, *54*(8), 1423–1440. DOI: 10.1057/s41267-023-00620-3 PMID: 37359753

Lux, S., Crook, T. R., & Woehr, D. J. (2011). Mixing business with politics: A meta-analysis of the antecedents and outcomes of corporate political activity. *Journal of Management*, *37*(1), 223–247.

Mark, J., & Roberts, D. T. (2023). United States–China Semiconductor Standoff: A Supply Chain under Stress. *Atlantic Council, 23*. https://www.atlanticcouncil.org/wp-content/uploads/2023/03/US-China-Semiconductor-Standoff.pdf

Marschlich, S. (2022). *Corporate diplomacy: How multinational corporations gain organizational legitimacy: A neo-institutional public relations perspective*. Springer Nature.

Martin, B., Baldwin, L. H., DeLuca, P., Henriquez Sanchez, N., Hvizda, M., Smith, C. D., & Whitehead, N. P. (2023). *Supply Chain Interdependence and Geopolitical Vulnerability: The Case of Taiwan and High-End Semiconductors*. RAND Corporation. https://www.rand.org/pubs/research_reports/RRA2354-1.html

Mazal, J. (2024). *The Dual Use of Civilian and Military Technologies in the Battlefield of the Future*. https://real.mtak.hu/210721/

Mende, J. (2023). Business authority in global governance: Companies beyond public and private roles. *Journal of International Political Theory*, *19*(2), 200–220. DOI: 10.1177/17550882221116924

Meyer, K. E., Li, C., & Schotter, A. P. (2020). Managing the MNE subsidiary: Advancing a multi-level and dynamic research agenda. *Journal of International Business Studies*, *51*, 538–576.

Miller, C. (2022). *Chip war: The fight for the world's most critical technology*. Simon and Schuster.

Mizrak, K. C. (2024). Crisis management and risk mitigation: Strategies for effective response and resilience. *Trends, Challenges, and Practices in Contemporary Strategic Management*, 254–278.

Moore, M., & Tambini, D. (Eds.). (2018). *Digital dominance: the power of Google, Amazon, Facebook, and Apple*. Oxford University Press.

Morales, J. (2024). Semiconductor analyst theorizes that China might want to destroy TSMC instead of capturing it, Chinese invasion of Taiwan would destroy supply chains, cripple South Korean chipmakers. *Tom's Hardware*. https://www.tomshardware.com/pc-components/cpus/semiconductor-analyst-theorizes-that-china-wants-to-destroy-tsmc-instead-of-capturing-it-a-chinese-invasion-of-taiwan-would-also-roil-supply-chains-removing-south-korean-chipmakers-from-contention

Morgenthau, H. J. (1948). *Politics among nations: The struggle for power and peace*. Alfred A. Knopf.

National Institute of Standards and Technology. (2023). Preventing the improper use of CHIPS Act funding (Final rule), 88 Fed. Reg. 65600–65620. https://www.govinfo.gov/content/pkg/FR-2023-09-25/pdf/2023-20471.pdf

National Intelligence Council. (2021). *Global trends 2040: A more contested world*. https://www.dni.gov/files/ODNI/documents/assessments/GlobalTrends_2040.pdf

Neill, A. (2023). Doubts grow over Taiwan's Silicon Shield. *GIS Reports*. Retrieved from https://www.gisreportsonline.com/r/china-taiwan-silicon-shield/

Office of the President Republic of China. (2020). *President Tsai designates TSMC founder Morris Chang as Leader's Representative at APEC Economic Leaders' Week* https://english.president.gov.tw/NEWS/6068

Porter, T., Spirlet, T., & Epstein, J. (2025). Musk said he wouldn't withdraw Starlink for Ukraine. Europe is looking for alternatives, but would struggle to replace it. *Business Insider*. https://www.businessinsider.com/musk-starlink-threats-europe-faces-obstacles-replace-eutelsat-ukraine-trump-2025-3

Pultarova, T. (2025). Starlink satellites: Facts, tracking and impact on astronomy. *Space.com*. https://www.space.com/spacex-starlink-satellites.html

Raswant, A., Nielsen, B. B., & Buckley, P. J. (2025). Space: A new frontier for international business. *Journal of International Business Studies*. Advance online publication. DOI: 10.1057/s41267-025-00783-1

Republic of China Ministry of National Defense. (2023). *ROC National Defense Report 2023*. https://www.mnd.gov.tw/newupload/ndr/112/112ndreng.pdf

Ruggie, J. G. (1982). International regimes, transactions, and change: Embedded liberalism in the postwar economic order. *International Organization*, *36*(2), 379–415.

Saner, R., Yiu, L., & Sondergaard, M. (2000). Business diplomacy management: A core competency for global companies. *The Academy of Management Perspectives*, *14*(1), 80–92.

Saxenian, A. L. (2006). *The New Argonauts: Regional Advantage in a Global Economy*. Harvard University Press.

Scherer, A. G., & Palazzo, G. (2007). Toward a political conception of corporate responsibility: Business and society seen from a Habermasian perspective. *Academy of Management Review*, *32*(4), 1096–1120.

Scherer, A. G., & Palazzo, G. (2011). The new political role of business in a globalized world: A review of a new perspective on CSR and its implications for the firm, governance, and democracy. *Journal of Management Studies*, *48*(4), 899–931.

Seawright, J., & Gerring, J. (2008). Case Selection Techniques in Case Study Research: A Menu of Qualitative and Quantitative Options. *Political Research Quarterly*, *61*(2), 294–308. DOI: 10.1177/1065912907313077

Shalal, A., & Roulette, J. (2025). US could cut Ukraine's access to Starlink internet services over minerals, say sources. *Reuters*. https://www.reuters.com/business/us-could-cut-ukraines-access-starlink-internet-services-over-minerals-say-2025-02-22/

Shattuck, T. J. (2021). Stuck in the Middle: Taiwan's Semiconductor Industry, the US-China Tech Fight, and Cross-Strait Stability. *Orbis*, *65*(1), 101–117.

Simma, B., Khan, D. E., Nolte, G., & Paulus, A. (2024). *The Charter of the United Nations: a commentary*. Oxford University Press.

Sun, P., Doh, J. P., Rajwani, T., & Siegel, D. (2021). Navigating cross-border institutional complexity: A review and assessment of multinational nonmarket strategy research. *Journal of International Business Studies*, *52*(9), 1818–1853. DOI: 10.1057/s41267-021-00438-x PMID: 34176993

Taiwan Ministry of Foreign Affairs. (2025) *SCIENCE AND TECHNOLOGY.* Government Portal of the Republic of China (Taiwan). Retrieved February 4, 2025, from https://www.taiwan.gov.tw/content_8.php

Teece, D. (2020). Fundamental issues in strategy: Time to reassess? *Strategic Management Review*, *1*, 103–144.

The Economic Times. (2024). How is Starlink Ukraine's strategic tool in the face of Russian invasion [Defence]. *The Economic Times (Online)*. https://economictimes.indiatimes.com/news/defence/how-is-starlink-ukraines-strategic-tool-in-the-face-of-russian-invasion/articleshow/107710900.cms

Timmers, P. (2024). Sovereignty in the digital age. In Werthner, H., Ghezzi, C., Kramer, J., Nida-Rümelin, J., Nuseibeh, B., & Prem, E. (Eds.), *Perspectives on digital humanism* (pp. 571–580). Springer.

U.S. Department of Commerce. (2024). Biden-Harris administration announces preliminary terms with TSMC, expanded investment from company to bring world's most advanced leading-edge technology to the U.S. U.S. Department of Commerce. https://www.commerce.gov/news/press-releases/2024/04/biden-harris-administration-announces-preliminary-terms-tsmc-expanded

TSMC. (2025) *Annual Reports*. Taiwan Semiconductor Manufacturing Company Limited. Retrieved February 4, 2025, from https://investor.tsmc.com/english/annual-reports

United Nations. (2022). *Treaty on Principles Governing the Activities of States in the Exploration and Use of Outer Space, including the Moon and Other Celestial*

U.S. Department of Defense. (2022). *National defense strategy of the United States of America.* https://media.defense.gov/2022/Oct/27/2003103845/-1/-1/1/2022-NATIONAL-DEFENSE-STRATEGY-NPR-MDR.PDF

U.S. Department of State. (2023). *Integrated Country Strategy: Ukraine.* https://www.state.gov/wp-content/uploads/2023/09/ICS_EUR_Ukraine_29AUG2023_PUBLIC.pdf

U.S. Government Accountability Office. (2020). *Defense acquisitions annual assessment: Drive to deliver capabilities faster increases importance of program knowledge and consistent oversight.* https://www.gao.gov/products/gao-20-439

Waltz, K. N. (1979). *Theory of international politics, communication.* Addison-Wesley.

Wendt, A. (1992). Anarchy is what states make of it: The social construction of power politics. *International Organization, 46*(2), 391–425.

Westermann-Behaylo, M. K., Rehbein, K., & Fort, T. (2015). Enhancing the Concept of Corporate Diplomacy: Encompassing Political Corporate Social Responsibility, International Relations, and Peace Through Commerce. *The Academy of Management Perspectives, 29*(4), 387–404. DOI: 10.5465/amp.2013.0133

Witt, M. A., Lewin, A. Y., Li, P. P., & Gaur, A. (2023). Decoupling in international business: Evidence, drivers, impact, and implications for IB research. *Journal of World Business, 58*(1), 101399.

Wong, C. Y., Yeung, H. W. C., Huang, S., Song, J., & Lee, K. (2024). Geopolitics and the changing landscape of global value chains and competition in the global semiconductor industry: Rivalry and catch-up in chip manufacturing in East Asia. *Technological Forecasting and Social Change, 209*, 123749.

WTO. (2023). *Global Value Chain Development Report 2023: Resilient and Sustainable Global Value Chains in Turbulent Times.* World Trade Organization., DOI: 10.30875/9789287075673

Wu, J.-m. (2024a). *Silicon Shield 2.0: A Taiwan perspective.* The Diplomat. https://thediplomat.com/2024/09/silicon-shield-2-0-a-taiwan-perspective/

Wu, R. (2024b). TSMC's role in the chip ecosystem. *Taipei Times.* Retrieved from https://www.taipeitimes.com/News/editorials/archives/2024/11/19/2003827117

Xiong, W., Wu, D. D., & Yeung, J. H. Y. (2024). Semiconductor supply chain resilience and disruption: Insights, mitigation, and future directions. *International Journal of Production Research*, •••, 1–24. DOI: 10.1080/00207543.2024.2387074

Yin, R. K. (2009). *Case study research: Design and methods* (Vol. 5). sage.

Zhang, J. Z. (2025). TSMC's market share reaches 64% in Q3 2024; 3nm process gains prominence. *United Daily News.* https://money.udn.com/money/story/5612/8486483

Chapter 2
Geopolitical Risk and Financial Markets:
Emerging Trends, Research Gaps, and Implications for International Trade

Valeria Caro
https://orcid.org/0009-0003-7691-9814
Universidad del Rosario, Colombia

Juan C. Espinosa
https://orcid.org/0000-0002-1643-2233
Universidad del Rosario, Colombia

ABSTRACT

When addressing international trade, the most commonly referenced concepts include imports, exports, exchange rates, customs tariffs, and, naturally, supply and demand. This chapter examines geopolitical risk (GPR) as a critical factor that significantly influences financial markets and, by extension, each of these trade-related indicators. It reviews the historical development of this concept within academic literature and analyzes its spillover effects across economies. Through an in-depth examination of the implications of geopolitical risk in international trade —supported by a comprehensive bibliometric analysis and literature review—this study identifies thematic and emerging trends, as well as research gaps that may inform future lines of inquiry.

DOI: 10.4018/979-8-3373-1265-1.ch002

INTRODUCTION

Throughout history, critical moments have been identified in global financial markets where the financial security of nations has been at risk. One of these critical moments was the well-known 2008 financial crisis, distinguished by deflation of the subprime mortgage bubble. This crisis paved the way for a field of study that necessitated a reconsideration of the approach taken to capital markets up to that point. This reconsideration arose once again 12 years later with the COVID-19 pandemic, which caused an 8,9% decline in global trade (Bank of England, 2021), thus marking the sharpest drop since the preceding crisis of 2008.

Just two years after the coronavirus outbreak, on February 24, 2022, when tensions between Russia and Ukraine escalated, the relationship between these geopolitical events and the global economy became obvious once again, as they resulted in a 1% decrease in world trade, leading to a 0.7% drop in global GDP (World Bank, 2022).

It is also worth mentioning events such as the Arab Spring, which began in 2011 and intensely affected the economies of multiple countries in the Middle East and North Africa. For example, Syria experienced an approximately 10% decline in its annual GDP from 2011 to 2014 (Ianchovichina, 2016), while Libya's economy contracted by 14% annually between 2013 and 2015.

Equally important is the Brexit case in 2016, which also had notable impacts on international economics and trade. One of these was a 14.9% (£18.9 billion) drop in UK exports to the European Union in the first quarter of 2021, accompanied by a 20.3% (£23.7 billion) decline in imports from the EU during the same time frame (Kren & Lawless, 2024).

Up to this point, we have been discussing political and international relations events that have had noteworthy geographical and economic impacts on a global scale, or vice versa. Without realizing it, throughout this commentary, we have been referring to geopolitics. "Geopolitics" refers to the study of how geography and economics influence politics and international relations (Hossain et al., 2024). As international business operations become increasingly complex, comprehensively understanding geoeconomics and geopolitics is essential. The subject of this chapter is a concept closely linked to geopolitics: Geopolitical Risk (GPR), which plays a crucial role in shaping stock market volatility, oil price fluctuations, and overall economic stability.

Scholars in the fields of finance and economics have been progressively researching how GPR is transmitted from one market to another or one economy to another. This rising interest reflects the need to understand how such risks can spread across borders, potentially disrupting global economic stability. All the previously stated pivotal moments in history have led the academic community to focus on analyzing mechanisms and alternatives to mitigate risks in financial markets associated with these events, aiming to predict their impact on the economy or even prevent them.

In the words of Bohl et al. (2017) and Engle and Campos-Martins (2020), the broad definition of GPR includes factors such as political unrest, religious disputes, anti-globalization movements, and natural disasters like heatwaves, earthquakes, and cyclones. Alternatively, Caldara and Iacoviello (2022) defined GPR from its narrower aspect as threats arising from terrorist attacks, military conflicts, and global crises. Transversely, the concept of geopolitical risk has been gaining relevance as policymakers, government officials, and global investors are gradually more concerned about it, which is directly related to the impact it has had on economic growth in the past few years.

With these notions as a starting point, a series of studies have been conducted on the correlation between geopolitical risk and numerous metrics of national economies, as well as the direct impact of geopolitical risk and the economy itself (Tamiselvan et al., 2024; Dong et al., 2023; Kumar et al., 2021; Bouri et al., 2023; Tran & Vo, 2023).

Simultaneously, in recent times, emerging markets have set the pace for rapid and stable economic growth driven by cooperation and integration. For example, the BRICS countries (Brazil, Russia, India, China, and South Africa) are among the most notable and rapidly expanding economic blocs, representing over 40 percent of the world's population and 29.5 percent of the global GDP (International Monetary Fund, 2014). These economic blocs often share objectives of economic expansion and opportunities for market and investment cooperation and integration, leading to resembling responses to diverse external shocks, with geopolitical events being one of them (Cheng & Chiu, 2018; Mamman et al., 2023; Zhang & Hamori, 2022).

That said, economic integration is not the only aspect that emerging markets share. Their inherent fragility and vulnerability partly define them as emerging markets, making them more exposed to global and domestic geopolitical risk and uncertainty than developed economies (Hoque et al., 2023). This exposure makes them more susceptible to steeper declines in asset prices than developed economies when global risk aversion increases (Yildirim, 2016). And it is due to this same volatility that emerging economies face more rigid controls in monetary policy (International Monetary Fund, 2016; World Bank, 2016), which alters interest rates and contributes to higher turbulence in investors' perception of risk. Thus, due to these distinct characteristics of emerging markets, their dynamics are significantly different from those of developed markets, calling for their separate study while also assessing their possible interconnectedness with developed markets.

The aforementioned points show not only that the concept of geopolitical risk is of utmost importance when examining financial market behavior dynamics, but also that these dynamics require separate examinations in emerging and developed markets. This chapter aims to explore these critical intersections, provide insights into how the influence of geopolitical risk on financial markets has been studied throughout the years, and identify research trends along with promising areas of inquiry.

By adding to the broader discussion on geoeconomics and geopolitics, this chapter prioritizes, based on the existing academic literature, the financial market implications of geopolitical risk. This chapter intends to identify existing research gaps, showcase the uneven academic contributions to this domain, and provide an inclusive perspective that accounts for both developed and emerging markets. By highlighting research trends, gaps, and opportunities, this work's objective is to enhance strategic decision-making for investors, business leaders, and policymakers steering through an increasingly uncertain global economic context. Understanding how geopolitical risk propagates across markets is a crucial aspect in mitigating potential disturbances and fostering economic stability worldwide.

To scrutinize these dynamics, this chapter aims to answer the following research questions: What thematic and methodological trends characterize the study of geopolitical risk in financial markets? How do emerging economies differ from developed economies? And what are their implications for financial stability and macroprudential policy design? To do so, it proposes a bibliometric analysis of publications retrieved from the Web of Science database, supplemented by an extensive literature review. This approach will lead us to the identification of key thematic areas and research trends related to geopolitical risk and the financial market by structurally reviewing existing scholarship, patterns, and gaps within the study area. As these become evident, valuable insights will be offered regarding emerging fields of interest.

The increasing relevance of the topic, the surfacing of research opportunities, the existing deficiencies in the development of identified thematic areas—such as the energy market—, and the remaining lack of extensive development regarding the spillover of volatility constitute intriguing findings included in this chapter that should be considered in future research related to geopolitical risk and its impact on financial markets.

STUDY OF GEOPOLITICAL RISK

Background

Before delving into the thematic trends and findings in recent geopolitical risk research, it is essential to examine how the concept of geopolitical risk emerged in academic literature and how its definition has evolved. Additionally, it is important to analyze the transformations in the methods used to interpret and assess this concept.

To do so, we must first revisit the concept of geopolitics following Flint (2016), as previously introduced. The term "Geopolitics" was first coined in the work *Stetn som Lifsform* (*The State as a Living Form*) by Swedish political scientist Rudolf Kjellén, published in 1916. Kjellén developed ideas originally proposed by Friedrich Ratzl (1844-1904), a German ethnographer and geographer, in his book *Politische Geographie* (1896). For Kjellén, *Geopolitik* was one of the five fundamental branches of the state, defining it as "the influence of geographical factors, in the broadest sense of the term, on the political development of nations and states." He synthesized various conceptual frameworks, arguing that the geographical characteristics of the state inherently shape political processes.

By the early 1920s, the academic study of geopolitics began to gain traction in Germany with the establishment of a research group led by General Karl Haushofer, a professor at the University of Munich. This group laid the epistemological foundations of geopolitics, culminating in the creation of *Zeitschrift für Geopolitik* (*Journal of Geopolitics*) in December 1923, co-founded by Haushofer and Ernst Obst.

In 1928, a collective of German geographers, including Ernst Obst, Hermann Lautensach, and Otto Maull (p.29-48), proposed the following definition of *Geopolitik*, which remains one of the most faithful to its original premises: "Geopolitics is the doctrine of the relationships between the earth and political developments (…) Geopolitics must be and will be the geographical consciousness of the state." Even so, the concept of geopolitics underwent a significant transformation by the mid-1920s as it was appropriated and reframed by the Nazi regime, a process initiated with the release of *Mein Kampf* by Adolf Hitler.

Written in 1924 and published in 1925 during Hitler's imprisonment in Landsberg, *Mein Kampf* integrated geopolitical ideas into the ideological framework of the Third Reich. While Hitler was incarcerated, he met Haushofer and his geopolitical theories, which he then reframed to link the concept of geopolitics to the expansionist policies of Nazi Germany, laying the groundwork for Nazi geopolitical doctrine by stating these ideas in Chapter XIV of *Mein Kampf*. Therefore, from that point onward, the term "geopolitics" became inextricably associated with the atrocities committed by the Nazi regime, causing a schism among geopolitical schools of thought. Nonetheless, Haushofer explicitly distanced himself from *Mein Kampf* in his later writings, asserting that he had refused to revise it and that its content bore little relation to the true essence of *Geopolitik*. He contended that *Mein Kampf* was nothing more than misinterpreted ideas and populist catchphrases that the Nazi regime skewed.

In search of asserting *Geopolitik* as a legitimate field of study, detaching it from the Nazi distortion, Haushofer published *Defense of German Geopolitics* in 1946. In this publication, he explained that the original intention of *Geopolitik* was to avoid conflicts like World War I through cooperation and development. However, *Geopolitik* was subjected to wide criticism, which triggered the appearance of new geopolitical perspectives that sought to isolate themselves from the Nazi influence while preserving the foundations in terms of epistemology and doctrine.

By the 1930s, schools of geopolitical thought outside Germany were beginning to gain recognition. Among them, the American school of geopolitics played a vital role, especially in the crafting of national security strategies. The U.S. geopolitical model ended up influencing geopolitical doctrines throughout Latin America and the Caribbean. These doctrines were initially adopted as strategies to maintain internal order despite perceived communist threats, exerting a considerable contribution to Latin American military regimes during the 1960s, 1970s, and 1980s.

Once the Cold War ceased, scholars began re-evaluating geopolitics, its role, and its significance in 20th-century history. At present, *Critical Geopolitics* (Ó Tuathail, 1996), *Modern Geopolitics* (Mackinder, 1904), *Postmodern Geopolitics* (Dalby, 1991), *Contemporary Geopolitics* (Flint, 2016), *New Geopolitics* (Krastev & Leonard, 2014), *Geopolitics of Chaos* (Ramonet, 1999), and *Geopolitics of Complexity* (Cuellar, 2012) constitute new approaches to the study of geopolitics.

In contemporary geopolitical thought, scholars have abandoned the notion that human behavior is rigidly shaped by geographical conditions. In contrast, the focus of modern geopolitics has been on analyzing how geography informs human decisions and strategies. This shift has reoriented geopolitical studies to an increasingly economic approach that stresses how societal improvement is contingent upon the availability of resources and the fulfillment of socioeconomic expectations. Hence, geopolitics has become profoundly intertwined with the economic dynamics that shape power structures globally.

Importance in International Trade

International business as a distinct academic discipline is fairly new and still developing in response to the increasing nuance of economic and political interactions around the globe (Anzo, 2012). Daniels et al. (2007) define international business as the field of study that assesses the processes of commercial exchange of goods and services between companies operating in different national contexts. In light of this definition, international business is intrinsically complex because it requires thorough comprehension of different economic, social, political, and cultural variables to mitigate risks while capitalizing on opportunities in global economies. This phenomenon explains why, while trade and commercial exchanges between countries have existed for centuries, the formal study of international business has only gained momentum in recent decades.

Over the last years, the interconnectedness of economies has intensified due to globalization, which makes international business a key driver of economic integration and global trade, as well as a highly multidisciplinary field in which businesses must evaluate and undergo various external factors such as market entry barriers, regulatory frameworks, financial risks, and political stability. The world is currently facing a context in which trade policies, diplomatic relations, and geopolitical strategies are gaining increasing relevance and shaping global commerce. This fosters the need to incorporate political and geopolitical considerations into international business decision-making.

This reality brings with it multiple challenges, among which the instability of protectionist policies and their impact on trade flows stand out as one of the most pressing. Historically, trade wars and economic crises have deeply molded the global economy. It is commonly acknowledged that across time, nations have used trade protectionism as a mechanism for economic defense, frequently resulting in disruptions to market volatility and supply chains (Irwin, 2012). A flagship example is the U.S. trade war, which has altered global trade patterns substantially, with impacts in industries spanning from technology to agriculture. John Lorié, Chief Economist at Atradius N.V., observed, "The trade war is having a profound effect on global trade. If it expands to other economies in Asia and Europe, which is very possible, we could see an even more pronounced slowing in trade" (Atradius, 2024). Likewise, financial crises such as the Eurozone crisis and the 2008 financial crisis had profound implications on global trade, reinforcing the necessity for businesses to integrate geopolitical risk audits into their strategic planning (Baena-Rojas & Bonilla-Calle, 2021).

Beyond its economic function, international business plays a pivotal role in shaping globalization. As companies expand across borders, they contribute to various forms of economic cooperation and integration, including:

- *Foreign Direct Investment (FDI):* International business fosters capital movement between nations, enabling economic growth and job creation in host countries (Rajagopal, 2007).
- *Technological Exchange and Innovation:* Cross-border business operations facilitate the transfer of knowledge, resources, patents, and technological advancements, enhancing productivity and industrial development (Baten, 2016).
- *Easing of protectionist policies:* Businesses' collaboration across borders tends to have a considerable impact on reducing the prevalence of restrictive tariffs.

- *Cultural and Economic Integration:* The internationalization of companies fosters cultural exchange and economic cooperation, reducing trade barriers and encouraging collaboration between nations.

With these aforementioned economic and social effects, it is clear that the reasoning behind international business is becoming an area of increasing academic interest, especially for policymakers. The global relevance of global trade regulations, foreign investment decisions, and cooperation and coordination between countries in terms of resources, technology, and knowledge highlights the need to integrate geopolitical analysis into international business research. Geopolitics is no longer confined to traditional concerns of territorial disputes or military strategy, and understanding the complexities of international business necessitates a robust integration of geopolitical analysis. In this context, examining geopolitics in regard to trade policy, supply chain stability, and investment security has become fundamental. Definitely, Bustillo (2022) rightly pointed out that geopolitics should be seen as a multidisciplinary analytical tool that examines how different economic, political, and geographical factors shape international business environments.

Now, to conclude this section by reaffirming the relevance of studying geopolitics in international trade, we will refer to some geopolitical risk examples that have prominently impacted global business strategies and international trade dynamics. Some of them include:

- *The ongoing trade war between the United States and China:* This latent risk showcases how geopolitical rivalries affect tariff schemes, supply chain structures, and market access (Góes & Bekkers, 2022). The impact of this ongoing competition between the U.S. and China has transcended to the point of forcing multinational firms to relocate production facilities, diversify suppliers, and reconsider investment destinations.
- *The Russia-Ukraine conflict:* This conflict has had serious repercussions for global energy markets, agricultural exports, and logistics routes. This conflict has pointed out the importance of supply chain resilience and diversification, as well as important strategies for companies such as vertical integration, along with other innovations that businesses might need to consider in order to mitigate consequences from these risks when structuring their global operations (Zhao et al., 2024).
- *Brexit:* The withdrawal of the United Kingdom from the European Union serves as a key example of how political decisions can impact trade agreements, foreign investment, and corporate strategies. Brexit has required the renegotiation of trade agreements and compliance structures, once again re-

instating the direct link between geopolitics and international business (Kren & Lawless, 2024).

- *Instability in regions such as the Middle East and Latin America:* Regions such as the Middle East and Latin America tend to present instability in terms of the political environment and exchange rates, as well as regulatory unpredictability. These conditions create additional layers of risk for businesses, since they must account for currency fluctuations, policy shifts, and security concerns when evaluating market entry strategies (Li et al., 2021).

These examples corroborate that geopolitical risks influence investment decisions, corporate expansion plans, and various indicators of the overall stability of international markets; without doubt, global economic trends cannot be fully understood without analyzing geopolitical factors. If a company fails to implement geopolitical risk assessments into its strategies, it may encounter operational disruptions, financial losses, and economic uncertainties.

With these challenges in mind, it becomes clear why the analysis of geopolitical risks has become an essential component in the design and implementation of international trade strategies. Ultimately, businesses must adopt adaptive and resilient strategies to face the increasing unpredictability of trade policies, regional stability, and political turmoil, which is only possible by integrating geopolitical risk analysis into corporate strategy and academic research. If successful, these firms will not only navigate uncertainties more efficiently but will also be able to seize new opportunities for growth and expansion, contributing to long-term resilience and competitive advantage in the unpredictable world of international business.

SPILLOVER EFFECTS OF GEOPOLITICAL RISK

When looking to comprehend how geopolitical forces shape international markets, it is of utmost necessity to understand that geopolitical events often have far-reaching consequences that extend beyond their immediate geographic boundaries. This reality leads us to a crucial concept worth exploring: spillover effects.

In economics, spillover effects refer to the unintended consequences of economic activities or events that affect third parties who are not directly involved in the original transaction or decision. According to the International Monetary Fund, "spillovers refer to the impact of shocks or policy changes in one country on another because of the large volume of trade or financial linkages" (International Monetary Fund, 2014, p.3). This definition emphasizes that economic shocks or policy decisions in one nation can have significant repercussions on other countries, particularly when there are strong trade or financial connections between them.

These effects can be either positive or negative and often occur because of the interconnected nature of economic systems. They can be transmitted through various channels, each with varying degrees of influence depending on the nature of the original shock and the vulnerability of the receiving entities. Understanding the typology of spillovers is essential for analyzing how geopolitical tensions, financial crises, or policy changes echo across borders.

Scholars commonly identify three principal factors that can trigger financial contagion: trade linkages, investor behavior, and financial linkages (Claessens & Forbes, 2001; Forbes & Rigobon, 2002; International Monetary Fund, 2016).

- *Trade Linkages*: In terms of financial contagion, trade linkages refer to the economic connections between countries through the exchange of goods and services, for example, in terms of the export/import dependence between them. They come to play when an economic shock in one country affects global supply chains and markets, leading to adverse effects in countries heavily reliant on trade. For example, a sharp decline in the demand for goods from a country experiencing economic distress can lead to lower exports and slower growth in other countries within the same region.
- *Investor behavior*: Investor sentiment often amplifies financial disruptions. When investors perceive that a crisis in one country will affect others, they may react by withdrawing capital or selling assets, even in countries that are not directly impacted by the initial shock. This behavior can create a ripple effect, where financial markets in multiple countries experience downturns as investors seek to minimize risk.
- *Financial Linkages:* In a globalized financial market, banking relationships and capital flows are profoundly interconnected. Consequently, a financial collapse in one region can lead to a domino effect, especially if it is a major financial center. This domino effect usually results in losses for institutions, banks, and international investors.

Two main examples of spillover effects are the 1997 Asian Financial Crisis and the Eurozone Crisis (2010-2012). The 1997 Asian Financial Crisis began in Thailand and quickly spread to neighboring countries, such as Indonesia, South Korea, and Malaysia. The rapid devaluation of currencies, the collapse of stock markets, and the sharp decline in investor confidence were all part of the spillover effects, which not only destabilized Asian economies but also impacted global financial markets. In terms of the Eurozone Crisis, the example of Greece is key, as it describes how fiscal problems in one or two countries can lead to broader instability across a whole region, such as the European Union. Claessens and Forbes analyze this phenomenon in *International Financial Contagion: Theory and Evidence*, where it is evident how spillover effects from other countries in a region have the power to intensify a crisis. In the Eurozone Crisis, concerns over sovereign debt led to declines in investor confidence and triggered capital flight, worsening the stability of the region.

Claessens and Forbes also emphasize in their discussion that the magnitude of spillover effects depends on the strength of said financial and trade linkages, as well as investors' confidence. Aspects that are deeply relevant in a globalized economy, where the risk of contagion is significant and the countries' ability to protect themselves from external shocks is often limited.

In this context, the importance of risk management and early warning systems arises to anticipate and mitigate the effects of spillovers from a financial crisis. Meaning, in the context of geopolitical risk, that companies, policymakers, and investors must consider not only local factors but also the broader, interconnected nature of the global economy when making decisions.

Having mentioned the three factors that can trigger financial contagion, it is now pertinent to continue with how these contagion effects manifest through different channels, impacting global financial markets, trade dynamics, investor behavior, and policy decisions. Understanding the pathways through which such risk spillover occurs is crucial for developing robust economic forecasts and building institutional resilience.

Financial Market Contagion

Financial contagion occurs when economic or political shocks in one country rapidly affect other countries through interconnected financial markets. This channel is particularly potent in the context of high-frequency trading, globalized portfolios, and tightly linked banking systems.

Contagion refers to significant co-movements in asset prices that are not explained by economic fundamentals. During periods of geopolitical stress, uncertainty, and risk aversion heighten, causing investors to rebalance their portfolios, triggering widespread volatility. For instance, the 1997 Asian Financial Crisis demonstrated how investor panic and herd behavior can transmit geopolitical shocks across seemingly unconnected markets (Claessens & Forbes, 2001).

Trade and Supply Chain Disruptions

Geopolitical events, such as sanctions, wars, and diplomatic breakdowns, often impede trade flows and disrupt global supply chains. The transmission mechanism here lies in physical and regulatory barriers to the movement of goods and services.

For example, the Russia-Ukraine war triggered global energy price spikes and shortages, which impacted not only Europe's access to natural gas but also influenced inflation and energy strategies in other continents. Industries reliant on cross-border inputs (e.g., automotive, agriculture, electronics) are particularly vulnerable to such disruptions. These shocks may lead companies to diversify suppliers or reshore production, altering both short- and long-term global trade patterns (Zhao et al., 2024).

Investor Sentiment and Capital Flows

Geopolitical risk also spreads through shifts in investor sentiment, particularly among international asset managers and institutional investors. Increased uncertainty typically results in risk-off behavior, triggering capital flight from emerging markets toward "safe havens" such as U.S. Treasury bonds or the Swiss franc.

During periods of elevated geopolitical tensions, stock markets often experience increased volatility, with emerging markets suffering sharper drawdowns. For example, in the early stages of the Russia-Ukraine conflict, several Eastern European stock indices saw weekly declines exceeding 10%. This response was not always proportionate to the countries' direct exposure to the conflict but was largely driven by changes in investor perception of regional risk (International Monetary Fund, 2025).

Policy and Regulatory Spillovers

This channel involves the indirect effects of geopolitical tensions on policy-making. When a major economy responds to geopolitical threats with regulatory or fiscal changes, other countries may be pressured to follow suit, either to protect domestic industries or to maintain competitiveness. Gallagher and Myers (2020), using the China–Latin America Finance Database, highlight how China's deepening financial ties with Latin America—especially in infrastructure, energy, and digital technology—have prompted governments in the region to reconsider their long-standing economic alignments. For instance, nations such as Brazil, Argentina, and Mexico have adopted more cautious and diversified trade and investment strategies to navigate the growing U.S.–China rivalry. This form of spillover reveals how geopolitical tensions can reshape global governance and regulatory norms, even in countries not directly involved in the conflict.

LITERATURE REVIEW AND BIBLIOMETRIC ANALYSIS

Altogether, these interconnected spillover effects underscore the complexity of navigating a world shaped by increasing geopolitical fragmentation. A deeper understanding of these channels is vital not only for anticipating risk but also for building resilient systems that can absorb and adapt to geopolitical shocks without reproducing cycles of instability.

At this point, we have already explored the historical background of geopolitical studies, as well as the relevance of this field in connection with international trade. Likewise, we confirmed that the contagion of geopolitical risk is not only real but also triggered by a range of catalysts, and that its effects are channeled through various transmission mechanisms. All this reaffirms that understanding geopolitical risks is not only essential but also constitutes a discipline that demands depth and close attention in research, since it relates not only to the prevention and mitigation of these risks but also to the potential development of mechanisms to counteract them. This is particularly valuable and promising when considering future crises that could disrupt the financial environment.

It is precisely in the pursuit of a deeper understanding of geopolitical risks that, in this section of the chapter, we move beyond the historical foundations of geopolitics as a term that is still somewhat distant from the fields of economics and international trade. We now turn our attention to how geopolitics has been studied in relation to financial markets, aiming to identify major research trends and, more importantly, gaps in the academic literature that may point toward promising opportunities for future inquiry. These opportunities, in turn, may contribute to our shared global pursuit of economic stability.

The study was conducted in two main stages. The first stage involved a literature review. It is important to highlight that the literature review in question is a narrative review that focuses on summarizing and identifying publications in the area to identify gaps in the existing literature and propose research opportunities. For the literature review, data was collected from the Web of Science[1] database. A total of 255 documents were obtained after cleaning the results by excluding articles unrelated to finance and related fields. In this stage, each article was carefully reviewed to propose a thematic classification and identify key conclusions in the academic production of recent years. In the second stage, a bibliometric analysis was conducted, allowing the identification of trends in scientific production regarding authors, countries, journals, and collaborations among countries.

Stage 1. Data Collection: The first step involved obtaining articles related to the spillover of geopolitical risk in emerging financial markets. To do so, a search was conducted in the mentioned database using keywords related to the topic, together with the terms "spillover(s)" and "finance" ("Geopolitical risk + spillovers"; "Geopolitical risk + finance"; "Geopolitical risk + emerging markets"). To refine the study, the equation was further refined to "Geopolitical risk + spillovers" and "Geopolitical risk + finance". From this process, 255 documents were identified and downloaded from the 2012 to 2024 time span. The search and download processes were completed on February 22, 2024.

Stage 2. Literature review: The objective of this second stage was to propose a classification of the articles to conduct a literature review. In this case, the documents were analyzed one by one, with an emphasis on three main topics: the relationship between geopolitical risk and financial markets, how geopolitical risk has been studied, and geopolitical risk in the context of emerging markets. From this analysis, recurring themes and notable conclusions were identified, which are detailed in the results section.

Stage 3. Statistical Analysis: In this step, a statistical analysis was performed on the results obtained from the initial search. For this purpose, the *Data table*, *DPLYR*, and *Bibliometrix* packages, which are available in R software, were used. Using these tools, the number of products associated with the topic of this study was identified, along with the leading authors, their nationalities, the journals in which the articles were published, author collaborations, and their respective countries. These inputs were analyzed and led to the findings presented in the next section.

Narrative Literature Review

By carrying out the process outlined in the previous section, a thematic classification of the literature was developed focusing on three primary areas. First, the relationship between geopolitical risk and financial markets is explored. Second, various approaches to studying geopolitical risk are identified, with particular attention to the financial indicators commonly examined. Finally, the specific impact of geopolitical risk on emerging markets is addressed, highlighting the unique challenges and vulnerabilities these economies face in the context of global political dynamics, while also examining the interconnections with developed economies and any potential differences.

The Relationship Between Geopolitical Risk and Financial Markets.

As previously established in this chapter, geopolitical events have been of utmost relevance during critical moments in history when nations' financial security has been impacted. The well-known 2008 financial crisis, the COVID-19 pandemic in 2020, and various market downturns or boosts during political tensions caused by wars or changes in the administration of countries whose economies dictate the economic direction of other nations are prime examples. Throughout the literature review, it has become evident that geopolitical events are not only directly related to the development of financial markets, but the study of this risk (GPR) is crucial because it has been consolidated as one of the main triggers of cross-risk contagion in global financial markets. In this context, it has been found that the volatility of financial markets brought about by geopolitical risk can easily result in significant financial risk contagion across larger financial markets (Acharya et al., 2020; Forbes & Warnock, 2021; Kim & Mehrotra, 2017; Mo et al., 2024), a claim later supported by Adil Shah in his study of the dynamics of connectedness across precious metals, exchange rates, and Crude in terms of frequency and time; where it is demonstrated that the level of contagion and risk reception in the stock market increased significantly during the global financial crisis and the COVID-19 pandemic (Shah et al., 2021).

In this way, we encounter two premises regarding geopolitical risk: that **it can easily impact market volatility and result in financial risk contagion across larger financial markets, implying effects on market liquidity** (Zhang & Hamori, 2022; Chiang, 2021; Le & Tran, 2021); and that **geopolitical events such as COVID-19 or the 2008 financial crisis increase levels of contagion and risk perception in stock markets, which would also ultimately result in an impact on investor sentiment** (Asai et al., 2020; Tiwari et al., 2021), as we are talking about risk perception, which is altered in the face of these tensions linked to geopolitical risk (Bernanke, 1983; Hedstrom et al., 2020; Rodrik, 1991).

These premises naturally lead to the conclusion that if one wishes to better understand the dynamics of the financial market, it is necessary to consider geopolitical risk as a fundamental aspect of this study, as the factors influencing stock market dynamics are not only limited to economic and financial aspects but also include uncertainty-induced factors (Antonakasis et al., 2017; Abel & Eberly, 1999), among which geopolitical risk prominently features (Bagirov & Mateus, 2019; Salisu et al., 2022).

If you recall, we had already—perhaps unknowingly—touched upon these premises in the section on spillover effects, which only serves to reinforce the conclusions we reached at the end of the previous section.

Approaches and Methodologies in Studying Geopolitical Risk

The study of geopolitical risk within the context of finance has undergone a thematic evolution throughout the period covered in the bibliometric analysis results. Among the articles identified in our search, a clear trend emerged that focused on the correlation between geopolitical risk and various economic indicators of nations, as well as the direct impact of geopolitical risk on the economy itself (Bouri et al., 2023; Dong et al., 2023; Kumar et al., 2021; Tamilselvan et al., 2024; Tran & Vo, 2023).

For this purpose, a trend of a series of specific indicators reflecting the financial health of a country was found, such as energy markets—measuring Crude (Gong et al., 2023; Qin et al., 2020) and Brent—, the stock market (Yang & Yang, 2021), the bond market (Lee et al., 2022), and gold (Li et al., 2021); to study the correlation between geopolitical risk and each of these indicators, resulting in five notable conclusions.

First, geopolitical risk has a net transmitter effect on energy markets particularly for natural gas since 2022 (Kumar & Singh, 2022). Second, geopolitical risk acts as a transmitter of risk in the gold market, and gold acts as the receiver of such risk (Baur & Smales, 2018). As a third conclusion, it is found that the impact of geopolitical risk on exchange rates is asymmetric in all cases (Hoque et al., 2023; Long et al., 2021). It has also been found that GPR has an asymmetric effect on returns and volatility in the global Crude market and that geopolitical threats and events have heterogeneous effects on Crude market volatility and returns (Gong et al., 2023). Finally, MIDAS regression models have been used to show that GPR has a lasting negative impact on stock markets (Yang et al., 2021).

Impact of Geopolitical Risk on Emerging Markets

Emerging markets, particularly the BRICS countries, have driven rapid economic growth, representing over 40% of the global population and nearly 30% of global GDP (International Monetary Fund, 2014). However, their vulnerability makes them more exposed to geopolitical risks and price declines, especially during periods of increased global risk aversion (Hoque, 2020; Wilkinson, 2013).

In this context, various studies have used MIDAS regression models (Salisu et al., 2022), Markov-switching models (Hoque, 2020), vector autoregression processes (Nguyen et al., 2022; Zhang & Hamori, 2022), and the panel GARCH model (Dong et al., 2023), among others, demonstrated that geopolitical risk has a considerable effect on emerging economies and influences the network system between these countries. Through connectivity analysis, it has been found that geopolitical risk in China and Russia significantly impacts their respective systems in terms of market volatility and returns. Furthermore, correlations have been found between shocks in terms of geopolitical risk in emerging economies and the macroeconomic system of developed countries, such as the United States (Bouri et al., 2023; Cheng & Chiu, 2018). It was found (Rao et al., 2023) that there is a strong relationship between geopolitical risk in Russia, Brazil, and India is strongly related to the financial market of the United States. A curious finding has been that geopolitical risk in China has lesser impacts on the U.S.'s macroeconomy than the other aforementioned countries (Yang et al., 2022), to the extent that investors and policymakers have found paying excessive attention to geopolitical risk in the Asian giant to be ineffective.

Now, concerning the strong relationship mentioned between geopolitical risk in Russia, Brazil, and India with the financial market of the United States, it is worth mentioning that the same studies that have found this relationship among these three BRICS countries and the US macroeconomy have identified a strong interdependence between the oil market and the stock market in these countries (Wang et al., 2021), with WTI and the S&P 500 being the major contributors to each other in terms of volatility and returns systems, and in turn, a strong interdependence between these two markets and geopolitical risk.

Bibliometric Analysis

Following the outlined stages, the next step after the literature review was a bibliometric analysis aimed at identifying patterns in the number of articles on geopolitical risk in financial markets between 2012 and 2024. This analysis also focused on the journals where this scientific production has been published, the nationalities of the authors, the collaboration between the countries of origin of these authors, and the development and relevance of the themes.

Regarding the number of published articles, a clear upward trend in scientific production on geopolitical risk in financial markets was observed (Figure 1), with a rapid acceleration starting in 2021. With an annual percentage growth rate of 44.52%, this growth serves as evidence that the study of the impact of geopolitical risk on financial markets is an increasingly relevant topic. Additionally, it can be speculated that the COVID-19 pandemic, which had significant global economic impacts, may have acted as a catalyst for the surge in studies related to this subject from 2021 onward.

Figure 1. Number of Articles per Year Related to Geopolitical Risk in Financial Markets.

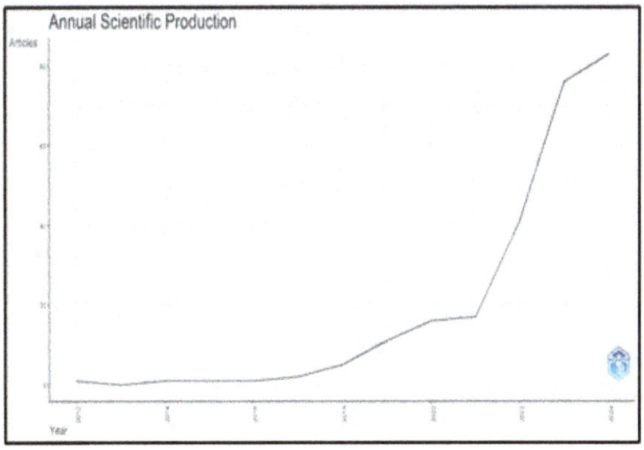

Source: Bibliometrix (2024).

The number of citations per year (Figure 2) has shown a significant increase compared with previous years, with average citations increasing since 2015. Notably, there were considerable peaks in 2020 and 2022 that could be linked to the impact of the COVID-19 pandemic on the scientific community, as noted in Figure

1. These spikes may reflect the growing attention to geopolitical risk studies as the global economic situation evolved in those years.

Figure 2. Number of Average Citations per Year.

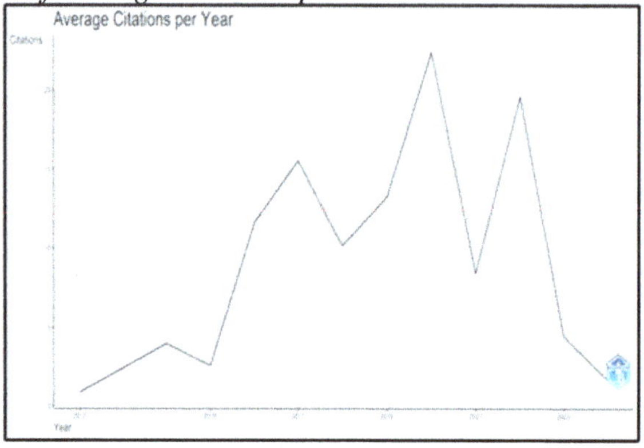

Source: Bibliometrix (2024).

Moving on to the author analysis, it was found that the most prolific authors, in terms of the number of articles, were Gupta R. and Bouri E., with 15 and 11 articles each, respectively (Figure 3). There is no significant concentration of publications among a few authors, as illustrated in Figure 4, with the top authors contributing only up to 15 articles (5.9% of the total sample). This aligns with the h-index analysis for leading authors, showing a direct correlation between authors with higher publication counts and greater citation impact (Figure 5).

Figure 3. Number of Articles per Author.

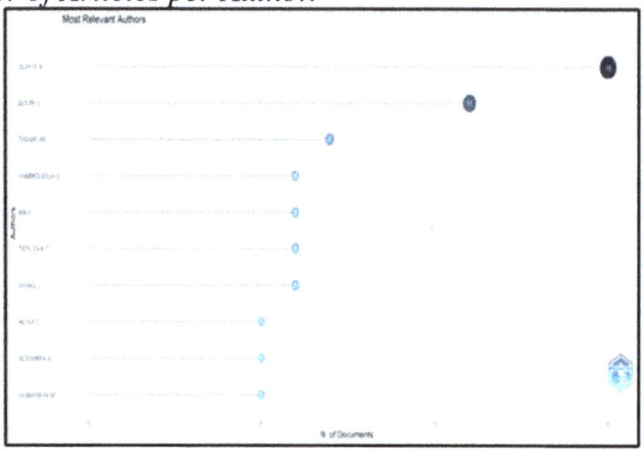

Source: Bibliometrix (2024).

Figure 4. Author Productivity Through Lotka's Law.

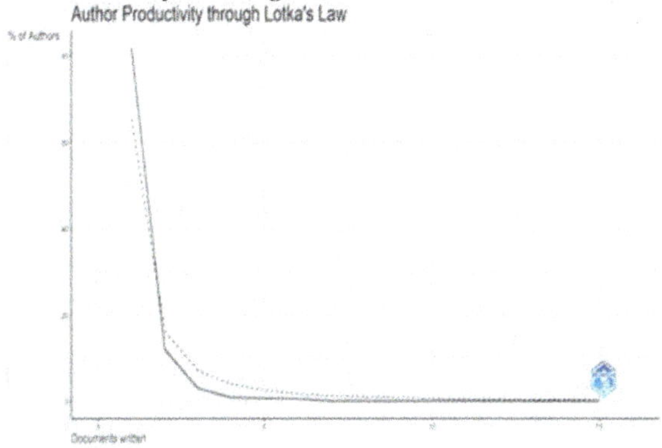

Source: Bibliometrix (2024).

Figure 5. H-index for Author's Local Impact.

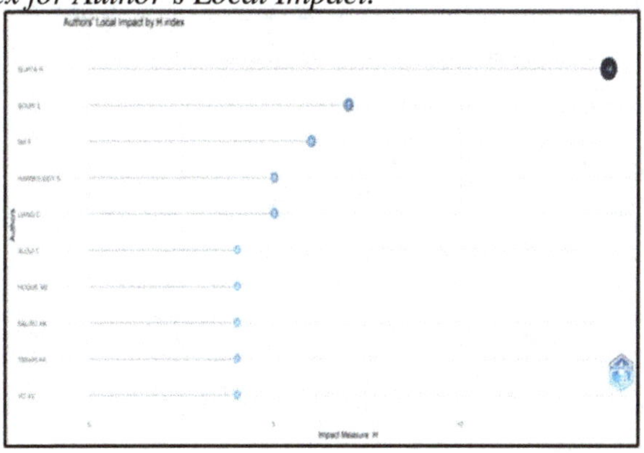

Source: Bibliometrix (2024).

Turning to the analysis of article counts by the authors' countries of origin, clear trends emerge in the scientific output on geopolitical risk and financial markets. In this case, as shown in Figure 6, authors from China, the United States, and the United Kingdom represent 70.3% of the total articles in the sample. It is worth noting that in most cases, articles authored from these countries involve contributions from individuals of a single nationality (Figure 7).

Figure 6. Number of Articles per Author's Corresponding Country.

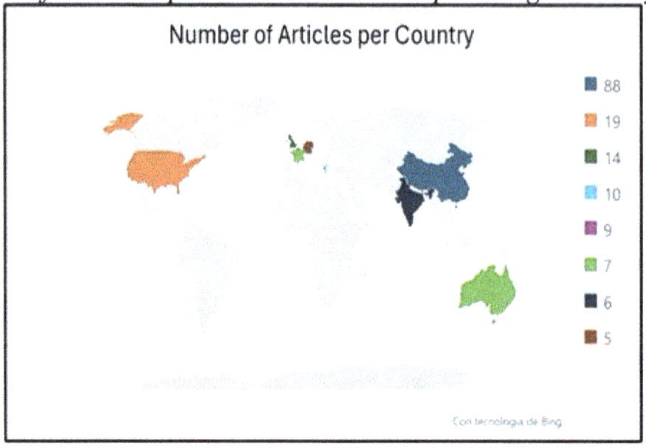

Source: Authors' own work.

Figure 7. Number of Articles per Author's Corresponding Country.

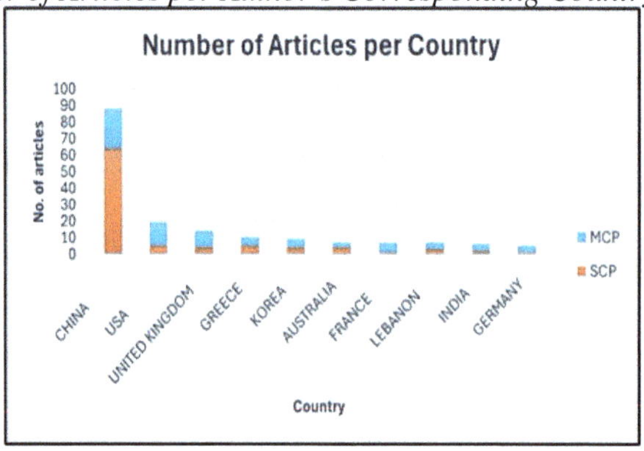

Source: Authors' own work.

Regarding impact, similar to the authors' analysis, the most frequently cited countries are those with a higher number of publications. This trend is clearly shown in Figure 8.

Figure 8. No. of Citations per Country.

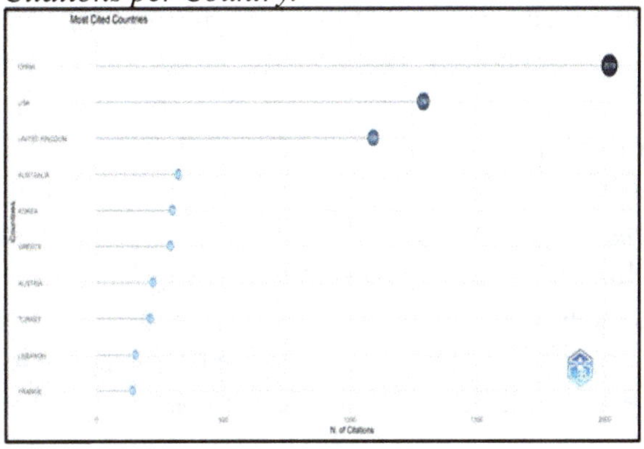

Source: Bibliometrix (2024).

The concentration of production by country is further supported by an analysis of the network of international collaborations in the article sample (Figure 9). China, the United Kingdom, and the U.S. show the highest levels of collaboration, particularly with other European and Asian countries such as France, Australia, and Greece, as well as South Africa.

Figure 9. Country Collaboration.

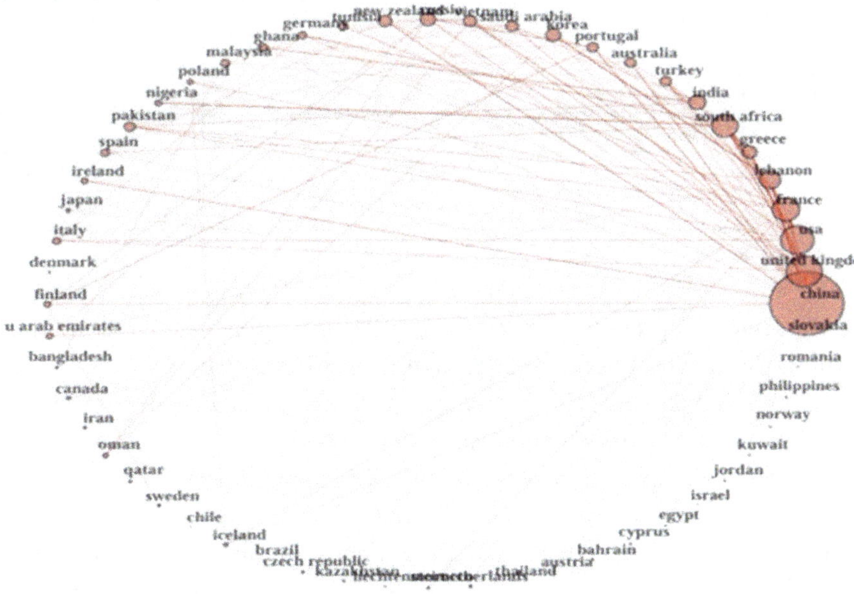

Source: Bibliometrix (2024).

Based on the recent analysis in Figures 8 and 9, there is a clear trend towards a high concentration of academic output on geopolitical risk and financial markets within a small group of countries. Given the importance of each nation's political factors in this area, along with the significance of scientific output in these studies, strengthening partnerships among countries and exploring new collaborations with authors from diverse nations is essential, as a fair amount of them remains unexplored.

Upon analyzing the various academic journals in which the reviewed articles are published (Table 1), it is evident that the vast majority of these journals, if not all, are directly related to economics and finance, with a particular emphasis on energy resources, markets, and technologies, which corresponds to the journal with the highest number of publications in *Energy Economics*.

Table 1. Number of Publications per Source.

Source	**# of PRODUCTS**	**%**
ENERGY ECONOMICS	37	14,51
FINANCIAL RESEARCH LETTERS	28	10,98
INTERNATIONAL REVIEW OF FINANCIAL ANALYSIS	20	7,84
INTERNATIONAL REVIEW OF ECONOMICS & FINANCE	13	5,10
DEFENCE AND PEACE ECONOMICS	12	4,71
NORTH AMERICAN JOURNAL OF ECONOMICS AND FINANCE	11	4,31
RESEARCH IN INTERNATIONAL BUSINESS AND FINANCE	11	4,31
APPLIED ECONOMICS	8	3,14
ECONOMIC ANALYSIS AND POLICY	7	2,75
EMERGING MARKETS FINANCE AND TRADE	7	2,75
OTHERS	101	39,61
TOTAL	255	100

Source: Authors' own work.

Finally, Figure 10 presents a thematic map illustrating the results of the study, which highlights the most developed and significant themes in the literature. Topics with high development and relevance are primarily associated with volatility and stock-market dynamics. Meanwhile, some themes—though relevant—are not as extensively developed in terms of scientific output, such as those related to oil and impulse-response analysis. Additionally, the map identifies a niche theme centered on terror attacks, which reveals a specialized interest in this area, although not as relevant-. There is also evidence of a declining trend in the focus on geopolitical risk within corporate environments, in contrast to its traditionally broader association with macroeconomic impacts.

Figure 10. Thematic Map.

SOURCE	# of PRODUCTS	%
ENERGY ECONOMICS	37	14,51
FINANCE RESEARCH LETTERS	28	10,98
INTERNATIONAL REVIEW OF FINANCIAL ANALYSIS	20	7,84
INTERNATIONAL REVIEW OF ECONOMICS & FINANCE	13	5,10
DEFENCE AND PEACE ECONOMICS	12	4,71
NORTH AMERICAN JOURNAL OF ECONOMICS AND FINANCE	11	4,31
RESEARCH IN INTERNATIONAL BUSINESS AND FINANCE	11	4,31
APPLIED ECONOMICS	8	3,14
ECONOMIC ANALYSIS AND POLICY	7	2,75
EMERGING MARKETS FINANCE AND TRADE	7	2,75
OTHERS	101	39,61
TOTAL	255	100

Source: Bibliometrix (2024).

EMERGENT TRENDS AND RESEARCH GAPS

As pointed out in the introduction of this chapter, the mission of this dissertation has been to explore how geopolitical risk impacts global financial markets while identifying possible emerging trends in the topic. It also aims to reveal key areas in which existing research is lacking and propose new avenues for investigation.

First, some research opportunities arise from the increasing relevance of the topic and are strengthened by the existing deficiencies in the development of certain thematic areas, such as the energy market, particularly the commodities market related to oil. The underexplored dynamics of energy markets, especially oil, in relation to geopolitical events is a significant gap in the literature. Despite the centrality of oil in global financial markets, a limited understanding exists of how geopolitical risk influences oil prices and the subsequent effects on global financial stability. This gap is even more pertinent in the context of recent events, such as the COVID-19 pandemic and geopolitical tensions, which have had a profound impact on oil production and global supply chains. Future studies could delve deeper into how geopolitical risks associated with energy-producing nations influence fluctuations in oil prices and market stability, offering valuable insights for investors and policymakers alike.

Additionally, there is still a lack of extensive development regarding the spillover of volatility, a topic that could yield interesting insights in future studies. Volatility spillovers refer to how shocks in one market, such as oil prices, can be transmitted to other markets, including equities, currencies, and bonds. While some research has explored these spillover effects (Diebold & Yilmaz, 2012; Kang et al., 2015), the literature remains limited in addressing the broader implications of geopolitical risks on volatility transmission. This gap presents an exciting opportunity for further exploration, particularly as the global interconnectedness of financial markets continues to evolve. For example, an analysis of volatility spillovers from recent energy crises, particularly disruptions caused by geopolitical tensions in the Middle East and Eastern Europe, could offer a deeper understanding of how financial markets respond to geopolitical shocks and their cascading effects across borders (Aloui et al., 2013; Antonakakis et al., 2017).

On the other hand, the bibliometric analysis revealed a significant concentration of academic production in developed economies, particularly in the United States, the United Kingdom, and China. These countries have historically been at the forefront of geopolitical risk research, largely due to their economic dominance and the global influence of their financial markets. However, emerging markets, particularly the BRICS countries—excepting China—and Latin American markets show almost negligible academic output. This geographic disparity in production indicates an area for future research to explore the reasons behind this imbalance and its potential implications for global financial markets. Several factors may contribute to this imbalance, including differences in research funding, institutional support, and the relative importance of geopolitical risk in these regions. A deeper exploration into the reasons for this geographic concentration could provide valuable insights into how emerging markets perceive and are impacted by geopolitical risks. Additionally, these findings highlight potential areas for greater international collaboration in research efforts (Jiménez, 2024).

Furthermore, when examining energy markets and oil, African countries present another promising avenue for research, particularly concerning the possible relationship between the internal policies of these nations and their effects on global oil prices. These countries, especially major oil exporters like Nigeria, Angola, and Libya, often face significant geopolitical challenges, including political instability, corruption, and internal conflict, which can directly impact global oil production and price volatility (Chen, 2023). The internal policies of these nations—such as nationalization efforts, fiscal reforms, and shifts in production-sharing agreements with international oil firms—frequently alter both output levels and market expectations. For instance, in Nigeria, the enactment of the Petroleum Industry Act (2021), which aimed to restructure the oil sector and attract foreign investment, has had far-reaching implications on production incentives and investor sentiment (Mo et al., 2024). Similarly, in Libya, recurring civil conflict and attacks on oil infrastructure have led to unpredictable supply disruptions that contribute to price spikes in global oil benchmarks like Brent Crude. These cases highlight the importance of understanding how domestic geopolitical risks in African oil-producing countries affect global markets. Such dynamics not only influence the pricing and supply of energy but also generate financial contagion through their effects on commodity-linked currencies, energy stocks, and sovereign bonds. This could lead to a more nuanced understanding of how geopolitical events in African nations can disrupt global energy markets and, in turn, affect financial markets worldwide.

Another important trend identified is the impact of geopolitical risk across different regions or market types. Comparative studies are just emerging, offering especially promising areas for further investigation. A clear example is the article "Geopolitical Risk and Trade Reorientation Dynamics: A Comparative Study" (Nazir et al., 2025), which assesses how geopolitical risk affects intrabloc trade in three major economic blocs: BRICS, G7 (advanced economies), and ASEAN (Southeast Asian bloc). In this study, the authors cover a time frame from January 2000 to June 2023 and use cross-quantilogram and partial cross-quantilogram techniques to detect dynamic and asymmetric effects across quantiles. The results (Table 2) demonstrate that geopolitical shocks strengthen intraregional trade integration in the BRICS bloc, while G7 countries show lower resistance and greater disruption—and ASEAN exhibits a cautious, short-run decline in trade integration. These carry clear implications for both policymakers and investors, illustrating the value of comparative frameworks in understanding differentiated GPR impacts across markets and guiding targeted policy and investment responses.

Table 2. Comparative Framework Findings.

Bloc	Trade Integration Response	Comparative Characteristics	Implications for Policy and Strategy
BRICS	Positive response to geopolitical risk – trade integration strengthened at low-to-medium levels of risk and within a 12–36-month lag.	Shared identity and mutual interest foster resilience.	May benefit from strategies that leverage shared geopolitical identity for trade resilience.
G7	Show lower resistance to geopolitical uncertainty, implying more disruption to trade integration compared to BRICS.	Less adaptative to geopolitical shocks.	Institutional frameworks to mitigate trade disruptions should be strengthened. Diversification, supply chain robustness, and coordinated diplomacy are advised approaches.
ASEAN	Cautious short-term response: higher risk leads to temporary declines in trade integration.	Sensitive to immediate risk changes.	Intervention to sustain integration during short-term upheaval might be considered.

Source: Author's own work.

These proposals have limitations that should be considered for future studies. First, the analysis was based solely on the Web of Science database for the bibliometric analysis and literature review. The Web of Science is a highly reputable source; however, incorporating additional databases, such as Scopus, could help confirm and strengthen the findings presented here. A broader search across multiple databases would increase the robustness of the findings and provide a more comprehensive view of the state of geopolitical risk research. Moreover, expanding the search criteria to include gray literature or working papers could further uncover new and emerging trends that may not yet be fully represented in peer-reviewed journals.

Additionally, it would be valuable to delve deeper into the dynamics of the scientific community in different countries to gain further insights into the concentration of academic production in specific countries with particular economies. Understanding motivations, funding structures and research priorities in these countries could help identify why certain regions are more active in researching geopolitical risk and its impact on financial markets. This could provide a more comprehensive understanding of the global research landscape, enabling the development of strategies to strengthen international collaboration on geopolitical risk and financial markets research. Exploring these dynamics would contribute to a more balanced and inclusive academic dialog, addressing the underrepresentation of emerging markets and fostering a more global approach to studying geopolitical risk.

CONCLUSIONS

This chapter explored the complex and multifaceted relationship between geopolitical risk (GPR) and its profound impact on international trade and financial markets. We began by tracing the origins and evolution of the concept of geopolitics, highlighting its transformation from early 20th-century academic thought to a modern discipline deeply intertwined with economic and political considerations. As geopolitical risk has increasingly shaped global trade dynamics, it has become evident that understanding this risk is no longer optional for businesses and policymakers; it is essential.

We then stated that the importance of geopolitical risk in international trade cannot be overstated because it directly influences key economic factors, including trade policies, market access, supply chain stability, and investment security. As evidenced by recent disruptions such as the Russia-Ukraine conflict, the U.S.-China trade rivalry, and the aftermath of Brexit, geopolitical factors are now fundamental drivers of market volatility. In this context, it is undeniable that companies and nations must adapt their strategies to account for the unpredictable shifts in political and economic landscapes. These historical and contemporary examples underscore the need for robust geopolitical risk analysis to navigate the complexities of global business environments.

In the third section of this chapter, it then became clear that the importance of understanding how geopolitical events influence financial markets has only grown, as these risks are no longer confined to isolated regions but have the potential to ripple across borders and disrupt global economic stability. Geopolitical events can have cascading effects, leading to volatility spillovers across various financial markets. These spillover effects, driven by both channels (such as financial market contagion, trade and supply chain disruptions, investor sentiment and capital flows, and policy and regulatory spillovers) and triggers (e.g., trade linkages, investor behavior, and financial linkages), show how one country's economic or political event can resonate across borders. In particular, disruptions in oil production, such as those seen in the Middle East and Eastern Europe, can cause significant volatility in global markets, affecting stock prices, exchange rates, and other commodities. However, while some studies have explored these spillover effects, much remains to be understood about the full breadth of how GPR triggers these dynamics, especially in emerging markets. This is a critical area for further research as global interconnectedness among markets continues to evolve, creating new potential for cross-border transmission of financial shocks.

Moving forward to the literature review and bibliometric analysis, we identified key trends in academic research related to GPR and financial markets. The findings pointed to a growing body of work, particularly after the year 2021, on the impact of geopolitical risks on energy markets, stock markets, and commodities like gold. However, there are significant gaps in research, particularly when it comes to emerging economies and regions like Africa, where geopolitical challenges directly influence oil production and prices. This geographic disparity in research underscores the need for further academic attention to these areas because their implications for global financial systems remain underexplored.

Finally, by examining emerging trends and research gaps, we identified the critical need for more comprehensive studies on volatility spillovers, particularly concerning the energy sector. Despite the growing body of work on GPR, there remains a lack of in-depth research into how these risks are transmitted across global markets. As energy markets continue to evolve and geopolitical tensions shape production and supply, the potential for volatility spillovers in markets like oil, gas, and renewables represent an exciting opportunity for future research. Understanding these contagion effects and the channels and triggers that amplify them is essential for mitigating risks and enhancing market resilience.

The future of research in this field offers promising opportunities to deepen our understanding of these dynamics and their implications for global economic stability. By addressing these gaps, scholars can contribute valuable insights into the complex nature of geopolitical risks and their far-reaching effects on international trade and financial systems.

In sum, this chapter illuminates the critical role of geopolitical risk in shaping international trade and financial markets. As the global interconnectedness of markets continues to evolve, the need for comprehensive geopolitical risk assessment in both academic and business contexts will only grow. The insights drawn from this exploration point to a promising avenue for future research that could help uncover the complexities of geopolitical risk transmission, its impact on global financial stability, and its profound influence on international trade dynamics. In conclusion, integrating GPR into trade and finance models is not just an academic necessity but also a practical imperative for policymakers, businesses, and investors to navigate the complexities of a volatile global landscape.

ACKNOWLEDGEMENTS

The authors are deeply grateful for the assistance provided by Jesús E. Molina, professor in the Department of Accounting and Finance at the Instituto Tecnológico y de Estudios Superiores de Monterrey. The authors are also profoundly appreciative of the support offered by Universidad del Rosario in proofreading.

REFERENCES

Abel, A. B., & Eberly, J. C. (1999). The effects of irreversibility and uncertainty on capital accumulation. *Journal of Monetary Economics*, *44*(3), 339–377. DOI: 10.1016/S0304-3932(99)00029-X

Acharya, V. V., Bhadury, S., & Surti, J. (2020). Financial vulnerability and risks to growth in emerging markets (CEPR Discussion Paper No. DP14962). https://ssrn.com/abstract=3638068

Aloui, R., Ben Aïssa, M. S., & Nguyen, D. K. (2013). Conditional dependence structure between oil prices and exchange rates: A copula-GARCH approach. *Journal of International Financial Markets, Institutions and Money*, *32*, 719–738. DOI: 10.1016/j.jimonfin.2012.06.006

Antonakakis, N., Gupta, R., Kollias, C., & Papadamou, S. (2017). Geopolitical risks and the oil-stock nexus over 1899-2016. *Finance Research Letters*, *23*, 165–173. DOI: 10.1016/j.frl.2017.07.017

Anzo, E. (2012). Negocios internacionales: Evolución, consolidación e identificación de los temas que lideran el campo de investigación. *Revista Ciencias Estratégicas*, *20*(27), 77–93.

Asai, M., Gupta, R., & McAleer, M. (2020). Forecasting volatility and co-volatility of crude oil and gold futures: Effects of leverage, jumps, spillovers, and geopolitical risks. *International Journal of Forecasting*, *36*(3), 933–948. DOI: 10.1016/j.ijforecast.2019.10.003

Atradius N.V. (February 21, 2024). *Trade War is Having a Profound Effect on Global Trade*. [Web article].

Baena-Rojas, J. J., & Bonilla-Calle, D. (2021). Revisión contextual para la interpretación del análisis de riesgo geopolítico. *Revista de Ciencias Sociales*, *27*(1), 12–28.

Bagirov, M., & Mateus, C. (2019). Oil prices, stock markets and firm performance: Evidence from Europe. *International Review of Economics & Finance, 61*, 270–288. DOI: 10.1016/j.iref.2019.02.007

Bank of England. (2021). *How Has COVID Affected Global Trade?* [Web article].

Baten, J. (Ed.). (2016). *A history of the global economy: From 1500 to the present.* Cambridge University Press.

Baur, D. G., & Smales, L. A. (2018). Gold and geopolitical risk: A safe haven? *The Quarterly Review of Economics and Finance, 70*, 279–288. DOI: 10.1016/j.qref.2018.07.004

Bernanke, B. S. (1983). Nonmonetary Effects of the Financial Crisis in the Propagation of the Great Depression. *The American Economic Review, 73*(3), 257–276. https://www.jstor.org/stable/1808111

Bohl, D. K., Hanna, T. L., Mapes, B. R., Moyer, J. D., Narayan, K., & Wasif, K. (2017). *Understanding and forecasting geopolitical risks and benefits.* Frederick S. Pardee Center for International Futures, Josef Korbel School of International Studies, University of Denver. https://doi.org/DOI: 10.2139/ssrn.3941439

Bouri, E., Hammoud, R., & Abou Kassm, C. (2023). The Effect of Oil Implied Volatility and Geopolitical Risk on GCC Stock Sectors Under Various Market Conditions. *Energy Economics, 106*, 106617. DOI: 10.1016/j.eneco.2023.106617

Bustillo, R. (2022, 13 de diciembre). Geopolítica y economía: imposible entender una sin la otra. *LISA News.*

Caldara, D., & Iacoviello, M. (2022). Measuring Geopolitical Risk. *The American Economic Review, 112*(4), 1194–1225. DOI: 10.1257/aer.20191823

Chen, X. (2023). Are the Shocks of EPU, VIX, and GPR Indexes on The Oil-stock Nexus Alike? A Time-frequency Analysis. *Applied Economics, 55*(29), 3587–3601. DOI: 10.1080/00036846.2022.2140115

Cheng, C. H. J., & Chiu, C. W. J. (2018). How important are global geopolitical risks to emerging countries? *Inter Economics, 156*, 305–325. DOI: 10.1016/j.inteco.2018.05.002

Chiang, T. C. (2021). Spillovers of U.S. market volatility and monetary policy uncertainty to global stock markets. *The North American Journal of Economics and Finance, 58*, 101523. DOI: 10.1016/j.najef.2021.101523

Claessens, S., & Forbes, K. J. (Eds.). (2001). *International Financial Contagion.* Springer., DOI: 10.1007/978-1-4757-3314-3

Dalby, S. (1991). Critical Geopolitics: Discourse, Difference, and Dissent. *Environment and Planning. D, Society & Space*, *9*(3), 261–283.

Daniels, J. D., Radebaugh, L. H., & Sullivan, D. P. (2007). *International business: Environments and operations* (11th ed.). Pearson Education.

Diebold, F. X., & Yilmaz, K. (2012). Better to give than to receive: Predictive directional measurement of volatility spillovers. *International Journal of Forecasting*, *28*(1), 57–66. DOI: 10.1016/j.ijforecast.2011.02.006

Dong, Q., Huo, D., & Wang, K. (2023). Risk Measurement and Application of the International Carbon Market in the Era of Global Conflict: A Data-driven Study Using FCM. *Journal of Environmental Management*, *345*, 118251. DOI: 10.1016/j.jenvman.2023.118251

Engle, R. F., & Campos-Martins, S. (2020). *Measuring and hedging geopolitical risk* (NIPE Working Papers No. 08/2020). NIPE – Universidade do Minho. https://doi.org/DOI: 10.2139/ssrn.3685213

Flint, C. (2016). *Introduction to geopolitics* (3rd ed.). Routledge.

Forbes, K. J., & Rigobon, R. (2002). No Contagion, Only Interdependence: Measuring Stock Market Comovements. *The Journal of Finance*, *57*(5), 2223–2261. DOI: 10.1111/0022-1082.00494

Forbes, K. J., & Warnock, F. E. (2021). Capital flow waves—Or ripples? Extreme capital flow movements since the crisis. *Journal of International Money and Finance*, *116*, 102394. DOI: 10.1016/j.jimonfin.2021.102394

Gallagher, K. P., & Myers, M. (2020). *China–Latin America Finance Database*. Inter-American Dialogue.

Góes, C., & Bekkers, E. (2022). *The Impact of Geopolitical Conflicts on Trade, Growth, and Innovation.* World Trade Organization https://www.wto.org/english/res_e/reser_e/ersd202209_e.htm

Gong, X.-L., Feng, Y.-K., Liu, J.-M., & Xiong, X. (2023). Study on international energy market and geopolitical risk contagion based on complex network. *Resources Policy*, *82*, 103495. DOI: 10.1016/j.resourpol.2023.103495

Hedstrom, A., Zelander, N., Junttila, J., & Uddin, G. S. (2020). Emerging Market Contagion under Geopolitical Uncertainty. *Emerging Markets Finance & Trade*, *56*(5), 1083–1099. DOI: 10.1080/1540496X.2018.1562895

Hoque, M. E. (2020). Global and country-specific geopolitical risk uncertainty and stock return of fragile emerging economies. *Journal of Economics and Business, 113*, 105926. DOI: 10.1016/j.jeconbus.2020.105926

Hoque, M. E., Soo-Wah, L., Uddin, M. A., & Rahman, A. (2023). International Trade Policy Uncertainty Spillover on Stock Market: Evidence from Five Fragile Economies. *Journal of International Financial Markets, Institutions and Money, 84*, 2072520. DOI: 10.1080/09638199.2022.2072520

Hossain, M. S., Voumik, L. C., Ahmed, T. T., Alam, M. B., & Tasmim, Z. (2024). Impact of Geopolitical Risk, GDP, Inflation, Interest Rate, and Trade Openness on Foreign Direct Investment: Evidence from Five Southeast Asian Countries. *Regional Sustainability, 5*(1), 100177. DOI: 10.1016/j.regsus.2024.100177

Ianchovichina, E. (2016). *Economic costs of post-Arab-Spring civil wars in the Middle East and North Africa*. Instituto Europeo del Mediterráneo (IEMed).

International Monetary Fund. (2014). *2014 Spillover Report*. [Web article].

International Monetary Fund. (2016). *2016 Spillover Chapter*. [Web article].

International Monetary Fund. (2025). *Global Financial Stability Report: Navigating Geopolitical Risks*. [Web article].

Irwin, D. A. (2012). *Trade policy disaster: Lessons from the 1930s*. MIT Press.

Jiménez, A. (2024, 10 de octubre). *Cómo afrontar un mundo de riesgos interconectados*. KPMG Tendencias.

Kang, W., Ratti, R. A., & Yoon, K. H. (2015). The impact of oil price shocks on the stock market return and volatility relationship. *Journal of International Financial Markets, Institutions and Money, 34*, 41–54. DOI: 10.1016/j.intfin.2014.11.002

Kim, S., & Mehrotra, A. (2017). *Effects of monetary and macro-prudential policies – evidence from inflation targeting economies in the Asia-Pacific region and potential implications for China* (BOFIT Discussion Papers No. 4/2017). Bank of Finland Institute for Economies in Transition (BOFIT). https://ideas.repec.org/p/zbw/bofitp/bdp2017_004.html

Krastev, I., & Leonard, M. (2014). *The New European Disorder*. European Council on Foreign Relations.

Kren, J., & Lawless, M. (2024). How Has Brexit Changed EU–UK Trade Flows? *European Economic Review, 161*, 104634. DOI: 10.1016/j.euroecorev.2023.104634

Kumar, P., & Singh, V. K. (2022). Does Crude Oil Fire the Emerging Markets Currencies Contagion Spillover? A Systemic Perspective. *Energy Economics*, *110*, 106384. DOI: 10.1016/j.eneco.2022.106384

Kumar, S., Khalfaoui, R., & Tiwari, A. K. (2021). Does Geopolitical Risk Improve the Directional Predictability from Oil to Stock Returns? Evidence from Oil-exporting and Oil-importing Countries. *Resources Policy*, *74*, 102253. DOI: 10.1016/j.resourpol.2021.102253

Le, T. P. T. D., & Tran, H. L. M. (2021). The contagion effect from U.S. stock market to the Vietnamese and the Philippine stock markets: The evidence of DCC–GARCH model. *The Journal of Asian Finance, Economics and Business*, *8*(2), 759–770. DOI: 10.13106/jafeb.2021.vol8.no2.0759

Lee, C.-C., Tang, H., & Li, D. (2022). The roles of oil shocks and geopolitical uncertainties on China's green bond returns. *Economic Analysis and Policy*, *74*, 494–505. DOI: 10.1016/j.eap.2022.03.008

Li, Y., Huang, J., & Chen, J. (2021). Dynamic Spillovers of Geopolitical Risks and Gold Prices: New Evidence from 18 Emerging Economies. *Resources Policy*, *71*, 101938. DOI: 10.1016/j.resourpol.2020.101938

Long, T. Q., Nguyen, L. H., & Morgan, P. J. (2021). Dynamic Connectedness of Financial Stress Across Advanced and Emerging Economies: Evidence from Time and Frequency Domains. *International Journal of Economics and Financial Issues*, *11*(6), 1–15. DOI: 10.1142/S0217590821410125

Mackinder, H. J. (1904). The Geographical Pivot of History. *The Geographical Journal*, *23*(4), 421–437.

Mamman, S. O., Wang, Z., & Iliyasu, J. (2023). Commonality in BRICS Stock Markets' Reaction to Global Economic Policy Uncertainty: Evidence from a Panel GARCH Model with Cross-Sectional Dependence. *Finance Research Letters*, *50*, 103877. DOI: 10.1016/j.frl.2023.103877

Mo, B., Zeng, H., Meng, J., & Ding, S. (2024). The Connectedness Between Uncertainty and Exchange Rates of Oil Import Countries: New Evidence from Time and Frequency Perspective. *Resources Policy*, *79*, 104398. DOI: 10.1016/j.resourpol.2023.104398

Nazir, S., Sohag, K., & Mariev, O. (2025). Geopolitical Risk and Trade Reorientation Dynamics: A Comparative Study. *Emerging Markets Finance & Trade*, *61*(8), 2338–2359. DOI: 10.1080/1540496X.2025.2451188

Nguyen, T. T. T., Pham, B. T., & Sala, H. (2022). Being an Emerging Economy: To What Extent Do Geopolitical Risks Hamper Technology and FDI Inflows? *Economic Analysis and Policy*, *74*, 123–134. DOI: 10.1016/j.eap.2022.04.005

Ó Tuathail, G. (1996). *Critical geopolitics: The Politics of Writing Global Space*. University of Minnesota Press.

Qin, Y., Hong, K., Chen, J., & Zhang, Z. (2020). Asymmetric effects of geopolitical risks on energy returns and volatility under different market conditions. *Energy Economics*, *90*, 104851. DOI: 10.1016/j.eneco.2020.104851

Rajagopal. (2007). *Dynamics of international trade and economy: An inquiry into emerging markets.* Nova Science Publishers Inc. ISBN 1-60021-171-9

Ramonet, I. (1999). *Géopolitique du chaos* [**The geopolitics of chaos**] (translation by the author). Paris: Éditions Gallimard. ISBN 978-2-07-041113-9

Rao, A., Lucey, B., & Kumar, S. (2023). Climate Risk and Carbon Emissions: Examining Their Impact on Key Energy Markets Through Asymmetric Spillovers. *Energy Economics*, *107*, 106970. DOI: 10.1016/j.eneco.2023.106970

Rodrik, D. (1991). Policy uncertainty and private investment in developing countries. *Journal of Development Economics*, *36*(2), 229–242. DOI: 10.1016/0304-3878(91)90034-S

Salisu, A. A., Ogbonna, A. E., Lasisi, L., & Olaniran, A. (2022). Geopolitical Risk and Stock Market Volatility in Emerging Markets: A GARCH-MIDAS Approach. *The North American Journal of Economics and Finance*, *59*, 101755. DOI: 10.1016/j.najef.2022.101755

Shah, A. A., Paul, M., Bhanja, N., & Dar, A. B. (2021). Dynamics of connectedness across crude oil, precious metals and exchange rate: Evidence from time and frequency domains. *Resources Policy*, *73*, 102154. DOI: 10.1016/j.resourpol.2021.102154

Tamilselvan, M., Halder, A., & Kannadhasan, M. (2024). Exploring the Ingredients, Mixtures, and Inclinations of Geopolitical Risk. *International Review of Economics & Finance*, *80*, 1–13. DOI: 10.1016/j.iref.2023.11.009

Tiwari, A. K., Mishra, B. R., & Solarin, S. A. (2021). Analysing the spillovers between crude oil prices, stock prices and metal prices: The importance of frequency domain in USA. *Energy*, *220*, 119732. DOI: 10.1016/j.energy.2020.119732

Tran, M. P.-B., & Vo, D. H. (2023). Market Return Spillover from the US to the Asia-Pacific Countries: The Role of Geopolitical Risk and the Information & Communication Technologies. *PLoS One, 18*(12), e0290680. DOI: 10.1371/journal.pone.0290680

Wang, L., Ma, F., Niu, T., & Liang, C. (2021). The importance of extreme shock: Examining the effect of investor sentiment on the crude oil futures market. *Energy Economics, 99*, 105319. DOI: 10.1016/j.eneco.2021.105319

Wilkinson, R., & Weiss, T. G. (Eds.). (2013). *International organization and global governance*. Routledge., DOI: 10.4324/9780203795972

World Bank. (2022). *The Impact of the War in Ukraine on Global Trade and Investment.*

Yang, C., Niu, Z., & Gao, W. (2022). The time-varying effects of trade policy uncertainty and geopolitical risks shocks on the commodity market prices: Evidence from the TVP-VAR-SV approach. *Resources Policy, 76*, 102600. DOI: 10.1016/j.resourpol.2022.102600

Yang, J., & Yang, C. (2021). The impact of mixed-frequency geopolitical risk on stock market returns. *Economic Analysis and Policy, 72*, 226–240. DOI: 10.1016/j.eap.2021.08.008

Yang, M., Zhang, Q., Yi, A., & Peng, P. (2021). Geopolitical Risk and Stock Market Volatility in Emerging Economies: Evidence from GARCH-MIDAS Model. *Journal of Applied Econometrics, 24*(3), 357–370. DOI: 10.1155/2021/1159358

Yildirim, Z. (2016). Global financial conditions and asset markets: Evidence from fragile emerging economies. *Economic Modelling, 57*, 208–220. DOI: 10.1016/j.econmod.2016.04.018

Zhang, Y., & Hamori, S. (2022). A Connectedness Analysis among BRICS's Geopolitical Risks and the US Macroeconomy. *Economic Analysis and Policy, 74*, 115–130. DOI: 10.1016/j.eap.2022.08.004

Zhao, Y., Chen, L., & Zhang, Y. (2024). Spillover Effects of Geopolitical Risks on Global Energy Markets: Evidence from CoVaR and CAViaR-EGARCH Model. *Energy, 289*, 119743. DOI: 10.1177/01445987231196617

[1] Other databases, such as Scopus, were not utilized because the Social Science Citation Index (SSCI) of the Web of Science encompasses the majority of the top journals featured in Scopus within the research area under analysis. Moreover, the data retrieved from the Web of Science was sufficiently com-

prehensive, providing ample information to conduct the analysis without the need for additional databases.

Chapter 3
Economic Growth, Political Stability, and Economic Globalization:
A Literature Review on BRICS Countries

Sibel Elif Özdilek
https://orcid.org/0000-0003-0907-8771
Ufuk University, Turkey

Sibel Elif Özdilek
Ufuk University, Turkey

ABSTRACT

Finally, it is clear that there is a parallel relationship between economic globalization and economic growth, which shows that the process of economic globalization positively affects growth. Although there are many studies on the relationship between political stability and economic growth, the fact that the relationship between political stability and economic growth and economic globalization; the limited number of literature review studies investigating the effect of political stability (political instability) on economic growth in the BRICS countries (Brazil, Russia, India, China and South Africa), which constitute 43% of the world population and approximately 30% of the world economy, made this study necessary. In this context, it is important for the study to explain the literature review of the BRICS countries that is covered in the study.

DOI: 10.4018/979-8-3373-1265-1.ch003

1. INTRODUCTION

Emerging market economies are a concept first put forward by Antoine W. Van Agtmael on behalf of the International Finance Corporation (IFC) in 1981 (Gürsoy and Eroğlu, 2016). Countries that decide to make reforms to eliminate many problems such as unfair income distribution, weak industrial and social infrastructure and overpopulation in the country, create long-term plans in this regard, put these plans into practice and increase their GNP per capita as a result of these activities are called emerging economies. Despite the similarities in their economic and social structures, emerging economies and developing countries are distinguished from each other by their determination to develop and their success in increasing the welfare of their citizens. Every emerging economy can be called a developing country, but not every developing country is included in the emerging economy class (Çivi and Çavuşgil, 2001).

It is quite difficult to provide a complete list of emerging economies. Many countries are classified as emerging economies in the classifications made by different institutions and organizations based on different criteria (Halisçelik, 2015). For example, while Morgan Stanley's Emerging Market Economies Index group (The MSCI Emerging Market Index) includes 21 countries, the S&P Global Broad Market Index (The S&P Global BMI) includes 19 countries. However, the FTSE Global Equity Index Series, Country Classification, which categorizes emerging economies as developed and secondary emerging economies, includes 22 countries. In addition, in the literature, while defining emerging markets or emerging markets, the BRIC economies, including Brazil, Russia, India and China, or the BRICS and BRICS-T (T-BRICS) economies, including South Africa and Turkey, are also used in the classifications made (Elmas et al., 2011). BRICS-T countries are rapidly developing countries covering 25% of the world in terms of total surface area (Narin and Kutluay, 2013; Akkoç et al., 2018).

Although there are many studies on the relationship between political stability and economic growth, the fact that the relationship between political stability and economic growth and economic globalization the limited number of literature review studies investigating the effect of political stability (political instability) on economic growth in the BRICS countries (Brazil, Russia, India, China and South Africa), which constitute 43% of the world population and approximately 30% of the world economy, made this study necessary. In this context, it is important for the study to explain the literature review of the BRICS countries that is covered in the study.

2. METHODOLOGY

This research adopts a qualitative approach to explore the use of literature review in BRICS countries. The study focuses on different passages under different headings. The research aims to identify common interaction between democratic political stability, economic growth and economic globalization information and procedures by analyzing the relationship between political stability and economic growth in the BRICS countries.

2.1 Data Collection

This research is a systematic review study in the documentary genre. The research conducted with this method examined the impact of political stability, economic growth and economic globalization on the BRICS countries in the literature. It also aims to reveal the impact of the current BRICS countries' results on people in a holistic way. The research data was obtained through document analysis. Document analysis is a systematic procedure used to examine or evaluate both printed and internet and computer-based materials. Systematic review is a research model in which research findings related to specific topics are identified and synthesized and carried out in a step-by-step manner (Corbin and Strauss, 2008: 47-48).

2.2 Data Analysis

The research analyzes various literature on political stability, economic growth and economic globalization. The research targets the methods and use of interactive features to engage people and their systems in BRICS countries. The analysis also considers how well these countries are aligned with their goals and how successful they are in influencing people.

3. LITERATURE REVIEW

3.1. Relationship between Political Stability and Economic Growth / Literature Review

The relationship between political stability and economic growth has been one of the important research topics analyzed by many economists using different methods. When analyzing economic growth, the relationship between growth and political stability is usually addressed through “political instability”. In studies conducted on this subject, there are different analyzes on whether the relationship between political instability and growth can be one-way, reciprocal or disconnected (Arslan, 2011).

In most studies emphasizing that political instability has a one-way and negative effect on economic growth, the relationship between instability and growth is explained through uncertainty and investment, and it is revealed that political stability affects growth through two different channels, direct and indirect. In the event of political instability, the decrease in investments and the withdrawal of foreign capital from the country have a direct negative effect on economic growth. On the other hand, the decrease in investments together with the decrease in employment area and the increase in unemployment rate cause growth to be negatively affected indirectly (Şanlısoy and Kök, 2010).

Table 1. Summary of Selected Literature

Author(s)	Data Range	Year	Result
	There are economists who argue that political stability does have a positive effect on economic growth.		
Alesina and Tabellina	-	1988	The uncertainty that occurs as a result of an unstable environment leads to a decrease in investments, and the decrease in investments negatively affects the economic growth process.
Barro	1960-1985	1991	Concluded that political instability negatively affected economic growth for 98 countries selected.
Grossman	-	1991	The existence of political stability plays an important role in ensuring the economic growth of the country.
Alesina and Rodrik	-	1994	The existence of political instability causes uncertainty in the markets and this uncertainty causes a decrease in foreign investments.
Alesina and Perotti	1960-1985	1995	Injustice in income distribution leads to political instability.
De Haan and Siermann	1963-1988	1996	As a result of the analysis, it was concluded that political instability negatively affects economic growth and political instability causes a decrease in investments in Asia.
Alesina et al.	1950-1982	1994	Alesina et al. (1996) stated that economies revealed the effect of political stability on growth.

continued on following page

Table 1. Continued

Author(s)	Data Range	Year	Result
	There are economists who argue that political stability does have a positive effect on economic growth.		
Benhabib and Rustichini	-	1996	Instability leads to a decrease in the income obtained as a result of investments and negatively affects economic growth.
Feng	1960-1980	1997	While irregular government changes such as coups cause economic growth to slow down, constitutional changes such as elections accelerate economic growth.
Asterio and Price	1961-1997	2001	Political instability leads to radical government changes. In this process, the stagnation and uncertainty prevailing in the market cause economic growth to slow down.
Berthélemy	-	2002	It was concluded that political instability directly negatively affected economic growth through investments.
Aisen and Veiga	1960-2004	2011	Political instability negatively affects the efficient use of resources. In unstable environments where violence and unrest exist, the production processes of firms are also negatively affected.
Gür and Akbulut	1986-2003	2012	They concluded that political stability had a positive effect on economic growth.
Özsağır	1923-2012	2013	It was stated that events that cause political instability such as military coups have a negative effect on economic growth.
Zureiqat	1985-2002	2015	It was stated that there is a significant relationship between democracy and economic growth.
Uddin	-	2017	Stated that political stability is important in order to be able to predict future risks within the country and to produce appropriate policies against these risks.

continued on following page

Table 1. Continued

Author(s)	Data Range	Year	Result
	There are economists who argue that political stability does have a positive effect on economic growth.		
Kamacı	2003-2017	2019	In summary, while political instability has a positive effect on economic growth in the short term, instability causes a decrease in economic growth in the long term for selected 20 OECD countries.
Yapraklı and Aslan	1992-2016	2020	It was concluded that variables such as political stability, effective functioning of institutions and trade openness affect economic growth positively; while corruption, inflation and unemployment affect it negatively for selected 23 countries.
	There are also economists who argue that political stability does not have a positive effect on economic growth.		
Olson	-	1982	Events that disrupt stability such as war and revolution negatively affect economic growth in the short term, but have an accelerating effect on economic growth in the medium term.
Goldsmith	1958-1967 1968-1977	1987	Since the dominant groups in the country prioritize their own interests, the existence of political stability does not have a positive effect on the country's economy.
Shabbir	-	2016	Increasing corruption and bribery would contribute to investors achieving faster results in their commercial.
	There are also studies in the literature that state that there is a bidirectional causality relationship between political instability and economic growth.		
Blomberg and Hess	1950-1992	2002	They emphasized that the occurrence of political unrest will cause the economy to deteriorate further. And as a result, the economy would be vibrant.
Belke and Al	1991-2016	2018	In summary, it has been stated that low economic growth is both a cause and a result of political instability.
	In the literature, the existence of a causal relationship from economic growth to political stability is also mentioned.		

continued on following page

Table 1. Continued

Author(s)	Data Range	Year	Result
	There are economists who argue that political stability does have a positive effect on economic growth.		
Paldam	1998		As a result of the income increase, the people of the country support the existing administration and this situation is effective in ensuring political stability.
	Among the studies indicating that there is no relationship between political stability and economic growth;		
Easterly and Rebelo	1993		It was concluded that there was no long-term relationship between political instability and growth.
Campos and Nugent	- 2002		As a result of their study, no long-term relationship was found between economic growth and political instability.
Biçen	- 2020		Political stability has a slightly positive effect on growth in Brazil, Russia, South Africa and Turkey.

3.2. Relationship between Political Stability and Economic Globalization (Trade Liberalization) / Literature Review

The relationship between economic globalization and political stability has been tried to be defined by different people in the literature using different methods (Kanık, 2016). In this context, the most recent academic and scientific studies on the globalization of the economy and its effects on political stability are summarized below. The studies aim to reveal the findings on how the economic opening of countries to the outside world affects political stability.

Economic globalization leads to income distribution inequality, which leads people to behaviors that will create instability such as revolution and political violence. In other words, it is stated that as a result of the removal of trade barriers between countries and the globalization of the economy, producers are shifting their production to countries with cheaper labor, and the demand for unskilled labor in these countries has increased. As a result of the shift of production to developing countries with cheap labor, it is predicted that workers in these countries will lose income since there will be no need for unskilled workers in developed countries. In this context, it is stated that the globalization of financial markets is a factor that increases income inequality. It is stated that the incomes of countries/individuals with the most productive and income-generating resources in global markets increase, and this situation fuels income inequality between countries and individuals. At the same time, it is seen that foreign direct investments (FDI) are mostly made in high-tech fields with high earnings. As a result, there is an increase in the demand and income of qualified individuals. This increase causes the income gap between skilled and unskilled workers to increase even more (Emin, 2016).

Table 2. Summary of Selected Literature

Author(s)	Data Range	Year	Result
Van de Walle	-	1998	The book states that states must assume great responsibilities in order to minimize the negative effects of economic globalization.
Yu-Rong		2003	State sovereignty and the right to self-control, strengthening the government's status as power, and adhering to the country's principles.
Nel	-	2003	. The findings revealed that high levels of inequality did not statistically significantly affect political instability.
Suliman	-	2005	The findings showed that a decisive tax reform is very important for fiscal consolidation and political stability.
Bussmann	-	2006	Economic globalization increases economic growth and that increased economic growth contributes to political stability.
Yu	1974-1998	2007	He stated that trade globalization reduces political liberalization, but political liberalization promotes trade globalization.
Oluwatosin	1986-2010	2013	Therefore, as a result of the study, it was emphasized that in order for the Nigerian economy to benefit from the gains of economic globalization.
	In the literature, the effect of political stability on economic growth is generally explained through foreign direct investments.		

continued on following page

Table 2. Continued

Author(s)	Data Range	Year	Result
Shahzad	-	2012	The existence of political instability has been one of the main reasons affecting FDI inflows in Pakistan.
Jewel	-	2015	There is no significant relationship between political stability and FDI in the short run.
Oransay and Mike	1990-2012	2016	A positive correlation was found between socio-political factors and FDI for selected 23 OECD countries.
Rashid	2000-2013	2017	It was emphasized that a stable economic and political environment should be provided to increase FDI flows.
Abdella	2002-2016	2018	
Kamowa and Arunasalam	-	2020	The findings showed that corruption does not have a significant impact on (FDIs) in BRIC countries.
Yakubu	1970-2016	2020	. As a result of the findings, it was determined that trade openness and political stability have a significant effect on FDIs In this context, it was stated that policy makers should ensure more liberalization of the capital account and maintain a stable political atmosphere.

3.3. Relationship between Economic Globalization (Trade Liberalization) and Economic Growth / Literature Review

When the international literature is examined, it is seen that the findings obtained according to the development levels of the countries are different. The general view in international studies is that trade liberalization positively affects the economies of developed countries.

In developing countries, the concept of trade liberalization can sometimes gain a speculative feature and lead countries to economic crisis and instability. When the national literature is examined, it is seen that the relationship between economic globalization (trade liberalization) and economic growth is investigated with different econometric models. There is also diversity in the findings obtained. While some studies find a positive effect of economic globalization on economic growth, some studies find a negative relationship. In other words, there is no consensus in the national literature on the relationship between economic globalization and economic growth.

Table 3. Summary of Selected Literature

Author(s)	Data Range	Year	Result
Ying, et al.	1970-2008	2014	It showed that economic globalization has a significant positive effect on economic growth.
Doğan	1970-2011	2017	In other words, it was determined in the study that economic globalization (such as foreign trade, foreign direct investments (FDI), portfolio investments, etc.) positively affected growth.
Gözgör and Can	1970-2010	2017	Export diversification and economic globalization are positively related to economic growth only in upper middle economies.
Özcan	1992-2015	2018	Results show that economic globalization affects economic growth at different levels according to countries.

continued on following page

Table 3. Continued

Author(s)	Data Range	Year	Result
Erkişi and Ceyhan	1995-2016	2019	In summary, it is stated that trade liberalization has a positive effect on economic growth.
Gündüz	1996-2016	2020	It was observed that there was a causality from the financial globalization index to economic growth and from economic growth to the financial globalization index.
	On the other hand, among the studies claiming that there is a negative relationship between economic globalization and economic growth.		
Özel	- 2012		As a result of the study, it was stated that there was a negative relationship between economic growth and financial liberalization.
Ahmed	1981-2009 2013		The negative effect occurs as follows: financial liberalization leads to instability, encourages domestic capital flight and increases the risk of financial fragility. In this case, it causes low economic growth.
Ayla and Karis	1985-2018 2020		It was determined that the trade openness rate negatively affected income justice in the short and long term.

Finally, there are also studies indicating that there is no relationship between economic growth and economic globalization.

Table 4. Summary of Selected Literature

Author(s)	Data Range	Year	Result
Çeştepe	-	2017	As a result, the impact of economic globalization on economic growth was examined.
Altıner	1990-2015	2018	According to the results obtained, no causal relationship was found between the economic globalization index and economic growth.
Ergin and Ünal	-	2019	The results showed that there is no long-term relationship between the variables.
Ersungur and Demirci	1998-2017	2020	As a result of this study, it was determined that there was no causal relationship between trade and financial openness and GDP.

4. DISCUSSION

Numerous studies conducted in recent years have frequently explored the correlation between policy and economic growth. These investigations suggest that the economic growth outcomes of nations cannot be solely attributed to economic factors; rather, political and institutional frameworks also play a significant role in shaping economic performance. It has been observed that countries characterized by robust political and institutional structures tend to be more developed, while those lacking such frameworks are often less developed. Furthermore, it is recognized that political stability—or its absence—within these structures significantly influences a country's economic growth performance, yielding various positive or negative effects. Research indicates a strong interconnection between political dynamics and economic conditions. Political instability, which poses a considerable threat and is a crucial factor in the policies enacted by governments, is of paramount importance to political actors and parties. Thus, defining the concepts of political stability and political instability is essential for a deeper understanding of this issue. Political stability serves as the cornerstone of sustainable economic development by mitigating uncertainties that may arise in the future. The research indicates that the primary driver of economic growth and heightened physical investment is the significant political stability present in the country. In nations characterized by political instability, future uncertainties tend to escalate, resulting in postponed investments. Such uncertainties represent a substantial barrier to the rational and long-term decision-making processes of the current government. Analysis of the interplay between political stability and economic growth reveals that political instability exerts both direct and indirect adverse effects on economic development. Furthermore, elevated levels of political instability heighten the likelihood of governmental changes within these countries. Despite the existence of numerous studies examining the correlation between political stability and economic growth, the lack of clarity in delineating this relationship, coupled with the limited research focused on the impact of political stability (or instability) on economic growth in BRICS-T nations (Brazil, Russia, India, China, South Africa, and Turkey)—which collectively account for 43% of the global population and approximately 30% of the world economy—underscores the necessity of this study.

Political instability is defined by economists as a serious problem that undermines the economic performance of countries. There are two main reasons behind this relationship. The first of these is that in an environment of uncertainty, decision makers' horizons narrow and thus they put forward suboptimal macroeconomic policies, and the second is that these suboptimal decisions negatively affect other actors in the economy.

The main factor underlying the theoretical basis of the political stability-economic performance relationship is the investments that show a direct proportional development with stability and the development of national income that is affected by this. This naturally has significant effects on the national income per capita and the level of welfare of the country.

Political economy is a branch of science that studies the relationships between national income and wealth distribution, production, trade and the state, tradition and law. In this respect, political economy uses economics, politics and sociology while explaining the interaction of political institutions, political environment and economic system (capitalist, socialist, communist or mixed). In the context of politics-economics interaction, it is possible to say that achieving political stability in a country brings economic stability. As a matter of fact, as a result of theoretical and econometric studies, it has been stated by many economists that political stability (instability) significantly affects the country's economy. Economic literature reveals results that political instabilities affect economic growth through human capital, natural resources, financial markets, capital, monetary and fiscal policies, investment and similar factors.

As a result, political stability creates an environment of predictability in a country, increases domestic and foreign investments, ensures the implementation of longer, more efficient projects, reduces the loss of human capital, increases public resources, and thus directly and positively affects economic growth. In fact, the policy recommendations that can be given in line with the findings obtained in the study are given below.

When the Turkish economy is examined in particular, it has structural problems such as the inability to substitute imports (import input dependency), foreign financial capital flows, growth based on financial investments, low savings and similar aspects that cause a current account deficit. These problems turn Turkey into a country that is more vulnerable and vulnerable to economic and political instability, especially from external sources. When it is examined in general in developing countries such as the BRICS countries, it is possible to say that even in times of political stability, economic instability can occur due to global shocks.

It is possible to list the policy recommendations regarding the relationship between political stability and GDP per capita as follows: Political stability increases the possibility of attracting employment-creating foreign investments by increasing economic growth for countries. In addition, political stability provides a more favorable environment for investments in infrastructure, education, health services and similar economic activities. Political instability can lead to economic instability in a country. The reason for this is that investors avoid investing in a country with uncertain political stability. This situation leads to a decrease in foreign investments and a decrease in economic growth. In addition, political instability increases corruption and negatively affects economic growth. It is possible to address the policy recommendations regarding the relationship between political stability and employment rate as follows: If there is political stability in a country, the possibility of businesses to make investments and expand their workforce increases. Thus, employment opportunities increase and the unemployment rate may decrease. In addition, political stability enables the development of policies that support employment creation, such as education programs, tax incentives, labor laws that protect workers' rights, and similar policies. Therefore, in the growth and development process for national economies, investments, production, and expenditures, especially regarding technological innovations, should be increased, and thus, external dependency should be reduced. In addition, economic growth should create an effect that increases the level of welfare in all segments of society with the policies implemented by the government. In addition, educational policies should be developed in order to train a well-equipped, qualified workforce for the digital age we are in. Indeed, in order to prevent the flight of physical investments and even human capital abroad (brain drain), it is extremely important to ensure political stability and therefore economic stability.

When all these policy recommendations are put into practice, a developing country can achieve sustainable economic growth and a political stability environment in which they interact. In this way, these developing countries will become stronger economically and politically, and will have a higher average level of welfare within the country and will become a leading country in the international arena. Otherwise, although economic growth is in favor of a certain segment, poverty begins to solidify, rights and freedoms are constantly regressed, and economic growth cannot be achieved. This situation can lead to political instability, chaos, an increase in crime, and the country becoming vulnerable to threats from foreign countries.

When the analysis results are evaluated in general, it is seen that the positive relationship between political stability and economic growth, as claimed in the literature, is also valid for developing countries. Therefore, the institutions responsible for structural transformation in developing countries should implement the policies they put into practice to realize these transformations by taking political stability into account and avoiding behaviors that increase instability. Therefore, the necessary legal arrangements for political stability should be made to ensure that economic growth is stronger and more sustainable.

5. CONCLUSION

When both economics and political science literature is examined, it is seen that, as far as is known, in the majority of studies examining the relationships between economic growth, economic globalization and political stability in the BRICS countries, these three concepts are not analyzed together. In this study, firstly, the definitions of the concepts of economic globalization, economic growth and political stability are made and the relationship between them is examined through literature review.

Although there are different definitions in the literature on globalization, in its most general sense, it is the spread of values belonging to everyone in the economic, political, social and cultural areas in the world we live in; the increase in mutual interactions of nations due to the easy mobility of capital and goods. Globalization has political, cultural and economic dimensions, but due to the scope of the study, economic globalization is discussed in this study. Economic globalization refers to the liberalization of international trade, the removal of obstacles to trade in goods and capital movements, and the gradual interconnection of economic activities between countries.

Although there is no consensus in the literature on the definition of political stability, it is generally defined as the continuity of political authority, the absence of violence within the state, and the existence of legitimate constitutional authority. Another concept discussed in the study is economic growth. Economic growth is defined as the increases in the capacity of goods and services produced within a country in a certain period.

In light of all these definitions, there are many studies in the literature that address the relationship between economic growth, political stability and economic globalization. When the relationship between political stability and economic growth is examined, it is seen that the relationship is generally established through "political instability". In most of the studies arguing that political instability has a negative effect on economic growth, it is argued that uncertainty reduces investments and that the decrease in investments has a negative effect on economic growth. Alesina and Tabellini (1988) explained the relationship between political instability and economic growth through this uncertainty channel. Uncertainty resulting from an unstable environment leads to a decrease in investments and the decrease in investments negatively affects the economic growth process. In addition to studies arguing that political instability negatively affects economic growth, there are also economists such as Olson who emphasize that an unstable environment has an increasing effect on growth. According to Olson (1982), destabilizing events such as war and civil unrest positively affect political stability in the long term. In addition, there are studies in the literature that conclude that there is no relationship between economic growth and political stability.

When the relationship between political stability and economic globalization is examined, it is seen that different results are reached by using different methods in the literature. According to the studies that argue that economic globalization has negative effects on political stability, economic globalization leads to injustice in income distribution and this injustice causes unrest within the society. On the other hand, there are also studies that claim that economic globalization increases economic growth and that increased growth provides political stability. In the literature, the effect of political stability on economic globalization is generally explained through investments. Many studies have stated that political instability in a country causes a decrease in foreign investments entering the country and negatively affects economic globalization. When the relationship between economic growth and economic globalization is examined, it is seen that many studies and econometric analyses have been conducted on this subject. While a positive relationship has been found between these two variables in some studies, a negative relationship has been detected in others. In addition to these, it has been seen that there are also studies in the literature that state that there is no relationship between the two variables.

When compared with the general literature, it was concluded that the evaluations made on the relationships between political stability and economic growth in BRICS countries are parallel to the findings obtained from the studies of Alesina and Tabellini (1988), De Haan and Siermann (1996), Alesina and Rodrik (1994), Benhabib and Rustichini (1996), Aisen and Veiga (2011), Berthélemy et al. (2002), Uddin et al. (2017) for India, Russia, Brazil and South Africa. It was observed that the observation made for China is consistent with the results obtained from the studies of Campos and Nugent (2002), Easterly and Rebelo (1993).

As a result of the observations made within the scope of the study, it was observed that the relationships between economic globalization and economic growth in BRICS countries were generally consistent with the results obtained from the studies of Tupy (2005), Doğan (2017), Özcan et al. (2018), and Gündüz (2020). In the study, it was observed that there was a weak relationship between economic globalization and economic growth for Russia and it was concluded that this observation was consistent with the findings obtained from the studies of Acaravci et al. (2018), Bumann et al. (2013), and Menyah et al. (2014).

Finally, it is not a coincidence that developed countries in the world are governed by democracy. On the contrary, it is a result of the two-way interaction of democracy on political, social and economic life. However, despite all these statements, it is still quite difficult to make a definitive judgment about the relationship between political stability and economic growth/development and economic globalization. Research in this direction is still needed to fully determine this relationship.

6. REFERENCES

Aisen, A., & Vega, F. J. (2011). How Does Political Instability Effect Economic Growth. IMF Working Paper, No:12.

Akkoç, G. K., Akkoç, U., & Yücel, Ö. F. (2018). BRICS-T Ülkelerinde Toplam Faktör Verimliliği & Teknoloji Transferi. *Uluslararası İktisadi & İdari İncelemeler Dergisi*, (21), 101–118.

Alesina, A., & Rodrik, D. (1994). Distributi& politics and economic growth. *The Quarterly Journal of Economics*, *109*(2), 465–490.

Alesina, A., & Tabellini, G. (1988). External Debt, Capital Flight and Politic Risk. *Working Paper Series (National Bureau of Economic Research)*, *2610*, 1–45.

Arslan, Ü. (2011). Siyasi istikrarsızlık & ekonomik performans: Türkiye örneği. *Ege Academic Review*, *11*(1).

Benhabib, J., & Rustichini, A. (1996). Social Conflict and Growth. *Journal of Economic Growth*, *1*(1), 125–142.

Berthélemy, J. C., Kauffmann, C., Renard, L., & Wegner, L. (2002). Political instability, political regimes and economic performance in African countries. Unpublished paper prepared for African Development Bank, African Economic Outlook.

Bumann, S., Hermes, N., & Lensink, R. (2013). Financial liberalization and economic growth: A meta-analysis. *Journal of International Money and Finance*, *33*, 255–281.

Campos, N. F., & Nugent, J. B. (2002). Who is Afraid of Political Instability? *Journal of Development Economics*, *67*(1), 157–172.

Çivi, E. & Çavuşgil, S. T. (2001). Yeni Dünya Düzeninde Güç Kazanan Ülkeler: Yükselen Ekonomiler. Celal Bayar Üniversitesi Yönetim & Ekonomi Dergisi, 7(1), ss. 113-128.

Corbin, J., & Strauss, A. (2008). *Basics of Qualitati& Research: Techniques and Procedures for Developing Grounded Theory* (3rd ed.). Sage.

De Haan, J., & Siermann, C. L. (1996). Political instability, freedom, and economic growth: Some further evidence. *Economic Development and Cultural Change*, *44*(2), 339–350.

Doğan, B. (2017). Ekonomik küreselleşme & büyüme ilişkisi: Türkiye örneği Toda-Yamamoto nedensellik analizi. *Finans Politik & Ekonomik Yorumlar*, *54*(628), 19–27.

Easterly, W., & Rebelo, S. (1993). Fiscal Policy and Economic Growth. *Journal of Monetary Economics, 32*, 417–458.

Elmas, B., Esen, Ö., & Yurttançıkmaz, Z. Ç. (2011). "Yeni Dünya Düzeniyle Başlayan Değişim; Yükselen Ekonomilerin Çağı", https://www.researchgate.net/publication/292775147_Yeni_Dunya_Duzeniyle_Baslayan_Degisim_Yukselen_Ekonomilerin_Cagi, (24.12.2016).

Emin, E. (2016). Küresel Adaletsizlik Dünya Yoksulluk & Eşitsizlik Raporu. İstanbul: İnsamer, https://insamer.com/rsm/icerik/dosya/dosya_389.pdf, Erisim Tarihi: 05.11.2024.

Gündüz, M. (2020). Financial Globalization and Economic Growth: Panel Causality Analysis for EU. In Handbook of Research on Social and Economic Development in the European Union (pp. 99-116). IGI Global.

Gürsoy, S. & Eroğlu, Ö. (2016). Yükselen Ekonomilerin Pay Piyasaları Arasında Getiri & Volatilite Yayılımı: 2006-2015 Yılları Arasında Yapılmış Bir Analiz. Mehmet Akif Ersoy Üniversitesi İİBF Dergisi, 3(5), ss. 16-33.

Halisçelik, E. (2015). *Binyıl Kalkınma Hedefleri & Yoksul Odaklı Büyüme: Yükselen Ekonomiler Üzerine Ampirik Bir Analiz.* Doktora Tezi, Hacettepe Üniversitesi Sosyal Bilimler Enstitüsü.

Kanık, İ. (2016). Küreselleşme Sürecinde Kültürel Melezleşme Örneği Olarak Yemek Kanalları & Programları. Folklor/Edebiyat, 22(86), 237-258.

Menyah, K., Nazlıoğlu, S., & Wolde-Rufael, Y. (2014). Financial development, trade openness and economic growth in African countries: New insights from a panel causality approach. *Economic Modelling, 37*, 386–394.

Narin, M., & Kutluay, D. (2013). *Değişen Küresel Ekonomik Düzen: BRIC, 3G & N-11 Ülkeleri.* Ankara Sanayi Odası Yayın Organı.

Olson, M. (1982). *The Rise and Decline of Nations: Economic Growth, Stagflation and Social Rigidities. New Heaven.* Yale University Press.

Şanlısoy, S. & Kök, R. (2010). Politik istikrarsızlık-ekonomik büyüme ilişkisi: Türkiye örneği (1987–2006). Dokuz Eylül Üniversitesi İktisadi İdari Bilimler Fakültesi Dergisi, 25(1).

Tupy, M. L. (2005). Trade liberalization and Poverty Reduction in Sub-Saharan Africa, CATO Analysis No.557.

Uddin, M. A., Ali, M. H., & Masih, M. (2017). Political Stability and Growth: An Application of Dynamic GMM and Quantile Regression. *Economic Modelling*, *64*, 610–625.

Chapter 4
Council of Europe:
Soft Power and Geopolitics

Sureyya Yigit
https://orcid.org/0000-0002-8025-5147
New Vision University, Georgia

ABSTRACT

The Council of Europe, established in 1949, promotes human rights, democracy, and the rule of law across its 46 member states. Inspired by Winston Churchill's vision, it fosters collaboration among European nations. The European Court of Human Rights ensures justice, while various treaties and expert bodies protect individuals and provide essential recommendations. The Council remains a cornerstone of European integration, promoting peace and cooperation across the continent. Through its comprehensive approach, the Council of Europe continues to be a vital institution in upholding shared values and standards across Europe.

INTRODUCTION

> *The main safeguard of democracy in Turkey as in any other democratic country is inevitably the people's attachment to democracy and freedom. But there had been times where our membership in the Council has served as a compass that helped to prevent us from losing our bearings.* **Bülent Ecevit - 10 May 1979**

The term "globalisation" gained prominence in the 1980s. However, the underlying phenomenon it describes—a continuous increase in economic, human, and financial interactions among a rapidly expanding network of global partners—has roots that extend much further back in history. The contemporary process of globalisation can be traced back to the late 19th century when advances in technology and transportation began to connect distant regions. Its resurgence after World

DOI: 10.4018/979-8-3373-1265-1.ch004

War II marked a significant turning point as nations sought to rebuild and foster international cooperation.

During this early phase, known as "internationalisation," trade intensified primarily among a limited group of countries. This was largely a reaction to the disruptions caused by previous global crises, as nations aimed to recover from the setbacks and restore economic stability. However, this era did not witness the emergence of strong transnational private actors; instead, state cooperation dominated the landscape, focusing on rebuilding economies while still constrained by the legacy of previous geopolitical tensions.

As the 20th century drew to a close, a profound wave of globalisation began to take shape, fundamentally altering the way we interact with the world. This transformative period was distinguished by groundbreaking technological innovations, an extraordinary acceleration of connections and exchanges, and a rapid proliferation of nations engaging in the complexities of global capitalism. Unlike earlier forms of trade, this new wave of globalisation encompassed not just the invisible aspects of commerce but also introduced an entirely new productive and societal framework that reshaped our daily lives.

From a geographical standpoint, globalisation represents a significant shift in scale, intricately woven into the broader tapestry of historical continuity. It encapsulates the emergence of a cohesive world system, marked by the compression of both space and time, leading to the fluidity of borders and the gradual diminishing of traditional national territories. This phenomenon does not merely denote a geographical transformation; it also signifies a pivotal change in our understanding and representation of the world around us.

This new era has given rise to post-Fordist, transnational, and financialised capitalism, which emphasises global networks and economic interdependence. As local communities grapple with the influences of these transnational trends, they often find their identities and cultures reshaped by the rising power of global cities, which serve as critical hubs of finance, commerce, and innovation; in this intricate dance of globalisation, local and global dynamics intertwine, creating a rich, complex landscape of relationships that redefine what it means to exist in a connected world.

In the aftermath of the Second World War, global leaders recognised the urgent need to prevent a resurgence of economic warfare, which had historically led to profound social and political upheavals both domestically and internationally. To foster a more stable and equitable global economy, they advocated for the establishment of free trade as the cornerstone of economic reconstruction. This initiative aimed to create a balanced remuneration system for factors of production, ensuring fairness in an open economy. Furthermore, it called for the development of institutions dedicated to this cause, particularly to reestablish a reliable currency exchange framework that could facilitate international trade and investment.

The Bretton Woods Conference, held in July 1944, emerged as a pivotal moment in this effort. Delegates from forty-four nations convened in Bretton Woods, New Hampshire, to chart a new course for the global economy. These discussions not only shaped the future of economic cooperation but also laid the groundwork for the creation of lasting institutions. The United Nations, which would soon be founded the following year by fifty-one member states, embodied this collective aspiration for cooperation and peace.

Notably, the Soviet Union participated as an observer at the conference but chose not to sign the final agreements. As a result, two major institutions were established: the International Bank for Reconstruction and Development (IBRD) and the International Monetary Fund (IMF). These organisations were designed with the dual purpose of financing the reconstruction of war-torn nations and assisting countries in maintaining the stability and parity of their currencies, thus fostering an environment conducive to economic growth and global collaboration.

The Bretton Woods Agreements, established in 1944 during a conference held in Bretton Woods, New Hampshire, aimed to create a stable international monetary system following World War II. This system was designed as a gold exchange standard, whereby the value of each participating currency was defined in terms of a specific amount of gold. Furthermore, the daily exchange rate of these currencies on the foreign exchange market was constrained, allowing them to fluctuate only within a range of plus or minus 1% from their defined gold parity. This mechanism was intended to promote exchange rate stability, which in turn would facilitate international trade and economic cooperation.

The establishment of this system reflected significant shifts in global power dynamics. At that time, the United States held approximately 70% of the world's monetary gold reserves, which gave the U.S. dollar a unique position. As a result, the dollar became the sole currency directly convertible into gold, thereby enhancing its status as the dominant global currency. This preference for the dollar was further reinforced by the establishment of key international financial institutions, including the International Monetary Fund (IMF) and the International Bank for Reconstruction and Development (IBRD), both of which were headquartered in Washington, D.C.

This geographical positioning was significant, as it underscored the immense economic influence of the United States, which, by the end of the war, was responsible for producing roughly half of the world's total Gross Domestic Product (GDP). The outcomes of the Bretton Woods Agreements not only shaped the post-war economic order but also laid the groundwork for what would become known as Cold War geoeconomics, a period marked by the strategic use of economic power in international relations and conflict. This era shifted the focus from merely military might to including economic influence as a vital component of national security and global diplomacy.

Another powerful means of influence was the spread of democratic values and ideas. In a momentous speech delivered at the University of Zurich on 19 September 1946, Winston Churchill passionately advocated for the unification of Europe, proposing a regional framework that he referred to as the "United States of Europe." In the aftermath of the Second World War, the wounds inflicted by years of conflict remained painfully fresh, leaving Europe in turmoil and uncertainty. Nations were grappling with the devastation of their economies, the loss of countless lives, and the urgent need for healing. Amidst this backdrop, Winston Churchill's powerful rhetoric struck a chord with many, as he passionately advocated for reconciliation and unity among the war-torn nations.

Churchill envisioned the establishment of a "Council of Europe," an ambitious initiative to foster collaboration and mutual understanding. He believed that such an institution would promote diplomatic dialogue and work toward rebuilding trust and strengthening the bonds frayed by years of animosity. This Council would ideally bring together various European countries, encouraging them to set aside their differences, collaborate on shared challenges, and ultimately foster a lasting peace across the continent. By promoting cooperation in various spheres, including economics, culture, and politics, Churchill hoped to lay the groundwork for a stable and prosperous Europe where the horrors of war would no longer overshadow the future.

His stirring call to action inspired devoted Europeans from approximately 20 countries to unite in The Hague two years later. There, they began to shape an organisation dedicated to fostering greater unity between its members, driven by a shared vision of a peaceful and cooperative Europe (Duffy, 1950). The collaborative efforts of various nations ultimately resulted in the creation of the Council of Europe, a significant milestone in European integration. The Council was officially established through a treaty signed in London on 5 May 1949 by ten founding member states: Belgium, Denmark, France, Ireland, Italy, Luxembourg, the Netherlands, Norway, Sweden, and the United Kingdom. This began a new chapter in European history to promote human rights, democracy, and the rule of law across the continent.

The Council of Europe established a decision-making body known as the Committee of Ministers, which is composed of government representatives from member states alongside a deliberative assembly of parliamentarians. While the organisation has a broad scope of action, its statute explicitly prohibits involvement in defence matters, which fall under the North Atlantic Treaty signed just a month earlier on 4 April 1949 (Yigit, 2024). Additionally, the Council of Europe holds a law-making function. It is responsible for drafting European conventions that require adoption by the Committee of Ministers and subsequent signature and ratification by individual member states.

LITERATURE REVIEW

Soriano provides an in-depth analysis of the Greek coup that took place in 1967, an event that not only caused significant turmoil within Greece but also raised critical questions about Greece's role and responsibilities within key international organisations, particularly the Council of Europe and the European Community (Soriano, 2019). Greece established a military dictatorship, prompting an urgent need for these organisations to respond to the challenges posed by an authoritarian regime, especially considering Greece's longstanding membership and the commitments it had made under existing treaties. Almost immediately following the coup, a group of proactive politicians within the parliamentary assemblies of both the Council of Europe and the European Community began to forge alliances. These politicians were resolutely determined to address the situation in Greece by implementing sanctions against the military regime and articulating their collective disapproval of its actions. A sense of urgency marked their response as they sought to uphold democratic values and human rights. The article provides a comprehensive examination of the pivotal relationship between the Council of Europe and the European Community during this pivotal moment in Greece's political history. Fernández Soriano argues that the European Community, in particular, not only condemned the Greek military regime but also adopted specific policy positions and normative frameworks derived from the Council of Europe's human rights standards. This collaboration and mutual support were instrumental in shaping a coherent response to the coup. Moreover, by taking a firm stand against the Greek regime, the European Community set a precedent that would influence its future human rights policies across Europe. The insights and lessons learned during this tumultuous period proved to be significant, laying the foundation for the Community's ongoing commitment to governance, democracy, and the protection of fundamental rights throughout the continent. This historical moment not only affected Greece but also had a lasting impact on the larger framework of European integration and human rights advocacy.

Greer and Williams focus on the European Convention on Human Rights, which was adopted by the Council of Europe in 1950 and remains a landmark document that has established an influential framework for the protection of human rights across Europe and beyond (Greer & Williams, 2009). It is widely recognised as the most successful experiment in providing transnational judicial protection for individuals' rights, setting a high standard that many other regions and countries strive to emulate. This Convention has been instrumental in addressing various human rights violations and has fostered a culture of accountability among its member states. In recent years, the European Union (EU) has increasingly prioritised human rights within its legal and political agenda. This growing interest has been met with enthusiasm, as many view it as a vital step toward enhancing the protection of fundamental rights in Europe. However, the relationship between the EU and the Convention system is not without complexity. While the crisis currently affecting the Convention system—including issues such as compliance and enforcement—has begun to garner attention, the challenges resulting from the increasing interdependence of the EU's human rights framework and that of the Convention have remained largely underexplored.

Among the limited number of scholars and practitioners who have addressed this interconnection, the prevailing view tends to be overly optimistic. A combination of good intentions and common sense will suffice to navigate the emerging challenges and find satisfactory resolutions. Nevertheless, the authors of this analysis express a more cautious perspective. They observe a looming crisis that threatens to intensify, particularly if the evolving relationship between the EU and human rights is not thoroughly examined and addressed. Greer and Williams argue that the core of this issue is deeply conceptual and outlines a critical question that, while seemingly simple, is fraught with complexities: Is the transnational protection of human rights in Europe fundamentally a matter of 'individual justice,' which emphasises the rights of the individual; 'constitutional justice,' which focuses on the application of these rights within the framework of constitutions and legal systems; or 'institutional justice,' which pertains to the roles and responsibilities of institutions in safeguarding these rights? This inquiry not only poses significant philosophical and legal implications but also challenges stakeholders to reevaluate their approaches to human rights protection in an increasingly interconnected European landscape.

Trommer and Chari articulate a nuanced critique of traditional literature on interest group behaviour, highlighting a prevailing assumption: that private interests strategically develop their lobbying approaches, primarily guided by the principle of effective resource allocation (Trommer & Chari, 2006). In practice, however, a notable paradox emerges. Nearly four hundred private interest groups are actively engaged in lobbying the Council of Europe, a prominent intergovernmental organisation characterised by its classical framework and limited decision-making authority. This raises a thought-provoking question: Why would these groups dedicate their efforts to influencing an institution that is frequently regarded as having minimal capacity to effect significant policy outcomes within the European political landscape? To unravel this complex puzzle, the analysis thoroughly investigates three well-documented explanations found in the existing literature. The first, 'policy overlap,' suggests that interest groups often lobby when their goals intersect with the policies being considered, creating opportunities for influence even in less powerful institutions. The second explanation, 'venue shopping,' refers to the strategic behaviour of interest groups as they seek out the most favourable arenas—whether national or international—where their advocacy efforts are likely to be most effective. Lastly, the concept of 'epistemic community' pertains to networks of experts who unite around specific issues, advocating for informed and specialised policy recommendations.

In addition to these established frameworks, Trommer and Chari present a fourth perspective—one that has not been extensively explored in prior literature—termed 'ideological motivation.' This explanation posits that the intrinsic beliefs and values held by interest groups significantly shape their lobbying behaviour and strategic choices. By acknowledging the ideological underpinnings that drive the actions of these groups, we can gain deeper insights into their preferences and the motivations that guide their lobbying efforts. By integrating the concept of ideological motivation into the analysis of lobbying strategies, the authors argue that we can gain a deeper understanding of certain preferences and actions that might otherwise appear counterintuitive or irrational within the traditional framework of interest representation. Ultimately, Trommer and Chari advocate for a more comprehensive approach that considers ideological motivations as a crucial element in examining the behaviour of any interest group, thus enriching the discourse on interest group dynamics and their role in influencing policy within the European context.

Stivachis and Habegger undertake a comprehensive examination of the historical trajectory of the Council of Europe, illuminating its pivotal role in the evolving post-enlargement European landscape (Stivachtis & Habegger, 2017). Their analysis meticulously traces the organisation's development, highlighting how its structural functions have adapted over time in response to the challenges and demands of a diverse membership, underscores the Council's ongoing commitment to cultivating a unified European regional international society, one that champions shared values and collaborative governance. The authors argue that the Council of Europe's process of liberal norm socialisation, which aims to instil democratic principles and human rights standards within its member states, remains partially incomplete. This remaining challenge is not merely an academic concern; it is integral to the organisation's overall legitimacy and effectiveness. The necessity for robust socialisation is inherent in the organisation's current context, as certain member states exhibit resistance or outright non-compliance with the core principles that the Council seeks to uphold. This dynamic presents significant obstacles to achieving the deepening of the European Regional International Society.

Moreover, Stivachis and Habegger emphasise the importance of the European Union's complementary roles and its institutions in supporting the Council's objectives. They illustrate how the two entities can work together synergistically, enhancing their collective efforts to promote democratic governance and human rights. This collaboration becomes even more crucial considering non-compliant states, as it bolsters a unified European response to these challenges. In the post-enlargement era, the Council of Europe has solidified its position as an indispensable player in the grand historical enterprise of Europeanization. This initiative aspires to weave together diverse nations under a common framework of democratic values and legal norms, thereby reinforcing the Council's vital role in shaping a harmonious and interconnected Europe. Through this, Stivachis and Habegger vividly illustrate the Council's ongoing mission and its significant impact on the continent's future.

In their comprehensive analysis, Simpson and Dervin examine the widespread and growing appeal of the intercultural concept, providing a close look at how it is understood and represented differently across various geographic and cultural contexts worldwide (Simpson & Dervin, 2019). They emphasize that the meanings attached to this notion are far from uniform; instead, they reveal a rich tapestry of interpretations that reflect the unique historical, social, and political backgrounds of different societies. The authors argue that this diversity stands in stark contrast to the concept of democracy, which is often perceived more superficially. Many approaches to democracy lean towards universal or absolutist frameworks that ignore local nuances and the complexities of cultural identity. Given these disparities, Simpson and Dervin contend that merging intercultural and democratic perspectives necessitates a careful and critical examination of both concepts. They illustrate their points by referencing The Council of Europe's Reference Framework of Competences for Democratic Culture. This influential document outlines the key competencies needed to nurture a democratic culture. It is expected to have a significant impact on educational systems not only across Europe but also in various educational contexts worldwide.

To dissect the intricate layers of the Framework, the authors employ a strategy known as intertextuality. This method allows them to draw connections between different texts and concepts, leading to a deeper understanding of the implications of the Framework's components. They focus their analysis on three crucial aspects identified within the document: identity competence, political competence, and intercultural competence. Through this lens, they expose how certain ideologies present in the Framework reflect Eurocentric narratives. Such ideologies can undermine the complexity of intercultural relations and contribute to the marginalization and stigmatization of those deemed “Other” or different.

Furthermore, Simpson and Dervin highlight how the sanitization of political discourse within the Framework can inadvertently promote a culture of depoliticization. This creates a landscape where individuals may feel compelled to conform and comply, stifling authentic engagement with democratic ideals. In light of these observations, the authors propose the concept of critical interculturality as a necessary framework for rethinking the intersections between culture and democracy. This approach aims to move beyond narrow, self-referential interpretations of the intercultural, arguing compellingly that the political and social dimensions of life are inextricably linked to intercultural interactions and discussions, particularly when considering the vitality and health of democratic societies.

Figure 1. Development of the Council of Europe

Source: *Council of Europe. (2024, February). Map of the Council of Europe 46 member States Eng/fra. Council of Europe Publishing. https://edoc.coe.int/en/map-of-the-member-states/11072-map-of-the-council-of-europe-46-member-states-engfra.html*

At first glance, one might believe that the Council of Europe fully embraces Winston Churchill's 1946 vision - a robust European organisation created to unite the continent and encourage cooperation among its members across diverse areas. It is important to recognise that the Council stands as a vital compromise among diverse and competing visions of Europe, clearly reflecting the intricate landscape of interests and aspirations held by its member nations.

These include a predominantly intergovernmental approach championed by the United Kingdom versus a more federalist perspective primarily supported by France and Italy. Furthermore, tension exists between the concept of a political Europe shaped by an overarching European organisation and an economic Europe focused on a large common market. Finally, the Council of Europe navigates the contrast between promoting a Europe founded on shared culture and values and one defined solely by geographic considerations.

Every individual from a Council of Europe member state has the profound right to seek justice from the European Court of Human Rights, a vital institution dedicated to safeguarding fundamental rights across the continent. The Council of Europe's Committee of Ministers champions the implementation of tens of thousands of judgments from the Court, positively transforming millions of lives.

Composed of foreign affairs ministers from each member state, the Committee is the Council's principal decision-making body, fostering collaboration and informed choices. The Parliamentary Assembly, with its 306 representatives from 46 member states, inspires democratic dialogue, elects key officials, and monitors elections, igniting meaningful conversations on pressing issues (Liechtenstein et al., 2024). Since its inception in 1994, the Congress of Local and Regional Authorities has been a beacon for enhancing local and regional democracy, uniting 612 elected officials to represent over 130,000 authorities (Council of Europe, 2006).

The Commissioner for Human Rights, established in 1999, advances human rights through awareness initiatives, regular country visits, and engagement with national authorities and civil society. This dynamic approach champions a robust commitment to human rights protection throughout Europe. The Council of Europe has established over 200 legally binding international treaties that effectively safeguard individuals from various threats, including torture, violence, and sexual abuse. Noteworthy initiatives include:

European Social Charter: With ratification by 42 member states, this charter is a critical framework for protecting essential economic and social rights. Sixteen countries have also embraced the collective complaints procedure before the European Committee of Social Rights.

Istanbul Convention: This groundbreaking treaty addressing violence against women and domestic violence has been signed by 45 countries and ratified by 37, ensuring its impactful entry into force.

Lanzarote Convention: Every one of the 46 member states has decisively ratified this convention, which focuses on protecting children from sexual exploitation and abuse. Tunisia's accession in 2019 as the first non-European signatory underscores the convention's global significance.

Council of Europe Convention on Action against Human Trafficking: All member states, along with Belarus and Israel, have signed and ratified this significant convention, demonstrating a united stance against human trafficking.

Cybercrime and Data Protection Conventions: These pivotal treaties encompass 68 countries, including the United States, Australia, and Japan. The data protection convention further extends its reach to 54 nations worldwide.

European Cultural Convention: This convention is vital in preserving Europe's rich cultural and natural heritage across approximately 50 countries.

Youth Policy: The Council has implemented a robust Youth Policy that actively engages youth representatives alongside public authorities, enhancing young people's representation and influence in the democratic process.

Sport-related Conventions: The Council has pioneered three essential conventions addressing match-fixing, doping, and safety and security at sporting events, reinforcing integrity in sports.

Artificial Intelligence Treaty: The Council has adopted the first legally binding international treaty to ensure human rights and democracy in artificial intelligence.

The Council of Europe is crucial in helping countries achieve shared European standards through its esteemed expert bodies. These include the Group of States against Corruption (GRECO), Committee for the Prevention of Torture (CPT), the Venice Commission, which advocates for democracy and the rule of law and the anti-money laundering and counter-terrorism financing body (MONEYVAL). Additionally, the European Commission against Racism and Intolerance (ECRI) diligently monitors trends in racism, discrimination, and hate speech, providing essential recommendations that empower member states to act.

Furthermore, the Council proactively safeguards the rights of individuals belonging to national minorities while promoting regional and minority languages. It has set exemplary educational standards that foster democratic citizenship and combat hate speech. Since its launch in 2015, the Platform for the Protection of Journalism and the Safety of Journalists has issued over 1,400 alerts for 42 member states, significantly raising awareness of threats to freedom of expression and underscoring the importance of protecting journalism as a pillar of democracy (Marcén, 2021).

Through its innovative HELP Programme, the Council stands out as a premier provider of online training on human rights for legal professionals, academics, and the public, reaching audiences throughout Europe and beyond. In response to the shrinking space for civil society in various regions, the Council actively champions democratic initiatives in Belarus through a dedicated Contact Group (Sahm, 2010, March). The Council of Europe and the European Union have forged a formidable political and strategic partnership, driving cooperation programs valued at over €230 million across numerous countries, both within and outside the European Union.

Enlargement

Over the decades, the Council expanded, and most members became part of European integration. The involvement of some non-EU member states in the Council of Europe can be seen as an example of the organisation's geopolitical pull or soft power. The states that, individually, have relied on the Council of Europe to assert their positions and interests are, unsurprisingly, primarily non-member states of the European Union, and more specifically, small states like Switzerland or very small ones like San Marino or Monaco, known as "micro-states" (Yigit, 2024a). The case of Turkey is different because while this state is currently taking advantage of the Council of Europe's role as an "antechamber to the EU" and "school of democracy" to assert its desire to join the EU, it is almost a founding member of the organisation and has long been involved partly related to the linkages of the Cold War (Yigit,

1996). How are these states' involvement and influence in the Council of Europe manifested? What are their interests and their strategies for asserting them?

Switzerland and Turkey are two very old members of the Council of Europe that are not, for different reasons, members of the EU. The case studies of these two states are interesting because they are historically and politically very different and, therefore, joined the Council of Europe with distinct interests. However, they are two very active states that cooperate with the organisation.

Why did Switzerland, known for being a neutral state, join this organisation, which was strongly influenced by its ideological affiliation with the Western camp during the Cold War? How does it perceive this organisation and its role? What is its involvement, and how does it assert its interests within the Council of Europe?

Turkey, whose membership in Europe is still contested in some quarters today, was nevertheless able to soon after joining the Council of Europe in 1950. Since this accession, Turkey has experienced two direct coups (in 1960 and 1980) and one indirect coup (in 1971) by its army. How has it reconciled an, at times, military regime with the values advocated by the Council of Europe without ever being excluded?

Switzerland: Accession of a Neutral

Switzerland's participation in the Council of Europe was not immediate, as it only joined the organisation on 6 May 1963, fourteen years after its creation. Switzerland would take another eleven years to ratify the European Convention on Human Rights in 1974. However, in Zurich, Churchill delivered his speech in 1946 on the need for European states to unite around Franco-German reconciliation. In Basel, the same year, one of Europe's great thinkers, the Swiss federalist Denis de Rougemont, created the Union of European Federalists (Domínguez Castro & Rodríguez Lago, 2022). It was also in Switzerland, in Gstaadt, that the European Parliamentary Union was founded by European parliamentarians, including Count Coudenhove-Kalergi, to impose the idea of a "European federation" with a constitution.

This marked the pro-European commitment of Switzerland at the end of the Second World War; however, it was quickly confronted by the tense international geopolitical context following the Prague coup and the Berlin blockade, which marked the beginning of the Cold War. Switzerland demonstrated itself as more reticent towards the projects of European unification, facing the dilemma of active solidarity with a group of powers – the Western democracies – to which its moral values and economic interests indisputably bound it or of asserting a policy of neutrality in the face of the two blocs being formed.

Officially neutral during both world wars, Switzerland only fully participated in the Organization for European Economic Cooperation (OEEC) to benefit from the Marshall Plan but expressed numerous reservations in 1948 due to this neutrality (Yigit, 2022). It ultimately chose to affirm its policy of neutrality concerning any attempt at European unification; as early as January 1949, the head of Swiss diplomacy explained to Robert Schuman, French Minister of Foreign Affairs, his country's desire to remain outside any political organisation and not to join any military alliance while collaborating with European countries at the economic level. It followed that Switzerland would not be invited to the Brussels Pact (later the WEU), the North Atlantic Treaty (NATO), nor the preparatory meeting for the creation of a European Union (later the Council of Europe).

Switzerland's choice of neutrality meant it rejected all political and military co-operation in Europe, but it remained heavily involved in other forms of cooperation, whether scientific or economic (Yigit, 2022a). At the same time as the creation of the Council of Europe, the Swiss government took the initiative of convening a meeting in Geneva on nuclear energy, which led to the creation of the European Council for Nuclear Research (CERN), located on the French-Swiss border near Geneva. They were also founding members of the ESRC in the space sector. Switzerland was keen for all Europeans to work together, but it was very wary of the potential political developments in these organisations.

In response to the signing of the Treaty of Rome in 1957, establishing the European Communities for economic and political purposes, Switzerland and six other states created the European Free Trade Association (EFTA) in 1960. This was simply an economic zone that posed no neutrality problems for them. From that moment on, the Council of Europe appeared to the Swiss to be much more legal than political, and they could join it. Switzerland's distrust of any form of political organisation has also been expressed towards the UN, whose European headquarters are based in Geneva, within the former structures of the League of Nations. As witnessed, Switzerland waited 57 years before becoming a full member in 2002.

The accession of another neutral state to the Council of Europe in 1956, Austria, must also have influenced Switzerland's decision, as the Austrian government considered that neutrality was not an obstacle to the membership of an organisation with no military competence. Swiss membership was not very popular with the population. When a "Committee for the Participation of Switzerland in the Council of Europe" was established in 1957, it collected only a little over 20,000 signatures in two years from a population of approximately six million (Fawcett, 1974). This explains why, despite the Swiss custom of holding a referendum on every international issue, there was no referendum on membership of the Council. However, despite the lack of interest that membership has aroused among the population, Swiss representatives were to play a very active role immediately.

The Swiss were very active within the Council of Europe, the only international political body they belonged to until 2002. Not involved in the EEC's supranational system, the Swiss quickly proved to be among the most active members of the

Council of Europe. Six years after accession, a Swiss parliamentarian, the Geneva Liberal National Councillor Olivier Reverdin, became President of the Parliamentary Assembly from 1969 to 1972 (Boulloche, Richter & Warren, 1976).

The first enlargement of the EEC, which increased from six to nine members, with the United Kingdom, Denmark, and Ireland joining in 1973, already raised the crucial question of the future of the Council of Europe. The Assembly's Political Affairs Committee then instructed Mr. Reverdin to prepare a report on the mission of the Council of Europe. This recourse to a Swiss parliamentarian was not accidental, as the organisation was referred to as the sleeping beauty, it was a politically serious issue; hence, they turned to the Swiss because they were the last resort for the Council of Europe. The neutral states had held the organisation back in the 1960s, especially in the Committee of Ministers, but did help later.

Mr Reverdin's report was debated in the Parliamentary Assembly, which adopted a recommendation to coordinate better the activities of the Council of Europe and the EEC (Chiti-Batelli, 1967). Four years later, a Swiss parliamentarian, Mr Pierre Aubert, presented a new report, which gave rise to a new recommendation from the Assembly following the EEC's decision to call direct elections for the European Parliament in 1979 (Blanc, 2013). Swiss parliamentarians, although few, were therefore very involved in questions relating to the future of the Council of Europe.

From November 1998 to January 2007, for more than eight years, the Swiss judge, Mr Luzius Wildhaber, was elected to the Parliamentary Assembly as the first President of the new ECHR and then re-elected twice more (Bruinsma & Parmentier, 2003). In the Committee of Ministers, Switzerland and Norway, non-EU members and comparable populations are among the most active. In contrast, in the Committee of Ministers, there are often common positions with Norway because it is not a member of the EU. They do not have any pre-organised consultation between non-EU countries, but this is secondary because, in meetings, they appear to support each other without prior consultation.

However, Switzerland's commitment at the highest level in the Committee of Ministers has diminished since it acceded to the UN in 2002, both financially, since Switzerland refuses any increase in the Council's budget, and also in terms of its representation. The foreign ministers of EU member states already meet regularly at the EU level, not to mention OSCE and NATO meetings, so they rarely attend the Council of Europe. However, Switzerland, unfortunately, has no lessons to teach since ministerial sessions are always attended by the Federal Minister of Foreign Affairs or his/her Secretary of State.

Therefore, Switzerland's new commitment to the UN has direct repercussions on its commitment to the Council of Europe. Although the Swiss delegation to the Parliamentary Assembly is small, comprising only six parliamentarians (three times fewer than France, Germany, or Italy), Swiss parliamentarians are far more engaged than most of their counterparts and serve as rapporteurs on several committees and the most sensitive issues.

Therefore, Switzerland has been fully committed to the Council of Europe since its accession, especially since it does not need this organisation as an "antechamber to the EU" since it already meets all the Copenhagen political criteria for membership. Invoking its "neutrality" vis-à-vis the EU also hides other issues. The Swiss, who benefit from one of the highest GDPs per capita in the world, fear that membership would have direct consequences on banking secrecy or the level of taxation. However, more than 70% of its foreign trade is with EU states, and Switzerland's entire border is contiguous with the EU, except for Liechtenstein. Therefore, for foreign trade, Switzerland must adopt laws that consider EU directives and acquis, developed without its participation in Brussels. It may be asked whether this situation will not be perceived as an obstacle to its national sovereignty, where the only solution would ultimately be membership. However, in the medium term, the Swiss do not seem ready for EU membership and are content with their membership of the Council of Europe.

Turkey: Military Regime Reconciling With The Council of Europe

Turkey is an interesting case study within the Council of Europe. This state's interests in the organisation are very old, dating back to when it initially became a member. However, its interests have evolved considerably since its formal application for membership in the EEC in 1987. The Council of Europe thus became an "antechamber" and "a school of democracy" for Turkey for twenty years (Bond, 2016).

Officially, Turkey and Greece were the first two states to accede to the Council of Europe and join its ten founding members on 9 August 1949, just three months after its creation by the Treaty of London. They were then co-opted by the other member states meeting within the Committee of Ministers without waiting for the green light from the Assembly since the latter would not hold its first session until the following day, on 10 August. For many, this choice did not pose any problems in the context of the Cold War. Since Turkey was part of the Western camp, the founders of the Council of Europe thought it would be a good idea to include it in this organisation. Hence, the invitation came from the Council of Europe, and the Turkish government, without hesitation, agreed to join because it was the organisation to which they felt they belonged throughout their history. It was not a difficult choice, and there were not all the problems encountered in the negotiations for accession to the European Union.

Even though only 3% of its territory is geographically located in Europe, Turkey's geographical or cultural belonging to Europe did not arise in the tense context of the Cold War, especially since concerns about potential threats linked to Islamism were non-existent. At its creation, the United States, one of the main political and financial supporters of the Council of Europe, has always supported Turkey's attachment to the Western camp and encouraged its accession among the founding countries. Due to its geostrategic position as a "shield" of the Western world against the expansionism of the Soviet Union, which wishes to access the Mediterranean through the Bosphorus Strait and the Dardanelles, Turkey occupies an important place within the Council.

This is probably why the Council of Europe symbolically admitted it on the same day as Greece, even though Turkey had not administratively prepared for it. The statute of the Council of Europe was only ratified by Turkey on 13 April 1950, and therefore, it only really became a member on that date, eight months after Greece and one month after Iceland, which joined on 7 March 1950 (Robertson, 1954). However, the Council of Europe still officially uses 9 August 1949 as the date of accession while specifying that Turkey is the 13th Member State, which causes a slight anachronism with Iceland, the 12th Member State. The Council of Europe has always been concerned and cared about maintaining its equidistant relations with Greece and Turkey. However, relations between Turkey and the Strasbourg-based organisation have never been simple, primarily because the Council of Europe was, until 1989, considered a club of Western democracies with a certain number of basic rules to be respected.

Between 1950 and 2008, Turkey violated the "club " rules several times without ever being excluded. It experienced two direct military coups, the first in 1960, only ten years after its accession, and the second in 1980, as well as two interventions (indirect coups) forcing democratically elected prime ministers to resign in 1971. Therefore, the army's role was considerable in Turkey, and it did not hesitate to temporarily seize power when it believed that the legacy of Mustafa Kemal Atatürk, founder of the Turkish Republic in 1923, was threatened. This legacy, called the "Kemalist Revolution" in Turkey, was to protect the Westernization of the state, notably through the adoption of the Latin alphabet to replace the Arabic alphabet, the relocation of the capital from Istanbul to Ankara, and the application of secularism on the model of French secularism.

1980 Coup d'Etat

The 1980 military coup occurred when three Southern European states, Greece, Spain and Portugal, emerged from long years of dictatorship and finally joined the organisation. However, few within the Council of Europe criticised Turkey, especially since the Turkish military had American support. This coup officially lasted only three years but left deep scars until the mid-1990s due to the mindset and the constitution it created. This legacy cost Turkey in Court before the European Court of Human Rights.

During the Cold War, neither France, the United Kingdom, nor Germany, within the Council of Europe, wanted to see human rights violations in Turkey but were less interested in pushing them to the forefront. Human rights became a prominent factor only after the Cold War ended. If, in the 1950s and 1960s, all member states of the Council of Europe had been asked to comply with the ECHR, Turkey, alongside other southern European states, would certainly have been excluded.

An exclusion procedure was initiated against Greece when the "Colonels" seized power and established a dictatorship in April 1967. Greece withdrew from the Council of Europe in 1969 under penalty of imminent exclusion and could only rejoin the organisation at the end of the dictatorship in 1974 (Kubas, 2022). Questions arose concerning whether the Council of Europe member states applied a policy of double standards towards the military intervention in Turkey.

Arguments were put forward justifying the conciliatory attitude of the organisation as Turkey was threatened with exclusion; the institution was always hesitant to go that far because the situation was so chaotic before the coup. There was much positive reaction in the Council of Europe when the generals took power in 1980, even though it was a military regime that was hardly compatible with the established values (Soyaltin-Colella, 2021). However, given the previous situation, the organisation were willing to accept the generals' promises to restore democracy quickly despite the poor human rights situation. They were more sympathetic, at times accused of being too lenient, to the Turkish military than the Greek colonels (Constas, 1982). However, the Greek colonels wanted to establish a regime of terror, which was not the case in Turkey.

One of the reasons undoubtedly concerned the dictatorship in Greece, which was very conservative. The far-right military junta, which enjoyed American support, was unlikely to fall into the Soviet camp, and the Council of Europe could, therefore, without too much risk, exclude it from the organisation (Okur, 2015). The situation in Turkey was quite different, since in the late 1970s, a radicalisation of the opposition between far-right and far-left groups caused several thousand victims until the military coup in September 1980. This military dictatorship was interpreted positively as a halt to a chaotic situation of terror.

Turkey was in a period of considerable instability, quite close to a full-blown civil war, with approximately thirty violent deaths every day. Ordinary non-political students taking a public bus to go to university would see corpses in the streets that had been machine-gunned from cars. Many who were progressive and anti-militarist, with no sympathy for any military regime, were relieved when the military took power and put an end to this situation, even though it did much damage afterwards.

Response of the Council of Europe's Institutions

The military, which historically enjoyed enormous popularity among the Turkish population, always assured the Council of Europe that it would restore democratic institutions and that Turkey's membership in the organisation would help them to do so (Dagi, 1996). While waiting for the situation to improve, they made concessions, such as relinquishing the chairmanship of the Committee of Ministers, thus skipping their turn. Aware of this situation and undoubtedly encouraged by the United States to engage in dialogue, the Council of Europe member states never initiated exclusion proceedings against Turkey, fearing it would fall into the Soviet camp. Only five states—Denmark, France, the Netherlands, Norway, and Sweden—mobilised and filed an inter-state complaint against Turkey with the European Court of Human Rights in June 1982 (Leckie,1988). This complaint was ultimately withdrawn following promises from the generals of a rapid return to democracy, which was kept.

The greatest pressure, however, came from the Parliamentary Assembly, which had no qualms about sanctioning the military coup by suspending the participation of the Turkish parliamentary delegation on 14 May 1981 (Donald & Speck, 2019, June). This suspension lasted just under three years since, following the Turkish parliamentary elections of November 1983, the Assembly ratified the credentials of the Turkish delegation in January 1984, thus normalising relations between Turkey and the organisation (Dagi, 2001). Relations between the Council of Europe and Turkey improved despite the criticism. Where would Turkey be if all the Parliamentary Assembly's missions and the inter-state complaint against Turkey had not occurred? Who would have both kept Turkey in a European institution where it wanted to be, with Atatürk's legacy, and at the same time helped train the authorities, help them evolve and be patient. They have often been attacked or accused of being overprotective or lax. Nevertheless, the procedures continued, and the Turks adhered to the rules, returning to the mindset of being held accountable. As part of its return to democracy and the values advocated by the Council of Europe, Turkey strategically pursued its normalisation with the organisation, with the more ambitious objective of joining the EEC.

Turkey's membership in the Council of Europe was more a desire to side with the democratic Western bloc at the start of the Cold War than a desire to claim to be an exemplary "European" state. However, in the early 1960s, Turkey sought closer ties with the EEC and signed an association agreement with it in 1963, which included the prospect of membership. It then undoubtedly asserted its early membership in the first European organisation. An interesting artefact demonstrating such a viewpoint can be found in passports issued during the 1960s. On the cover of these passports, it says: 'Republic of Turkey. Member of the Council of Europe,' exactly as it says 'European Union' on member states passports decades later.

Such evidence indicates the importance the Council of Europe held for Turkey and its external image at the time. In 1970, Turkey and the EEC strengthened their association by signing an additional financial protocol. However, in the 1980s, the military dictatorship squelched any prospect of Turkish membership in the EEC. Sanctioned by the Parliamentary Assembly, Turkish generals strengthened their presence in other areas at the Council of Europe, starting with culture, by organising a major European art exhibition under the organisation's auspices. The Turks' European commitment, even under the dictatorship, was clear. Despite the dictatorship in Turkey, the generals tried to get closer to Europeans. In December 1983, a huge effort was mobilised to organise an exhibition called "Anatolian Civilizations." With this exhibition, Turkey wanted to prove, through objects of civilisation, that it had assimilated, developed, and respected everything on its territory before the arrival of the Turks.

However, this did not mean there were no other pressing problems. An important issue related to women. While this exhibition was prepared largely by women who had invested a lot in it, on the day of the exhibition's opening at Topkapi Palace, they were pushed into a nearby room, and there were only men at the opening. Nevertheless, Turkey did open up culturally thanks to the Council of Europe, and two years after this exhibition, they organised another major exhibition, "Suleiman the Magnificent," which toured the world and was deemed a huge success (Kljajić & Lapaine, 2013).

Return to Democracy

Such initiatives are interesting because they highlight how difficult it was for Turkey to comply with European standards despite its desire to present itself culturally as a major European power, even under an authoritarian regime. Emerging from authoritarianism, Turkey sought a strong gesture to erase the memory of it and to move politically closer to the EEC and the democratic standards in force in the other member states of the Council of Europe. After the coup, Turkey was absent from the European scene for several years. The liberal Turkish government of Premier Özal decided to submit an official application for membership in the EEC to make people look to the future and not dwell on the past. Behind the scenes, the European states advised Turkey to be realistic, especially after emerging from such a worrisome past. However, European leaders also suggested to Turkey that it would facilitate its candidacy if it recognised its citizens' right to file a complaint against the Turkish state with the European Court of Human Rights.

This explains why Turkey granted the right of individual petition to the Court on 28 January 1987, three months before formally submitting its application to the EEC on 14 April. This decision was difficult as the Turks were very concerned about their sovereignty and wanted to control everything in their territory. Hence, it was not easy to accept the control of a supranational body, especially after a military regime. This decision was not taken lightly, as Turkey was still experiencing many difficulties. The Court had many problems, but it also assisted in democratisation. The Court was able to highlight how to find a balance between the fight against terrorists and the safeguarding of human rights. The reforms of the 2000s in Turkey were prepared with maximum regard to the Court's rulings that they were obliged to implement, and their criticism of Turkey was much more comprehensive than the criticism from the EU or other bodies.

Turkey also ratified the European Convention for the Prevention of Torture and its mechanism for monitoring all places of detention in 1988 (Cassese, 1989). However, accepting the right of individual petitions and ratifying this convention was not sufficient in the eyes of the European Commission, which issued a negative opinion on the opening of accession negotiations in 1989 due to Turkey's economic and political context and its poor situation regarding human rights and minority rights.

In March 1995, Turkey's economic integration with the EU continued with the signing of a customs union agreement that took effect in 1996 and abolished import duties on products from the EU. However, at the same time, Turkey intensified its fight against the separatist Kurdistan Workers' Party (PKK), which had been waging a guerrilla war against it in the southeastern quarter of Turkey since 1984 until the arrest of their leader Abdullah Öcalan in 1999. Faced with accusations of repression and torture practised by the Turkish military, the Parliamentary Assembly raised such issues and placed Turkey under its monitoring procedure, along with the new democracies emerging from Eastern Europe. To avoid harming its application for EU membership, Turkey accepted this monitoring procedure, observing its obligations to Council of Europe standards.

Turkey's official application was finally accepted by the EU at the Helsinki Summit in 1999, although the EU tightened the conditions for its entry. In June 2001, the Parliamentary Assembly's Monitoring Committee published its first monitoring report on Turkey. It adopted a resolution urging it to change its constitution, drawn up under the 1982 military dictatorship, and calling for the abolition of the death penalty. Turkey then radically amended its constitution in October to meet its obligations to the Council of Europe and fulfil the political criteria set by the EU. It also abolished the death penalty in 2002. The effectiveness of the joint pressure from the Council of Europe and the EU was palpable.

Turkey demonstrated its goodwill by even allowing the publication of all reports of the Committee for the Prevention of Torture, which is responsible for monitoring compliance with the convention of the same name, which visits the country every year and publishes a report. In its second monitoring report on Turkey in 2004, the Parliamentary Assembly welcomed all the progress made by the Turkish authorities.

It adopted a resolution that expressed its confidence in the Turkish authorities to implement and consolidate the reforms concerned and, therefore, decided to close the monitoring procedure, which had operated since 1996. Turkey was, therefore, placed in a post-monitoring dialogue procedure to encourage reforms on certain points.

In his speech to the Parliamentary Assembly in October 2004, Turkish Prime Minister Erdoğan recalled the extent of the reforms carried out in recent years by drawing up an exhaustive list (Aydindag, 2021). He described them as a "silent revolution" and welcomed the Assembly's decision to close the monitoring process. He also welcomed the positive conclusions of its latest report, which it described as important for Turkey in its EU accession process. Despite the end of the monitoring procedure, Turkey continued to demonstrate goodwill by following the Parliamentary Assembly's recommendations by adopting a new penal code in 2005, which was more in line with the standards of individual freedoms required by the Council of Europe. There was widespread domestic acknowledgement that improvements had taken place in Turkey, notably thanks to the numerous condemnations of Turkey by the ECHR. Turkey has, however, accumulated the largest number of judgments handed down by the Court since 2004. Despite this, there has been a clear evolution in freedom of thought in the practice of torture, which is no longer systematic. The role of the Court is very positive because its judgments have a strong influence on Turkey. They have served as a mirror, showing its negative practices.

In response to all these positive developments, the EU began accession negotiations with Turkey in October 2005. The Council of Europe played a major role in the accession to the EU. Its monitoring mechanisms were very effective, such as the European Court of Human Rights, the Monitoring Committee, and the Committee for the Prevention of Torture. Moreover, when Turkey cooperated with the Council of Europe, the EU could appreciate that Turkey was active because representatives of the European Commission often came to the Council of Europe to verify the results of its expertise.

EU membership, however, is conditional on Turkey resolving many unresolved issues. These issues particularly affect relations between Turkey and its neighbouring states, notably Greece, Armenia, Syria, and the Greek Cypriots. Turkey imposed a border blockade on Armenia in 1993 following the Nagorno-Karabakh conflict between Armenia and Azerbaijan. Syria claimed the Hatay region (ceded to Turkey by France in 1938) from Turkey. It criticised Turkey for its water flow management at the Euphrates Dam, upstream of the Turkish-Syrian border. However, the biggest problem to be resolved for Turkey's EU membership remained the unresolved Cyprus problem, with its detractors focusing on the island's division in 1974.

Micro-States in the Council of Europe

Among the member states of the Council of Europe, microstates represent a special category. The world has relatively few microstates, but most are concentrated in Europe. Due to their small size and small population, they represent a form of confetti in European territory (Yigit, 2024). However, they are sovereign states represented in the Parliamentary Assembly, the Committee of Ministers, and other international organisations such as the UN. Why did these microstates, more often famous for the royal or princely families that reign there or for their attractive tax systems and banking facilities than for their role in foreign policy, want to become members of the Council of Europe? What were their interests and influence in the organisation?

The smallest of the European microstates but certainly the most influential, Vatican City in Rome, is not a member of the Council of Europe. However, the Holy See is an observer on the Committee of Ministers, along with the United States, Japan, Mexico, and Canada. The oldest observer is Israel, though only in the Parliamentary Assembly. Why did these states want to be observers? Are they active, and what weight do they carry in the Council of Europe?

There is no precise definition of what a microstate is, and it remains subjective by definition. In 1967, the UN Secretary-General, U Thant, proposed a definition for the term "microstate" as "entities that are extremely small in terms of their area, population, human and economic resources." Due to a lack of consensus, this definition is not based on any numerical statistics of population or territory as delimitation criteria.

The common trait of all microstates is that they are neither an economic nor a military power. Europe has almost ten of them, which are very different from each other in size and population: Andorra, Liechtenstein, Luxembourg, Malta, Monaco, San Marino, and the Vatican. These microstates are all remnants of the feudal era and, for some, have not always had a continuous existence, depending on the era. Despite its size comparable to that of Portugal, Iceland is also sometimes considered a microstate due to its very small population - barely 300,000 inhabitants - comparable to that of Malta.

European microstates range in size from 0.5 km^2 for the Vatican to 2,586 km^2 for Luxembourg, and their populations are always less than half a million, or between 1,000 inhabitants for the Vatican and 473,000 for Luxembourg. Luxembourg's largest and most populous microstate is 260 times smaller than France and 136 times less populated. This contrast also exists between microstates since Monaco is 1,300 times smaller than Luxembourg and 15 times less populated.

Since Monaco's accession in 2004, all European microstates have become members of the Council of Europe, except the Vatican, which cannot be a full member due to its undemocratic functioning, according to the Council's standards. Why did these microstates, often with few diplomatic representations abroad, want to join an international organisation? Moreover, what was the Council of Europe's reaction to these states' desire to join?

The answer depends on the state's situation and the geopolitical context. Luxembourg is the only microstate that is one of the organisation's founding members. It is historically closely linked to Belgium and the Netherlands, with which it created a free-trade customs union in 1948, the Benelux (for Belgium, Netherlands, Luxembourg), with a common tax on foreign products. This initiative is often considered one of the cores of European construction, and it is, therefore, with this perspective of European integration, Luxembourg wished to participate in the creation of the Council of Europe from the negotiation phase. Luxembourg's weight is, therefore, much greater than that of the other microstates.

Malta was, therefore, the first micro-state to join the Council of Europe in 1965, seven months after the United Kingdom recognised its independence (Willems, 2007). However, the island remained ruled by Queen Elizabeth II until 1974. Situated in the middle of the Mediterranean basin, between Sicily, Tunisia and Libya, Malta was long disputed between Arabs and Christians, and its desire to join the Council of Europe can be explained as much by the desire to assert its recently acquired sovereignty as by the demonstration of its belonging to Europe. Due to its relative demographic importance, with nearly 540,000 inhabitants, Malta's membership was not contested within the Council of Europe, unlike that of Liechtenstein, when it joined in 1978.

The Principality of Liechtenstein, which is significantly less populated than Malta, Luxembourg and Iceland, made it necessary to deal comprehensively with the issue of very small states in 1978 within the Council of Europe. After a long and cautious approach and exciting debates in the Parliamentary Assembly, the Council of Europe approved the admission of the principality and, in doing so, also decided on the question of its future policy towards the smallest European countries (Fawcett, 1974).

After Liechtenstein, three other micro-states joined the Council of Europe: San Marino in 1988, Andorra in 1994 and Monaco in 2004. For these four states, the main objective was to confirm their state sovereignty. For a long time, San Marino had a somewhat unfair image at the international level as an Italian protectorate, even though their sovereignty dated back more than seventeen centuries. Hence, their participation in the Council of Europe in 1988 fulfilled this whole affirmation and confirmation of sovereignty and the role they could play within this organisation since other small states were already part of it. It was very interesting for them to join at that time because they obtained the chairmanship of the Committee of Ministers in 1990 and joined the UN two years later. Their policies often conflict with Italian policy because other factors determine the latter. Italy is a large country, almost a great power, since it is part of the G8 and does not have the same interests as a small state.

This desire to distance itself from the "powerful" neighbouring state is strongly felt in San Marino, a state of barely 61 km^2 and 33,000 inhabitants. It is completely landlocked within Italy (5,000 times larger and 2,000 times more populated), with which a customs union links. Other micro-states, such as Andorra or Liechtenstein, are between two large states. This situation logically leads to solidarity within the Council as they have excellent relations with all small states. They strongly supported the accession of Andorra and then Monaco because they were very sensitive to what was happening in other small states. Although they face different geopolitical situations, they have common budgetary problems.

Small states, however, do not constitute a homogeneous interest group within the Council of Europe and generally prioritise their relations with their neighbours, such as Luxembourg with Belgium (and to a lesser extent with France and Germany) or Liechtenstein with Switzerland and Austria. The Council of Europe also allows micro-states to maintain diplomatic ties with all other member states at little cost, even though they often have few diplomatic representations (embassies, consulates) abroad due to their limited resources.

Micro-states sometimes try to outdo each other to make themselves heard at the Council of Europe. Malta, which enjoyed a strategic position during the Cold War, used the organisation to assert its positions and demands, accompanied by ultimatums and threats, including the threat of allying itself with Libya or the USSR if it did not obtain satisfaction. Prime Minister Mintoff, who appeared at the Parliamentary Assembly in 1978 during the Maltese Presidency of the Committee of Ministers, clearly demonstrated this double game (Pace, 1999). Such an attitude reveals a clear desire to assert its sovereignty in the face of the major European powers, as was recently observed during Monaco's accession in 2004.

The Principality of Monaco is, after Vatican City, the smallest state in the world. With 38,000 inhabitants spread over 2 km^2, it is landlocked on the French Mediterranean coast. Like Andorra and Liechtenstein, Monaco is gradually becoming a free zone, attracting large amounts of foreign capital and companies thanks to its tax advantages. These three states are among the three non-cooperative tax havens listed in the world by the OECD, which has, therefore, made no commitments regarding transparency and effective exchange of information. As for its two predecessors, this situation did not prevent it from joining the Council of Europe in 2004, six years after it applied for membership. This relative slowness in the accession process can be explained by the democratisation of power that the principality had to undertake to meet the conditions for membership.

In addition to a revision of its constitution in 2002 and the reform of the electoral law aimed at ensuring greater political pluralism within the Monaco Parliament, Monaco and France had to revise the 1930 Franco-Monaco Convention, which ensured access for the Monegasque to certain public offices in France and senior Monegasque civil service positions for French citizens. The two states also had to review the 1918 treaty governing Monaco and France's ties. This treaty stipulated that Monaco would become an integral part of France if the Crown Prince failed to inherit. The amendment to this treaty stipulates that France would be informed in the event of a change in the order of succession in Monaco, which considerably strengthens the principality's sovereignty. The first article of the new 2002 treaty stated that the French Republic assured the Principality of Monaco the defence of its independence and sovereignty and guaranteed the integrity of Monegasque territory under the same conditions as its own. For the Principality of Monaco, membership symbolises the acquisition of a pledge of credibility and international respectability, as did the membership of previous microstates. This international brand is also fuelled by the overrepresentation of microstates within the Council of Europe relative to their population and contribution.

In theory, each state has one representative on the Committee of Ministers and, therefore, one vote to make decisions. The states' votes are not weighted as they are in the EU Council of Ministers. Therefore, the vote of a microstate with a population of 29,000, like San Marino, counts as much as that of the Russian Federation, with over 143 million inhabitants. The overrepresentation of micro-states is also noticeable in the Parliamentary Assembly. Despite their very low contribution to the Council of Europe's budget, the total share of the six micro-states being only 0.5% of the organisation's total budget, they are nevertheless very well represented in the Assembly since they have at least two parliamentarians, regardless of their population and contribution. There is one parliamentarian for every 16,000 Monegasques in the Parliamentary Assembly, compared to one for every 3.6 million French people. Therefore, the distribution of votes in the Assembly reflects the interests of the micro-states.

This situation explains why micro-states take their participation in this organisation very seriously and generally send their foreign ministers to the meetings of the Committee of Ministers, while the larger states often send a diplomat to replace the foreign minister. The Council of Europe is an important carrot for some states because it allows their ministers to meet when they do not have the opportunity elsewhere. Small or recently joined states are more interested in travelling to Strasbourg than larger ones. Not surprisingly, states such as San Marino, Monaco, Andorra, and Liechtenstein have few opportunities to meet apart from relatively rare bilateral relations.

For micro-states, institutional issues at the Council of Europe are of paramount importance, and any attempt to challenge the principle of equality of states provokes strong resistance on their part. They often insist on the principle of equality between member states so that in the Committee of Ministers, the principle of one state equals one vote. In any case, micro-states try to obtain consensus in the Committee of Ministers so as not to resort to a two-thirds majority vote.

Although, in theory, all states enjoy the same rights at the Council of Europe and San Marino, like Italy just before it, chaired the Council of Europe for six months (from November 2021 to May 2022), in practice, states are not equal (Baukhage, 2010, April). Their influence logically depends on their contribution to the organisation's budget. While there is no problem considering positions because they are informal, the number of experts in the working groups and rapporteurs who create the conventions depends on what states contribute to finances. The power distribution in the Committee of Ministers and the Council of Europe means that the big financial contributors are much more influential than the others. Therefore, The principle that one country equals one vote does not correspond to reality because a country such as Germany, in effect, has much more than 1/46th of votes in the Committee of Ministers.

A microstate like San Marino has no civil servants within the Council of Europe, except for a judge at the European Court of Human Rights, which de facto limits their influence. The other problem for microstates within the Council of Europe is that they sometimes struggle to respect the rules of democratic values the organisation advocates. With great reluctance, Prince Rainier III finally agreed to bequeath more legislative power to the parliament, called the National Council, and was forced to accept political alternation after the 2003 elections. The situation has been more problematic in Liechtenstein since Prince Hans-Adam II pushed through a reform bill in 2003, threatening to leave Liechtenstein for Austria if he did not get his way. He then obtained 65% of the vote to implement his reforms, considerably strengthening his power to make him resemble an absolute monarch, able to dismiss the government and parliament at will (Turmer, 2008). The Council of Europe then strongly opposed these constitutional reforms, which the Venice Commission described as a clear step backwards. The Secretary-General Schwimmer even warned Liechtenstein that it was exposing itself to a monitoring process in Turkey's mould or even being excluded from the organisation at the same level as Belarus (Fawn &Fawn, 2013). This type, however, is a clash in that micro-states generally seek to prioritise the best relations with the organisation, which holds a primordial place in their foreign policy.

CONCLUSION

The Council of Europe represents the "European idea," which has inspired efforts for unity since the 19th century. The phrase "United States of Europe," popularized by Winston Churchill, originally came from 1848. Victor Hugo imagined a future where Europe and America would work together. Between the world wars, different groups promoted ideas for European unity. They suggested various ways to bring countries closer, such as cultural, economic, or political integration. The Council of Europe was established after 1945 to start making this idea a reality.

Any comprehensive examination of the Council of Europe's development from 1949 to 2025 must confidently acknowledge the narrative shift. The Council was established as a crucial part of the post-1945 Europe-building process during the Cold War, with a clear focus on economic recovery. The United States launched the Marshall Plan in June 1947, which led to the formation of the Organisation for European Economic Cooperation (OEEC) on April 16, 1948, effectively managing American aid distribution among European nations.

Simultaneously, military alliances emerged in response to the Prague coup in February 1948, which brought communists to power in Czechoslovakia. This division of Europe was solidified by the signing of the Brussels Pact on March 17, 1948, by five Western European countries, establishing a firm mutual support and defence treaty. On April 4, 1949, Western Europe took a bold step by forming military ties with the United States through the North Atlantic Treaty, paving the way for establishing the North Atlantic Treaty Organization (NATO) in 1950. This monumental alliance was soon complemented by the establishment of the Council of Europe just one month later, on May 5, 1949, signalling a commitment to unity and cooperation. A year later, on May 9, 1950, Robert Schuman envisioned a groundbreaking proposal to pool coal and steel production, which became the foundation for the Treaty of Paris. This pivotal treaty, signed on April 18, 1951, created the European Coal and Steel Community (ECSC), marking a transformative moment in fostering economic collaboration and peace in Europe.

The narrative of the Council of Europe is intricately connected to several other European and Atlantic organizations, such as the European Economic Community (EEC), NATO, and the European Coal and Steel Community (ECSC), which were established in rapid succession between 1948 and 1951. A pivotal element of this story is the evolving relationship between "Greater Europe," represented by the Council of Europe's ten member states, and "Smaller Europe," which comprises the ECSC's six member states—commonly referred to as "the Six"—all of which are also Council members.

As time progressed, however, the smaller group, which became increasingly integrated within the EEC in 1957 and subsequently evolved into the European

Union (EU) in 1992, began to overshadow the Council. Consequently, the Council of Europe was largely diminished in prominence and even forgotten by specialists in European affairs and the general public. Today, it is important to recognize that Europe still exists in two forms: "smaller" (the 27-member EU) and "greater" (the 47-member Council of Europe).

One must consider the Council of Europe, as it represents a crucial aspect of Europe that extends beyond the EEC and EU. The Council embodies a vision centred on fundamental values such as human rights, democracy, and the rule of law rather than merely serving as an economic market. Europe's boundaries encompass countries like Russia and Turkey, frequently arising in "Community" Europe " discussions. By examining the history of the Council of Europe, one gains a more comprehensive understanding of European integration that transcends the economic focus of the EU. Hence, non-EU member states are important to the Council of Europe. This organisation occupies a large place in its foreign policy for various reasons, from asserting its sovereignty in the face of large neighbouring states or former colonisers to asserting its European identity.

The Council of Europe is an organisation that creates European law through the treaties it adopts and the monitoring mechanisms it establishes to enforce them, including the European Court of Human Rights. Small states benefit from the legal protection this system offers, the equal treatment afforded to larger states in the Committee of Ministers, and the favourable treatment afforded to the Parliamentary Assembly about their population and contribution. Some small states, even microstates like Cyprus and Malta, joined the EU in 2004. However, most, often for fiscal or neutrality reasons, such as Switzerland, do not wish to join, and their participation in the Council of Europe remains their priority.

Turkey was one of the states that, along with the Russian Federation before its expulsion, most clearly marked the difference between the Council of Europe and the EU, and which allowed the Council to retain a certain influence in European integration. This influence is all the stronger as Turkey, engaged in a long and uncertain process of accession to the EU, increasingly scrupulously respects the standards and commitments entered into with the Council of Europe to facilitate its candidacy. If this process results in Turkey's full membership of the EU, the Council of Europe will undoubtedly no longer play such an important role and thus lose much of its added value. However, due to its large population and economic instability, alongside questions regarding the functioning of its judicial system, Turkey is likely to remain one of the main clients of the European Court of Human Rights in the short term.

Observer states' influence has changed over time depending on their interests. While they have given real importance to the organisation for its role as a "school of democracy" in the Balkans, they were still interested in it for some of its technical cooperation activities, particularly concerning the fight against terrorism, cybercrime, bioethics, and health. However, these states favoured organisations of which they were full members, such as NATO, the OSCE, or the OECD, especially since the Council of Europe is often very critical of those who do not respect its democratic standards, notably by refusing to abolish the death penalty.

In the final analysis, the compression of space-time linked to globalization and new technologies relativizes the boundary between the national and international spheres, blurring our perception of foreignness. More broadly, while the notion of international relations is subject to a series of approximations and confusions, these stem from an intrinsic duality. On the one hand, the expression designates an empirical reality. This corresponds primarily to all interstate relations. This is the original meaning of the epithet "international," a word coined by the British philosopher Jeremy Bentham in the early 19th century: it literally refers to relations "between nations," that is, between states. This original conception has been the subject of an expansion linked to the emergence and development of interstate (international organizations) and trans-state or transnational (non-state internal subjects that fall under and operate within the territories of different states). International relations therefore include interstate relations and transnational relations, that is, any cross-border relationship, public or private, regardless of the nature or status of the actors capable of acting beyond the sole national-state sphere.

The expansion of international organisations such as the Council of Europe further questions the main conceptions of international relations regarding the "anarchic" nature of the international system with near unanimity concerning "anarchy" as the structuring concept of the system (Yigit, 2023). It should be noted that this notion is understood here not as a synonym for chaos or disorder, but in the etymological sense of the word (from the Greek anarkhia) meaning "absence of (higher) authority" capable of imposing its will or decision, its arbitration. Since all states are by definition "sovereign," no higher, transcendent authority is conceivable (Yigit, 2023a). This fundamental fact immediately limits the analogy between national society and international society. This characteristic of international relations does not, however, allow for the delineation of its "boundaries."

The traditionally state-centric and Western-centric nature of the system is being (re)challenged by the multidimensional effects of decolonization, the end of the Cold War, and globalization. Not reducible to the classic themes of war and peace, the subject and field of international organisations are constantly expanding. Reconstructing all of its constituent elements requires a systematization of knowledge, approaches, and structuring concepts. Such an endeavour thus stems from a construct (and not a "given"), which has its roots in a long history.

Figure 2. Council of Europe: 2022

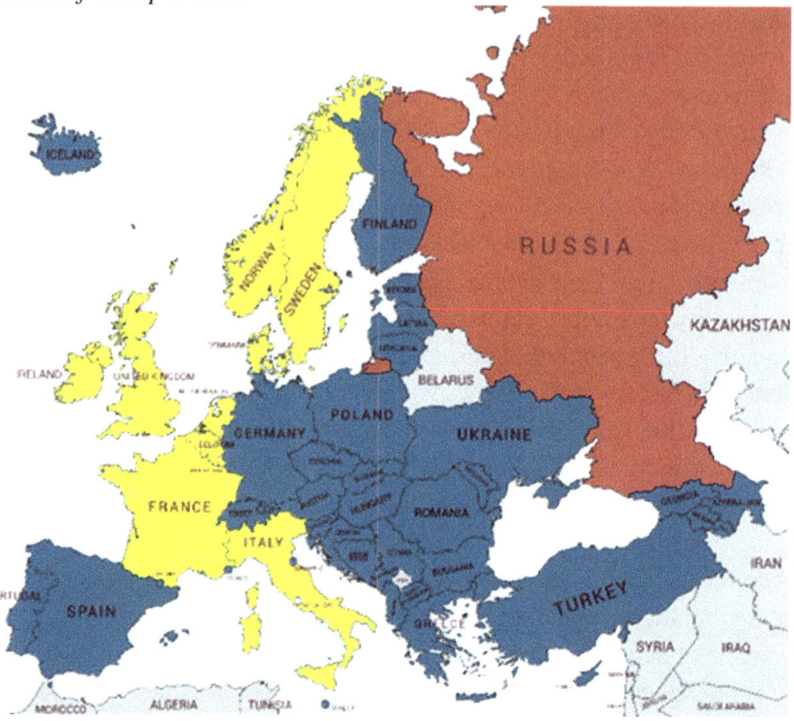

Source: *JayCoop. (2022, March 7). File:map of council of europe member states by founding and later members.svg. Wikimedia Commons. https://commons.wikimedia.org/wiki/File:Map_of_Council_of_Europe_member_states_by_founding_and_later_members.svg*
Yellow: *Founding Members*
Blue: *Newer Members/Enlargements*
Red: Former Member

The soft power of the Council of Europe was evident in its relationship with Russia. Russia had to demonstrate its democratic credentials before being permitted to become a member, and it was only on February 28, 1996, that Russia formally joined the Council of Europe, underlying the fact that it remained a significant political and legal institution dedicated to promoting human rights, democracy, and the rule of law throughout Europe. This membership represented Russia sent to align itself with European standards and foster cooperation with other member states. However, the landscape shifted dramatically after February 2022 when Russia launched a military invasion of Ukraine, another sovereign member state of the Council (Yigit, 2022b).

In response to this blatant act of aggression, the Council of Europe swiftly mobilised its mechanisms to uphold its core principles. On February 25, following extensive consultations and discussions among its members and the Parliamentary Assembly, the Committee of Ministers convened to address the serious breach of international norms. During this meeting, the Committee decided to initiate the procedure laid out in Article 8 of its Statute, which allows for the suspension of a member state's rights. This pivotal decision marked a significant step in demonstrating the Council's resolve to maintain stability and security in Europe.

The Committee agreed to suspend the Russian Federation's representation within the Council, effectively limiting its ability to participate in the decision-making processes of the resolution. It also outlined the legal and financial repercussions that would arise from such a suspension, emphasising the severity of the situation and the Council's commitment to upholding the values that bind its members. On March 10, as the situation continued to unfold, the Committee of Ministers sought to further engage with the Parliamentary Assembly regarding the ongoing implications of the Russian situation. They consulted the Assembly on the potential further application of Article 8, signalling a collective and democratic approach to governance in the wake of international crises.

By March 15, the Parliamentary Assembly reached an urgent consensus. It unanimously adopted a formal opinion stating that the Russian Federation could no longer remain a member of the Council of Europe—this unanimous decision was a consensus on the need to uphold the Council's standards and values, which Russia's membership had fundamentally undermined. On the same day, the Government of the Russian Federation took a decisive step by informing the Secretary General of its intention to withdraw from the Council of Europe. This notification was made by the provisions outlined in the Statute of the Council. The Russian government also expressed its intention to denounce the European Convention on Human Rights, further exacerbating the rift between Russia and European institutions. This sequence of events not only highlighted the deteriorating relations between Russia and the Council of Europe but also underscored the profound implications for human rights protection and European security in the broader geopolitical context.

REFERENCES

Aydindag, D. (2021). *The role of language in power and politics (case study: Erdoğan speeches between 2002-2020)*. Revista EntreLinguas.

Baukhage, C. (2010, April). San Marino. In Elections in Europe (pp. 1669-1698). Nomos Verlagsgesellschaft mbH & Co. KG.

Blanc, I. (2013). Essence of indecision-explaining Veto Player structures and Agenda Setting processes in Swiss Foreign Policy.

Bond, M. (2016). The EU and the Council of Europe: Difference, duplication or delegation? In Cooperation or Conflict? (pp. 11-28). Routledge.

Boulloche, A., Richter, K., & WARREN, K. (1976). The Sciences and Democratic Government. Palgrave Macmillan Limited.

Bruinsma, F. J., & Parmentier, S. (2003). Interview with Mr. Luzius Wildhaber, President of the ECHR. *Netherlands Quarterly of Human Rights*, *21*(2), 185–201.

Cassese, A. (1989). A new approach to human rights: The European convention for the prevention of torture. *The American Journal of International Law*, *83*(1), 128–153.

Chiti-Batelli, A. (1967). European assemblies and space. *The International Spectator*, *2*(3), 248–262.

Constas, D. C. (1982). Turkish Affair: A Test Case for the Council of Europe, The. Legal Issues of Eur. *Integration (Tokyo, Japan)*, *9*, 69.

Council of Europe. The Congress of Local, Regional Authorities, Congress of Local, Regional Authorities of Europe (CLRAE), & National Association of Portuguese Municipalites. (2006). The European Charter of Local Self-Government--20th Anniversary: Proceedings: Lisbon (Portugal), 8 July 2005: International Conference Organised by the Congress of Local and Regional Authorities of the Council of Europe, in Co-operation with the National Association of Portuguese Municipalities (Vol. 8). Council of Europe.

Council of Europe. (2024, February). Map of the Council of Europe 46 member States Eng/fra. Council of Europe Publishing. https://edoc.coe.int/en/map-of-the-member-states/11072-map-of-the-council-of-europe-46-member-states-engfra.html

Dagi, I. (2001). Human rights and democratization: Turkish politics in the European context. *Southeast European and Black Sea Studies*, *1*(3), 51–68.

Dagi, I. D. (1996). Democratic transition in Turkey, 1980–83: The impact of European diplomacy. *Middle Eastern Studies*, *32*(2), 124–141.

Domínguez Castro, L., & Rodríguez Lago, J. R. (2022). Denis de Rougemont: An Europos Federalist. In *The European Union and its Political Leaders: Understanding the Integration Process* (pp. 97–110). Springer International Publishing.

Donald, A., & Speck, A. K. (2019, June). Wholehearted? Half-hearted? The response from the Parliamentary Assembly of the Council of Europe to recent developments in Turkey. In FU Berlin/Hertie School of Governance Workshop on Responses to the Decay of the Rule of Law and Human Rights Protections in Turkey: Exceptional or Symptomatic.

Duffy, C. G. (1950). Can Europe Unite? *The Irish Monthly*, *78*(930), 580–589.

Fawcett, J. E. S. (1974). The Council of Europe and integration. International Affairs (Royal Institute of International Affairs 1944-), 50(2), 242-250.

Fawn, R., & Fawn, R. (2013). The Birth of Internal Conditionality: The Conception and Evolution of the Council of Europe and the Organization for Security and Cooperation in Europe. International Organizations and Internal Conditionality: Making Norms Matter, 20-55.

Greer, S., & Williams, A. (2009). Human rights in the council of Europe and the EU: Towards 'Individual','Constitutional'or 'Institutional'justice? *European Law Journal*, *15*(4), 462–481.

JayCoop. (2022, March 7). File:map of council of europe member states by founding and later members.svg. Wikimedia Commons. https://commons.wikimedia.org/wiki/File:Map_of_Council_of_Europe_member_states_by_founding_and_later_members.svg

Kljajić, I., & Lapaine, M. (2013). Piri Reis–Cartographer of Suleiman the Magnificent, Exhibition in Croatia. Kartografija i geoinformacije (Cartography and Geoinformation), 12(20), 88-91.

Kubas, S. (2022). Suspension, Withdrawal and Expulsion of a Member State from the Council of Europe. *Biuletyn Stowarzyszenia Absolwentów i Przyjaciół Wydziału Prawa Katolickiego Uniwersytetu Lubelskiego*, *17*(19 (1)), 171–179.

Leckie, S. (1988). The inter-state complaint procedure in international human rights law: Hopeful prospects or wishful thinking? *Hum. Rts. Q.*, *10*, 249.

Liechtenstein, A., Luxembourg, A., Macedonia, C. N., & Serbia, F. (2024). Council of Europe. *Organization*.

Marcén, A. G. (2021). The Platform for the Protection of Journalists: A Mechanism for Cooperation between Non-Governmental Organisations and the Council of Europe. *Utrecht Law Review*, *17*(2).

Okur, M. A. (2015). The American geopolitical interests and turkey on the eve of the september 12, 1980 coup. *Journal of Modern Turkish History*, *11*(21), 199–222.

Pace, R. (1999). Malta's Foreign Policy in the 1990s. In *The Foreign Policies of the European Union's Mediterranean States and Applicant Countries in the 1990s* (pp. 195–249). Palgrave Macmillan UK.

Robertson, A. H. (1954). The Council of Europe, 1949–1953—I. *The International and Comparative Law Quarterly*, *3*(2), 235–255.

Sahm, A. (2010, March). Belarus at the Crossroads? Prospects for Co-operation with the EU, Council of Europe, and OSCE. In OSCE Yearbook 2009 (pp. 123-137). Nomos Verlagsgesellschaft mbH & Co. KG.

Simpson, A., & Dervin, F. (2019). The Council of Europe Reference Framework of competences for democratic culture: Ideological refractions, othering and obedient politics. *Intercultural Communication Education*, *2*(3), 102–119.

Soriano, V. F. (2019). Facing the Greek junta: the European Community, the Council of Europe and the rise of human-rights politics in Europe. In *Multiple Connections in European Cooperation* (pp. 22–40). Routledge.

Soyaltin-Colella, D. (2021). (Un) Democratic change and use of social sanctions for domestic politics: Council of Europe monitoring in Turkey. *International Political Science Review*, *42*(4), 484–500.

Stivachtis, Y. A., & Habegger, M. (2017). The Council of Europe: the institutional limits of contemporary European International Society? In Europe After Enlargement (pp. 59-77). Routledge.

Trommer, S. M., & Chari, R. S. (2006). The council of Europe: Interest groups and ideological missions? *West European Politics*, *29*(4), 665–686.

Willems, W. J. (2007). The work of making Malta: The Council of Europe's archaeology and planning committee 1988–1996. *European Journal of Archaeology*, *10*(1), 57–71.

Yigit, S. (1996). From here to eternity—Turkey, the European Union and the Customs Union. *Cambridge Review of International Affairs*, *10*(1), 51–60.

Yiğit, S. (2022). Swiss-EU Relations: The Cold War Years, El Ruha 10th International Conference "Social Sciences & Humanities", Eds: Mercimek & Tan, Iksad Publications November 27-28, 2022, ISBN: 978-625-6380-76-9, pp.476-499.

Yiğit, S. (2022a). Switzerland and the European Union: No Union, Only Close Relations, I. International Anglo-American Cultural and Literary Studies Symposium Proceedings Book, Eds: Tanritanir & Aykac, Iksad Publications, 15.12.2022, ISBN: 978-625-6380-74-5, pp.215-232.

Yigit, S. (2022b). Russia's Invasion of Ukraine: The First Seven Months. in Aydın, M., Şiriner, İ., & Koç, Ş. A. *Global Agenda in Social Sciences: Global Studies*, *9*, 417.

Yiğit, S. (2023). Power, Polarity and the Present. The Zambakari Advisory Special Issue: Spring 2023 The Great Power Competition in Eurasia, 146-159.

Yiğit, S. (2023). 2022: Unipolar Delusion, Bipolar Illusion and Multipolar Aspiration. Diplomacy and Security, Volume VI, Number 1/2023. Page: 79-99.

Yigit, S. (2024). Miscalculated Cause-and-Effect: The Russian Invasion of Ukraine and Finland's Accession to NATO. In Analyzing Global Responses to Contemporary Regional Conflicts (pp. 39-51). IGI Global.

Yigit, S. (2024a). The Vulnerability of Small States in Europe, International Scientific Conference "European Studies: Past-Present-Future" 13 December 2024, Proceedings of the conference #5, ISSN 2960-9976, p.206-215.

Chapter 5
Key Regional Conflicts in Northeast India:
The Koch Rajbongshi Tribe's Role in Geoeconomics and Geopolitics

Surjit Singha
https://orcid.org/0000-0002-5730-8677
Kristu Jayanti University, India

Ranjit Singha
https://orcid.org/0000-0002-3541-8752
Christ University, India

ABSTRACT

This chapter explores the complex regional conflicts in Northeast India through the lens of historical statehood movements, ethnic assertions, and cross-border cultural continuities. Focusing on the Koch-Rajbongshi community, the proposed Kamatapur state, and tribalhood, it analyzes the geo-ethno-political landscape involving Assam, North Bengal, and the bordering areas of Bangladesh, Bhutan, and Nepal. Drawing from the Kamata and Koch kingdom's historical legacies, the chapter situates the demand for Kamatapur within broader frameworks of linguistic rights, tribal autonomy, and national security concerns. Koch Rajbongshi, an Indigenous tribe tracing their lineage to the ancient Koch civilization and rightfully meets the criteria for Scheduled Tribe status, has long been denied their rightful recognition due to regional political intricacies. Through interdisciplinary insights, this study argues for a more nuanced understanding of regional self-determination, identity politics, and governance reforms in Eastern South Asia.

DOI: 10.4018/979-8-3373-1265-1.ch005

INTRODUCTION

Northeast India, which includes eight states — Arunachal Pradesh, Assam, Manipur, Meghalaya, Mizoram, Nagaland, Tripura, and Sikkim — is one of India's most culturally rich and strategically important regions. Surrounded by international frontiers with China, Nepal, Bhutan, Bangladesh and Myanmar and linked to the Indian mainland by the narrow Siliguri corridor, called the "Chicken's Neck," it is India's only remaining land corridor to Southeast Asia. However, notwithstanding its geo-strategic significance and putative promise for connectivity through instruments such as the Act East Policy, Northeast India remains trapped by chronic underdevelopment, political deprivation and conflicting ethnic tensions that remain under the surface (Baruah, 2012). There is a demand from the natives of the entire north Bengal area, which was earlier part of the greater Koch Behar Princely state and the Kamatapur Kingdom, to be included under the North East India region.

The Koch Rajbongshi community traces its origin to the ancient Koch civilization, which played a significant role in the political and cultural history of the eastern Indian subcontinent. The Koch civilization flourished under the Koch rulers like Maharaja Biswa Singha and Maharaja Naranarayan, significantly influencing pre-colonial Northeast India's political, cultural, and religious fabric.

With more than 200 indigenous communities with their languages, belief systems, and social order, the region's rich ethnic tapestry is a strength and a political tinderbox. Successive Indian administrations have battled with developing a governance architecture that is inclusive and meets the aspirations of these communities in a significant way. Consequently, the area has experienced periodic outbursts of ethnic violence, secessionist activities, and uneven patterns of development (Misra, 2000).

The Koch Rajbongshis are one of the indigenous communities of Assam, a state in Northeast India. Historically, they were rulers of the Kamata Kingdom and then subsequently joined the Cooch (Koch) Behar state. They have held sway in what are now the Indian states of Assam, West Bengal, and Bihar and have influenced the entire region. However, colonial border-making and reorganization of the post-independence state dismembered their ancestral land and rendered their community politically and culturally marginal (Roy, 2014). Such a loss of control became the root of the longstanding assertion of a separate Kamatapur state and their Scheduled Tribe (ST) status demands (Roy, 2014).

The Koch Rajbongshi's demand for ST status, which started in the mid-60s but intensified in the 90s, is led by the All Koch Rajbongshi Students' Union (AKRSU). Ordinance No. 9 of the Government of India came into force in 1996, conferring ST (Plains) status on the community. It was re-promulgated by succeeding re-promulgations—Ordinances No. 19 or 30 in 1996 and No. 3 in 1997. These ordinances were, however, never enacted into law, and as a result, the community lost its recognition due to a lack of activity by the parliament (Lok Sabha, 1997; Times of India, 2014; Singha, 2018). Through these pushes and pulls, the movement has persevered aggressively, illustrated in the demand memorandum of 2025 submitted by the Koch-Rajbongshi Sanmilita Joutha Mancha, comprising 12 organizations, repeating the claim for ST status and the state of Kamatapur (India Today NE, 2025; IAS Gyan, 2025).

The Koch Rajbongshi community has a culture and social practices which conform to the constitutional and anthropological aspects of a Scheduled Tribe. Besides, they have a deeply rooted traditional way of life, with animistic rituals, and traditional livelihoods include agriculture, shifting cultivation, and subsistence in the forest. Their religion revolves around the worship of the sun, the moon, trees, rivers, groves, an indigenous breed of bamboo, and particular kinds of plants that are considered holy, practices that predate Hindu beliefs. Their respect for nature and ancestral spirits is embodied in practices and festivities like Baas Puja and Kati Bihu (Saikia & Senapoti, 2019). After centuries of contact with other religious expressions, their basic practices are unassimilated and distinctive as a part of their tribal heritage.

The indigenous communities also communicate in Kamatapuri or Rajbanshi, which is an oral literature-rich language that is the expression of the culture of the community. Koch Rajbongshi of Assam has been placed in the (More Other Backwards Class) MOBC (Roy, 2014). Koch Rajbongshi are known as Rajbansi in West Bengal, while they are known as Koch Rajbongshi in Assam. Moreover, in West Bengal, they were recognized as a Scheduled caste.

Throughout history, the Koch Rajbongshi identity has undergone many linguistic and political transformations, and multiple names have been applied to the community in various regions. The community reasserts itself as Koch Rajbongshi in Assam, while in West Bengal, some sections of political and social elites deliberately drop the "Koch" term from "Rajbanshi" or "Rajbongshi" (Roy, 2014). The name of the former princely state (Koch State) and its few parts are now part of the entire Northbengal, Koch Behar (or Cooch Behar) still upholds the original "Koch" prefix, indicating the ancient ties of the community with the place.

However, the Koch population in Meghalaya is still identified as a Scheduled Tribe (ST). This recognition has historical underpinnings: when Meghalaya was part of Assam (it was created as an autonomous hill state of Assam in 1970 and became a state in full-fledged status in 1972), the Koch were scheduled tribes (ST) in the State of Assam. Following the statehood formation of Meghalaya, the Koch in Meghalaya have sustained their constitutional status as a tribal group, so far as the Scheduled Tribes Order, 1950 (as amended) is concerned (Government of India, 1950; Ministry of Tribal Affairs, n.d.). After the bifurcation, legal recognition of Koch communities in Assam diminished over time despite their consistency in cultural, linguistic and anthropological attributes with their counterparts in Meghalaya and West Bengal (Roy, 2014; Saikia & Senapoti, 2019). Some Koch people in Assam have obtained Scheduled Tribe (ST) status by affiliating with the Rabha tribe and are officially categorized as "Kocha-Rabha." While such affiliations have enabled certain Koch groups to gain tribal recognition, the larger Koch Rajbongshi community continues to seek official ST status. The underlying issue is that the recorded Koch population remains low—partly due to these subgroup classifications. Consequently, the number of Kocha-Rabha increases, even though they and the Koch Rajbongshi share a common ancestral lineage. The Koch Rajbongshi trace their roots directly to the Koch.

There have been profound socio-political implications from this lack of consistent classification. The Meghalaya Kochs are STs at par with their state brethren, but those settled in Assam have been clubbed with the Other Backwards Classes (OBCs), thereby restricting their access to reserved jobs and tribal welfare programmes. The eradication of the "Koch" identity in West Bengal and the differential treatment with that in Assam have divided the identity and obstructed its cohesive move toward a collective follow-up of political representation and socio-economic advancement.

The Koch case in India brings out the arbitrary and locality-dependent nature of the classification of tribes, where similar communities may get classified differently across state lines despite their having the exact ethno-cultural origin. This also reiterates the justice of the Koch Rajbongshi community's ST demand in Assam, as their exclusion is not on any objective criterion but due to administrative apathy and political inertia (India Today NE, 2025).

. The Koch Rajbongshi people are descended from the Koch, an Indigenous group heavily associated with the formation of the Koch dynasty. The kingdom that they ruled, Kamata Kingdom, Koch Behar (Cooch Behar), rose as a powerful political entity in the early 16th century by Biswa Singha, its glory days by his two sons — Naranarayan and Chilarai. This dominant regional power encompassed much modern-day Assam, West Bengal, and portions of Bihar and Bangladesh (Roy, 2014; Saikia & Senapoti, 2019).

Koch Behar was a princely state during the British Raj and maintained a status of political recognition as a feudatory state associated with British India. Afterwards, when India reached independence, 'Koch Behar' was a princely state and formed a part of a Part C state in the Constitution of India (1950) in the First Schedule. However, that did not last for long. Koch Behar was integrated and included under the Indian Union on January 1, 1950, with the signing of the Merger Agreement, which was executed on August 28, 1949 (Government of India, 1950a).

Today, the former principality of Koch Behar is now part of the Indian states of West Bengal and Assam. The process of being a state to a district-level administrative unit has impacted the identity of the Koch Rajbongshi community. Most locals experience this metamorphosis as symbolizing their loss of political sovereignty and former grandeur. One of the key forces driving the quest of creating a Kamata state and bestowal of ST status (Roy, 2014; India Today NE, 2025).

This historical story of statehood, indigenous governance and cultural sovereignty heavily influences the community's recent socio-political mobilization. The acknowledgement of Koch Behar as erstwhile a princely state and then a constitutional state of the Part C category also adds credence to the continued political assertions of the community against enforced disavowal of political identity and equal recognition of collective rights in the Indian Union.

The Koch Rajbongshi community—this very day—strives for their rights and demands through peaceful protests, cultural activism and lobbying. Their struggle is not just for ST status but for restoring their historical identity, preserving their cultural heritage, and a fair share in India's development visionary journey. The perseverance of this movement can be seen as an expression of the limitations of present policy paradigms in making space for homegrown realities in the Indian Northeast.

The chapter accordingly attempts to unpack the socio-political and economic dimensions of the Koch Rajbongshi movement and reflect on its potential for regional development and international collaboration. Its goal is to offer a multifaceted understanding of how unaddressed ethnic claims can constitute significant structural obstacles to national consolidation and peace in regions. In so doing, the chapter makes a case for a type of policy inclusivity and understanding conducive to meeting the aspirations of the indigenous peoples on the one hand while dovetailing them with the larger developmental and foreign policy goals of India on the other.

BACKGROUND

A Complex Narrative Northeast India's experience of Marginalization is inextricably connected to its geographical remoteness, colonial trajectories, and policy lacunae following India's independence. Surrounded by international boundaries — and attached to the rest of the country by the narrow strip of Siliguri Corridor, known as the "Chicken's Neck"— the region has been physically and politically insulated from national policy debates (Baruah, 2012). In early colonial times, the British considered the area the ungoverned frontier of their resources rather than a unified area for governance. The colonizer's interest in resource extraction (tea, oil, timber, etc.) superseded their immediate concern for developing any governance structure, eventually leaving the existing social organization in despair (Misra, 2000).

This colonial desuetude prepared the way for permanent political fragmentation. The imposition of fixed state borders has broken up many interspersed ethnolinguistic groups like the Koch Rajbongshi, disrupting their traditional governance systems. State reorganization on linguistic lines after independence has since marginalized smaller ethnic communities. India's partition occurred, but the India-Bangladesh border was subsequently delineated, thereby seriously dislocating the socio-cultural and economic ties of the Koch with others (who were in the erstwhile Kamata kingdom) (Roy, 2014).

During extended periods of rule of Kamata and then the flame of the princely state of Cooch Behar, after independence, the Koch Rajbongshi community did not hold on to their autonomy and cultural recognition. Their ancestral land — "Kamatapur" — now covers portions of Assam, West Bengal, Bihar, and Rangpur of Bangladesh. Instead of political accommodation, they were "sunk" within larger administrative entities controlled by other ethnic majorities and were once again marginalized and excluded (Roy, 2014).

In the late 1990s, the Koch Rajbongshi people began the Kamatapur movement in reaction to these developments, demanding a separate state to protect their culture, language (Kamatapuri/Rajbanshi), and identity. These demands were mobilized by the All Koch Rajbongshi Students' Union (AKRSU) (Saikia & Senapoti, 2019). However, state reactions to the movement have been mainly dismissive or cosmetic, from militarizing the area to moving in paramilitary forces to offering small development packages that do not meet the movement's central demands.

Acts, such as the AFSPA, only further alienate the local people by enacting a militarized state (Hazarika, 1994). Although some tribal development councils and economic assistance programs have been initiated, such measures rarely are autonomous in function, are only token in funding, and are not generally supported by the local people or supported only in limited ways, and are, therefore, perceived as largely superficial and irrelevant to the people of the region.

The region also has much untapped economic potential, exacerbating these problems. With rich biodiversity and close access to international markets, Northeast India has not, however, managed to exploit cross-border trade opportunities with Bangladesh, Bhutan, and Myanmar. Security concerns and exclusionary planning have also marginalized communities such as the Koch Rajbongshi, who inhabit these strategic border areas, from the gains of trade and infrastructure projects (Kuame, 2022).

The Koch Rajbongshi meet the criteria for Scheduled Tribe (ST) status in India. They are people with different cultures who are impoverished and politically marginalized. Their animistic beliefs, worship of natural forces like the sun, moon, rivers, and bamboo, and peculiar language and traditions distinguish them from mainstream religion and society (Saikia & Senapoti, 2019; Singh, 2010). However, they are listed inconsistently, state by state, with OBC status in Assam and similar tribal equivalents in adjoining regions, pointing to the lack of coordination and state aversion (Roy, 2014).

Their economic background is complicated over here. Rural poverty, low literacy percentage, lack of medical facilities, lack of political exposure, and so on still prevail (Singha & Singha, 2025). ST recognition would open the doors for affirmative action, educational and employment reservations, benefits, and financial assistance as per constitutional protections such as those outlined under the Fifth and Sixth Schedules.

Although it has been repeatedly raised in the Indian Parliament and committee reports that have acknowledged the validity of their claim, the government has not taken any firm action for ST status (India Today NE, 2025). This prolonged lapse has, in turn, generated more pressure, triggering demands again for the statehood of Kamatapur.

The enforced farce of Koch Rajbongshis is part of the larger structural flaws governing the relations between the Centre and Northeast India. In seeking ST status and an autonomous administrative identity, they are not secessionists; they only want recognition, dignity, and a share in India's idea of progress. Meeting this demand with empathetic, inclusive policies will unlock the region's economic, political, and social potential.

THEORETICAL FRAMEWORK

This research is grounded in ethnic conflict, geoeconomics and native autonomy. Ethnic mobilization theory is based on the belief that ethnic mobilization for political and economic rights is strongest when ethnic groups feel relatively deprived compared to the privileged or dominant groups (Horowitz, 1985). In contrast, geoeconomic frames highlight the influence and condition of political will on economic behaviours (Blackwell & Harris, 2016). Lastly, Indigenous Rights Theory focuses on cultural recognition and political representation to achieve sustainable peace and development (Anaya 2004). These frameworks make sense in understanding the politics of conflict in the Koch Rajbongshi tribe and the potential of inclusive governance and economic reforms in resolving conflicts.

CONCEPTUAL FRAMEWORK

This chapter draws from four dimensions to allow the conceptual integration:

Historical Marginalization – understanding the legacy of exclusion and identity oppression.

Geopolitical importance – Retrieved on the region's strategic relevance for regional security and diplomacy.

Geo-economic Integration – untouched potential for trade and development because of conflicts.

Indigenous Agency – the initiative of Indigenous peoples to reclaim reparation, autonomy, and identity.

Thus, the 4D framework approach accounts for structural and agency-based factors to analyze regional conflict and development processes.

HISTORICAL BACKGROUND OF REGIONAL CONFLICTS

Northeast India is one of Asia's most ethnically varied regions, comprising more than 200 ethnic groups, 220 languages and dialects (Misra, 2000). The volatile mix of ethnicities has been a cultural treasure and a chronic source of political tension. The region's demographic diversity results from centuries of migration, kingdom formation, and colonial boundary-drawing that often took no account of ethnic and linguistic boundaries. The Indian Constitution provides space for this diversity by linking all-India political formations to protective devices such as the Sixth Schedule. However, protection has not been uniform, resulting in unequal political representation and governance.

The Koch-Rajbongshi community occupies a unique position among the various ethnic communities. They claim descent from the ancient Kamata Kingdom and the subsequent Cooch Behar principality that included parts of Assam, West Bengal and Bihar (Barman, 2005). Their political independence had also eroded under British colonial rule. Partition in 1947 led to the separation of the territorial and cultural integrity of the Koch Rajbongshis, as the Koch Rajbongshis' historical homeland was partitioned between India and East Pakistan (now Bangladesh).

The marginalization of the Koch-Rajbongshi people continued even during the independence period. They were recategorized into different administrative groups. First, they were listed as a Scheduled Caste in West Bengal and an OBC in Assam (Roy, 2014). With the political hegemony of Assamese in all official interactions and the increasing identity politics of other advanced and developed tribes like the Boro Kochari and Dimasas, the Koch Rajbongshi found it impossible to articulate its aspirations.

The origin of the region's autonomy movement, including the Kamatapur movement, was rooted in these historical grievances and based on successful campaigns by movements like other Territorial Councils. The Koch Rajbongshi community increased their demand for a separate Kamatapur state in the late 1990s. All Koch

Rajbongshi Students' Union (AKRSU) was one of the top players in demanding recognition for the language, political autonomy and cultural resurgence (Roy, 2014).

The state's reaction to these demands has largely been reactive, relying more on mollification or repression. Though the state government did constitute some development councils and granted language recognition at the district level, these were considered too little, too late, and symbolic. In addition, the movement has occasionally splintered into fundamentally different groups that have taken more radical or violent lines, further complicating its legitimacy (Saikia & Senapoti, 2019).

The failure of economic development also plays a role in perpetuating local warfare. Many tribal populations, such as the Koch Rajbongshi people, are confined to the jungle terai and have little or no access to good education, healthcare, and employment opportunities. This developmental gap breeds discontent and strengthens the aspiration for self-governing entities that prefer local requirements and conserving traditions and cultures (Sharma, 2020).

The historical background of regional conflicts in Northeast India is traced back to colonial frontiers, post-independence administrative lacuna, and lack of recognition and accommodation of the aspirations of indigenous people. The Koch Rajbongshi community exemplifies how ambiguous ethnicity, debate on classification and economic deprivation can converge through time towards a longstanding demand for autonomy.

GEOPOLITICAL SIGNIFICANCE OF NORTHEAST INDIA

One highlighted aspect in the geopolitical discussion is the geographic position of Northeast India, which is meaningful not only as a culturally rich region with beautiful diversity but also being connected with neighbouring countries such as Bhutan, Nepal, Bangladesh, Myanmar and China (In Southeast Asia and East Asia) a land of cultural diversity near international borders. Geographically, it has been a germinal area connecting the bridge between mainland India and South East Asia. International land borders with China, Bangladesh, Bhutan, Myanmar and Nepal along its four corners make it a crucial point in India's foreign policy, regional security and foreign trade architectures (Baruah, 2020). This strategic geographic situation of the region is gaining significance, particularly considering India's efforts to connect with the global and other regional economies through its connectivity corridors and regional cooperation ventures.

The strategic significance of North-East India is primarily due to the narrow Siliguri corridor (also known as Chicken's Neck), an area between the northeastern states and the rest of India, just 22 km at its narrowest point. This corridor is an economic and logistics lifeline and a serious security nightmare. In the case of regional turmoil or war, disruption of this corridor may be enough to effectively detach the northeast from the mainland, with significant national security implications (Singh, 2025).

The international borders in the northeast have increased their geo-strategic value. These neighbouring countries also have historical, cultural and economic ties to ethnic groups in the area. For example, the Koch Rajbongshi community shares transcultural commonality with the East Bengal, Nepal, and Bhutan communities. Hence, it is illustrative that regional geopolitics can never be delinked from local ethnic dynamics (Roy, 2014).

Bangladesh is still a principal player in Northeast India's cross-border strategy. With transit and trade agreements with Bangladesh already in place, options to reduce the region's dependence on the Siliguri Corridor have been made available. Thus, ports such as Chittagong and Mongla in Bangladesh are available for Indian goods in transit through Northeast India, opening up the possibilities for regional trade and connectivity (MEA, 2023). Even Bhutan has a hugging international border with India, and its surreptitious consent for executing hydro-power projects and greenery-conscious activities has always served mutual interests.

Another strategic axis for the region is the India-Myanmar border. It is a linchpin of India's “Act East Policy,” a plan to enhance economic and strategic ties with Southeast Asia. The India-Myanmar-Thailand Trilateral Highway and the Kaladan Multi-Modal Transport Project are critical connectivity and trade projects expected to facilitate seamless trade and robust connectivity and strengthen cultural exchanges through Northeast India (Ministry of External Affairs, 2023). Nevertheless, border insurrections and ethnic rivalries commonly throttle the smooth implementation of such endeavours, reemphasizing the necessity of inclusive governance and conflict-sensitive development planning.

The India-Nepal border, though peaceful, is of strategic significance in terms of the movement of people, goods and culture. The ethnic community of Sikkim and North West Bengal has marital and cultural relations with various groups of Nepal. These links can be used for soft diplomacy, tourism and economic cooperation.

The strategic significance of Northeast India is also apparent from India's Act East policy, which is to transform the area into a corridor of connectivity with ASEAN countries. The Act East Policy – The Continuation of India's “Look East Policy”, which was established in the 1990s, was a policy formulated to cultivate and develop strategic, cultural, and social relations between India and all the East and Southeast Asian countries. Peace and political stability in Northeast India are essential for materializing this vision. Hence, ethnic grievances and secessionist movements—such as those of the Koch Rajbongshi— are not only a domestic matter but also a significant challenge to regional diplomacy and economic expansion (Singh, 2020).

What can only be underlined is the geopolitical importance of northeast India. The strategic location, proximity to significant international boundaries, and pattern of India's east foreign policy make the region more critical in internal security and outer world engagement. The identification and inclusion of the aspirations of indigenous people, such as the Koch Rajbongshi, is imperative to operationalize India's regional and global ambitions fully.

INTERNATIONAL BUSINESS IMPLICATIONS

Global Geopolitical and Geo-economic Relevance of the Koch Rajbongshi Tribe

While the Koch Rajbongshi tribe's immediate concerns center around identity recognition and socio-political marginalization within India and its neighboring states, their geopolitical and geo-economic significance extends beyond these regional confines into global policy, trade, and strategic diplomacy.

1. Ethno-Strategic Location and Global Connectivity

The areas historically inhabited by the Koch Rajbongshi people—including parts of Assam, West Bengal, and North Bengal in India, including Bhutan, Nepal and Bangladesh—lie at the crossroads of major inter-regional corridors such as the Bangladesh-Bhutan-India-Nepal (BBIN) initiative and the India-Myanmar-Thailand Trilateral Highway. These corridors are part of wider global supply chain integration and act as critical arteries in India's *Act East Policy*, which aims to economically and strategically integrate with ASEAN and Indo-Pacific nations (Srisangnam & Devendrakumar, 2018; Ministry of External Affairs, 2023). The tribe's territories thus occupy strategic spaces that mark transnational movement and logistics planning.

2. Cultural Diplomacy and Soft Power

The tribe's cultural legacy—especially their linguistic and ritualistic heritage tied to Kamatapuri/Rajbanshi—creates opportunities for India to leverage cultural diplomacy in the region. Soft power initiatives, such as cross-border cultural festivals or language exchange programs, could integrate the tribe into India's broader cultural outreach in South and Southeast Asia (Nandi, 2014; Barman, 2009; Ray, 2023; Roy, 2014). Such efforts have been employed globally, as seen in promoting China's Confucius Institutes or Japan's "Cool Japan" initiative.

3. Sustainable Development and Global SDGs

The Koch Rajbongshi's traditional practices—such as bamboo craft, eco-friendly farming, and water-based rituals—align closely with global sustainability discourses. Their indigenous knowledge systems offer locally viable solutions for achieving the UN's Sustainable Development Goals (SDGs), especially SDG 13 (Climate Action), SDG 15 (Life on Land), and SDG 8 (Decent Work and Economic Growth). Inclusion of their economic and cultural practices in international frameworks like UNESCO's Intangible Cultural Heritage could raise their global profile.

4. Diaspora and Transnational Identity Politics

With historical Koch communities spread across present-day India, Bangladesh, Bhutan, and even parts of Nepal, their demand for cultural and political recognition speaks to broader conversations in global diaspora politics and stateless nations—similar to the Kurdish, Basque, or Rohingya cases. These comparative ethnic-nationalist movements are increasingly discussed in the context of human rights law, global governance, and conflict resolution (Anaya, 2023).

5. Security and International Risk Assessment

The unresolved demands of communities such as the Koch Rajbongshi are increasingly considered in international risk analyses and FDI evaluations. According to Arenla (2023), foreign investors view ongoing ethnic tensions and demands for autonomy as political risk indicators, thereby affecting cross-border investments from India and ASEAN, EU, and Indo-Pacific strategic partners.

GEOSPATIAL MAPPING OF THE KOCH RAJBONGSHI HOMELAND

State- and country-wise list of districts and regions where the Koch Rajbongshi / Rajbanshi / Koch community resides. The information includes Indian states (Assam, West Bengal, Bihar, Meghalaya) and neighbouring countries (Bangladesh, Nepal, Bhutan) based on historical habitation, socio-linguistic distribution, and ethnographic research.

Understanding the Koch Rajbongshi's locational spread—also called Rajbanshi or Koch—is critical for contextualizing their socio-political identity, cultural continuity, and role in regional development. The community's historical and cultural presence extends across multiple administrative and geopolitical territories, intersecting with

South Asia's most strategically significant corridors. This section offers a detailed geospatial overview of the districts and regions where the Koch Rajbongshi people are predominantly found, spanning several Indian states—including Assam, West Bengal, Bihar, and Meghalaya—as well as neighbouring countries such as Bangladesh, Nepal, and Bhutan.

The mapping draws from ethnographic research, historical state formations (such as the Kamata and Cooch Behar kingdoms), linguistic continuity in the Kamatapuri/Rajbanshi language, and contemporary demographic trends. These spatial insights ground the community's political and cultural claims and demonstrate the tribe's relevance in cross-border development, regional diplomacy, and international business strategies. The chapter highlights how identity, heritage, and territory converge through this geospatial lens to inform broader discourses of inclusion, governance, and transnational engagement.

India

1. Assam

Koch Rajbongshis are concentrated primarily in Lower Assam, especially in districts bordering West Bengal and Bangladesh.

Key Districts:

- Kokrajhar, Bongaigaon, Chirang, Baksa, Dhubri, Goalpara, Barpeta, Nalbari, South Salmara–Mankachar, Kamrup (especially Kamrup Rural), Kamrup Metropolitan (urban migration), Udalguri, Darrang, Morigaon, Sonitpur, Lakhimpur etc.

2. West Bengal

They are known as Rajbanshi here and form a significant group in North Bengal, particularly in areas of the former Cooch Behar State and Jalpaiguri Division.

Key Districts:

- Cooch Behar, Alipurduar, Jalpaiguri, Darjeeling, Kalimpong, Uttar Dinajpur, Dakshin Dinajpur, Malda etc.

3. Bihar

Rajbanshis (a sub-group of Koch origin) live in northern parts bordering Nepal.

Key Districts:

- Kishanganj, Purnia, Araria, Katihar, etc.

4. Meghalaya

In Meghalaya, Koch people (classified as ST) are scattered in districts bordering Assam and Bangladesh.

Key Districts:

- West Garo Hills, South West Garo Hills, South Garo Hills, North Garo Hills, East Garo Hills, etc.

In Meghalaya, many Koch are recognized as Scheduled Tribes under the name "Koch."

Bangladesh

In Bangladesh, Koch Rajbongshi people are mainly called Rajbanshi and reside in the northwestern region.

Key Districts:

- Rangpur, Lalmonirhat, Kurigram, Nilphamari, Dinajpur, Thakurgaon, Panchagarh, Gaibandha, etc.

Historically, this area was part of the Kamata Kingdom, and cultural-linguistic continuity with Indian Rajbanshis is strong.

Nepal

Rajbanshis are officially recognized as one of Nepal's Indigenous Nationalities (Adivasi Janajati) and are mainly found in the Kochila or southeastern Terai region.

Key Districts:

- Jhapa, Morang, Sunsari, etc.

Referred to as Kochila Rajbanshi in Nepal, they speak a dialect closely related to Kamatapuri.

Bhutan

There is no formal recognition or categorization of Koch/Rajbanshi in Bhutan, but there are small undocumented communities (possibly mixed) near the Indian border in southern Bhutan.

Likely Areas:

- Sarpang, Samdrup Jongkhar, Phuentsholing (Chukha District), etc.

These areas share borders with West Bengal (Alipurduar, Jalpaiguri) and Assam.

Table 1. Summary Table

Country	State/Region	Key Districts
India	Assam	Kokrajhar, Bongaigaon, Chirang, Baksa, Dhubri, Goalpara, Barpeta, Nalbari, South Salmara–Mankachar, Kamrup (especially Kamrup Rural), Kamrup Metropolitan (urban migration), Udalguri, Darrang, Morigaon, Sonitpur, Lakhimpur etc.
	West Bengal	Cooch Behar, Alipurduar, Jalpaiguri, Darjeeling, Kalimpong, Uttar Dinajpur, Dakshin Dinajpur, Malda **etc.**
	Bihar	Kishanganj, Purnia, Katihar, Araria **etc.**
	Meghalaya	West Garo Hills, South West Garo Hills, South Garo Hills, North Garo Hills, East Garo Hills **etc.**
Bangladesh	Rangpur Division	Rangpur, Lalmonirhat, Kurigram, Nilphamari, Dinajpur, Thakurgaon, Panchagarh, Gaibandha **etc.**
Nepal	Eastern Terai	Jhapa, Morang, Sunsari **etc.**
Bhutan	Southern Bhutan	Sarpang, Samdrup Jongkhar, Phuentsholing (Chukha District) **etc.**

Figure 1. Map of Northeast India showing borders with Bhutan, Nepal, Bangladesh, China, and Myanmar.

(Source: Google Maps, accessed June 5, 2025) (Google, 2025).

Kamatapur Kingdom: Historical and Geopolitical Context

The Kamatapur Kingdom, ruled by the Koch dynasty, emerged as a formidable polity in the early 16th century under King Biswa Singha (r. 1515–1540), who unified fragmented principalities across the northeast of the Indian subcontinent. Its capital was Kamatapur, now Gosanimari in North Bengal. The kingdom's territorial expanse stretched from the Karatoya River in the west to the Barnadi River in the east, extending south into Rangpur and Mymensingh (present-day Bangladesh), westward into Mithila in Bihar, northward to the lower Himalayas, and south to Chattagram (Padmapati, 2022; Roychowdhury, 2024)

The kingdom reached its zenith under Koch King Nara Narayan (r. 1540–1587) and his younger brother and military commander Chilarai (1510–1571). Sukladhwaj, popularly known as Chilaray, literally translates to “Falcon” for his swiftness in battle; like a falcon, Chilarai is regarded as one of India's greatest military strategists. British historian Arnold J. Toynbee (1889–1975) ranked Chilarai among the three greatest generals in world history, alongside Napoleon Bonaparte and Chatrapati Shivaji Maharaj. Chilarai commanded an estimated 600,000-strong army, including 4,000 cavalry, 200,000 infantry, 700 war elephants, and 1,000 war boats, as recorded in the *Akbarnama* (Ali, 2017). Remarkably, he is credited with launching India's first naval warfare strategy—preceding Mughal Emperor Akbar—when he led a naval assault on the Brahmaputra River during his 1562 AD campaign against Assam (Nag, 2015).

Chilarai's military expeditions consolidated Koch's rule across Assam and Bengal and introduced advanced military logistics, including unparalleled riverine defence and supply chains. His leadership expanded Koch's sovereignty into Assam, West Bengal, Bihar, Meghalaya (including parts of present-day Garo Hills, formerly undivided Goalpara), Bhutan, and Bangladesh. His campaigns decisively shaped regional power dynamics and repelled external invasions.

The Koch rulers were known for their pluralistic administration, which respected local traditions. The Koch Rajbongshi tribe practised animistic rituals centred on natural elements like the sun, moon, rivers, sacred groves, and native bamboo species, distinguishing them from orthodox Vedic practices.

The enduring legacy of Kamatapur continues to resonate today in regional identity movements across Assam, West Bengal, and the eastern Himalayan region. The historical narratives of Koch kings and Chilarai form the foundation of modern-day demands for Scheduled Tribe status, creating a separate Kamatapur State (Borah, 2016).

Figure 2. Historical map showing the extent of the Kamarupa Kingdom during the reign of Maharaja Nara Narayan. (Source: Chaudhuri, 1903; Pinterest, n.d.)

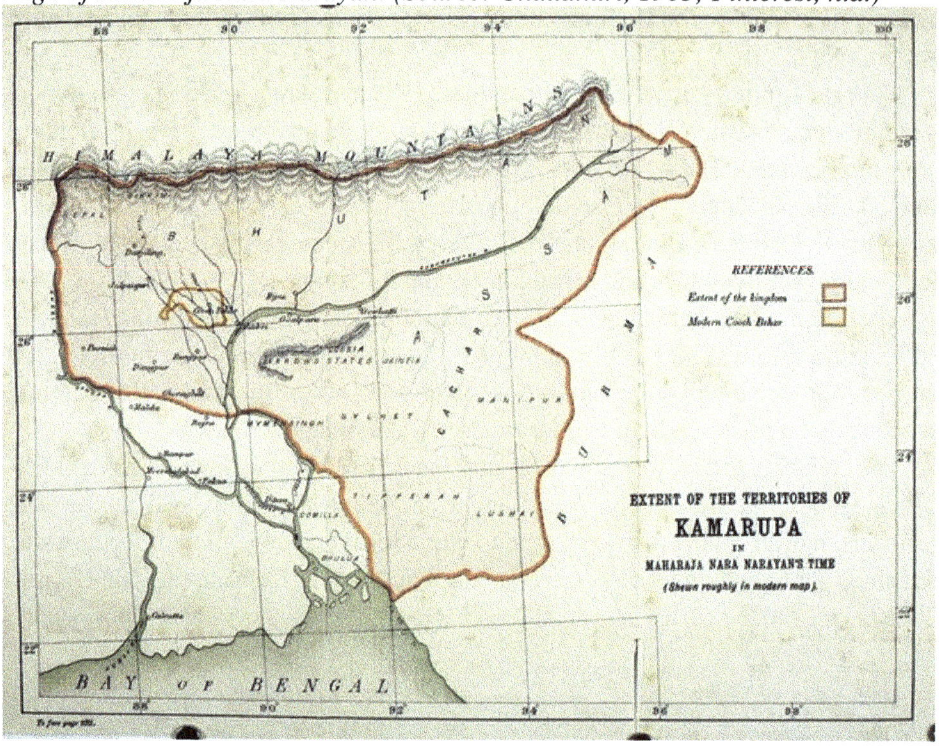

Proposed Kamatapur State Map within the territory of India

Figure 3. Proposed Kamatapur State Map (Borah, 2016).

The proposed Kamatapur State is a political and ethnolinguistic demand primarily advanced by the Koch-Rajbanshi community across Assam and West Bengal, India. Rooted in the historical legacy of the Kamatapur Kingdom, which flourished from the 13th to 16th century under Koch rulers like Biswa Singha and Naranarayan, the demand seeks to restore a distinct regional identity that predates colonial territorial reconfigurations (Nandi, 2014; Ray, 2023).

The proposed state aims to include districts such as Kokrajhar, Bongaigaon, Chirang, Baksa, Dhubri, Goalpara, Barpeta, Nalbari, South Salmara–Mankachar, Kamrup (especially Kamrup Rural), Kamrup Metropolitan (urban migration), Udalguri, Darrang, Morigaon, Sonitpur, Lakhimpur in Assam, and Cooch Behar, Alipurduar, Jalpaiguri, Darjeeling, Kalimpong, Uttar Dinajpur, Dakshin Dinajpur, Malda in West Bengal. Advocates argue that this region represents the historical homeland of the Koch-Rajbanshi people and is characterized by a shared linguistic and cultural heritage centered around the Kamtapuri/Rajbanshi language.

The demand is further justified on linguistic grounds, emphasizing the constitutional right to language preservation and promotion under Articles 29 and 30 of the Indian Constitution. The Kamtapuri language has long been marginalized in state education and administration despite being spoken by millions across the region.

Proponents have also called for its recognition under the Eighth Schedule of the Indian Constitution.

The movement for Kamatapur gained significant momentum with the emergence of organizations such as the All Koch Rajbongshi Students' Union (AKRSU), which served as a student-led platform for mobilization, and the Kamtapur People's Party (KPP), which sought political representation for the Koch-Rajbongshi community. In parallel, armed factions like the Kamtapur Liberation Organisation (KLO) also surfaced, symbolizing the community's deeper grievances related to cultural marginalization, linguistic suppression, and political neglect (Borah, 2016; Barman, 2005; Nag, 2015).

In essence, the demand for Kamatapur represents a quest for historical justice, linguistic preservation, and political autonomy, grounded in a distinct civilizational identity that the community believes has been subsumed under broader Assamese and Bengali nationalist frameworks.

GEO-ECONOMIC CHALLENGES AND OPPORTUNITIES

The economic opportunity in Northeast India is enormous. However, its potential is almost entirely unrealized because of a tangled web of infrastructure shortfalls, neglectful policy and regional conflicts that endure. While it is rich in natural resources – oil, tea, coal, forests and hydroelectric potential – the area remains behind the national average in many important socio-economic indicators like per capita income, industrial growth and infrastructure (World Bank, 2007; Sharma, 2020). The region's strategic location offers tremendous potential for trade and investment and the benefits of geoeconomics, the rewards of which have yet to materialize fully, especially for indigenous communities such as the Koch Rajbongshi.

Economic marginalization of tribal and indigenous peoples is one of the leading issues. Communities like the Koch Rajbongshi have always been bypassed in the planning and execution of development projects. Although located next door to new economic corridors and global transportation ways, these communities usually do not have the institutional representation, educational opportunity, or resource ownership to join regional growth. Also, differing classifications–Scheduled Caste in West Bengal and OBC in Assam–had limited access to reservation benefits that could ease economic mobility (Roy, 2014).

Bottleneck to economic integration, infrastructural development has continued. The dominated area has sparse road, rail, and digital infrastructure, limiting market access and connectivity. Although big projects such as the Kaladan Multi-Modal Transit Project and the India-Myanmar-Thailand Trilateral Highway promise enhanced connectivity, connectivity is contingent on regional peace and cooperation, which are frequently interrupted by ethnic tensions and autonomy movements (Ministry of External Affairs, 2023). Protests, strikes and insurgency also deter investment and add to the transaction cost for trade and logistics.

Regional conflicts can also have a profound effect on cross-border trade. The international border in northeast India runs to over 5300 km, and it is home to the lush Khasi hills with a high commercial potential. However, the ethnic violence and militarisation in border districts make it insecure for trade flows and investment confidence. Trade, for example, between Assam, Meghalaya and Bangladesh, has not been seamless; it is volatile due to political developments and border issues (Kuame, 2022). Intermittent operations by insurgents have also threatened to disrupt the functioning of envisaged trading routes along the Indo-Myanmar border.

However, the area has great potential for sustainable economic growth. Agricultural productivity, for example, can be enhanced with modern practices, agro-processing units and stronger market linkages. The development of these sectors also holds significant export potential with the right policies and skills training – many tribal communities, including the Koch Rajbongshi, have traditional skills in bamboo and handicrafts (Sharma, 2020).

The tourism industry is still untapped as well. One way to draw nationals and foreigners to the region could be through cultural tourism, eco-tourism or historical circuits. Koch Rajbongshi's legacy, which partly includes the historical interiors of the Kamata kingdom, can be incorporated into the larger umbrella of tourism agendas, bringing money and jobs to the people and ensuring cultural preservation.

To seize these opportunities, an inclusive economic planning process must put Indigenous communities at the forefront. Participatory development, tribal entrepreneurship, and a cooperative business model may be used to make economic growth inclusive and sustainable. This representation should even include the community in the planning process of Special Economic Zones (SEZs) and border trade centres to ensure place-based infrastructure development.

Another critical area is access to finance. Augmenting the banking and digital payment infrastructure in tribal regions can create better access to credit, savings and insurance, thereby lessening economic vulnerability. Considering the local socio-cultural setting, community-based skill enhancement schemes can train youth to become employable in these new sectors.

While the geo-economic potential of Northeast India is extensive, to harness it, the historical exclusions need to be addressed, infrastructural connectivity needs to be improved, and development needs to be conflict-sensitive and culturally inclusive. Meanwhile, indigenous communities such as the Koch Rajbongshi must be key stakeholders in designing their economic future.

SOCIO-POLITICAL ASPIRATIONS OF THE KOCH RAJBONGSHI TRIBE

The Koch Rajbongshi community, indigenous to Assam, West Bengal and some parts of Bihar, has long fought for socio-political recognition and autonomy. Their goals range from statehood and cultural protection to a strong role in regional politics. These grievances are based on their historical experience and feelings of marginalization within the current socio-political framework.

The Koch Rajbongshi political movement centres on demands for a separate state, Kamatapur. The proposed state covers areas with a substantial Koch Rajbongshi population, who were the rulers of a historical kingdom. The Kamtapur movement for the recognized state is based on the burning issues of political marginalization, a fratricidal war among activists, and deprivation and neglect in the economy and culture.

The All Koch Rajbongshi Students' Union (AKRSU) spearheaded this agitation, demanding the creation of Kamatapur and including the Koch Rajbongshi in the ST category in Assam. The ST tag is crucial because it would give the community affirmative action benefits, enabling their upliftment. However, even as these demands continued, the community's quest for the ST tag ran into bureaucratic and political roadblocks, with many in the community nursing a grievance that they had been denied for too long.

The Koch Rajbongshi people attach great significance to preserving their culture, embodying animistic faith, customs, dialects, language, and history. The community speaks Kamatapuri or Rajbanshi, which is integral to their identity. Attempts have since been made to include the language in the Eighth Schedule of the Indian Constitution, the aim of which is to enable the language to be an official language and be used in educational and administrative contexts.

Preserving culture involves celebrating traditional festivals, supporting folk arts, and documenting oral histories. They are an effort to combat alien forces, keep traditions and ways of life alive, play a part in a larger narrative, and a manifestation of identity against a hegemonic culture. In essence, the community preserves its culture for generations by resisting historical invisibility and recovering its narrative fortified by a national narrative larger than itself.

The participation of the Koch Rajbongshi community in local governance has also been minimal, resulting in demands for more political representation and administrative independence. One of these efforts is the creation of the Kamatapur Autonomous Council in Assam. This council is intended to help the Koch Rajbongshi community develop, both socially and economically, and to give their community a voice in the governance of this region.

However, the effectiveness of these councils would depend on sufficient devolution of powers and resources and, more importantly, genuine political will. Civil society has been demanding greater participation in decision-making, arguing that participation in governance is crucial to their immediate problems and aspirations.

Leaving no stone unturned for its statehood, cultural preservation, and partaking in governance, some of the socio-political aspirations of the community are understood here. The indigenous groups argue for Kamatapur as their historical motherland. These are all interlocked with their historical and present realities. It is essential to deal with these demands in a way that respects their distinct identity, rights, and the wrongs of history and promotes an inclusive development model. Dialogue and policy-making with the Koch Rajbongshi population are essential if they are to be integrated into the broader social and political reality. There is little trust in the state government, so such dialogue becomes imperative.

INTERNATIONAL BUSINESS IMPLICATIONS

Northeast India occupies a strategically significant location with substantial potential for international business through trade, investment, and transnational economic cooperation. However, persistent ethnic conflicts and deep-rooted structural challenges continue to hinder the region's promise, diminishing its appeal for foreign direct investment (FDI) and stifling the growth of local enterprises. This dynamic is particularly evident in the case of the Koch Rajbongshi community, whose ancestral lands lie at the intersection of several key inter-regional economic corridors.

Risk-averse foreign investors appreciate political stability, regulatory certainty and infrastructural reliability when considering where to put their money. Growing ethnic tensions, secessionist movements and insurgency in Northeast India seriously erode investors' confidence in this region. The existence of acts such as the Armed Forces (Special Powers) Act (AFSPA), which has been applied in many areas of the region, is perceived as a sign of insecurity and has provided a deterrent against long-term investing (Baruah, 2012).

Furthermore, unpredictable and partial policy implementation and frequent interruptions, including strikes, demonstrations and road blockades, create logistical difficulties, add to the cost of transactions and impede the movement of goods and services. Insufficient security infrastructure, government land acquisition challenges, and inter-state coordination issues exacerbate these problems. Therefore, many potential MNCs that can benefit from the region's proximity to ASEAN invest elsewhere.

Opportunities for Indigenous Enterprise Development

Despite operating under constrained and adverse conditions, considerable scope remains for advancing indigenous enterprise development. Communities such as the Koch Rajbongshi have an indigenous innovation ecosystem with traditional skills of weaving, bamboo craft, and organic agriculture, which can be nurtured for scaling up with a conducive policy and markets global demand for green, ethical and handcrafted products. The demand for eco-readymade has led to a small but growing segment of the local community that has developed economies of scale in international markets (Sharma, 2020).

Local entrepreneurship should be supported by development organizations and microfinance institutions, using capacity-building programmes, financial inclusion programmes and market access programmes. For example, Self-Help Groups (SHGS) and cooperatives are potential micro-enterprise clusters oriented towards SDGs, provided they are networked and have proper training. E-commerce and digital platforms also provide opportunities to expand the market access for local products further, which in turn connects rural production to the global consumer.

Policy Recommendations for Inclusive Economic Growth

To unlock the international business potential of the region and ensure inclusive growth, a multi-pronged policy strategy is required:

1. **Peace-building and Governance Reforms**: Conflict resolution and peace-building must be prioritized. Initiatives such as peace accords, autonomous councils, and ethnic representation in governance should be strengthened to foster trust and stability (Sen, 2013).
2. **Infrastructure and Connectivity**: Accelerating the completion of key infrastructure projects like the Kaladan Multi-Modal Transit Project and the India-Myanmar-Thailand Trilateral Highway can enhance regional integration. Improving digital and financial infrastructure in tribal areas is also essential.
3. **Skill Development and Education**: Tailored vocational training programs for Indigenous youth can align local skills with global market demands. Education policies should incorporate cultural content to strengthen identity and resilience.
4. **FDI Incentives and Investor Protection**: These countries can attract international investments, including through foreign direct investments (FDI), by establishing special economic zones (SEZs) with investor-friendly policies, providing risk insurance against potential losses caused by violence, and offering single-window clearances.

5. **Support for Tribal Enterprises**: Government and private sector partnerships will help scale up indigenous products involving branding, quality certification, and international trade fairs.

Northeast India is hampered by regional conflicts and governance challenges that have kept it from being integrated with global economic networks elsewhere in the country. Still, these obstacles can be turned into opportunities, given specific interventions and inclusive policies. With investments in indigenous enterprise and peace, it can be the blueprint for sustainable international business engagement in a post-conflict society.

CONFLICT RESOLUTION AND DEVELOPMENT STRATEGIES

Northeast India, a tapestry of ethnicities and cultures, has long experienced violent intergroup clashes driven by historical grievances, identity politics, and economic competition. Such challenges call for a multi-dimensional approach, combining the efforts of civil society groups on the ground with anticipatory government policies and the concerted action of the international community to achieve long-term peace and sustainable development.

Across North-East India, societies and communities have exchanged and transformed conflict into resolution. Local means, such as village courts and customary legal guidelines, have long supplied mediation for conflicting interests. Recently, for example, the Naga Mothers' Association (NMA) has played a frontline role in peace-building initiatives to help dialogue and reconciliation between warring factions.

Likewise, Indigenous women play a vital role by using their extraordinary societal position to pursue peace and development. More than that, though, as the "dream maps" in Odisha (where Adivasi women imagined and realized ecological conditions in their villages) reveal, a transformative possibility places the responsibility on grassroots movements.

Slowly, the international community has recognized Northeast India's strategic role in regional stability. The Bay of Bengal Initiative for Multi-Sectoral Technical and Economic Cooperation (BIMSTEC) is a multilateral grouping whose member states pursue several common objectives, such as economic and security ones. India is trying to connect the North Eastern Region (NER) with the Mainland Economic Region (MER) through BIMSTEC to strengthen the regional economy and contribute to the infrastructural development and conflict meditation forums as the regional cooperation mechanism unfolds.

At the national level, the Indian government has also launched several initiatives to address the regional issues. The general mindset of the state to resolve longstanding issues through discussion and political agreements, as illustrated by initiatives like the Naga Peace Accord 2015 and the Mizoram Peace Accord 1986, depicts the overall political developments. Autonomous councils and development schemes seeking to ameliorate socio-economic disparities are available; it has been suggested that these communities' autonomy provides a degree of empowerment.

This, in turn, requires governance which considers the needs and aspirations of the indigenous peoples of Northeast India for a healthy resolution of conflict. It is essential to have collaborative initiatives with the role of government agencies, civil society organizations, and local leaders so that mutual understanding and problem-solving can occur.

The North Eastern Council (NEC) can be described as a statutory advisory body which aims towards inter-state planning and development in the North Eastern Region, which is working towards a proper sync of resources and appropriate, balanced growth so that one region does not overpower the other. Similarly, various civil society organizations might help address the existing divide between the state and communities by advocating appropriate state policies and social norms needed for the specificity of local socio-cultural contexts.

The only way to fix the twisted web of Northeast India is through mobilization at the grassroots level, responsive government, and international cooperation, only by opening paths to empower local communities, preserving traditional conflict resolution pathways, and encouraging inclusive development.

RECOMMENDATIONS AND SOLUTIONS

The northeast remains complex for many reasons, and a multi-faceted approach is required to overcome this crisis. Still, the indigenous peoples, such as the Koch Rajbongshi tribe, must be empowered. First, the Assam government should show utmost respect and ensure the rights of indigenous people are restored as soon as possible by granting ST status to the Koch Rajbongshi for the entire geography of India to get constitutional safeguards and socio-economic development.

Conflict sensitivity should be used in development interventions, and every major project should undergo a full-fledged impact assessment to ensure that local grievances are not further inflamed and that communities are part of the decision-making process. Indeed, strengthening local-level governance (traditional councils and tribal advisory bodies) will allow for more localized decision-making and conflict resolution. Simultaneously, boosting indigenous enterprises with skill development and targeted funding in conventional sectors such as handloom, agriculture, eco-tourism, crafts, etc., can integrate local economies with the global chain. Increasing regional connectivity, including fast-tracking infrastructure projects such as the India-Myanmar-Thailand Trilateral Highway and upgrading road, rail, and digital infrastructure, is also necessary to mitigate isolation and realize commercial potential. Also, the so-called autonomous bodies and institutions, such as the Kamatapur Autonomous Council, would need to be streamlined and given more financial and administrative power with extended territory while incorporating systems of transparency and accountability. Finally, long-term peace-building must be based on inter-ethnic dialogue, education for coexistence and reconciliation initiatives with the help of schools, NGOs, religious associations and local structures as brokers of peace and mutual commitment.

FUTURE RESEARCH DIRECTIONS

Uniting knowledge across disciplines is the basic and urgent step to gaining a better understanding of the multifarious dynamics of the socio-political field of Northeast India, especially the tribe of the Koch Rajbongshi. Prospective studies may also need a longitudinal approach, which can trace the changes in the indigenous autonomy movements, such as the Kamatapur demand, regarding social, political, and economic impacts. Further studies on the impacts of other types of regional trade arrangements, such as the Bangladesh-Bhutan-India-Nepal (BBIN) corridor, on tribal economies would provide insights into how cross-border integration affects indigenous livelihoods and regional cohesion. The nexus between regional conflict and business environments, and particularly how the intensity of conflict influences foreign direct investment and market confidence, is a further key research need. Assessing the delivery and impact of government-sponsored welfare programmes and autonomous councils will generate an evidence-based understanding of effectiveness and inform policy revisions. Comparative lessons from forms of autonomy like the Sixth Schedule in Meghalaya and Tripura could identify such flexible governance models for the Koch Rajbongshi. Finally, it would be more fruitful to understand how access, especially to technology, can empower young people through education, entrepreneurship, and participation in governance.

DISCUSSION

The chapter has provided us a window to the intricacies of north-east India by using the socio-political experience of the Koch Rajbongshi community within the meditative material culture of the different ethnic groups of north-east India under the intersection of ethnicity and geopolitics and geoeconomics. The study highlighted the historical roots of marginalization, identity politics, and limited access to policy processes that continue to shape regional conflicts and dynamic opportunities for its development. This is not merely a tale of local grievances but part of systems of governance that have long ignored the complex life of Indigenous peoples.

The longstanding demands of the Koch Rajbongshi tribe for a separate Kamatapur state and the status of the Scheduled Tribe illustrate the intertwined connections between an ethnic group and political representation. The pressure to demand identity recognition and separate geography rises from the sole purpose of identity recognition and self-governance, including preserving culture and inclusion of history, culture and language in the educational board and university curriculum for greater dignity and survival in the rapidly industrialized India and global world. These demands and aspirations should not be labelled as separatist or divider as they want dignity and participate equally like other mainland Indians. The pleas, requests, and voices of the natives have been continuously discarded by India's bureaucrats and policymakers, which led to various revolts and the rise of movements led by ordinary people to survive in this complex world.

The discussion highlights Northeast India's developmental challenges. The natives' actions might be seen as a threat (perceived as the threat to integration), which resulted in the extended implementation of the Armed Forces (Special Powers) Act (AFSPA) in various parts of Northeast India. These factors may suppress conflict in the short term, circumvent the root causes of discontent, and likely make local populations feel even more disenfranchised. No matter how many economic initiatives are implemented, policies and acts unfavourable to the natives will be seen as distrust and isolation from mainland India.

The geographical significance of the area, especially being a transit zone to Southeast Asia, makes it an essential part of India's foreign policy and trade interests. However, this chapter shows that such aspirations cannot be realized without domestic peace and tranquillity. Predictability, safety and social cohesion are prerequisites for investment, national and international, and cannot be ensured without systemic conflict resolution and governance. In this respect, the economic disempowerment of the Koch Rajbongshi and other communities constitutes a danger to local order and India's larger regional and global aspirations.

The participation of the Koch Rajbongshi community in small-scale industries, agriculture and crafts shows that economic development can be a bridge to peace as long as it is done with empathy. Inclusive policies, improved access to finance, and market integration can help communities to help themselves, reduce dependence on state assistance and promote a sense of ownership over development. This, however, will only work if institutions are prepared to devolve power and resources to local and autonomous organizations.

Further, this chapter highlights that analysis needs to shift from ethnocentric or top-down exploration within academic and policy debate. Future approaches must be grounded in cultural understanding, intersectionality, and local engagement. Local knowledge practices of indigenous traditions, culture and governance models, and mechanisms for traditional conflict resolution can be key in the design of context-specific interventions.

It becomes evident that regional conflicts in Northeast India, especially those involving intra-community tensions among groups like the Koch Rajbongshi, warrant a perspective beyond the conventional law-and-order framework. Deep-seated sociopolitical struggles need durable, long-lasting, and engaged responses. With inclusive governance, peace-building and development processes driven by justice and equity, Arunachal has the potential to become more than a mere bridge to South East Asia, but instead a gateway to the peaceful coexistence of multiple cultures. Such a change would serve national imperatives and global development objectives, reinforcing that peace and prosperity are not mutually exclusive. Nonetheless, one is linked with the other. The Northbengal corridor, which was once an integral part of the Koch Behar Princely State and Kamatapur Kingdom, can be an exclusive gateway to Bhutan, Nepal, China, and Bangladesh provided the demand of the native to form a separate Kamatapur State or Koch State is respected by India.

CONCLUSION

The region's multi-ethnic, conflict-prone socio-political landscape, characterized by strategic borders and different cultures, has immense implications for such plans. By focusing on the particular case of the Koch Rajbongshi community, the chapter has demonstrated how past dispossession, cultural debasement and political aspirations for recognition are transformed into contemporary regional tensions impeding transboundary economic connectivity and international collaboration.

Demand for identity recognition, the status of a state, and socio-economic integration is rooted in the remotest aspirations of Indigenous peoples of the region and the broader Koch Rajbongshi struggle speaks similar aspirations of other ethnic groups of the region. Although these claims are historically conditioned, they articulate longings for dignity, cultural integrity and equal participation in the domains of political power and development in manners that are relevant to contemporary aspirations. Meeting these demands of locals is essential for peace and broader regional stability and development.

While India positions Northeast India at the centre of the Act East Policy and strives to establish cross-border trade and connectivity, it has to first contend with the domestic causes of disaffection. International business opportunities, an influx of foreign capital, and regional diplomacy will only prosper when there is peace, equity, and inclusive governance. Some of the keys to any sustainable resolution are development's sensitivity to conflict, work in the local communities of the populations, and collaboration between states, international organizations, and local actors—Act East Policy – A Strategic Initiative of the Government of India. Officially launched in 2014, it was a more proactive successor to the earlier Look East Policy initiated in the early 1990s.

The experience of the Koch Rajbongshi case can be beneficial for areas of similar ethnic assertion, regional development discontent and geopolitical divergence. Northeast India stands at a crossroads. By linking local aspirations and initiatives to national and global economic and political agendas, the region can be a reference point for inclusive growth and sustainable peace. Effective use of combined policy, broader inclusion and respect for the rights of the indigenous majorities would be necessary to change India and its periphery from a potential conflict zone into a thriving Indian and beyond gateway.

REFERENCES

Anaya, S. J. (2023). *Indigenous peoples in international law* (2nd ed.). Oxford University Press., https://academic.oup.com/book/50412

Arenla. (2023). *FDI inflow in Northeast India: Policy reforms, trends and prospects.* Asian Confluence. https://www.asianconfluence.org/publication-details-full/fdi-inflow-in-northeast-india-policy-reforms-trends-and-prospects

Barman, R. K. (2005). *From tribalism to independent state: Reflection on the emergence of Kamate Koch Kingdom c. 15th century AD–1773 AD* (Doctoral dissertation, University of North Bengal). Shodhganga. http://hdl.handle.net/10603/149146

Barman, R. K. (2009). Partition of Bengal and Struggle for Existence of the Scheduled Castes: Impact of the Partition (1947) on the Rajbanshis of North Bengal. *Voice of Dalit*, *2*(2), 141–164. DOI: 10.1177/0974354520090202

Baruah, S. (2012). *Durable Disorder: Understanding the Politics of Northeast India.* Oxford University Press., https://academic.oup.com/book/5580

Baruah, S. (2020). *In the Name of the Nation: India and Its Northeast.* Stanford University Press., https://www.sup.org/books/asian-studies/name-nation

Borah, P. (2016). *Ethnic movements in Assam: A study of Koch Rajbanshis* (M.Phil. dissertation). Sikkim University. http://14.139.206.50:8080/jspui/bitstream/1/4571/1/Paresh%20Borah.pdf

Chaudhuri, H. N. (1903). *The Cooch Behar state and its land revenue settlements.* Cooch Behar State Press., https://archive.org/download/coochbeharstatei00chaurich/coochbeharstatei00chaurich.pdf

Google. (2025). *Map of Northeast India showing borders with Bhutan, Nepal, Bangladesh, China, and Myanmar* [Map]. Google Maps. https://maps.app.goo.gl/aYbszNgdWkgEPFbS8 *(Accessed on June 5, 2025, at 9:22 AM IST, from Assam, India)*

Government of India. (1950). *The Constitution of India, Scheduled Tribes Order.* https://legislative.gov.in

Government of India. (1950a). *The Constitution of India: First Schedule.* Part C States.

Gyan, I. A. S. (2025). *Koch-Rajbongshi.* IAS Gyan. https://www.iasgyan.in/daily-current-affairs/koch-rajbongshis

Hazarika, S. (1994). *Strangers of the Mist: Tales of War and Peace from India's Northeast.* Penguin Books. https://www.caluniv.ac.in/global-mdia-journal/BR_JUNE_DEC_2015/BookReview1.pdf

India Today, N. E. (2025). *Assam: Koch-Rajbongshi Mancha submits a 15-point memorandum, demanding ST status and Kamatapur state.* https://www.indiatodayne.in/assam/story/assam-koch-rajbongshi-mancha-submits-15-point-memorandum-demands-st-status-and-kamatapur-state-1181318-2025-03-09

Kuame, C. (2022). Cross border trade in Northeast India: Critical analysis. *International Journal of Research in Engineering, Science and Management,* 5(4), 232–236. https://journal.ijresm.com/index.php/ijresm/article/download/1945/1885

Lok Sabha. (1997). *The Constitution (Scheduled Tribes) Order (Amendment) Bill, 1996: Report of the Select Committee.* Government of India. https://eparlib.nic.in/bitstream/123456789/757628/1/jcb_11_1997_scheduled_tribes.pdf

Ministry of External Affairs. (2023). *Question No-1456: India's Act East Policy.* Government of India. https://www.mea.gov.in/lok-sabha.htm?dtl/36927/QUESTION+NO1456+INDIAS+ACTEAST+POLICY Ministry of Tribal Affairs. *Scheduled Tribes Profile.* https://tribal.nic.in/Statistics.aspx

Misra, U. (2000). *The Periphery Strikes Back: Challenges to the Nation-State in Assam and Nagaland.* Indian Institute of Advanced Study. http://14.139.58.199:8080/jspui/handle/123456789/449

Nag, S. N. (2015). *Kamtapur movement in North Bengal: Geo-ethno-environmental and historical perspective* (Doctoral dissertation, University of North Bengal). Shodhganga. http://hdl.handle.net/10603/174126

Nandi, R. (2014). Spectacles of Ethnographic and Historical Imaginations: Kamatapur Movement and the Rajbanshi Quest to Rediscover their Past and Selves. *History and Anthropology, 25*(5), 571–591. DOI: 10.1080/02757206.2014.928776

Padmapati, R. K. (2022). *General Chilarai.* The Sentinel. https://www.sentinelassam.com/more-news/editorial/general-chilarai-578610

Pinterest. (n.d.). *Map of Kamata Kamarupa* [Image]. Pinterest. https://in.pinterest.com/pin/map-of-kamata-kamarupa--531424824773446898/ *(Accessed on June 5, 2025)*

Ray, S. (2023). Koch Rajbanshis and the Kamatapur Movement: Azadi in Eastern India? In Ranjan, A., & Chattoraj, D. (Eds.), *Migration, Regional Autonomy, and Conflicts in Eastern South Asia.* Palgrave Macmillan., DOI: 10.1007/978-3-031-28764-0_10

Roy, A. (2014). *Koch Rajbongshi and the Politics of Belonging*. Eastern Book House.

Roy, H. (2014). Politics of Janajatikaran: Koch Rajbanshis of Assam. *Economic and Political Weekly*, *49*(47). https://www.epw.in/journal/2014/47/reports-states-web-exclusives/politics-janajatikaran.html

Roychowdhury, A. (2024). *The Rajbanshis and the history of their statehood demand*. The Indian Express. https://indianexpress.com/article/research/the-rajbanshis-and-the-history-of-their-statehood-demand-9263934/

Saikia, G., & Senapoti, I. (2019). Autonomy movements in North East India: A study of Koch Rajbongshi autonomy movement (Kamatapur movement) in Assam. *IOSR Journal of Humanities and Social Science (IOSR-JHSS)*, *24*(3), 10–14. https://www.iosrjournals.org/iosr-jhss/papers/Vol.%2024%20Issue3/Series-8/C2403081014.pdf

Singh, K. S. (2010). *People of India: An Introduction*. Anthropological Survey of India. https://archive.org/details/people-of-india-intro

Singh, M. P. (2025). *Siliguri Corridor: India's strategic lifeline and a growing concern*. The Times of India. https://timesofindia.indiatimes.com/blogs/voices/siliguri-corridor-indias-strategic-lifeline-and-a-growing-concern

Singha, R., & Singha, S. (2025). The Case for Granting Scheduled Tribe Status to the Koch Rajbongshi Community. *SSRN*. https://ssrn.com/abstract=5236639

Singha, S. (2018). *Koch or Koch Rajbongshi: Tribal by birth*. The Native Tribe. https://www.thenativetribe.org/blog/koch-or-koch-rajbongshi-tribal-by-birth

Srisangnam, P., & Devendrakumar, A. (2018). Unlocking the Northeast Region of India: An ASEAN Connectivity Perspective. In Sarma, A., & Choudhury, S. (Eds.), *Mainstreaming the Northeast in India's Look and Act East Policy*., DOI: 10.1007/978-981-10-5320-7_5

Times of India. (2014). *Clarify stand on ST tag to Koch Rajbongshis: HC*. The Times of India. https://timesofindia.indiatimes.com/city/guwahati/clarify-stand-on-st-tag-to-koch-rajbongshis-hc/articleshow/29293726.cms

KEY TERMS AND DEFINITIONS

Cross-Border Trade: The exchange of goods, services, and capital across international borders or territories. In the context of Northeast India, it refers to trade between India and neighbouring countries such as Bangladesh, Bhutan, Myanmar, and Nepal, which can be significantly influenced by regional stability and infrastructure development.

Geoeconomics: The study and application of economic instruments to achieve geopolitical objectives. It uses trade, investment, and economic policy to influence regional and international relations. Northeast India's economic integration with Southeast Asia is a prime example of a geo-economic strategy.

Geopolitics: The analysis of the effects of geography (human and physical) on international politics and relations. It includes territorial disputes, border security, and strategic influence. Northeast India's location at the intersection of multiple international borders makes it geopolitically significant.

Indigenous Autonomy: The right of indigenous peoples to self-govern, preserve their cultural identity, manage resources, and make decisions affecting their communities. For the Koch Rajbongshi tribe, autonomy includes demands for statehood or special constitutional status to protect their heritage and ensure development.

Koch Rajbongshi Tribe: An Indigenous community with historical roots in the Kamata kingdom spread across Assam, West Bengal, and Bihar. The tribe has been actively seeking recognition, cultural preservation, and political representation through movements like the demand for Kamatapur state.

Northeast India: A region comprising eight Indian states, known for its ethnic diversity, strategic location, and developmental challenges. Bordered by five countries, it is pivotal to India's Act East Policy and prone to ethnic conflicts and economic exclusion.

Regional Conflicts: Localized disputes often involve ethnic, cultural, or political grievances within a specific region. In Northeast India, these conflicts frequently involve demands for autonomy, opposition to migration, and historical injustices, impacting governance and regional development.

Chapter 6
Geopolitical Risk and Uncertainty in Mexico's Foreign Direct Investment

Minerva E. Ramos
https://orcid.org/0000-0001-8399-6058
Universidad de Monterrey, Mexico

Cristina G. González
https://orcid.org/0009-0001-3542-1601
Universidad de Monterrey, Mexico

Regina García
https://orcid.org/0009-0003-5791-6669
Universidad de Monterrey, Mexico

Enid A. Sáenz
https://orcid.org/0009-0006-0386-3786
Universidad de Monterrey, Mexico

Roberto A. De los Santos
https://orcid.org/0009-0003-0707-1143
Universidad de Monterrey, Mexico

ABSTRACT

Geopolitical risk, the strength and direction of association with uncertainty factors, and new foreign direct investment (FDI) investments by country of origin as a measure of nearshoring in Mexico led to the objective of this chapter: to analyze the relationship between new FDI investments in Mexico by country of origin and Mexico's geopolitical risk, the United States' trade policy uncertainty, and Mexico's

DOI: 10.4018/979-8-3373-1265-1.ch006

economic policy uncertainty, during the period from the first quarter of 2006 to the second quarter of 2024. The methodology was based on an analysis of Pearson and Spearman correlation coefficients, selected using the Shapiro-Wilk normality test. The main results establish that changes in Mexico´s new FDI investments by country of origin are associated with changes in Mexico's geopolitical risk index, the United States' trade policy uncertainty index, and Mexico´s economic policy uncertainty index. Consequently, by reducing risk and uncertainty, it is possible to establish public policies that increase new FDI investments and, therefore, nearshoring in Mexico.

INTRODUCTION

Globalization, geopolitical risk, trade policy uncertainty, economic policy uncertainty, and investment through nearshoring have become increasingly prominent factors, particularly in terms of their potential benefits for countries looking to relocate their production operations (Pietrobelli & Seri, 2023). Given its close geographical location to the United States and its existing trade agreement with that country, Mexico can capitalize on the advantages offered by foreign investment from nearshoring companies (IMCO, 2024; Santillán et al., 2024). Companies that engage in nearshoring adopt a strategy that involves relocating a portion of their production and supply chains to regions that are geographically closer to their target market (IMCO, 2024; Santillán et al., 2024). Companies involved in nearshoring have gained significant strength due to the rising logistics costs resulting from events such as the COVID-19 pandemic and the trade war between the United States and China (Santillán et al., 2024).

In this case, companies can choose to relocate their production chains inshore within the same country, nearshore to a nearby country, offshore to a distant country (Pietrobelli & Seri, 2023), or friendshoring to a friendly country (Nedumpara, 2024).

Following research by Carrasco (2024), Garrido (2022), Hernández & Estay (2018), and Pietrobelli & Seri (2023), companies consider several key factors when establishing subsidiaries in either nearby or distant foreign locations. These factors include labor costs, marketing strategies, logistics costs, skilled workforce availability, digital infrastructure, trade openness, economic and political stability, and geopolitical tensions.

This chapter examines the association between geopolitical risk, trade policy uncertainty, and economic policy uncertainty, employing new foreign direct investment (NFDI) as a metric for nearshoring companies. In this regard, Al-Mustofa & Risyad (2025) revealed both a direct and inverse relationship between geopolitical risk and foreign direct investment (FDI) in Muslim economies. However, Bussy

& Zheng (2023) highlighted an inverse relationship between geopolitical risk and FDI in Latin America, Asia, and Africa, among other regions. On the other hand, Coën & Desfleurs (2024) reveal in their findings that geopolitical risk and economic policy uncertainty have a detrimental impact on investments in the United States.

According to Okara (2023), there is a direct relationship between the risk of political instability and FDI in developing countries, including Mexico. Meanwhile, Dutta et al. (2017) and Maharmah (2023) found a direct relationship between trade openness and FDI in Asian countries.

Other studies have examined the relationship between geopolitical risk and economic policy uncertainty in the United States (Adeosun et al., 2024), as well as the relationship between geopolitical risk and trade flows in Latin American, Asian, and African countries (ÖzçeliK, 2023; Singh et al., 2024).

In the case of Mexico, Banco de México (2017) noted that its trade openness with its main trading partner, the United States, depends on U.S. trade policy. However, these studies do not consider FDI in relation to both political stability and trade policy together.

Consequently, the objective is to analyze the strength and direction of the association between Mexico's new FDI investments by country of origin and Mexico's geopolitical risk, the United States' trade policy uncertainty, and Mexico's economic policy uncertainty.

Therefore, Mexico and the United States' decisions to leverage nearshoring among companies are critically important.

Context

FDI is an attractive mechanism that establishes connections between multinational companies (Jha et al., 2024) by providing an inflow of capital into the host country (Jadhav et al., 2016; Simelyte & Antanaviciene, 2014) and facilitating the transfer of advanced technologies, which improve productivity and innovation in the host country (Bozsik et al., 2023; Jadhav et al., 2016). It also contributes to economic growth by enhancing the productive capacity of the host country (Baci et al., 2022; Kumar, 2016; Marchewka, 2023). Furthermore, Jha et al. (2024) noted that the influx of FDI benefits developed economies through efficient resource utilization, while developing economies gain advantages from capital, diversification, and knowledge. Therefore, some factors that drive or discourage FDI are outlined below.

TRADE POLICY UNCERTAINTY (TPU) AND FDI

Promoting trade integration through the signing of free trade agreements and changes in tariff policies can generate moderate economic impacts in the short term but more significant effects in the long-term, including an expansion of FDI flows (Dávila et al., 2018). For example, Africa positively impacted FDI inflows by reducing trade costs and tariffs (Cantah et al., 2018; Obuobi et al., 2021), whereas Costa Rica did so through the signing of regional trade agreements such as the Central American Free Trade Agreement (CAFTA) (Frutos et al., 2011). However, China has focused on developing a specific sector, such as the agrifood sector, with soybean processing (Wang, 2012).

By nearshoring, Mexico has boosted new FDI investments due to the economic integration between the United States and Mexico (Phillips & Slijk, 2015; Reynolds, 2019; Sanderson, 2014) (see Figure 1), the United States' investment in key Mexican economic sectors (Reynolds, 2019), Mexico's young workforce (Phillips & Slijk, 2015), and Mexico's geographic location (Quintana & Salgado, 2016). Notably, the notable growth in Mexico's new FDI investments comes from companies from China and South Korea (Romero, 2024).

Figure 1. US goods imports to goods imports of the World (seasonally adjusted) by country of origin.

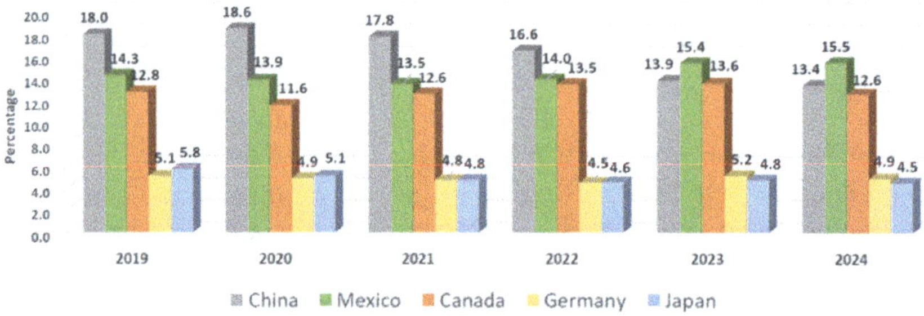

Source: Authors' elaboration with data from the U.S. Census Bureau (2024).

However, why and how might companies choose to offshore their operations? It is not only about gaining a competitive advantage through geographic location (Carmel & Abbott, 2007) but also about attracting new investment through logistics and supply chain aspects by ensuring efficiency and sustainability (Bednarski et al., 2023; Piña-Barcenas et al., 2024), shortening delivery times (Wang et al., 2024), and guaranteeing regional production networks (Yin et al., 2023).

In fact, increased uncertainty in trade policies generally has a negative impact on FDI inflows; that is, it makes the expected returns on investment projects less predictable, leading to a decrease in FDI flows (Azzimonti, 2019; Bao et al., 2022; Choi et al., 2021). The effect of trade policy uncertainty on the unpredictability of investment returns can vary by sector and over time, highlight the complex nature of the relationship (see Table 1).

Table 1. Impact of FDI and trade policy uncertainty.

Factor	Impact on FDI	Details
General impact	Negative	Lower FDI inflows due to unpredictability in returns (Azzimonti, 2019; Bao et al., 2022; Choi et al., 2021).
Sector-specific effects	Negative	Reducing trade policy uncertainty can increase FDI in high-export industries (Bao et al., 2022).
Temporal dynamics	Positive/Negative	Outwardly, FDI peaks three-quarters after a domestic shock in the domestic economic policy uncertainty index and decreases after the host economic policy uncertainty index shock (Hsieh et al., 2019).
Global Context	Negative	Similar negative impacts have been observed in other countries like China (Su et al., 2022; Gao et al., 2024).

Source: Authors' elaboration.

Therefore, new FDI investments (see Figure 2) are highlighted not only by strategic decision-making but also by risk management (Guedes & Pereira, 2024) and economic vulnerability in developing economies (Nguyen & Le, 2021).

Figure 2. Behavior of Mexico's FDI by type of investment.

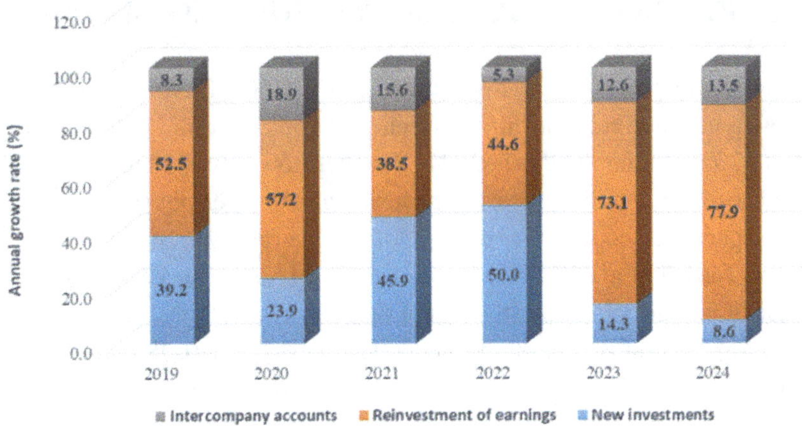

Source: Authors' elaboration with data from Secretaría de Economía (2024a).

However, 70% of FDI in Mexico, from new investments, reinvested earnings, and intercompany accounts, is concentrated in only three economic sectors: manufacturing, financial and insurance services, and mining (see Figure 3).

Figure 3. Behavior of Mexico's FDI by economic sector.

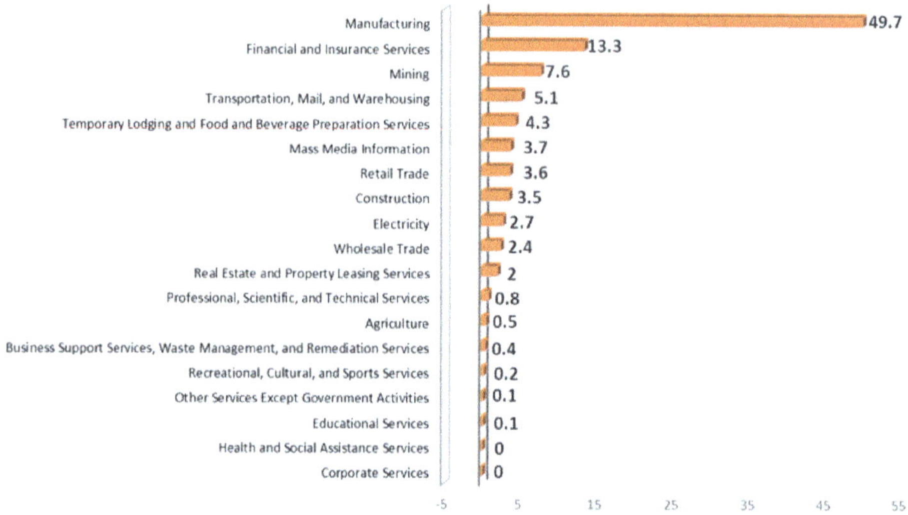

Source: Authors' elaboration with data from Secretaría de Economía (2024a).

ECONOMIC POLICY UNCERTAINTY (EPU) AND FDI

Economic policy uncertainty discourages FDI inflows. Cases such as China and India show a negative relationship between FDI and economic policy uncertainty (Gao et al., 2024; Sinha & Ghosh, 2021). Furthermore, lower FDI inflows are due to domestic economic policy uncertainty during election periods (Chen et al., 2019) and sector-specific effects, such as energy policy uncertainty in Brazil, Russia, India, and China (Tabash et al., 2024). Mexico has also seen lower FDI inflows due to high levels of volatility in domestic economic policy uncertainty resulting from the cancelation of large infrastructure projects (Canh et al., 2020; Woo-Mora, 2025).

However, global uncertainty caused by the United States' economic policy may establish a causal relationship with FDI from another country (Olanipekun & Olasehinde-Williams, 2022). The Mexican economy is particularly sensitive to changes in the United States' policies because of its high dependence on U.S. exports (Alam & Istiak, 2020; Seker, 2023). However, Olanipekun & Olasehinde-Williams

(2022) argued that no causal relationship existed between the United States' economic policy uncertainty and Mexico's FDI inflows.

Furthermore, among the factors contributing to Mexico's economic policy uncertainty are the electoral processes and the different governing parties in 2000, 2006, and 2024 (Paolino, 2009; Sánchez, 2024), the reluctance to provide quality infrastructure in state-owned companies with high financial costs, such as Comisión Federal de Electricidad (CFE) and Petróleos Mexicanos (PEMEX) (Vargas, 2024), and the sensitivity of stock and currency markets, as experienced during the 2008 crisis (Muñoz & Gálvez-Gamboa, 2022).

The high fixed costs associated with FDI make it particularly sensitive to uncertainty because investors seek stable investment environments (Choi et al., 2021). Hence, the importance of stable and predictable economic policies is not only to attract but also to retain FDI.

Table 2. Impact of FDI and economic policy uncertainty.

Factor	Impact on FDI	Details
Local EPU	Negative	Reduced FDI inflows due to increased uncertainty (Choi et al., 2021; Gao et al., 2024; Sosa et al., 2023).
International EPU	Negative	Affects Mexican economic activities and FDI because of its close economic ties (e.g., with the United States) (Alam & Istiak, 2020).
Economic reforms	Positive	Attracts FDI by creating a more predictable environment (e.g. North American economic integration: NAFTA/USMCA) (Colyer, 2004; Nagy & Navarro, 2025; Villarreal, 2020).
Financial market sensitivity	Negative	Financial variables react quickly to economic policy uncertainty, and the broader economic impact is slower (Mo, 2024; Sosa et al., 2023).

Source: Authors' elaboration.

Although policymakers have attempted to mitigate the adverse effects of economic policy uncertainty and foster economic stability, geopolitical risk must also be considered. Surprisingly, Mexico's economic policy uncertainty is less sensitive to shocks in economic variables (Sosa et al., 2023). However, Mexico's geopolitical risk and populist policies affect investor risk aversión (Choi & Hadad, 2025; Woo-Mora, 2025).

GEOPOLITICAL RISK (GPR) AND FDI

Geopolitical risk increases and decreases FDI inflows. Truong et al. (2024) stated that it creates an unstable environment that discourages investor decisions in the long-term, but in the short-term, the relationship between geopolitical risk and FDI is positive.

On the other hand, Soussane et al. (2023) established that the relationship between geopolitical risk and FDI is direct and inverse, depending on the economic sector. Yu & Wang (2023) showed that the relationship between geopolitical risk and FDI is low to highly significant, depending on the country's level of economic development.

Consequently, Cetín & Yaman (2023) pointed out that to achieve an inverse relationship between geopolitical risk and FDI, economies must improve institutional quality, the rule of law, and a more equitable distribution of resources. However, geopolitical risks are leading to an increase in trade protectionism, as countries, including Mexico, apply trade restrictions to safeguard their industries during growing uncertainty (Shen & Yang, 2024). In Mexico, geopolitical risk is primarily affected by the coordination of trade relations with the United States (Sweidan, 2023), supply chain disruptions (Atacan & Açık, 2023), the harm posed by organized crime to public safety (Molinar & Carrillo, 2024; Rodríguez, 2019), limited confidence in the economy due to fluctuations in oil and natural gas prices (Cervantes & Rivera, 2021; Shahbaz et al., 2024), and fluctuating sovereign credit risk (Naifar & Aljarba, 2023), among other factors.

Therefore, geopolitical risk significantly inhibits Mexico's FDI inflows by creating an unstable environment that discourages foreign investors (Kapopoulos et al., 2024; Yu & Wang, 2023). Mexico's geopolitical stability is crucial for long-term investments in specific sectors, such as energy (Lu & Liu, 2024).

Table 3. Impact of FDI and geopolitical risk.

Factor	Impact on FDI	Details
Sectoral analysis	Positive/Negative	Positive in the primary sector and negative in the secondary and tertiary sectors (Soussane et al., 2023).
Emerging vs. advanced economies	Negative	Greater variations in emerging economies (Feng et al., 2023).
Short-term effects	Positive/Negative	Short-term increase in FDI, although its effect on long-term decrease in FDI (Truong et al., 2024).

Source: Authors' elaboration.

GEOPOLITICAL RISK (GPR) AND ECONOMIC SECTORS

Geopolitical risk has been analyzed by sector, such as agricultural sector (Sohag et al., 2023; Sun & Su, 2024), electricity sector (Su et al., 2021; Sweidan, 2021;

Zhao et al., 2023), mining of metallic minerals sector (Adeosun et al., 2024; Zhou & Liang, 2025), real estate and property leasing services sector (Coën & Desfleurs, 2024), and tourism services sector (Yilanci et al., 2023), analyzing periods in which geopolitical tension events have occurred, such as Russia-Ukraine gas conflict, U.S.-China trade war, Brexit referendum, Iran-U.S. conflicts, Covid-19 pandemic, Russia's invasion of Ukraine, among others.

Instead, Sivaprasad et al. (2025) studied geopolitical risk in the financial services sector in Georgia, Kazakhstan, Russia, Ukraine, and Uzbekistan. Al-Mustofa & Risyad (2025) also studied geopolitical risk in the financial services sector across 42 economies, including Indonesia, Saudi Arabia, Türkiye, Malaysia, Kazakhstan, Uganda, Egypt, Nigeria, Azerbaijan, and others (excluding Mexico). Additionally, Alqahtani et al. (2022) examined geopolitical risk in the financial services sector in Bahrain, Kuwait, Oman, Qatar, Saudi Arabia, and the United Arab Emirates. However, Iacoviello et al. (2024) demonstrated that the financial services sector has a special relevance in addressing the rise in global inflation across 44 economies (including Mexico) as geopolitical risk increases.

GEOPOLITICAL RISK (GPR) AND MACROECONOMIC INDICATORS

This section presents three important macroeconomic indicators and their relationship to geopolitical risk. The first macroeconomic indicator is oil production from the countries that comprise the Organization of the Petroleum Exporting Countries (OPEC), particularly Saudi Arabia, and its relation to the geopolitical risk index (Alqahtani et al., 2022). In this sense, Mignon & Saadaoui (2024) demonstrated a positive relationship between geopolitical risk and oil prices when supply declines.

In Figure 4, the OPEC and West Texas Intermediate (WTI) oil prices exhibit similar behavior from January 2019 to May 2025. This period was characterized by global geopolitical risk following the declaration of the COVID-19 pandemic. Additionally, two regional geopolitical risks emerged: Russia's invasion of Ukraine and the election of Mexico's first female president. According to Figure 4, global geopolitical risk appears to have a trend of increasing oil prices per barrel, whereas regional geopolitical risk shows a trend of decreasing oil prices per barrel. This decrease in oil prices is consistent with the findings of Zhang et al. (2022), who attributed it to expectations of reduced demand.

Figure 4. OPEC and WTI oil prices per barrel.

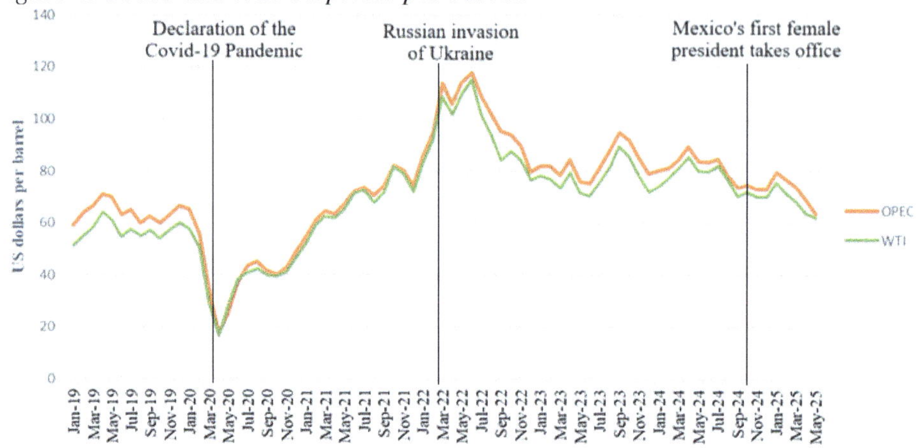

Source: Authors' elaboration with data from Datosmacro (2025a) (2025b).

The second macroeconomic indicator is the consumer price index (CPI), which is positively influenced by economic uncertainty and negatively impacted by geopolitical risk in the case of Türkiye (Bilgili et al., 2022).

The CPI trend observed in both Mexico and Türkiye exhibits a notable similarity, implying that an inverse relationship between the CPI and geopolitical risk may be expected in Mexico, as depicted in Figure 5.

Figure 5. CPI in Mexico and Türkiye (1998-2024).

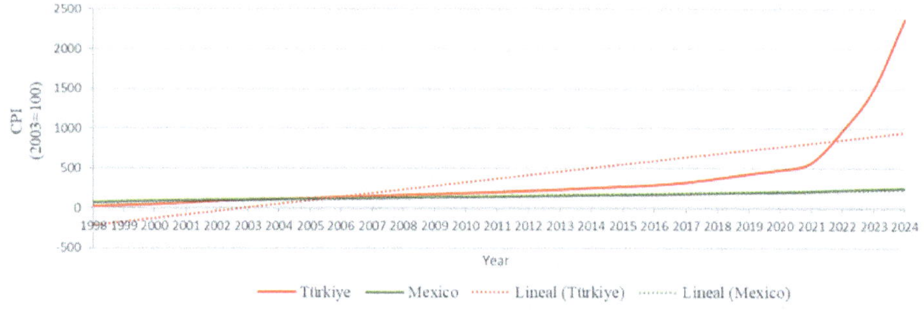

Source: Authors' elaboration with data from IMF (2025).

The third macroeconomic indicator is the exchange rate, which experiences currency devaluation as geopolitical risk increases in India, Indonesia, Malaysia, Morocco, Russia, Romania, Tunisia, Türkiye, Ukraine, and Vietnam (Hachicha, 2024).

Table 4 illustrates the number of times each of the nine countries analyzed by Hachicha (2024) experienced currency devaluation concerning the US dollar from the start of Russia's invasion of Ukraine to the present. It is worth noting that Mexico was included as a comparative country in our analysis.

Table 4. Period and number of times the currency has devalued during the period February 2022-May 2025.

Country and currency	Period	Number of times
India (Indian Rupee)	2022: November 2023: January, March, April, June, December 2024: January, February, June, September 2025: March, April	12
Indonesia (Indonesian Rupiah)	2022: March, July, December 2023: January, March, April, November, December 2024: February, May, July, August, September 2025: March, May	15
Malaysia (Malaysian Ringgit)	2022: November, December 2023: January, March, July, November, December 2024: March, May, July, August, September 2025: January, March, April, May	16
Morocco (Moroccan Dirham)	2022: May, November, December 2023: January, March, April, June, July, October, November, December 2024: April, May, July, August, September 2025: January, February, March, April, May	21
Russia (Russian Rouble)	2022: March, April, May, June, August, November 2023: January, October, November 2024: May, June 2025: January, February, March, April, May	16
Romania (Romanian New Leu)	2022: February, May, August, October, November, December 2023: January, March, April, June, July, October, November, December 2024: May, July, August, September 2025: January, February, March, April,	22
Türkiye (Turkish Lira)	2022: November 2023: August 2024: May	3
Ukraine (Ukraine Hryvnia)	2022: March, May, June 2023: October, November 2024: January, August 2025: January, March	9

continued on following page

Table 4. Continued

Country and currency	Period	Number of times
Vietnam (Vietnamese Dong)	2022: November, December 2023: January, March, April, November 2024: July, August, September 2025: January	10
Mexico (Mexican Peso)	2022: April, June, July, December 2023: August, September, October 2024: January, April, June, July, August, October, November, December	15

Note: Tunisia was excluded due to not available data.
Source: Authors' elaboration with data from Banco de México (2025).

GEOPOLITICAL RISK (GPR) AND GOVERNANCE

However, reducing geopolitical risk for countries attracting foreign direct investment (FDI) involves more than controlling macroeconomic indicators; it also requires implementing governance mechanisms.

Trade agreements can lead to policy reforms, integrating efforts around the establishment of common frameworks and the elimination of institutional barriers, aimed at reducing geopolitical risk (Hou et al., 2024; Shen & Yang, 2024). The effectiveness of trade agreements in reducing tensions between regions is largely dependent on the political stability of the participating countries (Baena-Rojas, 2024). For example, the European Union trade agreements have played a crucial role in promoting international cooperation and stability (Baena-Rojas, 2024). South Korea has also used its free trade agreements with the United States and China to maintain positive relations and prevent potential conflicts (Choi, 2018). Similarly, the Belt and Road Initiative has demonstrated its ability to mitigate the adverse effects of geopolitical risk on economic relations, serving as a landmark example of economic cooperation offsetting the impact of geopolitical risk on trade (Wang et al., 2025).

Figure 6 illustrates the relative position of Mexico in terms of perceived governance quality among the United States-Mexico-Canada Agreement (USMCA). According to Kaufmann & Kraay (2024) six dimensions, Mexico exhibited the lowest performance, with percentile ranks below 50. In contrast, Canada and the United States outperformed at least 75% of the evaluated countries in each dimension in terms of perceived governance quality.

Figure 6. Dimensions of governance in the USMCA countries, 2023.

Source: Authors' elaboration with data from World Bank Group (2025).

Other mechanisms that reduce tensions between countries include fostering economic interdependence, providing platforms for dialog, and promoting regional stability. These measures also involve promoting environmental, social, and governance practices to mitigate external risks within companies (Cheng et al., 2025; Erzurumlu et al., 2025; Reyad et al., 2024). Furthermore, international collaboration and dialog are facilitated for critical infrastructure protection (Gehringer, 2025), and robust institutions and resilient financial systems are established (Al-Mustofa & Risyad, 2025). Additionally, mechanisms for coordinating working conditions are developed (Gitterman, 2003), and technologies such as convolutional neural networks have been leveraged for enhanced market analysis and decision-making (Gehringer, 2025).

The following section examines the methodology used to analyze the correlation of Mexico's new FDI investments with trade policy uncertainty, economic policy uncertainty, and geopolitical risk.

METHODOLOGY

The analysis focuses on measuring and evaluating the strength and direction of the association between Mexico's new FDI investment variables and the United States' trade policy uncertainty, Mexico's economic policy uncertainty, and Mexico's geopolitical risk (see Table 5). Data were obtained from secondary sources, such as the Ministry of Economy of Mexico and the Economic Policy Uncertainty.

Due to data availability, the study period was from the first quarter of 2006 to the second quarter of 2024.

Table 5. Study variables

Variable		Source
Dependent variable	**Mexico's new Foreign Direct Investment (NFDI)**	**Secretaría de Economía (2024b)**
Independent variable	The United States' Trade Policy Uncertainty Index (USATPU)	Economic Policy Uncertainty (2024a), (2024b), (2024c)
	Mexico's Economic Policy Uncertainty Index (MEXEPU)	
	Mexico's Geopolitical Risk Index (MEXGPR)	

Source: Authors' elaboration.

Regarding the flows of Mexico's new FDI investments by country of origin, the Ministry of Economy (Secretaría de Economía, 2024b) records the following countries: Argentina, Australia, Austria, Belgium, Belize, Brazil, Canada, Chile, China, Colombia, Costa Rica, the Czech Republic, Denmark, Ecuador, El Salvador, Finland, France, Germany, Guatemala, Hong Kong, India, Indonesia, Ireland, Israel, Italy, Japan, Luxembourg, Malaysia, the Netherlands, New Zealand, Nicaragua, Norway, Panama, Peru, the Philippines, Poland, Portugal, Puerto Rico, Russia, Singapore, South Africa, South Korea, Spain, Sweden, Switzerland, Taiwan, the United Kingdom, the United States, Uruguay, and Venezuela.

On the other hand, Economic Policy Uncertainty constructed the United States Monthly Trade Policy Uncertainty (USATPU) index (Economic Policy Uncertainty, 2024c) and the Economic Policy Uncertainty (EPU) index for Mexico (Economic Policy Uncertainty, 2024b) using the method proposed by Baker et al. (2016), which consists of a search for articles in national newspapers. In the case of the United States, the search was conducted in the following newspapers: Chicago Tribune, Los Angeles Times, The Boston Globe, The New York Times, The Wall Street Journal, and The Washington Post. In Mexico, a search was made for newspapers such as El Norte, Mural, and Reforma. The method consists of selecting articles by identifying keywords for trade policy uncertainty, such as *"Doha Round"*, *"dumping"*, *"GATT"*, *"government subsidies"*, *"import barriers"*, *"import duties"*, *"import tariffs"*, *"trade agreement"*, *"trade law"*, *"trade policy"*, *"trade treaty"*, *"Uruguay Round"*, *"WTO"*, etcetera.; and for economic policy uncertainty, keywords such as *"budgets"*, *"deficit"*, *"economic"*, *"regulation"*, *"tariffs"*, *"taxes"*, *"uncertainty"*, etcetera.

The geopolitical risk (GPR) index (Economic Policy Uncertainty, 2024a) was constructed by Caldara & Iacoviello (2022), searching for keywords such as *"army"*, *"attack"*, *"bomb"*, *"conflict"*, *"geopolitical"*, *"guerrilla"*, *"military"*, *"peace"*, *"revolution"*, *"tension"*, *"threat"*, *"truce"*, *"war"*, *"weapons"*, etcetera. This search was performed for articles from the Chicago Tribune, Financial Times, Los Angeles Times, The Globe and Mail, The Guardian, The New York Times, The Telegraph, The Wall Street Journal, The Washington Post, and USA Today.

However, to measure and evaluate the strength and direction of the association between variables, Etaga et al. (2021) recommend using correlation analysis. Thus, the correlation coefficient assumes a linear relationship between the variables. If the relationship is not linear, the correlation coefficient may not accurately represent the strength or direction of the association between the variables (Janse et al., 2021).

Consequently, the strength of the correlation coefficient can vary between -1 and 1, with values close to 1 indicating that the variables have a strong negative relationship, while values close to 0 indicate no linear relationship, and values close to 1 indicating that the variables have a strong positive relationship (Yay, 2022).

In contrast, the sign reflects the direction of the association between variables (Etaga et al., 2021). A positive sign means that the values of both variables change in the same direction; that is, as the value of one variable increases, so does the value of the other, and vice versa. A negative sign means that the values of both variables change in opposite directions; that is, as the value of one variable increases, the value of the other variable decreases. It should be clarified that this does not imply causality because a third variable influences both variables (Shugan, 2007).

As a first step, Dambolena et al. (2006) and Lütkepohl & Xu (2012) proposed stabilizing the variance of a series that is not expressed as a percentage or index and linearizing the nonlinear relationships between the variables. Therefore, the series of Mexico's new FDI investments available by country of origin are transformed logarithmically.

In the second step, the missing values were replaced using the *SPSS Statistics* (2022) program using the series mean method. In the third step, due to the sample size (N = 74), the Shapiro-Wilk test was selected (Borbats & Shkolina, 2021; Huang et al., 2007), and its purpose was to determine whether the data follow a normal distribution or not (Thakur et al., 2023). In the fourth step, the selection of the parametric or nonparametric correlation was selected, that is, the Pearson correlation (r_p) if the distribution is normal (when the degree of significance in the Shapiro-Wilk test is greater than 0.05 or the Spearman correlation (r_s) if it does not follow a normal distribution (when the degree of significance in the Shapiro-Wilk test is less than or equal to 0.05) (Winter et al., 2016).

Mathematically, based on El-Hashash & Shiekh (2022) and Xiao et al. (2016), Pearson's correlation coefficient and Spearman's correlation coefficient are calculated as follows:

Pearson

$$r_p = \frac{\sum_{i=1}^{n}(X_i - \bar{X})(Y_i - \bar{Y})}{\sqrt{(\sum_{i=1}^{n}(x_i - \bar{x})^2)(\sum_{i=1}^{n}(y_i - \bar{y})^2)}} \tag{1}$$

Where:
y = averages of the measurements of observations X and Y.

Spearman

$$r_s = 1 - \frac{6\sum d_i^2}{N((N^2 - 1)} \tag{2}$$

Where:
di = square of the difference between the ranges of the i-th observations of X and Y.
N = sample size.

Therefore, *SPSS Statistics* (2022) was used for the statistical analysis of both correlation coefficients. In the fifth step, once the value of the correlation coefficient was obtained, the strength of the association was determined, for which Xiao et al. (2016) indicated that it is considered strong if the coefficient is between -1 to -0.5 or 0.5 to 1, moderate if the coefficient is between -0.5 to -0.3 or 0.3 to 0.5, weak if the coefficient is between -0.3 to -0.1 or 0.1 to 0.3, and very weak or no strength -0.1 to 0.1. The results of the correlation analysis are presented in the following section.

RESULTS

The results obtained from the correlation analysis are presented below, which allows us to measure and evaluate the strength and direction of the association between the variables of Mexico's new investments in foreign direct investment (NFDI) by country of origin, the United States' trade policy uncertainty (USATPU) index, Mexico's economic policy uncertainty (MEXEPU) index, and Mexico's geopolitical risk (MEXGPR) index.

The first results correspond to the Shapiro-Wilk normality test, which measures whether Mexico's NFDI by country of origin conforms to a normal distribution, that is, accepting the null hypothesis (H_0) if the significance level is greater than 0.05 (see Table 6).

Table 6. Shapiro-Wilk normality test.

Mexico's NFDI by country of origin	Statistics	Level of significance	Null hypothesis of normality (H_0)
Argentina	0.957	0.013	Rejected
Australia	0.940	0.002	Rejected
Austria	0.924	<0.001	Rejected
Belgium	0.892	<0.001	Rejected
Belize	0.269	<0.001	Rejected
Brazil	0.985	0.521	Accepted
Canada	0.989	0.747	Accepted
Chile	0.978	0.219	Accepted
China	0.990	0.856	Accepted
Colombia	0.845	<0.001	Rejected
Costa Rica	0.896	<0.001	Rejected
Czech Republic	0.497	<0.001	Rejected
Denmark	0.967	0.049	Rejected
Ecuador	0.510	<0.001	Rejected
El Salvador	0.840	<0.001	Rejected
Finland	0.818	<0.001	Rejected
France	0.913	<0.001	Rejected
Germany	0.943	0.002	Rejected
Guatemala	0.314	<0.001	Rejected
Hong Kong	0.730	<0.001	Rejected
India	0.878	<0.001	Rejected
Indonesia	0.382	<0.001	Rejected
Ireland	0.928	<0.001	Rejected
Israel	0.666	<0.001	Rejected
Italy	0.981	0.342	Accepted
Japan	0.916	<0.001	Rejected
Luxembourg	0.873	<0.001	Rejected
Malaysia	0.687	<0.001	Rejected
Netherlands	0.881	<0.001	Rejected
New Zealand	0.763	<0.001	Rejected
Nicaragua	0.759	<0.001	Rejected
Norway	0.755	<0.001	Rejected
Panama	0.810	<0.001	Rejected

continued on following page

Table 6. Continued

Mexico's NFDI by country of origin	Statistics	Level of significance	Null hypothesis of normality (H_0)
Peru	0.910	<0.001	Rejected
Philippines	0.674	<0.001	Rejected
Poland	0.798	<0.001	Rejected
Portugal	0.888	<0.001	Rejected
Puerto Rico	0.511	<0.001	Rejected
Russia	0.878	<0.001	Rejected
Singapore	0.612	<0.001	Rejected
South Africa	0.384	<0.001	Rejected
South Korea	0.843	<0.001	Rejected
Spain	0.929	<0.001	Rejected
Sweden	0.916	<0.001	Rejected
Switzerland	0.885	<0.001	Rejected
Taiwan	0.907	<0.001	Rejected
United Kingdom	0.946	0.003	Rejected
United States	0.971	0.091	Accepted
Uruguay	0.763	<0.001	Rejected
Venezuela	0.826	<0.001	Rejected

Note: Sample size N = 74
Source: Authors' elaboration in *SPSS Statistics* (2022).

The results of the Spearman (r_s) and Pearson (r_p) correlation coefficients are presented below. The null hypothesis of normality (H_0) was rejected, and calculated for México's NFDI investments from Argentina, Australia, Austria, Belgium, Belize, Colombia, Costa Rica, the Czech Republic, Denmark, Ecuador, El Salvador, Finland, France, Germany, Guatemala, Hong Kong, India, Indonesia, Ireland, Israel, Japan, Luxembourg, Malaysia, the Netherlands, New Zealand, Nicaragua, Norway, Panama, Peru, the Philippines, Poland, Portugal, Puerto Rico, Russia, Singapore, South Africa, South Korea, Spain, Sweden, Switzerland, Taiwan, the United Kingdom, Uruguay, and Venezuela.

The null hypothesis of normality (H_0) was accepted and calculated for Mexico's NFDI investments from Brazil, Canada, Chile, China, Italy, and the United States (see Table 7).

Table 7. Correlation coefficient values and the level of significance.

Mexico's NFDI by country of origin	USATPU	MEXEPU	MEXGPR
Argentina	0.197* (0.093)	0.256** (0.028)	0.085 (0.473)
Australia	0.048 (0.684)	0.288** (0.013)	0.090 (0.447)
Austria	0.124 (0.291)	-0.093 (0.430)	-0.016 (0.891)
Belgium	-0.266** (0.022)	0.033 (0.779)	-0.112 (0.343)
Belize	-0.010 (0.930)	-0.149 (0.205)	0.057 (0.627)
Brazil	-0.0147 (0.212)	-0.053 (0.654)	-0.249** (0.033)
Canada	-0.007 (0.956)	0.221* (0.058)	0.114 (0.335)
Chile	-0.275** (0.018)	-0.031 (0.796)	-0.181 (0.123)
China	-0.033 (0.781)	0.205* (0.080)	0.055 (0.643)
Colombia	-0.124 (0.292)	0.086 (0.466)	-.042 (0.721)
Costa Rica	-0.082 (0.488)	-0.004 (0.970)	0.006 (0.962)
Czech Republic	-0.116 (0.327)	-0.155 (0.188)	-0.046 (0.700)
Denmark	-0.239** (0.040)	-0.049 (0.680)	-0.115 (0.328)
Ecuador	-0.087 (0.462)	0.019 (0.874)	-0.111 (0.348)
El Salvador	-0.100 (0.397)	0.000 (0.997)	-0.086 (0.465)
Finland	-0.027 (0.821)	-0.132 (0.261)	-0.068 (0.567)
France	-0.080 (0.501)	-0.068 (0.565)	-0.166 (0.158)
Germany	0.226* (0.053)	-0.164 (0.162)	-0.124 (0.294)
Guatemala	0.028 (0.811)	0.070 (0.553)	-0.079 (0.503)
Hong Kong	0.022 (0.850)	0.118 (0.319)	-0.049 (0.681)

continued on following page

Table 7. Continued

Mexico's NFDI by country of origin	USATPU	MEXEPU	MEXGPR
India	-0.226* (0.053)	-0.113 (0.337)	-0.203* (0.083)
Indonesia	0.007 (0.955)	0.141 (0.230)	-0.114 (0.332)
Ireland	-0.203* (0.083)	-0.069 (0.558)	-0.156 (0.184)
Israel	-0.084 (0.475)	-0.039 (0.741)	-0.144 (0.220)
Italy	0.285** (0.014)	-0.048 (0.682)	-0.249** (0.033)
Japan	0.096 (0.415)	-0.206* (0.078)	-0.042 (0.720)
Luxembourg	-0.102 (0.387)	0.065 (0.582)	-0.223* (0.056)
Malaysia	0.095 (0.418)	0.168 (0.153)	0.181 (0.123)
Netherlands	-0.074 (0.531)	0.035 (0.766)	0.097 (0.412)
New Zealand	-0.207* (0.077)	-0.042 (0.722)	0.057 (0.630)
Nicaragua	-0.100 (0.395)	-0.187 (0.110)	0.064 (0.591)
Norway	0.080 (0.497)	0.010 (0.934)	0.159 (0.176)
Panama	-0.186 (0.112)	-0.075 (0.527)	-0.320** (0.005)
Peru	-0.020 (0.866)	-0.086 (0.464)	-0.175 (0.136)
Philippines	-0.176 (0.134)	-0.110 (0.352)	-0.228* (0.051)
Poland	0.113 (0.337)	0.137 (0.244)	0.029 (0.806)
Portugal	0.078 (0.507)	0.161 (0.172)	0.176 (0.134)
Puerto Rico	-0.096 (0.416)	-0.109 (0.353)	0.089 (0.451)
Russia	0.076 (0.520)	0.129 (0.275)	0.271** (0.020)
Singapore	-0.179 (0.127)	0.078 (0.511)	0.080 (0.497)

continued on following page

Table 7. Continued

Mexico's NFDI by country of origin	USATPU	MEXEPU	MEXGPR
South Africa	0.002 (0.990)	0.008 (0.947)	0.195* (0.096)
South Korea	-0.165 (0.159)	-0.259** (0.026)	-0.177 (0.131)
Spain	0.087 (0.462)	0.055 (0.639)	-0.124 (0.294)
Sweden	0.088 (0.455)	0.108 (0.359)	0.048 (0.684)
Switzerland	0.062 (0.602)	-0.070 (0.551)	0.036 (0.763)
Taiwan	0.028 (0.813)	0.323** (0.005)	0.087 (0.459)
United Kingdom	0.051 (0.667)	0.258** (0.027)	-0.057 (0.628)
United States	0.049 (0.676)	-0.014 (0.908)	-0.152 (0.195)
Uruguay	0.009 (0.940)	-0.019 (0.870)	-0.179 (0.126)
Venezuela	-0.130 (0.271)	-0.151 (0.198)	-0.096 (0.414)

Note: Sample size N = 74
* = Correlation is significant at the 0.10 level (two-tailed)
** = Correlation is significant at the 0.05 level (two-tailed)
Source: Authors' elaboration in *SPSS Statistics* (2022).

Next, statistically significant correlation coefficients were found for Mexico's NFDI investments from Belgium, Chile, Denmark, Ireland, and New Zealand, which changed in the same direction as the USATPU index with weak strength. However, Mexico's NFDI investments from Germany changed in the opposite direction from the USATPU index with weak strength (see Figure 7).

Figure 7. Strengths and directions of the correlation of Mexico's NFDI investments by country of origin with the USATPU.

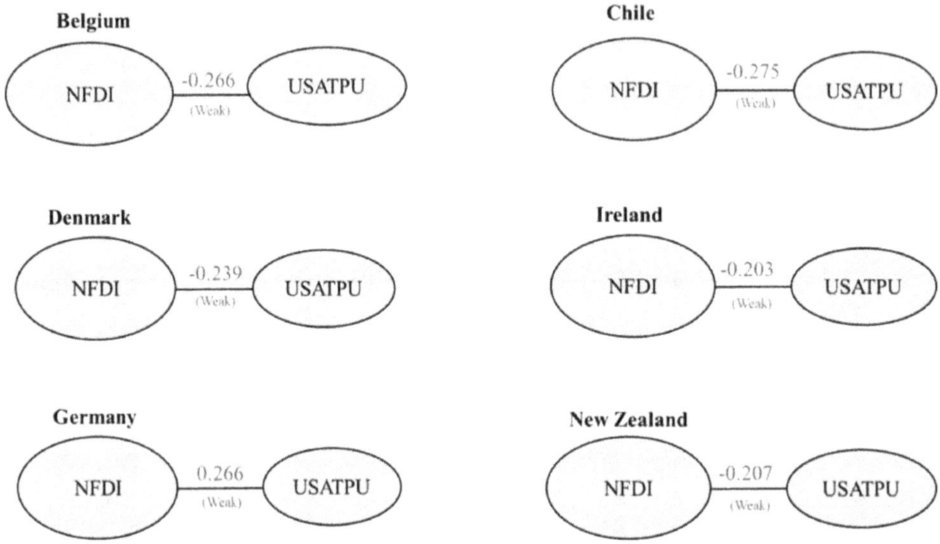

Source: Authors' elaboration.

However, Mexico's NFDI investments from Taiwan change in the same direction as the MEXEPU index, with moderate strength. Meanwhile, Mexico's NFDI investments from Australia, Canada, China, and the United Kingdom change in the same direction as the MEXEPU index, showing weak strength. Conversely, Mexico's NFDI investments from South Korea and Japan change in the opposite direction from the MEXEPU index, showing weak strength (see Figure 8).

Figure 8. Strengths and directions of the correlation of Mexico's NFDI investments by country of origin with the MEXEPU.

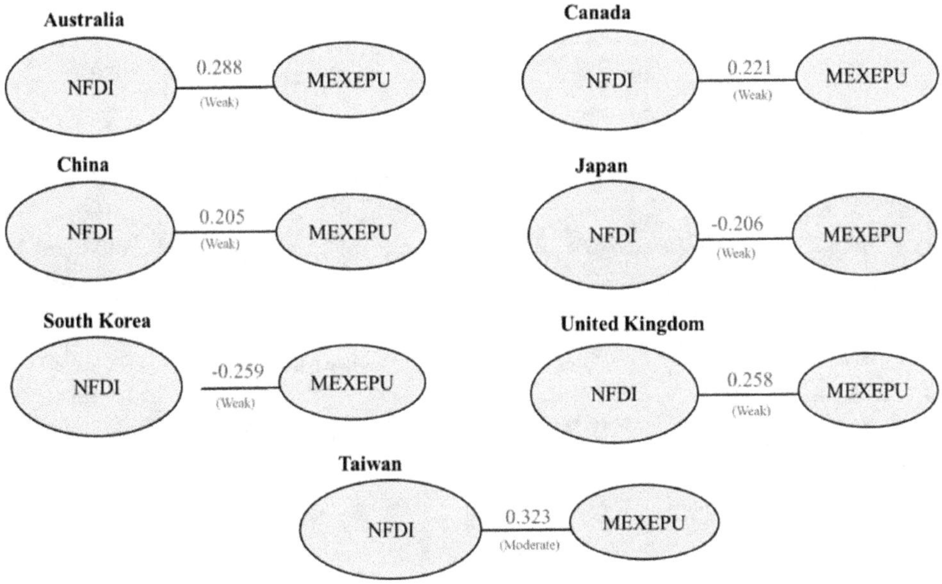

Source: Authors' elaboration.

However, Mexico's NFDI investments from Panama change in the opposite direction from the MEXGPR index with moderate strength. Meanwhile, Mexico's NFDI investments from Brazil, the Philippines, Panama, and Luxembourg change in the opposite direction from the MEXGPR index, showing weak strength. Conversely, Mexico's NFDI investments from Russia and South Africa change in the same direction as the MEXGPR index, showing weak strength (see Figure 9).

Figure 9. Strengths and directions of the correlation of Mexico's NFDI investments by country of origin with the MEXGPR.

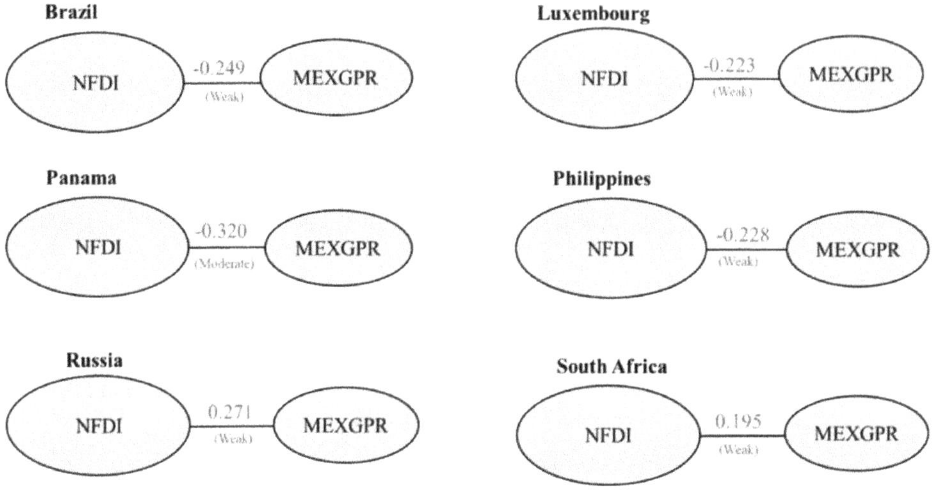

Source: Authors' elaboration.

While Mexico's NFDI investments from Argentina change in the same direction as the USATPU and MEXEPU indexes, with weak strength, Mexico's NFDI investments from India change in the opposite direction from the USATPU and MEXGPR indexes, with weak strength. In contrast, Mexico's NFDI investments from Italy change in the same direction as the USATPU index and in the opposite direction from the MEXGPR index, with weak strength (see Figure 10).

Figure 10. Strengths and directions of the correlation of Mexico's NFDI investments by country of origin with the USATPU, MEXEPU, and MEXGPR.

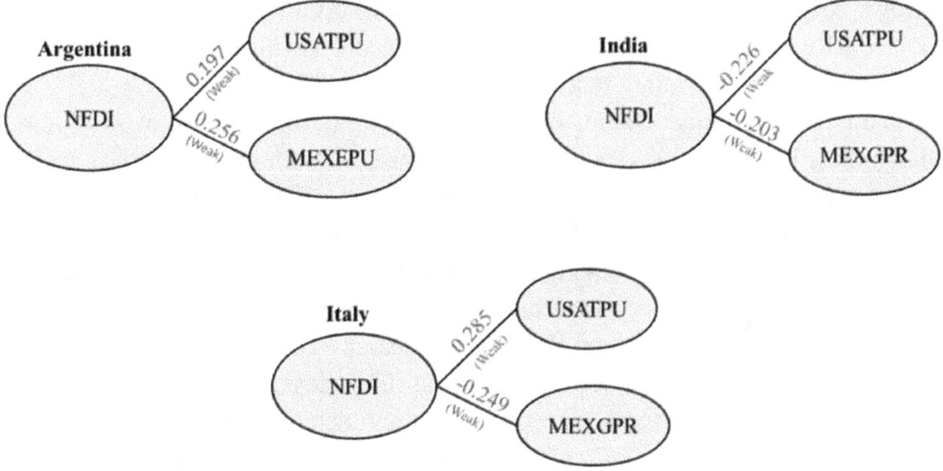

Source: Authors' elaboration.

Thus, Mexico's NFDI investments by country of origin exhibit direct and opposite associations with the USATPU, MEXEPU, and MEXGPR indexes.

CONCLUSIONS

The strength and direction of the association between Mexico's geopolitical risk, the United States' trade policy uncertainty, and Mexico's economic policy uncertainty affect Mexico's new FDI investment by country of origin. Consequently, risk and uncertainty can highlight the nearshoring effects of Mexico's new FDI investments.

Due to the data distribution for the USATPU, MEXEPU, MEXGPR indices, and Mexico's new FDI investment, the correlation between these variables was estimated using the Pearson and Spearman methods. This highlights the importance of performing the Shapiro-Wilk normality test.

The correlation coefficient results show that Mexico's new FDI investments from Belgium, Chile, Denmark, Ireland, India, and New Zealand tend to increase, whereas the USATPU uncertainty index decreases. Conversely, Mexico's new FDI investments from Germany, Argentina, and Italy tend to rise as the USATPU uncertainty index increases.

In contrast, Mexico's new FDI investments from Japan and South Korea tend to rise while the MEXEPU uncertainty index declined. However, Mexico's new FDI investments from Argentina, Australia, Canada, China, the United Kingdom, and Taiwan tend to increase as the MEXEPU uncertainty index rises.

Mexico's new foreign direct investment (FDI) from countries such as Brazil, the Philippines, India, Italy, Luxembourg, and Panama exhibits a trend of increasing inflows, concurrent with a decline in the country's MEXGPR risk index. Conversely, FDI from Russia and South Africa has been rising, albeit in tandem with an increase in the MEXGPR uncertainty index.

The policy recommendations of Bussy & Zheng (2023), Gamso et al. (2024), Mahjoubi & Henchiri (2024), and Oanh & Hoang (2021) for mitigating the adverse effects of geopolitical risk on foreign direct investment (FDI) suggest that adequate governance is crucial. This can be achieved through the implementation of risk management strategies within companies, investment in corporate social responsibility initiatives, and the use of cryptocurrencies for currency hedging.

Finally, the recommendation for future research is to model the association between the variables of Mexico's geopolitical risk index, the United States' trade policy uncertainty index, Mexico's economic policy uncertainty index, and Mexico's new FDI investments by country of origin through a regression analysis that allows for predictive modeling, such as the panel vector autoregression (PVAR) model.

REFERENCES

Adeosun, O. A., Anagreh, S., Tabash, M. I., & Vo, X. V. (2024). Return and volatility transmission among economic policy uncertainty, geopolitical risk and precious metals. *Studies in Economics and Finance, 41*(5), 1057–1084. DOI: 10.1108/SEF-10-2023-0586

Al-Mustofa, M. U., & Risyad, M. H. (2025). Geopolitical risk and foreign direct investment: the role of liberalization, institutions and financial markets. *Studies in Economics and Finance, ahead-of-print.* DOI: 10.1108/SEF-09-2024-0621

Alam, M. R., & Istiak, K. (2020). Impact of US policy uncertainty on Mexico: Evidence from linear and nonlinear tests. *The Quarterly Review of Economics and Finance, 77*, 355–366. DOI: 10.1016/j.qref.2019.12.002

Alqahtani, A., Hammoudeh, S., & Selmi, R. (2022). Relationship between different sources of geopolitical risks and stock markets in the GCC region: A dynamic correlation analysis. *Review of Behavioral Finance, 14*(2), 296–316. DOI: 10.1108/RBF-07-2019-0099

Atacan, C., & Açık, A. (2023). Impact of Geopolitical Risk on International Trade: Evidence from Container Throughputs. *Transactions on Maritime Science, 12*(2). Advance online publication. DOI: 10.7225/toms.v12.n02.019

Azzimonti, M. (2019). Does partisan conflict deter FDI inflows to the US? *Journal of International Economics, 120*, 162–178. DOI: 10.1016/j.jinteco.2019.06.001

Baci, N., Mulla, G., Millo, D., & Xhyheri, K. (2022). Foreign direct investment and its drivers: An empirical comparative study on developed and developing countries. *WSEAS Transactions on Environment and Development, 18*, 992–1004. DOI: 10.37394/232015.2022.18.95

Baena-Rojas, J. J. (2024). La Unión Europea dentro de la OMC: ¿paradigma de liderazgo geopolítico en las relaciones internacionales? *Novum Jus, 18*(1), 431–459. DOI: 10.14718/NovumJus.2024.18.1.15

Baker, S. R., Bloom, N., & Davis, S. J. (2016). Measuring Economic Policy Uncertainty. *The Quarterly Journal of Economics, 131*(4), 1593–1636. DOI: 10.1093/qje/qjw024

Banco de México. (2017). *Estimación del Efecto de la Incertidumbre Relativa a la Política Comercial sobre la Inversión Extranjera Directa en México* (Extracto del Informe Trimestral Julio – Septiembre No. 2; pp. 38-41). Banco de México. https://www.banxico.org.mx/publicaciones-y-prensa/informes-trimestrales/recuadros/%7BDF3E752F-A739-FA28-5750-91FE1AE24085%7D.pdf

Banco de México. (2025, mayo 30). *Tipos de cambio y resultados históricos de las subastas*. Sistema de Información Económica. https://www.banxico.org.mx/SieInternet/consultarDirectorioInternetAction.do?accion=consultarCuadroAnalitico&idCuadro=CA113&sector=6&locale=es

Bao, X., Deng, J., Sun, H., & Sun, J. (2022). Trade policy uncertainty and foreign direct investment: Evidence from China's WTO accession. *Journal of International Money and Finance, 125*, 102642. DOI: 10.1016/j.jimonfin.2022.102642

Bednarski, L., Roscoe, S., Blome, C., & Schleper, M. C. (2023). Geopolitical disruptions in global supply chains: A state-of-the-art literature review. *Production Planning and Control, 36*(4), 536–562. DOI: 10.1080/09537287.2023.2286283

Bilgili, F., Ünlü, F., Gençoğlu, P., & Kuşkaya, S. (2022). Modeling the exchange rate pass-through in Turkey with uncertainty and geopolitical risk: A Markov regime-switching approach. *Applied Economic Analysis, 30*(88), 52–70. DOI: 10.1108/AEA-08-2020-0105

Borbats, N. M., & Shkolina, T. V. (2021). Comparing the test power for the normal distribution of the direct multiple measurements. *Journal of Physics: Conference Series, 1889*, 052036. DOI: 10.1088/1742-6596/1889/5/052036

Bozsik, N., Ngo, D. M., & Vasa, L. (2023). The effects of foreign direct investment on the performance of small-medium enterprises: The case of Vietnam. *Journal of International Students, 16*(1), 57–70. DOI: 10.14254/2071-8330.2023/16-1/4

Bussy, A., & Zheng, H. (2023). Responses of FDI to geopolitical risks: The role of governance, information, and technology. *International Business Review, 32*(4), 102136. DOI: 10.1016/j.ibusrev.2023.102136

Caldara, D., & Iacoviello, M. (2022). Measuring Geopolitical Risk. *The American Economic Review, 112*(4), 1194–1225. DOI: 10.1257/aer.20191823

Canh, N. P., Binh, N. T., Thanh, S. D., & Schinckus, C. (2020). Determinants of foreign direct investment inflows: The role of economic policy uncertainty. *Inter Economics, 161*, 159–172. DOI: 10.1016/j.inteco.2019.11.012

Cantah, G. W., Brafu-Insaidoo, G. W., Wiafe, E. A., & Adams, A. (2018). FDI and Trade Policy Openness in Sub-Saharan Africa. *Eastern Economic Journal, 44*, 97–116. DOI: 10.1057/eej.2016.9

Carmel, E., & Abbott, P. (2007). Why 'nearshore' means that distance matters. *Communications of the ACM, 50*(10), 40–46. DOI: 10.1145/1290958.1290959

Carrasco, C. A. (2024). Perspectives on nearshoring: Recent developments and the challenges for Mexico. *Latin American Policy, 15*(2), 339–350. DOI: 10.1111/lamp.12340

Cervantes, M. M., & Rivera, R. G. (2021). Law and economics challenges of natural gas—The hard case of Mexico. *Journal of World Energy Law and Business, 14*(3), 205–214. DOI: 10.1093/jwelb/jwab017

Cetín, M. A., & Yaman, I. (2023). The Importance of Geopolitical Risk and Institutional Quality Indicators on Foreign Direct Investment to BRICS Countries. *Romanian Journal of Economic Forecasting, 26*(4), 107–127. https://www.scopus.com/pages/publications/85186539130

Chen, K., Nie, H., & Ge, Z. (2019). Policy uncertainty and FDI: Evidence from national elections. *The Journal of International Trade & Economic Development, 28*(4), 419–428. DOI: 10.1080/09638199.2018.1545860

Cheng, P., Wang, M., Li, K., Choi, B., & Chen, W. (2025). The impact mechanism of geopolitical risks on ESG performance: The moderating effects of investor attention and government subsidies. *PLoS One, 20*(1), e0311659. DOI: 10.1371/journal.pone.0311659

Choi, S., Furceri, D., & Yoon, C. (2021). Policy uncertainty and foreign direct investment. *Review of International Economics, 29*(2), 195–227. DOI: 10.1111/roie.12495

Choi, S.-Y., & Hadad, E. (2025). The dynamic relationship among economic and monetary policy, geopolitical risk, sentiment, and risk aversion: A TVP-VAR approach. *Finance Research Letters, 72*, 106532. DOI: 10.1016/j.frl.2024.106532

Choi, Y. (2018). A middle power's trade policy under U.S.-China FTA competition: South Korea's double hedging FTA diplomacy. *Contemporary Politics, 24*(2), 233–249. DOI: 10.1080/13569775.2017.1416735

Coën, A., & Desfleurs, A. (2024). The relative importance of economic policy uncertainty and geopolitical risk on U.S. REITs returns. *Journal of Property Investment & Finance, 42*(6), 576–590. DOI: 10.1108/JPIF-05-2024-0064

Colyer, D. (2004). Foreign Direct Investment in the Primary Sector of Mexico. In Kehal, H. S. (Ed.), *Foreign Investment in Developing Countries* (pp. 223–237). Palgrave Macmillan., DOI: 10.1057/9780230554412_12

Dambolena, I., Eriksen, S. E., & Kopcso, D. P. (2006). Assessing the Appropriateness of Transformations Using Simulation. *Problems, Resources, and Issues in Mathematics Undergraduate Studies*, *16*(2), 105–120. DOI: 10.1080/10511970608984139

Datosmacro. (2025a, may 29). *Precio del petróleo OPEP por barril.* Expansion/Datosmacro.com. https://datosmacro.expansion.com/materias-primas/opec?anio=2025

Datosmacro. (2025b, may 30). *Precio petróleo tipo West Texas Intermediate (WTI). Spot. $USA por barril.* Expansion/Datosmacro.com. https://datosmacro.expansion.com/materias-primas/petroleo-wti?anio=2025

Dávila, F. A., Sobarzo, F. H. E., & Valdés, I. M. (2018). México y el TLCAN: Escenarios de política comercial. Simulaciones con un modelo de equilibrio general aplicado. *El Trimestre Economico*, *85*(340), 703–744. DOI: 10.20430/ete.v85i340.699

Dutta, C. B., Haider, M. Z., & Das, D. K. (2017). Dynamics of Economic Growth, Investment and Trade Openness: Evidence from Bangladesh. *South Asian Journal of Macroeconomics and Public Finance*, *6*(1), 82–104. DOI: 10.1177/2277978717695150

Economic Policy Uncertainty. (2024a). *Geopolitical Risk Index.* Economic Policy Uncertainty. https://www.policyuncertainty.com/gpr.html

Economic Policy Uncertainty. (2024b). *Mexico Monthly Index.* Economic Policy Uncertainty. https://www.policyuncertainty.com/mexico_monthly.html

Economic Policy Uncertainty. (2024c). *US Monthly Trade Policy Uncertainty Index.* Economic Policy Uncertainty. https://www.policyuncertainty.com/trade_uncertainty.html

El-Hashash, E. F., & Shiekh, R. H. A. (2022). A Comparison of the Pearson, Spearman Rank and Kendall Tau Correlation Coefficients Using Quantitative Variables. *Asian Journal of Probability and Statistics*, *20*(3), 36–48. DOI: 10.9734/ajpas/2022/v20i3425

Erzurumlu, Y. O., Gozgor, G., Lau, C. K. M., Soliman, A. M., & Turkkan, M. (2025). The effects of geopolitical and political risks on corporate ESG practices. *Journal of Environmental Management*, *386*, 125747. DOI: 10.1016/j.jenvman.2025.125747

Etaga, H. O., Okoro, I., Aforka, K. F., & Ngonadi, L. O. (2021). Methods of Estimating Correlation Coefficients in the Presence of Influential Outlier(s). *African Journal of Mathematics and Statistics Studies, 4*(3), 157–185. DOI: 10.52589/AJMSS-LLNZXUOZ

Feng, C., Han, L., Vigne, S., & Xu, Y. (2023). Geopolitical risk and the dynamics of international capital flows. *Journal of International Financial Markets, Institutions and Money, 82*, 101693. DOI: 10.1016/j.intfin.2022.101693

Frutos, D., Teekasap, P., & Samii, M. (2011). CAFTA-DR Effects on FDI Inflows, Growth, and Distribution of the Workforce in Costa Rica: A System Dynamics Approach. *Guoji Maoyi Wenti, 25*(3), 372–393. DOI: 10.1080/08853908.2011.581612

Gamso, J., Inkpen, A., & Ramaswamy, K. (2024). Managing geopolitical risks: The global oil and gas industry plays a winning game. *The Journal of Business Strategy, 45*(3), 190–198. DOI: 10.1108/JBS-04-2023-0081

Gao, H., Chen, W., Li, J., & Zhou, T. (2024). Economic policy uncertainty and foreign direct investment: Evidence from China. *Structural Change and Economic Dynamics, 70*, 178–191. DOI: 10.1016/j.strueco.2024.01.014

Garrido, C. (2022). *México en la fábrica de América del Norte y el nearshoring* (Sede Subregional de la CEPAL en México (Estudios e Investigaciones); pp. 1-95). Comisión Económica para América Latina y el Caribe (CEPAL). https://hdl.handle.net/11362/48056

Gehringer, A. (2025). The Challenging Terrain of Critical Infrastructures–A Geopolitical Perspective. *Journal of Homeland Security and Emergency Management. ahead-of-print.* DOI: 10.1515/jhsem-2024-0014

Gitterman, D. P. (2003). European Integration and Labour Market Cooperation: A Comparative Regional Perspective. *Journal of European Social Policy, 13*(2), 99–120. DOI: 10.1177/0958928703013002001

Guedes, J., & Pereira, L. (2024). Unlocking the full potential of nearshoring - a conceptual delivery model for proximity offshoring services. *International Journal of Productivity and Quality Management, 41*(4), 510–528. DOI: 10.1504/IJPQM.2024.137884

Hachicha, F. (2024). Sentiment investor, exchange rates, geopolitical risk and developing stock market: Evidence of co-movements in the time-frequency domain during RussiaUkraine war. *Review of Behavioral Finance, 16*(3), 486–509. DOI: 10.1108/RBF-04-2023-0119

Hernández, M. J. E., & Estay, R. J. (2018). Determinantes de la Inversión Extranjera Directa en México, 2005-2012. *Ensayos de Economía, 28*(53), 65–91. DOI: 10.15446/ede.v28n53.75074

Hou, Y., Xue, W., & Zhang, X. (2024). The Impact of Geopolitical Risk on Trade Costs. *Global Economic Review, 53*(1), 1–24. DOI: 10.1080/1226508X.2024.2305464

Hsieh, H.-C., Boarelli, S., & Vu, T. H. C. (2019). The effects of economic policy uncertainty on outward foreign direct investment. *International Review of Economics & Finance, 64*, 377–392. DOI: 10.1016/j.iref.2019.08.004

Huang, S., Yeo, A. A., & Li, S. D. (2007). Modification of Kolmogorov-Smirnov test for DNA content data analysis through distribution alignment. *Assay and Drug Development Technologies, 5*(5), 663–672. DOI: 10.1089/adt.2007.071

Iacoviello, M., Caldara, D., Penn, M., & Conlisk, S. (2024). Do Geopolitical Risks Raise or Lower Inflation? Available at *SSRN*. https://ssrn.com/abstract=4852461 or http://dx.doi.org/*SSRN*. DOI: 10.2139/ssrn.4852461

IMCO. (2024). *Nearshoring: El impacto sobre la Inversión Extranjera Directa* (pp. 1-60). Instituto Mexicano para la Competitividad, A.C. https://imco.org.mx/nearshoring-el-impacto-sobre-la-inversion-extranjera-directa/

IMF. (2025). *Inflation, average consumer prices*. World Economic Outlook Database: April 2025, International Monetary Fund. https://www.imf.org/en/Publications/WEO/weo-database/2025/april/weo-report?c=273,186,&s=PCPI,&sy=1998&ey=2024&ssm=0&scsm=1&scc=0&ssd=1&ssc=0&sic=0&sort=country&ds=.&br=1

Jadhav, P., Katti, V., & Choudhury, R. N. (2016). Trends, determinants and challenges of foreign direct investment in emerging markets. In *Trade, Investment and Economic Development in Asia* (1st ed., pp. 234-246). Routledge.

Janse, R. J., Hoekstra, T., Jager, K. J., Zoccali, C., Tripepi, G., Dekker, F. W., & Diepen, M. V. (2021). Conducting correlation analysis: Important limitations and pitfalls. *Clinical Kidney Journal, 14*(11), 2332–2337. DOI: 10.1093/ckj/sfab085

Jha, S., Awate, S., & Mudambi, R. (2024). A multilateral network perspective on inward FDI. *Journal of International Business Studies, 55*, 303–325. DOI: 10.1057/s41267-023-00650-x

Kapopoulos, T., Sakkas, A., & Drakos, K. (2024). Geopolitical Risk and Foreign Direct Investment Inflows: The Moderating Role of Water and Energy Risks. *International Journal of Finance & Economics*, •••, 1–24. DOI: 10.1002/ijfe.3106

Kaufmann, D., & Kraay, A. (2024, november). *The Worldwide Governance Indicators. Methodology and 2024 Update*. Policy Research Working Paper (WPS10952). World Bank Group. https://documents.worldbank.org/curated/en/099005210162424110

Kumar, D. (2016). A Study of Economic Growth and Foreign Direct Investment: An Econometric Approach in SAARC Region. *International Journal of Economics and Management Studies, 3*(12), 18–22. DOI: 10.14445/23939125/IJEMS-V3I6P117

Lu, B., & Liu, W. (2024). Does Comprehensive Geopolitical Risk Deter FDI Outflows: Evidence from China. *Defence and Peace Economics, 35*(3), 383–399. DOI: 10.1080/10242694.2022.2160140

Lütkepohl, H., & Xu, F. (2012). The role of the log transformation in forecasting economic variables. *Empirical Economics, 42*, 619–638. DOI: 10.1007/s00181-010-0440-1

Maharmah, M. H. (2023). Does The Foreign Direct Investment Affect Economic Growth in Jordan in Light of Commercial Openness. *International Journal of Professional Business Review, 8*(5), e02088. DOI: 10.26668/businessreview/2023.v8i5.2088

Mahjoubi, M., & Henchiri, J. E. (2024). The effect of policy uncertainty on the volatility of bitcoin. *Journal of Financial Economic Policy, 16*(4), 429–441. DOI: 10.1108/JFEP-08-2023-0222

Marchewka, A. (2023). Application of multi-criteria Vector Measure Construction Method (VMCM) to assess importance of foreign direct investment (FDI) to host country's regional economy. *Procedia Computer Science, 225*, 2497–2506. DOI: 10.1016/j.procs.2023.10.241

Mignon, V., & Saadaoui, J. (2024). How do political tensions and geopolitical risks impact oil prices? *Energy Economics, 129*, 107219. DOI: 10.1016/j.eneco.2023.107219

Mo, H. (2024). A Critical Analysis of Economic, Political, and Financial Determinants Influencing Location Choices of Foreign Direct Investments. *Financial Economics Research, 1*(1), 83–89. DOI: 10.70267/pnbt8t44

Molinar, C. M. A., & Carrillo, I. M. (2024). Crime and Insecurity as Factors of Uncertainty and Erosion of the Tourist Image of Mexico. In *Tourism in a VUCA World: Managing the Future of Tourism* (pp. 187-201). Emerald Publishing Limited. DOI: 10.1108/978-1-83753-674-020241013

Muñoz, H. E., & Gálvez-Gamboa, F. (2022). Efecto de la incertidumbre de la política económica internacional sobre los mercados financieros latinoamericanos. *Estudios Gerenciales, 38*(165), 519–528. DOI: 10.18046/j.estger.2022.165.5383

Nagy, S. G., & Navarro, M. (2025). North American Economic Integration (NAFTA7USMCA). In *The Economics of Regional Integration* (1st ed., pp. 169-194). Routledge.

Naifar, N., & Aljarba, S. (2023). Does Geopolitical Risk Matter for Sovereign Credit Risk? Fresh Evidence from Nonlinear Analysis. *Journal of Risk and Financial Management*, *16*(3), 148. DOI: 10.3390/jrfm16030148

Nedumpara, J. J. (2024). Editorial: Friendshoring, Nearshoring, Greenshoring and Resshoring: Changing Faces of Global Supply Chains and its Impact on International Economic Law - Introduction to the Special Issue. *Global Trade and Customs Journal*, *19*(3), 125–128. DOI: 10.54648/GTCJ2024035

Nguyen, C. Q., & Le, T.-H. (2021). The Nexus Between Trade Openness and Foreign Direct Investment Amid Structural Economic Vulnerability in Developing Countries. In *Globalization, Deglobalization, and New Paradigms in Business* (pp. 61-86). Palgrave Macmillan. DOI: 10.1007/978-3-030-81584-4_4

Oanh, H. K., & Hoang, K. (2021). The bright side of geopolitical risk: Evidence from Chinese firms. *Journal of Financial Economic Policy*, *13*(3), 353–370. DOI: 10.1108/JFEP-04-2020-0076

Obuobi, N. K., Gatsi, J. G., Appiah, M. O., Kawor, S., Amoah, E. K., & Abeka, M. J. (2021). Trade liberalization policies and foreign direct investment inflows in Africa: Evidence from new measures of trade liberalization. *The Journal of International Trade & Economic Development*, *31*(3), 394–409. DOI: 10.1080/09638199.2021.1983009

Okara, A. (2023). Does foreign direct investment promote political stability? Evidence from developing economies. *Economic Modelling*, *123*, 106249. DOI: 10.1016/j.econmod.2023.106249

Olanipekun, I. O., & Olasehinde-Williams, G. (2022). Unveiling the causal interactions among the US monetary policy uncertainty, exchange market pressure, and FDI-flows in large emerging market economies. *Journal of Public Affairs*, *22*(4), e2684. DOI: 10.1002/pa.2684

Özçeli, K. O. (2023). Effects of Geopolitical Risks on Countries' Trade Flows: A Nonlinear ARDL Analysis. [Ege Academic Review]. *Ege Academic Review*, *23*(3), 519–530. DOI: 10.21121/eab.1065493

Paolino, P. (2009). La posición del PRI en la política mexicana. *Política y Gobierno*, *16*(2), 321–348. https://www.scielo.org.mx/scielo.php?script=sci_arttext&pid=S1665-20372009000200003&lng=es&tlng=es

Phillips, K. R., & Slijk, C. (2015). Border Economic Recovery Lags Rest of State. In *Ten-Gallon Economy* (1st ed., pp. 199-212). Palgrave Macmillan, New York. DOI: 10.1057/9781137530172_13

Pietrobelli, C., & Seri, C. (2023). Reshoring, nearshoring and development. Readiness and implications for Latin America and the Caribbean. *Transnational Corporations, 30*(2), 37–70. DOI: 10.18356/2076099x-30-2-2

Piña-Barcenas, J., Cedillo-Campos, M. G., Moreno-Quintero, E., & Covarrubias, D. (2024). Graph Theory to Achieve the Digital Transformation in Managing Freight Transportation Corridors. *Mobile Networks and Applications, 29*, 201–210. DOI: 10.1007/s11036-023-02283-8

Quintana, L., & Salgado, U. (2016). Internal migration in Mexico from 1990-2010: A new economic geography approach. *Problemas del Desarrollo, 47*(184), 137–162. DOI: 10.1016/j.rpd.2016.01.007

Reyad, H. M., Ayesha, M., Iqbal, M. M., & Zariyawati, M. A. (2024). The role of ESG in enhancing firm resilience to geopolitical risks: An eastern European perspective. *Business Strategy & Development, 7*(4), e70027. DOI: 10.1002/bsd2.70027

Reynolds, C. (2019). A United States View. In *Industrial Strategy and Planning in Mexico and The United States* (1st ed., pp. 231–243). Routledge., DOI: 10.4324/9780429041129

Rodríguez, S. A. (2019). Mexico's National Security Paradoxes and Threats in a Geopolitical Context. *Politics & Policy, 47*(1), 207–232. DOI: 10.1111/polp.12287

Romero, A. J. R. (2024). El nearshoring en México y su relación con China, Corea del Sur y Japón. *PORTES, Revista Mexicana de Estudios sobre la Cuenca del Pacífico, 2*, 31-54. DOI: 10.53897/RevPortes.2024.02.02

Sánchez, T. M. (2024). Old and New Polarization: Democracy, Elections and Conflict in Mexico. *Foro Internacional, 64*(2), 183–187. DOI: 10.24201/fi.v64i2.3099

Sanderson, M. R. (2014). Free trade, food-processing, and migration: An analysis of Mexican immigration in the U.S. Great Plains Region. *The Social Science Journal, 51*(3), 474–482. DOI: 10.1016/j.soscij.2013.11.001

Santillán, L. I., Ceja, P. J. J., & Pineda, D. D. (2024). Practical Strategies for The Economic Development of Mexico: Nearshoring Trend. *Mercados y Negocios, 52*(25), 105–126. DOI: 10.32870/myn.vi52.7727

Secretaría de Economía. (2024a). *Comisión Nacional de Inversiones Extranjeras: Cuarto Trimestre 2024* (No. 2024 enero-diciembre; p. 22). Gobierno de México. https://www.gob.mx/se/acciones-y-programas/competitividad-y-normatividad-inversion-extranjera-directa?state=published

Secretaría de Economía. (2024b). *Inversión Extranjera Directa. Gobierno de México.* https://www.gob.mx/se/acciones-y-programas/competitividad-y-normatividad-inversion-extranjera-directa?state=published

Seker, O. (2023). The contagious effect of economic policy uncertainty in the post-crisis period. *Economía, 24*(2), 205–218. DOI: 10.1108/ECON-06-2022-0046

Shahbaz, M., Sharif, A., Soliman, A. M., Jiao, Z., & Hammoudeh, S. (2024). Oil prices and geopolitical risk: Fresh insights based on Granger-causality in quantiles analysis. *International Journal of Finance & Economics, 29*(3), 2865–2881. DOI: 10.1002/ijfe.2806

Shen, M., & Yang, M. (2024). Are Geopolitical Risks Fuelling Trade Protectionism? *Defence and Peace Economics, 35*(8), 1120–1140. DOI: 10.1080/10242694.2024.2364320

Shugan, S. M. (2007). Editorial-Causality, Unintended Consequences and Deducing Shared Causes. *Marketing Science, 26*(6), 731–741. DOI: 10.1287/mksc.1070.0338

Simelyte, A., & Antanaviciene, J. (2014). Formation of Foreign Direct Investment Policy: Case of Estonia. *The Engineering Economist, 25*(2), 177–185. DOI: 10.5755/j01.ee.25.2.4263

Singh, V., Correa da Cunha, H., & Mangal, S. (2024). Do Geopolitical Risks Impact Trade Patterns in Latin America? *Defence and Peace Economics, 35*(8), 1102–1119. DOI: 10.1080/10242694.2023.2299072

Sinha, A., & Ghosh, T. (2021). Impact of Economic Policy Uncertainty on FDI Inflows: Evidence from India. In *Recent Developments in Asian Economics International Symposia in Economic Theory and Econometrics* (Vol. 28, pp. 157–167). Emerald Publishing Limited., DOI: 10.1108/S1571-038620210000028009

Sivaprasad, S., Adami, R., Malki, I., Ibragimova, D., & Yodgorova, F. (2025). Spillover effects of geopolitical risk on the banking sectors of post-Soviet countries. *Review of Behavioral Finance, 17*(3), 544–562. DOI: 10.1108/RBF-01-2025-0026

Sohag, K., Islam, M. M., Žiković, I. T., & Mansour, H. (2023). Food inflation and geopolitical risks: Analyzing European regions amid the Russia-Ukraine war. *British Food Journal, 125*(7), 2368–2391. DOI: 10.1108/BFJ-09-2022-0793

Sosa, C. M. M., Ortiz, E., & Cabello-Rosales, A. (2023). Economic Policy Uncertainty Impact on Mexican Economic Activity and Stock and Currency Markets: A DCC Approach. *Lecturas de Economía, 98,* 39–65. DOI: 10.17533/udea.le.n98a349886

Soussane, J. A., Fakhouri, M. Y., & Mansouri, Z. (2023). The effect of geopolitical risks on TNC location decision from antagonizing countries in the Russian Federation in light of the Ukrainian crisis. *Transnational Corporations Review, 15*(4), 90–99. DOI: 10.1016/j.tncr.2023.01.002

SPSS Statistics (Versión 29.0.0.0). (2022). [Software]. IBM.

Su, C.-W., Khan, K., Umar, M., & Zhang, W. (2021). Does renewable energy redefine geopolitical risks? *Energy Policy, 158,* 112566. DOI: 10.1016/j.enpol.2021.112566

Su, C.-W., Umar, M., & Chang, H.-L. (2022). Nonlinear Dependence between Economic Policy Uncertainty and FDI Inflows in China. *Economic Computation and Economic Cybernetics Studies and Research, 56*(3), 153–168. DOI: 10.24818/18423264/56.3.22.10

Sun, T.-T., & Su, C. W. (2024). How is geopolitical risk associated with food prices? *International Journal of Emerging Markets, ahead-of-print*(ahead-of-print). DOI: 10.1108/IJOEM-01-2023-0004

Sweidan, O. D. (2021). The geopolitical risk effect on the US renewable energy deployment. *Journal of Cleaner Production, 293,* 126189. DOI: 10.1016/j.jclepro.2021.126189

Sweidan, O. D. (2023). The effect of the US macroeconomic indicators on the international geopolitical risk. *Defence and Peace Economics, 34*(4), 495–511. DOI: 10.1080/10242694.2022.2034103

Tabash, M. I., Farooq, U., & Issa, S. S. (2024). BRIC in flux: Understanding the influence of energy policy uncertainty on foreign direct investment flows. *OPEC Energy Review, 48*(4), 246–260. DOI: 10.1111/opec.12311

Thakur, R., Malik, S. C., & Nandal, N. (2023). Normality Testing under Neutrosophic Statistics. *Neutrosophic Sets and Systems, 58,* 149–158. DOI: 10.5281/zenodo.10070527

Truong, L. D., Friday, H. S., & Pham, T. D. (2024). The Effects of Geopolitical Risk on Foreign Direct Investment in a Transition Economy: Evidence from Vietnam. *Journal of Risk and Financial Management, 17*(3), 101. DOI: 10.3390/jrfm17030101

U.S. Census Bureau. (2024). *U.S. Trade in Goods by Country* [Dataset]. https://www.census.gov/foreign-trade/balance/index.html#C

Vargas, M. J. (2024). Paquete económico* 2024 del gobierno de López Obrador en el marco de la incertidumbre económica mundial. *Economía Informa, 446*, 4-25. http://www.libros.unam.mx/economia-informa-446-mayo-junio-2024-6560000002184-libro.html

Villarreal, M. A. (2020). U.S.-Mexico Economic Relations: Trends, Issues, and Implications. *Congressional Research Service,* CRS Report RL32934, 1-28. https://sgp.fas.org/crs/row/RL32934.pdf

Wang, C., Yao, X., & Kim, C. Y. (2025). Is a friend in need a friend indeed? Geopolitical risk, international trade of China, and Belt & Road Initiative. *Applied Economics Letters*, *32*(7), 1021–1028. DOI: 10.1080/13504851.2023.2299275

Wang, M., Amiri-Aref, M., Klibi, W., & Babai, M. Z. (2024). Global multi-sourcing network design with inventory planning under uncertainty. *International Journal of Production Research*, *62*(21), 7660–7686. DOI: 10.1080/00207543.2024.2323068

Wang, Y. (2012). The interaction between foreign direct Investment and Trade in China's agro-food sector. *2012 International Conference on Information Management, Innovation Management and Industrial Engineering*, Sanya, 179-183. DOI: 10.1109/ICIII.2012.6339627

Winter, J. C. F., Gosling, S. D., & Potter, J. (2016). Comparing the Pearson and Spearman correlation coefficients across distributions and sample sizes: A tutorial using simulations and empirical data. *Psychological Methods*, *21*(3), 273–290. DOI: 10.1037/met0000079

Woo-Mora, L. G. (2025). Populism's original sin: Short-term populist penalties and uncertainty traps. *European Economic Review*, *172*, 104917. DOI: 10.1016/j.euroecorev.2024.104917

World Bank Group. (2025, junio 9). *Worldwide Governance Indicators*. Interactive Data Access. https://www.worldbank.org/content/publication/worldwide-governance-indicators/en/interactive-data-access.html

Xiao, C., Ye, J., Esteves, R. M., & Rong, C. (2016). Using Spearman's correlation coefficients for exploratory data analysis on big dataset. *Concurrency and Computation*, *28*(14), 3866–3878. DOI: 10.1002/cpe.3745

Yay, M. (2022). Relationship between right atrial pressure and the Model For End-Stage Liver Disease (MELD) score in patients with advanced heart failure: Correlation analysis and ROC curve method. *Turkish Journal of Thoracic and Cardiovascular Surgery*, *30*(1), 8–10. DOI: 10.5606/tgkdc.dergisi.2022.40073

Yilanci, V., Hopoğlu, S., & Eryüzlü, H. (2023). The impact of the economic policy uncertainty and geopolitical risks on tourism demand of Mexico. *Theoretical & Applied Economics, 30*(3), 147-164. https://www.ectap.ro/the-impact-of-the-economic-policy-uncertaintyand-geopolitical-risks-on-tourism-demand-of-mexico-veli-yilanci_serta-hopolu_hakan-eryuzlu/a1682/

Yin, S., Xing, L., Zhang, P., & Duan, Y. (2023). Stability analysis of production networks in the ASIA-pacific region based on nested structure theory. *Xitong Gongcheng Lilun Yu Shijian*, *43*(11), 3214–3229. DOI: 10.12011/SETP2022-2758

Yu, M., & Wang, N. (2023). The Influence of Geopolitical Risk on International Direct Investment and Its Countermeasures. *Sustainability*, *15*(3), 2522. DOI: 10.3390/su15032522

Zhang, Z., He, M., Zhang, Y., & Wang, Y. (2022). Geopolitical risk trends and crude oil price predictability. *Energy*, *258*, 124824. DOI: 10.1016/j.energy.2022.124824

Zhao, Z., Gozgor, G., Lau, M. C. K., Mahalik, M. K., Patel, G., & Khalfaoui, R. (2023). The impact of geopolitical risks on renewable energy demand in OECD countries. *Energy Economics*, *122*, 106700. DOI: 10.1016/j.eneco.2023.106700

Zhou, H., & Liang, C. (2025). Geopolitical risk and gold price bubbles. *Review of Accounting and Finance*, *24*(3), 353–374. DOI: 10.1108/RAF-09-2024-0369

Chapter 7
How Foreign Investments by Multinational Enterprises Become National Security Threats:
An Organizational Field Perspective

Keyan Lai
https://orcid.org/0000-0001-7388-1986
Business School, University of Edinburgh Business School, UK

ABSTRACT

Recent years have witnessed a surge in national security concerns associated with foreign direct investments (FDI). However, International Business research has hitherto paid limited attention to this phenomenon. While scholars in International Relations and International Law have examined the institutional and policy-level dimensions of FDI securitization, existing research remains predominantly macro-level and fails to explain how and why specific multinational enterprises' (MNEs) investments become national security threats. To address this gap, I draw on organizational field theory and develop the Dual-Field Framework (DFF) to introduce a field-level approach to demonstrate that the securitization of FDI is a field-driven process. This study highlights the central role of domestic politics and geopolitics in shaping how FDI translate into a national security threat. This chapter further outlines key directions for future research on FDI-related national security concerns, and offers managerial implications for MNEs from a field perspective.

DOI: 10.4018/979-8-3373-1265-1.ch007

1. INTRODUCTION

In recent years, the politicized nature of international business has drawn significant attention from scholars (e.g. Beugelsdijk & Luo, 2024; Lai & Fortwengel, 2025; Luo & Van Assche, 2023; Witt, 2019; Witt, Li, Valikangas, & Lewin, 2021). Interconnected events such as Donald Trump's presidency in the United States (US) in 2016 and 2025, the beginning of the China–US trade war in 2018, and the Western allies' collective backlash against the Chinese telecommunications giant Huawei since 2019 on the grounds of national security have brought to the fore the complex relationship between geopolitics and international business. Against this backdrop, this chapter examines a critical yet underexplored phenomenon at the intersection of geopolitics and international business: national security concerns related foreign direct investments (FDI).

News media in recent years have extensively covered stories about some firms being labeled as national security threats. Among these, Huawei has been one of the most high-profile cases, with the US government classifying it as a national security threat and subsequently banning it from the US market. Similar bans followed in other countries, particularly US allies. For example, in the United Kingdom (UK), the British government decided to remove Huawei from its 5G network by 2027, citing national security concerns. Beyond Huawei, other companies flagged as "national security threats" include the Chinese companies ByteDance (owner of TikTok), Beijing Kunlun (former owner of the dating app Grindr), Midea Group (a household appliances company), and Addsino (a subsidiary of the state-owned China Aerospace and Industry Group) and the Russian companies Gazprom, Rosneft, and Kaspersky. Since 2017, Kaspersky software products have been banned across all government departments in the US and the UK on the grounds that they could be under the influence of the Kremlin and pose a threat to national security (Solon, 2017), and in 2019 Beijing Kunlun was pressured by the US government national security panel CFIUS to sell Grindr, a West Hollywood, California-based dating app Kunlun owned since2016 (O'Donnell, et al., 2019) .

While the recent surge in media coverage and social media discussions may have amplified public awareness of national security concerns associated with multinational enterprises (MNEs) and their foreign investments, the practice of labeling FDI as a national security threat and subsequently blocking or expropriating it has a much longer history. During World War I, concerns over German FDI—particularly its dominance in the US chemical industry—prompted the US Congress to pass sector-specific restrictions on foreign investments, including the Trading with the Enemy Act (TWEA) in 1917, which granted the president broad powers to block or expropriate foreign assets (Graham & Marchick, 2006). In the 1970s, the sharp rise in oil prices and the accumulation of petrodollars by members of the Organization of Petroleum Exporting Countries (OPEC) led to fears that Arab investors might use their wealth to acquire key US assets. This anxiety resulted in the establishment of Committee of Foreign Investment in the United States (CFIUS) in 1975 to monitor the security implications of foreign investments in the US (Hasnat, 2015). In the late 1980s and early 1990s, Japanese electronics firms became the new focal point of security concerns, as "the increasing competitiveness of Japanese companies and their acquisition of US firms were seen as threats to national security" (Hasnat, 2015, p.187).

In these FDI- related national security concerns, the targeted industries and the national origins of the targeted firms may vary over time, but two constants remain: national security is inherently subjective (Williams, 2003; Wæver, 1995), and the assessment of whether an FDI poses a security risk is more shaped by political and strategic considerations than by objective criteria (Lai, 2021). Scholars from the fields of international relations and international laws (e.g. Bauerle Danzman & Meunier, 2023, Esplugues, 2018; Feng, 2009; 2023 Lenihan, 2018) have provided valuable insights into the interplay between FDI and national security, primarily focusing on macro-level institutions and policies. Similarly, international business research has largely concentrated on macro-level dynamics. For instance, Godsell, Lel, and Miller (2023) examined whether the US's Foreign Investment and National Security Act of 2007 (FINSA) has contributed to de-globalization trends, while Li, Shapiro, Ufimtseva, and Zhang (2024) explored how technology policies, such as China's Made in China 2025 (MIC2025) and the US's Foreign Investment Risk Review Modernization Act (FIRRMA) of 2018, are used to develop and maintain geopolitical advantages. Despite these macro-level contributions, we still lack an understanding of how national security concerns impact MNEs' foreign investment activities. Several key questions remain unanswered: How do FDI translate into national security risks? Why do certain MNEs pose a greater national security threat to host countries through their investments than others? Why are specific FDI projects—such as those made by Chinese firms—more likely to be perceived as security risks?

In this study, I move beyond the macro-level analyses and develop the Dual-Field Framework (DFF) to introduce a field-level approach to understanding FDI-related national security concerns. This framework examines the mechanisms through which national security concerns materialize. As I will further discuss in the Research Directions section, the DFF offers a valuable lens for analyzing FDI-related national security concerns by bridging macro, meso, and micro levels of analysis. This multi-level perspective allows researchers to examine how national security threats associated with FDI are constructed, contested, and responded to across different levels of actors and institutions.

Drawing on insights from organizational field theory, I conceptualize the inflow of FDI as MNEs entering a field, in which diverse actors exist and interact to shape the general perception of the nature of FDI and their impact on national security. To analyze the interaction and dynamics in the field, the Dual-Field Framework integrate two fields in the analysis: the exchange field and the issue field (Zietsma et al., 2017). MNE investments in the exchange field—wherein they interact with their competitors, customers, regulators, and others in physical proximity—are perceived to pose a national security threat to the host countries owing to the perception that their entry could disrupt the established field composition (i.e., field *positions, understandings,* and *rules*). Such disruptions create opportunities for a particular type of security risk, such as dominance of supply, technology transfer, or espionage. Second, in the level of issue field, which "is formed around the issues that become important to the interests and objectives of a specific collective of organizations" (Hoffman, 1999, p.352), home and host countries emerge as critical actors in the field, engaging in the process of conflict, negotiation, and contestation, thereby transforming FDI into an issue of national security. In this sphere, politics and international relations between the home and host countries shape the perceptions about MNEs and the nature and impact of their investments; this, in turn, shapes the dynamics in the exchange field. Figure 1 illustrates my arguments and guides the discussion in the following sections. By illuminating the processes through which FDI are perceived as national security risks, this study highlights the central role of politics in international business, including the domestic politics of both home and host countries as well as their broader international relations.

Figure 1. The Dual-Field Framework

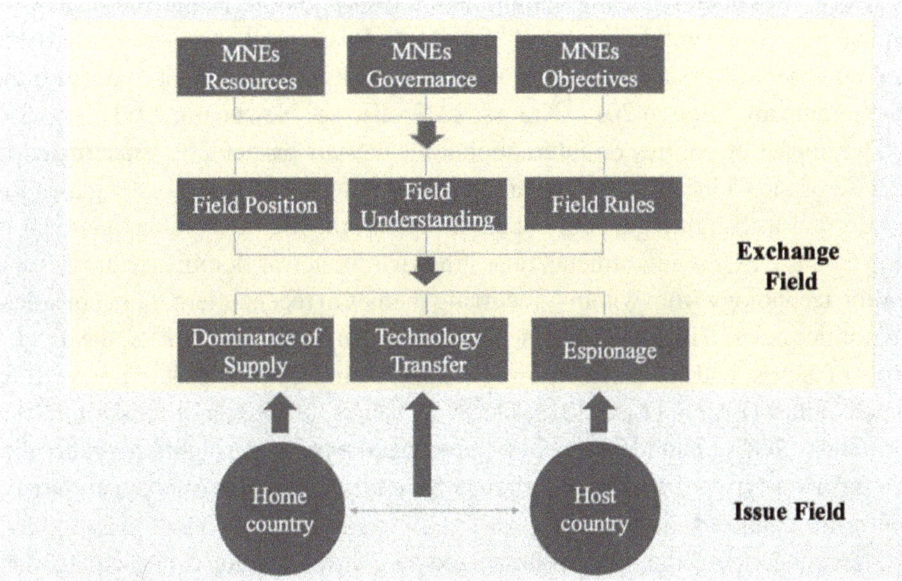

This study makes a novel contribution toward understanding of FDI-related national security concerns and, more generally, the impact of geopolitics on international business. By introducing the Dual-Field Framework, this research offers a multi-level perspective that connects political, institutional, and organizational dynamics, providing a foundation for future research on the intersection of national security, FDI, and international business and management.

In this chapter, I use state-owned enterprises (SOEs) as a representative example for theorization. This is based on two reasons: First, there is a well-established and vast body of literature on the unique nature of SOEs (Lawson, 1994; Levy, 1987; Lindsay, 1976), which reveals that SOEs, particularly those from emerging markets, are treated with suspicion, censure, and disapproval by host governments and societies during internationalization (Cuervo-Cazurra, 2018; Cui & Jiang, 2012; Meyer et al., 2014). Second, given state ownership and SOEs' inherent political connections with the states, they can be viewed as an extreme case to illustrate the dynamics of politics and international business, specifically for those from emerging markets. Research has demonstrated the prominence of SOEs in emerging markets and their complex relationship with their home countries; such close ties tend to generate suspicion that SOEs are neither market-oriented nor profit-driven but politically motivated, serving certain strategic national goals on behalf of their governments. Globerman and Shapiro (2009), for instance, observe that acquisitions by Chinese companies have emerged as a concern for policymakers in the US and other developed countries because of the belief that Chinese multinational corporations acquire companies to "pursue non-commercial objectives." Similarly, Russian oil company Rosneft has been considered Russia's "foreign policy tool" in its failed attempt to acquire the US oil company Citgo in 2017 (Krauss, 2017; also see Newnham, 2011).

The impact of politics on international business is particularly exacerbated in the case of the Chinese SOEs that are involved in technology sectors. Against the backdrop of a changing geopolitical environment, the high-technology element in these Chinese SOEs' investments raises the twin issues of dominance and who is stealing technology from whom—recurring themes in recent international business and politics news. Given the prominence of SOEs in emerging markets, the diverse forms of SOEs, and the difficulties in clearly defining a company's ties with its home country (Bruton et al., 2015; Cuervo-Cazurra, 2018), the discussion in this study treats SOEs as an ideal type; I believe that the present insights are generalizable for other types of MNEs, which may have different levels of connection with their home countries.

The remainder of the paper is organized as follows. Section 2 presents the key concepts from organizational field theory to show how the entry of SOEs into a field may be perceived as a challenge to the status quo and a threat to the established hierarchy of status, the shared meaning system, and commonly followed rules. In Section 3, I discuss the key features of SOEs and the three types of national security risks associated with FDI, i.e., dominance of supply, technology transfer, and espionage, arguing that the SOEs' unique characteristics exacerbate the perceived national security risks. In Section 4, I discuss how domestic politics in the home and host countries and their international relations affect the perceptions of the nature and impact of SOE investments on national security. In Section 5 I reflect on the value of the present framework and indicate future research directions for the study of national security, FDI, and international business and management. I conclude this chapter with a discussion on the managerial implications.

2. THE ORGANIZATIONAL FIELD PERSPECTIVE

Organizational field theory provides valuable insights on how a newcomer in a field may challenge the status quo and change field dynamics. These insights can help us analyze how SOEs' investments are perceived as national security risks. In this paper, I suggest that it is necessary to examine the exchange field and the issue field as two levels of the same field, rather than two unique field types, to comprehend the complexity of the national security issue in the context of SOEs' FDI. Considering SOE investments into the host country as a process of simultaneous entry into exchange field and issue field enables the assessment of the potentially conflicting relationship between SOEs and local field constituents, as well as that between the host and home countries.

An organizational field is also referred to as an institutional field (Hardy & Maguire, 2010). DiMaggio and Powell's (1983, p. 148) widely adopted definition of fields focuses on the exchange field, stating that fields comprise "a recognized area of institutional life: key suppliers, resource and product consumers, regulatory agencies and other organizations that produce similar services or products." Similarly, Scott (2001) defines a field as "a community of organizations". These definitions mainly represent fields in the physical proximity of actors (Wooten & Hoffman, 2008), that is "exchange fields," where actors are engaged in interaction and exchange with their partners (Zietsma et al., 2017, p. 396).

However, a field need not always comprise actors in physical proximity. The concept of an issue field, as introduced by Hoffman (1999, p. 352), argues that "a field is formed around the issues that become important to the interests and objectives of a specific collective of organizations." While existing conceptualizations of an exchange field center around networks, typically of companies that produce similar products and in the same market, the concept of an issue field centers around issues because "issues define what the field is." Two key features distinguish an issue field from an exchange field. First, the physical proximity of actors or field constituents becomes irrelevant in an issue field. According to Hoffman (1999, p. 352), whether an organization is part of the field is defined by social interaction patterns; as such, even if two actors are not physically proximate, they can still become constituents of the same field. Second, the conflictual element in the interactions between actors is intensified. Although there is no lack of conflict in an exchange field, issue fields are more contested because an issue can bring together various actors with diverse identities and interests. While exchange fields revolve around conflicts between competitors for resources, status, and market shares, issue fields aim to compete over meanings and practices (Zietsma et al., 2017). In this context, fields are characterized with more contestation and struggles (Wooten & Hoffman, 2008).

An organizational field comprises three key components: *positions, understandings,* and *rules* (Hardy & Maguire, 2010). First, a field is a structured space of *positions* (Hardy & Maguire, 2010). Different actors occupy these *positions*, involve themselves with other actors, and establish mutual relationships (Bourdieu & Wacquant, 1992; Wooten & Hoffman, 2008). As all actors are not created equal, a hierarchy of status and influence comes into being (Zietsma et al., 2017). Second, a field comprises common *understandings* and meaning systems (Hardy & Maguire, 2010). Actors within a field apply the same set of cultural expectations, cognitions, and beliefs as frames to make sense of the social reality (Scott, 2001). Such shared meaning systems and common *understandings* "shape what is considered appropriate behavior" and "give meaning to actions" (Hardy & Maguire, 2010, p. 1366). Greenwood & Suddaby (2006, p. 28) interpret this as "shared institutional logics" that define and stabilize field boundaries, identities, and interactions. Third, a field is characterized by formal *rules* such as laws and professional standards (Hardy & Maguire, 2010). Within a field, actors are expected to follow these *rules*, with the imposition of penalties for noncompliance (Hoffman, 1999; Scott, 2001).

Field *positions, understandings,* and *rules* imply a shared identity among organizations within the field (Zietsma et al., 2017), which occupy clear places in a defined power relation, follow common meaning systems, and respect the same norms. This is particularly true within a mature field, wherein relationships tend to be more stable and well defined, and field constituents tend to have stronger sense of mutual understandings (David et al., 2013). Due to the pressure of isomorphism, members in a mature field tend to follow the same institutional logic, and their behaviors are guided by similar values and beliefs (DiMaggio & Powell, 1983). They also have strong mutual awareness of their roles and positions in the dominant hierarchy within the field (DiMaggio & Powell, 1983; Greenwood & Suddaby, 2006). Such homogeneity has important implications for new entrants, particularly when they represent new organizational forms, defined by David et al. (2013, p. 356) as "those that are underpinned by novel logics, that project new social identities, and that carve out new roles in exchange networks." Accordingly, when a new organizational form enters a mature field, its legitimacy is often met with doubt, criticism, and opposition, as witnessed in the cases of vocational community colleges emerging in a field dominated by academically- focused colleges (Brint & Karabel, 1989); the emergence of specialty coffee retailers in the US coffee industry (Rindova & Fombrun, 2001); and the entry of a multidisciplinary firm in the accounting field (Greenwood et al., 2002). Xhauflair et al.'s (2018) study, for instance, shows that when a community-based labor market intermediary entered the highly institutionalized Belgian labor market system, it faced strong opposition from established field actors such as trade unions. It was not considered a good fit for the established cognitive field categories, and its alternative practices were thought to challenge the established actors' positions of power.

Based on the insights from the existing field literature, I develop two arguments regarding the perception of certain FDI as national security risks. First, I argue that SOEs are characterized by some unique features that constitute a new organizational form; as such, when they invest and enter a field abroad, they are likely to be perceived as challenging and disrupting field *positions, understandings,* and *rules,* thus posing three types of national security risks to the host country. Second, I argue that FDI can be considered an issue field, in which the home countries of SOEs become important actors in the field despite the lack of physical proximity or direct business transactions with local firms; their potentially cooperative, competitive, or conflictual relationships with the host country considerably impact the SOEs' perceived threat to the host country's national security.

3. THE ENTRY OF SOES IN AN EXCHANGE FIELD

SOEs are a global phenomenon (Bruton et al., 2015). Although liberalization and privatization policies in most countries in the 1980s and 1990s have reduced the number of SOEs worldwide, they persist in almost all countries, including those of the Organisation for Economic Co-operation and Development (OECD; Cuervo-Cazurra, 2018; Musacchio et al., 2015; Okhmatovskiy, 2010). In particular, state ownership is an enduring feature in China, Russian, India, Brazil, and other emerging markets (Inoue, 2020). However, as important and active global investors, SOEs from these countries are often met with censure by the host governments and societies (Cuervo-Cazurra, 2018; Cui & Jiang, 2012; Meyer et al., 2014), to the extent of being accused of posing a threat to national security. To understand this phenomenon, I conceptualize SOEs' FDI as their entry into a field. In this section, I focus on the exchange field to demonstrate how the three key features of SOEs can be associated with the three types of national security risk. I argue that the unique characteristics of SOEs exacerbate the perception that their entry could disrupt established field *positions, understandings,* and *rules*, thereby leading to security risks such as the dominance of supply, technology transfer, and espionage.

All SOEs, including those from emerging markets, share certain common features. As entities owned by the state, SOEs are created as a mechanism to tackle domestic market imperfections (Lawson, 1994; Levy, 1987; Lindsay, 1976) and a political tool to represent state ideology, achieve non-economic goals, and solve other social problems (Cuervo-Cazurra et al., 2014; Goldeng et al., 2008). This implies that SOEs inherently differ from private enterprises in three major aspects.

First, compared with their private counterparts, SOEs are more resourceful. On the one hand, SOEs, by default, have exclusive control over those assets that the government does not want to privatize, such as natural resources and railroad infrastructure (Okhmatovskiy, 2010). On the other hand, SOEs tend to have preferential access to financial and non-financial support from the governments, ranging from cheap loans and subsidies to overseas diplomatic representations and political networks (Buckley et al., 2007; Duanmu, 2014). Second, corporate governance in SOEs tends to be more ambiguous and less effective. The agency problem is acute within SOEs, because as owners, governments have weaker abilities and incentives than private owners to monitor the behavior of politicians, who, despite being responsible for the firm's operations, may focus on political rent-seeking than efficiency (Grøgaard et al., 2019; Mariotti & Marzano, 2019). Furthermore, SOEs are also less transparent about their finances, operations, and objectives (Cannizzaro & Weiner, 2018). Due to these specific failures of corporate governance, studies indicate that SOEs are less efficient and deliver poorer performance than privately-owned firms (Cui & Jiang, 2012; Goldeng et al., 2008). Third, SOEs are endowed with a broader range of objectives, which not only concern profits, but also non-commercial objectives such as social, political, or even ideological goals (Grøgaard et al., 2019). SOEs may thus use their ownership control to strategically utilize their resources to achieve these goals and take not only economic but political factors into account when making strategic choices (Okhmatovskiy, 2010). Owing to these three key features, SOEs have a different organizational form compared with the private firms dominant in the field, with the following clear implications regarding their perceived impact field *positions,* field *understandings,* and field *rules,* thereby leading to national security risks.

First, SOEs' exclusive control over unique assets and their access to preferential support from the home country (Buckley et al., 2007; Duanmu, 2014) imply that their entry into a field potentially changes the established hierarchy of status. SOEs have greater resources than other private actors in the field, thereby challenging the position and status enjoyed by private actors. SOEs can pose a threat to local businesses because of the unfair competitive advantage arising from the support of their home government (Christiansen & Kim, 2014). In the event of SOEs leveraging their resources and abusing their market power, the disruption of existing field *positions* can lead to the first type of national security risk: dominance of supply. In this scenario, the foreign company, with the support of its home country, gains a foothold in certain strategically important industries and exercises its market power to deny the provision of goods or services that are critical to the functioning of the host economy (Moran, 2009; 2017). During a bilateral crisis, the foreign company's home government could use the provision of such goods or services as a bargaining chip. For instance, concerns about the Chinese energy company CNOOC stopping energy provision to the US and diverting energy supplies to China was partly the rationale for blocking its acquisition of the American company Unocal in 2006 (Moran, 2017). A high-profile case is that of the China General Nuclear Power Group (CGN), which has generated a heated debate on the threat to UK's national security, since the beginning of the firm's involvement in the construction of the Hinkley Point nuclear plant in 2012. There are apprehensions that China may shut down the energy supply should China and UK fall out over diplomatic issues. Senior British Conservative politician Nick Timothy strongly opposed CGN's involvement, claiming, "[t]he government is selling our national security to China," in his article published on the Conservatives' website in October 2015. He also stated that "the Chinese could use their role to build weaknesses into computer systems which will allow them to shut down Britain's energy production at will" (Timothy, 2015).

Second, the logic driving SOEs is not as clear as that of their private counterparts (Cuervo-Cazurra et al., 2014). Driven by various economic, social, and ideological objectives, whether SOEs operate for profitmaking or the achievement of other goal is unpredictable; the inability to assess how they may affect other constituents in the field and erode "shared institutional logics" (Greenwood & Suddaby, 2006) is a concern. Owned by and serving the interests of the home country, SOEs have been perceived by host countries not only as economic agents, but also as political actors representing their home government, thereby undermining the national interests of host countries (Meyer et al., 2014). Accordingly, when SOEs enter foreign markets, they may be suspected of hidden motives. For instance, certain SOEs may engage in merger and acquisitions; however, such behavior may not be guided by the general principles of capacity building or maximizing market opportunities, but by an unknown logic that serves the home country's objectives. SOEs' deviation from the common *understandings* and meaning systems may imply the pursuit of certain non-commercial goals. This issue is further worsened by SOEs' ambiguous corporate governance; the operations of SOEs lack transparency, and their behaviors are not well regulated (Grøgaard et al., 2019).

Accordingly, SOEs' divergent behaviors in the field can lead to the other two types of national security risks: technology transfer and espionage. In the first scenario, an SOE may transfer technology, expertise, or capability to its home country, which can then be used in a way that jeopardizes the host country's national interests (Moran, 2009; 2017). A recent example is the proposed acquisition of German communication technology firm IMST by Chinese firm Addsino (a subsidiary of the state-owned China Aerospace and Industry Group). The deal was blocked by the German government in December 2020, fearing that IMST's key know-how and technology in the fields of radio system, satellite communication, and 5G could spill over and be used to enhance the military capability of China, a non-ally of the West, thereby endangering IMST's supply to the German Armed Forces (Nienaber, 2020). More generally, some argue that a foreign firm's acquisition of cutting-edge technology could help its government weaken their rivals and strengthen themselves. For example, Elisabeth Braw, leader of the think tank Royal United Services Institute for Defence and Security Studies (RUSI), argues that cutting-edge technology takeovers are a strategic threat to the West, whereby "rivals can weaken their adversaries and strengthen themselves" (Braw, 2019). In the second scenario, espionage, there is an apprehension that foreign acquisition may afford the new ownership's government a platform for infiltration, surveillance, and sabotage. For instance, it is feared that foreign SOEs and their respective governments will insert malware into government and military information technology systems for monitoring and surveillance. Therefore, in June 2020, Chinese state-owned telecommunication equipment maker ZTE, as well as Huawei, were designated as "national security threats" by the US Federation Communications Commission (FCC), which believed that both companies' equipment provided backdoor access for espionage by the Chinese state: "[T]he Chinese government could go through the companies' equipment to spy on traffic around the world or sabotage networks and the technologies they power" (McCabe, 2020).

4. THE ENTRY OF HOME & HOST COUNTRIES IN AN ISSUE FIELD

So far, I have discussed how the key features of SOEs could lead to a negative perception regarding their likelihood to disrupt the estabblished field *positions, understandings,* and *rules* upon entry, thereby generating three types of security risks to the host country. My analytical focus is mainly on the exchange field, wherein SOEs interact with local actors in their physical proximity, such as merger and acquisitions target firms, competitors, customers, suppliers, and regulators. SOEs may rely on their strong resource base, eliminate competitors, and dominate the market and supply, posing a threat to the host's national security. In the exchange field, the host country's agencies mainly function as regulators, whereas the home country is large absent or plays a behind-the-scenes role. However, the exchange field perspective may not provide a complete picture of how SOEs become national security concerns. A question arises as to why only Chinese and Russian SOEs tend to be considered as threats to national security by the West, and not, for instance, Indian or Brazilian SOEs. Only by considering FDI as an issue field and including SOEs' home countries in the discussion can this phenomenon be fully understood. In this section, I use key insights from the field of international relations to examine how domestic politics in the home and host countries and the relations between them affect the perceptions of the nature and impact of SOEs' investments on national security.

National security is intersubjective in nature. In the field of international relations, securitization theorists (Buzan et al., 1998; Wæver, 1995) convincingly argue that national security issues are not objective conditions, but socially constructed by securitizing actors (Williams, 2003). As suggested by Wæver (1995, p. 550), security is a speech act, and 'by saying it, something is done.' In recent decades securitizing actors have increasingly used security language to turn unconventional issues into security issue, such as energy, religion, and migration, and there has been a move toward dramatizing issues and presenting them as supreme priorities, thereby obtaining national prominence and financial support (Hudson, 2009; Karyotis & Patrikios, 2010; Williams, 2003). These attributes of national security have important implications for the key role that politics and international relations play in the issue field of FDI.

In the three scenarios discussed in Section 3—dominance of supply, technology transfer, and espionage—the national security risks associated with FDI fundamentally involve two nations. When a foreign firm is considered as threats to the national security of its host country, the worry is not about the firm *per se* but about the firm's home government, and the firm's relation with its government. This implies that when the host country scrutinizes foreign investments, the process and outcome are likely to be subject to the relations with the foreign firms' home country. In other words, the treatment of certain FDI as a national security risk is subjective and may be contingent upon international relations (Lai, 2021). A telling example here is that of the change in perception about CGN's national security threat in the past decade amid the evolution of China–UK relations.

CGN's involvement in the Hinkley nuclear project was considered a major deal that promoted a "new golden decade" between the UK and China. During David Cameron's tenure as the British Prime Minister (May 2010–June 2016), the then Chancellor George Osborne and Cameron himself were among the prominent cheerleaders of Chinese investments into the UK. A series of meetings occurred between top officials from China and the UK during this period to promote economic collaborations, as exemplified by Osborne's China visit in October 2013, Cameron's meeting with the Chinese Premier Li Keqiang in Beijing in December 2013, Chinese Premier Li Keqiang's three-day state visit to the UK in June 2014, and Chinese President Xi Jinping's state visit to the UK in October 2015. In its honeymoon period with China, the Cameron government evaluated the national security risk posed by CGN's involvement as minimal and controllable, as indicated by Osborne's call for the British people's openness to Chinese investments: "We have to confront any anxieties that exist out there about Chinese investment in British civil nuclear power." He also stated:

> *"The truth is this: the reactor - which is actually a French reactor - can only go ahead if it is signed off by our nuclear safety experts and there are plenty of rules that exist to protect the British people from the misuse of civil nuclear power and to make sure that our nuclear power stations are completely safe." (Phillips et al., 2015).*

However, the British Conservative government's stance on the national security risk associated with CGN's involvement changed after Theresa May took over as Prime Minister following the Brexit vote. Prime Minister May's decision on July 29, 2016 to review and delay the Hinkley project signaled a re-evaluation of CGN's national security risk, as stated by the Times article titled *Chinese Spies are Biggest Threat to Nuclear Power Deal:* "Intelligence sources confirmed that the key issue in the review of Hinkley and its related projects is China, not cost, the future price of its electricity nor the reliability of the reactors" (Evans et al., 2016). The May government eventually approved the project on September 15, 2016, reiterating the absence of a national security risk associated with CGN. However, in July 2021, various media sources reported that the UK government was planning to remove CGN from all nuclear projects in the country on the grounds of national security. This dramatic change coincided with worsening relations between China and the UK, as rightly pointed out by the Financial Times:

> *"It [the removal of CGN] follows the chilling in relations between London and Beijing in recent years over issues including China's clampdown on dissent in Hong Kong, its repression of the Uyghurs and other Muslim minorities in Xinjiang and its handling of the initial Covid-19 outbreak in Wuhan." (Pickard & Thomas, 2021)*

The impact of international relations on the host country's handling of FDI from specific countries is strongly supported by the literature, which notes that there is a hierarchy of nations based on power, and nations take action to restore the balance of power if another nation threatens their survival (Waltz, 1979); accordingly, government intervention in FDI is one of those tools of statecraft to achieve this objective (Lenihan, 2018). As a case in point, given the worsening China–US relations in recent years, the Foreign Investment Risk Review Modernization Act of 2018 (FIRRMA) in the US is considered by many as ''born out of the nexus of increased fear regarding China's growing strategic and economic clout and the potential loss of American technology supremacy'' (Zimmerman, 2019, p. 1269). In this sense, the recent crackdown on Chinese technology firms may be considered a move to protect US technological supremacy and relative power.

Domestic politics and international relations are intertwined. The existing international relations literature has shown how domestic politics influence states' foreign policies and thus their international relations (Fearon, 1998), such as with respect to trade policy (Milner, 1997) and international cooperation (Downs & Rocke, 1995). As Schultz (2012, p. 478) states, "[t]he idea that politics within states influences politics among states is as old as the study of international relations." While it is beyond the scope of this study to illustrate how domestic politics influence international relations between the home and host countries, two issues are key here: first, the effect of domestic politics in the host country on the creation and handling of FDI-related national security issues (focusing on the host country's perception of SOEs and their investments); and second, the effect of domestic politics in the home country on the motives, behaviors, and strategies of SOEs, which in turn may alter the dynamics in the issue field (focusing on SOEs themselves).

Owing to the intersubjective nature of the national security issue, powerful actors, such as politicians and corporate elites, could emerge as securitizing actors who rely on their powers and transform a particular issue into one of national security. Research has showed how the process of FDI review on the grounds of national security has become a notoriously politicized process (Feng, 2009; Graham & Marchick, 2006; Hasnat, 2015). Commenting on the obscurity of FDI policies in most countries with regard to national security, Lai (2021) suggests that policy ambiguity facilitates the securitization of FDI and enables securitizing actors to achieve their agendas. He argues:

> *"In this sense, a policy with broad wording and vagueness becomes an important prerequisite for these powerful actors to engage in the FDI securitization process when necessary. As such, the processes of screening and FDI securitization become power struggles, where various actors exercise their power to designate specific issues as security threats, and to deal with these as they wish."*

Therefore, although it is key to balance openness to FDI and national security interests, whether certain FDI constitute a national security threat is nevertheless a highly politicized. From this perspective, domestic politics influence field dynamics, because politics can lead to government instability in the form of personnel change (e.g., change in the head of government), factional change (e.g., change in the controlling party), or even systemic change (e.g., change from a civilian to a military regime). Any such changes could entail policy revisions (Brewer, 1983), leading to a new definition and interpretation of national security and a new policy paradigm governing foreign investments. As Brewer (1983, p. 147) observes:

> *"The essence of a national political process is a struggle over which individuals and groups get to exercise governmental power so that their policy preferences can be implemented. The struggle for power reflects the conflicting ideologies and interests of participants in the political process. Changes in governments therefore entail changes in the power of individuals and groups and in their ability to promote their ideologies and interests through government policies."*

The case of CGN is not only a striking example of the role of international relations in shaping the perceptions of national security risks posed by MNEs, but also a case that shows how domestic politics can lead to dramatic changes in party ideologies and FDI policies. While Prime Minister Cameron's government appeared to downplay the national security risks and embrace Chinese investments, his successors, Theresa May and Boris Johnson, adopted a much more skeptical stance, with the latter's government introducing the *National Security and Investment Act 2021,* a move widely considered to be targeting Chinese investments (Pickard et al., 2020).

My arguments about the impact of domestic politics on field dynamics and the resulting security implications for SOEs' FDI are in line with what international business scholars (Brewer, 1983; Jones, 1984; Kobrin, 1979; Simon, 1984) label as political risk. This strand of research indicates that political risk is a significant determinant of FDI decisions. For instance, due to their association with uncertainty and extra costs, political risks such as electoral uncertainty, political instability, and social unrest are believed to affect MNEs' FDI decisions and entry strategies (e.g. Chung & Beamish, 2005; Delios & Henisz, 2000; García-Canal & Guillén,

2008). In particular, foreign investments tend to be affected by the host country's policy changes, which Holburn and Zelner (2010) label as "policy risk". Delios and Henisz (2003) and Chung and Beamish (2005) highlight that FDI policy uncertainty in host countries has driven Japanese MNEs to change their entry strategies; Julio and Yook (2016) reveal that policy uncertainty deters cross border flows of capital. This presents another perspective to show how domestic politics can create a challenging institutional environment for SOEs when they enter a foreign market.

Finally, I argue that domestic politics in the SOEs' home country may change the dynamics in the issue field by influencing the motives, behaviors, and strategies of SOEs and the other actors' perceptions about SOEs and their investments. Given their political embeddedness (Michelson, 2007, p. 352), SOEs are readily subject to the impact of domestic political changes and developments. At a macro level, SOEs function as tools of social and economic policy (Bruton et al., 2015; Wang & Luo, 2019), for example, to promote economic development in certain region (Amsden, 1992). However, domestic politics induce changes in the state's goals and policies; as a result, SOEs' priorities "will likely fluctuate according to the political ambitions of state officials" (Inoue, 2020, p. 678). At a micro level, politicians may interfere with SOEs' decision-making (Okhmatovskiy, 2010), and the actions of SOEs may be manipulated by state officials to obtain political benefits (Inoue, 2020). Under these circumstances, the behaviors and nature of SOEs' investments assume new bearings and lead to different interpretations. The recent developments in China's domestic political landscape, wherein President Xi Jinping is strengthening the power of SOEs to expand China's global influence (Leutert, 2018; Shullman, 2019), is a good example. As expected, Chinese SOEs and their investments are increasingly being scrutinized by many host countries, given their close links with the Chinese government and the possibility that they may be used to achieve political objectives.

5. RESEARCH DIRECTIONS

The recent years have witnessed a new wave of tighter FDI screening in many western countries, such as the UK, with its new *National Security and Investment Act 2021,* and the European Union (EU), with the new EU Foreign Direct Investment Screening Regulation, effective since October 2020. Against the backdrop of a surge in populist and anti-globalization sentiments (Witt, et al. 2021), I expect the rise in FDI-related national security concerns and accusations to continue. This study addresses this increasingly relevant issue in international business. Using SOEs as a representative case, I develop the Dual-Field Framework (DFF) to analyze how FDI made multinational enterprises become national security threats. By applying a field-level perspective, this study reveals the political embeddedness of international business, demonstrating that FDI is not merely an economic activity but one deeply embedded in domestic politics, international relations, and geopolitical tensions.

The Dual-Field Framework (DFF), which I develop in this chapter, contributes to the study of FDI-related national security concerns by bridging macro, meso, and micro levels of analysis. Traditional research on national security has primarily focused on macro-level factors, such as national policies and geopolitical dynamics, while largely overlooking how security concerns materialize at the field level. The DFF addresses this gap by incorporating both institutional and organizational perspectives, offering a multi-level approach that enhances our understanding of how FDI is constructed as a security threat. As an under-researched phenomenon, the national security issue deserves more attention from international business scholars. To this end, I propose the following future research directions across three levels.

At the macro level, researchers can extend this study by further theorizing how politics and international relations play a role in the development of the FDI-related national security issue. Some important research questions include: (i) How is the issue of national security socially constructed by news media, politicians, and other actors?; (ii) how should the host country's government deal with FDI that have national security implications?; and (iii) how has the national security issue forced the FDI policy regime to change?

At the meso level, researchers can focus on MNEs' market and non-market strategies. A key question to explore here is how MNEs respond to national security threat accusations. Such accusations may lead to strategic changes by the firms, including entry strategies and location choices, global value chain configurations, and corporate political activities. For instance, Kaspersky is reportedly diversifying its current cyber security software business "in an attempt to rehabilitate a business hit with spying allegations" (Warrell, 2020); furthermore, in 2020, it moved key parts of its data-processing business from Moscow to Switzerland as a part of the Global Transparency Initiative, commonly recognized as a move to evade the allegation of being vulnerable to Moscow's interference (Woo & McMillan, 2018).

At the micro level, researchers can investigate the impact of national security accusations on the MNEs' current employees, job seekers, and other individual stakeholders. It would be interesting, for example, to examine how job seekers and current employees evaluate MNEs that have been accused of posing a national security threat, and how their evaluations impact their joining decisions and attrition rates. Based on social identity theory, our affiliation with a particular company partly defines who we are, and we feel a sense of pride from being affiliated with a good company (Tajfel & Turner, 1986). Research has revealed that being associated with a good company can enhance self-esteem and help us gain social approval and impress others (Highhouse et al., 2007). However, when a firm is accused of posing national security threat, key question arises as to whether current employees and job seekers want to be associated with this firm, particularly when, in the case of SOEs, its owner (e.g. the Chinese and Russian states) is often perceived as authoritarian and is frequently plagued by such accusations as human rights abuse, intellectual property theft, and cyber hacking. Empirically addressing such question as how national security threat accusations impact organizational attractiveness could provide significant insights for theory building in this unchartered territory.

In this study, I use SOEs as a representative example to theorize how FDI becomes a national security concern. I do not distinguish between SOEs based on ownership structure because, in my opinion, in many cases, perceived connectedness to the home state matters more than legal classification. However, it is important to acknowledge that not all SOEs are the same—some are wholly state-owned, while others are partially privatized but retain strong government influence through ownership stakes, board appointments, or regulatory interventions (Cuervo-Cazurra, 2018).

The degree of state ownership and control may play a role in shaping national security perceptions. For example, wholly state-owned SOEs are typically subject to the highest scrutiny, particularly when operating in strategic industries such as energy, telecommunications, defense, and technology. Host governments often suspect these firms of serving their home country's geopolitical interests, raising concerns about dominance of supply, technology transfer, and espionage. For instance, Chinese state-owned energy firms, including CNOOC and CGN, have faced resistance in Western markets due to fears that their operations could be leveraged for political or economic coercion. Meanwhile, partially privatized SOEs, though structurally distinct, may still raise concerns if they receive preferential treatment, state subsidies, or maintain informal political ties, as their presence in foreign markets may be perceived as disrupting the fields. A case in point is Huawei; although legally a private firm —not even a partially privatized SOE—it is widely perceived by the West as having close ties with the Chinese government. As a result, it has been accused of posing national security threats and has faced restrictions in countries such as the US and the UK. These variations illustrate that national security concerns are not solely determined by a firm's ownership structure but rather by the broader political and geopolitical context in which these firms operate.

6. CONCLUSIONS

National security in the context of international business is a complex and evolving issue, shaped by interactions among MNEs, regulators, policymakers, media, local businesses, and both home and host country governments. The Dual-Field Framework (DFF) developed in this study highlights how national security concerns materialize within and across fields, emphasizing the interplay between the exchange field and the issue field. The dynamic nature of these fields—driven by factors such as technological advancements (e.g., 5G, AI), the entry of new market players, domestic political shifts, and intensifying geopolitical tensions—continuously reshapes how FDI is framed as a security risk and underscores impacts of geopolitics on international business.

For MNEs, the field-level nature of national security concerns requires a context-sensitive approach to risk management, strategy formulation, and stakeholder engagement. First, MNEs must recognize that national security risks are not intrinsic to their operations but are constructed within fields. The exchange field determines how firms' market activities, ownership structures, and industry positioning are interpreted, while the issue field shapes how political and institutional actors frame these activities as security threats. Firms that fail to anticipate shifts in these fields risk being caught in the crossfire of geopolitical conflicts and regulatory tightening. To mitigate this, MNEs must develop field-awareness strategies, continuously monitoring how their industry, host-country policies, and geopolitical relationships evolve.

Second, MNEs need to engage with and shape the institutional logics governing the fields. Since national security concerns are socially constructed, firms can proactively influence narratives about their role in the host country by engaging regulators, industry groups, policymakers, and media. Transparent engagement, participation in policy discussions, and collaboration with local institutions allow firms to engage in institutional entrepreneurship (Battilana, Leca, & Boxenbaum, 2009), enabling them to shape regulatory frameworks, shift field dynamics, and reposition themselves as contributors to national interests rather than as security threats.

Third, MNEs must adapt their positioning in the exchange field to reduce perceptions of field disruption. In industries where MNEs from politically sensitive home countries are viewed with suspicion, MNEs should adjust their entry strategies, governance structures, and local partnerships to avoid triggering security concerns. For example, rather than entering a market through full acquisitions, firms could opt for joint ventures or minority stakes, signaling a commitment to cooperation rather than control. Similarly, organizational restructuring—such as creating distinct regional subsidiaries with local leadership—may help dissociate the firm from home-state influence narratives.

In conclusion, the securitization of FDI is a field-driven process, rather than a fixed regulatory issue. The Dual-Field Framework (DFF) provides a multi-level perspective to understand how MNEs' foreign investments become national security threats. It is argued that market disruptions in the exchange field and political contestation in the issue field jointly shape the security perceptions and narratives about firms.

REFERENCES

Amsden, A. H. (1992). *Asia's Next Giant: South Korea and Late Industrialization*. Oxford University Press.

Battilana, J., Leca, B., & Boxenbaum, E. (2009). 2 how actors change institutions: Towards a theory of institutional entrepreneurship. *The Academy of Management Annals*, *3*(1), 65–107.

Bauerle Danzman, S., & Meunier, S. (2023). Naïve no more: Foreign direct investment screening in the European Union. *Global Policy*, *14*, 40–53.

Beugelsdijk, S., & Luo, Y. (2024). The politicized nature of international business. *Journal of International Business Studies*, *55*(3), 281–284.

Bourdieu, P., & Wacquant, L. (1992). *Invitation to Reflexive Sociology*. University of Chicago Press.

Braw, E. (2019). Cutting-edge tech takeovers are a strategic threat to the west. *Financial Times*, October 7, 2019. https://www.ft.com/content/763cae4e-e5ed-11e9-b8e0-026e07cbe5b4. Accessed September 10, 2021

Brewer, T. (1983). The instability of governments and the instability of controls on funds transfers by multinational enterprises: Implications for political risk analysis. *Journal of International Business Studies*, *14*(3), 147–157.

Brint, S., & Karabel, J. (1989). *The Diverted Dream: Community Colleges and the Promise of Educational Opportunity in America*. Oxford University Press.

Bruton, G. D., Peng, M. W., Ahlstrom, D., Stan, C., & Xu, K. (2015). State-owned enterprises around the world as hybrid organizations. *The Academy of Management Perspectives*, *29*(1), 92–114.

Buckley, P. J., Clegg, L. J., Cross, A. R., Liu, X., Voss, H., & Zheng, P. (2007). The determinants of Chinese outward foreign direct investment. *Journal of International Business Studies*, *38*(4), 499–518.

Buzan, B., Wæver, O., & De Wilde, J. (1998). *Security: A new framework for analysis*. Lynne Rienner Publishers.

Cannizzaro, A. P., & Weiner, R. J. (2018). State ownership and transparency in foreign direct investment. *Journal of International Business Studies*, *49*(2), 172–195.

Christiansen, H., & Kim, Y. (2014). *State-Invested Enterprises in the Global Marketplace : Implications for a Level Playing Field* (OECD Corporate Governance Working Papers, Issue 14).

Chung, C. C., & Beamish, P. W. (2005). The impact of institutional reforms on characteristics and survival of foreign subsidiaries in emerging economies. *Journal of Management Studies, 42*(1), 35–62.

Cuervo-Cazurra, Alvaro, Inkpen, A., Musacchio, A., & Ramaswamy, K. (2014). Governments as owners: State-owned multinational companies. *Journal of International Business Studies, 45*(8), 919–942.

Cuervo-Cazurra, A. (2018). Thanks but no thanks: State-owned multinationals from emerging markets and host-country policies. *Journal of International Business Policy, 1*(3–4), 128–156.

Cui, L., & Jiang, F. (2012). State ownership effect on firms' FDI ownership decisions under institutional pressure: A study of Chinese outward-investing firms. *Journal of International Business Studies, 43*(3), 264–284.

David, R. J., Sine, W. D., & Haveman, H. A. (2013). Seizing opportunity in emerging fields: How institutional entrepreneurs legitimated the professional form of management consulting. *Organization Science, 24*(2), 356–377.

Delios, A., & Henisz, W. (2000). Japanese firm investment strategies in emerging economies. *Academy of Management Journal, 43*, 305–323.

Delios, A., & Henisz, W. J. (2003). *Policy uncertainty and the sequence of entry by Japanese firms, 1980 – 1998*. 227–241.

DiMaggio, P. J., & Powell, W. W. (1983). The iron cage revisited: Institutional isomorphism and collective rationality in organizational fields. *American Sociological Review, 48*(2), 147–160.

Downs, G., & Rocke, D. (1995). *Optimal Im- perfection? Domestic Uncertainty and In- stitutions in International Relations*. Princeton University Press.

Duanmu, J. L. (2014). State-owned MNCs and host country expropriation risk: The role of home state soft power and economic gunboat diplomacy. *Journal of International Business Studies, 45*(8), 1044–1060.

Esplugues, C. (2018). *Foreign Investment, Strategic Assets and National Security*. Intersentia.

Evans, M., O'Neil, S., & MacLeod, C. (2016). Chinese spies are biggest threat to nuclear power deal. *The Times*. August 13, 2016. https://www.thetimes.co.uk/article/chinese-spies-are-biggest-threat-to-nuclear-power-deal-kp75t36kf. Accessed September 12, 2021.

Fearon, J. D. (1998). Domestic politics, foreign policy, and theories of international relations. *Annual Review of Political Science*, *1*(1), 289–313.

Feng, Y. (2009). "We Wouldn't Transfer Title to the Devil": Consequences of the Congressional Politicization of Foreign Direct Investment on National Security Grounds. *Journal of International Law and Politics*, *42*(1), 253–310.

García-Canal, E., & Guillén, M. F. (2008). Risk and the strategy of foreign location choice in regulated industries. *Strategic Management Journal*, *29*(10), 1097–1115.

Godsell, D., Lel, U., & Miller, D. (2023). US national security and de-globalization. *Journal of International Business Studies*, *54*(8), 1471–1494.

Goldeng, E., Grünfeld, L. A., & Benito, G. R. (2008). The performance differential between private and state owned enterprises: The roles of ownership, management and market structure. *Journal of Management Studies*, *45*(7), 1244–1273.

Graham, E., & Marchick, D. (2006). *US National Security and Foreign Direct Investment*. Peterson Institute for International Economics.

Greenwood, R., Suddaby, R., & Hinings, C. R. (2002). Theorizing Change : The Role of Professional Associations in the Transformation of Institutionalized Fields A. *Academy of Management Journal*, *45*(1), 58–80.

Grøgaard, B., Rygh, A., & Benito, G. R. G. (2019). Bringing corporate governance into internalization theory: State ownership and foreign entry strategies. *Journal of International Business Studies*, *50*(8), 1310–1337.

Hardy, C., & Maguire, S. (2010). Discourse, field-configuring events, and change in organizations and institutional fields: Narratives of DDT and the Stockholm Convention. *Academy of Management Journal*, *53*(6), 1365–1392.

Hasnat, B. (2015). US National Security and Foreign Direct Investment. *Thunderbird International Business Review*, *57*(3), 185–196.

Highhouse, S., Thornbury, E. E., & Little, I. S. (2007). Social-identity functions of attraction to organizations. *Organizational Behavior and Human Decision Processes*, *103*(1), 134–146.

Hoffman, A. J. (1999). Institutional Evolution and Change: Environmentalism and the U.S. Chemical Industry. *Academy of Management Journal*, *42*, 351–371.

Holburn, G. L., & Zelner, B. A. (2010). Political capabilities, policy risk, and international investment strategy: Evidence from the global electric power generation industry. *Strategic Management Journal, 31*(12), 1290–1315.

Hudson, N. F. (2009). *Gender, Human Security and the United Nations: Security Languages as a Political Framework for Women*. Routledge.

Inoue, C. (2020). Election cycles and organizations: How politics shapes the performance of state-owned enterprises over time. *Dministrative Science Quarterly, 65*(3), 677–709.

Jones, R. (1984). Empirical Models of Political Risks in U. S. Oil Production Operations in Venezuela. *Journal of International Business Studies, 15*(1), 81–95.

Julio, B., & Yook, Y. (2016). Policy uncertainty, irreversibility, and cross-border flows of capital. *Journal of International Economics, 103*, 13–26.

Karyotis, G., & Patrikios, S. (2010). Religion, securitization and anti-immigration attitudes: The case of Greece. *Journal of Peace Research, 47*(1), 43–57.

Kobrin, S. (1979). Political risk: A review and reconsideration. *Journal of International Business Studies, 10*(1), 67–80.

Krauss, C. (2017). Russian uses its oil giant, Rosneft, as a foreign policy tool. The New York Times. October 29, 2017. https://www.nytimes.com/2017/10/29/business/energy-environment/russia-venezula-oil-rosneft.html. Accessed September 12, 2021

Lai, K. (2021). National security and FDI policy ambiguity: A commentary. *Journal of International Business Policy, 4*(4), 496–505.

Lai, K., & Fortwengel, J. (2025). Constructing an organizational identity with political ideology: The case of Huawei, 1987-2020. *Strategic Organization*. Advance online publication. DOI: 10.1177/14761270251327988

Lawson, C. (1994). The theory of state-owned enterprises in market economies. *Journal of Economic Surveys, 8*(3), 283–309.

Lenihan, A. T. (2018). *Balancing Power without Weapons: State Intervention into Cross-Border Mergers and Acquisitions*. Cambridge University Press.

Leutert, W. (2018). Firm control: governing the state-owned economy under Xi Jinping. *China Perspectives*. June 1, 2018. 27-36. https://journals.openedition.org/chinaperspectives/7605

Levy, B. (1987). A theory of public enterprise behavior. *Journal of Economic Behavior & Organization, 8*(1), 75–96.

Li, J., Shapiro, D. M., Ufimtseva, A., & Zhang, P. (2024). Techno-nationalism and cross-border acquisitions in an age of geopolitical rivalry. *Journal of International Business Studies*, *55*, 1190–1203.

Lindsay, C. M. (1976). A theory of government enterprise. *Journal of Political Economy*, *84*(5), 1061–1077.

Luo, Y., & Van Assche, A. (2023). The rise of techno-geopolitical uncertainty: Implications of the United States CHIPS and Science Act. *Journal of International Business Studies*, *54*(8), 1423–1440.

Mariotti, S., & Marzano, R. (2019). Varieties of capitalism and the internationalization of state-owned enterprises. *Journal of International Business Studies*, *50*(5), 669–691.

McCabe, D. (2020). F.C.C. designates Huawei and ZTE as national security threats. *The New York Times*. June 20, 2020. https://www.nytimes.com/2020/06/30/technology/fcc-huawei-zte-national-security.html. Access September 10, 2021.

Meyer, K. E., Ding, Y., Li, J., & Zhang, H. (2014). Overcoming distrust: How state-owned enterprises adapt their foreign entries to institutional pressures abroad. *Journal of International Business Studies*, *45*(8), 1005–1028.

Michelson, E. (2007). Lawyers, political embeddedness, and institutional continuity in China's transition from socialism. *American Journal of Sociology*, *113*, 352–414.

Milner, H. (1997). *Interests, Institutions, and Information: Domestic Politics and International Relations*. Princeton University Press.

Moran, T. (2017). *CFIUS and National Security: Challenges for the United States, Opportunities for the European Union*. https://www.piie.com/commentary/speeches-papers/cfius-and-national-security-challenges-united-states-opportunities

Moran, T. H. (2009). *Three threats: An analytical framework for the CFIUS process*. Peterson Institute.

Newnham, R. (2011). Oil, carrots, and sticks: Russia's energy resources as a foreign policy tool. *Journal of Eurasian Studies*, *2*(2), 134–143.

Nienaber, M. (2020). Germany blocks Chinese takeover of satellite firm on security concerns. *Reuters*. December 8, 2020. https://www.reuters.com/article/uk-germany-china-m-a-idUKKBN28I1U0. Accessed September 10, 2021

O'Donnell, C., Baker, L., & Wang, E. (2019). Exclusive: Told U.S. security at risk, Chinese firm seeks to sell Grindr dating app. *Reuters*. March 27, 2019. https://www.reuters.com/article/us-grindr-m-a-exclusive/exclusive-u-s-pushes-chinese-owner-of-grindr-to-divest-the-dating-app-sources-idUSKCN1R809L. Accessed September 10, 2021

Okhmatovskiy, I. (2010). Performance implications of ties to the government and SOEs: A political embeddedness perspective. *Journal of Management Studies, 47*(6), 1020–1047.

Phillips, T., Allen, K., & Macalister, T. (2015). Kinkley Point: Osborne seeks to ease doubts with £2bn guarantee. *The Guardian*. September 21, 2015. https://www.theguardian.com/business/2015/sep/21/nuclear-plant-project-osbornes-commits-2bn-guarantee. Accessed September 12, 2021

Pickard, J., Thomas, D., Massoudi, A., & Mitchell, T. (2020). UK takes aim at China with revamp of takeover rules, *Financial Times*, November 11, 2020. https://www.ft.com/content/55f848d8-92f8-4c42-9775-dd9d6c55ee91. Accessed September 10, 2021

Pickard, L., & Thomas, D. (2021). UK looks to remove China's CGN from nuclear power projects. *Financial Times*. July 25, 2021. https://www.ft.com/content/c4a3fe02-8535-45a4-aacf-0c4fbce8409d. Accessed September 12, 2021

Rindova, V., & Fombrun, C. (2001). Entrepreneurial action in the creation of the specialty coffee niche. In S. CB & R. E (Eds.), *The Entrepreneurship Dynamic: Origins of Entrepreneurship and the Evolution of Industries* (pp. 236–26). Stanford University Press.

Schultz, K. (2012). Domestic politics and international relations. In Carlsnaes, W., Risse, T., & Simmons, B. A. (Eds.), *Handbook of International Relations* (pp. 478–502). SAGE.

Scott, W. R. (2001). Institutions and Organizations. *Sage (Atlanta, Ga.).*

Shullman, D. (2019). Protect the Party: China's growing influence in the developing world. January 22, 2019. https://www.brookings.edu/articles/protect-the-party-chinas-growing-influence-in-the-developing-world/. Access September 12, 2021.

Simon, J. (1984). A Theoretical Perspective on Political Risk. *Journal of International Business Studies, 15*(3), 123–143.

Solon, O. (2017). US government bans agencies from using Kaspersky software over spying fears. *The Guardian.* September 13, 2017. https://www.theguardian.com/technology/2017/sep/13/us-government-bans-kaspersky-lab-russian-spying. Accessed September 13, 2021.

Tajfel, H., & Turner, J. C. (1986). The social identity theory of intergroup behavior. In Worchel, S., & Austin, W. G. (Eds.), *Psychology of intergroup relations* (pp. 7–24). Nelson-Hall.

Timothy, N. (2015). Nick Timothy: The Government is selling our national security to China. October 20, 2015. *Conservativehome.* https://www.conservativehome.com/thecolumnists/2015/10/nick-timothy-the-government-is-selling-our-national-security-to-china.html. Accessed September 12, 2021.

Wæver, O. (1995). Securitization and Desecuritization. In Lipschitz, R. D. (Ed.), *On Security.* Columbia University Press.

Waltz, K. N. (1979). *Theory of International Politics.* McGraw Hill.

Wang, D., & Luo, X. R. (2019). Retire in peace: Officials' political incentives and corporate diversification in China. *Administrative Science Quarterly, 77*(3), 773–809.

Warrell, H. (2020). Kaspersky diversifies from cyber security after spying allegations. *Financial Times.* December 5, 2020. https://www.ft.com/content/d8f27227-bdc4-4b8d-a361-345d3de0738a. Accessed September 12, 2021.

Williams, M. C. (2003). Words, images, enemies: Securitization and international politics. *International Studies Quarterly, 47*(4), 511–531.

Witt, M. A. (2019). China's challenge: Geopolitics, de-globalization, and the future of Chinese business. *Management and Organization Review, 15*(4), 687–704.

Witt, M. A., Li, P. P., Välikangas, L., & Lewin, A. Y. (2021). De-globalization and decoupling: Game changing consequences? *Management and Organization Review, 17*(1), 6–15.

Woo, S., & McMillan, R. (2018). Kaspersky to relocate some operations out of RUssia amid tampering suspicions. *The Wall Street Journal.* May 15, 2018. https://www.wsj.com/articles/kaspersky-to-relocate-some-operations-out-of-russia-amid-tampering-suspicions-1526367600. Accessed Septemner 12, 2021.

Wooten, M., & Hoffman, A. J. (2008). Organizational Fields: Past, Present and Future. In *The Sage Handbook of Organizational institutionalism* (pp. 55–74).

Xhauflair, V., Huybrechts, B., & Pichault, F. (2018). How Can New Players Establish Themselves in Highly Institutionalized Labour Markets? A Belgian Case Study in the Area of Project-Based Work. *British Journal of Industrial Relations*, *56*(2), 370–394.

Zietsma, C., Groenewegen, P., Logue, D. M., & Hinings, C. R. (2017). Field or fields? Building the scaffolding for cumulation of research on institutional fields. *The Academy of Management Annals*, *11*(1), 391–450.

Zimmerman, E. J. (2019). The Foreign Investment Risk Review Modernization Act: How CFIUS Became a Tech Office. *Berkeley Technology Law Journal*, *34*, 1267–1303.

Chapter 8
The Power of Consumer Boycotts in Geoeconomics and Geopolitical Conflicts

Merve Kır
https://orcid.org/0000-0001-8883-180X
Istanbul University, Turkey

Süphan Nasir
https://orcid.org/0000-0002-2302-334X
Istanbul University, Turkey

ABSTRACT

In recent years consumer boycotts have gained renewed attention as a form of political and ethical expression, particularly in response to international conflicts and humanitarian crises.The objective of this study is to explore consumers' attitudes and behavioral responses to boycott calls against Israeli products as well as certain multinational brands perceived to support Israel in the context of the recent humanitarian crisis in Gaza.Specifically the research aims to identify the levels of participation in the boycott, the motivations and perceived barriers to compliance with boycott, generational differences in boycott engagement, perceived effectiveness of the boycott, the influence of social pressure and public visibility and the social and psychological factors influencing consumer behavior in this context. The research seeks to examine the extent and patterns of boycott participation by segmenting consumers into three groups: non-boycotters, strict boycott compliers and partial boycott compliers.It further aims to investigate the generational differences in boycott behavior.

DOI: 10.4018/979-8-3373-1265-1.ch008

INTRODUCTION: THE INTERSECTION OF GEOECONOMICS, GEOPOLITICS, AND INTERNATIONAL BUSINESS

In recent years, geopolitical developments have significantly influenced the international business environment, affecting trade flows, investment patterns, and consumer behavior. Conflicts such as the Russia– Ukraine war, the U.S.- China trade tensions, and instability in the Middle East have generated political and economic effects. These tensions are no longer limited to diplomatic or governmental domains; they increasingly affect consumer markets and multinational corporations operating across borders. Global value chains, foreign direct investment, and supply chain structures have come under pressure as companies attempt to navigate politically sensitive contexts while maintaining operational continuity.

One outcome of this shifting landscape is the increased visibility and frequency of consumer boycotts, which have become a form of consumer driven response to geopolitical events. These boycotts, particularly those targeting multinational corporations perceived to support controversial regimes, represent a bottom-up form of economic protest (Mulyono & Rolando, 2025). Rather than being organized through state institutions, such actions are initiated and sustained by consumers, who use their purchasing choices to express disapproval and demand accountability.

In different parts of the world, consumer boycotts have been used as a reaction to political tensions and international conflicts. Cases such as the boycott of French products in the U.S. during the Iraq War, the South Korean boycott of Japanese goods in 2019, and the recent boycott campaigns targeting Israeli-linked brands after the Gaza conflict show how consumers express political views through market choices. These examples reflect the growing global role of boycott behavior in shaping public responses to international issues.

This trend highlights an important transformation in the relationship between politics and consumption. Companies that fail to consider the geoeconomic dimensions of politically motivated consumer behavior risk losing the support of key market segments, especially younger consumers who are more politically and socially engaged. For example Generations Z and Generation Y, frequently align their purchasing decisions with their ethical or political values, and use collective economic pressure to influence corporate behavior and public discourse (Francis & Hoefel, 2018; Kim et al., 2021).

In the context of ongoing geopolitical tensions, the prevalence of consumer activism is predicted to increase, thereby impacting global business dynamics. To operate effectively in this environment, companies need to understand the political and social contexts of the markets in which they are present. Recognizing and addressing the political motivations of consumers is essential for developing resilient strategies capable of withstanding disruptions linked to international conflicts (Gong et al., 2025; Misiewicz & Stepaniuk, 2024; Tsougkou et al., 2025).

Furthermore, the increasing tendency for moralisation of markets in the post globalisation era has resulted in the elevation of the importance of consumer boycotts. Purchasing decisions are now shaped not only by price or functionality, but also by consumers' ethical values and desire for symbolic expression (Kailash et al., 2023; Kutaula et al., 2024). Brands are viewed not only as providers of products but as entities that carry social and political meaning. As a result, companies are increasingly held accountable for their positions on geopolitical issues, labor standards, and cultural associations (Budhathoki et al., 2019; Papaoikonomou et al., 2012; Rindell et al., 2014). This transition towards values-based consumption has resulted in the marketplace becoming a space where ethical and political concerns are actively negotiated. In this context, geopolitical events such as the Israel–Gaza conflict have the potential to significantly impact consumer-brand relationships.

The humanitarian crisis in Gaza and the perceived support of certain global brands for Israeli policies have triggered widespread calls for boycott across many countries, including Türkiye. This chapter introduces a geoeconomic perspective that considers consumer action as a soft tool of influence in global political contexts. In this context, this study explores Turkish consumers' behavioral and attitudinal responses to the Israel-related boycott campaigns, aiming to provide a comprehensive understanding of the motivations, limitations, and generational dynamics that shape boycott participation. The research categorizes consumers into three main groups based on their degree of compliance: full adherents, who strictly comply with the boycott by avoiding all targeted brands; partial adherents, who express support for the boycott in principle but face difficulties in full compliance due to reasons such as brand loyalty, lack of alternatives, and the overwhelming number of brands involved; and non-boycotters, who neither support nor participate in the boycott. It further aims to investigate the generational differences in boycott behavior. Lastly, it introduces a geoeconomic perspective that considers consumer action as a soft tool of influence in global political contexts.

The chapter is structured to reflect both the conceptual and empirical foundations of the research. It begins by reviewing the theoretical background on consumer boycotts, including definitions, historical evolution, and classification frameworks. This is followed by a discussion of key motivations and barriers influencing participation, using interdisciplinary literature in marketing, sociology, and political consumerism. The chapter then integrates a geoeconomic and geopolitical lens, positioning consumer boycotts as strategic responses within broader international market and political systems.

The methodology section outlines the design of the empirical study conducted in Türkiye in December 2023, detailing the sampling strategy, data collection tools, and demographic profile of the 1,383 valid respondents. The findings section presents quantitative results on levels of boycott participation, perceived effectiveness, generational patterns, emotional motivations, brand-switching behavior, and the role of social influence.

The chapter concludes by considering the implications of the findings for international business strategy, consumer research, and geopolitical risk analysis. It emphasizes the growing role of consumers as political and moral agents, whose collective decisions increasingly affect brand reputation, market positioning, and corporate strategy in politically sensitive environments.

Geoeconomics provides a central framework throughout the chapter, illustrating how economic instruments, such as trade restrictions, sanctions, and consumer boycotts, are used to advance or resist political objectives. Within this context, the chapter raises a key question: how do geopolitical conflicts translate into changes in consumer behavior? More specifically, how do individual consumers come to view their purchasing decisions as meaningful actions in global affairs? Addressing these questions helps illuminate the link between micro-level consumer choices and macro-level geopolitical developments.

This study contributes to the literature by focusing on two areas that have received limited attention. First, although consumer boycotts are often examined in relation to ethical or political consumption, there is a lack of research that approaches them from a geoeconomic perspective, linking consumer actions to global political and economic developments. Second, few empirical studies explore how different generations respond to politically motivated boycotts, especially in emerging markets like Türkiye. By addressing these gaps, the study offers a timely analysis of Turkish consumers' responses to the 2023 Israel-related boycott campaigns, connecting moral values, political conflict, and consumer behavior.

1.UNDERSTANDING CONSUMER BOYCOTTS

Boycotts are organized attempts to influence the behavior of a target by encouraging them to refrain from making specific purchases in the marketplace.The term originates from the 1880s when Charles C. Boycott, a land agent in Ireland, was collectively avoided as part of a protest. Since then, the term has evolved to describe a strategic form of resistance in which individuals or groups refuse to maintain economic or social relations with a target organization or nation. Consumer boycotts are a form of consumer activism that uses purchasing decisions to express disapproval. At its core, a boycott is a voluntary act of refraining from consumption with the aim of bringing about change in the behavior or policies of the targeted party. (Friedman, 1999).

Among the various types of boycotts, consumer boycotts have become increasingly prominent as a tool for social and political expression. Defined as organized attempts to influence the behavior of a target by encouraging consumers to refrain from making specific purchases in the marketplace, consumer boycotts differ from individual ethical consumption choices in their collective, strategic, and often publicly organized nature (Friedman, 1985). Unlike private acts of ethical consumption, consumer boycotts are collective and strategically planned efforts that often involve public calls to action. They typically arise in response to corporate misconduct, labor violations, human rights abuses, or broader political issues, and aim to align consumer behavior with personal or shared values (Klein et al., 2004).

Consumer boycotts are a form of protest in which consumers attempt to influence a company's behavior by refusing to make purchases. Rather than being purely instrumental, this behavior often reflects individuals' desire to act in accordance with their moral beliefs. According to John and Klein (2003), some consumers participate in boycotts not only to achieve change, but also to avoid feelings of complicity and to maintain a sense of ethical consistency. In this way, the act of withholding consumption serves both as a means of expressing personal values and as a symbolic effort to hold companies accountable.

1.1. Classification of Consumer Boycotts

The literature presents several frameworks for classifying consumer boycotts based on their origins, objectives, and strategies. One of the most widely cited typologies is offered by Friedman (1999), who categorizes boycotts according to their scope (local, national or international), duration (short, medium, or long term), target (brand, firm, product category or sector), and function (instrumental or expressive). Instrumental boycotts aim to achieve specific and measurable outcomes, such as policy change, product removal, or a public apology. These campaigns are usually structured around clear demands and, in some cases, involve negotiation with the target entity. In contrast, expressive boycotts are primarily symbolic actions that allow participants to express ethical or emotional dissatisfaction, even when no direct outcome is expected. These boycotts function more as declarations of values than as tools for concrete change. Friedman (1999) also distinguishes between direct boycotts, where the targeted entity is the source of grievance, and surrogate boycotts, where a related party is targeted to apply indirect pressure on another actor, often in geopolitical contexts.

Building on Friedman's framework, Sen, Gürhan-Canlı, and Morwitz (2001) propose a classification based on consumer motivation. They differentiate between economically or policy driven boycotts, which are guided by rational decision making and cost-benefit assessments, and ethically or socially driven boycotts, which are rooted in moral values, identity expression, or solidarity with a cause. This distinction shows that while some consumers aim to achieve tangible change, others participate to remain consistent with their ethical beliefs or to affirm their membership in a value-based community. In such cases, the act of boycotting serves an expressive function, regardless of its actual impact (Klein et al., 2004).

In addition to functional classifications, boycotts can also be categorized based on the underlying issues that motivate them. Cause-based typologies offer insight into the moral and political drivers of consumer activism by linking specific grievances to targeted market actions. Friedman (1999) provides a framework that identifies five primary categories: economic, minority, labor-related, religious, and ecological boycotts. Each type reflects a distinct source of discontent and serves as a mobilizing force, often shaped by broader structural conditions or historical contexts.

Economic boycotts typically arise in response to macroeconomic policies, global trade inequalities, or perceived foreign domination of local markets. These campaigns often challenge economic dependency or exploitation, such as in protests against World Trade Organization policies or structural adjustment programs.

Minority boycotts are initiated by or on behalf of marginalized ethnic, racial, or cultural groups and aim to address systemic exclusion, discrimination, or symbolic disrespect. Targets are often companies accused of discriminatory practices or lacking representation of minority identities.

Labor-related boycotts focus on workers' rights and are frequently supported by unions or advocacy organizations. They seek to expose exploitative labor conditions, inadequate wages, or unsafe work environments.

Religious boycotts are motivated by faith-based concerns and typically target brands perceived to violate religious norms or support morally objectionable causes. These boycotts can gain momentum due to the strong moral cohesion within religious communities.

Ecological boycotts are driven by environmental concerns such as sustainability, climate change, and animal welfare. They often target firms involved in environmentally harmful practices like deforestation, pollution, or unethical sourcing (Friedman, 1999).

Building on Friedman's typology, Cruz (2015; 2017) introduces two additional categories of boycotts that reflect the evolving nature of consumer activism: relational boycotts and social boycotts. Relational boycotts target not only specific products or actions, but also the underlying relational structures within organizations—such as dependency, hierarchy, or perceived betrayal (Cruz, 2015). In these cases, consumers withhold consumption as a way to challenge the power dynamics or trust breaches embedded in institutional relationships. In contrast, social boycotts are grounded in group identity and emphasize collective values and solidarity. Here, abstention is used to affirm social alignment and is often shaped by peer expectations and shared moral norms (Cruz, 2017). These two forms illustrate how boycotts can function not only as economic pressure but also as socially situated expressions of group identity and relational protest.

1.2. Motivations Behind Consumer Boycotts

Motivations to participate in consumer boycotts are typically complex and involve a combination of factors. Klein, Smith and John (2004) found that most consumers are driven by a mix of instrumental, expressive, and self-enhancement motivations. Instrumental motivations are based on the belief that participation can contribute to concrete outcomes, such as stopping unethical business practices or shaping public opinion (Granström, 2014). In contrast, expressive motivations are rooted in emotional responses like anger, frustration, or moral outrage, often without a clear expectation of change. Boycotts may also serve self-enhancement functions, allowing individuals to act in line with their values and maintain a sense of personal or social integrity (Granström, 2014; Klein & John, 2001).

Another commonly cited motivation is the desire to maintain what has been referred to as "clean hands", a wish to avoid complicity in unethical behavior by refusing to support the offending company (Klein et al., 2004). The perceived relevance of the issue also plays a role; consumers are more likely to participate in a boycott when the cause aligns with their personal identity, cultural background, or political beliefs (Granström, 2014; Hoffmann, 2013). In some cases, boycott participation is shaped by broader ideological commitments, such as religious or political convictions. These faith based and politically driven boycotts tend to be more enduring and emotionally intense, often continuing beyond the specific event that triggered them (Al-Hyari et al., 2012; Swimberghe et al., 2011).

1.3. Barriers to Boycott Participation

While motivations offer a strong basis for engagement, various structural, contextual, and psychological factors can limit whether supportive attitudes lead to actual boycott behavior. One of the most frequently cited barriers is the perception of ineffectiveness, the belief that individual action will not produce meaningful change or influence the target. When the likelihood of success appears low, consumers are less willing to incur personal inconvenience, even if they agree with the cause (Sen et al., 2001). This barrier is particularly relevant in large scale or international boycotts, where an individual's contribution may feel insignificant within a broader consumer base.

A related issue is the free-rider problem. In this case, individuals support the goals of the boycott but choose not to participate, assuming that the collective action of others will be sufficient. They believe their personal abstention will go unnoticed and that others will bear the burden of change (Sen et al., 2001).

In addition to psychological factors, practical barriers also limit participation in consumer boycotts. A lack of accessible or affordable product alternatives, ingrained consumption habits, or limited knowledge about which brands are implicated often discourages consumers from engaging in boycott behavior (Granström, 2014). These challenges are particularly pronounced in markets dominated by a few multinational firms or in contexts where consumer protection is weak. In such cases, individuals may wish to participate but feel constrained by a lack of viable choices, leading to a sense of dependency and frustration.

Psychological mechanisms further contribute to non-participation. Cognitive dissonance, the discomfort that arises when actions conflict with personal beliefs, can lead consumers to rationalize inaction. They may minimize the significance of the issue, question the credibility of boycott organizers, or frame their purchasing behavior as neutral or unavoidable (Hoffmann, 2013).

Social pressure, though often considered a key driver of boycott behavior, appears to have a variable influence. While earlier research emphasized its role, more recent studies suggest that intrinsically motivated consumers, especially those concerned with environmental or ethical issues, are more likely to act based on personal values than on external expectations (Granström, 2014). This highlights the complex interaction between internal moral convictions and social influence in shaping participation decisions.

1.4. Effectiveness of Consumer Boycotts

The effectiveness of consumer boycotts is generally evaluated along two key dimensions: the extent to which they reduce the target's sales (effectiveness) and whether they achieve their stated objectives (success). However, assessing such impact is often challenging. Companies may be unwilling to disclose detailed sales figures, and behavioral change can occur indirectly or gradually (Friedman, 1999; Klein & John, 2001). In many cases, firms respond to boycott campaigns with symbolic gestures or public relations strategies rather than implementing substantive changes. Some may even preemptively alter their messaging or restructure operations to avoid reputational damage, making it difficult to determine whether consumer demands have truly been addressed (Friedman, 1999; Garrett, 1987; Klein et al., 2004).

Despite these challenges, the literature identifies several conditions that increase the likelihood of a boycott's success. These include the clarity and credibility of campaign goals, broad public support, extensive media coverage, and the perceived reputational risk to the targeted company (Garrett, 1987). Boycotts that articulate specific, realistic objectives tend to be more effective than diffuse campaigns driven primarily by emotion or vague moral appeals. One often-cited example is the international boycott against Shell's Brent Spar platform disposal plan, which led not only to a reversal of company policy but also to significant shifts in public perception, highlighting how organized consumer action can produce both material and symbolic outcomes (Klein et al., 2004).

However, not all boycotts result in such clear victories. Many achieve only partial or delayed outcomes, and some remain largely symbolic. Companies with strong brand loyalty or market dominance may withstand temporary sales losses without addressing the underlying cause of protest. Notably, Klein et al. (2004) emphasize that even when immediate financial effects are limited, boycotts can still inflict long-term reputational harm. Negative shifts in brand perception may erode consumer trust and leave companies vulnerable to sustained criticism. This suggests that the true impact of a boycott lies not only in disrupting consumption, but also in shaping public discourse, altering brand narratives, and redefining stakeholder expectations over time.

1.5. The Role of Social Media in Consumer Boycotts

In the digital age, social media has profoundly reshaped how consumer boycotts are initiated, organized, and sustained. Unlike traditional activism, modern boycotts often gain traction through digital platforms that enable rapid information exchange, emotional engagement, and coordinated action (Mulyono & Rolando, 2025). These platforms serve not only as channels for mobilization but also as interactive spaces where expressive and instrumental motivations converge and evolve.

Platforms such as Twitter, Instagram, and TikTok play a critical role in amplifying individual dissatisfaction into widespread campaigns. For instance, Yüksel, Thai, and Lee (2019) found that online petitions circulated via social media significantly increased support for boycotts against ethically questionable brands. However, the abundance of simultaneous campaigns can create a sense of "choice overload," potentially leading to perceived inefficacy and reduced engagement.

Empirical evidence by Prastiwi and Harsoyo (2025) further supports the role of social media in shaping consumer boycott participation. Digital spaces amplify not only public sentiment and moral outrage but also foster new forms of sociopolitical solidarity that transcend offline affiliations. Dalakas et al. (2023) offer a typology of social media boycott actors, identifying categories such as "crusaders," "moral elites," and "threat-makers," who drive engagement by performing identity and moral alignment rather than relying solely on rational appeals. These roles underscore the dual expressive and strategic nature of digital boycott activism.

Suraji et al. (2023) distinguishing between "hot" (emotion-driven) and "cold" (goal-oriented) phases of participation. Social media often facilitates the shift from the initial emotional response, rooted in values such as religious belief, political anger, or perceived injustice, toward a more outcome-focused engagement. This transition is mediated through ongoing discussions in comment threads, reposts, and hashtag movements, which help sustain participation and maintain campaign visibility.

The case study by Nazahra (2024) provides a concrete illustration of these dynamics. Following public support for Israel by the owners of beauty brands Rose All Day and Esqa, Indonesian consumers leveraged social media not only to express disapproval but also to disseminate brand alternatives and scrutinize supply chains. This shows that digital platforms enable both symbolic protest and tactical redirection of consumption behavior.

For companies, the reputational risks posed by social media-driven boycotts are immediate and far-reaching. Brands that fail to respond adequately to online backlash risk significant losses in consumer trust and financial performance (Mulyono & Rolando, 2025). Conversely, firms that engage transparently and address concerns proactively may mitigate reputational harm and even rebuild public perception.

In summary, social media is not merely a medium for message dissemination; it actively shapes the pace, structure, and emotional tone of consumer activism. Therefore, any comprehensive analysis of modern consumer boycotts—especially those occurring within geopolitical and geoeconomic contexts—must consider the central and transformative role of digital platforms.

2. THE GEOECONOMIC IMPACT OF CONSUMER BOYCOTTS: EVIDENCE FROM GLOBAL CASES AND FIRM-LEVEL REACTIONS

2.1. Geopolitical Triggers and Global Cases of Boycotts

Consumer boycotts, defined as collective and deliberate refusals to purchase specific goods or services in order to express political or social opposition, have increasingly emerged as geoeconomic events with significant implications for global markets and international relations. Empirical evidence suggests that such boycotts can impose considerable economic pressure on targeted firms and countries, influencing their economic performance and global positioning (Tomlin, 2019; Kim, Yan, & Park, 2021; Song, 2020).

Their geoeconomic relevance becomes particularly evident when the target is a multinational corporation or a product strongly associated with a specific national identity. In such cases, consumer action may extend beyond symbolic protest to materially affect trade volumes and bilateral economic relations. One well-documented example is the 2003 U.S. boycott of French goods following France's opposition to the Iraq War. Chavis and Leslie (2009) report that this campaign led to a 13% decline in French wine sales in the United States over a six-month period. Beyond its immediate economic effect, the boycott also influenced broader U.S.–France trade relations and illustrated how consumer sentiment can shape international economic dynamics.

Boycotts initiated as a consequence of geopolitical tensions are frequently characterised by emotional and ideological motivations, which serve to amplify their reputational impact on the targeted countries and industries. The 2019 South Korean boycott of Japanese products, rooted in historical and political grievances, provides a striking example. Kim, Yan, and Park (2021) demonstrate that this boycott resulted in steep reductions in the import of key Japanese consumer goods, including tobacco (−91%), alcoholic beverages (−79%), groceries (−36%), electronics (−35%), and cosmetics (−29%). These changes not only disrupted trade flows but also signaled a shift in consumer identity and national economic alignment.

The South Korean boycott also exemplifies the crucial role of small businesses as actors in boycott dynamics. The involvement of small business owners in boycott campaigns not only reinforced national solidarity but also intensified the economic consequences. Consumers showed a clear preference for stores that openly supported the boycott, turning retail spaces into platforms for expressing collective identity and nationalist sentiment (Song, 2020). These dynamics illustrate the strong link between socio-political contexts and market behavior, and underscore how global supply chains and multinational corporations can be vulnerable to nationalism-driven consumer activism.

One of the most prominent and recent examples of consumer boycotts driven by geopolitical tensions is the global boycott of Israeli-linked products following the outbreak of violence in Gaza in October 2023. This movement was not only a response to perceived Israeli aggression but also served as a form of international solidarity with the Palestinian cause. The boycott had global repercussions, particularly for companies perceived as financially or politically aligned with Israeli interest (Sarjono et al., 2024; Ihssane & Wang, 2024).

In Indonesia, the campaign against Israeli-affiliated products gained considerable traction, driven by a combination of religious authority, social influence, and moral outrage. Key religious institutions, such as the Indonesian Ulema Council, explicitly called on consumers to avoid brands associated with Israel, lending moral weight to the boycott and framing it as a religious obligation (Husaeni & Ayoob, 2025; Awaludin & Al-Khaidar, 2023). Major multinational corporations, including Unilever, faced significant backlash, as consumers shifted their preferences toward local alternatives in response to sustained calls for ethical and nationalistic consumption (Lestari & Jazil, 2024).

The intensity of the Indonesian boycott can be attributed to several overlapping factors: strong religious identification, emotional responses to the conflict, and perceived national duty. Religious leaders were instrumental in legitimizing boycott participation by framing it within a broader narrative of collective responsibility and moral resistance, consistent with previous research on faith-based consumer activism in the Muslim world (Al-Hyari et al., 2012).

In addition, the campaign activated high levels of consumer ethnocentrism, the belief that buying domestic products is morally superior to supporting foreign brands. Indonesian consumers not only chose local alternatives out of availability but also as a form of symbolic resistance and cultural affirmation. This behavior aligns with findings from prior studies that link ethnocentric attitudes with increased boycott participation in times of geopolitical conflict (De Nisco et al., 2020; Sharma et al., 1994).

2.2. Economic and Reputational Impacts of Boycotts

Consumer boycotts also influence financial markets, particularly by affecting shareholder value. Using event study methods, Tomlin (2019) found that boycott announcements had a negative impact on the shareholder wealth of U.S. firms, particularly in cases related to labor disputes, animal rights, and political or religious controversies. Companies operating in highly competitive markets or relying heavily on brand reputation suffered greater losses, highlighting the sensitivity of financial outcomes to shifts in consumer perception and public sentiment.

Beyond financial implications, consumer boycotts can also contribute to broader policy change. Their effectiveness in this regard depends largely on sustained consumer engagement and media visibility. For instance, the anti-Israeli boycotts triggered by Middle East conflicts and the Danish goods boycott following the prophet Muhammad cartoon controversy both illustrate how consumer movements can influence diplomatic relations, trade flows, and even national policies (Tomlin, 2019). These cases show that boycotts are not merely tools of economic pressure but also mechanisms of geopolitical signaling.

In sum, the geoeconomic impact of consumer boycotts reflects a complex interaction between consumer action, political conflict, and economic structure. While their immediate aim may be to punish or pressure a specific target, their broader consequences include altered international trade patterns, shifting corporate strategies, and reputational reconfigurations. As globalization continues to deepen interdependencies, understanding the political dimensions of consumer behavior is essential for firms, policymakers, and global governance actors seeking to manage reputational and economic risk in an increasingly polarized world.

2.3. Corporate Responses to Boycott Campaigns

Companies targeted by boycotts often adopt a range of strategies to manage reputational risk and restore consumer trust. These may include public relations campaigns, clarification statements, temporary disengagement from controversial partnerships, or increasing visibility of local affiliations. In some cases, firms choose to remain silent to avoid escalating political sensitivities, while others attempt to localize their brand image or emphasize corporate social responsibility. For example, in response to public backlash, certain multinational brands operating in Indonesia emphasized their local employment practices and community support programs to mitigate reputational harm (Lestari & Jazil, 2024; Prastiwi & Harsoyo, 2025).

Research shows that these responses vary significantly depending on market conditions, consumer sentiment, and the nature of the boycott. Mulyono and Rolando (2025) argue that companies that respond quickly and transparently to boycotts are more likely to retain consumer goodwill, while firms that fail to acknowledge public concern risk long-term damage to brand equity. Understanding corporate response patterns is essential for evaluating the full impact of consumer activism in politically charged environments.

3. METODOLOGY OF THE STUDY

In recent years, consumer boycotts have gained renewed attention as a form of political and ethical expression, particularly in response to international conflicts and humanitarian crises. The objective of this study is to explore consumers' attitudes and behavioral responses to boycott calls against Israeli products as well as certain multinational brands perceived to support Israel in the context of the recent humanitarian crisis in Gaza. Specifically, the research aims to identify the levels of participation in the boycott, the motivations and perceived barriers to compliance with boycott, generational differences in boycott engagement, perceived effectiveness of the boycott, the influence of social pressure and public visibility and the social and psychological factors influencing consumer behavior in this context. The research seeks to examine the extent and patterns of boycott participation by segmenting consumers into three groups: non-boycotters, strict boycott compliers, and partial boycott compliers. It further aims to investigate the generational differences in boycott behavior.

Data were collected through a structured questionnaire administered via Google Forms during December 2023, a period marked by intense public attention to the Israel- Gaza crisis. The survey link was distributed via social media platforms to maximize reach and ensure a diverse demographic representation across age groups and regions.

A total of 1,545 individuals participated in the survey. After excluding inconsistent entries, 1,383 valid responses were retained for analysis. The demographic profile of the final sample is presented in Table 1. As indicated, the majority of participants are male, born between 1980 and 1995 (classified as Generation Y), married, and hold a bachelor's degree.This profile reflects a digitally literate and socially engaged population segment, likely to encounter and interact with boycott-related content online. The demographic distribution thus provides a suitable basis for analyzing generational dynamics.

Table 1. Demographic Profile of Participants

Demographic features of participants		**Number of Participants**
Gender	Woman	375
	Man	1008
Year of The Birth	1945 - 1965 (Baby Boomers)	254
	1966 - 1979 (Generation X)	494
	1980 - 1995 (Generation Y)	535
	1996 - 2005 (Generation Z)	100
Marital status	Married	1021
	Single	362
Education status	Middle school and below	23
	High school	130
	Associate Degree	86
	Bachelor degree	779
	Master's degree / PhD degree	365

4. FINDINGS OF THE STUDY

The findings of this study reveal that approximately 35% of participants reported some level of engagement in the consumer boycott targeting Israeli products. 65%

of the respondents stated that they had not participated in the boycott and did not intend to do so in the near future. Among the participants, 14% reported that they are actively boycotting all the brands targeted by the campaign. The proportion of those partially participating in the boycott was approximately 21%.

Respondents were categorized into three groups: **strict boycott compliers, partial boycott compliers** and **non-boycotters**. Non-boycotters represent the segment of consumers who did not participate in the boycott and expressed no intention to do so in the future, often citing skeptical about the boycott's effectiveness. Full adherents strictly complied with the boycott, avoiding all listed brands without exception. The strict boycott compliers viewed their consumption as a form of political action, maintaining full alignment with the boycott campaign. Partial adherents expressed support for the boycott in principle but reported difficulties in fully complying. Partial boycott compliers avoided only a portion of the listed brands, they support the boycott ideologically but face barriers to full adherence due to factors like brand loyalty, perceived lack of alternatives, or confusion over extensive boycott lists.

Table 2 shows that regarding generational differences, approximately 50% of Generation Z and 45% of Generation Y respondents strictly or partially complied with the boycott. This rate drops to around 25% among Generation X and Baby Boomer responders.

Table 2. Distribution of Participants by Boycott Participation Status

			1945 - 1965 Baby Boomers	**1966 - 1979 Generation X**	**1980 - 1995 Generation Y**	**1996- 2005 Generation Z**
Are you boycotting Israeli products or products of multinational brands that are claimed to support Israel by not purchasing them?	I have never participated in the boycott and do not plan to do so in the near future. **(non-boycotters)**	% of respondents	74.0%	75.1%	55.3%	51.0%
	I am actively boycotting the brands targeted by the campaign **(strict boycott compliers)**	% of respondents	6.7%	9.5%	20.0%	24%
	I am partially boycotting the brands targeted by the campaign. **(partial boycott compliers)**	% of respondents	19.3%	15.4%	24.7%	26%
Total		% of respondents	100.0%	100.0%	100.0%	100.0%

As illustrated in Table 3, the effectiveness of boycotts is perceived differently depending on the level of participation. An overwhelming majority, exceeding 75%, of those who strictly or partially complied with the boycott perceived the current boycott initiative as lacking both strategic organization and tangible impact. Importantly, this perception varied significantly according to the level of individual engagement. While approximately 90% of non-boycotters regarded the boycott as ineffective, only 23% of strict boycott compliers shared this sentiment, suggesting that engagement may reinforce a belief in efficacy, or alternatively.

Table 3. Perceptions of Boycott Effectiveness by Level of Participation

			Non-boycotters	**Strict boycott compliers**	**Partial boycott compliers**
Do you think the ongoing boycott is effectively organized and impactful?	Yes	%of respondents	1.2%	23.2%	4.6%
	No	% of respondents	90.1%	22.7%	65.4%
	Partially	% of respondents	8.7%	54.1%	30%
Total		% of respondents	100.0%	100.0%	100.0%

As shown in Table 4, a substantial majority of respondents (76.2%) reported that the boycott lists included brands or products they regularly consume. This intersection between personal consumption habits and boycott targets emerges as a structural barrier, making it more difficult for consumers to disengage from brands that are deeply embedded in their daily routines and market environments. The habitual use and widespread availability of these products appear to reduce the likelihood of full boycott participation, even among individuals who are morally or politically supportive of the cause.

Table 4. Prevalence of Frequently Used Brands Among Boycotted Brands

		% of respondents
Are there any brands/products that you frequently purchase among those that have been boycotted?	Yes	76.2%
	No	23.8%

When responders were asked, *"Do the people around you, whose opinions you value, actively participate in the boycott?"*, approximately one-third (32.4%) responded affirmatively. This suggests that social context and the perceived behaviors of trusted individuals may influence consumer attitudes toward boycott participation. However, the presence of supportive peers does not necessarily guarantee individual engagement, indicating that personal motivations and constraints still play a critical role. Table 5 presents the distribution of responses to this question.

Table 5. Perceptions of Boycott Participation in Respondents' Immediate Social Environment

		% of respondents
Do the people around you, whose opinions you value, actively participate in the boycott?	Yes	32.4%
	No	67.6%

Moreover, as shown in Table 6, approximately 28.5% of respondents reported receiving explicit encouragement from trusted individuals to participate in the boycott. While this figure indicates a modest level of normative pressure, it also implies that boycott participation is largely self motivated rather than socially imposed, an observation consistent with theories emphasizing intrinsic over extrinsic motivations in ethical consumption.

Table 6. Perceived Encouragement to Participate in the Boycott by Trusted Contacts

		% of respondents
Have people whose opinions you value encouraged you to participate in the boycott?	Yes	28.5%
	No	71.5%

Approximately 67% of responders stated that the boycott against Israel is not important to them, whereas 24% indicated that they consider the boycott important. The level of importance attributed to the boycott significantly differs by participation status: those who strictly complied with boycott rate its importance very high (mean value: 4.78/5.00), while non-boycotters rate it very low (mean value: 1.30/5.00). Another striking result is that members of Generation Z and Generation Y attach more importance to the boycott than Generation X and Baby Boomers.

Consistent with the perceived importance of the boycott, around 67% of responders stated they would not feel uncomfortable being seen purchasing or consuming products from the boycotted brands. On the other hand, 23% expressed discomfort when seen consuming boycotted products. Those who strictly complied with boycott reported significantly higher levels of discomfort when seen purchasing these brands (mean value: 3.85/5.00) compared to non-boycotters (mean value: 1.62/5.00). Among generational groups, Generation Z reported the highest discomfort in such scenarios. The findings related to perceived importance of the boycott and discomfort in purchasing boycotted brands are presented in Tables 7 and Table 8.

Table 7. Perceived Importance of the Boycott and Discomfort in Purchasing Boycotted Brands by Boycott Participation Status

	Non-boycotters	**Strict boycott compliers**	**Partial boycott compliers.**	**Total**
	Mean Value	**Mean Value**	**Mean Value**	**Mean Value**
I would feel uncomfortable if other boycott participants saw me purchasing or consuming products from the boycotted brands	1.62	3.85	2.8	2.18
Please indicate how important this boycott is to you.	1.30	4.78	3.23	2.19

Table 8. Perceived Importance of the Boycott and Discomfort in Purchasing Boycotted Brands by Generation

	1945-1965 Baby Boomers	1966-1979 Generation X	1980-1995 Generation Y	1996-2005 Generation Z	Total
	Mean Value	Mean Value	Mean Value	Mean Value	Mean Value
I would feel uncomfortable if other boycott participants saw me purchasing or consuming products from the boycotted brands	1.84	1.97	2.41	2.74	2.18
Please indicate how important this boycott is to you.	1.75	1.90	2.53	2.87	2.19

Non-Boycotters' Reasons for Not Participating in the Boycott

Among non-boycotters, individuals who have never participated in the boycott and do not intend to do so, the primary reasons for non-participation include the belief that the boycott will not help resolve the humanitarian crisis in Gaza (45%) and the perception that it will not be effective (36%). Other reasons cited include the excessive number of brands included in the boycott list (4%), the fact that they do not use the listed products in the first place (4%), and the lack of available alternatives to the boycotted brands (3%).

Partial Boycott Compliers' Reasons for Limited Participation

Among partial boycott compliers, individuals who only partially participate in the boycott, the main reasons for limited participation include the belief that the boycott will not resolve the issues in Gaza (29%) and the perception that it is unlikely to be effective (17%). However, these reasons are less prominent compared to those reported by non-boycotters. Additionally, the large number of brands included in the boycott list (17%) and the absence of suitable alternatives to the boycotted brands (14%) are also key factors contributing to partial participation.

Strict Boycott Compliers' Main Motivations

Similar to non-boycotters and partial boycott compliers, strict boycott compliers are also aware that the boycott may not resolve the humanitarian crisis in Gaza. Nevertheless, 29% stated that they participate to express their reaction and contribute to the boycott, even if only in a small way. Additionally, 25% of strict boycott compliers expressed a desire to financially disadvantage the supporting brands, while an additional 25% participated with the intention of expressing their discontent towards brands that provide support to Israel.

Table 9 shows that 89.2% of those who strictly complies with the boycott stated that they have stopped purchasing brands they frequently used during the boycott period. An additional 9.2% reported that, in response to the boycott call, they have significantly reduced their consumption or purchasing of these brands.

Table 9. Change in Purchasing Behavior of Frequently Used Brands During the Boycott Period

		% of respondents
During the boycott period, have you stopped purchasing brands that you frequently used before the boycott?	Yes	89.2%
	Reduced consumption / purchasing	9.2%
	No	1.6%

Approximately 80% of those who strictly or partially complied with the boycott stated that they are able to refrain from purchasing the brands included in the boycott. Around 70% reported feeling good about participating in the boycott, while 60% indicated that they would feel guilty if they purchased boycotted brands. Additionally, 65% believe they can find alternative brands to replace the boycotted ones, 62% are willing to compromise on quality to avoid buying from those brands, and 60% are willing to pay more for alternative products.

Table 10 shows that generation Z, in particular, showed higher levels of agreement with these statements compared to other generations. They are more likely to report feeling good about participating in the boycott, feeling guilty if they purchase boycotted brands, being willing to pay more for alternatives, and being prepared to sacrifice quality rather than purchase from boycotted brands.

Table 10. Mean Value by Generation for Statements Related to Boycott Behavior

	1945-1965 Baby Boomers	1966-1979 Generation X	1980-1995 Generation Y	1996-2005 Generation Z	Total
	Mean Value	Mean Value	Mean Value	Mean Value	Mean Value
I can refrain from purchasing brands included in the boycott	3.83	4.26	4.32	4.29	4.23
I would feel guilty if I purchased products from the boycotted brands.	2.98	3.68	3.76	4.19	3.68
I feel better when I participate in the boycott	3.29	3.99	4.13	4.38	4.00
I am willing to compromise on quality rather than purchase boycotted brands.	3.35	3.89	3.91	4.02	3.84
I am confident that I can find alternative brands to replace the boycotted ones..	3.64	3.85	3.90	3.96	3.86
I would pay more to buy alternatives instead of products from the boycotted brands.	3.02	3.67	3.75	4.13	3.67

As demonstrated in Table 11, approximately 45.3% of respondents who strictly or partially complied with the boycott indicated that, due to the substantial number of brands to be boycotted and to avoid confusion, they frequently preferred local brands during the designated boycott period.

Table 11. Local Brand Preference Among Boycott Participants to Avoid Brand Confusion

		% of respondents
During the boycott period, do you prefer local brands in order to avoid confusion caused by the large number of brands included in the boycott?	Yes	28.1%
	Frequently	45.3%
	No	26.6%

5.DISCUSSION

The findings of this study offer important insights into the motivations, perceptions, and behavioural patterns of Turkish consumers in response to the boycott of Israeli-affiliated products amid ongoing geopolitical conflict. Beyond contributing to the literature on consumer boycotts, this chapter enhances our understanding of how geoeconomic and geopolitical dynamics increasingly intersect with consumer behaviour, highlighting the strategic importance of consumer agency in shaping international business environments.

5.1. Generational Differences in Boycott Participation

A key observation is the clear generational divide in boycott participation. As shown in Table 12, Generation Z and Generation Y report the highest levels of boycott participation, both strict and partial. They also score highest in perceived importance of the boycott and discomfort when buying boycotted brands. In contrast, Generation X and Baby Boomers exhibit lower levels across these measures. These values are relative and based on mean scores reported in Findings. "High" indicates significantly higher averages compared to other groups.

Table 12. Generational Differences in Boycott Participation and Attitudes

	1945-1965 Baby Boomers	1966-1979 Generation X	1980-1995 Generation Y	1996-2005 Generation Z
Boycott Participation	Low	Low–Moderate	Moderate–High	High
Discomfort When Buying Boycotted Brands	Low	Low–Moderate	Moderate–High	High
Importance Attributed to Boycott	Low	Low–Moderate	Moderate–High	High

This finding aligns with prior research highlighting that younger consumers tend to be more politically engaged, ethically oriented and responsive to social justice issues. For instance, Kim, Yan, and Park (2021) demonstrate that younger generations in South Korea were the most active participants in the boycott of Japanese products, driven by national identity and moral conviction. Similarly, Francis and Hoefel (2018) describe Generation Z as "True Gen," emphasizing their heightened awareness of social, political, and environmental issues, as well as their tendency to align consumption with personal values. Their higher levels of emotional engagement and willingness to pay more for alternatives or compromise on product quality indicate a strong alignment between moral identity and consumer behavior, reinforcing the expressive function of boycotts outlined by Friedman (1999).

5.2. Barriers and Motivational Tensions

Despite this, the overall participation rate in the boycott remains moderate, with over 65% of respondents reporting no engagement and no future intention to participate. The main barriers cited, perceived ineffectiveness of the boycott and the belief that it will not resolve the situation in Gaza, correspond to the well-documented free-rider problem and perceived lack of individual impact (John & Klein, 2003; Sen et al., 2001; Zheng, 2019). These barriers appear particularly prevalent among older generations, who also report significantly lower levels of discomfort when purchasing boycotted brands.

In addition to generational differences, the study also reveals the nuanced role of subjective norms in shaping boycott behavior. Approximately one-third of participants observed boycott participation among their social environmentsocial and nearly 29% reported receiving direct encouragement to participate. While these numbers suggest that social influence is present, it is not dominant, particularly when compared to the strength of internalized motivations observed among younger generations. This nuance aligns with Granström's (2014) findings that intrinsic drivers may outweigh social pressures in ethically charged consumer contexts.

5.3. Structural Constraints and Brand Confusion

Another striking finding is the discrepancy between consumer intentions and structural constraints. Although many strictly or partially complied with the boycott report moral or emotional motivation, practical issues, such as the ubiquity of targeted brands, the lack of alternatives, and brand confusion due to extensive boycott lists, hinder fully adhere to the boycott. This highlights the tension between consumer ideals and market realities, echoing Cruz's (2015; 2017) concepts of relational and social boycotts, where protest operates not only through rational calculation but also through symbolic and communal acts of identity expression.

5.4. Preference for Local Brands as Resistance

The preference for local brands observed among those who strictly or partially complied with the boycott appears to be a calculated and pragmatic response to the complexity of boycott implementation. Faced with long and sometimes ambiguous boycott lists, consumers may turn to domestic brands as a way to simplify decision-making and avoid potential inconsistencies. This behavior also reflects a symbolic alignment with national values and collective identity. Prior studies have shown that in politically charged contexts, consumers often choose local products as expressions of resistance and solidarity (Song, 2020). This tendency is strongly associated with consumer ethnocentrism, the belief that domestic products are morally superior and more appropriate than foreign alternatives (Sharma, Shimp, & Shin, 1994). Lekakis (2017) similarly argues that consumption becomes a form of political expression during geopolitical crises. De Nisco et al. (2020) further demonstrate that national image and cultural affinity play a critical role in shaping consumer preferences during times of conflict. These findings suggest that consumer boycotts can foster a type of economic nationalism, with implications that extend beyond individual purchase decisions to broader geoeconomic trends.

5.5. Cross-Cultural Comparison

While this study focuses on the case of Türkiye, placing its findings alongside other geopolitical boycott cases helps highlight how cultural, historical, and institutional contexts shape consumer activism. In South Korea, the 2019 boycott of Japanese goods was rooted in unresolved historical tensions and framed as a nationalistic act of collective memory, resulting in widespread public participation and support from local businesses (Kim et al., 2021). In contrast, the Indonesian boycott of Israeli-affiliated brands during the Gaza conflict was primarily driven by religious authority and moral obligation, with strong endorsement from Islamic organizations and opinion leaders (Husaeni & Ayoob, 2025). The United States' boycott of French goods in 2003, triggered by political disagreement over the Iraq War, was more symbolic and short-lived, reflecting a different form of diplomatic consumer protest (Chavis & Leslie, 2009).

Compared to these cases, the Turkish boycott campaign exhibits a hybrid profile. It combines emotional and moral motivations with structural limitations such as brand dependence and market concentration. Unlike the centralized religious influence in Indonesia or the high degree of national unity observed in South Korea, the Turkish case is characterized by digital mobilization, generational fragmentation, and ambivalence about boycott efficacy. These cross-cultural differences underscore the importance of context in shaping how consumers respond to geopolitical crises and how activism is expressed through market behavior.

5.6. Symbolic and Political Dimensions of Consumer Agency

Consumer boycotts should be understood not only as economic actions but as symbolic expressions of moral and political agency. Among younger, ideologically motivated consumers, in particular, boycotts serve as a means of enacting values and demanding accountability from corporations and governments. Rather than functioning solely as transactional tools of protest, they contribute to shaping brand legitimacy, influencing international trade relations, and pressuring multinational firms to revise their global strategies. For scholars, policymakers, and business leaders, recognizing the multi-layered nature of contemporary boycott behavior is essential to navigating an increasingly politicized and value-driven consumer landscape.

The empirical evidence collated in this study goes beyond merely documenting a localised consumer reaction; it demonstrates how micro-level consumer sentiment can evolve into a form of informal geoeconomic intervention. In politically volatile contexts, such as the Israel–Gaza conflict, it has been demonstrated that boycott campaigns transcend the boundaries of ethical consumption and emerge as citizen-led mechanisms of geopolitical signalling. These acts, while decentralised and often spontaneous, effectively generate economic pressure and convey sociopolitical resistance without state mediation. This phenomenon is especially pertinent in emerging markets such as Türkiye, where civil society engagement is becoming increasingly digital, value-driven, and emotionally resonant.

5.7. Structural Constraints and Strategic Implications for Business

The intersection of market structure and the practical viability of boycotts ultimately unveils a pivotal paradox concerning consumer agency within the context of hyper-globalised economies. Despite the fact that digital platforms have enhanced the capacity for mobilisation of consumer boycotts, the dominance of a small number of multinational brands often constrain consumers' ability to act in accordance with their political or ethical intentions. This disjunction between symbolic resistance and structural limitations reflects a broader geoeconomic reality in which consumers possess increased ideological agency but remain embedded within systems that restrict their behavioural options. For firms operating in geopolitically sensitive markets, this underscores the importance of viewing consumer sentiment not merely as a reputational concern, but as a strategic geopolitical variable with the potential to influence market dynamics, investment decisions, and supply chain configurations. In this context, companies must proactively assess boycott risks as part of their political risk management strategies, develop culturally adaptive communication plans, and monitor localised consumer sentiment to pre-empt reputational fallout or shifts in demand. Region-specific sensitivity and responsiveness to activist consumer behaviour will be essential to maintaining brand resilience across divergent political landscapes

Ultimately, recognising consumer boycotts as strategic, affective, and ideologically motivated instruments will be essential for interpreting the evolving logic of global markets in an era of geopolitical uncertainty.

5.8.Limitations of the Study

This study has several limitations that should be acknowledged. First, the research is geographically limited to Türkiye, which constrains the generalizability of its findings. A comparative approach including consumers from other countries would provide broader insights into the global dynamics of boycott behavior. Second, the study is based on data collected during a specific period of heightened public attention following the escalation of the Gaza conflict. As such, it does not capture the long-term effects or behavioral shifts that may occur as public interest fluctuates. Third, the exclusive use of an online survey for data collection may have resulted in the underrepresentation of certain demographic groups, particularly older individuals or those with limited internet access, thus potentially skewing the sample toward younger, more digitally engaged respondents. This methodological limitation may restrict the diversity of perspectives reflected in the data.

5.9. Suggestions for Future Research

Future research could benefit from a comparative and cross-cultural design to explore how consumer boycotts unfold in different geopolitical and socio-cultural contexts. Specifically, analyzing responses to similar geopolitical events across multiple countries would help illuminate variations in consumer activism driven by cultural, political, or economic factors. Longitudinal studies are also recommended to assess the durability of boycott participation and track changes in consumer attitudes over time. In addition, greater emphasis should be placed on the role of digital platforms in mobilizing and sustaining boycott campaigns. Further investigation is needed into how social media dynamics shape the spread, emotional tone, and impact of boycott participation. Looking ahead, emerging technologies such as artificial intelligence, blockchain, and algorithmic content curation may transform the way boycotts are organized and amplified. These tools could enhance the personalization and speed of mobilization, but also introduce new challenges such as misinformation, digital manipulation, or ethical concerns related to surveillance and data privacy. Future studies should consider how these technological shifts might reshape the scope, strategy, and consequences of consumer activism in increasingly digital political environments.

REFERENCES

Al-Hyari, K., Alnsour, M., Al-Weshah, G., & Haffar, M. (2012). Religious beliefs and consumer behaviour: From loyalty to boycotts. *Journal of Islamic Marketing, 3*(2), 155–174. DOI: 10.1108/17590831211232564

Awaludin, A. A., & Al-Khaidar, M. A. (2023). Opinion leaders and boycott intentions: Factors influencing consumer behavior in support of Israel Boycott. *Journal of Digital Marketing and Halal Industry, 5*(2), 243–264. DOI: 10.21580/jdmhi.2023.5.2.20166

Budhathoki, P., Adhikari, K., & Koirala, R. (2019). The Gap between Attitudes and Behavior in Ethical Consumption: A Critical Discourse. *Quest Journal of Management and Social Sciences, 1*(2), 285–295. DOI: 10.3126/qjmss.v1i2.27446

Chavis, L., & Leslie, P. (2009). Consumer boycotts: The impact of the Iraq war on French wine sales in the U.S. *Quantitative Marketing and Economics, 7*(1), 37-67. https://doi.org/y Cruz, B.d.P.A. and Botelho, D. (2015), "Proposition of the relational boycott", Management Research, Vol. 13 No. 3, pp. 315-333. https://doi.org/DOI: 10.1007/s11129-008-9043-

Cruz, B. D. P. A. (2017). Social boycott. *Revista brasileira de gestão de negocios, 19*, 05-29. https://doi.org/DOI: 10.7819/rbgn.v0i0.2868

Dalakas, V., Melancon, J. P., & Szczytynski, I. (2023). Brands in the eye of the storm: Navigating political consumerism and boycott calls on social media. *Qualitative Market Research, 26*(1), 1–18. DOI: 10.1108/QMR-07-2021-0089

De Nisco, A., Massi, M., & Papadopoulos, N. (2020). Partners or foes? Cross-country consumer animosity, ethnocentrism, and nationalism in times of international crisis. *Journal of Global Marketing, 33*(3), 207–222. DOI: 10.1080/08911762.2020.1744209

Francis, T., & Hoefel, F. (2018). True Gen': Generation Z and its implications for companies. *McKinsey & Company, 12*(2), 1-10.

Friedman, M. (1985). Consumer boycotts in the United States, 1970–1980: Contemporary events in historical perspective. *The Journal of Consumer Affairs, 19*(1), 96–117. DOI: 10.1111/j.1745-6606.1985.tb00346.x

Friedman, M. (1999). *Consumer boycotts: Effecting change through the marketplace and the media*. Routledge., DOI: 10.4324/9780203900406

Garrett, D. E. (1987). The effectiveness of marketing policy boycotts: Environmental opposition to marketing. *Journal of Marketing, 51*(2), 46–57. DOI: 10.1177/002224298705100204

Gong, Y., Tang, X., Chang, E. C., & Wan, F. (2025). EXPRESS: Corporate Sociopolitical Activism and Language Strategies for Mitigating Animosity in a Host Country. *Journal of International Marketing*. Advance online publication. DOI: 10.1177/1069031X251319018

Granström, J. (2014). *Consumer motivations to boycott: Focus on non-green products. Master*. Aalborg University.

Hoffmann, S. (2013). Are boycott motives rationalizations? *Journal of Consumer Behaviour, 12*(3), 214–222. DOI: 10.1002/cb.1418

Husaeni, U. A., & Ayoob, M. A. (2025). Determinants of Muslim's intention to boycott Israel-affiliated products: Evidence from Indonesia. *Jurnal Ekonomi & Keuangan Islam, 11*(1), 14–28. DOI: 10.20885/JEKI.vol11.iss1.art2

Ihssane, A., & Wang, W. (2024). Boycotting effects on the Europe and America corporates amid Gaza-Israel conflict. *International Journal of Research Publication and Reviews, 5*(4), 5150–5157. DOI: 10.55248/gengpi.5.0424.1057

John, A., & Klein, J. (2003). The boycott puzzle: Consumer motivations for purchase sacrifice. *Management Science, 49*(9), 1196–1209. DOI: 10.1287/mnsc.49.9.1196.16569

Kailash, M. S. R., Joshi, C., Desai, P. R., Teferra, N. B., & Radhakrishnan, S. (2023). The Rise of Ethical Consumerism. *Marketing Strategies for the Conscious Buyer., 44*(8), 1329–1337.

Kim, C., Yan, X., & Park, S. (2021). Do consumer boycotts really matter with global companies? The moderating effect of gender differences. *International Journal of Emerging Markets, 18*(12), 5707–5726. DOI: 10.1108/IJOEM-03-2021-0312

Klein, J. G., & John, A. (2001). *Exploring motivations for participation in a consumer boycott* (Working Paper No. 01-701). INSEAD.

Klein, J. G., Smith, N. C., & John, A. (2004). Why we boycott: Consumer motivations for boycott participation. *Journal of Marketing, 68*(3), 92–109. DOI: 10.1509/jmkg.68.3.92.34770

Kutaula, S., Gillani, A., Gregory-Smith, D., & Bartikowski, B. (2024). Ethical consumerism in emerging markets: Opportunities and challenges. *Journal of Business Ethics, 191*(4), 651–673. DOI: 10.1007/s10551-024-05657-4

Lekakis, E. J. (2017). Economic nationalism and the cultural politics of consumption under austerity: The rise of ethnocentric consumption in Greece. *Journal of Consumer Culture, 17*(2), 286–302. DOI: 10.1177/1469540515586872

Lestari, P., & Jazil, T. (2024). The role of religiosity, consumer animosity, and ethnocentrism in explaining the boycott motivation. *Journal of Islamic Economics and Finance Studies*, *5*(1), 134–152. DOI: 10.47700/jiefes.v5i1.7755

Misiewicz, C., & Stepaniuk, K. (2024). CONSUMER ACTIVISM ON SOCIAL MEDIA DURING GEOPOLITICAL CONFLICT. *Scientific Papers of Silesian University of Technology. Organization & Management / Zeszyty Naukowe Politechniki Slaskiej. Seria Organizacji i Zarzadzanie*, (208). Advance online publication. DOI: 10.29119/1641-3466.2024.208.19

Mulyono, H., & Rolando, B. (2025). Consumer boycott movements: Impact on brand reputation and business performance in the digital age. *Multidisciplinary Reviews*, *8*, e2025291. DOI: 10.31893/multirev.2025291

Nazahra, G. N. (2024). Analysis of public responses to political controversies in the beauty industry: A case study of Rose All Day and Esqa Brand owners in support of Israel. *Gema Wiralodra*, *15*(1), 350–354. DOI: 10.31943/gw.v15i1.630

Papaoikonomou, E., Valverde, M., & Ryan, G. (2012). Articulating the Meanings of Collective Experiences of Ethical Consumption. *Journal of Business Ethics*, *110*, 15–32. DOI: 10.1007/s10551-011-1144-y

Prastiwi, A., & Harsoyo, T. D. (2025). Analysis of the Influence of Consumer Animosity, Religiusity, and Social Media Sentiment on Product Boycott Decisions. *East Asian Journal of Multidisciplinary Research*, *4*(1), 255–270. DOI: 10.55927/eajmr.v4i1.12980

Rindell, A., Strandvik, T., & Wilén, K. (2014). Ethical consumers' brand avoidance. *Journal of Product and Brand Management*, *23*(2), 114–120. DOI: 10.1108/JPBM-09-2013-0391

Sarjono, H., Khairunnisa, A. S., Sandy, C. A. N., Leono, M., Melisa, & Soeratin, B. S. (2024). The effect of the Israeli and Palestinian war boycott on Starbucks finances. *Jurnal Ekonomi dan Statistik Indonesia*, *4*(1), 13–22. https://doi.org/DOI: 10.11594/jesi.04.01.02

Sen, S., Gürhan-Canli, Z., & Morwitz, V. (2001). Withholding consumption: A social dilemma perspective on consumer boycotts. *The Journal of Consumer Research*, *28*(3), 399–417. DOI: 10.1086/323729

Sharma, S., Shimp, T. A., & Shin, J. (1994). Consumer ethnocentrism: A test of antecedents and moderators. *Journal of the Academy of Marketing Science*, *23*(1), 26–37. DOI: 10.1177/0092070395231004

Song, E. (2020). South Korean Consumers' Attitudes toward Small Business Owners Participating in the 2019 Anti-Japan Boycott. *Social Sciences*, *9*(5), 74. DOI: 10.3390/socsci9050074

Suraji, R., Haque, M., Yasir, M., & Istianingsih, I. (2023). Dynamics of consumer boycotts: Exploring the interplay of expressive and instrumental factors. *Dinasti International Journal of Digital Business Management*, *1*(2), 50–57. DOI: 10.38035/dit.v1i2.309

Swimberghe, K., Flurry, L. A., & Parker, J. M. (2011). Consumer Religiosity: Consequences for Consumer Activism in the United States. *Journal of Business Ethics*, *103*, 453–467. DOI: 10.1007/s10551-011-0873-2

Tomlin, K. M. (2019). Assessing the Efficacy of Consumer Boycotts of U.S. Target Firms: A Shareholder Wealth Analysis. *Southern Economic Journal*, *86*(2), 503–529. DOI: 10.1002/soej.12389

Tsougkou, E., Sykora, M., Elayan, S., Ifie, K., & Oliveira, J. S. (2025). Peace brand activism: Global brand responses to the war in Ukraine. *Journal of Public Policy & Marketing*, *44*(1), 100–121. DOI: 10.1177/07439156241289079

Yüksel, Ü., Thai, N. T., & Lee, M. S. W. (2019). Boycott them! No, boycott this! Do choice overload and small-agent rationalization inhibit the signing of anti-consumption petitions? *Psychology and Marketing*, *36*(9), 1–15. DOI: 10.1002/mar.21293

Zheng, Y. (2020). Non-organized boycott: Alliance advantage and free riding incentives in uneven wars of attrition. *Eurasian Econ Rev*, *10*, 123–141. DOI: 10.1007/s40822-019-00138-w

Chapter 9
New Space as a Geopolitical and Economic Frontier:
Space Security and International Business Dynamics

Gianni De Bruyn
https://orcid.org/0000-0002-4517-1140
San Diego State University, USA

Jingning Ao
https://orcid.org/0000-0003-1866-8415
Morgan State University, USA

ABSTRACT

The emerging space economy is being reshaped by and reshaping the current geopolitical and geoeconomic landscape, with significant implications for international business. As governments and commercial actors compete for strategic dominance in outer space, shifts in space governance, technological advancements, and the rise of private space ventures are influencing global trade and investment. The dual-use (military and commercial) nature of many space technologies introduces both risks and opportunities for businesses. We discuss the evolution of space as a geopolitical and economic frontier, highlighting its historical context, technological developments, and the interplay between public and private actors. We propose a theoretical framework that analyzes space security through a geopolitical lens, emphasizing the cyclical relationship between technology, governance, and inter-

DOI: 10.4018/979-8-3373-1265-1.ch009

national relations. Additionally, we incorporate interdisciplinary theories to deepen understanding of space governance complexities and their implications for global business strategies and policymaking.

INTRODUCTION

The rapid growth of the New Space sector—fueled by advancements in artificial intelligence (AI) technologies, reusable rockets, frequent spaceflight launches, and a surge in private investment, 72% of which occurred between 2015 and 2020 (Klein & Boensch, 2024)—has transformed the space economy into a dynamic geopolitical and economic frontier. Space technologies, with approximately 95% possessing dual-use capabilities for both commercial and military purposes (Johnson-Freese, 2007), now support critical global infrastructures, including GPS for precision navigation, communication networks, and disaster response mechanisms (Cobb, 2024; Zhou & Wang, 2024). New Space—the commercialization of space driven by private investment and market expansion (Klein & Boensch, 2024)—is reshaping global business strategies, cross-border investments, and international security dynamics. Despite the sector's growing importance, space technologies and their geopolitical implications remain underexplored in international business literature.

Technological innovations, especially dual-use technologies with both civilian and military applications, blur the lines between commercial and defense activities, heightening the need for space security. Studying the dynamics between space security and international business is crucial, as the unique physical environment of outer space presents significant challenges and unparalleled opportunities (Sweijs & Ellison, 2024). Governments and commercial actors are locked in fierce competition for space dominance, viewing it as a pathway to technological supremacy, military power, and economic leadership (Archinard, 2024). Recognizing the strategic importance of space is essential for scholars, policymakers, and business leaders to address challenges and seize opportunities in this rapidly evolving domain.

Therefore, this chapter investigates how multinational enterprises (MNEs) and New Space actors can adapt their strategies to address escalating geopolitical tensions while leveraging technological innovation and fostering sustainable growth. We propose a theoretical framework that analyzes space security from a geopolitical perspective, highlighting the interplay between government and commercial actors and the pivotal role of emerging technologies in shaping New Space. Additionally, we outline the theoretical implications from interdisciplinary perspectives, incorporating complexity theory, securitization theory, and hegemonic stability theory to better illuminate the geopolitical and economic dynamics of space as a frontier.

SPACE AS A GEOPOLITICAL AND ECONOMIC FRONTIER

Historical Context: Peaceful Use of Space

Space has long captured the imagination of humanity, and its role as a geopolitical and economic domain has evolved significantly since the mid-20th century. Initially, the era of space exploration was marked by an emphasis on peaceful collaboration, embodied in the Outer Space Treaty (OST) of 1967. The OST established the foundational legal framework for space activities, designating outer space as the global commons to be used for peaceful purposes. This commitment to cooperation was further exemplified in key milestones of international collaboration, such as the Apollo-Soyuz Test Project in 1975 (US-Soviet Union) and the development of the International Space Station in an effort to advance scientific knowledge. These laid the groundwork for a vision of space as a shared domain, although subsequent geopolitical and economic shifts would introduce new complexities and challenges to this ideal.

While the OST provides a robust framework for the peaceful use of outer space, it faces significant limitations in addressing the complexities of the current geopolitical and technological landscape. One prominent gap lies in its inability to regulate novel strategic advancements, such as anti-satellite weapons. Another shortcoming is the OST's lack of provisions for addressing advancements in AI. The increasing integration of AI in space systems raises questions about accountability, ethical use, and the potential for AI-driven conflict escalation.

Finally, the OST is silent on the commercialization and privatization of space resources. With private companies spearheading initiatives to extract resources from celestial bodies, the treaty's prohibition against national sovereignty over celestial bodies does not explicitly address commercial ownership, complicating property rights (Foss & Foss, 2005). This legal ambiguity risks creating conflicts between governments and commercial entities.

The Ongoing U.S.-China Rivalry in Space

The commercialization of space has transformed traditional alliances, with private actors and emerging powers now shaping global space governance (Archinard, 2024; Zhou & Wang, 2024). This evolving landscape creates a divide in views: while China and Russia advocate for binding treaties to prevent space weaponization, the U.S. and its allies favor non-binding guidelines that acknowledge weaponization as inevitable (Zhou & Wang, 2024). These competing views illustrate the geopolitical complexities surrounding space governance.

While China's space diplomacy positions it as a collaborative global leader (Pollpeter, 2024), the U.S. and its allies focus on new technologies and private innovation to challenge China's goals and maintain competitiveness in space governance. China has rapidly advanced its space capabilities since 2000, becoming a leader in space launches and holding the second-largest number of satellites in orbit after the U.S. (Pollpeter, 2024). Through initiatives like the "Space Silk Road," an extension of its Belt and Road Initiative (BRI), China leverages its Beidou satellite system to integrate precision navigation and timing services into its geopolitical strategy (The Strategist, 2017). This initiative could make BRI states reliant on Chinese space services, cementing Beijing's influence over their economies and locking out Western companies from critical markets (The Strategist, 2017). Meanwhile, the U.S. space ecosystem thrives on diversity, with a robust mix of large corporations and innovative start-ups that dominate both traditional and emerging space sectors, such as space mining and space tourism (Morin & Tepper, 2023). Private organizations (including publicly traded or privately owned companies, non-profit organizations, universities, and business associations) comprise 92.7% of U.S. space entities, compared to 61.5% in China, reflecting the U.S.'s lead in fostering commercial space innovation (Morin & Tepper, 2023). As shown in Figure 1, Morin and Tepper (2023) state that there is currently no evidence to indicate that China will reach the same level as the United States in the near future.

Figure 1. Cumulative public and private organizations in the U.S. and China, 1960–2020 (Picture source: Morin & Tepper, 2023)

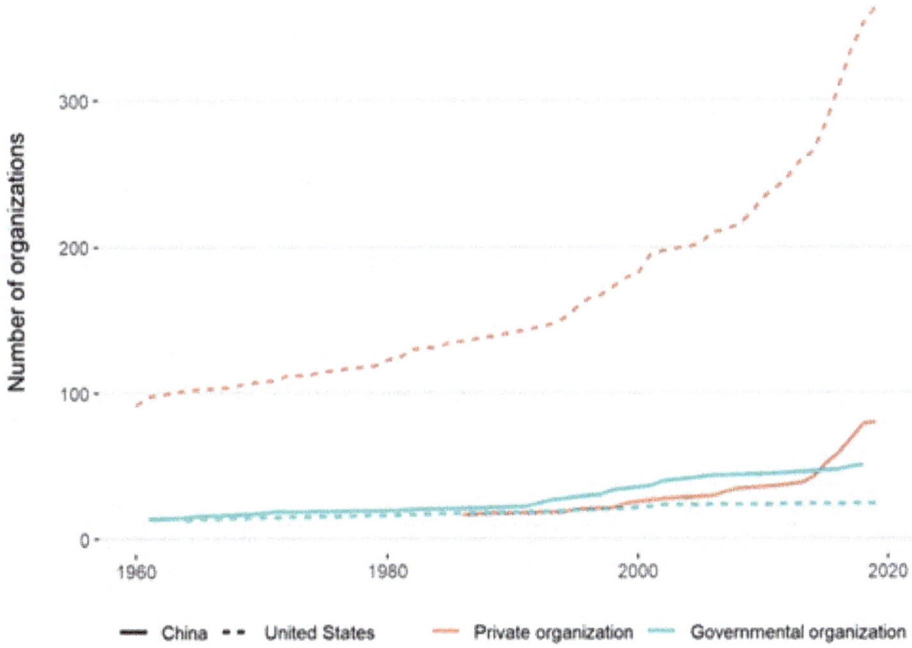

Space is becoming the "new high ground" of military and economic competition, and the U.S.-China rivalry highlights both risks and opportunities for commercial actors. The risks include geopolitical tensions arising from regulations driven by the U.S.-China rivalry in space, as well as the challenges for international firms to adapt to shifting government priorities when aligning with one country's space strategy. On the other hand, significant opportunities exist, such as the U.S.'s leadership in private organizations involved in space innovation, space tourism, and satellite communications. Additionally, as multiple countries develop space infrastructure, the growing global demand is expected to create new opportunities for international businesses to engage with and capitalize on these advancements.

Recent Technological Innovations and The Need for Space Security

Recent technological advancements in space have heightened geopolitical tensions, particularly as innovations blur the lines between commercial and military applications. Enhanced satellite capabilities for spying and surveillance now facilitate precise intelligence gathering, raising concerns over espionage and the potential for covert operations to destabilize international relations.

However, some research suggests that improved reconnaissance and spying capabilities could actually stabilize relations and deter geopolitical escalations (Early & Gartzke, 2021). The authors argue that the presence of spying satellites can prevent military disputes between nations for two reasons. First, potential aggressors can conduct surveillance from space, eliminating the need for invasion, which would compromise the strategic advantage provided by reconnaissance (recon) satellites. Second, if a potential target possesses a recon satellite, the element of surprise diminishes, increasing the costs associated with military conflict.

Table 1. Presence of reconnaissance (recon) satellites in military disputes (1950–2010), emphasizing their potential deterrent effect.

Recon Satellite Presence	Number of Disputes	Percentage of Total (n = 139)
Aggressor had recon satellite	14	10.1%
Target had recon satellite	9	6.5%
Both had recon satellites	1	0.7%

Among the 139 military disputes that occurred between 1950 and 2010 (see Table 1), we notice that for only 10% involved an aggressor with a recon satellite, and just 6.5% involved a target with one, indicating the deterrent effect of these dual-use technologies. Notably, only 0.7% of disputes arose when both nations had recon satellites. When we replicate the authors' study and analyze the relationship between military disputes and the presence of reconnaissance satellites, along with several key covariates (e.g., GDP, military capacity), we find a negative association between the presence of these satellites and the likelihood of military conflict. Figure 2 illustrates the coefficients for these regressions along with their 95% confidence intervals.

Figure 2. Recon satellites reduce the likelihood of military disputes (1950–2010), controlling for GDP, military capacity, and other factors, as shown by regression coefficients with 95% confidence intervals.

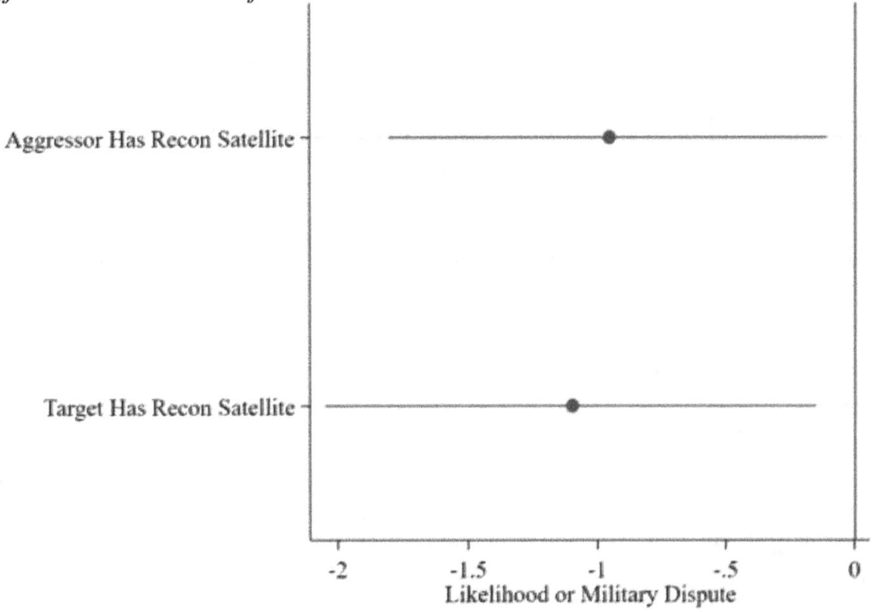

Additionally, the rapidly expanding commercial space sector, with its shorter turnaround times, enables firms to exercise greater influence over geopolitics. Space security, defined as "the ability to place and operate assets outside the Earth's atmosphere without external interference, damage, or destruction" (Moltz, 2019, p. 11), has become increasingly vital as globalization intensifies interdependence among nations. Space assets have become indispensable for national security, providing critical infrastructure for communication, navigation, and surveillance. Private actors are central to this security paradigm, as they own and operate much of the commercial space infrastructure that governments rely on. Ensuring the security of these systems requires collaboration between state and commercial entities, fostering a unified approach to resilience against cyberattacks, physical threats, and orbital congestion. This partnership underscores the necessity of integrating commercial actors into national and international frameworks for space security, ensuring their investments align with broader geopolitical and economic stability.

Framework for Understanding Space Security in the Context of Geopolitics

Our chapter proposes a theoretical framework (see Figure 3) to examine space security through the lens of geopolitics, focusing on the interplay between government and commercial actors and technological advancements. The framework analyzes how geopolitical competition and collaboration shape geopolitical relations, space security, and the broader space economy.

Figure 3. The conceptual model of space security in the context of geopolitics.

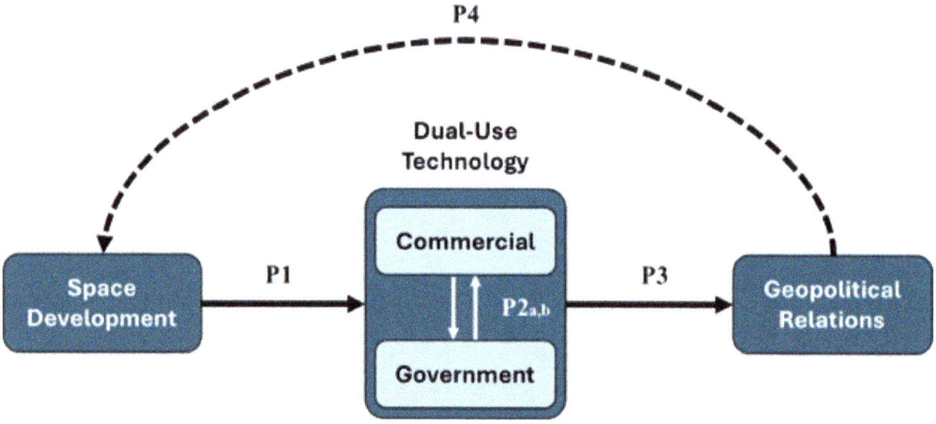

The framework illustrates the cyclical relationship between space technology development, commercial and government applications, and geopolitical relations. Advances in space technologies, such as the shift from large, single-use satellites to networks of small, cost-effective satellites launched via reusable rockets, have driven innovations in commercial and civilian uses like GPS and monitoring systems, as well as military applications like missile systems. This overlap allows for the cross-pollination of innovations from commercial and government actors.

The dual-use nature of space technologies generates fears of espionage and attacks, influencing geopolitical dynamics by raising concerns over airspace sovereignty and surveillance capabilities (Luo & Van Assche, 2023). In response, geopolitical tensions drive further space development as nations invest in anti-satellite technologies, soft-kill systems, and adversarial AI to secure their interests. The framework emphasizes a feedback loop that perpetuates both innovation and tension.

Space Development and Dual-Use Technology (P1)

Historical Context

The dual-use nature of space technologies, capable of serving both civilian and military purposes, has posed significant challenges to the peaceful use of outer space since its early development (Johnson-Freese, 2007). Following the end of the Cold War, the boundaries between military, scientific, and commercial space applications became increasingly blurred, transforming the dynamics of space activity (Tachibana, 2024). For example, military satellites initially designed for defense began supporting civilian purposes like weather forecasting and environmental monitoring. Conversely, scientific missions, such as JAXA's Hayabusa spacecraft, demonstrated dual-use capabilities by collecting asteroid samples while showcasing technological advancements with potential military applications (Tachibana, 2024). This interconnection between civilian and military uses has complicated global efforts to govern space activities and maintain peace, as technologies developed for scientific progress often carry latent military potential (Johnson-Freese, 2007).

Current Trends

Nowadays, the dual-use nature of space technologies remains deeply embedded across the spectrum of space activities, from launch systems to satellite operations and the data they produce (Hilborne, 2024). Of the 169 satellites currently in orbit, over 100 are either dedicated to military use or serve dual purposes (UCS, 2022), reflecting the extensive overlap between defense and civilian applications. The growing participation of commercial entities in the space sector further complicates the distinction between military, civilian, and commercial endeavors. For instance, technologies like satellite servicing and debris removal can simultaneously meet commercial needs while fulfilling military objectives (Klein & Boensch, 2024). In addition, the dominance of the New Space sector by the United States and its allies has intensified global competition, creating potential instability as state-led space powers like China and Russia work to catch up (Klein & Boensch, 2024). These advancements in space technology are not only reshaping national security strategies and economic opportunities but also amplifying concerns about sustainability and governance in outer space.

Implications for International Business

Space possesses unique characteristics (Wang, 2024), which have the potential to significantly impact international business in various ways. The dual-use nature of space technologies, combined with the increasing complexity of space activities, presents important implications for international business. The intersection of military, civilian, and commercial applications of space technologies has blurred traditional industry boundaries, creating both opportunities and challenges for businesses operating in this evolving domain. Rapid advancements in New Space initiatives, largely driven by the United States and its allies, have accelerated the commercialization of space through activities like satellite servicing, space mining, 3D bioprinting, and space-based solar power (Lee & Jeong, 2024). While these innovations open lucrative avenues for businesses to engage in the global space economy, they also raise pressing concerns about regulatory oversight, market stability, and long-term sustainability.

Moreover, emerging global competition in space adds another layer of complexity, impacting supply chains and elevating geopolitical risks. As spacefaring nations such as China and Russia work to catch up with advancements led by Western powers, businesses must navigate a fractured global landscape marked by diverging national interests and uneven international cooperation (Klein & Boensch, 2024). This fragmented environment reflects the critical need for clear governance frameworks to manage dual-use technologies effectively and ensure sustainable practices in space operations. For international businesses, thriving in this competitive and high-stakes arena will require balancing economic opportunities with compliance, security considerations, and strategic partnerships across an increasingly interconnected global order.

Interplay between Government and Commercial Actors (P2a, P2b) and Geopolitical Relations (P3)

The line between military and commercial activities in space is increasingly indistinct. Security experts predict that entrepreneurial investments and innovations in space technology will significantly impact civil, military, and commercial sectors alike. This transformation is marked by the incorporation of commercial expertise in cutting-edge fields like machine learning and AI, where private-sector innovation is pivotal. Today, defense innovation is no longer driven exclusively by traditional military-industrial corporations. Instead, advanced technologies such as 3D printing, nanotechnology, AI, drones, and space systems are often first developed in the commercial sector and later adapted—or "spun on"—for military use.

Commercial-to-Government/Military Spillovers (P2a)

Advancements in small satellites have been accelerated by cost reductions resulting from reusable rocket technology. For example, the Space Shuttle in the 1980s and

1990s had a launch cost of $1.7 billion ($65,400 per kilogram of payload), compared to the SpaceX Falcon 9 Heavy at $95 million ($1,500 per kilogram) and the projected SpaceX Starship Super Heavy at just $10 million per launch (O'Callaghan, 2022; Roberts & Kaplan, 2022). Small satellites play a vital role in national security by enabling AI-driven maritime surveillance, GPS, threat detection, and strategic operations (Pekkanen, Aoki, & Mittleman, 2022). They also have dual-use applications, such as enhancing operational efficiency, preventing collisions, and countering adversarial strategies. Furthermore, autonomous small satellite constellations in low Earth orbit or medium Earth orbit significantly improve global situational awareness and enable multi-domain operations. Some examples include SpaceX's Starlink, which provides global satellite-based broadband internet, and Amazon's Project Kuiper, a competing satellite internet initiative supported by Arianespace, United Launch Alliance, and Blue Origin (Amazon, 2022).

The U.S. research and development priorities emphasize early warning systems, command and control networks, space and electronic warfare, cyber capabilities, and autonomous weapons, often developed or based on intellectual property from commercial actors. Commercial dominance in space is exemplified by SpaceX, which regularly launches U.S. Air Force satellites using reusable Falcon 9 rockets. Cost-effective access to space has enabled a broader range of state and non-state actors to participate in space operations. Emerging business models, such as "Space as a Service," allow operators to manage satellite constellations through integrated ground stations and cloud-based data storage, reducing reliance on traditional ground infrastructure. Additionally, the convergence of AI, satellite technology, and defense innovations is ushering in a new era of interconnected and intelligent military capabilities. Commercial advancements like AI are increasingly adapted for defense applications, including AI-enabled autonomous weapon systems (e.g., LAWS), which are reshaping traditional warfare by reducing direct human involvement (Jensen & Pashkewitz, 2019). Algorithms and data now play a growing role in decision-making processes, particularly in autonomous weapon systems.

To summarize, commercial-to-government and military spillovers highlight the growing integration of private-sector innovations into defense strategies. Technologies originally developed for commercial purposes, such as reusable rockets and satellite constellations, are enabling governments to achieve cost efficiency and operational flexibility. This cross-sector collaboration accelerates advancements in dual-use technologies, facilitating the seamless application of commercial innovations to meet complex military and national security demands.

Government/Military-to-Commercial Spillovers (P2b)

Historically, many dual-use technologies initially developed for military applications have transitioned into widespread commercial use, delivering significant societal and economic benefits. The evolution of small satellite technology, along with its civilian and commercial applications, exemplifies this transition. Traditional military satellites were large, complex, and prohibitively expensive, often costing millions or even billions of dollars. These systems were central to major defense projects, such as Australia's Defence SATCOM System, which plans to deploy geosynchronous satellites under Project JP-9102 (Yeo, 2019). However, since the 1990s, there has been a significant shift toward small satellites. These smaller, cost-effective, and rapidly deployable satellites have revolutionized both military and civilian operations, enhancing operational flexibility, lowering barriers to access, and enabling frequent technological upgrades. Small satellite constellations now provide critical services across multiple domains. Examples include global broadband internet access through systems like SpaceX's Starlink, Earth observation for climate monitoring and disaster response, agricultural monitoring to enhance crop yields and sustainability, and environmental data collection to address pressing global challenges. Moreover, small satellites have found diverse commercial uses, such as environmental monitoring to track deforestation, pollution, and climate change impacts. Precision farming has been transformed through satellite imaging, enabling more efficient and sustainable agricultural practices. Satellite-based broadband services are expanding connectivity to remote areas, while real-time satellite data deployment plays a vital role in disaster response and emergency management. Many of these applications were originally initiated by military or government organizations but have since been adopted and further developed by commercial actors and NGOs.

Beyond satellite technology, military investment in other technological innovations, such as AI, has been a key driver of advancements in secure communication, surveillance, and data processing. Defense-led advancements have created scalable and adaptable solutions that foster economic growth. Military-funded research continues to drive rapid innovation cycles, bridging the defense and commercial sectors and enabling solutions that address global challenges.

Government and military investments have historically catalyzed commercial innovations, with technologies such as small satellites and secure communication systems transitioning from defense-specific uses to broader civilian and commercial applications. This process has not only revolutionized industries like telecommunications, agriculture, and environmental monitoring but also demonstrated the ability of defense innovations to drive global economic growth and address critical societal challenges.

Implications for International Business

First, the growing intersection of dual-use technologies in international business presents significant regulatory challenges as it blurs the line between civilian and military applications. Ensuring compliance with international humanitarian law (*jus in bello*) is essential to prevent misuse and maintain global security. This raises important questions about the implications of commercial actors, driven by profit motives, playing a role in matters of national and international security.

Second, ethical dilemmas emerge as commercial satellite constellations, while advancing innovation, also expose military assets and undermine states' traditional monopoly on intelligence. Transparency and privacy concerns further complicate this landscape. With private companies increasingly involved in defense-related activities, issues of accountability become critical, particularly regarding liability and ethical responsibility. These firms are under scrutiny for compliance with international law and sustainability standards when deploying dual-use technologies. Additionally, trust and transparency are important for businesses navigating these complexities. Companies must strike a balance between fostering innovation and maintaining public trust by adhering to ethical codes and demonstrating transparency in their technological applications. Operating in the defense sector poses reputational risks, especially if companies are linked to unethical practices or regulatory violations. Adversarial threats add another layer of complexity. Technologies such as adversarial AI can be manipulated by both state and non-state actors, potentially undermining predictions and decision-making processes. These vulnerabilities pose significant risks to business operations tied to these technologies. To counter such threats, companies must develop resilient frameworks to withstand cyberattacks, environmental disruptions, or adversarial actions. Investments in technological adaptability are crucial to ensuring operational continuity in contested and unpredictable environments.

Third, sustainability in the rapidly evolving New Space economy also presents critical implications. The rapid expansion of satellite constellations, like Starlink and Project Kuiper, raises concerns about orbital congestion and debris. Interestingly, commercial operators often outpace governments in debris mitigation and active removal efforts (ESA, 2021). Autonomous systems and predictive analytics are proving essential for collision avoidance and operational efficiency. However, governments, particularly in the U.S., face criticism for their slow progress in advancing space sustainability policies, placing additional responsibility on commercial actors (Weeden, 2020). Hence, collaboration among governments, private actors, and international organizations is necessary to ensure balanced progress in this field. Coordinated efforts are needed to establish ethical standards for space governance, develop frameworks that balance innovation with responsibility, and align commercial interests with global security and environmental goals. These partnerships are critical for fostering sustainable and secure advancements in space and related industries.

The intersection of dual-use technologies in international business introduces regulatory challenges, ethical dilemmas, and security risks as the boundaries between civilian and military applications blur. Commercial involvement in defense activities raises critical questions about liability, compliance, and public trust, particularly as transparency and privacy concerns grow. Businesses face reputational and operational risks, including vulnerabilities to adversarial threats such as manipulated AI systems. Meanwhile, the rapid growth of satellite constellations amplifies concerns about orbital debris and sustainability, highlighting the need for stronger government policies and commercial responsibility. Achieving balanced progress requires collaboration among governments, private actors, and international organizations to establish ethical standards, ensure compliance, and align innovation with global security and environmental goals.

Feedback Loop: Geopolitical Relations and Space Development (P4)

Geopolitical Relations Advancing Space Development (P4)

Geopolitical tensions are driving significant advancements in space development, with countries like the United States and organizations such as NASA leading these efforts. Key initiatives include the establishment of the U.S. Space Force and the development of innovative technologies such as deep learning for Earth observation and biomimicry-inspired engineering to tackle scientific and operational challenges (NASA, 2024). These advancements reflect a broader shift in the balance of power, as space emerges as a critical arena for both national security and technological leadership.

This transformation affects the dynamics between nation-states and commercial actors, with commercial entities often serving as tools for their home countries or even foreign states. Such developments introduce changes to the global power balance, potentially reshaping alliances. For example, Japan's evolving position in the global space landscape reflects how shifting relations and uncertainties influence geopolitical strategies (Pekkanen, 2024). In response to these changes, nation-states are compelled to further develop their space capabilities, either as protectionist measures or as reactive strategies. Countries like South Korea exemplify this trend, as they enhance their space programs to navigate the uncertain dynamics of shifting global power relations. These developments indicate the complex interplay between geopolitical tensions and the rapid evolution of space technology.

Implications for International Business

The evolving landscape of space development, driven by geopolitical tensions, presents significant implications for international business. As nations and organizations such as NASA advance their capabilities, businesses increasingly play a pivotal role in shaping the global space economy. The involvement of influential commercial actors like Elon Musk (SpaceX), Jeff Bezos (Blue Origin), Richard Branson (Virgin Galactic), and South Korea's Hanwha Group highlights the crucial contributions of private enterprise in this domain. These businesses are not only key drivers of innovation but also instruments of geopolitical influence, as they often align with the strategic interests of their home countries. For example, U.S.-based companies like SpaceX and Blue Origin support American leadership in space technology and security, while South Korea's Hanwha Group strengthens its nation's position in the regional and global space race. As commercial entities collaborate with or operate on behalf of nation-states, they help shape the balance of power, contributing to technological advancements and strengthening national security frameworks.

However, this growing interdependence between businesses and governments also brings challenges. The global power balance continues to shift as nations like South Korea and Japan enhance their space capabilities to adapt to evolving geopolitical dynamics. These uncertainties force businesses to navigate complex regulatory environments and align their operations with national and international policies.

For international businesses, the geopolitical tensions advancing space development underscore the importance of strategic partnerships, investment in cutting-edge technologies, and alignment with global governance frameworks. As the space industry becomes an arena for both economic opportunity and geopolitical maneuvering, businesses must balance innovation with compliance and responsibility.

DISCUSSION

Space Security and International Business Dynamics

New Space offers opportunities but also significant challenges as space security and geopolitical tensions increasingly shape this domain. Once seen as the global commons under the OST, space is now contested by geopolitical rivalries, strategic competition, and commercial interests, undermining its original spirit of cooperative governance and collaboration (Archinard, 2024). Recognized as an independent warfighting domain, space disrupts traditional military doctrines while playing a critical role in supporting terrestrial operations (Sweijs & Ellison, 2024). As geopolitical competition intensifies (Beugelsdijk & Luo, 2024), MNEs and firms' foreign investment decisions face a fragmented regulatory landscape where commercial and military objectives often overlap. Balancing innovation with strategic risk management is crucial to mitigate disruptions from security tensions or hostile actions.

International relations scholars provide diverse perspectives (Bowen, 2020; Cobb, 2021; Deudney, 2020; Moltz, 2024; Paikowsky, 2017) on space security, offering valuable insights for international businesses to navigate these complex dynamics better. The full chapter will include an overview of the disparate perspectives. By fostering collaboration and advocating for responsible space behavior, MNEs can play a pivotal role in ensuring a secure and sustainable space economy while exploiting the new space economy for innovation, strategic advantage, and long-term economic growth.

The Importance of Space Diplomacy

Space diplomacy refers to the processes of dialogue, communication, and bargaining among state and non-state actors to manage cooperation and conflict in space activities. It involves creating norms, establishing governance frameworks, and addressing dual-use technology challenges while balancing scientific, economic, and security interests (Cross & Pekkanen, 2023). As geopolitical tensions increase, space diplomacy becomes critical in preventing space from becoming a domain of conflict. It fosters collaboration on issues like space debris, international exploration missions, and satellite regulation. The growing role of the commercial sector, such as private companies managing satellite constellations and reusable launch technologies, adds complexity and urgency to diplomatic efforts, as economic interdependence in space can act as both a stabilizing force and a point of contention in great power competition. By leveraging mechanisms like **communication**, **persuasion**, and **bargaining**, space diplomacy can help align commercial and military objectives, ensuring the peaceful and sustainable use of space.

Communication in space diplomacy involves the exchange of information, framing of narratives, and dissemination of norms among a diverse range of actors to foster collaboration and shape perceptions of space activities (Cross & Pekkanen, 2023). This mechanism includes both public and private dimensions. Public communication often takes the form of outreach initiatives highlighting the shared benefits of space exploration, building public support, and creating an environment for collaboration. For example, the International Space Station exemplifies how consistent communication among epistemic communities, such as scientists and diplomats, can establish mutual goals and reinforce shared objectives. Private communication, on the other hand, occurs through informal verbal and non-verbal signaling and diplomatic rituals, which build trust and understanding among stakeholders. These engagements within epistemic communities or coalitions are critical in fostering dialogue and advancing shared knowledge, ultimately laying the groundwork for cooperative ventures in space.

Persuasion in space diplomacy goes beyond communication by actively seeking to change the perspectives or actions of other actors through the use of evidence, reasoning, and normative arguments (Cross & Pekkanen, 2023). It relies heavily on trust, prior cooperation, and mutual understanding to align interests and facilitate agreements. This mechanism is often employed by epistemic communities and experts, who leverage their technical knowledge to influence policy and decision-making. Persuasion was pivotal in fostering international consensus on the Artemis Accords, where the United States successfully encouraged other nations to adopt common principles for lunar exploration. By framing these agreements around shared values such as sustainability and peaceful cooperation, persuasion served as a bridge between differing interests, enabling alignment on critical issues, and will do so going forward.

Bargaining, in contrast, represents a more strategically focused mechanism of space diplomacy, where actors engage in negotiations driven by self-interest to reach agreements that balance national, international, and commercial objectives (Cross & Pekkanen, 2023). This mechanism often involves tit-for-tat exchanges, where states trade commitments or resources to achieve mutually beneficial outcomes. Bargaining reflects the material interests and power dynamics that underpin state interactions in space governance. Establishing the ISS is a prime example of successful bargaining, as countries agreed to share resources, responsibilities, and technologies in exchange for access to a shared scientific platform. Through these negotiations, nations navigated competing interests to create a lasting framework for international collaboration in space exploration.

Together, these mechanisms—communication, persuasion, and bargaining—illustrate the nuanced processes through which space diplomacy facilitates cooperation and mitigates conflict in an increasingly complex and interconnected domain. In addition, this no longer falls under the purview of nation-states and professional diplomats alone. Commercial actors are increasingly playing an important role in shaping space diplomacy.

Theoretical Implications: Interdisciplinary Theoretical Lenses

Because space represents a fundamentally unique domain, existing theoretical frameworks fall short of capturing its complex dynamics (Sweijs & Ellison, 2024), particularly within the field of international business. Building on the proposed framework, this chapter also explores interdisciplinary theoretical perspectives to provide a more comprehensive understanding of geopolitics in the context of new space. We highlight several promising theoretical lenses that offer valuable insights for both scholars and practitioners in international business (Luo, 2024; Luo & Van Assche, 2023). This interdisciplinary approach aims to not only deepen the analysis of geopolitical dynamics in new space but also lay a robust foundation for future academic research. By leveraging these frameworks, we hope to inspire actionable insights and contribute to a more nuanced understanding of the forces shaping geopolitical relationships in this emerging era of space exploration and global competition. Table 2 provides an overview.

Table 2. Overview of interdisciplinary theoretical lenses.

Broad field	Theory	Core concepts	Assumptions
Organizational theory, strategic management	Configurational theory	Organizations achieve performance through specific combinations (configurations) of strategies, structures, and processes. Multiple configurations can lead to success.	There is no single optimal strategy; success depends on aligning multiple factors within a specific context. Configurations evolve with technological and environmental changes.
Systems theory, organizational theory, and physics	Complexity theory	Systems are composed of interdependent components that interact dynamically, often leading to unpredictable outcomes. Non-linear interactions and emergent properties are central.	Systems are inherently complex and cannot be fully predicted or controlled. Small changes can lead to large-scale effects, often giving the impression of chaos.
Security studies, innovation	Techno-nationalism	Technological innovation in space is driven by external threats, state intervention, and civil-military integration. Self-reliance and national security concerns play pivotal roles.	National security threats catalyze innovation. States believe technological superiority in space is crucial for security and economic competitiveness.
International political economy	Structural power theory	Power is distributed unevenly within the international system due to economic structures and institutions, which reinforce the dominance of certain states.	Economic and institutional structures determine power dynamics. States that control these structures exert influence over others, shaping global norms and policies.
International relations	Securitization theory	Issues can be framed as existential threats to justify extraordinary measures, often bypassing normal political procedures.	Security is a socially constructed concept. States and actors can "securitize" topics like space exploration to prioritize them politically and allocate resources accordingly.

continued on following page

Table 2. Continued

Broad field	Theory	Core concepts	Assumptions
International relations, political economy	Commercial space peace theory	Economic interdependence through commercial space activities reduces the likelihood of conflict. Space commercialization fosters cooperation.	States and corporations prioritize economic gains over political or military competition. Commercialization creates shared interests that discourage conflict.
International political economy	Hegemonic stability theory	A single dominant power (hegemon) creates stability in the international system by enforcing rules and norms, reducing uncertainty for other actors.	Stability is contingent on the presence of a hegemon capable of maintaining order. The decline of the hegemon may lead to disorder or the rise of competing powers.
Security studies, war studies	Deterrence theory	States deter aggression by demonstrating their capability and willingness to respond with overwhelming force, including in the space domain.	Rational actors avoid conflict when the costs outweigh the benefits. Space deterrence relies on demonstrating resilience and the ability to respond effectively to attacks.
War theory, military strategy	Clausewitzian war theory	War is a continuation of politics by other means. The use of space assets in conflict is an extension of terrestrial political and strategic objectives.	War is driven by political motives, and space is an extension of the battlefield. States will leverage space assets strategically to achieve their terrestrial political goals.

While each framework offers distinct insights, they collectively highlight the importance of aligning strategic, organizational, and systemic factors to address the complexity and dual-use nature of New Space technologies. These theories also underscore the value of interdisciplinary approaches, demonstrating how concepts from different fields could be integrated to provide insights into the intersection of New Space and geopolitics. By integrating these perspectives, we aim to encourage future research that refines and expands on these theoretical contributions to better address the challenges and opportunities in the geopolitics of New Space.

Configurational Theory. Configurational theory posits that organizational performance results from specific combinations of strategies, structures, and processes that align with the environmental context (Fiss, 2007; Furnari et al., 2021; Misangyi et al., 2017). This theory assumes there is no universally optimal configuration, as success depends on achieving fit across multiple dimensions. However, critics argue that it may oversimplify dynamic changes and neglect the role of power and agency. At the intersection of geopolitics and New Space, configurational theory highlights the importance of aligning strategic goals, technological capabilities, and governance frameworks to achieve success. For instance, spacefaring nations may adopt distinct configurations to balance military, commercial, and scientific objectives. In our framework, these configurations evolve dynamically in response to geopolitical shifts, technological advancements, and competitive pressures.

Complexity Theory. Complexity theory views systems as composed of interdependent components whose interactions generate non-linear dynamics and emergent behaviors (Anderson, 1999; Beck & Plowman, 2014; Brown & Eisenhardt, 1997). It assumes systems are inherently unpredictable and evolve through feedback loops, where small changes can cascade into significant effects. Critics of complexity theory often cite its challenges in providing actionable predictions. In the context of New Space, complexity theory underscores the unpredictable interplay of state, corporate, and international actors in a rapidly evolving technological landscape. For example, innovations in satellite constellations or space mining may create unintended geopolitical consequences. In our framework, complexity theory illustrates how the convergence of commercial and military interests in space can generate emergent patterns, such as shifts in alliances or unexpected vulnerabilities in space infrastructure.

Techno-Nationalistic Perspective. Techno-nationalism frames technological advancement as a tool for national security and global competitiveness, driven by external threats, state intervention, and civil-military integration (Godsell, Lel, & Miller, 2023; Luo, 2021; Luo & Van Assche, 2023). It assumes that states prioritize self-reliance and technological superiority to mitigate security risks, though critics argue this perspective may overstate state capacity and neglect global interdependence. In New Space, techno-nationalism explains the pursuit of indigenous capabilities in space exploration, satellite systems, and launch technology. For instance, South Korea's recent space efforts are built on the notion that the future of the US-ROK alliance is uncertain. In our framework, techno-nationalism is a driving force behind dual-use innovations, shaping the geopolitical landscape by fostering competition over technologies that blur the lines between civilian and military applications.

Structural Power Theory. Structural power theory posits that global power dynamics are shaped by underlying economic and institutional structures, which reinforce the dominance of certain states and marginalize others (Strange, 2015). It assumes that power is embedded in these structures, enabling hegemonic states to shape global norms and rules. Critics of structural power theory often highlight its lack of focus on agency and resistance by smaller states. In New Space, structural power theory explains how established spacefaring nations use governance frameworks, such as the Artemis Accords or the Outer Space Treaty, to maintain dominance while marginalizing emerging actors. In our framework, structural power shapes access to resources and technology, creating asymmetries in space exploration and commercial activities that reinforce existing geopolitical hierarchies.

Securitization Theory. Securitization theory (Balzacq, 2010) posits that security threats are socially constructed through social discourse. Problems and conflicts are "securitized" when they are framed as existential threats that need extraordinary solutions. It assumes security is shaped by those who can shape narratives and public discourse. However, it has faced criticism for a lack of focus on material threats. At the intersection of geopolitics and New Space, securitization drives militarization and dual-use applications, such as satellites for communication and surveillance. Narratives about adversaries like China or Russia influence space policy and geopolitics. In our framework, securitization could be a source of feedback loops, driving new military technologies and commercial-military integration.

Commercial Space Peace Theory. Commercial Space Peace Theory posits that economic interdependence in space discourages conflict by raising the costs of disruption and promoting stability (Keohane & Nye, 1977). It assumes states and firms act rationally to protect investments, though conflicts may still arise over ideology or resources. In New Space, commercial activities like satellite constellations and space tourism create shared dependencies and encourage cooperation. Innovations driven by geopolitics further shape the behavior of military and commercial sectors. In our framework, commercial integration might reduce conflict potential through economic interdependence as these commercial actors provide services across borders on a global scale.

Hegemonic Stability Theory. Hegemonic Stability Theory proposes that a dominant power (hegemon) maintains global stability by providing public goods like security and trade norms (Kindleberger, 1973). It posits the hegemon as the keeper of order and balance, though overemphasis on one power may overlook cooperation between smaller states. In geopolitics and New Space, the U.S. acts as a hegemon, shaping governance norms (e.g., Artemis Accords) and driving competition with emerging rivals like India and China. This competition fuels innovation in dual-use technologies like reconnaissance satellites. Our framework reflects how hegemonic competition advances military space technologies, which in turn has consequential impacts on the supra-national structure of geopolitical alignments.

Deterrence Theory. Deterrence theory seeks to prevent adversaries from harmful actions by demonstrating that retaliation costs outweigh the benefits (Schelling, 1966), building on the similar cost-benefit logic of commercial space peace theory. It assumes rational actors weigh the costs and benefits of actions (aggressive and defensive). Deterrence is enhanced by novel dual-use innovations such as recent developments in AI technologies (e.g., real-time surveillance and autonomous defense systems).

Clausewitzian War Theory. Clausewitzian War Theory takes a political perspective of war, equating it to "politics by other means," emphasizing the uncertainties associated with both war and politics under the concept of the "fog of war" (Clausewitz, 2003). In this framework, success requires balancing rational planning, chance, and human factors. In our framework, the commercial-military integration in

New Space can both increase or decrease the fog of war. An increase is possible as this integration instills uncertainty and fear in other actors, who are therefore more likely to act irrationally. In contrast, increased surveillance and enhanced decision-making through novel technologies (e.g., AI) could provide additional insights and intelligence that reduce uncertainty by enhancing situational awareness.

UNSOLVED QUESTIONS AND FUTURE RESEARCH OPPORTUNITIES

Research grounded in **configurational theory** could explore how spacefaring nations align their strategic goals, technological capabilities, and governance frameworks to achieve competitive advantages in the New Space economy. For example, scholars could investigate the distinct configurations adopted by countries to balance military, commercial, and scientific objectives in response to geopolitical shifts and technological advancements. Additionally, private-sector configurations, such as partnerships between aerospace firms, may evolve dynamically as competitive and cooperative pressures change. Understanding these configurations can reveal how nations and firms achieve "fit" in this complex multi-level landscape. Policymakers can use such insights to design governance models that promote synergies between public and private space actors while ensuring alignment with national security and economic goals.

Complexity theory highlights the unpredictable and emergent patterns arising from interactions between commercial and governmental actors in the space economy. Research could examine how small-scale technological innovations, such as advances in nanosatellites, cascade into larger geopolitical and economic shifts, creating new alliances or exposing vulnerabilities in space infrastructure. Feedback loops between space technologies and geopolitical tensions are particularly ripe for study, as these dynamics can result in unintended consequences such as arms races or destabilization of alliances. Policymakers could benefit from these studies by developing adaptive strategies that account for non-linear effects, enhancing resilience against destabilizing influences in the space domain.

The **techno-nationalistic** perspective offers fertile ground for examining how states prioritize indigenous space capabilities while navigating the challenges of international cooperation. Research could focus on the role of external threats in driving state investments in dual-use technologies and how these policies influence global space governance. Additionally, scholars might investigate how techno-nationalism shapes competition among nations and fosters innovation in civilian and military applications. Findings from this line of inquiry could inform policies that balance domestic capacity-building with international collaboration, reducing the risks of techno-nationalistic rivalries escalating into conflict while maintaining competitive advantages.

Drawing from **structural power theory**, scholars could investigate the mechanisms by which smaller or emerging space nations attempt to challenge these structural inequalities, particularly in their access to resources and technology. Additionally, understanding how global economic and institutional structures shape the distribution of benefits from space activities could shed light on long-term geopolitical dynamics. These findings could help reform international governance frameworks, making them more inclusive and equitable for developing space nations.

Securitization theory emphasizes the role of narratives in framing security threats and shaping space policies. Research could analyze how framing nations like China or Russia as existential threats influence both military and commercial space decisions. Such studies might also explore the implications of these narratives for long-term international cooperation and investment. Policymakers could use these insights to craft communication strategies that de-escalate tensions and foster cooperative narratives, mitigating the risks of securitization-driven arms races in space.

Commercial space peace theory posits that economic interdependence in space can discourage conflict by creating shared dependencies. Research could examine how commercial ventures, such as satellite constellations or space tourism, act as stabilizing forces in geopolitics and under what conditions such interdependence may fail due to ideological or resource-based disputes. Insights from this research could encourage the development of policies that promote cross-border economic integration, such as multinational joint ventures or shared resource exploration initiatives, fostering stability in the space domain.

Hegemonic stability theory suggests that dominant powers, like the United States, maintain order in the New Space economy by setting governance norms and driving innovation. Research could explore how competition with emerging rivals, such as China and India, influences the development of dual-use technologies and impacts the sustainability of the current hegemonic order. These studies could also assess the extent to which hegemonic stability dynamics hinder or encourage multilateral space governance. Policymakers and international organizations could use this research to evaluate and adapt governance strategies to maintain global stability in the face of rising competition.

Deterrence theory provides a framework for investigating the role of novel technologies, such as AI-driven surveillance systems, in preventing adversarial actions in space. Research could explore the effectiveness of such deterrence strategies and their unintended consequences, such as escalating arms races or destabilizing alliances. Additionally, studies could examine how commercial actors contribute to or disrupt deterrence dynamics in the space domain. Policymakers might leverage these findings to design strategies that minimize the risks of escalation while maintaining stability in the increasingly militarized space environment.

Clausewitzian war theory emphasizes the uncertainties and human factors involved in the integration of commercial and military space technologies. Research could focus on how this integration affects uncertainty in geopolitical conflicts and decision-making processes, particularly during crises. For example, scholars might explore whether advancements in surveillance and AI technologies reduce uncertainty by enhancing situational awareness or exacerbate it by increasing fear and mistrust among nations. Such insights could help policymakers anticipate and manage the risks of miscalculations or unintended escalations in the militarized space domain.

These research opportunities, spanning multiple theoretical lenses, offer a rich array of pathways for further exploration. Collectively, they aim to deepen the understanding of the dynamic interplay between geopolitics and the New Space economy, providing actionable insights for scholars, policymakers, and practitioners.

Opportunities for Interdisciplinary Research

This chapter has examined the intersection of geopolitics and New Space, developing a novel dynamic framework that connects the two through innovation. However, several related fields are also crucial to understand. While a full exploration of these areas is beyond the scope of this chapter and the overall focus of the book, we highlight key interconnected disciplines that should closely monitor the dynamics of geopolitics in space: sustainability, emerging countries and alliances, scientific and technological cooperation, and international law.

Sustainability in space has become increasingly critical, especially with the growing issue of space debris and its long-term environmental impact. The Kessler Syndrome—a scenario where the density of objects in low Earth orbit (LEO) becomes so high that collisions generate more debris—poses a significant risk to both commercial and government satellites. As space activity escalates, the accumulation of debris could lead to a self-perpetuating cycle of collisions, creating a hazardous environment for satellite operations and future missions. Efforts to mitigate space debris, including active debris removal, collision avoidance strategies, and stricter regulations on satellite deorbiting, are essential to ensure sustainable space exploration and utilization. Countries and private companies must address these environmental concerns to keep space accessible for future generations.

In the realm of emerging countries and strategic alliances, the geopolitical landscape in space is shifting. Emerging nations are leveraging space capabilities for both soft and hard power. A prime example is the India-Vietnam satellite partnership, where space collaboration serves as a tool for asserting sovereignty and enhancing regional influence. This partnership integrates civil and military applications, providing real-time surveillance over contested regions like the South China Sea. It illustrates how emerging powers are using space to bolster strategic autonomy without engaging in traditional military confrontations. India's space agency, ISRO, and Vietnam's VNSC are establishing a hybrid network that combines Earth observation (EO) and radar technologies, which not only enhances Vietnam's security but also extends India's strategic influence eastward. This collaboration exemplifies how space can be utilized for counter-coercion and soft power, fostering a rules-based order in the Indo-Pacific region. Furthermore, the increasing involvement of the private sector in these space initiatives—through technology, analytics, and dual-use applications—indicates a future where commercial companies play a pivotal role in geopolitical strategy, further blurring the lines between state and private contributions to space power.

Scientific cooperation in space has led to groundbreaking advancements. The unique environment of space has proven instrumental in pharmaceutical innovations, with microgravity facilitating the development of new drugs and therapies that cannot be replicated on Earth. For instance, the creation of advanced protein crystals in microgravity has resulted in improved drug efficacy and delivery. Additionally, space-based research in materials science, fluid dynamics, and combustion has produced innovations benefiting various industries, from healthcare to manufacturing. The International Space Station (ISS) has been central to many of these breakthroughs, serving as a hub for international scientific collaboration. The value of space for scientific and technological advancements extends beyond medical applications, influencing fields such as advanced manufacturing, communication technologies, and environmental monitoring. This cooperation underscores the importance of international partnerships in space, as the combined expertise and resources of multiple nations and private entities continue to drive global progress. Notably, scientific collaboration in space often transcends earthly tensions (Fewer, Ma, & Coraiola, 2025).

As space activity expands, international law faces increasing pressure to adapt. The 1967 Outer Space Treaty (OST), while revolutionary at its inception, is now considered outdated in the context of modern space exploration and commercialization. One critical area in need of reform is the legal framework governing space resource exploitation and militarization. The OST's ambiguity regarding private-sector involvement and military use of space highlights the necessity for new governance structures. Moreover, international export controls related to space technologies and dual-use technologies require clearer definitions to ensure compliance with agreements like the Wassenaar Arrangement, which regulates the export of sensitive technologies. The growing number of space actors also calls for more robust international liability and dispute resolution mechanisms. As the risks of space debris escalate—especially with the Kessler Syndrome—the issue of end-of-life disposal becomes increasingly urgent. Effective protocols must be established to ensure responsible deorbiting of satellites, minimizing the risk of further debris generation. The challenges posed by the commercialization and militarization of space necessitate a comprehensive update to the OST, along with the establishment of more specific, enforceable international agreements to address these emerging concerns.

The Next 20 Years of Geopolitics in Space

In our previous discussions, we concentrated on three key areas: 1) establishing a theoretical framework with relevant propositions; 2) presenting various theoretical perspectives; and 3) emphasizing the potential for interdisciplinary research. Throughout this process, we aimed for objectivity, offering a neutral assessment of the current landscape. Now, we shift to a more subjective perspective, examining the next 20 years of geopolitics in space and identifying what we view as critical issues.

Space Traffic Management (STM) and Space Situational Awareness (SSA). As space activity increases, effective STM and SSA become crucial. Space debris poses not only a hazard to satellites and astronauts but also a growing threat to national security and geopolitical stability. Nations must collaborate to establish global standards for space traffic management and debris mitigation. A unified international body, similar to the International Civil Aviation Organization (ICAO) for air traffic, could oversee the development of universal guidelines for collision avoidance, tracking, and debris removal. However, the politicization of space assets may obstruct these initiatives, as space-faring nations could hesitate to share sensitive SSA data due to national security concerns, fearing that information on space activities might be weaponized. The establishment of an international regulatory body to standardize STM could help alleviate these worries, but the challenge lies in balancing the need for cooperation with national security interests. If not addressed, the lack of universal standards could worsen the militarization of space, leading to conflicts over orbital dominance and access.

Dark and Quiet Skies. The increasing number of satellites and space debris threatens not only the physical security of space assets but also scientific research. Satellites, especially those in low Earth orbit (LEO), create visible and electromagnetic signatures that pollute the night sky, hampering astronomical observations and making it difficult for scientists to study the universe. The issue of "dark and quiet skies" requires urgent attention from both scientific and geopolitical perspectives. As nations and private companies launch thousands of satellites, the risk of overcrowding and pollution in space grows, affecting both research and the natural beauty of the night sky. The weaponization of space could further complicate this issue, as military satellites designed for strategic advantages may contribute to the degradation of the night sky. International dialogue and regulations, possibly through the United Nations or specialized space agencies, are essential to protect the night sky from becoming a conflict arena while accommodating the growing demand for space-based technologies.

Space Resources and Interpretation of Article II in the OST. Space resources, including water and minerals on celestial bodies and asteroid materials, represent a potential frontier for economic development and geopolitical competition. As nations and private companies begin to explore and mine space, defining and governing space resources will become critical. Article II of the OST states that space shall be free for exploration and use but prohibits any nation from claiming sovereignty over celestial bodies. This clause's ambiguity has sparked debate over the ownership and utilization of space resources. Are these resources genuinely "common heritage," as outlined by the treaty, or can they be privately owned and exploited? A clearer interpretation of Article II is necessary. Geopolitically, space resource extraction could shift power balances, as countries with access to asteroids and the Moon may gain significant strategic advantages, potentially leading to competition or conflict over these resources, where space becomes a battleground for both military control and economic dominance.

Development of Remote Sensing and Imagery Policies. The proliferation of satellite constellations is greatly increasing access to remote sensing and imagery data. While this benefits sectors such as agriculture, climate monitoring, and disaster management, it also raises security and privacy concerns. Commercial access to high-resolution imagery could enable monitoring of sensitive locations worldwide, including military installations and critical infrastructure. This capability could be weaponized, with states using imagery for strategic advantages or political pressure. Establishing international norms for remote sensing and imagery use is crucial to ensuring that space remains a peaceful domain. As commercial satellites become more powerful and numerous, regulating access to and the use of satellite data will be vital to prevent it from becoming a tool for geopolitical manipulation. Creating international policies governing the use and dissemination of remote sensing data is essential to managing the risks associated with these advanced capabilities.

Cybersecurity. Cybersecurity in space is an increasing concern as nations and private entities rely more on space-based infrastructure for military, communications, and economic purposes. Integrating commercial satellites into military strategies, along with using space for critical national security functions, makes space an attractive target for cyberattacks. Weaponizing space through cyberattacks could disrupt communications, navigation systems, and intelligence gathering by crippling adversaries' satellite networks. As space systems become more interconnected, the potential for hacking, jamming, and other forms of digital interference increases, destabilizing both space and global security. In response, robust cybersecurity frameworks and international agreements to safeguard space-based infrastructure are necessary to prevent space from becoming a new domain of warfare. Future policies must address the cross-border nature of cyber threats, as attacks may originate from anywhere in the world, complicating geopolitical tensions in space.

Legislation on Orbital Carrying Capacity. As the number of satellites and space debris continues to rise, there is a critical need for legislation addressing Earth's orbital carrying capacity. Each orbit has a finite capacity, and launching more satellites increases the risk of collisions, interference, and congestion. Orbital congestion could exacerbate the risks of space debris, potentially triggering a cascade of collisions that further reduces available orbital space and degrades the safety of space operations. Geopolitically, a nation controlling prime orbital slots could gain strategic military and commercial advantages, leading to competition over access to key orbital regions. Establishing a legal framework that limits the number of satellites and the types of activities in each orbital region could prevent space from becoming overcrowded and hostile. Such legislation could involve setting international quotas or guidelines on satellite launches, ensuring that all space-faring nations have equal access to orbital positions while preventing military overreach and space monopolization.

In-Space Servicing, Assembly, and Manufacturing. The development of in-space servicing, assembly, and manufacturing (ISAM) is set to revolutionize space operations by enabling satellite repair, assembly of large structures, and on-orbit production. These advancements could transcend earthly geopolitics by democratizing space exploration and allowing more nations, including emerging powers, to access and utilize space-based infrastructure. However, the geopolitical implications of ISAM cannot be overlooked. As private companies and nations develop the capabilities to maintain and construct satellites or entire space stations, the strategic value of these technologies could be weaponized. Nations may seek to control the technologies or infrastructure to ensure their dominance in space, while private companies may operate in ways that blur the lines between civil and military applications. Additionally, ISAM's potential to facilitate military space infrastructure construction adds a layer of complexity to the geopolitics of space. As these technologies develop, international agreements will be necessary to govern their use, ensuring they do not become a tool for escalating space-based conflicts.

CONCLUSION

This chapter explores the intersection of geopolitics, space security, and the emerging commercial space economy. We argue that space has transformed into a geopolitical and economic frontier, driven by rapid advancements in technology and the emergence of private commercial ventures. The commercialization of space—New Space—as a critical area of interest is dual-use (commercial and governmental/military) in nature and has an impact on global trade, investment, and security dynamics. We notice significant gaps between the historical framework of space as a domain for peaceful use and the modern challenges driven by AI, space debris, and commercialization. These gaps leave unresolved issues that could fuel geopolitical rivalries and strain cooperative norms. Hence, we propose a theoretical framework to discuss space security through the lens of geopolitics, emphasizing the interplay between government, commercial actors, and technological advancements. This framework introduces interdisciplinary theoretical perspectives—such as complexity theory, securitization theory, and hegemonic stability theory—to illuminate the dynamics of space as a geopolitical and economic frontier.

For researchers and practitioners in international business, we discuss the importance of navigating regulatory challenges, balancing ethical considerations with innovation, and addressing sustainability issues like orbital debris. Businesses are urged to align with global governance frameworks and invest in adaptive strategies to thrive in this volatile environment. In particular, we highlight the role of diplomacy in managing conflicts and fostering cooperation in space activities. Mechanisms such as communication, persuasion, and bargaining are suggested tools to bridge differences among nations and commercial actors.

Furthermore, we offer numerous opportunities for interdisciplinary research on subjects intricately connected to the geopolitics of space. Finally, we project into the future and articulate a call for attention to what we deem essential topics for scholars, practitioners, and policymakers to engage with in the realm of space.

To conclude, New Space presents unprecedented opportunities while simultaneously challenging traditional geopolitical norms and governance frameworks. As commercial and government actors navigate a complex landscape marked by dual-use technologies, fragmented regulations, and intensifying rivalries, collaboration and innovation become vital. Businesses and policymakers must strike a balance between leveraging space's economic potential and safeguarding its security and sustainability. By fostering partnerships and adopting adaptive strategies, stakeholders can ensure that the space frontier remains a domain for innovation, peace, and shared prosperity. Together, we can unlock the full potential of New Space as a transformative force in global business and international relations.

REFERENCES

Amazon. (2022). *Amazon secures up to 83 launches from Arianespace, Blue Origin, and United Launch Alliance for project Kuiper*. Retrieved from: https://press.aboutamazon.com/2022/4/amazon-secures-up-to-83-launches-from-arianespace-blue-origin-and-united-launch-alliance-for-project-kuiper

Anderson, P. (1999). Perspective: Complexity theory and organization science. *Organization Science*, *10*(3), 216–232.

Archinard, N. (2024). The future of global space governance. In Pekkanen, S. M., & Blount, P. J. (Eds.), *The Oxford handbook of space security* (pp. 807–823). Oxford University Press.

Balzacq, T. (2010). *Securitization theory: How security problems emerge and dissolve* (1st ed.). Routledge.

Beck, T. E., & Plowman, D. A. (2014). Temporary, emergent interorganizational collaboration in unexpected circumstances: A study of the Columbia space shuttle response effort. *Organization Science*, *25*(4), 1234–1252.

Beugelsdijk, S., & Luo, Y. (2024). The politicized nature of international business. *Journal of International Business Studies*, *55*(3), 281–284.

Bowen, B. (2020). *War in space: Strategy, spacepower, geopolitics*. Edinburgh University Press.

Brown, S. L., & Eisenhardt, K. M. (1997). The art of continuous change: Linking complexity theory and time-paced evolution in relentlessly shifting organizations. *Administrative Science Quarterly*, •••, 1–34.

Clausewitz, C. (2003). *On war*. (Original work published 1832)

Cobb, W. N. W. (2021). *Privatizing peace: How commerce can reduce conflict in space*. Routledge.

Cobb, W. N. W. (2024). Commercial space peace theory. In Pekkanen, S. M., & Blount, P. J. (Eds.), *The Oxford handbook of space security* (pp. 93–107). Oxford University Press.

Cross., & Pekkanen, S. M. (2023). Introduction. Space Diplomacy: the final frontier of theory and practice. *The Hague Journal of Diplomacy*, 18(2-3), 193-217.

Deudney, D. (2020). *Dark skies: Space expansionism, planetary geopolitics, and the ends of humanity*. Oxford University Press.

Early, B. R., & Gartzke, E. (2021). Spying from space: Reconnaissance satellites and interstate disputes. *The Journal of Conflict Resolution, 65*(9), 1551–1575.

ESA. (2021). *ESA's annual space environment report.* European Space Agency (ESA) Space Debris Office. Retrieved from https://www.sdo.esoc.esa.int/environment_report/Space_Environment_Report_latest.pdf

Fewer, T. J., Ma, D., & Coraiola, D. M. (2025). Working with the "Enemy": Supervised Space, Free Space, and Cross-Border Collaboration amid Geopolitical Rivalry. *Organization Science.*

Fiss, P. C. (2007). A set-theoretic approach to organizational configurations. *Academy of Management Review, 32*(4), 1180–1198.

Foss, K., & Foss, N. J. (2005). Resources and transaction costs: How property rights economics furthers the resource-based view. *Strategic Management Journal, 26*(6), 541–553.

Furnari, S., Crilly, D., Misangyi, V. F., Greckhamer, T., Fiss, P. C., & Aguilera, R. V. (2021). Capturing causal complexity: Heuristics for configurational theorizing. *Academy of Management Review, 46*(4), 778–799.

Godsell, D., Lel, U., & Miller, D. (2023). US national security and de-globalization. *Journal of International Business Studies, 54*(8), 1471–1494.

Hilborne, M. (2024). UK space policy: A quest for coherence. In Pekkanen, S. M., & Blount, P. J. (Eds.), *The Oxford handbook of space security* (pp. 400–414). Oxford University Press.

Jensen, B., & Pashkewitz, J. (2019). *Mosaic warfare: small and scalable are beautiful.* War on the Rocks. 23 December. Available from: https://warontherocks.com/2019/12/mosaic-warfare-small-and-scalable-are-beautiful/

Johnson-Freese, J. (2007). *Space as a strategic asset.* Columbia University Press.

Keohane, R., & Nye, J. S. (1977). *Power and interdependence.* World Politics in Transition.

Kindleberger, C. P. (1973). *The world in depression, 1929-1939.* Cambridge University Press.

Klein, J. J., & Boensch, N. J. (2024). NewSpace and new risks in space security. In Pekkanen, S. M., & Blount, P. J. (Eds.), *The Oxford handbook of space security* (pp. 761–782). Oxford University Press.

Lee, S., & Jeong, H. (2024). The dynamics of South Korea's space trajectories. In Pekkanen, S. M., & Blount, P. J. (Eds.), *The Oxford handbook of space security* (pp. 511–532). Oxford University Press.

Luo, Y. (2021). Illusions of techno-nationalism. *Journal of International Business Studies, 53*(3), 550. PMID: 34511654

Luo, Y. (2024). Paradigm shift and theoretical implications for the era of global disorder. *Journal of International Business Studies, 55*(2), 127–135.

Luo, Y., & Van Assche, A. (2023). The rise of techno-geopolitical uncertainty: Implications of the United States CHIPS and Science Act. *Journal of International Business Studies, 54*(8), 1423–1440. PMID: 37359753

Misangyi, V. F., Greckhamer, T., Furnari, S., Fiss, P. C., Crilly, D., & Aguilera, R. (2017). Embracing causal complexity: The emergence of a neo-configurational perspective. *Journal of Management, 43*(1), 255–282.

Moltz, J. C. (2019). *The politics of space security: Strategic restraint and the pursuit of national interests*. Stanford University Press.

Moltz, J. C. (2024). The future of space security: Assessing the Prospects for Peaceful Outcomes. In Pekkanen, S. M., & Blount, P. J. (Eds.), *The Oxford handbook of space security* (pp. 824–838). Oxford University Press.

Morin, J.-F., & Tepper, E. (2023). The empire strikes back: Comparing US and China's structural power in outer space. *Global Studies Quarterly, 3*(4).

NASA. (2024). *NASA FY24 AI inventory*. Retrieved December 17, 2024, from https://www.nasa.gov/ai-inventory/

Paikowsky, D. (2017). *The power of the space club*. Cambridge University Press.

Pekkanen, S. M., Aoki, S., & Mittleman, J. (2022). Small satellites, big data: Uncovering the invisible in maritime security. *International Security, 47*(2), 177–216.

Pekkanen, S. M., Aoki, S., & Takatori, Y. (2024). Japan in the new lunar space race. *Space Policy, 69*, 101577.

Pollpeter, K. (2024). Neo classical realism as a framework for understanding China's rise as a space power. In Pekkanen, S. M., & Blount, P. J. (Eds.), *The Oxford handbook of space security* (pp. 293–311). Oxford University Press.

Roberts, T. G., & Kaplan, S. (2022). *Space launch to low Earth orbit: How much does it cost. Center for Strategic and International Studies*. Retrieved from https://aerospace.csis.org/data/space-launch-to-low-earth-orbit-how-much-does-it-cost/

Schelling, T. C. (1966). *Arms and influence*. Yale University Press.

Strange, S. (2015). States and markets. *States and Markets*, 1-304.

Sweijs, T., & Ellison, D. (2024). The next frontier: Strategic theory for the space domain. In Pekkanen, S. M., & Blount, P. J. (Eds.), *The Oxford handbook of space security* (pp. 155–171). Oxford University Press.

Tachibana, K. (2024). Ethics in space security: Virtue and the future of cosmopolitanism. In Pekkanen, S. M., & Blount, P. J. (Eds.), *The Oxford handbook of space security* (pp. 248–274). Oxford University Press.

The Strategist. (2017). The coming of China's space silk road. Link: https://www.aspistrategist.org.au/coming-chinas-space-silk-road/ accessed on 2025-Jan-17.

UCS. (2022). UCS satellite database. https://www.ucsusa.org/resources/satellite-database

Wang, G. (2024). Space sustainability: Balanced space security global governance. In Pekkanen, S. M., & Blount, P. J. (Eds.), *The Oxford handbook of space security* (pp. 633–649). Oxford University Press.

Weeden, B. (2020). The United States is losing its leadership role in the fight against orbital debris. *The Space Review*. Retrieved from https://www.thespacereview.com/article/3889/1

Yeo, M. (2019). ADF to acquire next generation satellite technology. Asia-Pacific Defence Reporter, 45(6), 12. Retrieved from https://asiapacificdefencereporter.com/jp-9102-adf-to-acquire-next-generation-satellite-technology/

Zhou, B., & Wang, G. (2024). The future of space security: Assessing the Prospects for Peaceful Outcomes. In Pekkanen, S. M., & Blount, P. J. (Eds.), *The Oxford handbook of space security* (pp. 839–852). Oxford University Press.

Chapter 10
The Interplay of Geopolitical Risk and Container Throughput:
A Panel Data Analysis in the Context of Global Shifts

Abdullah Açık
https://orcid.org/0000-0003-4542-9831
Dokuz Eylül University, Turkey

Nergis Özispa
Mersin University, Turkey

ABSTRACT

This chapter explores how geopolitical risks affect international trade, with a specific focus on container throughput. Given the inherently global nature of maritime logistics, geopolitical shocks have intensified disruptions in trade flows. The study investigates whether the causal relationship between geopolitical risk and trade performance differs between advanced and emerging economies. Using non-causality tests on panel data from 39 countries between 2007 and 2022, the analysis reveals significant differences. In advanced economies, declining container traffic is found to increase geopolitical risk, whereas in emerging economies, rising geopolitical risk leads to a reduction in container traffic. These findings underscore the need for differentiated policies: advanced economies should closely monitor trade indicators to anticipate tensions, while emerging economies should prioritize political stability and trade infrastructure. The chapter provides empirical insights for policymakers navigating the complex interplay between geopolitical uncertainty and global maritime trade.

DOI: 10.4018/979-8-3373-1265-1.ch010

INTRODUCTION

Geopolitical risk is a situation related to the formation of both local and global effects of increasing risk on a regional basis, influenced by many factors. These factors can be generally divided into eight groups. First, political instability, which can arise from government changes, political unrest, civil wars, and coups, significantly heightens the risk. Second, international conflicts, driven by tensions between countries, trade wars, border issues, and military conflicts, further escalate the risk. Third, terrorism and extremism destabilize regions, affecting economic activities, trade, and investments, thus increasing the risk. Fourth, global economic factors, such as economic crises, inflation, currency wars, and recessions, contribute to the risk by generate economic instability. Fifth, competition and struggles over global strategic resources generate instability, thereby amplifying the risk. Sixth, social uprisings and protests can disrupt national stability and strain international relations, leading to increased risk. Seventh, shifts in power dynamics among globally influential countries can cause the breakdown of traditional alliances, raising the risk. Finally, disruptions in trade and supply chains impact workflows and efficiency, further intensifying geopolitical risk.

Regardless of its source, geopolitical risk has inevitable effects on international trade and some of them can be listed as follows. (i) Increasing geopolitical risk can cause disruptions in the global supply chain and cause problems in reaching both final products and intermediate goods to their locations on time. (ii) Increasing geopolitical risk can cause changes in international trade routes and especially maritime transport routes, leading to increased costs. (ii) Increasing geopolitical risk can lead to economic sanctions and restrict countries' market access, leading to a decrease in trade volume. (iii) Increasing geopolitical risk can increase market uncertainty, increasing volatility. (iv) Increasing geopolitical risk can cause changes in trade flows by changing global trade agreements and unions. (v) Increasing geopolitical risk can cause an increase in risk management and insurance costs, leading to an increase in total costs. (vi) Since energy resources are generally concentrated in geopolitically risky regions, increasing risk can cause problems in energy supply and increase costs.

In this study, we aimed to determine whether the relationship between geopolitical risk and international trade, measured through container volumes, differs between Advanced and Emerging economies. We believe that this relationship will differ because Advanced and Emerging economies exhibit distinct characteristics in several key areas, including (i) economic structure and diversification, (ii) political stability and governance, (iii) integration and impact on global trade, (iv) infrastructure and technological capability, (v) trade dependency and market access, (vi) economic resilience and adaptation, (vii) investor confidence and risk perception, (viii) and the geographical location. Geopolitical risks can significantly affect trade, especially in emerging countries, where the factors mentioned above are less developed. Also, trade wars can exacerbate geopolitical risks and lead to a decline in trade volumes, as they also undermine the economic stability of countries.

To deepen the understanding of this relationship, the study draws on several theoretical perspectives that help explain the asymmetrical dynamics between geopolitical risk and international trade. World Systems Theory, which was developed in the 1970s by Immanuel Wallerstein, and Dependency Theory, which was developed by Paul A. Baran in 1957, provide a foundational lens to interpret how systemic inequalities between advanced and emerging economies shape their exposure to geopolitical disruptions. These frameworks suggest that emerging economies, often positioned on the periphery of the global system, are more vulnerable to external shocks due to structural dependencies and economic fragility. Conversely, advanced economies, operating from a position of relative autonomy and influence, may experience geopolitical fluctuations as a consequence of economic shifts, such as changes in trade performance (Wallerstein, 1974; Chirot, 2001; Chirot, 2015; Burhanuddin, 2015; Turhan, 2018; Glosh, 2019). Complex Interdependence Theory, developed by Keohane and Nye in 1977, further emphasizes the intricate and reciprocal linkages among states (economic, political, and security-related) demonstrating how trade flows can act as both a stabilizing force and a source of geopolitical tension (Keohane and Nye, 1987; Rogerson, 2000; Rana, 2015). Additionally, Institutional Theory underscores the importance of robust governance structures, legal frameworks, and policy stability in shaping a country's ability to manage risk and sustain trade activity. From this perspective, the resilience of advanced economies in the face of geopolitical shocks can be partly attributed to institutional maturity, while the greater vulnerability of emerging economies reflects weaker institutional capacities (Meyer and Rowan, 1977; Dimaggio and Powell, 2002). By grounding the empirical analysis in these theoretical frameworks, the study contributes to both the empirical literature on maritime trade and geopolitical risk, and to broader academic debates on global asymmetry, interdependence, and institutional resilience.

Granger non-causality test proposed by Juodis et al. (2021), which is robust to cross-sectional dependence and heterogeneity, was applied to examine the relationship between variables according to country groups. Countries are classified as Advanced Economies and Emerging and Developing Economies to see possible differentiation in the relationship. Classification of the countries are made according to the Country Composition of WEO Groups published by IMF (IMF, 2024). The results showed a two-way interaction in the analyses conducted on the entire sample, whereas a one-way interaction was found when the countries were clustered. In Advanced economies, the direction of this interaction was from Container Throughput to Geopolitical Risk, while in Emerging economies, it flowed from

Geopolitical Risk to Container Throughput. This confirmed that the relationship between these variables differs based on the economic structures of the countries. Consequently, it is suggested that countries adopt policies tailored to their specific economic conditions to mitigate the effects of Geopolitical Risk.

Section 2 provides an overview of global events that influence geopolitical risk and their implications for maritime transportation. Section 3 reviews the relevant literature on the subject, highlighting key findings and theoretical perspectives. Section 4 outlines the data sources and methodology employed in the empirical analysis. Section 5 presents the results and discusses their implications. Finally, Section 6 concludes the paper and offers policy recommendations based on the findings.

GLOBAL EVENTS THAT AFFECT GEOPOLITICAL RISK AND MARITIME TRANSPORTATION

Geopolitical shocks are a major concern for the business community, the international trade sector, financial markets and participants of these markets, policy makers, etc. It is possible to exemplify these geopolitical shocks as wars, military attacks, global diseases, terrorist acts or diplomatic conflicts occurring anywhere in the world (Wang et al., 2023). When it comes to the maritime sector, the highly international nature of the sector makes it sensitive to such geopolitical risks. Although some geopolitical tensions may be preceded by early warning signs, such events are relatively rare, often abrupt, and their impacts are difficult to fully anticipate in scale and direction (Georgoulas et al., 2024).

The maritime sector has been significantly affected by geopolitical events from past to present, both positively and negatively. For example, the new market opportunity that emerged with the closure of the Suez Canal in 1956 increased the profitability of tanker owners, while the Yom Kippur War in 1973 caused the tanker market to collapse, and the Gulf War in 1991 increased the demand for tankers again. When we examine more recent examples, it is observed that the Russia-Ukraine war that started in 2022 created serious difficulties for shipping companies and crew changes, while creating opportunities for LNG ships and tankers to increase their margins (Georgoulas et al., 2024).

In the academic literature, eight key drivers are frequently identified as sources of geopolitical risk, each contributing to both localized and global impacts. These are political instability, international conflicts, terrorism and extremism, global economic factors, competition of energy resources, social protests, power changes of global actors and disruptions in global supply chains.

Political Instabilities

Political instabilities are among the issues that affect and even shape the international maritime industry. In addition to geopolitical risks, economic and trade policy risks can have significant consequences that have negative effects on international maritime trade. Political turmoil increases market friction in financial markets and hampers economic decision-making. The literature suggests that instability elevates firms' credit risk, increases private borrowing costs, and raises the cost of public debt financing. In response, firms often reduce capital expenditures, limit dividend payments, cut financial expenses, and decrease financial leverage to manage their exposure to heightened uncertainty (Kotcharin & Maneenop, 2020).

There are numerous examples of political instability events around the world that have disrupted trade flows, increased economic uncertainty, and influenced maritime activities. One prominent example is the Arab Spring, a wave of protests and uprisings that began in late 2010 and spread across several countries in the Middle East and North Africa. In Egypt, the 2011 uprisings created uncertainty for traders and temporarily paralyzed institutional functions, leading to a significant demand shock in wheat imports—an essential staple tied closely to national food security. During the period of instability, Egypt's wheat trade patterns deviated markedly from seasonal norms, indicating the fragility of import-dependent supply chains during domestic unrest (Veninga & Ihle, 2018). The effects of political turmoil are not limited to trade flows but also extend to financial markets. During the Arab Spring, abnormal returns in major stock market indices of affected countries averaged −1.1%, while credit default spreads increased by 1.4%. These shifts reflect how investors reprice assets based on both local and regional unrest, with protests in neighboring countries influencing perceptions of domestic risk. Once unrest breaks out locally, investor attention shifts inward, amplifying volatility in asset prices and raising financing costs (Tanyeri et al., 2022).

Another major example of political instability with significant trade implications is Brexit, which introduced considerable uncertainty and structural change in the UK's trade relations, particularly with the European Union. Following the implementation of the EU–UK Trade and Cooperation Agreement (TCA), the UK experienced a substantial and persistent decline in its export performance. There was a statistically significant and long-lasting negative impact on UK exports, including a contraction in the diversity of goods exported—raising serious concerns about the UK's long-term productivity and trade capacity (Du et al., 2023). Complementary findings indicate that Brexit reduced trade flows between the UK and the EU by nearly 20% in both directions, with notable measurement and structural effects that further complicate trade logistics and reporting accuracy (Kren and Lawless, 2024).

These effects are particularly visible in the maritime sector, where political uncertainty can raise capital acquisition costs and delay investment decisions. Maritime companies, highly sensitive to global developments, respond cautiously during such periods to mitigate long-term financial and operational risk. For example, political tensions in the South and East China Seas have triggered trade frictions between China and its trading partners, particularly the United States, leading to retaliatory tariffs and trade barriers. These frictions, while rooted in regional disputes, have had broad implications for international trade flows and market stability (Wang et al., 2023).

International Conflicts

In today's world, where the effects of globalization can be clearly seen in all their aspects, it is necessary to accept that the entire world is interconnected. Any event that happens at one end of the world (even the seizure of a single commercial ship) has the potential to directly affect the entire world economy. In short, a geopolitical risk/tension at one end of the world can create a butterfly effect and hit a different point at the other end of the world (Capolongo & Kühl, 2024).

The global political landscape has been characterized by a heightened frequency of geopolitical tensions in recent years, including Sino-American trade disputes, the United Kingdom's withdrawal from the European Union, the Russia-Ukraine conflict, and territorial contentions between China and India. Critical infrastructure sabotage incidents, such as the Nord Stream pipeline explosion and the Crimean Bridge attack arising from the Russia-Ukraine hostilities, have further exacerbated international tensions. These developments have catalyzed the proliferation of nationalist and populist ideologies, introduced significant uncertainty into the global political economy, diminished multilateral capacity to address the COVID-19 pandemic effectively, generated novel geopolitical friction points, exposed structural vulnerabilities in the international relations framework, and precipitated a global economic contraction (Yu & Wang, 2023).

For example, the tension between Israel and Hamas that began in the Middle East in late 2023 resulted in ships moving on the Red Sea having to seek safe routes, and while the usage rate of the Suez Canal, one of the most active channels in the world, decreased, commercial ships changed their routes to the Cape of Good Hope. This change of route made by commercial ships extended the voyage times of ships sailing in international waters, causing more fuel consumption, more harmful emissions, higher freight rates and port congestion in different parts of the world (Capolongo & Kühl, 2024; Pseftogkas et al. 2024)

Take two agricultural exporting countries, Russia and Ukraine, for example, both of which play important roles in delivering agricultural products and foodstuffs to global markets. And the Russia-Ukraine tensions that emerged in early 2022 have caused congestion at certain ports, as well as delays in grain shipments, disruptions in maritime logistics connections, jeopardizing maritime security and, of course, increased freight rates (Dawar & Bai, 2024).

Terrorism and Extremism

Terrorism has emerged as a critical global security challenge, permeating virtually all regions worldwide since the late twentieth and early twenty-first centuries. The geographical distribution of terrorist activity has exhibited significant shifts over the past two decades. While Latin America, the Caribbean, Europe, and Central Asia previously constituted primary epicenters of terrorist incidents, contemporary patterns reveal a pronounced concentration in South Asia, the Middle East, North Africa, and sub-Saharan Africa, indicating a substantial reorientation of the global terrorism landscape (Khan, 2024).

Terrorism and extremism alter global trade dynamics through broader security-driven distortions. Increased security measures near regions associated with terrorist activity tend to suppress trade volumes, not only in the affected country but also in its neighboring economies. Proximity to transnational terrorism often leads to heightened controls, delays, and inspections that reduce trade efficiency in surrounding regions, while more distant countries may experience increased trade due to rerouting and diversion (De Sousa et al., 2018).

Terrorism's impact also varies by product type and trade direction. While trade in primary commodities tends to remain relatively stable, manufactured goods—especially those requiring complex and time-sensitive supply chains—face pronounced declines in both imports and exports. Domestic terrorism is associated with reduced manufactured exports and increased primary exports, while transnational terrorism is more likely to reduce primary exports, disrupting global supply patterns and altering comparative advantages across regions (Bandyopadhyay et al., 2018).

The shipping industry has always been a vulnerable and lucrative target for terrorists by its nature. There are multiple risk factors in the shipping industry that can attract terrorist attacks. These risk factors can be divided into two main groups: misuse of containers and misuse of ships. Some of the factors that constitute terrorist risk factors in the shipping industry include the use of containers to carry weapons or similar prohibited items, the use of ships to launder money, to attack the other party or to damage infrastructure and to threaten people (Kotcharin & Maneenop, 2020).

In the past, the 9/11 attacks on the United States tightened security regimes internationally and these tightening policies in security processes significantly affected the global transportation sector all around the world (Kotcharin & Maneenop, 2020). Similarly, the attack on the tanker Limberg in October 2002, which caused the death of 1 seafarer and the injuries of 12 seafarers (The BBC News, 2014), caused insurance companies to change their risk assessments and demand three times more premiums from ships calling at Yemeni ports (Kotcharin & Maneenop, 2020), significantly increasing maritime transportation costs.

These dynamics demonstrate that terrorism, whether through targeted attacks or broader geopolitical consequences, creates logistical, financial, and psychological burdens on international trade. The maritime sector, given its role in handling over 80% of global trade, remains particularly susceptible to these disruptions, which often lead to long-term changes in trade routes, insurance practices, and global supply chain structures.

Global Economic Factors

Global uncertainties cause global economic activities to contract. The 7-11 attacks that took place in the USA in 2001 are among the main events that created a situation of global uncertainty in the world. These attacks in 2001 caused a rapid contraction in world markets, but just as the demand for oil decreased in line with the supply-demand balance, causing a decrease in oil prices, the maritime sector, which started to revive in 2002, reacted in a similar way (Khan et al., 2021).

As an example, although the 2009 financial crisis was seen as a systemic failure of the world banking system, the financial crisis it left behind has remained a source of concern worldwide for many years. The impact of the crisis was felt most the proverb "When America sneezes, the rest of the world gets cold" has once again become a haven for economists, and they have spent a lot of time trying to predict how the financial flu diagnosis in the US will affect the rest of the world (Glod et al., 2009).

While global uncertainties cause economic growth to slow down, the slowdown in economic growth reduces the demand for transport and the demand for the maritime sector, which is a derived demand industry, and the BDI starts to show a downward trend. Similar to the Iran-US tension that started in 2012, the US-China trade conflict that took place in 2018 and the COVID-19 crisis that emerged in 2020 are some of the geopolitical risk factors that affect global economic factors and drag the world economy into uncertainty. While these uncertainties cause phenomena such as stagnation, quarantine, and social isolation in the markets, global trade declines rapidly and the global trade slowdown manifests itself with the BDI entering a downward trend (Khan et al., 2021).

Freight rates in the shipping industry are directly related to demand for global economic factors/activities. The shipping industry accounts for 80 to 90 percent of global trade, adding approximately $380 billion to the global economy. The truly global nature of the shipping industry makes the industry vulnerable to geopolitical risks. In addition to geopolitical risks, shocks resulting from uncertainties in global policies are causing a decrease in global production activities and thus a decrease in demand for shipping (Drobetz et al., 2021).

Competition of Energy Resources

Energy constitutes the fundamental resource for economic vitality, with consistent energy availability being essential for maintaining economic development and safeguarding national security interests. The strategic control of energy resources, particularly fossil fuels, provides significant geopolitical leverage during both conflict and peace periods, owing to their finite availability. The geopolitical dimensions of energy are predominantly associated with the vulnerabilities inherent to fossil fuel dependencies (oil, gas, and coal). Significantly, fossil fuel reserves are characterized by their limited nature and their concentration in regions experiencing political instability. The emphasis on fossil fuels in geopolitical discourse reflects their continued predominance in the global energy portfolio, constituting 86% of worldwide energy consumption (Su et al., 2021). Geopolitical risk and natural resource dynamics constitute critical variables that substantially influence the energy landscape within economic systems. Escalating geopolitical tensions generate energy price volatility, supply disruptions, and investment contraction, profoundly impacting the equilibrium of energy demand and supply mechanisms. Recent years have witnessed a strategic reorientation from fossil fuel consumption toward renewable energy production, driven by the expanding growth potential of renewable technologies as viable fossil energy alternatives that facilitate sustainable development objectives. Nevertheless, intensifying geopolitical tensions continue to adversely affect energy markets and impede renewable development trajectories, as heightened geopolitical risk environments demonstrably diminish investment returns and constrain capital allocation opportunities (Zhang et al., 2023).

Although geopolitical risks are an important reality for the entire world, the regions where geopolitical tensions occur today are also strategically separate regions that pose a separate risk. For example, Venezuela and the Middle East are oil producing regions and geopolitical tensions in these regions will significantly disrupt global oil supply. While the decrease in supply causes fuel prices to increase, which directly affects transportation costs, shipping companies will have to reflect this increase in fuel prices in freight rates (VS&B Containers Group., 2024).

In today's interconnected world, escalating tensions between Russia and Ukraine in early 2022 and between Israel and Hamas in late 2023 could has caused significant problems in energy supplies. The Strait of Hormuz, through which 30% of the world's oil and over 20% of global liquefied natural gas trade are carried, is of critical importance for global energy transport. Therefore, disruptions along this route would not only increase global oil and natural gas prices, but would also cause even more significant problems for European countries that are heavily dependent on this region for energy supplies. Although eurozone countries have signed multiple contracts with Qatar for the delivery of 10 million tons of LPG per year starting in 2026 and have made a strategic move by phasing out Russian gas, they continue to be dependent on other countries for energy resources and face the risk of longer transportation times due to Middle East tensions (Capolongo & Kühl, 2024).

Social Protests

Recently, as societies are increasingly exposed to the effects of globalization and crises cannot or are difficult to contain within their original areas due to changes in the structure of social communication, analyses of the world's political, economic and social situation and the way it is evolving have increased (Suarez-de Vivero & Mateos, 2017).

The US National Intelligence Council, listed social tensions and extremist movements in the general category of lack of trust in its 2004 report named Mapping the Global Future (Suarez-de Vivero & Mateos, 2017). However, when examining the social dimension of geopolitical risks, the concept of food comes to the fore. Rising food prices due to lack of food supply or food security can lead to increased inflation as well as inaccessibility to food. Failure to ensure food supply or security, in turn, leads to loss of labor, disruption of livelihoods, and income levels. Food shortages, which can lead to social unrest and protests, are also factors that disrupt supply chains and question the stability of governments (S&P Global, 2024).

Since around 2007, rising food prices and volatility in international food markets have brought the issue of the "global food crisis" to the forefront. Global concerns about this food crisis have been addressed through measures such as the creation of capital by various international institutions to counter this geopolitical risk and the creation of public awareness to highlight agricultural development plans and opportunities (Sommerville et al., 2014). However, the war between Ukraine and Russia that started in 2022 has affected world markets with many items such as commodity markets, financial flows, population displacement and trade, while also negatively affecting the world in terms of access to food and food security. The prices of goods such as energy, wheat and fertilizer exported from Russia and Ukraine to the world have increased by 30% to 60% since the beginning of the war. In addition to all these, the increase in energy prices and the disruptions in logistics systems throughout Europe are causing the prices of basic foodstuffs to increase rapidly and still continue to increase (Saâdaoui et al., 2022).

Power Changes of Global Actors

Tensions and shifts in power direction between the world's great powers are another important geopolitical risk. The increasing tensions between the world's two great powers, the US and China, in recent years have caused collateral damage to weaker countries whose survival depends largely on their relationships with these powerful countries (Lin & Meng, 2024). In times of high tensions between countries considered to be among the world's great powers, neutrality or bridging strategies are not possible for weaker countries, and survival interests take precedence. In such cases, weaker countries become territorial acquisitions, buffer zones, economic exploitation bases, battlefields or power projections for strong countries, and the chances of survival of weaker countries are significantly reduced. When looking at early history, the damages inflicted on weaker countries in developed and developing countries during the Cold War and the periods of increasing tensions between the US and the Soviet Union are presented as examples of how tensions between great powers affect the world (Can, 2024).

One of the important threats of today is the tension based on competition between the US and China. Discussions that started on the grounds of global leadership during the Covid-19 pandemic have forced a lot of countries, which considered a secondary power, especially the US ally, to cope with powers that are larger than itself (Lin & Meng, 2024). In recent years, China has significantly narrowed its power gap with the US, affecting almost every aspect of international politics and causing significant power realignments. For example, while the US and China competed for world dominance, important pieces have been moved, while countries such as the European Union, India and Russia have remained relatively independent and emerged as separate powers. Therefore, in today's conditions, the US cannot be seen as the world's sole power as it used to be, while China cannot be shown as the world's sole power in the same way. This situation has been summarized by a Chinese academic as "the world structure has changed from a single superpower, from many great powers, to two superpowers, to many great powers" (Zhao, 2022).

The tensions between Washington and Beijing, which began in recent years and continue today, have received a "high" risk score of 1.5 in the BlackRock Investment Institute's geopolitical risk reports. For comparison, a risk level of 1.5 is twice the score of a possible major terrorist attack (Gu, 2023). In contrast, the same institution assigned a score of 0.65 for Hamas' attacks on Israel, while the score assigned for an escalation of conflict in the Middle East after a war between Russia and NATO was 0.37 (The Business Times, 2023).

This strategic competition has been described by BlackRock as the biggest geopolitical risk that all world markets have to endure. Despite the efforts of both sides to stabilize the relationship, it is stated that these geopolitical events, especially

China's actions in the South China Sea and Beijing's desire to pressure Taiwan, have now become a structural risk (The Business Times, 2023).

Disruptions in Global Supply Chain

Since 2016, a surge in nationalism and protectionism has disrupted global supply chains through a series of compounding geopolitical events. Brexit initiated prolonged commercial uncertainty in the UK, while the US-China trade conflict under President Trump redirected manufacturing primarily to Southeast Asia rather than the US. The COVID-19 pandemic subsequently triggered protectionist policies globally, exposing vulnerabilities in the established global value chain model. Russia's 2022 invasion of Ukraine created an energy crisis throughout Europe, where Russian gas had constituted 40% of EU consumption, necessitating extensive governmental interventions. These consecutive interstate conflicts have fundamentally challenged supply chain resilience, compelling organizations to reconsider their global network designs (Bernardski et al., 2025).

Geopolitical risks cause supply chain disruptions because they create various challenges in maritime supply chains, such as economic, logistical, and security (Dawar & Bai, 2024). Maritime transportation, which is of vital importance in global world trade, also has a fragile nature that can be easily disrupted by being directly affected by global events. Since supply chains affected by these geopolitical risks negatively affect economic growth and financial stability, the whole world is seeking to diversify supply chains, find new energy sources and develop strategies that will make supply chains more resilient (Capolongo & Kühl, 2024).

Geopolitical risks have always been important for supply chain logistics. However, in recent years, due to the Russia-Ukraine and Israel-Hamas tensions, they have played a major role that will probably continue into the foreseeable future and have even reached a level that will affect world trade routes (Dawar & Bai, 2024).

Due to the war between Israel and Palestine, the upheavals in the Red Sea and the Gulf of Aden have significantly affected the global maritime supply chain, with merchant ships turning to the Cape of Good Hope instead of the Suez Canal. The change in route has increased the freight rates of ships, lengthened voyages, delayed delivery dates, and in addition to all this, increased greenhouse gas emissions (Peng et al., 2024).

LITERATURE REVIEW

A review of the current literature reveals that the concept of geopolitical risk has been explored globally, regionally, and locally across various sectors and for different purposes. Although the scope and variables of these studies vary, they are interconnected because the markets examined influence one another. The prominent areas of examination in the studies examined in this section are investments decisions, cash holding decisions, oil prices, various shipping related indices and stock markets.

In maritime transportation, the effects of geopolitical risk are inevitable because critical energy resources (such as oil and natural gas), essential agricultural commodities (like grains and fertilizers), and strategic transit points—including major shipping canals (such as the Suez Canal and Panama Canal) and key straits (like the Strait of Hormuz, Bab-El-Mandeb, and Malacca)—are frequently located in regions prone to political instability, conflict, or territorial disputes. In this regard, Dawar and Bai (2024) examined the relationship between geopolitical risks and disruptions in maritime supply chains, conducted a comprehensive analysis using case studies, data analysis, and data from current events. As a result of the study, it was concluded that trade disputes, terrorism, global conflicts, and political instability could lead to disruptions in global supply chains through effects such as port closures, increased security concerns and agreements, changes and irregularities in shipping routes, and increased insurance costs. The study argues that all these disruptions will increase transportation costs, increase security risks, and significantly damage international trade flows. As evidenced by the impacts discussed in the previous study, rising geopolitical risk will also be reflected in an increase in freight rates.

Depending on the source of the risk, geopolitical instability can impact freight rates through various channels, including disruptions in trade routes, higher insurance premiums, port closures, delays in port operations, increased fuel price volatility, heightened risk of piracy, reduced trade volumes, increased uncertainty, and reduced available tonnage due to longer, rerouted voyages. In this context, Khan et al. (2021) examined the relationship between geopolitical risk and oil prices and the Baltic Dry Index. As a result of the study, in cases where geopolitical risk occurs, they concluded that the connection between oil prices and the Baltic Dry Index is more pronounced. The study emphasized the importance of oil prices for the transportation sector, while it was determined that geopolitical risk is the determining factor for oil prices and the Baltic dry index. The study found that the performance of the transportation sector is affected by the oil markets and geopolitical risk. Similarly, Monge et al. (2023), who aimed to determine the effect of geopolitical risks on crude oil prices and shipping freight rates, conducted analyses using Baltic Dry index (BDI) and West Texas Intermediate (WTI) data between 1985 and 2021. As a result of the analyses they conducted using statistical methods, they concluded that geopolitical risk and BDI will return to their original trends in case of exogenous shocks. In the LNG and LPG freight markets, Michael and Melas (2022) investigated the impact of geopolitical shocks and found that such events significantly increased the spot charter rates for LNG and LPG carriers. Their study highlights the critical importance of natural resources for economic development and energy security, particularly for resource-importing nations. The authors argue that geopolitical shocks not only elevate prices and costs but also disrupt the global flow of natural resources, potentially triggering a downward economic spiral and exacerbating the risk of recession.

Given the clear impact of geopolitical risk on maritime supply chains and freight markets, shipping companies are naturally influenced by these factors in their financial decision-making. In this context, Kotcharin and Maneenop (2020) explored the relationship between shipping companies' cash holding decisions and geopolitical risk. Their findings suggest that during periods of heightened geopolitical risk, shipping companies tend to increase their cash reserves. The study also revealed that geopolitical risk has a positive and significant impact on the container and dry cargo sectors, while it does not significantly affect the tanker market. As evident, the impact of geopolitical risk varies across different sectors. Moreover, the effects of geopolitical risk are not confined to maritime companies alone but extend to businesses across various industries. Wang et al. (2023) found a strong negative relationship between firm-level corporate investment and geopolitical risk in their study, which examined the impact of geopolitical risk on the investments of U.S. companies. The results show that when the geopolitical risk index doubles, corporate investment in the following quarter decreases by 14% of its sample mean. The study also suggests that this effect is more pronounced for firms with greater market power.

The effects of political risk at the firm level often stem from its broader influence on a country's macroeconomic variables. Political instability can lead to fluctuations in interest rates, inflation, exchange rates, and overall economic growth, which in turn affect corporate profitability, investment decisions, and long-term planning. Tuna and Çalışkan (2022) investigated the impact of geopolitical risks on macroeconomic variables in Turkey. Using monthly data from 1994 to 2022 and employing a causality test in the frequency domain, the authors found that inflation rates and real effective exchange rates were significantly influenced by geopolitical risks in the medium and long term. Their study, focused specifically on Turkey, concluded that the country's geographical location makes it particularly vulnerable to geopolitical risks, which directly affect its economy. Building on the notion that geopolitical risks influence all financial markets as key determinants of investment decisions, Üçler and Özşahin (2020) conducted a Bootstrap Panel Causality analysis to explore the causal relationship between geopolitical risk and stock market indices in developing countries. Analyzing data from nine developing nations between 1987 and 2018, they found evidence of a unidirectional causality from geopolitical risk to the stock market indices in Argentina, Brazil, Mexico, and Thailand.

The study most closely related to our research in the literature was conducted by Atacan and Açık (2023), who applied asymmetric panel causality analysis to 15 countries. Their findings indicated that geopolitical risks of the countries spread to other countries and positive shocks in geopolitical risk had a negative impact on the container traffic of these countries. For this reason, they emphasized that the geopolitical risks of other countries, in addition to a country's own geopolitical risks, are crucial for its economic stability and overall well-being.

The existing literature on geopolitical risk and its economic implications can be broadly grouped into several thematic areas. A significant body of research has focused on the financial dimensions of geopolitical risk, exploring its effects on investment decisions, corporate cash holdings, and stock market behavior. Another major group of studies examines the commodity and energy markets, particularly the impact of geopolitical tensions on oil prices, natural gas markets, and shipping indices such as the Baltic Dry Index. A third stream of research has investigated macroeconomic and trade-related outcomes, analyzing how geopolitical instability influences exchange rates, inflation, and international trade flows. More recently, a growing number of studies have addressed the maritime transportation sector, considering how geopolitical risks disrupt supply chains, affect freight rates, and alter strategic shipping routes. While each of these thematic groups provides valuable insights into the multifaceted nature of geopolitical risk, there remains a lack of integrative studies that link these dimensions with country-level heterogeneity, especially in the context of maritime trade.

While previous studies have examined the impact of geopolitical risk on trade and maritime markets, few have explicitly considered how these relationships may differ systematically between advanced and emerging economies, despite clear theoretical grounds for such differentiation. Drawing on World Systems Theory and Dependency Theory, it is evident that emerging economies, positioned on the periphery of global trade networks, face higher vulnerability to geopolitical disruptions due to structural dependencies and limited economic diversification, making their trade volumes more susceptible to external shocks. Conversely, advanced economies, operating from a position of economic strength and institutional maturity, may experience geopolitical tensions as a consequence of trade fluctuations, consistent with Complex Interdependence Theory, where trade flows act as stabilizers or signals influencing geopolitical dynamics. Institutional Theory further suggests that advanced economies are better equipped to buffer geopolitical shocks due to robust governance structures, whereas emerging economies' weaker institutional frameworks exacerbate their exposure to risk. Despite these clear theoretical underpinnings, empirical literature has yet to systematically test whether and how the causal dynamics between geopolitical risk and international trade differ by a country's development level within the maritime context. This gap underscores the importance of the current study, which explicitly examines these asymmetrical relationships using a differentiated advanced-emerging economy perspective within the maritime trade framework, thereby advancing scholarly understanding in this field.

Despite the increasing number of studies exploring the impact of geopolitical risk on financial markets, energy prices, and trade-related variables, there remains a notable gap in the literature regarding the asymmetrical effects of geopolitical risk on international trade across different country groups, particularly through the lens of container throughput. Most existing studies either focus on a single country or analyze geopolitical risk in aggregate without distinguishing between advanced and emerging economies, which differ significantly in terms of institutional structure, trade dependency, and resilience to external shocks. This study addresses this gap by examining whether the direction and nature of the relationship between geopolitical risk and international trade vary depending on a country's level of development. By employing the Granger non-causality test proposed by Juodis et al. (2021), which accounts for cross-sectional dependence and heterogeneity, this research contributes methodologically as well. Furthermore, the use of container throughput as a proxy for trade activity provides a direct and sector-specific measure of the maritime economy's sensitivity to geopolitical developments. This dual contribution—differentiating country groups and using maritime trade as a focal point—makes this study uniquely positioned to inform both academic debates and policy discussions in the field of international trade and maritime economics.

DATA AND METHODOLOGY

The panel dataset includes 39 countries covering the period between 2007 and 2022 and consists of 624 (39x16) annual observations. In selection of countries, countries that have both the Geopolitical Risk Index and Container Throughput variables were preferred. The included countries are Argentina, Australia, Belgium, Brazil, Canada, Chile, China, Colombia, Denmark, Egypt, Finland, France, Germany, Hong Kong, India, Indonesia, Israel, Italy, Japan, Malaysia, Mexico, Netherlands, Norway, Peru, Philippines, Poland, Portugal, Russian Federation, Saudi Arabia, South Africa, South Korea, Spain, Sweden, Thailand, Tunisia, Türkiye, United Kingdom, United States, and Viet Nam in alphabetical order.

Geopolitical Risk Index developed by Caldara and Iacoviello (2022). The relevant index variable was obtained from Policyuncertainty (2024). Container Throughput volumes of the countries were obtained from the World Bank (2024) and the missing year years were completed by UNCTAD (2024).

Countries are classified as Advanced Economies and Emerging and Developing Economies to see possible differentiation in the relationship. Classification of the countries are made according to the Country Composition of WEO Groups published by IMF (IMF, 2024). The list of countries included in our study sample because they have both GPR and Container throughput data is presented in Table 1.

Table 1. Classified Countries Based on IMF

Developed Economies	Emerging and Developing Economies
Australia, Belgium, Canada, Denmark, Finland, France, Germany, Hong Kong, Israel, Italy, Japan, Netherlands, Norway, Portugal, South Korea, Spain, Sweden, United Kingdom, United States	Argentina, Brazil, Chile, China, Colombia, Egypt, India, Indonesia, Malaysia, Mexico, Peru, Philippines, Poland, Russia, Saudi Arabia, South Africa, Thailand, Tunisia, Türkiye, Vietnam

Source: IMF (2024).

The different colored presentations and geographical locations of the countries included in our study according to their IMF classifications are presented in Figure 1. General assessments can be made by considering the geographical locations of the countries. Advanced economies tend to be more integrated into the global economy through trade, investment, and the presence of multinational corporations. Many of these countries have also strengthened their global trade relationships by being part of organizations like the OECD. In addition, advanced economies typically enjoy stable political systems and well-established legal frameworks, which generate a reliable environment for both businesses and governments. On the other hand, many developing economies face challenges such as weak governance, political instability, and economic volatility. While advanced economies boast advanced industrial sectors and robust service industries, developing countries often rely on low value-added industries, which can limit their economic growth potential. Most advanced countries were early participants in the Industrial Revolution, which allowed them to enjoy prolonged periods of economic growth and industrial development. In contrast, developing countries generally joined this revolution later and are now striving to "catch up" with developed nations by pursuing new industrial and economic advancements. The stability challenges faced by these countries contribute to elevated geopolitical risks on a regional level.

Individual scatter plot graphs illustrating the relationships between Container Throughput and Geopolitical Risk for each country over the 16-year period are provided in Appendix 1. While the relationship between the series appears to be positive for most countries, it would be premature to draw this conclusion without first considering the results of unit root tests, which will be applied in later stages of the analysis. Theoretically, it is not reasonable to argue that increased Geopolitical Risk would lead to higher Container Throughput.

Figure 1. Geographical Locations of the Countries

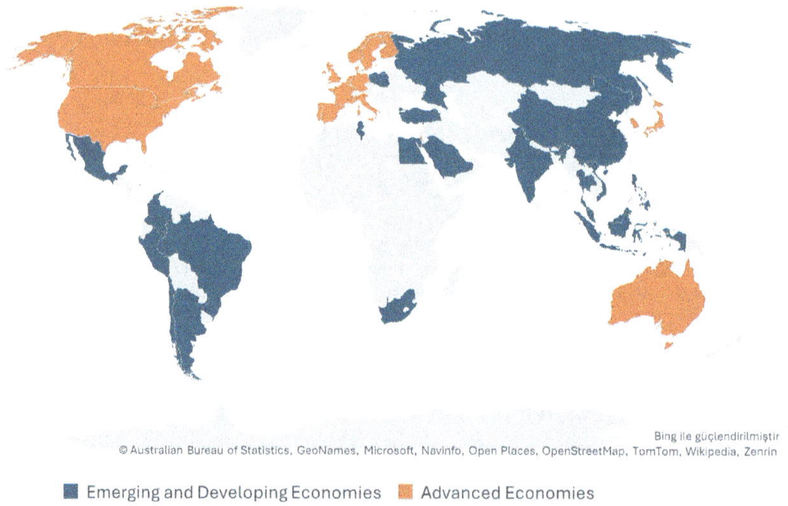

Descriptive statistics for two variables from the panel data set, which includes 39 countries and 16 years, are presented in Table 2. Detailed descriptive statistics for individual countries' Container Throughput values are provided in Appendix 2, while the detailed statistics for Geopolitical Risk values can be found in Appendix 3. When we investigate the table, mean container throughput is significantly higher in emerging economies (16 million TEUs) compared to advanced economies (11.2 million TEUs), despite the perception that advanced economies dominate global trade. This is largely driven by the presence of major exporting countries like China and large-volume transit hubs in developing regions. However, the median container throughput is much higher in advanced economies, indicating that the distribution in emerging economies is heavily skewed due to a few outliers with extremely high volumes. The standard deviation of container throughput is also higher in emerging economies (42.2 million) than in advanced ones (11.4 million), suggesting greater disparity among emerging countries in terms of trade volume. This variability likely reflects structural differences in port infrastructure, trade dependency, and economic scale.

Regarding the Geopolitical Risk (GPR) index, advanced economies have a higher mean GPR score (3.74) than emerging economies (1.77). However, skewness and kurtosis values indicate more extreme and infrequent GPR shocks in emerging economies — the GPR distribution in these countries is sharply right-skewed and highly leptokurtic, with a kurtosis of 75.79, suggesting the presence of rare but extreme geopolitical events. All series show significant non-normality, as confirmed by the

Jarque-Bera test statistics (all p-values = 0.00), which justifies the need for robust and non-parametric econometric approaches, such as the Granger non-causality test employed in this study. These statistics highlight the heterogeneity between country groups in terms of both trade performance and exposure to geopolitical risk.

Table 2. Descriptive Statistics

	ALL		ADVANCED		EMERGING	
	CONT	**GPR**	**CONT**	**GPR**	**CONT**	**GPR**
Mean	13714004	2.734969	11282954	3.743768	16023501	1.77661
Median	6786766.	0.903754	9442883	1.555696	5845416	0.544261
Maximum	269000000	44.28464	62214119	42.3823	269000000	44.284
Minimum	318924.0	0.051	318924	0.093	418883.9	0.051
Std. Dev.	31339395	5.02	11397884	6.11	42234511	3.44
Skewness	5.88	4.13	1.876621	3.08	4.50	6.85
Kurtosis	40.16	24.54	7.224521	13.53	22.78	75.79
Jarque-Bera	39505.15	13847.54	404.49	1889.17	6301.52	73147.96
Probability	0.00	0.00	0.00	0.00	0.00	0.00
Observations	624	624	304	304	320	320

Source: UNCTAD (2024); World Bank (2024).

The most widely used tests for detecting cross-sectional dependence include the LM test (Breusch and Pagan, 1980), CD LM test (Pesaran, 2004a), CD test (Pesaran, 2004b), and the LM adjusted test (Pesaran, Ullah, and Yamagata, 2008). The choice among these tests depends on the relative sizes of the cross-sectional dimension (N) and the time dimension (T) in the panel data set. The LM Test is used when N is relatively small compared to T; the CD LM test is used when N is large compared to T; and the CD and LM Adjusted tests are used when both N is larger than T and when T is larger than N. The null hypotheses of all these tests indicate that there is no cross-sectional dependence in the series.

LLC (Levin, Lin, & Chu Test) (Levin et al., 2002), IPS (Im, Pesaran, & Shin Test) (IM et al., 2003), ADF Fisher (Fisher-type Augmented Dickey-Fuller Test) (Maddala & Wu, 1999), PP Fisher (Fisher-type Phillips-Perron Test) (Choi, 2001), and Hadri (Hadri, 2000) tests were applied to the series. While the LLC test is suitable for homogeneous variables, all other tests are suitable for heterogeneous variables. In addition, Hadri is a stationarity test, and its null hypothesis indicates that the series is stationary, while all other tests are unit root tests and their null hypotheses indicate the existence of a unit root.

We chose the homogeneity test developed by Pesaran and Yamagata (2008) to assess the homogeneity of the series. This test provides both Delta and Delta Adjusted outputs. The Delta Adjusted version is an improved and more reliable version of the Delta test, particularly for small samples and in cases where the time dimension (T) is not large enough. The null hypotheses of these tests indicate that the series are homogeneous.

In this study, we employ the Granger non-causality test proposed by Juodis et al. (2021), which is specifically designed to be robust to cross-sectional dependence and heterogeneity in panel data—features that are critical when analyzing macroeconomic relationships across countries with diverse structures and interconnected markets. This method allows us to reliably test directional predictability without imposing restrictive assumptions of homogeneity across units, making it particularly well-suited for our sample of 39 countries over 16 years. By using this advanced causality framework, we ensure that the identified relationships between geopolitical risk and container throughput are not artifacts of unaddressed dependencies or heterogeneity, thereby strengthening the validity and credibility of our findings. This methodological choice supports our study's objective to provide nuanced insights into the asymmetric dynamics between geopolitical risk and maritime trade across advanced and emerging economies.

To ensure transparency, we report each methodological choice and its rationale explicitly: the Juodis et al. (2021) Granger non-causality test was selected for its robustness to cross-sectional dependence and heterogeneity, which is critical in macro panel structures like ours (N=39, T=16). Tests for cross-sectional dependence (LM, CD, CD LM, LM adjusted) were applied to determine the appropriate generation of unit root tests, and homogeneity tests guided the choice between LLC and IPS tests. Lag lengths were selected using information criteria and consistency with prior literature, ensuring credible inference within the panel structure.

RESULTS

The empirical analysis is initially conducted using the full sample of countries to examine the overall relationship between Geopolitical Risk (GPR) and Container Throughput. Subsequently, to account for potential structural differences arising from varying levels of economic development, the sample is divided into two subgroups: Advanced Economies and Emerging and Developing Economies, as classified by the International Monetary Fund (IMF). This disaggregated approach allows for a comparative assessment of the dynamics between GPR and trade activity across distinct economic contexts, enabling the identification of group-specific patterns and potential asymmetries in the causal relationship.

Full Sample

To detect possible cross-sectional dependencies in variables, LM Test (Breusch-Pagan, 1980), CD LM Test (Pesaran, 2004a), CD Test (Pesaran, 2004b), LM adj Test (PUY, 2008) were applied to both Container and GPR variables, and the results are presented in Table 3. According to the cross-sectional dependency tests implemented with GAUSS software with maximum lag of 2, the null hypothesis of no cross-sectional dependence was rejected in LM and CD LM tests but could not be rejected in CD and LM Adjusted tests at 95% confidence level. Since T was 16 and N was 39 in our sample, it was decided that there was no cross-sectional dependence in the series based on the results of the CD and LM Adjusted tests.

Table 3. Cross-Section Dependence and Homogeneity Tests

Test	Container	GPR
Breusch-Pagan LM	1067.13 [0.00]	1244.64 [0.00]
Pesaran CD LM	8.47 [0.00]	13.08 [0.00]
Pesaran CD	-1.53 [0.06]	-1.25 [0.10]
LM Adj.	-2.74 [0.99]	-2.42 [0.99]
Delta Tilde	1.89 [0.02]	3.72 [0.00]
Delta Tilde Adjusted	2.20 [0.01]	4.12 [0.00]

Since there is no cross-sectional dependency in our data set, first-generation unit root tests should be applied. The selection of these tests depends on whether the distributions of the variables are homogeneous. According to the results presented in Table 3, the null hypothesis of homogeneity is rejected for both variables. Therefore, the appropriate tests to use are the IPS, ADF Fisher, PP Fisher, and Hadri tests, whose results were presented in Table 4. At the 95% confidence level in the constant models, the IPS and ADF Fisher tests indicate that the null hypothesis of a unit root is accepted, while the Hadri test indicates that the null hypothesis of stationarity is rejected for both variables. Based on these results, it was concluded that both series contain a unit root and are not stationary.

Table 4. Unit Root and Stationarity Test Results

		Container		GPR	
		Constant	**Constant & Trend**	**Constant**	**Constant & Trend**
LLC	Level	-4.23 [0.00]	-6.65 [0.00]	-0.05 [0.47]	-2.65 [0.00]
	First Diff.	-15.10 [0.00]	-21.63 [0.00]	-6.76 [0.00]	-2.80 [0.00]
IPS	Level	1.47 [0.92]	-0.70 [0.24]	-0.61 [0.27]	-2.67 [0.00]
	First Diff.	-15.10 [0.00]	-13.55 [0.00]	-10.39 [0.00]	-6.42 [0.00]
ADF Fisher	Level	58.41 [0.95]	100.44 [0.04]	90.12 [0.16]	113.75 [0.00]
	First Diff.	-11.49 [0.00]	313.27 [0.00]	254.94 [0.00]	177.70 [0.00]
PP Fisher	Level	101.83 [0.03]	102.62 [0.32]	95.85 [0.08]	121.53 [0.00]
	First Diff.	276.50 [0.00]	456.76 [0.00]	423.07 [0.00]	394.24 [0.00]
Hadri	Level	13.28 [0.00]	9.86 [0.00]	8.81 [0.00]	16.01 [0.00]
	First Diff.	4.85 [0.00]	37.70 [0.00]	5.75 [0.00]	27.93 [0.00]

While bootstrapping provides robust inference in certain contexts, it can lead to conservative estimates that reduce test power in panels with small T relative to N, as in our study (T=16, N=39). Given that the Granger non-causality test by Juodis et al. (2021) is designed to be robust to heterogeneity and cross-sectional dependence without requiring resampling for consistency, and following practice in similar macroeconomic panel studies, we report the asymptotic results for our causality tests. This choice maintains test power while retaining methodological rigor, ensuring reliable interpretation of the causal dynamics between geopolitical risk and container throughput.

We implemented the Granger non-causality test using the xtgrangert package in Stata (Juodis et al., 2021), which provides a heteroskedasticity-robust test for panel Granger causality while accounting for cross-sectional dependence and heterogeneity. The tests were conducted in Stata, employing xtgrangert with maxlags(2) and the het option to allow for heteroskedasticity across panels.

The results of the panel causality test applied to all sample countries are presented in Table 5. The findings reveal significant bidirectional causality at the 10% significance level, indicating that Container Throughput and Geopolitical Risk mutually influence each other. In both models, the optimum lag was determined to be 1, suggesting that changes in Container Throughput impact Geopolitical Risk after 1 year, and similarly, changes in Geopolitical Risk affect Container Throughput after a 1-year lag. Moreover, the fact that the coefficients of both dependent variables are negative indicates the presence of a feedback loop between the two variables. An increase in Geopolitical Risk leads to a decrease in Container Throughput, which in turn triggers a further rise in Geopolitical Risk. Conversely, an increase in Container

Throughput results in a reduction in Geopolitical Risk, which subsequently leads to a further increase in Container Throughput.

When examining the magnitude of the coefficients, it becomes evident that the effect of Container Throughput on Geopolitical Risk is significantly stronger than the reverse. This suggests that, when considering the entire sample, the impact of a country's economic structure on geopolitical risks is greater than the influence of geopolitical risks on the country's economy.

An increase in Geopolitical Risk can lead to disruptions, delays, uncertainties, and political instability along global trade routes, potentially resulting in a decline in container traffic at ports (Dawar and Bai, 2024; Capolongo and Kühl, 2024). Conversely, a reduction in Geopolitical Risk may indicate improved conditions, which could contribute to a rise in container traffic. On the other hand, a decrease in container traffic may signal weakening economic activity. This can lead to rising unemployment, reduced government revenues, and increased social unrest, which, in turn, could elevate geopolitical tension (Kotcharin & Maneenop, 2020; Wang et al., 2023).

Table 5. Results for the Panel Causality Test

Dependent Variable	Container	GPR
Independent Variable	$gpr_{(-1)}$	$container_{(-1)}$
Coefficient	-0.020	-0.444
Std Error.	0.010	0.173
Z [prob]	-1.92 [0.055]	-2.56 [0.010]
HPJ Walt Test [prob]	3.688 [0.0548]	6.571 [0.0104]

However, analyses conducted using the entire sample may not be valid for every country, as potential differences in their economic structures are not considered. Countries with stronger economic foundations may be less vulnerable to the effects of Geopolitical Risk. To address this, separate analyses were performed for each cluster by classifying countries according to their levels of economic development.

By Cluster

When the countries were classified according to the IMF classification, the Advanced cluster included 19 cross-sectional units (countries) observed over 16 time periods (T = 16, N = 19), while the Emerging cluster included 20 cross-sectional units observed over the same 16 time periods (T = 16, N = 20). This classification allowed for a more nuanced analysis of the relationship between Container Throughput and Geopolitical Risk, considering the differences in economic development levels between countries. To determine whether there is cross-sectional dependencies in the variables, LM Test (Breusch-Pagan, 1980), CD LM Test (Pesaran, 2004a), CD Test (Pesaran, 2004b), LM adj Test (PUY, 2008) were applied to both variables in each cluster and the results were presented in Table 6. Since N is relatively large in both clusters according to T, the most appropriate tests are CD and LM Adjusted tests. When the results are examined at the 95% confidence level, the null hypothesis of no cross-sectional dependence in all variables is accepted according to the CD test in both clusters. In the LM adjusted test, the null hypothesis is accepted in the container variables in Advanced countries and the GPR variables in Emerging countries. Accordingly, based on the CD test results, it was decided that there is no cross-sectional dependence in all variables in both clusters. According to the Pesaran and Yamagata (2008) homogeneity test results presented in Table 6, the null hypothesis of homogeneity was accepted for Container variables in both Advanced and Emerging countries, while it was rejected for GPR variables in both clusters at %95 confidence level.

Table 6. Cross-Section Dependence and Homogeneity Tests

	Advanced		Emerging	
Test	**Container**	**GPR**	**Container**	**GPR**
Breusch-Pagan LM	265.66 [0.00]	250.67 [0.00]	290.37 [0.00]	333.64 [0.00]
Pesaran CD LM	5.11 [0.00]	4.30 [0.00]	5.14 [0.00]	7.36 [0.00]
Pesaran CD	-0.60 [0.47]	-1.55 [0.06]	-0.70 [0.24]	-1.41 [0.08]
LM Adj.	1.20 [0.11]	3.57 [0.00]	5.78 [0.00]	-2.162 [0.98]
Delta Tilde	0.31 [0.37]	2.88 [0.00]	-0.37 [0.64]	1.77 [0.03]
Delta Tilde Adjusted	0.34 [0.36]	3.20 [0.00]	-0.41 [0.65]	1.97 [0.02]

Since there is no cross-sectional dependence in the series, the first-generation unit root and stationarity tests were applied, and the results are presented in Table 7. According to the homogeneity test results, since the Container variable is homogeneous in both clusters, the LLC test results should be applied. According to the results obtained, the null of unit root hypothesis in the Container variable in Advanced countries was rejected at a 95% confidence level. On the other hand, in the GPR variable, while the null of unit root hypothesis was accepted in the IPS, ADF Fisher, and PP Fisher unit root tests, the null of stationarity hypothesis was rejected in the Hadri stationarity test at the constant and 95% confidence level. Thus, in the Advanced countries cluster, the Container variable was determined as I(0) and the GPR variable as I(1).

Table 7. Advanced Economies Unit Root and Stationarity Test Results

		Container		GPR	
		Constant	**Constant & Trend**	**Constant**	**Constant & Trend**
LLC	Level	-1.63 [0.05]	-7.57 [0.00]	1.53 [0.93]	-2.08 [0.02]
	First Diff.	-13.94 [0.00]	-17.50 [0.00]	-3.68 [0.00]	-1.55 [0.06]
IPS	Level	1.62 [0.94]	-3.69 [0.24]	0.56 [0.71]	-3.39 [0.00]
	First Diff.	-10.10 [0.00]	-10.33 [0.00]	-7.38 [0.00]	-79.23 [0.00]
ADF Fisher	Level	29.61 [0.83]	82.95 [0.04]	35.85 [0.56]	69.73 [0.00]
	First Diff.	166.75 [0.00]	164.48 [0.00]	125.25 [0.00]	142.12 [0.00]
PP Fisher	Level	25.86 [0.93]	60.73 [0.01]	32.43 [0.72]	59.71 [0.01]
	First Diff.	189.95 [0.00]	184.83 [0.00]	171.83 [0.00]	394.24 [0.00]
Hadri	Level	8.67 [0.00]	6.49 [0.00]	8.58 [0.00]	12.01 [0.00]
	First Diff.	3.75 [0.00]	24.99 [0.00]	4.22 [0.00]	19.12 [0.00]

Given that the Container variable is homogeneous and the GPR variable is heterogeneous within the cluster of Emerging economies, the most appropriate unit root test for the Container variable was identified as the LLC test. The results from the LLC test indicate that the null hypothesis of a unit root is rejected at the 95% confidence level under the constant model. For the GPR variable, the IPS and ADF Fisher tests fail to reject the null hypothesis of a unit root, while the Hadri test rejects the null hypothesis of stationarity at the 95% confidence level under the constant model. Based on these test results, the Container variable is determined to be stationary at level, I(0), whereas the GPR variable is identified as integrated of order one, I(1), within the cluster of Emerging economies.

Table 8. Emerging Economies Unit Root and Stationarity Test Results

		Container		GPR	
		Constant	**Constant & Trend**	**Constant**	**Constant & Trend**
LLC	Level	-3.97 [0.00]	-1.27 [0.10]	1.56 [0.06]	-1.71 [0.04]
	First Diff.	-6.57 [0.00]	-12.79 [0.00]	-5.82 [0.00]	-2.38 [0.06]
IPS	Level	0.46 [0.68]	2.62 [0.99]	-1.40 [0.08]	-0.42 [0.33]
	First Diff.	-6.21 [0.00]	-8.85 [0.00]	-7.31 [0.00]	-5.13 [0.00]
ADF Fisher	Level	28.89 [0.90]	17.49 [0.99]	54.27 [0.07]	44.01 [0.30]
	First Diff.	109.74 [0.00]	148.78 [0.00]	129.68 [0.00]	98.46 [0.00]
PP Fisher	Level	75.97 [0.00]	41.89 [0.38]	63.42 [0.01]	61.82 [0.02]
	First Diff.	249.67 [0.00]	271..93 [0.00]	251.24 [0.00]	252.12 [0.00]

continued on following page

Table 8. Continued

		Container		GPR	
		Constant	**Constant & Trend**	**Constant**	**Constant & Trend**
Hadri	Level	10.09 [0.00]	7.60 [0.00]	3.95 [0.00]	10.65 [0.00]
	First Diff.	3.12 [0.00]	28.29 [0.00]	3.91 [0.00]	20.37 [0.00]

The results of the panel causality analysis, conducted separately for the clusters of Advanced and Emerging economies, are presented in Table 9. Notable differences were observed between the two clusters. In Advanced economies, no significant causality was found from Geopolitical Risk to Container Traffic. However, a significant causality from Container Traffic to Geopolitical Risk was identified at the 90% confidence level. The negative coefficient suggests that a decline in container traffic increases geopolitical tensions, whereas increased trade volumes may contribute to geopolitical stability. This finding aligns with the argument that in developed countries, maritime trade performance is a critical indicator of broader economic health and geopolitical leverage. A drop in container throughput may signal an economic slowdown, reducing a country's global influence and potentially intensifying internal political pressures and international vulnerabilities (Kotcharin & Maneenop, 2020; Wang et al., 2023).

In contrast, the analysis for Emerging economies reveals a significant causal effect of Geopolitical Risk on Container Traffic, while no significant relationship was detected from Container Traffic to Geopolitical Risk. The negative coefficient reveals that rising geopolitical risk leads to a decline in container traffic. This is consistent with previous literature suggesting that emerging economies, due to their limited economic diversification, institutional fragility, and dependence on vulnerable trade routes, are more susceptible to external shocks (Dawar and Bai, 2024; Capolongo and Kühl, 2024). Increased geopolitical tensions in such regions can lead to logistical disruptions—such as port closures, rerouting, heightened insurance premiums, and delayed shipping operations—which directly reduce container flows (Pseftogkas et al., 2024; Peng et al., 2024).

These asymmetrical results highlight the importance of considering country-specific dynamics when assessing the economic impact of geopolitical shocks. While Advanced economies appear more resilient to geopolitical disturbances but sensitive to trade fluctuations, Emerging economies are more directly affected by political instability, which can severely hinder trade performance. This underscores the relevance of tailored policy responses aimed at either enhancing trade resilience or reducing geopolitical exposure, depending on the development level of the country.

Table 9. Results for the Panel Causality Test by Cluster

	Advanced Economies		Emerging and Developing Economies	
Dependent Variable	**Container**	**GPR**	**Container**	**GPR**
Independent Variable	$gpr_{(-1)}$	$container_{(-1)}$	$gpr_{(-1)}$	$container_{(-1)}$
Coefficient	0.0074	-0.180	-0.028	0.062
Std Error.	0.013	0.097	0.012	0.129
Z [prob]	0.57 [0.56]	-1.86 [0.06]	-2.29 [0.022]	0.49 [0.62]
HPJ Walt Test [prob]	0.3252 [0.568]	3.46 [0.062]	5.230 [0.0222]	0.2358 [0.627]

CONCLUSION

This study investigated the relationship between geopolitical risk and international trade, as proxied by container throughput, in the context of Advanced and Emerging economies. Using the Granger non-causality test by Juodis et al. (2021), which accounts for cross-sectional dependence and heterogeneity, the results reveal distinct dynamics between the two groups. In Advanced economies, container throughput Granger-causes geopolitical risk, while in Emerging economies, the causality runs in the opposite direction. These findings confirm the asymmetric nature of the interaction depending on countries' economic structures.

We expect this relationship to vary because Advanced and Emerging economies differ significantly in several critical aspects, such as (i) their economic structure and diversification, (ii) political stability and governance, (iii) integration with and influence on global trade, (iv) infrastructure and technological capabilities, (v) dependency on trade and access to markets, (vi) economic resilience and adaptability, (vii) investor confidence and perceived risk, and (viii) geographical location.

In Emerging economies, the significant influence of geopolitical risk on container throughput can be attributed to their greater vulnerability to external shocks, limited economic diversification, and weaker institutional resilience. Heightened geopolitical risk in such contexts tends to disrupt trade logistics, raise transportation costs, and reduce international investor confidence, all of which contribute to reduced maritime trade volumes. Conversely, in Advanced economies, the significant effect of container throughput on geopolitical risk underscores the importance of trade activity as a reflection of economic strength and stability. A decline in container volumes may signal an economic slowdown or reduced global competitiveness, potentially weakening geopolitical positioning and increasing domestic and international tensions. These findings underscore the necessity for differentiated policy approaches: Emerging economies should prioritize geopolitical stability to secure trade continuity, while Advanced economies may need to safeguard trade volumes to maintain international influence and internal stability. As shown in Figure 1, many developing countries are situated in regions characterized by high levels of political instability, conflict, and territorial disputes. Consequently, the impact of Geopolitical Risk on Container Trade is more pronounced in these environments, where risks fluctuate more frequently. This is evident in the average Geopolitical Risk values, as shown in Table 2. The average for Advanced countries is 1.78, whereas Emerging countries have a significantly higher average of 3.74. Naturally, the effects of elevated risk levels are expected to be more pronounced.

Given the asymmetrical relationship between geopolitical risk and international trade observed across Advanced and Emerging economies, differentiated policy strategies are essential to mitigate risk exposure and enhance trade resilience. For Emerging and Developing Economies, where geopolitical risk exerts a significant negative influence on container throughput, policymakers should prioritize the following:

- Strengthen Political Stability and Governance: Establishing a predictable and transparent political environment is essential to reduce investor uncertainty and attract sustainable trade flows.
- Invest in Infrastructure: Enhancing port facilities, transport networks, and logistics capabilities will improve trade efficiency and reduce the vulnerability of maritime operations to external shocks.
- Diversify Trade Partnerships: Reducing dependence on a limited set of trade partners and routes can buffer economies from geopolitical disruptions.
- Explore Alternative Trade Corridors: Developing inland connectivity or participating in regional trade initiatives can provide redundancy in case of maritime disruptions.
- Enhance Crisis Management and Risk Mitigation: Establishing strategic reserves, enhancing risk insurance mechanisms, and improving institutional response capacities can reduce the impact of trade shocks.

For Advanced Economies, where container throughput was found to influence geopolitical risk, the focus should be on preserving trade volumes and safeguarding economic influence:

- Monitor Trade Activity as a Strategic Indicator: Recognizing container traffic as a proxy for economic vitality can help anticipate geopolitical shifts and adapt proactively.
- Secure and Modernize Supply Chains: Investments in digitalization, automation, and traceability can increase resilience to geopolitical disturbances.

- Promote Multilateral Cooperation and Strong Alliances: Reinforcing diplomatic and trade alliances can help stabilize trade routes and reduce the political risks associated with economic downturns.
- Foster Innovation and Competitive Trade Practices: Supporting technological advancement and diversification in maritime trade ensures continued global relevance and influence.

By tailoring risk mitigation strategies to the structural realities of each group, countries can better manage the effects of geopolitical uncertainty and ensure more stable integration into the global trade system.

The findings of this study, which reveal divergent causal relationships between geopolitical risk and container throughput in advanced and emerging economies, can be meaningfully interpreted through multiple theoretical lenses. World Systems Theory and Dependency Theory help explain why emerging economies, often situated on the periphery of the global economic system, exhibit heightened sensitivity to geopolitical disruptions. These nations depend heavily on external markets and global political stability, making their trade volumes more vulnerable to risk shocks. In contrast, advanced economies, typically occupying the core of global trade networks, are less dependent and more capable of projecting economic strength outward. This aligns with Complex Interdependence Theory, which suggests that economic performance, especially trade flows, can serve as both a cause and consequence of geopolitical dynamics. In such interdependent systems, disruptions in trade not only reflect underlying geopolitical tensions but can also amplify or diffuse them depending on institutional responses. Here, Institutional Theory provides further explanatory power: the ability of advanced economies to absorb and respond to external shocks is underpinned by strong institutions, legal frameworks, and governance capacities. Emerging economies, with weaker institutional infrastructures, are less able to buffer the impacts of geopolitical uncertainty. Together, these frameworks offer a coherent theoretical foundation for understanding the asymmetrical relationships revealed in this study, and they underscore the importance of differentiated policy strategies tailored to the structural and institutional realities of each country group.

Beyond these theoretical lenses, the divergent causal relationships identified in this study can be traced to practical mechanisms embedded within trade and political systems. In Emerging Economies, geopolitical risks such as regional conflicts, instability, or sanctions directly disrupt logistics networks, increase insurance costs, and deter foreign investment, leading to immediate declines in container throughput. For example, tensions in the Red Sea region have forced vessels to reroute around the Cape of Good Hope, extending transit times and raising freight costs, which directly reduces trade volumes for African and Middle Eastern countries dependent on timely imports and exports. Conversely, in Advanced Economies, container throughput serves as an indicator of economic vitality, with declines signaling broader economic slowdowns that can erode government revenues and elevate domestic social unrest, indirectly increasing geopolitical tensions. The post-Brexit decline in the UK's trade volumes and its link to subsequent political instability and social fragmentation exemplifies this pathway. By clarifying these mechanisms, our study highlights that geopolitical risk and trade flows are not only statistically linked but are also embedded in the operational and institutional realities of countries, reinforcing the necessity for policy strategies that address these channels to ensure both trade resilience and geopolitical stability.

While the study offers valuable insights, it is subject to several limitations. First, the geopolitical risk index may not fully capture localized or short-term tensions. Second, container throughput may not reflect all dimensions of international trade, particularly in landlocked or service-heavy economies. Third, the country classification based on IMF's WEO groups, while widely accepted, may overlook internal heterogeneity within each group.

Future research could incorporate more granular trade data (e.g., port-level or commodity-specific flows) and examine sectoral variations. Moreover, integrating additional geopolitical dimensions, such as cyber risk or climate-induced political instability, may enrich understanding. Methodologically, employing machine learning or time-varying causality models could capture evolving dynamics more precisely. Finally, a comparative case study approach may offer contextual insights complementing the panel-based findings.

REFERENCES

Atacan, C., & Açık, A. (2023). Impact of geopolitical risk on international trade: Evidence from container throughputs. *Transactions on Maritime Science*, *12*(2). Advance online publication. DOI: 10.7225/toms.v12.n02.019

Bandyopadhyay, S., Sandler, T., & Younas, J. (2018). Trade and terrorism: A disaggregated approach. *Journal of Peace Research*, *55*(5), 656–670. DOI: 10.1177/0022343318763009

Breusch, T. S., & Pagan, A. R. (1980). The Lagrange multiplier test and its applications to model specification in econometrics. *The Review of Economic Studies*, *47*(1), 239–253. DOI: 10.2307/2297111

Burhanuddin, A. (2015). Rethinking world system theory: A historical and conceptual analysis. *WANUA: Jurnal Hubungan Internasional*, *1*(1), 1–16.

Caldara, D., & Iacoviello, M. (2022). Measuring geopolitical risk. *The American Economic Review*, *112*(4), 1194–1225. DOI: 10.1257/aer.20191823

Can, C. M. (2024). Small power strategies under great power competition. *International Politics*, *61*, 296–321. DOI: 10.1057/s41311-023-00552-7

Capolongo, A., & Kühl, M. (2024, August 30). The butterfly effect of geopolitical conflicts. *European Stability Mechanism, Economic and Market Analysis*. https://www.esm.europa.eu/blog/butterfly-effect-of-geopolitical-conflicts

Chirot, D. (2001). World Systems Theory. In Smelser, N. J. & Baltes, P.B. (Eds.), *International Encyclopedia of the Social & Behavioral* Sciences (pp. 16609-16613), Pergamon. https://doi.org/DOI: 10.1016/B0-08-043076-7/01891-X

Chirot, D. (2015). World Systems Theory. In Wright, J. D. (Ed.), *International Encyclopedia of the Social & Behavioral Sciences* (pp. 748–752). Elsevier., DOI: 10.1016/B978-0-08-097086-8.32172-9

Choi, I. (2001). Unit root tests for panel data. *Journal of International Money and Finance*, *20*(2), 249–272. DOI: 10.1016/S0261-5606(00)00048-6

Dawar, A., & Bai, Y. (2024). Impact of geopolitical risk on the maritime supply chain: A regional analysis of the effects on global trade. *International Journal of Supply Chain Management*, *13*(3), 42–53. DOI: 10.59160/ijscm.v13i3.6245

De Sousa, J., Mirza, D., & Verdier, T. (2018). Terror networks and trade: Does the neighbor hurt? *European Economic Review*, *107*, 27–56. DOI: 10.1016/j.euroecorev.2018.05.001

DiMaggio, P. J., & Powell, W. W. (2002). Institutional isomorphism and collective rationality in organizational fields. *Strategy: Critical Perspectives on Business and Management*, 1(1983), 283-306.

Drobetz, W., Gavriilidis, K., Krokida, S. I., & Tsouknidis, D. (2021). The effects of geopolitical risk and economic policy uncertainty on dry bulk shipping freight rates. *Applied Economics*, *53*(19), 2218–2229. DOI: 10.1080/00036846.2020.1857329

Du, J., Satoglu, E. B., & Shepotylo, O. (2023). How did Brexit affect UK trade? *Contemporary Social Science*, *18*(2), 266–283. DOI: 10.1080/21582041.2023.2192043

Georgoulas, D., Tsioumas, V., Stavroulakis, P. J., & Papadimitriou, S. (2024). Geopolitical risk and sustainable shipping: A quantitative approach. *Australian Journal of Maritime and Ocean Affairs*, •••, 1–13. DOI: 10.1080/18366503.2024.2325270

Glod, M., Boone, G., Huang, J., De Spiegeleire, S., & Sweijs, T. (2009). Looking ahead. In *Economic crisis: Examining the security implications* (pp. 15–18). Hague Centre for Strategic Studies., https://www.jstor.org/stable/resrep12576.6

Gu, J. (2023, October 23). US-China tensions are top geopolitical risk, BlackRock says. *Bloomberg Screentime*. https://www.bloomberg.com/news/articles/2023-10-23/blackrock-says-us-china-tensions-are-top-geopolitical-risk?embedded-checkout=true

Hadri, K. (2000). Testing for stationarity in heterogeneous panel data. *The Econometrics Journal*, *3*(2), 148–161. DOI: 10.1111/1368-423X.00043

Im, K. S., Pesaran, M. H., & Shin, Y. (2003). Testing for unit roots in heterogeneous panels. *Journal of Econometrics*, *115*(1), 53–74. DOI: 10.1016/S0304-4076(03)00092-7

IMF. (2024). *Country composition of WEO groups*. https://www.imf.org/en/Publications/WEO/weo-database/2023/April/groups-and-aggregates

Keohane, R. O., & Nye, J. S.Jr. (1987). Power and interdependence revisited. *International Organization*, *41*(4), 725–753.

Khan, H. U. (2024). An analytical investigation of consequences of terrorism in the Middle East. *Journal of Economic Criminology*, *4*, 100067. DOI: 10.1016/j.jeconc.2024.100067

Khan, K., Su, C. W., Tao, R., & Umar, M. (2021). How do geopolitical risks affect oil prices and freight rates? *Ocean and Coastal Management*, *215*, 105955. DOI: 10.1016/j.ocecoaman.2021.105955

Kotcharin, S., & Maneenop, S. (2020). Geopolitical risk and corporate cash holdings in the shipping industry. *Transportation Research Part E, Logistics and Transportation Review, 136*, 101862. DOI: 10.1016/j.tre.2020.101862

Kotcharin, S., & Maneenop, S. (2020). Geopolitical risk and shipping firms' capital structure decisions in Belt and Road Initiative countries. *International Journal of Logistics Research and Applications, 23*(6), 544–560. DOI: 10.1080/13675567.2020.1766003

Kren, J., & Lawless, M. (2024). How has Brexit changed EU–UK trade flows? *European Economic Review, 161*, 104634. DOI: 10.1016/j.euroecorev.2023.104634

Levin, A., Lin, C. F., & Chu, C. S. J. (2002). Unit root tests in panel data: Asymptotic and finite-sample properties. *Journal of Econometrics, 108*(1), 1–24. DOI: 10.1016/S0304-4076(01)00098-7

Lin, F., & Meng, X. (2024). Stuck between the great powers: Secondary countries' responses to soft power competition between the US and China during the COVID-19 pandemic. *Journal of Chinese Political Science, 29*(2), 233–256. DOI: 10.1007/s11366-023-09862-2

Maddala, G. S., & Wu, S. (1999). A comparative study of unit root tests with panel data and a new simple test. *Oxford Bulletin of Economics and Statistics, 61*(S1), 631–652. DOI: 10.1111/1468-0084.0610s1631

Meyer, J. W., & Rowan, B. (1977). Institutionalized organizations: Formal structure as myth and ceremony. *American Journal of Sociology, 83*(2), 340–363.

Monge, M., Rojo, M. F. R., & Gil-Alana, L. A. (2023). The impact of geopolitical risk on the behavior of oil prices and freight rates. *Energy, 269*, 126779. DOI: 10.1016/j.energy.2023.126779

Peng, H., Wang, M., & An, C. (2024). Implied threats of the Red Sea crisis to global maritime transport: Amplified carbon emissions and possible carbon pricing dysfunction. *Environmental Research Letters, 19*(7), 074053. DOI: 10.1088/1748-9326/ad59b7

Pesaran, M. H. (2004a). General diagnostic tests for cross-section dependence in panels. *CESifo Working Paper Series No. 1229; IZA Discussion Paper No. 1240.* https://doi.org/DOI: 10.2139/ssrn.572504

Pesaran, M. H. (2004b). A simple panel unit root test in the presence of cross-section dependence. *Journal of Applied Econometrics, 22*(2), 265–312. DOI: 10.1002/jae.951

Pesaran, M. H., Ullah, A., & Yamagata, T. (2008). A bias-adjusted LM test of error cross-section independence. *The Econometrics Journal, 11*(1), 105–127. DOI: 10.1111/j.1368-423X.2007.00227.x

Pesaran, M. H., & Yamagata, T. (2008). Testing slope homogeneity in large panels. *Journal of Econometrics, 142*(1), 50–93. DOI: 10.1016/j.jeconom.2007.05.010

PolicyUncertainty. (2024). *Geopolitical risk index.* https://www.policyuncertainty.com/gpr.html

Pseftogkas, A., Stavrakou, T., Müller, J. F., Koukouli, M. E., Balis, D., & Meleti, C. (2024). Shifts in maritime trade routes as a result of Red Sea shipping crisis detected in TROPOMI NO2 data. *Geophysical Research Letters. ESS Open Archive.* https://doi.org/DOI: 10.22541/au.171893482.21861538/v1

Rana, W. (2015). Theory of complex interdependence: A comparative analysis of realist and neoliberal thoughts. *International Journal of Business and Social Science, 6*(2), 290–297.

Rogerson, K. S. (2000). Information Interdependence: Keohane and Nye's complex interdependence in the information age. *Information Communication and Society, 3*(3), 415–436. DOI: 10.1080/13691180051033379

Saâdaoui, F., Jabeur, S. B., & Goodell, J. W. (2022). Causality of geopolitical risk on food prices: Considering the Russo–Ukrainian conflict. *Finance Research Letters, 49*, 103103. DOI: 10.1016/j.frl.2022.103103

Sommerville, M., Essex, J., & Le Billon, P. (2014). The 'global food crisis' and the geopolitics of food security. *Geopolitics, 19*(2), 239–265. DOI: 10.1080/14650045.2013.811641

S&P Global. (2024). *Top geopolitical risks of 2024.* S&P Global, Research and Insights. https://www.spglobal.com/en/research-insights/market-insights/geopolitical-risk

Su, C. W., Khan, K., Umar, M., & Zhang, W. (2021). Does renewable energy redefine geopolitical risks? *Energy Policy, 158*, 112566. DOI: 10.1016/j.enpol.2021.112566

Suárez-de Vivero, J. L., & Mateos, J. C. R. (2017). Forecasting geopolitical risks: Oceans as source of instability. *Marine Policy, 75*, 19–28. DOI: 10.1016/j.marpol.2016.10.009

Tanyeri, B., Savaser, T., & Usul, N. (2022). The stock and CDS market consequences of political uncertainty: The Arab Spring. *Emerging Markets Finance & Trade, 58*(7), 1821–1837. DOI: 10.1080/1540496X.2021.1937116

The BBC News. (2014). Guantanamo prisoner al-Darbi admits MV Limburg attack. *BBC*. https://www.bbc.com/news/world-us-canada-26277556

The Business Times. (2023). US-China tensions are top geopolitical risk, BlackRock says. *The Business Times*. https://www.businesstimes.com.sg/international/us-china-tensions-are-top-geopolitical-risk-blackrock-says

Tuna, F., & Çalışkan, H. (2022). Jeopolitik risklerin makroekonomik göstergeler üzerindeki etkisi: Türkiye örneği. *Gaziantep University Journal of Social Sciences, 21*(4), 1989–2003. DOI: 10.21547/jss.1151714

Turhan, R. (2018). The Effect of Dependency Theory on Discussions of 'Underdevelopment' in Turkey. In Roldán, C., Brauer, D., & Rohbeck, J. (Eds.), *Philosophy of Globalization* (pp. 269–286). De Gruyter., DOI: 10.1515/9783110492415-020

Üçler, G., & Özşahin, Ş. (2020). Jeopolitik risk ve borsa endeksinin nedensellik analizi: Gelişmekte olan ülkeler üzerine bootstrap panel nedensellik testi. *Muhasebe ve Finansman Dergisi*, (87), 167–180. DOI: 10.25095/mufad.756266

UNCTAD. (2024). *Container port throughput, annual*. https://unctadstat.unctad.org/datacentre/dataviewer/US.ContPortThroughput

Veninga, W., & Ihle, R. (2018). Import vulnerability in the Middle East: Effects of the Arab Spring on Egyptian wheat trade. *Food Security*, *10*, 183–194. DOI: 10.1007/s12571-017-0755-2

VS&B Containers Group. (2024). The impact of geopolitical tensions and conflicts on container shipping and shipping rates. *VS&B*. https://www.vsnb.com/impact-geopolitical-tensions-and-conflicts-container-shipping-and-shipping-rates

Wallerstein, I. (1974). Dependence in an interdependent world: The limited possibilities of transformation within the capitalist world economy. *African Studies Review*, *17*(1), 1–26.

Wang, G., Gu, X., Shen, X., Uktamov, K. F., & Ageli, M. M. (2023). A dual risk perspective of China's resources market: Geopolitical risk and political risk. *Resources Policy*, *82*, 103528. DOI: 10.1016/j.resourpol.2023.103528

Wang, X., Wu, Y., & Xu, W. (2023). Geopolitical risk and investment. *Journal of Money, Credit and Banking*. Advance online publication. DOI: 10.1111/jmcb.13110

World Bank. (2024). *Container port traffic (TEU: 20-foot equivalent units)*. https://data.worldbank.org/indicator/IS.SHP.GOOD.TU

Yu, M., & Wang, N. (2023). The influence of geopolitical risk on international direct investment and its countermeasures. *Sustainability*, *15*(3), 2522. DOI: 10.3390/su15032522

Zhang, S., Shinwari, R., Zhao, S., & Dagestani, A. A. (2023). Energy transition, geopolitical risk, and natural resources extraction: A novel perspective of energy transition and resources extraction. *Resources Policy*, *83*, 103608. DOI: 10.1016/j.resourpol.2023.103608

Zhao, S. (2022). The US–China rivalry in the emerging bipolar world: Hostility, alignment, and power balance. *Journal of Contemporary China*, *31*(134), 169–185. DOI: 10.1080/10670564.2021.1945733

KEY TERMS AND DEFINITIONS

Advanced Economies: Economically developed countries with stable political systems, high-income levels, and diversified industrial structures.

Container Throughput: A measure of trade activity, referring to the total volume of container units (usually in TEUs) handled by a country's ports within a given period.

Cross-Sectional Dependence: A statistical condition where units in a panel data model (e.g., countries) are not independent, indicating shared shocks or global spillovers.

Economic Resilience: A country's ability to absorb external shocks—such as geopolitical instability—while maintaining stable growth and trade performance.

Emerging Economies: Countries experiencing rapid growth and industrialization but still facing structural vulnerabilities and political instability.

Freight Rate Volatility: The fluctuation of shipping prices due to changing market conditions, often influenced by demand, fuel costs, and geopolitical tensions.

Geopolitical Risk: The likelihood of political events, conflicts, or instability disrupting the global or regional economy, trade flows, and supply chains.

Global Supply Chain Disruptions: Interruptions in the normal flow of goods and services across countries due to political, logistical, or environmental shocks.

Granger Non-Causality Test: An econometric technique used to determine whether one time series can predict another, while controlling for temporal and structural characteristics.

Panel Data: A dataset that includes multiple entities (like countries) observed over time, allowing for richer modeling of dynamics across both dimensions.

APPENDIX 1

Figure 2. Countries' Geopolitical Risk and Container Throughput Values

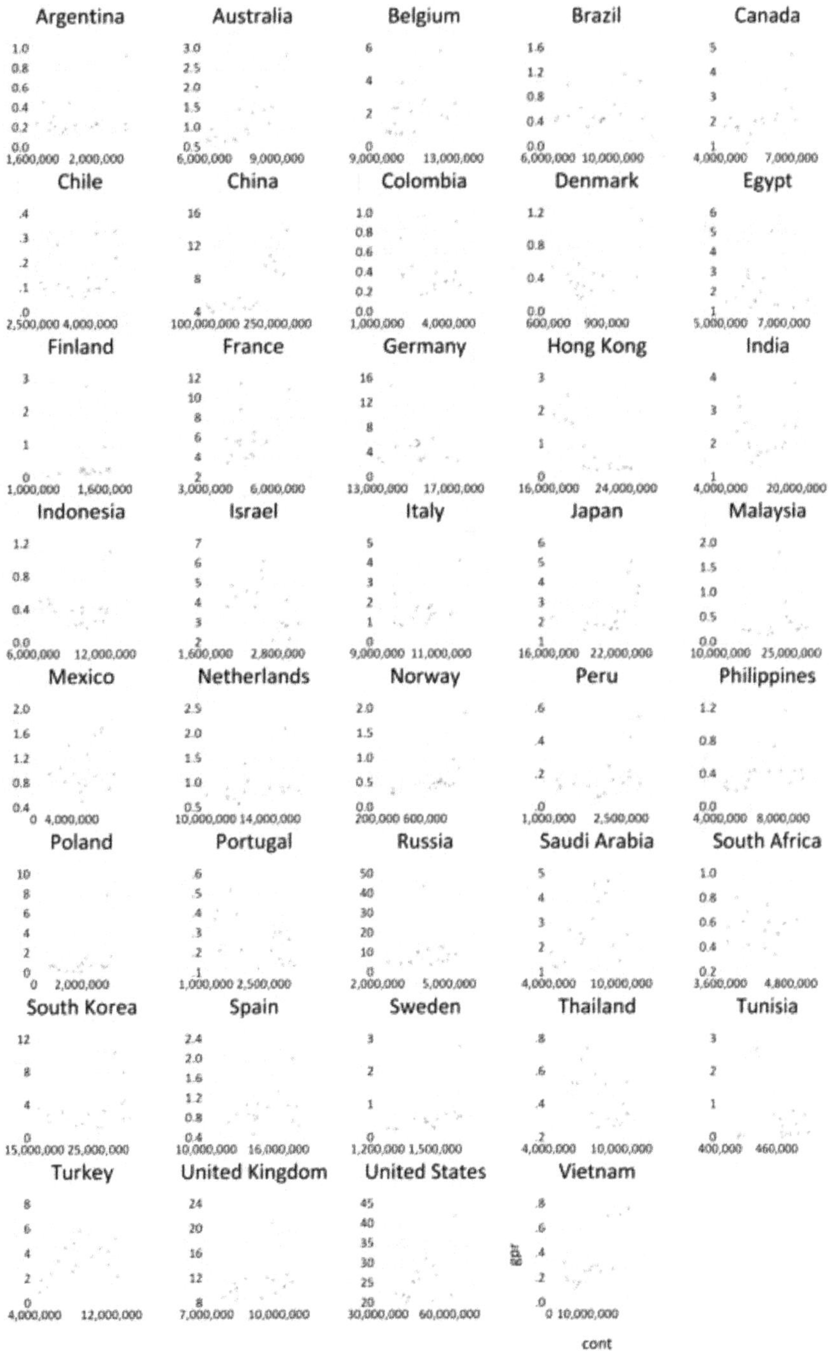

APPENDIX 2

Table 10. Country-Based Descriptive Statistics of Container Throughput

ID	Mean	Max	Min.	Std. Dev.	Skew.	Kurt.	Obs.
Argentina	1875734.	2184625.	1626835.	188557.0	0.516074	1.957276	16
Australia	7546543.	9375992.	6102342.	1000606.	0.087337	1.973276	16
Belgium	10812380	13075891	9528054.	1199312.	0.719233	2.014826	16
Brazil	9051755.	11801530	6464724.	1659058.	0.030218	2.081454	16
Canada	5671336.	7169607.	4191568.	999451.0	0.128607	1.653355	16
Chile	3835864.	4661306.	2725218.	638565.4	-0.370665	1.932520	16
China	1.91E+08	2.69E+08	1.04E+08	54530467	-0.231200	1.835835	16
Colombia	3412303.	4901510.	1969316.	929943.9	-0.209875	1.876904	16
Denmark	809599.8	1079649.	621546.0	123844.2	0.971095	3.256424	16
Egypt	6240371.	7765482.	5181581.	670945.9	0.719285	3.053345	16
Finland	1461245.	1630089.	1125533.	139073.5	-0.936432	3.533937	16
France	4717707.	6467242.	3865087.	648982.4	1.111945	4.403194	16
Germany	14987885	17183042	13056019	1096914.	0.041411	2.808295	16
Hong Kong	21006423	24494229	16573000	2568007.	-0.131755	1.765322	16
India	12978037	19937138	7398211.	4339242.	0.288551	1.672454	16
Indonesia	9981424.	12380584	6582910.	1879639.	-0.442774	1.967028	16
Israel	2585174.	3133000.	1957328.	367831.2	-0.254092	1.903161	16
Italy	10404552	11577495	9532462.	590558.4	0.151895	2.456361	16
Japan	21106620	23424446	16285918	1833633.	-1.107234	4.044378	16
Malaysia	22151325	28261849	14828836	4278773.	-0.323291	1.891479	16
Mexico	5298378.	8307884.	1661288.	1855396.	-0.193968	2.278874	16
Netherlands	12924695	15781756	10066374	1727300.	0.243668	1.789770	16
Norway	682187.5	933300.0	318924.0	193337.1	-0.970034	2.807692	16
Peru	2130456.	2874109.	1177925.	586181.2	-0.411761	1.883683	16
Philippines	6726155.	9249451.	4306965.	1747682.	0.018040	1.598947	16
Poland	1987345.	3187943.	671552.0	870722.4	-0.104830	1.697783	16
Portugal	2387126.	3276794.	1233482.	731627.0	-0.425636	1.619754	16
Russia	4090336.	5260825.	2427744.	802428.7	-0.452998	2.286593	16
Saudi Arabia	7209760.	10459765	4208854.	1972748.	-0.035817	1.868638	16
South Africa	4306010.	4892423.	3726313.	356733.5	-0.249372	1.940805	16
South Korea	24113500	29786900	15699663	4712127.	-0.480094	1.891321	16
Spain	14920592	17712459	11803192	1872695.	0.137102	1.780756	16
Sweden	1483160.	1635394.	1251424.	126324.9	-0.454534	2.086027	16

continued on following page

Table 10. Continued

ID	Mean	Max	Min.	Std. Dev.	Skew.	Kurt.	Obs.
Thailand	8588508.	10497112	5897935.	1543957.	-0.288128	1.763045	16
Tunisia	461697.7	493366.0	418883.9	23950.77	-0.680610	2.261971	16
Türkiye	8512486.	12591327	4521713.	2747036.	0.043359	1.720420	16
United Kingdom	9157284.	10508000	7671300.	972746.2	-0.093757	1.451898	16
United States	47598126	62214119	37353575	7285105.	0.651202	2.423601	16
Vietnam	10619710	20518926	4009066.	5088025.	0.453476	2.116848	16
All	13714004	2.69E+08	318924.0	31339395	5.881746	40.16247	624

APPENDIX 3

Table 11. Country-Based Descriptive Statistics of Geopolitical Risk Index

ID	Mean	Max	Min.	Std. Dev.	Skew.	Kurt.	Obs.
Argentina	0.307616	0.941445	0.164666	0.191029	2.505199	8.752453	16
Australia	1.196555	2.850462	0.671910	0.599107	1.460187	4.644833	16
Belgium	2.092433	5.908877	0.867379	1.363006	1.453325	4.864155	16
Brazil	0.608566	1.195263	0.339532	0.261357	1.295952	3.229573	16
Canada	2.232672	4.793196	1.165663	0.833031	1.955611	6.836356	16
Chile	0.152627	0.333991	0.067673	0.088361	1.137848	2.810287	16
China	7.022761	14.11712	4.196613	3.036867	0.952153	2.708801	16
Colombia	0.382371	0.930481	0.184672	0.200427	1.655248	5.030515	16
Denmark	0.413144	1.128218	0.170842	0.228789	1.926172	7.037473	16
Egypt	2.160990	5.123260	1.254350	1.006963	1.668350	5.597508	16
Finland	0.441428	2.803781	0.093407	0.659997	3.153654	11.71950	16
France	6.290131	11.58939	3.624022	2.344620	1.205829	3.449227	16
Germany	5.112992	15.03666	2.661398	2.973878	2.407872	8.944898	16
Hong Kong	0.785000	2.498965	0.249385	0.743457	1.183661	2.888984	16
India	2.339713	3.877525	1.457007	0.682132	0.903798	2.865239	16
Indonesia	0.427158	1.121845	0.189991	0.213525	2.168533	8.196123	16
Israel	4.002995	6.174804	2.157044	1.213937	0.094920	1.996599	16
Italy	1.673474	4.203915	0.901639	0.801322	2.051221	7.332987	16
Japan	2.604613	5.134217	1.660168	1.089120	1.238587	3.198351	16
Malaysia	0.434545	1.826790	0.173615	0.404056	2.804898	10.12323	16
Mexico	1.065804	1.727543	0.525039	0.368864	0.559273	2.114542	16
Netherlands	0.938323	2.146786	0.589945	0.376879	2.267586	7.829965	16
Norway	0.610120	1.940622	0.308839	0.395373	2.602371	9.258877	16
Peru	0.192960	0.560342	0.070515	0.130568	1.784915	5.399064	16
Philippines	0.434864	1.187962	0.208649	0.241485	2.068399	7.099481	16
Poland	1.303019	8.083865	0.265325	1.859721	3.291563	12.59308	16
Portugal	0.270136	0.525723	0.128322	0.115666	0.644200	2.541754	16
Russia	10.72136	44.28464	4.629515	9.429198	3.030310	11.46033	16
Saudi Arabia	2.678750	4.763302	1.251880	1.170245	0.548244	2.063821	16
South Africa	0.572231	0.814213	0.349881	0.125368	0.104612	2.502383	16
South Korea	3.649714	10.53666	1.476721	2.459635	1.762238	5.312965	16
Spain	0.989053	2.033132	0.504300	0.346594	1.664955	6.314723	16

continued on following page

Table 11. Continued

ID	Mean	Max	Min.	Std. Dev.	Skew.	Kurt.	Obs.
Sweden	0.680342	2.810930	0.289954	0.592072	3.132342	11.97193	16
Thailand	0.443861	0.747974	0.270455	0.151574	0.546076	2.084515	16
Tunisia	0.467336	2.712551	0.051251	0.655863	2.685701	9.833209	16
Türkiye	3.484075	5.961057	1.072129	1.420708	-0.014302	2.034761	16
United Kingdom	11.46190	21.26430	8.710391	2.895096	2.518125	9.490749	16
United States	25.68657	42.38230	20.37513	5.588029	1.734603	5.949223	16
Vietnam	0.331591	0.770162	0.128996	0.208707	1.311197	3.195608	16
All	2.734969	44.28464	0.051251	5.021640	4.135743	24.54484	624

Chapter 11
Three Summits Plus One in 2024:
The World Is Still Seeking the Best Pathway for Sustainable Development

Isidore E. Agbokou
https://orcid.org/0000-0003-1225-9311
Ecole des Hautes Etudes Internationales et Politiques de l'Académie de Paris, France

ABSTRACT

This chapter critically examines five major international summits held in 2024—COP29, COP16 on Biodiversity, COP16 on Desertification, the High-Level Political Forum, and the Summit of the Future—to understand why global sustainability efforts remain stalled. Despite ambitious declarations, these forums revealed persistent challenges: fragmented governance, imbalanced financing, and weak political continuity. The chapter calls for integrated reforms, including streamlined funding, renewed diplomatic mandates, and digital tools like AI and blockchain to improve transparency and accountability. It offers a timely reflection on how multilateral action might finally close the gap between global ambition and implementation.

INTRODUCTION

The pursuit of global sustainability remains one of the most pressing imperatives of the 21st century. Despite decades of environmental diplomacy and a growing consensus on the urgency of ecological preservation, tangible progress continues

DOI: 10.4018/979-8-3373-1265-1.ch011

to lag behind rhetorical commitments. In 2024, the international community witnessed an unprecedented convergence of high-level summits—including COP29 on climate change, COP16 on biodiversity, COP16 of the Convention to Combat Desertification, the High-Level Political Forum on Sustainable Development, and the Summit of the Future—each of which sought to reaffirm global ambitions for environmental stewardship and social equity. These events unfolded amid intensifying climate crises, persistent inequalities, and mounting skepticism about the efficacy of multilateral action.

While five major summits took place in 2024—including COP29 on climate change, COP16 of the Convention on Biological Diversity, COP16 of the Convention to Combat Desertification, the High-Level Political Forum (HLPF), and the Summit of the Future—this chapter adopts the phrase "Three Summits Plus One" as a narrative and analytical lens. The "three summits" refer to the pillar conventions of the Rio Process—climate, biodiversity, and land—whose convergence symbolizes the sectoral architecture of global environmental governance. The "plus one" refers to the Summit of the Future, conceived as a systemic event transcending MEA silo and aiming to reimagine the institutional landscape of multilateralism. This framing emphasizes the contrast between thematic fragmentation and the emerging imperative for holistic sustainability diplomacy.

This chapter approaches these summits not merely as isolated diplomatic events but as reflective of deeper structural dynamics within global environmental governance. It interrogates the philosophical, legal, financial, and technological dimensions that shape international sustainability discourse, while highlighting the challenges of policy fragmentation, political inconsistency, and inadequate accountability mechanisms.

The primary objective of this chapter is to critically examine the limitations and prospects of contemporary environmental diplomacy, particularly through the lens of synergy among multilateral environmental agreements. It aims to propose forward-looking strategies—including integrated summits, digital innovation, and redefined diplomatic missions—that can bridge the gap between ambition and action in global sustainability efforts.

Although five major summits occurred in 2024, the framing of "Three Summits Plus One" reflects a deliberate analytical emphasis. The three Rio Conventions (climate, biodiversity, land) are treated as thematically interlinked pillars of the environmental governance structure, while the Summit of the Future is analyzed as a systemic inflection point aimed at transcending the siloed architecture of MEAs. The High-Level Political Forum (HLPF), though significant, is subsumed under the Rio conventions' implementation review mechanisms. This narrative choice facilitates a more focused discussion on structural reform imperatives.

Analytical Approach and Methodology

This chapter adopts a qualitative and interdisciplinary analytical approach, combining critical discourse analysis, policy review, and theoretical reflection. It draws upon a targeted literature review of scholarly publications, intergovernmental reports (UNFCCC, UNEP, OECD, IPCC), summit declarations, and official communiqués from the 2024 global summits (COP29, COP16, HLPF, and the Summit of the Future). The chapter also engages with philosophical constructs such as political existentialism to interrogate the dissonance between sustainability rhetoric and diplomatic practice. Methodologically, the chapter emphasizes comparative institutional analysis, examining synergies and gaps among multilateral environmental agreements (MEAs). Furthermore, it integrates forward-looking insights on artificial intelligence, blockchain, and stakeholder roles, informed by case-based illustrations and reflective synthesis. While not based on primary fieldwork, the analysis is grounded in policy triangulation and normative critique, making it suitable for both theoretical elaboration and strategic policy dialogue.

This chapter contributes to the field of international sustainability governance by offering a critical and integrative analysis of four major summits held in 2024, while proposing structural and diplomatic innovations to enhance MEA synergy. By introducing the lens of political existentialism, the chapter offers a novel critique of diplomatic contradictions. Its emphasis on artificial intelligence, blockchain, and stakeholder-driven reforms adds to the growing discourse on technological diplomacy. It also bridges philosophical, legal, and policy perspectives in proposing forward-looking pathways for reform.

While the chapter adopts a rigorous interdisciplinary lens, it is limited by the absence of primary fieldwork or empirical datasets. The findings are thus grounded in secondary analysis and reflective synthesis rather than statistical inference. Furthermore, while the summits discussed reflect global tendencies, regional divergences—especially in Asia-Pacific and Latin America—require further contextualization in future studies. These limitations notwithstanding, the chapter's contribution lies in its conceptual reframing and normative interrogation of global environmental diplomacy.

Given the conceptual density of this chapter, key terms are defined here to establish a shared understanding. These clarifications also serve to standardize terminologies across interdisciplinary audiences—including law, international relations, environmental studies, and technology policy.

BACKGROUND

The discourse on global sustainability has evolved from a developmental ideal into an existential imperative, driven by the escalating threats of climate change, biodiversity loss, and environmental degradation. Since the 1992 Earth Summit in Rio de Janeiro, the international community has developed a complex architecture of multilateral environmental agreements (MEAs), legal instruments, and institutional mechanisms aimed at advancing sustainable development. Yet, persistent implementation gaps have cast doubt on the effectiveness of these frameworks, especially as global emissions continue to rise and vulnerable populations bear disproportionate burdens of ecological collapse (UNEP, 2019; IPCC, 2023).

Central to this debate is the concept of policy coherence, which the OECD (2019) defines as the alignment and mutual reinforcement of policies across sectors to achieve common objectives. Scholars such as Nilsson et al. (2018) and Biermann et al. (2009) argue that the lack of coherence between climate, energy, and economic strategies undermines sustainability outcomes. Fragmented governance, overlapping mandates, and institutional silos contribute to duplication of efforts and inefficiencies in implementation (Raustiala & Victor, 2004). The literature suggests that synergies among MEAs—such as the UNFCCC, CBD, and UNCCD—are both conceptually appealing and practically elusive due to diverging priorities and power asymmetries among states (Chasek et al., 2016).

A growing body of work has highlighted the rhetoric–action gap in environmental diplomacy. According to Dimitrov (2010), the climate regime suffers from chronic underperformance because national self-interest often overrides collective environmental goals. Similarly, Falkner (2016) underscores that voluntary pledges and non-binding instruments, while politically expedient, have limited normative power in enforcing compliance. These critiques are echoed in recent assessments of COP negotiations, which reveal that despite increasing participation and financial pledges, legally binding obligations remain rare and accountability mechanisms weak (UNFCCC, 2023; WEF, 2024).

The chapter also engages with the philosophical dimension of political existentialism, drawing on thinkers such as Jean-Paul Sartre and scholars like Flynn (2006), who apply existentialist principles to political decision-making. In this context, political existentialism refers to the paradox of world leaders acknowledging the existential threat of environmental collapse while simultaneously pursuing policies that perpetuate ecological harm. This dissonance reveals a crisis of political authenticity and calls into question the integrity of international diplomacy as a tool for transformative action.

Further, recent literature emphasizes the transformative potential of innovation and digital technologies in environmental governance. Artificial intelligence, blockchain, and satellite monitoring are increasingly seen as tools to enhance transparency, track emissions, and reduce transaction costs in carbon markets (UNDP, 2023; Göpel, 2016). However, scholars also warn against techno-optimism that ignores structural inequities and the political economy of technology diffusion (Jasanoff, 2018; Sovacool et al., 2020).

In summary, the background of this chapter is situated at the intersection of environmental law, diplomatic studies, global governance, and political philosophy. It builds on an interdisciplinary review of literature to argue that despite institutional proliferation and normative advancement, sustainable development remains constrained by incoherence, inconsistency, and inadequate innovation in diplomatic practice. This necessitates a paradigmatic rethinking of both the structure and spirit of global sustainability efforts.

Table 1. Comparative Matrix of 2024 Summits

Summit	Key Theme	Major Declarations	Structural Gaps	Future Potential
COP29	Climate Action	$100B reiterated; Net-zero pledges	Weak enforceability; mitigation bias	Scope for AI tracking, finance alignment
CBD COP16	Biodiversity	30x30 commitments reaffirmed	Overlap with REDD+; lack of data	Synergy with indigenous knowledge
UNCCD COP16	Desertification	Land degradation neutrality targets	Low visibility; underfunded	Nexus with food and migration policies
Summit of the Future	Multilateral Reform	Pact for the Future; Digital Compact	High abstraction; institutional lag	Potential to realign MEA architecture
HLPF	SDG Review & Policy Coherence	Voluntary National Reviews; Global SDG progress evaluation	Weak enforcement; lacks binding power; overlap with MEAs	Could act as integrative platform for MEA monitoring and SDG alignment

MAIN FOCUS OF THE CHAPTER

Issues, Controversies, Problems

Despite the widespread acknowledgment of sustainability as a shared global objective, environmental diplomacy remains hindered by systemic incoherence, political inconsistency, and fragmented multilateral frameworks. The 2024 cycle of summits—including COP29, COP16, the High-Level Political Forum (HLPF), and the Summit of the Future—has once again exposed the discrepancy between international declarations and the realities of implementation. These events, while ambitious in rhetoric, have largely failed to resolve long-standing structural problems that undermine sustainable development goals.

One of the core issues addressed in this chapter is the incoherence between international agreements and national implementation strategies. Although multilateral environmental agreements (MEAs) such as the UNFCCC, CBD, and UNCCD share common goals, their parallel trajectories and differing reporting mechanisms create inefficiencies and regulatory overlaps. This fragmentation reduces the overall effectiveness of global governance and weakens collective impact. In contrast to the integrated logic required by the Sustainable Development Goals (SDGs), many countries continue to approach environmental, social, and economic challenges in silos (UNEP, 2023; OECD, 2024).

A second controversy is the over-reliance on non-binding commitments, which, while politically convenient, dilute the enforceability of global environmental targets. Voluntary national contributions (e.g., under the Paris Agreement) often fall short of scientific recommendations, and few legal mechanisms exist to ensure compliance. The reliance on symbolic declarations, particularly at high-profile summits, contributes to what this chapter terms the "ritualization of sustainability discourse"—a pattern in which negotiation becomes a form of performance rather than a catalyst for transformation (Falkner, 2016; Ruggie, 1998).

Thirdly, the chapter interrogates the misalignment of financial flows and sustainability priorities. The 2024 summits reiterated longstanding funding pledges—such as the $100 billion annual commitment for climate finance—but failed to operationalize credible pathways for disbursement, especially to developing countries. This results in a persistent trust deficit, particularly among nations in the Global South who bear the brunt of climate impacts but receive inadequate support for adaptation and resilience. Innovative financing tools such as carbon markets, green bonds, and debt-for-nature swaps remain underutilized due to regulatory barriers and political reluctance.

In addition to institutional and financial challenges, the chapter explores the philosophical and normative tension within environmental diplomacy, using the lens of political existentialism. This framework suggests that global leaders often deploy sustainability rhetoric as a strategic tool to project moral leadership without confronting the existential contradictions embedded in their own policy choices—such as continued fossil fuel subsidies or weak environmental regulations. This political dualism contributes to what many scholars describe as "climate hypocrisy," eroding public trust and weakening diplomatic credibility (Flynn, 2006; Heywood, 2019).

Finally, the chapter contrasts current practices with emerging models of diplomatic innovation. For example, some scholars and practitioners have proposed integrating MEAs into a biannual summit framework to promote synergy, reduce transaction costs, and enhance cross-sectoral coordination. Others have advocated for AI-powered governance platforms to improve monitoring, transparency, and accountability. While such proposals remain at the margins of official negotiations, they point toward alternative architectures of global environmental governance that are more agile, inclusive, and technologically adaptive.

In comparison with existing approaches, this chapter asserts that addressing the sustainability crisis requires not just more negotiations, but a paradigm shift in how diplomacy is conceptualized and practiced. A critical reading of the 2024 summits reveals both the urgency and the inertia that characterize international relations today highlighting the need for more courageous, coherent, and cooperative pathways toward sustainable futures.

Barriers to Synergy in Multilateral Environmental Agreements

Despite the proliferation of international environmental treaties over the past three decades, efforts to foster synergy among Multilateral Environmental Agreements (MEAs) have been persistently undermined by structural, political, and institutional barriers. These constraints compromise the coherence and effectiveness of global environmental governance and inhibit the ability of international summits to produce integrated, cross-cutting solutions. Two primary sets of barriers merit critical attention: institutional fragmentation and political asymmetry among signatory states.

a. Fragmentation of Governance Structures Across Conventions

The first barrier is the institutional fragmentation of global environmental governance, characterized by parallel legal regimes, discrete reporting obligations, and poorly coordinated secretariats. Since the early 1990s, MEAs such as the *United Nations Framework Convention on Climate Change* (UNFCCC), the *Convention on Biological Diversity* (CBD), and the *United Nations Convention to Combat Desertification* (UNCCD) have developed in relative isolation, each with its own governing body, monitoring apparatus, and strategic plans. While these agreements share thematic intersections—such as ecosystem resilience, carbon sequestration, and land use—they often operate on separate diplomatic tracks with minimal cross-reference in their implementation protocols (UNEP, 2023).

A major manifestation of this fragmentation lies in the independent reporting systems and incompatible legal mandates of each MEA. States are required to submit distinct national reports, often using differing metrics, timeframes, and verification methodologies. This lack of harmonization not only imposes administrative burdens—especially on low-capacity states—but also prevents the synthesis of data necessary for integrated global assessments. Moreover, contradictions between legal mandates can generate conflicting obligations. For instance, afforestation projects promoted under the UNFCCC's REDD+ framework may inadvertently undermine biodiversity goals if they involve monoculture plantations not aligned with CBD criteria (Miles & Kapos, 2008).

Additionally, the siloed nature of MEA secretariats constrains institutional learning and policy alignment. Despite ad hoc attempts to promote joint work programs—such as the "Rio Conventions Pavilion"—there remain few formal mechanisms that oblige secretariats to coordinate their decision-making processes, budget allocations, or scientific advisory inputs. This institutional isolation is compounded by competitive funding dynamics and the absence of a unifying oversight body within the UN system to ensure coherence across conventions (Raustiala & Victor, 2004).

b. Asymmetrical Political Will and Resource Capacity Among Signatory States

The second major barrier stems from asymmetries in political will and institutional capacity among parties to the MEAs. In practice, the degree of engagement with environmental agreements varies considerably between industrialized and developing countries, leading to uneven implementation and persistent north-south tensions.

Developing nations often face significant constraints in both technical and financial implementation. These countries, particularly Least Developed Countries (LDCs) and Small Island Developing States (SIDS), struggle to meet their obligations due to limited human resources, outdated infrastructure, and dependency on external funding. As noted in repeated Global Environment Outlook reports, these systemic limitations impede timely reporting, enforcement, and the scaling-up of best practices (UNEP, 2019). Moreover, the disbursement of climate finance—nominally pledged to alleviate these burdens—remains inconsistent and entangled in complex eligibility criteria that deter access (OECD, 2023).

These inefficiencies are particularly evident in the case of the Green Climate Fund (GCF), which has faced recurrent delays in project approvals and disbursement, especially in Sub-Saharan Africa. Countries like Benin, Malawi, and the Democratic Republic of Congo have encountered protracted cycles of proposal revisions and financial closure, often due to insufficient in-country technical capacity to meet the Fund's rigorous documentation standards. Such delays contribute not only to missed implementation windows but also to frustration among national stakeholders, who perceive the climate finance architecture as structurally biased against the very countries it purports to serve.

These inefficiencies are well-documented in the operations of the Green Climate Fund (GCF), particularly across Sub-Saharan Africa. The GCF has acknowledged recurrent delays in both project approvals and disbursements, prompting the need for reforms in its operational modalities. According to the UNFCCC (2020), despite high approval volumes, disbursement has often lagged due to administrative and procedural bottlenecks, particularly affecting readiness support and adaptation finance.

Countries such as the Democratic Republic of Congo (DRC), Malawi, and Benin have benefited from readiness programs intended to strengthen technical capacity, a reflection of broader difficulties in meeting the GCF's complex documentation and fiduciary requirements. For instance, the DRC signed a readiness grant agreement in 2015, receiving USD 300,000 to strengthen institutional coordination and build capacity for effective climate finance absorption (Green Climate Fund, n.d.-a).

Moreover, the GCF Secretariat has highlighted the need to simplify access for countries with limited institutional capabilities. The Board's decision in B.36/12 underscores the structural difficulties encountered by many developing countries and calls for expedited and programmatic access to funds (Green Climate Fund, 2023). These challenges contribute not only to missed implementation timelines but also to perceptions among stakeholders that the climate finance architecture is disproportionately complex and burdensome for countries it aims to support.

In response, regional coalitions such as the African Group of Negotiators on Climate Change (AGN) and the Alliance of Small Island States (AOSIS) have emerged as collective platforms to enhance negotiating power, coordinate technical inputs, and push for more equitable procedural reforms at UNFCCC COPs. Similarly, CELAC (Community of Latin American and Caribbean States) has advocated for regional access mechanisms to climate finance that are adapted to the structural specificities of the Global South.

These trust asymmetries are further exacerbated during high-level negotiations. Developing countries often point to the repeated failure of developed nations to fulfill landmark pledges—such as the $100 billion climate finance commitment—as emblematic of climate duplicity. This perceived hypocrisy undermines diplomatic goodwill and fosters a climate of skepticism and procedural defensiveness that hampers consensus on deeper institutional reforms.

Conversely, developed countries often prioritize short-term economic or geopolitical interests over global environmental commitments, thereby eroding the collective ambition of MEAs. While these nations possess greater institutional capacity, they frequently resist binding commitments or meaningful financial transfers, preferring non-binding pledges that preserve policy flexibility. For example, the withdrawal of major economies from agreed protocols (such as the United States from the Kyoto Protocol or delays in fulfilling the $100 billion climate finance commitment) illustrates a persistent reluctance to align domestic policy with international responsibility (UNFCCC, 2023).

This asymmetry deepens the trust deficit between global North and South, making it difficult to secure consensus on reforms that would enhance MEA synergy—such as integrated reporting, joint compliance mechanisms, or pooled funding platforms.

Without mutual accountability and equitable burden-sharing, the structural incoherence of the MEA system is likely to persist.

Core Areas of Diplomatic Reform

The reform of environmental diplomacy requires more than procedural adjustments; it demands a fundamental reconfiguration of both the mission of diplomacy and the architecture of multilateral negotiations. As climate change, biodiversity collapse, and resource conflicts increasingly transcend national boundaries, the traditional state-centric, interest-based model of diplomacy proves insufficient. The current global context calls for a new diplomatic ethos—one that is anticipatory, inclusive, interdisciplinary, and implementation-driven.

a. Reconfiguration of the Diplomat's Role in Environmental Governance

The first area of reform is the redefinition of the diplomat's role within the environmental governance landscape. Historically, diplomats functioned primarily as representatives of national sovereignty and negotiators of bilateral or multilateral agreements. In the sustainability context, however, this representational model falls short of addressing the interdependent and science-driven nature of environmental challenges.

A necessary shift is the transition from representation to co-construction and implementation. Diplomats must increasingly act as conveners, facilitators, and brokers of cooperative action—engaging not only in formal negotiations but also in the design, resourcing, and monitoring of solutions. This reconceptualization aligns with the evolving expectations that diplomats play proactive roles in aligning national development plans with global sustainability goals (Cooper, 2013). It also implies that embassies and missions should serve not only political but also technical and capacity-building functions within recipient countries and multilateral fora.

A number of real-world diplomatic initiatives illustrate the viability of this expanded mandate. For instance, Sweden's network of climate attachés—stationed in key embassies worldwide—actively supports climate negotiations, bilateral partnerships on green transition, and technical exchanges on sustainability innovation. Similarly, the European Union's Green Diplomacy initiative, launched in 2020, mandates EU delegations to integrate climate considerations across all foreign policy instruments, from trade negotiations to development cooperation and security dialogue.

At the institutional level, a more systemic approach involves cross-postings and rotational schemes between ministries of foreign affairs, environment, and planning, allowing for mutual learning and coherence between international and domestic sustainability agendas. This model has begun to take shape in countries like Germany, where climate and development attachés are embedded within both foreign and sectoral ministries, promoting interministerial coordination.

In terms of training, organizations such as UNITAR, UNEP, and the Clingendael Institute have developed specialized modules on climate diplomacy, negotiation strategy, science-policy interfaces, and stakeholder engagement. These programs not only equip diplomats with the technical and normative literacy required for MEA negotiations but also promote a culture of anticipatory, multilevel diplomacy attuned to the complexity of sustainability governance.

This transformation also entails the integration of science diplomacy, digital diplomacy, and economic diplomacy into the core competencies of environmental negotiators. Science diplomacy ensures that foreign policy is grounded in empirical evidence, particularly regarding climate risks and biodiversity metrics. Digital diplomacy enhances outreach, transparency, and real-time responsiveness using platforms, data visualization tools, and AI-enabled tracking systems (Bjola & Holmes, 2015). Economic diplomacy, finally, allows diplomats to engage with green investment flows, carbon pricing mechanisms, and sustainable finance instruments—thus linking environmental integrity to market transformation. The convergence of these domains reflects the complexity of today's sustainability imperatives, and the multidimensional skill set required to address them.

b. Reorientation of Multilateral Negotiation Formats

The second axis of reform focuses on the structural reconfiguration of multilateral environmental negotiations. Current summit formats—often formalistic, state-dominated, and constrained by diplomatic protocol—fail to reflect the participatory and integrated nature of sustainable development as outlined in Agenda 2030.

An essential starting point is the promotion of inclusive summit designs that go beyond governmental delegates to incorporate civil society, indigenous representatives, youth networks, and subnational actors as legitimate stakeholders. Inclusion must go beyond symbolic consultation to active participation in agenda-setting, drafting, and follow-up mechanisms. The case of the Escazú Agreement in Latin America, which institutionalizes environmental defenders and public access to environmental justice, offers a precedent for such inclusion (UN ECLAC, 2018). Only through broadening the diplomatic table can summits reflect the plural perspectives and experiences necessary for equitable sustainability outcomes.

Additionally, this chapter, based on the recurrent synergy concern, proposes the institutionalization of biannual integrated environmental summits, replacing the current siloed model of MEA-specific conferences. Such summits would bring together the UNFCCC, CBD, UNCCD, and other MEAs into a single, thematically clustered event that allows cross-convention alignment of targets, funding priorities, and monitoring systems. The aim is not administrative consolidation but strategic coherence. A biannual format—unlike the annual pace of COPs—would allow more meaningful intersessional implementation and technical preparation, avoiding the fatigue and performative nature of yearly negotiations. The use of AI and shared reporting infrastructure could further support integrated follow-up, thus moving from fragmented commitments to systemic delivery.

It should be recalled that, during the sixteenth session of the Conference of the Parties (COP 16) to the United Nations Convention to Combat Desertification (UNCCD), held in Riyadh from 2 to 13 December 2024, the United States submitted a strategic proposal aimed at institutionalizing an integrated cycle of environmental summits. This proposal, included in the official document ICCD/COP (16)/21, emerged in a context marked by overlapping environmental crises and the growing need to reform global environmental governance. The initiative seeks to address the institutional fragmentation among the three principal environmental conventions established at the 1992 Earth Summit in Rio de Janeiro—namely the United Nations Framework Convention on Climate Change (UNFCCC), the Convention on Biological Diversity (CBD), and the UNCCD.

Indeed, according to the United States, this fragmentation results in functional redundancies, institutional inefficiencies, and a lack of strategic coherence across international environmental action. As the world confronts converging crises related to climate change, biodiversity loss, and land degradation, a more integrated and predictable multilateral governance framework is seen as indispensable (UNCCD, 2024a).

The core of the U.S. proposal revolves around the creation of a rotating three-year calendar of conferences of the parties. Under this structure, the first year would focus on the biodiversity agenda (CBD), the second year on climate change (UNFCCC), and the third year on desertification and land degradation (UNCCD). Each three-year cycle would culminate in a joint high-level summit bringing together heads of state, UN agencies, and international financial institutions to deliver coordinated strategic guidance and renewed political commitment. The proposal also includes harmonized reporting frameworks across the three conventions, alignment of budget cycles, and the establishment of a Joint Implementation Platform. This platform would aim to reduce duplication, streamline technical and financial resources, and facilitate coherent access to multilateral funding instruments such as the Global Environment Facility (GEF) and the Green Climate Fund (GCF).

The expected benefits of such a reform include improved policy coherence across global environmental agendas, more efficient deployment of technical and financial resources, increased political visibility of cross-cutting issues such as land, climate, and biodiversity, and streamlined coordination for national focal points, particularly in developing countries. The proposal also envisions a unified monitoring system based on shared indicators aligned with the Sustainable Development Goals (SDGs) (UNCCD, 2024b).

The initiative was met with mixed reactions. Several delegations—including small island developing states (SIDS), African countries, and members of the scientific community—welcomed the proposal as a bold step toward systemic coherence. They acknowledged that it responded to long-standing calls for greater synergy among the Rio Conventions (IISD, 2024). However, concerns were raised by other Parties regarding the potential dilution of the individual mandates of each convention, particularly the UNCCD, which already suffers from relatively low political and financial attention. Additional apprehensions included the logistical complexity of synchronizing multiple high-level processes and the risk of overly centralized decision-making. Consequently, COP 16 deferred a final decision and mandated the UNCCD Secretariat to prepare a feasibility report for consideration at COP 17 (UNCCD, 2024a).

The U.S. proposal aligns with broader calls for reforming multilateral environmental governance, including recommendations made in the United Nations Secretary-General's *Our Common Agenda* report, which advocates for more coherent and networked international cooperation (United Nations, 2021). It also echoes discussions from the Stockholm+50 conference and debates at the 2023 United Nations General Assembly regarding the need to modernize the institutional architecture governing environmental action. Fundamentally, the proposal can be understood as a structural response to the planetary boundaries framework, which calls for institutions capable of addressing complex and interconnected ecological challenges (Rockström et al., 2009).

Although still at the exploratory stage, the U.S. initiative introduced at COP 16 represents a potentially transformative inflection point. It invites Parties to move beyond siloed approaches and engage in a paradigm shift toward integrated multilateralism—one that is better equipped to confront the systemic threats of the Anthropocene with coherence, agility, and shared purpose.

The proposal introduced by the United States at COP 16 of the United Nations Convention to Combat Desertification (UNCCD), aiming to institutionalize an integrated cycle of environmental summits, drew a spectrum of responses ranging from thematic endorsement to procedural caution. While the proposal was not adopted in its entirety, it catalyzed substantive discussions on enhancing synergies between the Rio Conventions—namely, the UNFCCC, the CBD, and the UNCCD—and prompted support from a variety of Parties who recognized the systemic nature of environmental crises and the need for more coherent multilateral governance frameworks.

Among the most vocal supporters of the principle underpinning the U.S. initiative were several small island developing states (SIDS) and African countries. These delegations have long advocated for stronger coordination between the three Rio Conventions, as their national and regional realities frequently involve overlapping vulnerabilities to climate change, biodiversity loss, and land degradation. For instance, island nations such as the Maldives, Saint Lucia, and Fiji expressed their support for integrated approaches during ministerial statements and thematic discussions, particularly emphasizing the benefits of reducing reporting burdens and improving policy coherence. Similarly, the African Group welcomed initiatives that could streamline environmental governance, enhance access to climate and biodiversity finance, and reinforce the capacity of national focal points (IISD, 2024).

Support was also articulated by scientific and technical constituencies, notably through the Science-Policy Interface (SPI) of the UNCCD and observer organizations such as the International Union for Conservation of Nature (IUCN). These bodies underscored the scientific rationale for integrated planning and monitoring systems. They highlighted that the interlinkages between land degradation, carbon cycles, and species habitats cannot be effectively addressed in isolation. Therefore, aligning the governance rhythms of the UNCCD, UNFCCC, and CBD was seen not only as administratively desirable, but as epistemologically necessary to reflect the interconnectedness of planetary systems (UNCCD, 2024a).

Nevertheless, expressions of support were nuanced. While many countries endorsed the thematic direction of the U.S. proposal—especially the idea of enhancing synergies and reducing inefficiencies—they diverged on the institutional mechanisms through which such integration should be achieved. Countries such as Brazil, India, and Mexico, for example, emphasized the need to preserve the legal autonomy and political independence of each Convention. They argued that any integration effort must be undertaken in full respect of the principles of subsidiarity and mandate differentiation. China, in particular, insisted that coordination must not lead to centralization or to a restructuring that could undermine the sovereign negotiation processes of each treaty body (IISD, 2024).

Additional caution was expressed by Latin American countries such as Uruguay, which raised substantive concerns about potential trade-offs in implementation. These Parties warned that unless carefully designed, joint programming across Rio Conventions could unintentionally privilege one set of goals—such as climate mitigation—at the expense of others, like land restoration or biodiversity preservation. Such scenarios, they argued, could emerge especially when project financing mechanisms fail to reflect the integrated benefits of nature-based solutions, which often fall outside narrow carbon accounting methodologies (UNCCD, 2024b).

The outcome of these divergent views was a negotiated compromise. The Parties at COP 16 chose not to adopt the U.S. proposal for a rotating, integrated cycle of environmental summits. Instead, they agreed to task the UNCCD Secretariat with conducting a feasibility assessment of enhanced institutional coordination across the three Conventions. This report is expected to be presented at COP 17, scheduled to be hosted by Mongolia in 2026. The request for further study reflects both the political sensitivity and the conceptual ambition of the proposal, and it preserves space for future deliberation without binding the Parties to immediate structural change (UNCCD, 2024a).

Importantly, the debate surrounding the U.S. proposal did not occur in isolation but resonated with broader currents of UN reform. The support expressed by numerous developing countries, scientific panels, and civil society actors aligned with recommendations articulated in the United Nations Secretary-General's report *Our Common Agenda* (United Nations, 2021). That report explicitly calls for more coherent and networked multilateralism in the face of planetary crises. The discussions at COP 16 also echoed positions advanced during the Stockholm+50 conference and the 2023 General Assembly dialogue on international environmental governance, where the need for integrated and synergistic approaches was repeatedly emphasized.

In conclusion, the U.S. proposal catalyzed an important political moment at COP 16, even in the absence of formal adoption. The support it received—especially from SIDS, African nations, and the scientific community—underscores the growing recognition that the fragmentation of the global environmental governance architecture is increasingly incompatible with the scale and complexity of the planetary crisis. While objections from other influential Parties reveal the institutional caution and sovereignty concerns that still shape international negotiations, the referral of the proposal to further study ensures that the conversation around integrated environmental summits remains open. The coming sessions, particularly COP 17, may prove decisive in determining whether this initiative will evolve into a cornerstone of environmental multilateralism or remain an aspirational blueprint.

In sum, diplomatic reform must operate at both the individual and institutional levels. By transforming how diplomats are trained and how negotiations are structured, the international community can reinvigorate environmental multilateralism and restore legitimacy to the sustainability agenda. The stakes are not merely diplomatic efficiency, but planetary survival and intergenerational equity.

Strategic Policy Reform Priorities

The credibility and effectiveness of global environmental governance depend not only on diplomatic processes and stakeholder engagement, but also on the capacity of international agreements to translate into enforceable, equitable, and operational policy outcomes. In light of the shortcomings observed during and after the 2024 cycle of global summits, this section identifies two strategic priorities for policy reform: strengthening legal enforceability and enhancing the effectiveness of climate finance mechanisms.

a. Development of Enforceable and Verifiable Commitments

One of the most persistent critiques of contemporary multilateral environmental agreements is their lack of legal teeth. While frameworks such as the Paris Agreement and the Kunming-Montreal Global Biodiversity Framework have fostered normative consensus, they often rely on voluntary national commitments that are not legally enforceable and that lack meaningful consequences for non-compliance. This voluntary architecture has contributed to a growing implementation gap and widespread public skepticism regarding the sincerity of governmental pledges (UNFCCC, 2023; WEF, 2024).

To remedy this, global sustainability agreements must evolve into legally binding frameworks with independent compliance mechanisms. This implies establishing juridical or quasi-juridical entities—such as environmental courts, treaty review panels, or ombuds institutions—tasked with monitoring progress, adjudicating disputes, and triggering remedial measures in case of breaches. These bodies must be independent of state parties and empowered to receive third-party complaints, including from civil society and affected communities. The precedent of the World Trade Organization's Dispute Settlement Body offers a model of how structured enforcement can incentivize compliance even among sovereign actors.

Complementing legal enforcement, the international system must also establish sanction regimes for non-compliance and greenwashing practices. Such sanctions may include reputational penalties (such as naming-and-shaming mechanisms), financial disincentives (withholding access to climate funds), or preferential treatment for compliant states (such as green trade corridors or concessional financing). Sanctions should also apply to corporations and financial institutions that falsely advertise sustainability credentials, thereby distorting markets and undermining public trust. A robust verification ecosystem—combining independent auditors, AI-based monitoring, and transparency platforms—is essential to make this accountability system operational and fair.

b. Alignment of Climate Finance with Equity and Implementation Efficiency

The second strategic reform priority concerns the structural reform of climate finance systems, which currently suffer from fragmentation, opacity, and accessibility challenges. Despite high-profile commitments—such as the $100 billion annual pledge under the UNFCCC—disbursements remain unpredictable, slow, and skewed toward mitigation at the expense of adaptation, particularly in vulnerable countries (OECD, 2023; World Bank, 2024).

To address these deficiencies, climate finance must be aligned with both equity and implementation efficiency. First, this requires the scaling up of innovative financial instruments, such as green bonds, carbon markets, and sustainability-linked loans. Green bonds offer a mechanism for financing public infrastructure and nature-based solutions with clear environmental criteria. Carbon markets—when properly regulated—can provide cost-effective mitigation pathways while generating revenue streams for conservation and reforestation. Sustainability-linked loans further align private sector incentives with climate goals by conditioning interest rates on performance indicators.

However, financial innovation alone is insufficient if access remains constrained. Therefore, a parallel objective must be the institutionalization of simplified access to climate finance for vulnerable states. Many developing countries, particularly in Sub-Saharan Africa and Small Island Developing States, lack the administrative capacity to navigate complex application procedures and co-financing requirements. Reform should include pre-approval templates, pooled application mechanisms for regional blocs, and fast-track modalities for urgent climate risks. The Green Climate Fund and Adaptation Fund could pilot such reforms, in collaboration with UNDP and regional development banks, to democratize financial access.

In sum, strategic policy reforms must tackle both the legal enforceability of global commitments and the equitable delivery of financial resources. Without such reforms, the ambitious visions articulated at summits risk becoming rituals of deferred responsibility. Strengthening these pillars is essential to restore faith in multilateralism and ensure that sustainability transitions are not only initiated but sustained and completed.

Practical Proposals for Diplomats

Reforming environmental diplomacy in the age of planetary crisis requires more than institutional realignment—it demands a recalibration of the operational role of diplomats. Traditional diplomatic functions, shaped by doctrines of sovereignty and bilateral interest, are increasingly ill-suited to the multidimensional, long-term, and intersectoral nature of sustainable development. In this context, diplomats must evolve into agents of ecological stewardship and normative innovation. Two practical proposals are essential: redesigning diplomatic training and transforming the mandates of foreign missions.

The first proposal is the integration of sustainability science and climate law into diplomatic training modules. While foreign service academies have historically focused on geopolitics, negotiation tactics, and consular affairs, the sustainability era requires a new core curriculum. Climate diplomacy is inherently interdisciplinary, drawing on earth system science, environmental economics, legal frameworks, and international cooperation instruments. As such, diplomats must be equipped with interdisciplinary skills that allow them to navigate the complex landscape of multilateral environmental negotiations—including the technical language of emissions reductions, adaptation finance, biodiversity targets, and land-use transitions.

Moreover, sustainability diplomacy is not purely technical; it is deeply participatory, involving a wide range of actors from indigenous communities and civil society organizations to private sector entities and youth networks. Therefore, diplomatic training must also emphasize stakeholder engagement and participatory governance methods. This includes developing listening capacities, cultural literacy, and the ability to co-design solutions with non-state actors. Empowering diplomats with these competencies will enhance the legitimacy and implementation potential of international commitments negotiated in forums like COP29 or the Summit of the Future.

The second proposal involves the redesign of mission mandates to prioritize long-term ecological security. Currently, most embassies and permanent missions focus on trade promotion, bilateral political relations, or consular services. Environmental issues—when addressed—are often relegated to specialized attachés or dealt with on an ad hoc basis. This fragmented approach is no longer sufficient. Diplomatic missions should expand their roles beyond symbolic representation to include continuous monitoring, domestic policy alignment, and international reporting obligations related to multilateral environmental agreements (MEAs).

In practice, this would mean embedding climate, biodiversity, and sustainability objectives into foreign policy toolkits. For example, ambassadors and consuls-general could be tasked with reporting on host country sustainability trends, liaising with local environmental stakeholders, or coordinating regional green finance partnerships. Environmental focal points could be institutionalized within each mission, linked directly to national sustainable development units and supported by data dashboards that track MEA compliance in real time. Such an approach would move sustainability from the periphery to the core of diplomatic operations.

These proposals are not merely functional adjustments—they represent a paradigm shift in how diplomacy is understood and practiced in the Anthropocene. By institutionalizing ecological literacy, participatory practice, and long-term thinking into the daily routines of diplomatic actors, the international system can better respond to the systemic and existential threats posed by environmental decline.

Key Innovations in AI for MEA Implementation

The implementation of Multilateral Environmental Agreements (MEAs) has long been hindered by opaque monitoring systems, fragmented data infrastructures, and institutional delays in verification and enforcement. As global sustainability challenges escalate in complexity and urgency, the deployment of artificial intelligence (AI) and blockchain technologies emerges as a transformative opportunity to enhance transparency, operational efficiency, and accountability in environmental governance.

One of the most promising applications of AI lies in the use of machine learning algorithms for predictive policy modeling and implementation tracking. Unlike conventional monitoring systems that rely on retrospective reporting and often incomplete data, AI can process vast volumes of real-time environmental, economic, and policy information to forecast compliance risks and identify implementation gaps. National submissions under frameworks such as the UNFCCC, CBD, or UNCCD could be systematically reviewed by intelligent agents trained to identify treaty violations, inconsistencies, or systemic inefficiencies—such as delays in financial disbursement, lack of alignment between national development plans and treaty goals, or emissions trajectories that diverge from pledged targets.

In addition, machine learning can automate cross-agreement performance analytics, enabling policymakers, researchers, and civil society actors to visualize and compare country progress across multiple MEAs. For instance, a country's deforestation trends under the REDD+ mechanism could be algorithmically correlated with its biodiversity metrics under the CBD, offering a more integrated understanding of environmental trade-offs and synergies. These tools also facilitate early warning systems that can flag areas at risk of non-compliance before violations occur, thereby strengthening the preventive dimension of environmental governance.

Several emerging initiatives already demonstrate the practical potential of AI in treaty implementation and environmental monitoring. The Climate TRACE coalition, for instance, harnesses satellite imagery and machine learning to track greenhouse gas emissions from individual facilities across the globe, offering an independent verification tool that can complement national reports under the UNFCCC. In India, AI-supported platforms such as e-Green Watch and forest monitoring tools developed by ISRO enable authorities to detect illegal logging and monitor afforestation efforts with unprecedented granularity. Likewise, the UNDP Climate Information for Resilient Development in Africa (CIRDA) initiative leverages AI and data modeling to enhance climate risk forecasting for vulnerable communities.

However, deploying such systems in the Global South raises critical concerns around algorithmic bias, data sovereignty, and infrastructural inequality. Most AI systems are trained on datasets generated in or by institutions from the Global North, which may not reflect the socio-environmental complexity of developing countries.

Furthermore, the absence of robust digital infrastructure, low levels of environmental data availability, and limited national technical capacity can hinder the effective adoption of AI solutions. Bridging this gap will require targeted investments in digital public goods, national AI literacy programs, and inclusive technology partnerships that prioritize local ownership and co-design.

Complementing AI, blockchain and smart contract technologies offer secure and transparent infrastructure to track climate finance flows and treaty commitments. Blockchain allows for the creation of immutable, time-stamped records that cannot be altered retroactively. In the context of MEAs, this means that funding pledges, project disbursements, and performance milestones can be permanently recorded on decentralized ledgers, reducing the risk of corruption, double-counting, or financial opacity.

Through smart contracts, disbursements of climate finance can be automatically triggered upon the verification of agreed results—thus linking performance directly to funding in real time. For example, a climate adaptation project in a vulnerable country could receive its second tranche of funding only when independent monitoring—facilitated by satellite data and AI verification—confirms that specified milestones have been achieved. This approach not only enhances trust between donor and recipient states but also ensures that funding mechanisms are outcome-oriented and less prone to political interference.

The application of these digital innovations is particularly relevant for addressing North–South asymmetries in environmental finance and compliance monitoring. By democratizing access to data, reducing transaction costs, and minimizing the influence of geopolitical power dynamics, AI and blockchain have the potential to rebalance the global implementation architecture in favor of equity and efficiency.

Nevertheless, their deployment must be guided by ethical principles, data governance standards, and capacity-building investments, especially in developing countries. Without inclusive digital literacy, there is a risk that these tools may reinforce existing inequalities or become instruments of technocratic dominance. Therefore, international cooperation and support from multilateral institutions are essential to ensure that AI and blockchain serve as enablers of sustainability, rather than as barriers to participation.

In sum, the integration of AI and blockchain into MEA implementation is not a luxury—it is a strategic necessity for a global governance system struggling to bridge the gap between ambition and action. When properly harnessed, these technologies can help convert global promises into measurable progress, offering a path forward in the age of digital diplomacy and data-driven sustainability.

Stakeholder Roles in Multilateral Environmental Governance

The implementation of Multilateral Environmental Agreements (MEAs) cannot succeed without the effective participation of a broad ecosystem of actors. While international treaties are negotiated primarily by sovereign states, their real-world impact depends on inclusive partnerships that bridge legal mandates, local realities, technological innovations, and financial flows. A multistakeholder approach is therefore essential—not only for legitimacy but also for effectiveness. This section delineates the complementary roles of key stakeholders: governments, civil society, the private sector, and multilateral institutions.

Governments as Legal Enablers and Resource Mobilizers

Governments hold the primary responsibility for translating international commitments into enforceable national frameworks. This begins with the harmonization of domestic legislation with MEA obligations and the broader targets of the Sustainable Development Goals (SDGs). National environmental laws, climate change acts, biodiversity regulations, and land-use policies must be updated to reflect treaty obligations and include clear enforcement provisions. Regulatory coherence at the national level is a prerequisite for global synergy.

In addition to legal alignment, governments must function as resource mobilizers, leveraging fiscal policy tools to stimulate sustainability-oriented investments. This includes the introduction of green incentives such as tax credits for renewable energy deployment, subsidies for sustainable agriculture, and preferential procurement for low-emission technologies. By redirecting public spending and de-risking private investments, states can create enabling environments that support MEA implementation while advancing national development objectives.

Civil Society Organizations and Indigenous Groups as Norm Shapers and Watchdogs

Civil society organizations (CSOs) and indigenous communities are vital for the democratization and contextualization of environmental governance. These actors play dual roles: as norm shapers who advocate for equitable, rights-based approaches, and as watchdogs who monitor government compliance and call out discrepancies between rhetoric and action.

CSOs contribute to the monitoring and review of national implementation plans, ensuring that environmental justice, gender equity, and intergenerational responsibility remain central to policy formulation. Their proximity to affected populations enables them to represent marginalized voices often excluded from official diplomatic processes. Moreover, indigenous knowledge systems offer critical insights into biodiversity protection, land stewardship, and climate resilience, making them indispensable for MEA operationalization.

The recognition of these knowledge systems has gained increasing prominence in multilateral frameworks. Notably, the Intergovernmental Science-Policy Platform on Biodiversity and Ecosystem Services (IPBES) has integrated indigenous and local knowledge into its assessment methodology, acknowledging their value in sustaining ecosystem resilience. Similarly, the Convention on Biological Diversity (CBD) promotes traditional knowledge as part of its Article 8(j), aiming to protect and respect indigenous contributions to conservation and sustainable use.

On the ground, indigenous coalitions such as the Coordination of Indigenous Organizations of the Amazon Basin (COICA) have effectively opposed deforestation and extractive projects through international advocacy and local resistance. Their mobilization has led to moratoria on oil exploration in ecologically sensitive areas and has inspired legal action that compels governments to consult indigenous populations, as exemplified by landmark rulings in Ecuador and Colombia.

Civil society organizations have also become instrumental in advancing climate litigation. The Urgenda Foundation's lawsuit against the Dutch government, which led to a historic ruling mandating stronger emission reduction, has inspired a wave of similar actions globally, including youth-led cases in the U.S., Germany, and South Korea. These legal strategies reinforce MEA norms through domestic courts, pushing states toward stronger compliance in the absence of binding international sanctions.

By serving as bridges between local realities and global commitments, civil society and indigenous networks enhance both the legitimacy and effectiveness of MEAs. Their involvement ensures that implementation is not just top-down but rooted in community participation and cultural relevance.

Private Sector and Financial Institutions as Innovation and Investment Drivers

The private sector is increasingly recognized as a catalyst for green transformation, particularly in domains such as renewable energy, carbon markets, sustainable infrastructure, and digital innovation. Corporations and financial institutions are uniquely positioned to develop market-based solutions aligned with MEA objectives. These include carbon trading schemes, nature-based solutions, green technology platforms, and circular economy models that reduce waste and promote resource efficiency.

In partnership with governments and development agencies, the private sector can co-finance adaptation and mitigation projects through public-private partnerships (PPPs). For example, banks and investment firms can issue sustainability-linked bonds or co-invest in resilient infrastructure projects in climate-vulnerable regions.

By aligning profitability with sustainability outcomes, businesses can shift from being part of the problem to becoming central to the solution.

However, this role requires regulation, transparency, and accountability. The effectiveness of the private sector's contribution depends on clear environmental standards, credible certification schemes, and mechanisms to prevent greenwashing. Regulatory frameworks should therefore both enable and constrain, ensuring that innovation serves public interest and planetary stability.

Multilateral Development Banks and UN Agencies as Conveners and Technical Support Hubs

Multilateral development banks (MDBs) and United Nations agencies play a pivotal intermediary role, bridging global agendas with national capacities. As conveners of knowledge, finance, and institutional partnerships, these organizations are uniquely equipped to facilitate MEA implementation, especially in low- and middle-income countries.

MDBs such as the World Bank, African Development Bank, and Asian Development Bank offer blended finance instruments, combining grants, loans, and guarantees to attract private investment into environmental sectors. Their long-term engagement with national governments allows them to support institutional reforms, build technical capacity, and scale up successful pilot initiatives. Similarly, UN agencies like UNEP, UNDP, and FAO provide technical assistance, policy advice, and knowledge platforms that promote best practices and facilitate peer learning.

Crucially, these institutions also help streamline MEA synergies, supporting integrated reporting systems, shared implementation frameworks, and cross-agency coordination platforms. Their convening power can be harnessed to push for more aligned planning cycles and monitoring tools across environmental conventions.

In conclusion, the success of MEA implementation hinges not on a single actor but on the productive interaction among multiple stakeholders, each bringing complementary assets—legal authority, community legitimacy, financial capital, or technical expertise. A stakeholder-inclusive approach transforms environmental governance from a closed intergovernmental domain into a collaborative global enterprise, capable of delivering on the promise of sustainable development.

SOLUTIONS AND RECOMMENDATIONS

Innovating Environmental Diplomacy

One of the most compelling avenues for reform lies in reimagining the institutional architecture of global environmental diplomacy. This chapter advocates for the establishment of biannual integrated summits that consolidate existing multilateral environmental agreement (MEA) forums. Such summits would reduce administrative duplication, encourage policy coherence, and foster synergies across climate, biodiversity, and pollution agendas. Rather than holding fragmented meetings under each convention, a harmonized platform could allow for cross-sectoral negotiations, improve funding efficiency, and increase political accountability.

Equally critical is the development of harmonized reporting frameworks. The current system of disjointed national communications across various MEAs contributes to inefficiencies and implementation fatigue. A unified, digital reporting protocol—anchored in agreed sustainability metrics—could streamline country obligations and foster real-time comparative analytics.

Finally, the deployment of artificial intelligence and blockchain technologies offers new frontiers for transparency and implementation tracking. AI can support pattern detection and predictive policy monitoring, while blockchain can provide immutable verification of climate finance flows, reducing corruption and increasing donor confidence.

Restructuring Diplomatic Missions

To align diplomacy with 21st-century sustainability challenges, a fundamental redefinition of diplomatic functions is required. The traditional model—based on state representation and bilateral interest negotiation—must evolve into a model of transformational diplomacy. In this model, diplomats not only advocate but also co-produce policy, mobilize cross-sectoral actors, and monitor MEA implementation on the ground.

This transformation necessitates new training paradigms. Diplomats must be equipped with knowledge in climate science, sustainable finance, systems thinking, and digital tools. Training should also include stakeholder engagement skills to effectively liaise with civil society, academia, and indigenous groups.

Beyond individual capacity, institutional redesign is needed to support synergy. Diplomatic missions should be embedded within national sustainable development frameworks, with specialized units focused on MEA compliance, climate finance mobilization, and local implementation support.

Strengthening MEA Implementation

Translating global environmental commitments into national action requires enforceable frameworks and inclusive mechanisms. Legal enforcement tools—including binding national targets, independent monitoring bodies, and judicial recourse—must replace the voluntary logic of past decades.

Equally important is the alignment of climate finance with national development strategies. Financial flows should respond not only to global priorities but also to local realities and institutional capacities. Ensuring predictability, accessibility, and equity in climate finance is key to restoring trust—especially among countries in the Global South.

Lastly, South-South and triangular cooperation should be strengthened as strategic pathways for knowledge exchange, technology transfer, and shared innovation. These modalities promote localized solutions, reduce dependency, and cultivate a global diplomatic culture rooted in mutual learning and solidarity.

FUTURE RESEARCH DIRECTIONS

The sustainability impasse calls for a new research frontier—one that merges political theory, behavioral science, and digital governance to understand and transform the practice of environmental diplomacy.

The need to critically reassess the theoretical and practical foundations of environmental diplomacy is more urgent than ever. First, scholars should deepen the exploration of political existentialism as a framework to understand the paradoxes of global sustainability discourse. How states acknowledge existential threats while pursuing ecologically destructive policies remains a fundamental tension that deserves further inquiry.

This paradox is particularly visible in cases like Norway, which champions international climate diplomacy while continuing to expand offshore oil exploration. Such contradictions exemplify what political existentialism identifies as a crisis of authenticity—where actors are conscious of ecological imperatives yet act in ways that betray that awareness. Future research could apply existentialist lenses to analyze how state narratives and diplomatic performances obscure or rationalize these contradictions. Qualitative discourse analysis and elite interviews could help reveal the psychological and ideological mechanisms behind these dualities.

Additionally, behavioral science provides useful insights into the cognitive and emotional drivers of climate inaction. Scholars like Cass Sunstein and Daniel Kahneman have shown how loss aversion, status quo bias, and temporal discounting distort political decision-making under environmental uncertainty. George Marshall argues that climate narratives often fail because they trigger anxiety without offering identity-compatible solutions. Empirical research combining mixed methods, participatory foresight, and narrative testing could illuminate how diplomatic strategies can be reframed to resonate with both policymakers and publics, strengthening MEA legitimacy and mobilization.

Second, research should focus on pilot models of integrated MEA summits. Experimental governance platforms that attempt thematic convergence, cross-institutional coordination, or joint financing could offer empirical insights into the feasibility of a biannual integrated summit structure.

Third, it is essential to measure the impact of artificial intelligence in treaty compliance, reporting accuracy, and decision-making efficiency. This includes ethical considerations related to data sovereignty and algorithmic bias.

Finally, scholars should explore behavioral science approaches to rebuilding public trust in sustainability governance. Understanding how narratives, emotions, and identity influence international negotiations and domestic support for MEAs could unlock more resonant and effective diplomatic strategies.

From a methodological standpoint, future research on sustainability diplomacy would benefit from interdisciplinary and multimethod approaches. Comparative case studies could illuminate how different states manage the contradictions of environmental rhetoric and extractive policy. Discourse analysis and narrative inquiry could reveal the framing techniques used by diplomats to reconcile global goals with national interests. For technological tools such as AI and blockchain, experimental pilot evaluations, data ethics audits, and human-centered design assessments are recommended. Additionally, participatory foresight methods—including scenario building and deliberative polling—can help model the institutional conditions for integrated MEA summits. Emphasizing both empirical validity and normative reflection, such methodological diversity is key to advancing the critical and constructive agenda outlined in this chapter.

CONCLUSION

This chapter has argued that the confluence of the 2024 summits, while historically significant, has reaffirmed the enduring gap between rhetorical ambition and operational reality in international sustainability governance. Despite an abundance of declarations and frameworks, structural fragmentation, financial disparities, and weak accountability mechanisms continue to undermine the potential of MEAs.

To overcome these deficits, a paradigm shift in diplomacy is required—one that prioritizes long-term ecological and social objectives over short-term political gains.

The transformation must be proactive, systemic, and grounded in enforceable legal instruments and innovative digital tools.

The 2024 summits mark not just a point of reflection but a call to action. The legacy of this diplomatic cycle will be measured not by its communiqués, but by whether it catalyzes structural reforms that bridge discourse and delivery. If the world is to meet the 2030 Agenda and ensure environmental resilience for future generations, diplomacy itself must be reinvented as a tool of inclusion, enforcement, and imagination.

The sustainability crisis requires more than iterative negotiations—it demands diplomatic reinvention, institutional synergy, and systemic accountability. This chapter underscores that future progress hinges not merely on the quantity of summits, but on their capacity to challenge structural inertia, harness innovation, and redistribute trust in global governance. As sustainability diplomacy evolves, so too must the actors, methods, and mindsets that define it.

The path forward requires not merely reform but reinvention—a collective reimagining of diplomacy as a tool not of posturing but of planetary stewardship. If the 2024 summits are to mark a rupture from the inertia of the past, they must become catalysts of an integrative, inclusive, and enforceable sustainability order. This will require new imaginaries, daring institutional experimentation, and an ethos of shared destiny that transcends geopolitical divides. Only then can sustainability cease to be a deferred ideal and become an enacted global contract.

What Future Generations Must Understand?

The struggle for sustainability is not merely technical or legal—it is civilizational. The paradoxes of political behavior, the inertia of institutions, and the allure of technocratic fixes must be confronted not only with data, but with courage, ethics, and imagination. Future leaders must remember that treaties alone do not sustain life—commitment, coherence, and accountability do.

REFERENCES

Bjola, C., & Holmes, M. (2015). *Digital diplomacy: Theory and practice*. Routledge., DOI: 10.4324/9781315767314

Chasek, P. S., Downie, D. L., & Brown, J. W. (2016). *Global environmental politics* (7th ed.). Routledge.

Cooper, A. F. (Ed.). (2013). *The Oxford handbook of modern diplomacy*. Oxford University Press., DOI: 10.1093/oxfordhb/9780199588862.001.0001

Dimitrov, R. S. (2010). Inside UN climate change negotiations: The Copenhagen conference. *The Review of Policy Research*, *27*(6), 795–821. DOI: 10.1111/j.1541-1338.2010.00472.x

Falkner, R. (2016). The Paris Agreement and the new logic of international climate politics. *International Affairs*, *92*(5), 1107–1125. DOI: 10.1111/1468-2346.12708

Flynn, T. R. (2006). *Existentialism: A very short introduction*. Oxford University Press.

Göpel, M. (2016). *The great mindshift: How a new economic paradigm and sustainability transformations go hand in hand*. Springer., DOI: 10.1007/978-3-319-43766-8

Green Climate Fund. (2023). *Decision B.36/12: Enhancing access to climate finance through simplified processes*. https://www.greenclimate.fund/sites/default/files/decision/b36/decision-b36-12-annex-vi.pdf

Green Climate Fund. (n.d.-a). *Democratic Republic of the Congo and the GCF*. https://www.greenclimate.fund/countries/dr-congo

Heywood, A. (2019). *Politics* (5th ed.). Macmillan International Higher Education.

IISD. (2024). UNCCD COP 16 Summary and Analysis: Riyadh, Saudi Arabia, 2–13 December 2024. Earth Negotiations Bulletin. https://enb.iisd.org/convention-combat-desertification-unccd-cop16-summary

IPBES. (2019). *Global assessment report on biodiversity and ecosystem services*. Intergovernmental Science-Policy Platform on Biodiversity and Ecosystem Services. https://ipbes.net/global-assessment

IPCC. (2023). [*Synthesis report*. Intergovernmental Panel on Climate Change. https://www.ipcc.ch/report/sixth-assessment-report-synthesis-report/]. *Climatic Change*, *2023*, •••.

Jasanoff, S. (2018). *The ethics of invention: Technology and the human future*. W. W. Norton & Company.

Miles, L., & Kapos, V. (2008). Reducing greenhouse gas emissions from deforestation and forest degradation: Global land-use implications. *Science*, *320*(5882), 1454–1455. DOI: 10.1126/science.1155358 PMID: 18556549

Nilsson, M., Chisholm, E., Griggs, D., Howden-Chapman, P., McCollum, D., Messerli, P., & Stafford-Smith, M. (2018). Mapping interactions between the sustainable development goals: Lessons learned and ways forward. *Sustainability Science*, *13*, 1489–1503. DOI: 10.1007/s11625-018-0604-z PMID: 30546483

OECD. (2019). *Policy coherence for sustainable development 2019: Empowering people and ensuring inclusiveness and equality*. OECD Publishing., DOI: 10.1787/a90f851f-

OECD. (2023). *Financing climate action: Progress and challenges*. Organisation for Economic Co-operation and Development. https://www.oecd.org/environment/cc/climate-finance.htm

OECD. (2024). *Policy coherence for sustainable development: Aligning policies in the decade of action*. OECD Publishing. [Pre-publication reference]

Raustiala, K., & Victor, D. G. (2004). The regime complex for plant genetic resources. *International Organization*, *58*(2), 277–309. DOI: 10.1017/S0020818304582036

Ruggie, J. G. (1998). *Constructing the world polity: Essays on international institutionalization*. Routledge.

UN ECLAC. (2018). *Regional agreement on access to information, public participation and justice in environmental matters in Latin America and the Caribbean (Escazú Agreement)*. United Nations Economic Commission for Latin America and the Caribbean. https://www.cepal.org/en/escazuagreement

UNCCD. (2024a). Report of the Conference of the Parties on its sixteenth session, held in Riyadh from 2 to 13 December 2024. ICCD/COP(16)/23/Add.1. https://www.unccd.int

UNCCD. (2024b). Annex to the Proposal on the Institutionalization of an Integrated Cycle of Environmental Summits. ICCD/COP(16)/21. https://www.unccd.int

UNDP. (2023). *Harnessing digital solutions for climate action*. United Nations Development Programme. https://www.undp.org/publications/digital-climate-solutions

UNEP. (2019). *Global environment outlook 6: Healthy planet, healthy people.* Cambridge University Press. https://www.unep.org/resources/global-environment-outlook-6

UNEP. (2023). *Emissions gap report 2023.* United Nations Environment Programme. https://www.unep.org/resources/emissions-gap-report-2023

UNFCCC. (2015). *The Paris Agreement.* United Nations Framework Convention on Climate Change. https://unfccc.int/process-and-meetings/the-paris-agreement/the-paris-agreement

UNFCCC. (2020). *Report of the Green Climate Fund to the Conference of the Parties and guidance to the Green Climate Fund (FCCC/CP/2020/5).* https://unfccc.int/sites/default/files/resource/cp2020_05E.pdf

UNFCCC. (2023). *Global stocktake synthesis report.* United Nations Framework Convention on Climate Change. https://unfccc.int/topics/global-stocktake

United Nations. (2021). Our Common Agenda – Report of the Secretary-General. United Nations. https://www.un.org/en/common-agenda

WEF. (2024). *The global risks report 2024.* World Economic Forum. https://www.weforum.org/reports/global-risks-report-2024

World Bank. (2024). (Forthcoming). Sustainable development outlook 2024: Charting resilient pathways. *World Bank Group.*

KEY TERMS AND DEFINITIONS

Accountability Mechanisms: Institutional arrangements, legal instruments, or procedural frameworks designed to monitor, report, verify, and enforce commitments made under multilateral environmental agreements. These may include review bodies, sanctions, or transparency protocols.

Blockchain: A decentralized ledger technology that, in governance contexts, can be used to track finance flows or verify compliance with environmental treaties.

Carbon Markets: Market-based systems where carbon emission allowances are bought, sold, or traded. These include compliance-based markets under the Kyoto Protocol or Paris Agreement (Article 6), as well as voluntary carbon markets used by private actors.

Climate Finance: Local, national, or transnational funding—drawn from public, private, and alternative sources—that is specifically earmarked to support mitigation and adaptation actions to address climate change. It includes both concessional and market-based instruments under frameworks like the UNFCCC and the Green Climate Fund.

Digital Diplomacy: The use of digital technologies—including data platforms, social media, and AI tools—by states and non-state actors to advance foreign policy, multilateral engagement, and international cooperation. In this chapter, it refers to the evolving toolkit of sustainability diplomacy.

Global Stocktake: A periodic assessment mechanism under the Paris Agreement (every five years), aimed at evaluating collective progress toward global climate goals and informing national contributions. The 2023 Global Stocktake is referenced in your chapter as a key moment of reflection.

Green Bonds: The debt instruments issued by governments, development banks, or corporations to finance projects with verified environmental benefits, such as renewable energy, sustainable transport, or ecosystem restoration.

Greenwashing: The practice by which institutions or corporations misrepresent environmental performance, often to gain reputational or financial advantage. The misrepresentation or exaggeration of environmental performance by states, corporations, or institutions in order to gain reputational, financial, or political advantage—often masking unsustainable practices.

Integrated Governance: A systems-based approach that seeks to align policy instruments, actors, and institutions across sectors and levels of governance to deliver coherent and synergistic outcomes. In sustainability, it implies breaking down silos between climate, biodiversity, land, energy, and finance agendas.

Loss and Damage: A principle under climate negotiations that refers to the irreversible consequences of climate change that cannot be prevented through mitigation or adaptation—requiring separate financial support. It highlights issues of historical responsibility and justice for vulnerable states.

Multilateral Environmental Agreements (MEAs): Formal treaties among three or more countries addressing specific environmental issues—such as climate change, biodiversity, or desertification—under international law.

Political existentialism: A philosophical framework inspired by thinkers such as Jean-Paul Sartre, which here refers to the paradox wherein political leaders acknowledge existential environmental threats while pursuing contradictory policies.

Ritualization of sustainability discourse: Used in this chapter to critique the repetitive, performative nature of international declarations that lack binding enforcement.

Summit Diplomacy: A form of high-level international negotiation involving heads of state, ministers, or multilateral representatives convening at summits to declare commitments, coordinate global strategies, or redefine diplomatic norms. Often criticized for being performative in the absence of binding outcomes.

Synergy among MEAs: The coordinated implementation of these treaties to avoid duplication, reduce costs, and maximize impact.

Techno-optimism: The belief that emerging technologies alone can solve structural sustainability challenges, sometimes without adequate attention to social or ethical risks.

Compilation of References

Abel, A. B., & Eberly, J. C. (1999). The effects of irreversibility and uncertainty on capital accumulation. *Journal of Monetary Economics*, *44*(3), 339–377. DOI: 10.1016/S0304-3932(99)00029-X

Abels, J. (2024). Private infrastructure in geopolitical conflicts: The case of Starlink and the war in Ukraine. *European Journal of International Relations*, *30*(4), 842–866. DOI: 10.1177/13540661241260653

Acharya, V. V., Bhadury, S., & Surti, J. (2020). Financial vulnerability and risks to growth in emerging markets (CEPR Discussion Paper No. DP14962). https://ssrn.com/abstract=3638068

Adeosun, O. A., Anagreh, S., Tabash, M. I., & Vo, X. V. (2024). Return and volatility transmission among economic policy uncertainty, geopolitical risk and precious metals. *Studies in Economics and Finance*, *41*(5), 1057–1084. DOI: 10.1108/SEF-10-2023-0586

Adler, E. (2013). Constructivism in international relations: Sources, contributions, and debates. *Handbook of International Relations, 2*, 112–144.

Aisen, A., & Vega, F. J. (2011). How Does Political Instability Effect Economic Growth. IMF Working Paper, No:12.

Aiyar, M. S., Chen, M. J., Ebeke, C., Ebeke, M. C. H., Garcia-Saltos, M. R., Gudmundsson, T., Ilyina, M. A., Kangur, M. A., Kunaratskul, T., & Rodriguez, M. S. L. (2023). *Geo-economic fragmentation and the future of multilateralism*. International Monetary Fund.

Akkoç, G. K., Akkoç, U., & Yücel, Ö. F. (2018). BRICS-T Ülkelerinde Toplam Faktör Verimliliği & Teknoloji Transferi. *Uluslararası İktisadi & İdari İncelemeler Dergisi*, (21), 101–118.

Alam, M. R., & Istiak, K. (2020). Impact of US policy uncertainty on Mexico: Evidence from linear and nonlinear tests. *The Quarterly Review of Economics and Finance*, *77*, 355–366. DOI: 10.1016/j.qref.2019.12.002

Alesina, A., & Rodrik, D. (1994). Distributi& politics and economic growth. *The Quarterly Journal of Economics*, *109*(2), 465–490.

Alesina, A., & Tabellini, G. (1988). External Debt, Capital Flight and Politic Risk. *Working Paper Series (National Bureau of Economic Research)*, *2610*, 1–45.

Al-Hyari, K., Alnsour, M., Al-Weshah, G., & Haffar, M. (2012). Religious beliefs and consumer behaviour: From loyalty to boycotts. *Journal of Islamic Marketing*, *3*(2), 155–174. DOI: 10.1108/17590831211232564

Al-Mustofa, M. U., & Risyad, M. H. (2025). Geopolitical risk and foreign direct investment: the role of liberalization, institutions and financial markets. *Studies in Economics and Finance, ahead-of-print.* DOI: 10.1108/SEF-09-2024-0621

Aloui, R., Ben Aïssa, M. S., & Nguyen, D. K. (2013). Conditional dependence structure between oil prices and exchange rates: A copula-GARCH approach. *Journal of International Financial Markets, Institutions and Money*, *32*, 719–738. DOI: 10.1016/j.jimonfin.2012.06.006

Alqahtani, A., Hammoudeh, S., & Selmi, R. (2022). Relationship between different sources of geopolitical risks and stock markets in the GCC region: A dynamic correlation analysis. *Review of Behavioral Finance*, *14*(2), 296–316. DOI: 10.1108/RBF-07-2019-0099

Amazon. (2022). *Amazon secures up to 83 launches from Arianespace, Blue Origin, and United Launch Alliance for project Kuiper*. Retrieved from: https://press.aboutamazon.com/2022/4/amazon-secures-up-to-83-launches-from-arianespace-blue-origin-and-united-launch-alliance-for-project-kuiper

Amsden, A. H. (1992). *Asia's Next Giant: South Korea and Late Industrialization*. Oxford University Press.

Anaya, S. J. (2023). *Indigenous peoples in international law* (2nd ed.). Oxford University Press., https://academic.oup.com/book/50412

Anderson, P. (1999). Perspective: Complexity theory and organization science. *Organization Science*, *10*(3), 216–232.

Antonakakis, N., Gupta, R., Kollias, C., & Papadamou, S. (2017). Geopolitical risks and the oil-stock nexus over 1899-2016. *Finance Research Letters*, *23*, 165–173. DOI: 10.1016/j.frl.2017.07.017

Anzo, E. (2012). Negocios internacionales: Evolución, consolidación e identificación de los temas que lideran el campo de investigación. *Revista Ciencias Estratégicas, 20*(27), 77–93.

Archinard, N. (2024). The future of global space governance. In Pekkanen, S. M., & Blount, P. J. (Eds.), *The Oxford handbook of space security* (pp. 807–823). Oxford University Press.

Arenla. (2023). *FDI inflow in Northeast India: Policy reforms, trends and prospects.* Asian Confluence. https://www.asianconfluence.org/publication-details-full/fdi-inflow-in-northeast-india-policy-reforms-trends-and-prospects

Arslan, Ü. (2011). Siyasi istikrarsızlık & ekonomik performans: Türkiye örneği. *Ege Academic Review, 11*(1).

Asai, M., Gupta, R., & McAleer, M. (2020). Forecasting volatility and co-volatility of crude oil and gold futures: Effects of leverage, jumps, spillovers, and geopolitical risks. *International Journal of Forecasting, 36*(3), 933–948. DOI: 10.1016/j.ijforecast.2019.10.003

Atacan, C., & Açık, A. (2023). Impact of Geopolitical Risk on International Trade: Evidence from Container Throughputs. *Transactions on Maritime Science, 12*(2). Advance online publication. DOI: 10.7225/toms.v12.n02.019

Atlantic Council. (2021). The Longer Telegram: Toward A New American China Strategy. Atlantic Council. https://www.atlanticcouncil.org/wp-content/uploads/2021/01/The-Longer-Telegram-Toward-A-New-American-China-Strategy.pdf

Atradius N.V. (February 21, 2024). *Trade War is Having a Profound Effect on Global Trade*. [Web article].

Autio, E., Mudambi, R., & Yoo, Y. (2021). Digitalization and globalization in a turbulent world: Centrifugal and centripetal forces. *Global Strategy Journal, 11*(1), 3–16. DOI: 10.1002/gsj.1396

Avant, D. D., Finnemore, M., & Sell, S. K. (Eds.). (2010). *Who governs the globe?* (Vol. 114). Cambridge University Press.

Awaludin, A. A., & Al-Khaidar, M. A. (2023). Opinion leaders and boycott intentions: Factors influencing consumer behavior in support of Israel Boycott. *Journal of Digital Marketing and Halal Industry, 5*(2), 243–264. DOI: 10.21580/jdmhi.2023.5.2.20166

Aydindag, D. (2021). *The role of language in power and politics (case study: Erdoğan speeches between 2002-2020).* Revista EntreLinguas.

Azzimonti, M. (2019). Does partisan conflict deter FDI inflows to the US? *Journal of International Economics*, *120*, 162–178. DOI: 10.1016/j.jinteco.2019.06.001

Baci, N., Mulla, G., Millo, D., & Xhyheri, K. (2022). Foreign direct investment and its drivers: An empirical comparative study on developed and developing countries. *WSEAS Transactions on Environment and Development*, *18*, 992–1004. DOI: 10.37394/232015.2022.18.95

Baena-Rojas, J. J. (2024). La Unión Europea dentro de la OMC: ¿paradigma de liderazgo geopolítico en las relaciones internacionales? *Novum Jus*, *18*(1), 431–459. DOI: 10.14718/NovumJus.2024.18.1.15

Baena-Rojas, J. J., & Bonilla-Calle, D. (2021). Revisión contextual para la interpretación del análisis de riesgo geopolítico. *Revista de Ciencias Sociales*, *27*(1), 12–28.

Bagirov, M., & Mateus, C. (2019). Oil prices, stock markets and firm performance: Evidence from Europe. *International Review of Economics & Finance*, *61*, 270–288. DOI: 10.1016/j.iref.2019.02.007

Baker, S. R., Bloom, N., & Davis, S. J. (2016). Measuring Economic Policy Uncertainty. *The Quarterly Journal of Economics*, *131*(4), 1593–1636. DOI: 10.1093/qje/qjw024

Balzacq, T. (2010). *Securitization theory: How security problems emerge and dissolve* (1st ed.). Routledge.

Banco de México. (2017). *Estimación del Efecto de la Incertidumbre Relativa a la Política Comercial sobre la Inversión Extranjera Directa en México* (Extracto del Informe Trimestral Julio – Septiembre No. 2; pp. 38-41). Banco de México. https://www.banxico.org.mx/publicaciones-y-prensa/informes-trimestrales/recuadros/%7BDF3E752F-A739-FA28-5750-91FE1AE24085%7D.pdf

Banco de México. (2025, mayo 30). *Tipos de cambio y resultados históricos de las subastas*. Sistema de Información Económica. https://www.banxico.org.mx/SieInternet/consultarDirectorioInternetAction.do?accion=consultarCuadroAnalitico&idCuadro=CA113&sector=6&locale=es

Bandyopadhyay, S., Sandler, T., & Younas, J. (2018). Trade and terrorism: A disaggregated approach. *Journal of Peace Research*, *55*(5), 656–670. DOI: 10.1177/0022343318763009

Bank of England. (2021). *How Has COVID Affected Global Trade?* [Web article].

Bao, X., Deng, J., Sun, H., & Sun, J. (2022). Trade policy uncertainty and foreign direct investment: Evidence from China's WTO accession. *Journal of International Money and Finance*, *125*, 102642. DOI: 10.1016/j.jimonfin.2022.102642

Barman, R. K. (2005). *From tribalism to independent state: Reflection on the emergence of Kamate Koch Kingdom c. 15th century AD–1773 AD* (Doctoral dissertation, University of North Bengal). Shodhganga. http://hdl.handle.net/10603/149146

Barman, R. K. (2009). Partition of Bengal and Struggle for Existence of the Scheduled Castes: Impact of the Partition (1947) on the Rajbanshis of North Bengal. *Voice of Dalit*, *2*(2), 141–164. DOI: 10.1177/0974354520090202

Baruah, S. (2012). *Durable Disorder: Understanding the Politics of Northeast India*. Oxford University Press., https://academic.oup.com/book/5580

Baruah, S. (2020). *In the Name of the Nation: India and Its Northeast*. Stanford University Press., https://www.sup.org/books/asian-studies/name-nation

Baten, J. (Ed.). (2016). *A history of the global economy: From 1500 to the present*. Cambridge University Press.

Battilana, J., Leca, B., & Boxenbaum, E. (2009). 2 how actors change institutions: Towards a theory of institutional entrepreneurship. *The Academy of Management Annals*, *3*(1), 65–107.

Bauerle Danzman, S., & Meunier, S. (2023). Naïve no more: Foreign direct investment screening in the European Union. *Global Policy*, *14*, 40–53.

Baukhage, C. (2010, April). San Marino. In Elections in Europe (pp. 1669-1698). Nomos Verlagsgesellschaft mbH & Co. KG.

Baur, D. G., & Smales, L. A. (2018). Gold and geopolitical risk: A safe haven? *The Quarterly Review of Economics and Finance*, *70*, 279–288. DOI: 10.1016/j.qref.2018.07.004

Beck, T. E., & Plowman, D. A. (2014). Temporary, emergent interorganizational collaboration in unexpected circumstances: A study of the Columbia space shuttle response effort. *Organization Science*, *25*(4), 1234–1252.

Bednarski, L., Roscoe, S., Blome, C., & Schleper, M. C. (2023). Geopolitical disruptions in global supply chains: A state-of-the-art literature review. *Production Planning and Control*, *36*(4), 536–562. DOI: 10.1080/09537287.2023.2286283

Benhabib, J., & Rustichini, A. (1996). Social Conflict and Growth. *Journal of Economic Growth*, *1*(1), 125–142.

Bernanke, B. S. (1983). Nonmonetary Effects of the Financial Crisis in the Propagation of the Great Depression. *The American Economic Review*, *73*(3), 257–276. https://www.jstor.org/stable/1808111

Berridge, G. R. (2022). *Diplomacy: Theory and practice*. Springer Nature.

Berthélemy, J. C., Kauffmann, C., Renard, L., & Wegner, L. (2002). Political instability, political regimes and economic performance in African countries. Unpublished paper prepared for African Development Bank, African Economic Outlook.

Beugelsdijk, S., & Luo, Y. (2024). The politicized nature of international business. *Journal of International Business Studies*, *55*(3), 281–284.

Bilchitz, D. (2021). *Fundamental rights and the legal obligations of business*. Cambridge University Press.

Bilgili, F., Ünlü, F., Gençoğlu, P., & Kuşkaya, S. (2022). Modeling the exchange rate pass-through in Turkey with uncertainty and geopolitical risk: A Markov regime-switching approach. *Applied Economic Analysis*, *30*(88), 52–70. DOI: 10.1108/AEA-08-2020-0105

Bjola, C., & Holmes, M. (2015). *Digital diplomacy: Theory and practice*. Routledge., DOI: 10.4324/9781315767314

Blanc, I. (2013). Essence of indecision-explaining Veto Player structures and Agenda Setting processes in Swiss Foreign Policy.

Bo Lillis, K., Bertrand, N., & Pleitgen, F. (2024). *Exclusive: US and Germany foiled Russian plot to assassinate CEO of arms manufacturer sending weapons to Ukraine*. CNN. https://edition.cnn.com/2024/07/11/politics/us-germany-foiled-russian-assassination-plot/index.html

Bohl, D. K., Hanna, T. L., Mapes, B. R., Moyer, J. D., Narayan, K., & Wasif, K. (2017). *Understanding and forecasting geopolitical risks and benefits*. Frederick S. Pardee Center for International Futures, Josef Korbel School of International Studies, University of Denver. https://doi.org/DOI: 10.2139/ssrn.3941439

Bond, M. (2016). The EU and the Council of Europe: Difference, duplication or delegation? In Cooperation or Conflict? (pp. 11-28). Routledge.

Borah, P. (2016). *Ethnic movements in Assam: A study of Koch Rajbanshis* (M.Phil. dissertation). Sikkim University. http://14.139.206.50:8080/jspui/bitstream/1/4571/1/Paresh%20Borah.pdf

Borbats, N. M., & Shkolina, T. V. (2021). Comparing the test power for the normal distribution of the direct multiple measurements. *Journal of Physics: Conference Series, 1889*, 052036. DOI: 10.1088/1742-6596/1889/5/052036

Boulloche, A., Richter, K., & WARREN, K. (1976). The Sciences and Democratic Government. Palgrave Macmillan Limited.

Bourdieu, P., & Wacquant, L. (1992). *Invitation to Reflexive Sociology*. University of Chicago Press.

Bouri, E., Hammoud, R., & Abou Kassm, C. (2023). The Effect of Oil Implied Volatility and Geopolitical Risk on GCC Stock Sectors Under Various Market Conditions. *Energy Economics, 106*, 106617. DOI: 10.1016/j.eneco.2023.106617

Bowen, B. (2020). *War in space: Strategy, spacepower, geopolitics*. Edinburgh University Press.

Bozsik, N., Ngo, D. M., & Vasa, L. (2023). The effects of foreign direct investment on the performance of small-medium enterprises: The case of Vietnam. *Journal of International Students, 16*(1), 57–70. DOI: 10.14254/2071-8330.2023/16-1/4

Braw, E. (2019). Cutting-edge tech takeovers are a strategic threat to the west. *Financial Times*, October 7, 2019. https://www.ft.com/content/763cae4e-e5ed-11e9-b8e0-026e07cbe5b4. Accessed September 10, 2021

Breusch, T. S., & Pagan, A. R. (1980). The Lagrange multiplier test and its applications to model specification in econometrics. *The Review of Economic Studies, 47*(1), 239–253. DOI: 10.2307/2297111

Brewer, T. (1983). The instability of governments and the instability of controls on funds transfers by multinational enterprises: Implications for political risk analysis. *Journal of International Business Studies, 14*(3), 147–157.

Brint, S., & Karabel, J. (1989). *The Diverted Dream: Community Colleges and the Promise of Educational Opportunity in America*. Oxford University Press.

Brown, S. L., & Eisenhardt, K. M. (1997). The art of continuous change: Linking complexity theory and time-paced evolution in relentlessly shifting organizations. *Administrative Science Quarterly*, •••, 1–34.

Bruinsma, F. J., & Parmentier, S. (2003). Interview with Mr. Luzius Wildhaber, President of the ECHR. *Netherlands Quarterly of Human Rights, 21*(2), 185–201.

Bruton, G. D., Peng, M. W., Ahlstrom, D., Stan, C., & Xu, K. (2015). State-owned enterprises around the world as hybrid organizations. *The Academy of Management Perspectives, 29*(1), 92–114.

Bryant, W. J. (2023). *When a CEO plays president: Musk, Starlink, and the war in Ukraine*. Irregular Warfare Initiative. https://irregularwarfare.org/articles/when-a-ceo-plays-president-musk-starlink-and-the-war-in-ukraine/

Bucheli, M., & DeBerge, T. (2024). Multinational enterprises' nonmarket strategies: Insights from History. *International Business Review*, *33*(2), 102198.

Buckley, P. J. (2021). Exogenous and endogenous change in global value chains. *Journal of International Business Policy*, *4*(2), 221.

Buckley, P. J. (2023). Corporate reactions to the fracturing of the global economy. *International Business Review*, *32*(6), 102014.

Buckley, P. J., Clegg, L. J., Cross, A. R., Liu, X., Voss, H., & Zheng, P. (2007). The determinants of Chinese outward foreign direct investment. *Journal of International Business Studies*, *38*(4), 499–518.

Budhathoki, P., Adhikari, K., & Koirala, R. (2019). The Gap between Attitudes and Behavior in Ethical Consumption: A Critical Discourse. *Quest Journal of Management and Social Sciences*, *1*(2), 285–295. DOI: 10.3126/qjmss.v1i2.27446

Bumann, S., Hermes, N., & Lensink, R. (2013). Financial liberalization and economic growth: A meta-analysis. *Journal of International Money and Finance*, *33*, 255–281.

Burhanuddin, A. (2015). Rethinking world system theory: A historical and conceptual analysis. *WANUA: Jurnal Hubungan Internasional*, *1*(1), 1–16.

Burnett, A., Arseneau, J. B., Darvishian, A., & Saigau, V. (2024). SpaceX: The independent investment guide Q1'24 update (Mach33 Capital Markets). https://spacedventure-marketing.s3.amazonaws.com/SpaceX+Public+Investment+Guide+M33+(Q1'24+Update).pptx+(4).pdf#page=46.25

Bussy, A., & Zheng, H. (2023). Responses of FDI to geopolitical risks: The role of governance, information, and technology. *International Business Review*, *32*(4), 102136. DOI: 10.1016/j.ibusrev.2023.102136

Bustillo, R. (2022, 13 de diciembre). Geopolítica y economía: imposible entender una sin la otra. *LISA News*.

Büthe, T., & Mattli, W. (2011). *The new global rulers: The privatization of regulation in the world economy*. Princeton University Press.

Buzan, B., Wæver, O., & De Wilde, J. (1998). *Security: A new framework for analysis*. Lynne Rienner Publishers.

Caldara, D., & Iacoviello, M. (2022). Measuring Geopolitical Risk. *The American Economic Review, 112*(4), 1194–1225. DOI: 10.1257/aer.20191823

Campos, N. F., & Nugent, J. B. (2002). Who is Afraid of Political Instability? *Journal of Development Economics, 67*(1), 157–172.

Can, C. M. (2024). Small power strategies under great power competition. *International Politics, 61*, 296–321. DOI: 10.1057/s41311-023-00552-7

Canh, N. P., Binh, N. T., Thanh, S. D., & Schinckus, C. (2020). Determinants of foreign direct investment inflows: The role of economic policy uncertainty. *Inter Economics, 161*, 159–172. DOI: 10.1016/j.inteco.2019.11.012

Cannizzaro, A. P., & Weiner, R. J. (2018). State ownership and transparency in foreign direct investment. *Journal of International Business Studies, 49*(2), 172–195.

Cantah, G. W., Brafu-Insaidoo, G. W., Wiafe, E. A., & Adams, A. (2018). FDI and Trade Policy Openness in Sub-Saharan Africa. *Eastern Economic Journal, 44*, 97–116. DOI: 10.1057/eej.2016.9

Capolongo, A., & Kühl, M. (2024, August 30). The butterfly effect of geopolitical conflicts. *European Stability Mechanism, Economic and Market Analysis.* https://www.esm.europa.eu/blog/butterfly-effect-of-geopolitical-conflicts

Carmel, E., & Abbott, P. (2007). Why 'nearshore' means that distance matters. *Communications of the ACM, 50*(10), 40–46. DOI: 10.1145/1290958.1290959

Carrasco, C. A. (2024). Perspectives on nearshoring: Recent developments and the challenges for Mexico. *Latin American Policy, 15*(2), 339–350. DOI: 10.1111/lamp.12340

Cassese, A. (1989). A new approach to human rights: The European convention for the prevention of torture. *The American Journal of International Law, 83*(1), 128–153.

Cervantes, M. M., & Rivera, R. G. (2021). Law and economics challenges of natural gas—The hard case of Mexico. *Journal of World Energy Law and Business, 14*(3), 205–214. DOI: 10.1093/jwelb/jwab017

Cetín, M. A., & Yaman, I. (2023). The Importance of Geopolitical Risk and Institutional Quality Indicators on Foreign Direct Investment to BRICS Countries. *Romanian Journal of Economic Forecasting, 26*(4), 107–127. https://www.scopus.com/pages/publications/85186539130

Chang, J. (2024). TSMC's advanced process remains strong and difficult to shake. *Yahoo Finance*. https://tw.stock.yahoo.com/news/%E5%8F%B0%E7%A9%8D%E9%9B%BB%E5%85%88%E9%80%B2%E8%A3%BD%E7%A8%8B%E5%A0%85%E6%8C%BA-%E9%9B%A3%E6%92%BC%E5%8B%95-201000970.html

Chang, J.-M. (2021). The future is small and fast: Assessing Taiwan's 2021 Quadrennial Defense Review and U.S. defense posture in the Indo-Pacific. *Institute for National Defense and Security Research*. https://indsr.org.tw/en/respublicationcon?uid=15&resid=44&pid=1501

Chasek, P. S., Downie, D. L., & Brown, J. W. (2016). *Global environmental politics* (7th ed.). Routledge.

Chaudhuri, H. N. (1903). *The Cooch Behar state and its land revenue settlements*. Cooch Behar State Press., https://archive.org/download/coochbeharstatei00chaurich/coochbeharstatei00chaurich.pdf

Chavis, L., & Leslie, P. (2009). Consumer boycotts: The impact of the Iraq war on French wine sales in the U.S. *Quantitative Marketing and Economics, 7*(1), 37-67. https://doi.org/y Cruz, B.d.P.A. and Botelho, D. (2015), "Proposition of the relational boycott", Management Research, Vol. 13 No. 3, pp. 315-333. https://doi.org/DOI: 10.1007/s11129-008-9043-

Cheng, C. H. J., & Chiu, C. W. J. (2018). How important are global geopolitical risks to emerging countries? *Inter Economics*, *156*, 305–325. DOI: 10.1016/j.inteco.2018.05.002

Cheng, P., Wang, M., Li, K., Choi, B., & Chen, W. (2025). The impact mechanism of geopolitical risks on ESG performance: The moderating effects of investor attention and government subsidies. *PLoS One*, *20*(1), e0311659. DOI: 10.1371/journal.pone.0311659

Chen, K., Nie, H., & Ge, Z. (2019). Policy uncertainty and FDI: Evidence from national elections. *The Journal of International Trade & Economic Development*, *28*(4), 419–428. DOI: 10.1080/09638199.2018.1545860

Chen, X. (2023). Are the Shocks of EPU, VIX, and GPR Indexes on The Oil-stock Nexus Alike? A Time-frequency Analysis. *Applied Economics*, *55*(29), 3587–3601. DOI: 10.1080/00036846.2022.2140115

Chiang, T. C. (2021). Spillovers of U.S. market volatility and monetary policy uncertainty to global stock markets. *The North American Journal of Economics and Finance*, *58*, 101523. DOI: 10.1016/j.najef.2021.101523

Chirot, D. (2001). World Systems Theory. In Smelser, N. J. & Baltes, P.B. (Eds.), *International Encyclopedia of the Social & Behavioral* Sciences (pp. 16609-16613), Pergamon. https://doi.org/DOI: 10.1016/B0-08-043076-7/01891-X

Chirot, D. (2015). World Systems Theory. In Wright, J. D. (Ed.), *International Encyclopedia of the Social & Behavioral Sciences* (pp. 748–752). Elsevier., DOI: 10.1016/B978-0-08-097086-8.32172-9

Chiti-Batelli, A. (1967). European assemblies and space. *The International Spectator*, *2*(3), 248–262.

Choi, I. (2001). Unit root tests for panel data. *Journal of International Money and Finance*, *20*(2), 249–272. DOI: 10.1016/S0261-5606(00)00048-6

Choi, S., Furceri, D., & Yoon, C. (2021). Policy uncertainty and foreign direct investment. *Review of International Economics*, *29*(2), 195–227. DOI: 10.1111/roie.12495

Choi, S.-Y., & Hadad, E. (2025). The dynamic relationship among economic and monetary policy, geopolitical risk, sentiment, and risk aversion: A TVP-VAR approach. *Finance Research Letters*, *72*, 106532. DOI: 10.1016/j.frl.2024.106532

Choi, Y. (2018). A middle power's trade policy under U.S.-China FTA competition: South Korea's double hedging FTA diplomacy. *Contemporary Politics*, *24*(2), 233–249. DOI: 10.1080/13569775.2017.1416735

Christiansen, H., & Kim, Y. (2014). *State-Invested Enterprises in the Global Marketplace : Implications for a Level Playing Field* (OECD Corporate Governance Working Papers, Issue 14).

Chung, C. C., & Beamish, P. W. (2005). The impact of institutional reforms on characteristics and survival of foreign subsidiaries in emerging economies. *Journal of Management Studies*, *42*(1), 35–62.

Çivi, E. & Çavuşgil, S. T. (2001). Yeni Dünya Düzeninde Güç Kazanan Ülkeler: Yükselen Ekonomiler. Celal Bayar Üniversitesi Yönetim & Ekonomi Dergisi, 7(1), ss. 113-128.

Claessens, S., & Forbes, K. J. (Eds.). (2001). *International Financial Contagion*. Springer., DOI: 10.1007/978-1-4757-3314-3

Clausewitz, C. (2003). *On war*. (Original work published 1832)

Cobb, W. N. W. (2021). *Privatizing peace: How commerce can reduce conflict in space*. Routledge.

Coën, A., & Desfleurs, A. (2024). The relative importance of economic policy uncertainty and geopolitical risk on U.S. REITs returns. *Journal of Property Investment & Finance*, *42*(6), 576–590. DOI: 10.1108/JPIF-05-2024-0064

Colyer, D. (2004). Foreign Direct Investment in the Primary Sector of Mexico. In Kehal, H. S. (Ed.), *Foreign Investment in Developing Countries* (pp. 223–237). Palgrave Macmillan., DOI: 10.1057/9780230554412_12

Constas, D. C. (1982). Turkish Affair: A Test Case for the Council of Europe, The. Legal Issues of Eur. *Integration (Tokyo, Japan)*, *9*, 69.

Cooper, A. F. (Ed.). (2013). *The Oxford handbook of modern diplomacy*. Oxford University Press., DOI: 10.1093/oxfordhb/9780199588862.001.0001

Corbin, J., & Strauss, A. (2008). *Basics of Qualitati& Research: Techniques and Procedures for Developing Grounded Theory* (3rd ed.). Sage.

Council of Europe. (2024, February). Map of the Council of Europe 46 member States Eng/fra. Council of Europe Publishing. https://edoc.coe.int/en/map-of-the-member-states/11072-map-of-the-council-of-europe-46-member-states-engfra.html

Council of Europe. The Congress of Local, Regional Authorities, Congress of Local, Regional Authorities of Europe (CLRAE), & National Association of Portuguese Municipalites. (2006). The European Charter of Local Self-Government--20th Anniversary: Proceedings: Lisbon (Portugal), 8 July 2005: International Conference Organised by the Congress of Local and Regional Authorities of the Council of Europe, in Co-operation with the National Association of Portuguese Municipalities (Vol. 8). Council of Europe.

Cross., & Pekkanen, S. M. (2023). Introduction. Space Diplomacy: the final frontier of theory and practice. *The Hague Journal of Diplomacy*, 18(2-3), 193-217.

Cruz, B. D. P. A. (2017). Social boycott. *Revista brasileira de gestão de negocios, 19*, 05-29. https://doi.org/DOI: 10.7819/rbgn.v0i0.2868

Cuervo-Cazurra, Alvaro, Inkpen, A., Musacchio, A., & Ramaswamy, K. (2014). Governments as owners: State-owned multinational companies. *Journal of International Business Studies*, *45*(8), 919–942.

Cuervo-Cazurra, A. (2018). Thanks but no thanks: State-owned multinationals from emerging markets and host-country policies. *Journal of International Business Policy*, *1*(3–4), 128–156.

Cui, L., & Jiang, F. (2012). State ownership effect on firms' FDI ownership decisions under institutional pressure: A study of Chinese outward-investing firms. *Journal of International Business Studies*, *43*(3), 264–284.

Cuthbertson, A. (2024). Elon Musk now controls two thirds of all active satellites. *The Independent*. https://www.independent.co.uk/tech/elon-musk-satellites-starlink-spacex-b2606262.html

Cutler, A. C. (2001). Critical reflections on the Westphalian assumptions of international law and organization: A crisis of legitimacy. *Review of International Studies*, *27*(2), 133–150.

Cutler, A. C., Haufler, V., & Porter, T. (Eds.). (1999). *Private authority and international affairs*. Suny Press.

Dagi, I. (2001). Human rights and democratization: Turkish politics in the European context. *Southeast European and Black Sea Studies*, *1*(3), 51–68.

Dagi, I. D. (1996). Democratic transition in Turkey, 1980–83: The impact of European diplomacy. *Middle Eastern Studies*, *32*(2), 124–141.

Dalakas, V., Melancon, J. P., & Szczytynski, I. (2023). Brands in the eye of the storm: Navigating political consumerism and boycott calls on social media. *Qualitative Market Research*, *26*(1), 1–18. DOI: 10.1108/QMR-07-2021-0089

Dalby, S. (1991). Critical Geopolitics: Discourse, Difference, and Dissent. *Environment and Planning. D, Society & Space*, *9*(3), 261–283.

Dambolena, I., Eriksen, S. E., & Kopcso, D. P. (2006). Assessing the Appropriateness of Transformations Using Simulation. *Problems, Resources, and Issues in Mathematics Undergraduate Studies*, *16*(2), 105–120. DOI: 10.1080/10511970608984139

Daniels, J. D., Radebaugh, L. H., & Sullivan, D. P. (2007). *International business: Environments and operations* (11th ed.). Pearson Education.

Datosmacro. (2025a, may 29). *Precio del petróleo OPEP por barril*. Expansion/Datosmacro.com. https://datosmacro.expansion.com/materias-primas/opec?anio=2025

Datosmacro. (2025b, may 30). *Precio petróleo tipo West Texas Intermediate (WTI). Spot. $USA por barril*. Expansion/Datosmacro.com. https://datosmacro.expansion.com/materias-primas/petroleo-wti?anio=2025

David, R. J., Sine, W. D., & Haveman, H. A. (2013). Seizing opportunity in emerging fields: How institutional entrepreneurs legitimated the professional form of management consulting. *Organization Science*, *24*(2), 356–377.

Dávila, F. A., Sobarzo, F. H. E., & Valdés, I. M. (2018). México y el TLCAN: Escenarios de política comercial. Simulaciones con un modelo de equilibrio general aplicado. *El Trimestre Economico*, *85*(340), 703–744. DOI: 10.20430/ete.v85i340.699

Dawar, A., & Bai, Y. (2024). Impact of geopolitical risk on the maritime supply chain: A regional analysis of the effects on global trade. *International Journal of Supply Chain Management*, *13*(3), 42–53. DOI: 10.59160/ijscm.v13i3.6245

De Haan, J., & Siermann, C. L. (1996). Political instability, freedom, and economic growth: Some further evidence. *Economic Development and Cultural Change*, *44*(2), 339–350.

De Nisco, A., Massi, M., & Papadopoulos, N. (2020). Partners or foes? Cross-country consumer animosity, ethnocentrism, and nationalism in times of international crisis. *Journal of Global Marketing*, *33*(3), 207–222. DOI: 10.1080/08911762.2020.1744209

De Sousa, J., Mirza, D., & Verdier, T. (2018). Terror networks and trade: Does the neighbor hurt? *European Economic Review*, *107*, 27–56. DOI: 10.1016/j.euroecorev.2018.05.001

De Villa, M. A. (2023). Assessing geopolitical risk: A multi-level approach for top managers of multinationals. *AIB Insights*, *23*(1), 1–7.

Deibert, R. J. (2019). The road to digital unfreedom: Three painful truths about social media. *Journal of Democracy*, *30*(1), 25–39.

Deitelhoff, N., & Wolf, K. D. (2010). Corporate Security Responsibility: Corporate Governance Contributions to Peace and Security in Zones of Conflict. In Deitelhoff, N., & Wolf, K. D. (Eds.), *Corporate Security Responsibility?* (pp. 1–25)., DOI: 10.1057/9780230277052_1

Delios, A., & Henisz, W. J. (2003). *Policy uncertainty and the sequence of entry by Japanese firms, 1980 – 1998*. 227–241.

Delios, A., & Henisz, W. (2000). Japanese firm investment strategies in emerging economies. *Academy of Management Journal*, *43*, 305–323.

Deudney, D. (2020). *Dark skies: Space expansionism, planetary geopolitics, and the ends of humanity*. Oxford University Press.

Diebold, F. X., & Yilmaz, K. (2012). Better to give than to receive: Predictive directional measurement of volatility spillovers. *International Journal of Forecasting*, *28*(1), 57–66. DOI: 10.1016/j.ijforecast.2011.02.006

DiMaggio, P. J., & Powell, W. W. (2002). Institutional isomorphism and collective rationality in organizational fields. *Strategy: Critical Perspectives on Business and Management*, 1(1983), 283-306.

DiMaggio, P. J., & Powell, W. W. (1983). The iron cage revisited: Institutional isomorphism and collective rationality in organizational fields. *American Sociological Review*, *48*(2), 147–160.

Dimitrov, R. S. (2010). Inside UN climate change negotiations: The Copenhagen conference. *The Review of Policy Research*, *27*(6), 795–821. DOI: 10.1111/j.1541-1338.2010.00472.x

Djeffal, C., Siewert, M. B., & Wurster, S. (2022). Role of the state and responsibility in governing artificial intelligence: A comparative analysis of AI strategies. *Journal of European Public Policy*, *29*(11), 1799–1821.

Doğan, B. (2017). Ekonomik küreselleşme & büyüme ilişkisi: Türkiye örneği Toda-Yamamoto nedensellik analizi. *Finans Politik & Ekonomik Yorumlar*, *54*(628), 19–27.

Dohale, V., Ambilkar, P., Gunasekaran, A., & Verma, P. (2022). Supply chain risk mitigation strategies during COVID-19: Exploratory cases of "make-to-order" handloom saree apparel industries. *International Journal of Physical Distribution & Logistics Management*, *52*(2), 109–129.

Doh, J. P., Lawton, T. C., & Rajwani, T. (2012). Advancing nonmarket strategy research: Institutional perspectives in a changing world. *The Academy of Management Perspectives*, *26*(3), 22–39.

Domínguez Castro, L., & Rodríguez Lago, J. R. (2022). Denis de Rougemont: An Europos Federalist. In *The European Union and its Political Leaders: Understanding the Integration Process* (pp. 97–110). Springer International Publishing.

Donald, A., & Speck, A. K. (2019, June). Wholehearted? Half-hearted? The response from the Parliamentary Assembly of the Council of Europe to recent developments in Turkey. In FU Berlin/Hertie School of Governance Workshop on Responses to the Decay of the Rule of Law and Human Rights Protections in Turkey: Exceptional or Symptomatic.

Dong, Q., Huo, D., & Wang, K. (2023). Risk Measurement and Application of the International Carbon Market in the Era of Global Conflict: A Data-driven Study Using FCM. *Journal of Environmental Management*, *345*, 118251. DOI: 10.1016/j.jenvman.2023.118251

Downs, G., & Rocke, D. (1995). *Optimal Im- perfection? Domestic Uncertainty and In- stitutions in International Relations*. Princeton University Press.

Drobetz, W., Gavriilidis, K., Krokida, S. I., & Tsouknidis, D. (2021). The effects of geopolitical risk and economic policy uncertainty on dry bulk shipping freight rates. *Applied Economics*, *53*(19), 2218–2229. DOI: 10.1080/00036846.2020.1857329

Du, Y., & Zhang, H. (2023). *Starlink militarization and its impact on global strategic stability*. Interpret: China, Center for Strategic and International Studies. https://interpret.csis.org/translations/starlink-militarization-and-its-impact-on-global-strategic-stability/

Duanmu, J. L. (2014). State-owned MNCs and host country expropriation risk: The role of home state soft power and economic gunboat diplomacy. *Journal of International Business Studies*, *45*(8), 1044–1060.

Duffy, C. G. (1950). Can Europe Unite? *The Irish Monthly*, *78*(930), 580–589.

Du, J., Satoglu, E. B., & Shepotylo, O. (2023). How did Brexit affect UK trade? *Contemporary Social Science*, *18*(2), 266–283. DOI: 10.1080/21582041.2023.2192043

Dutta, C. B., Haider, M. Z., & Das, D. K. (2017). Dynamics of Economic Growth, Investment and Trade Openness: Evidence from Bangladesh. *South Asian Journal of Macroeconomics and Public Finance*, *6*(1), 82–104. DOI: 10.1177/2277978717695150

Early, B. R., & Gartzke, E. (2021). Spying from space: Reconnaissance satellites and interstate disputes. *The Journal of Conflict Resolution*, *65*(9), 1551–1575.

Easterly, W., & Rebelo, S. (1993). Fiscal Policy and Economic Growth. *Journal of Monetary Economics*, *32*, 417–458.

Economic Policy Uncertainty. (2024a). *Geopolitical Risk Index*. Economic Policy Uncertainty. https://www.policyuncertainty.com/gpr.html

Economic Policy Uncertainty. (2024b). *Mexico Monthly Index*. Economic Policy Uncertainty. https://www.policyuncertainty.com/mexico_monthly.html

Economic Policy Uncertainty. (2024c). *US Monthly Trade Policy Uncertainty Index*. Economic Policy Uncertainty. https://www.policyuncertainty.com/trade_uncertainty.html

Eisenhardt, K. M., & Graebner, M. E. (2007). Theory Building From Cases: Opportunities And Challenges. *Academy of Management Journal*, *50*(1), 25–32. DOI: 10.5465/amj.2007.24160888

El-Hashash, E. F., & Shiekh, R. H. A. (2022). A Comparison of the Pearson, Spearman Rank and Kendall Tau Correlation Coefficients Using Quantitative Variables. *Asian Journal of Probability and Statistics*, *20*(3), 36–48. DOI: 10.9734/ajpas/2022/v20i3425

Elmas, B., Esen, Ö., & Yurttançıkmaz, Z. Ç. (2011). "Yeni Dünya Düzeniyle Başlayan Değişim; Yükselen Ekonomilerin Çağı", https://www.researchgate.net/publication/292775147_Yeni_Dunya_Duzeniyle_Baslayan_Degisim_Yukselen_Ekonomilerin_Cagi, (24.12.2016).

Emin, E. (2016). Küresel Adaletsizlik Dünya Yoksulluk & Eşitsizlik Raporu. İstanbul: İnsamer, https://insamer.com/rsm/icerik/dosya/dosya_389.pdf, Erisim Tarihi: 05.11.2024.

Engle, R. F., & Campos-Martins, S. (2020). *Measuring and hedging geopolitical risk* (NIPE Working Papers No. 08/2020). NIPE – Universidade do Minho. https://doi.org/DOI: 10.2139/ssrn.3685213

Erzurumlu, Y. O., Gozgor, G., Lau, C. K. M., Soliman, A. M., & Turkkan, M. (2025). The effects of geopolitical and political risks on corporate ESG practices. *Journal of Environmental Management*, *386*, 125747. DOI: 10.1016/j.jenvman.2025.125747

ESA. (2021). *ESA's annual space environment report*. European Space Agency (ESA) Space Debris Office. Retrieved from https://www.sdo.esoc.esa.int/environment_report/Space_Environment_Report_latest.pdf

Esplugues, C. (2018). *Foreign Investment, Strategic Assets and National Security*. Intersentia.

Etaga, H. O., Okoro, I., Aforka, K. F., & Ngonadi, L. O. (2021). Methods of Estimating Correlation Coefficients in the Presence of Influential Outlier(s). *African Journal of Mathematics and Statistics Studies*, *4*(3), 157–185. DOI: 10.52589/AJMSS-LLNZXUOZ

Evans, M., O'Neil, S., & MacLeod, C. (2016). Chinese spies are biggest threat to nuclear power deal. *The Times*. August 13, 2016. https://www.thetimes.co.uk/article/chinese-spies-are-biggest-threat-to-nuclear-power-deal-kp75t36kf. Accessed September 12, 2021.

Falkner, R. (2016). The Paris Agreement and the new logic of international climate politics. *International Affairs*, *92*(5), 1107–1125. DOI: 10.1111/1468-2346.12708

Farrell, H., & Newman, A. L. (2019). Weaponized interdependence: How global economic networks shape state coercion. *International Security*, *44*(1), 42–79.

Fawcett, J. E. S. (1974). The Council of Europe and integration. International Affairs (Royal Institute of International Affairs 1944-), 50(2), 242-250.

Fawn, R., & Fawn, R. (2013). The Birth of Internal Conditionality: The Conception and Evolution of the Council of Europe and the Organization for Security and Cooperation in Europe. International Organizations and Internal Conditionality: Making Norms Matter, 20-55.

Fearon, J. D. (1998). Domestic politics, foreign policy, and theories of international relations. *Annual Review of Political Science*, *1*(1), 289–313.

Feng, C., Han, L., Vigne, S., & Xu, Y. (2023). Geopolitical risk and the dynamics of international capital flows. *Journal of International Financial Markets, Institutions and Money*, *82*, 101693. DOI: 10.1016/j.intfin.2022.101693

Feng, Y. (2009). "We Wouldn't Transfer Title to the Devil": Consequences of the Congressional Politicization of Foreign Direct Investment on National Security Grounds. *Journal of International Law and Politics*, *42*(1), 253–310.

Fewer, T. J., Ma, D., & Coraiola, D. M. (2025). Working with the "Enemy": Supervised Space, Free Space, and Cross-Border Collaboration amid Geopolitical Rivalry. *Organization Science*.

Fiss, P. C. (2007). A set-theoretic approach to organizational configurations. *Academy of Management Review*, *32*(4), 1180–1198.

Fitzgerald, M., & Thompson, C. (2022). What does Starlink's participation in Ukrainian defense reveal about U.S. space policy? *Lawfare*. https://www.lawfaremedia.org/article/what-does-starlinks-participation-ukrainian-defense-reveal-about-us-space-policy

Flint, C. (2021). *Introduction to geopolitics*. Routledge.

Flynn, T. R. (2006). *Existentialism: A very short introduction*. Oxford University Press.

Forbes, K. J., & Rigobon, R. (2002). No Contagion, Only Interdependence: Measuring Stock Market Comovements. *The Journal of Finance*, *57*(5), 2223–2261. DOI: 10.1111/0022-1082.00494

Forbes, K. J., & Warnock, F. E. (2021). Capital flow waves—Or ripples? Extreme capital flow movements since the crisis. *Journal of International Money and Finance*, *116*, 102394. DOI: 10.1016/j.jimonfin.2021.102394

Fort, T. L. (2000). A Review of Donaldson and Dunfee's "Ties That Bind: A Social Contracts Approach to Business Ethics.". *Journal of Business Ethics, 28*(4), 383–387. https://www.jstor.org/stable/25074428

Foss, K., & Foss, N. J. (2005). Resources and transaction costs: How property rights economics furthers the resource-based view. *Strategic Management Journal, 26*(6), 541–553.

Francis, T., & Hoefel, F. (2018). True Gen': Generation Z and its implications for companies. *McKinsey & Company, 12*(2), 1-10.

Friedman, M. (1985). Consumer boycotts in the United States, 1970–1980: Contemporary events in historical perspective. *The Journal of Consumer Affairs, 19*(1), 96–117. DOI: 10.1111/j.1745-6606.1985.tb00346.x

Friedman, M. (1999). *Consumer boycotts: Effecting change through the marketplace and the media*. Routledge., DOI: 10.4324/9780203900406

Frutos, D., Teekasap, P., & Samii, M. (2011). CAFTA-DR Effects on FDI Inflows, Growth, and Distribution of the Workforce in Costa Rica: A System Dynamics Approach. *Guoji Maoyi Wenti, 25*(3), 372–393. DOI: 10.1080/08853908.2011.581612

Frynas, J. G., & Stephens, S. (2015). Political Corporate Social Responsibility: Reviewing Theories and Setting New Agendas. *International Journal of Management Reviews, 17*(4), 483–509. DOI: 10.1111/ijmr.12049

Furnari, S., Crilly, D., Misangyi, V. F., Greckhamer, T., Fiss, P. C., & Aguilera, R. V. (2021). Capturing causal complexity: Heuristics for configurational theorizing. *Academy of Management Review, 46*(4), 778–799.

Gallagher, K. P., & Myers, M. (2020). *China–Latin America Finance Database*. Inter-American Dialogue.

Gamso, J., Inkpen, A., & Ramaswamy, K. (2024). Managing geopolitical risks: The global oil and gas industry plays a winning game. *The Journal of Business Strategy, 45*(3), 190–198. DOI: 10.1108/JBS-04-2023-0081

Gao, H., Chen, W., Li, J., & Zhou, T. (2024). Economic policy uncertainty and foreign direct investment: Evidence from China. *Structural Change and Economic Dynamics, 70*, 178–191. DOI: 10.1016/j.strueco.2024.01.014

García-Canal, E., & Guillén, M. F. (2008). Risk and the strategy of foreign location choice in regulated industries. *Strategic Management Journal, 29*(10), 1097–1115.

Garrett, D. E. (1987). The effectiveness of marketing policy boycotts: Environmental opposition to marketing. *Journal of Marketing*, *51*(2), 46–57. DOI: 10.1177/002224298705100204

Garrido, C. (2022). *México en la fábrica de América del Norte y el nearshoring* (Sede Subregional de la CEPAL en México (Estudios e Investigaciones); pp. 1-95). Comisión Económica para América Latina y el Caribe (CEPAL). https://hdl.handle.net/11362/48056

Gawer, A. (2014). Bridging differing perspectives on technological platforms: Toward an integrative framework. *Research Policy*, *43*(7), 1239–1249.

Gehringer, A. (2025). The Challenging Terrain of Critical Infrastructures–A Geopolitical Perspective. *Journal of Homeland Security and Emergency Management. ahead-of-print.* DOI: 10.1515/jhsem-2024-0014

Georgoulas, D., Tsioumas, V., Stavroulakis, P. J., & Papadimitriou, S. (2024). Geopolitical risk and sustainable shipping: A quantitative approach. *Australian Journal of Maritime and Ocean Affairs*, •••, 1–13. DOI: 10.1080/18366503.2024.2325270

Gibbert, M., Ruigrok, W., & Wicki, B. (2008). What passes as a rigorous case study? *Strategic Management Journal*, *29*(13), 1465–1474. DOI: 10.1002/smj.722

Gigliuto, G. (2023). The relevance of semiconductors manufacturing in Taiwan's foreign policy. https://unive.unitesi.cineca.it/handle/20.500.14247/12680

Gilpin, R. (2016). *The political economy of international relations*. Princeton University Press.

Gitterman, D. P. (2003). European Integration and Labour Market Cooperation: A Comparative Regional Perspective. *Journal of European Social Policy*, *13*(2), 99–120. DOI: 10.1177/0958928703013002001

Glod, M., Boone, G., Huang, J., De Spiegeleire, S., & Sweijs, T. (2009). Looking ahead. In *Economic crisis: Examining the security implications* (pp. 15–18). Hague Centre for Strategic Studies., https://www.jstor.org/stable/resrep12576.6

Godsell, D., Lel, U., & Miller, D. (2023). US national security and de-globalization. *Journal of International Business Studies*, *54*(8), 1471–1494.

Góes, C., & Bekkers, E. (2022). *The Impact of Geopolitical Conflicts on Trade, Growth, and Innovation.* World Trade Organization https://www.wto.org/english/res_e/reser_e/ersd202209_e.htm

Goldeng, E., Grünfeld, L. A., & Benito, G. R. (2008). The performance differential between private and state owned enterprises: The roles of ownership, management and market structure. *Journal of Management Studies, 45*(7), 1244–1273.

Gong, X.-L., Feng, Y.-K., Liu, J.-M., & Xiong, X. (2023). Study on international energy market and geopolitical risk contagion based on complex network. *Resources Policy, 82*, 103495. DOI: 10.1016/j.resourpol.2023.103495

Gong, Y., Tang, X., Chang, E. C., & Wan, F. (2025). EXPRESS: Corporate Sociopolitical Activism and Language Strategies for Mitigating Animosity in a Host Country. *Journal of International Marketing*. Advance online publication. DOI: 10.1177/1069031X251319018

Google. (2025). *Map of Northeast India showing borders with Bhutan, Nepal, Bangladesh, China, and Myanmar* [Map]. Google Maps. https://maps.app.goo.gl/aYbszNgdWkgEPFbS8 *(Accessed on June 5, 2025, at 9:22 AM IST, from Assam, India)*

Göpel, M. (2016). *The great mindshift: How a new economic paradigm and sustainability transformations go hand in hand.* Springer., DOI: 10.1007/978-3-319-43766-8

Government of India. (1950). *The Constitution of India, Scheduled Tribes Order.* https://legislative.gov.in

Government of India. (1950a). *The Constitution of India: First Schedule.* Part C States.

Graham, E., & Marchick, D. (2006). *US National Security and Foreign Direct Investment.* Peterson Institute for International Economics.

Granström, J. (2014). *Consumer motivations to boycott: Focus on non-green products. Master.* Aalborg University.

Green Climate Fund. (2023). *Decision B.36/12: Enhancing access to climate finance through simplified processes.* https://www.greenclimate.fund/sites/default/files/decision/b36/decision-b36-12-annex-vi.pdf

Green Climate Fund. (n.d.-a). *Democratic Republic of the Congo and the GCF.* https://www.greenclimate.fund/countries/dr-congo

Green, J. F. (2013). Order out of chaos: Public and private rules for managing carbon. *Global Environmental Politics, 13*(2), 1–25.

Greenwood, R., Suddaby, R., & Hinings, C. R. (2002). Theorizing Change : The Role of Professional Associations in the Transformation of Institutionalized Fields A. *Academy of Management Journal, 45*(1), 58–80.

Greer, S., & Williams, A. (2009). Human rights in the council of Europe and the EU: Towards 'Individual','Constitutional'or 'Institutional'justice? *European Law Journal*, *15*(4), 462–481.

Grøgaard, B., Rygh, A., & Benito, G. R. G. (2019). Bringing corporate governance into internalization theory: State ownership and foreign entry strategies. *Journal of International Business Studies*, *50*(8), 1310–1337.

Gu, J. (2023, October 23). US-China tensions are top geopolitical risk, BlackRock says. *Bloomberg Screentime*. https://www.bloomberg.com/news/articles/2023-10-23/blackrock-says-us-china-tensions-are-top-geopolitical-risk?embedded-checkout=true

Guedes, J., & Pereira, L. (2024). Unlocking the full potential of nearshoring - a conceptual delivery model for proximity offshoring services. *International Journal of Productivity and Quality Management*, *41*(4), 510–528. DOI: 10.1504/IJPQM.2024.137884

Gündüz, M. (2020). Financial Globalization and Economic Growth: Panel Causality Analysis for EU. In Handbook of Research on Social and Economic Development in the European Union (pp. 99-116). IGI Global.

Gurantz, R. (2024). *Satellites in the Russia-Ukraine War*. https://press.armywarcollege.edu/monographs/971/

Gürsoy, S. & Eroğlu, Ö. (2016). Yükselen Ekonomilerin Pay Piyasaları Arasında Getiri & Volatilite Yayılımı: 2006-2015 Yılları Arasında Yapılmış Bir Analiz. Mehmet Akif Ersoy Üniversitesi İİBF Dergisi, 3(5), ss. 16-33.

Gyan, I. A. S. (2025). *Koch-Rajbongshi.* IAS Gyan. https://www.iasgyan.in/daily-current-affairs/koch-rajbongshis

Hachicha, F. (2024). Sentiment investor, exchange rates, geopolitical risk and developing stock market: Evidence of co-movements in the time-frequency domain during RussiaUkraine war. *Review of Behavioral Finance*, *16*(3), 486–509. DOI: 10.1108/RBF-04-2023-0119

Hadri, K. (2000). Testing for stationarity in heterogeneous panel data. *The Econometrics Journal*, *3*(2), 148–161. DOI: 10.1111/1368-423X.00043

Halisçelik, E. (2015). *Binyıl Kalkınma Hedefleri & Yoksul Odaklı Büyüme: Yükselen Ekonomiler Üzerine Ampirik Bir Analiz*. Doktora Tezi, Hacettepe Üniversitesi Sosyal Bilimler Enstitüsü.

Hall, R. B., & Biersteker, T. J. (Eds.). (2002). *The emergence of private authority in global governance* (Vol. 85). Cambridge University Press.

Hardy, C., & Maguire, S. (2010). Discourse, field-configuring events, and change in organizations and institutional fields: Narratives of DDT and the Stockholm Convention. *Academy of Management Journal, 53*(6), 1365–1392.

Hasnat, B. (2015). US National Security and Foreign Direct Investment. *Thunderbird International Business Review, 57*(3), 185–196.

Haufler, V. (2013). *A public role for the private sector: Industry self-regulation in a global economy*. Carnegie Endowment.

Hazarika, S. (1994). *Strangers of the Mist: Tales of War and Peace from India's Northeast*. Penguin Books. https://www.caluniv.ac.in/global-mdia-journal/BR_JUNE_DEC_2015/BookReview1.pdf

Hedstrom, A., Zelander, N., Junttila, J., & Uddin, G. S. (2020). Emerging Market Contagion under Geopolitical Uncertainty. *Emerging Markets Finance & Trade, 56*(5), 1083–1099. DOI: 10.1080/1540496X.2018.1562895

Henisz, W. J. (2016). The Dynamic Capability of Corporate Diplomacy. *Global Strategy Journal, 6*(3), 183–196. DOI: 10.1002/gsj.1121

Henisz, W. J. (2017). *Corporate diplomacy: Building reputations and relationships with external stakeholders*. Routledge.

Hernández, M. J. E., & Estay, R. J. (2018). Determinantes de la Inversión Extranjera Directa en México, 2005-2012. *Ensayos de Economía, 28*(53), 65–91. DOI: 10.15446/ede.v28n53.75074

Heywood, A. (2019). *Politics* (5th ed.). Macmillan International Higher Education.

Highhouse, S., Thornbury, E. E., & Little, I. S. (2007). Social-identity functions of attraction to organizations. *Organizational Behavior and Human Decision Processes, 103*(1), 134–146.

Hillman, A. J., & Hitt, M. A. (1999). Corporate political strategy formulation: A model of approach, participation, and strategy decisions. *Academy of Management Review, 24*(4), 825–842.

Hoffman, A. J. (1999). Institutional Evolution and Change: Environmentalism and the U.S. Chemical Industry. *Academy of Management Journal, 42*, 351–371.

Hoffmann, S. (2013). Are boycott motives rationalizations? *Journal of Consumer Behaviour, 12*(3), 214–222. DOI: 10.1002/cb.1418

Holburn, G. L., & Zelner, B. A. (2010). Political capabilities, policy risk, and international investment strategy: Evidence from the global electric power generation industry. *Strategic Management Journal, 31*(12), 1290–1315.

Hoque, M. E. (2020). Global and country-specific geopolitical risk uncertainty and stock return of fragile emerging economies. *Journal of Economics and Business, 113*, 105926. DOI: 10.1016/j.jeconbus.2020.105926

Hoque, M. E., Soo-Wah, L., Uddin, M. A., & Rahman, A. (2023). International Trade Policy Uncertainty Spillover on Stock Market: Evidence from Five Fragile Economies. *Journal of International Financial Markets, Institutions and Money, 84*, 2072520. DOI: 10.1080/09638199.2022.2072520

Hossain, M. S., Voumik, L. C., Ahmed, T. T., Alam, M. B., & Tasmim, Z. (2024). Impact of Geopolitical Risk, GDP, Inflation, Interest Rate, and Trade Openness on Foreign Direct Investment: Evidence from Five Southeast Asian Countries. *Regional Sustainability, 5*(1), 100177. DOI: 10.1016/j.regsus.2024.100177

Hou, Y., Xue, W., & Zhang, X. (2024). The Impact of Geopolitical Risk on Trade Costs. *Global Economic Review, 53*(1), 1–24. DOI: 10.1080/1226508X.2024.2305464

Hsieh, H.-C., Boarelli, S., & Vu, T. H. C. (2019). The effects of economic policy uncertainty on outward foreign direct investment. *International Review of Economics & Finance, 64*, 377–392. DOI: 10.1016/j.iref.2019.08.004

Huang, S., Yeo, A. A., & Li, S. D. (2007). Modification of Kolmogorov-Smirnov test for DNA content data analysis through distribution alignment. *Assay and Drug Development Technologies, 5*(5), 663–672. DOI: 10.1089/adt.2007.071

Hudson, N. F. (2009). *Gender, Human Security and the United Nations: Security Languages as a Political Framework for Women*. Routledge.

Husaeni, U. A., & Ayoob, M. A. (2025). Determinants of Muslim's intention to boycott Israel-affiliated products: Evidence from Indonesia. *Jurnal Ekonomi & Keuangan Islam, 11*(1), 14–28. DOI: 10.20885/JEKI.vol11.iss1.art2

Iacoviello, M., Caldara, D., Penn, M., & Conlisk, S. (2024). Do Geopolitical Risks Raise or Lower Inflation? Available at *SSRN*. https://ssrn.com/abstract=4852461 or http://dx.doi.org/*SSRN*. DOI: 10.2139/ssrn.4852461

Ianchovichina, E. (2016). *Economic costs of post-Arab-Spring civil wars in the Middle East and North Africa*. Instituto Europeo del Mediterráneo (IEMed).

Ihssane, A., & Wang, W. (2024). Boycotting effects on the Europe and America corporates amid Gaza-Israel conflict. *International Journal of Research Publication and Reviews*, *5*(4), 5150–5157. DOI: 10.55248/gengpi.5.0424.1057

IISD. (2024). UNCCD COP 16 Summary and Analysis: Riyadh, Saudi Arabia, 2–13 December 2024. Earth Negotiations Bulletin. https://enb.iisd.org/convention-combat-desertification-unccd-cop16-summary

IMCO. (2024). *Nearshoring: El impacto sobre la Inversión Extranjera Directa* (pp. 1-60). Instituto Mexicano para la Competitividad, A.C. https://imco.org.mx/nearshoring-el-impacto-sobre-la-inversion-extranjera-directa/

IMF. (2024). *Country composition of WEO groups*. https://www.imf.org/en/Publications/WEO/weo-database/2023/April/groups-and-aggregates

IMF. (2025). *Inflation, average consumer prices*. World Economic Outlook Database: April 2025, International Monetary Fund. https://www.imf.org/en/Publications/WEO/weo-database/2025/april/weo-report?c=273,186,&s=PCPI,&sy=1998&ey=2024&ssm=0&scsm=1&scc=0&ssd=1&ssc=0&sic=0&sort=country&ds=.&br=1

Im, K. S., Pesaran, M. H., & Shin, Y. (2003). Testing for unit roots in heterogeneous panels. *Journal of Econometrics*, *115*(1), 53–74. DOI: 10.1016/S0304-4076(03)00092-7

India Today, N. E. (2025). *Assam: Koch-Rajbongshi Mancha submits a 15-point memorandum, demanding ST status and Kamatapur state*. https://www.indiatodayne.in/assam/story/assam-koch-rajbongshi-mancha-submits-15-point-memorandum-demands-st-status-and-kamatapur-state-1181318-2025-03-09

Inoue, C. (2020). Election cycles and organizations: How politics shapes the performance of state-owned enterprises over time. *Dministrative Science Quarterly*, *65*(3), 677–709.

International Chamber of Commerce. (2016). *ICC Business Charter for Sustainable Development 2015*. ICC - International Chamber of Commerce. https://iccwbo.org/news-publications/policies-reports/icc-business-charter-for-sustainable-development-2015/

International Monetary Fund. (2014). *2014 Spillover Report*. [Web article].

International Monetary Fund. (2016). *2016 Spillover Chapter*. [Web article].

International Monetary Fund. (2025). *Global Financial Stability Report: Navigating Geopolitical Risks*. [Web article].

IPBES. (2019). *Global assessment report on biodiversity and ecosystem services*. Intergovernmental Science-Policy Platform on Biodiversity and Ecosystem Services. https://ipbes.net/global-assessment

IPCC. (2023). [*Synthesis report*. Intergovernmental Panel on Climate Change. https://www.ipcc.ch/report/sixth-assessment-report-synthesis-report/]. *Climatic Change*, *2023*, •••.

Irwin, D. A. (2012). *Trade policy disaster: Lessons from the 1930s*. MIT Press.

Isaacson, W. (2023). *Elon Musk*. Simon and Schuster.

Ivanov, D., & Dolgui, A. (2022). Stress testing supply chains and creating viable ecosystems. *Operations Management Research*, *15*(1–2), 475–486. DOI: 10.1007/s12063-021-00194-z

Jadhav, P., Katti, V., & Choudhury, R. N. (2016). Trends, determinants and challenges of foreign direct investment in emerging markets. In *Trade, Investment and Economic Development in Asia* (1st ed., pp. 234-246). Routledge.

James, L. (2021). Supply chains critical to Taiwan's security. *East Asia Forum*. https://eastasiaforum.org/2021/03/10/geoeconomics-and-the-security-of-taiwan/

Janse, R. J., Hoekstra, T., Jager, K. J., Zoccali, C., Tripepi, G., Dekker, F. W., & Diepen, M. V. (2021). Conducting correlation analysis: Important limitations and pitfalls. *Clinical Kidney Journal*, *14*(11), 2332–2337. DOI: 10.1093/ckj/sfab085

Jasanoff, S. (2018). *The ethics of invention: Technology and the human future*. W. W. Norton & Company.

JayCoop. (2022, March 7). File:map of council of europe member states by founding and later members.svg. Wikimedia Commons. https://commons.wikimedia.org/wiki/File:Map_of_Council_of_Europe_member_states_by_founding_and_later_members.svg

Jensen, B., & Pashkewitz, J. (2019). *Mosaic warfare: small and scalable are beautiful*. War on the Rocks. 23 December. Available from: https://warontherocks.com/2019/12/mosaic-warfare-small-and-scalable-are-beautiful/

Jha, S., Awate, S., & Mudambi, R. (2024). A multilateral network perspective on inward FDI. *Journal of International Business Studies*, *55*, 303–325. DOI: 10.1057/s41267-023-00650-x

Jiménez, A. (2024, 10 de octubre). *Cómo afrontar un mundo de riesgos interconectados*. KPMG Tendencias.

John, A., & Klein, J. (2003). The boycott puzzle: Consumer motivations for purchase sacrifice. *Management Science*, *49*(9), 1196–1209. DOI: 10.1287/mnsc.49.9.1196.16569

Johnson, J. (2025). Why Elon Musk is a headache for broadband bosses. *Thomson Reuters.* https://www.reuters.com/breakingviews/why-elon-musk-is-headache-broadband-bosses-2025-02-11/

Johnson-Freese, J. (2007). *Space as a strategic asset.* Columbia University Press.

Jones, R. (1984). Empirical Models of Political Risks in U. S. Oil Production Operations in Venezuela. *Journal of International Business Studies*, *15*(1), 81–95.

Julio, B., & Yook, Y. (2016). Policy uncertainty, irreversibility, and cross-border flows of capital. *Journal of International Economics*, *103*, 13–26.

Kailash, M. S. R., Joshi, C., Desai, P. R., Teferra, N. B., & Radhakrishnan, S. (2023). The Rise of Ethical Consumerism. *Marketing Strategies for the Conscious Buyer.*, *44*(8), 1329–1337.

Kang, W., Ratti, R. A., & Yoon, K. H. (2015). The impact of oil price shocks on the stock market return and volatility relationship. *Journal of International Financial Markets, Institutions and Money*, *34*, 41–54. DOI: 10.1016/j.intfin.2014.11.002

Kanık, İ. (2016). Küreselleşme Sürecinde Kültürel Melezleşme Örneği Olarak Yemek Kanalları & Programları. Folklor/Edebiyat, 22(86), 237-258.

Kapopoulos, T., Sakkas, A., & Drakos, K. (2024). Geopolitical Risk and Foreign Direct Investment Inflows: The Moderating Role of Water and Energy Risks. *International Journal of Finance & Economics*, •••, 1–24. DOI: 10.1002/ijfe.3106

Karyotis, G., & Patrikios, S. (2010). Religion, securitization and anti-immigration attitudes: The case of Greece. *Journal of Peace Research*, *47*(1), 43–57.

Kaufmann, D., & Kraay, A. (2024, november). *The Worldwide Governance Indicators. Methodology and 2024 Update*. Policy Research Working Paper (WPS10952). World Bank Group. https://documents.worldbank.org/curated/en/099005210162424110

Keohane, R. O., & Nye, J. S. (2011). *Power and interdependence* (4th ed.). Longman.

Keohane, R. O., & Nye, J. S.Jr. (1987). Power and interdependence revisited. *International Organization*, *41*(4), 725–753.

Kerr, P., & Wiseman, G. (2017). *Diplomacy in a globalizing world.* Oxford University Press.

Khan, H. U. (2024). An analytical investigation of consequences of terrorism in the Middle East. *Journal of Economic Criminology*, *4*, 100067. DOI: 10.1016/j.jeconc.2024.100067

Khan, K., Su, C. W., Tao, R., & Umar, M. (2021). How do geopolitical risks affect oil prices and freight rates? *Ocean and Coastal Management*, *215*, 105955. DOI: 10.1016/j.ocecoaman.2021.105955

Kim, S., & Mehrotra, A. (2017). *Effects of monetary and macro-prudential policies – evidence from inflation targeting economies in the Asia-Pacific region and potential implications for China* (BOFIT Discussion Papers No. 4/2017). Bank of Finland Institute for Economies in Transition (BOFIT). https://ideas.repec.org/p/zbw/bofitp/bdp2017_004.html

Kim, C., Yan, X., & Park, S. (2021). Do consumer boycotts really matter with global companies? The moderating effect of gender differences. *International Journal of Emerging Markets*, *18*(12), 5707–5726. DOI: 10.1108/IJOEM-03-2021-0312

Kindleberger, C. P. (1973). *The world in depression, 1929-1939*. Cambridge University Press.

Klein, J. G., & John, A. (2001). *Exploring motivations for participation in a consumer boycott* (Working Paper No. 01-701). INSEAD.

Klein, J. G., Smith, N. C., & John, A. (2004). Why we boycott: Consumer motivations for boycott participation. *Journal of Marketing*, *68*(3), 92–109. DOI: 10.1509/jmkg.68.3.92.34770

Kljajić, I., & Lapaine, M. (2013). Piri Reis–Cartographer of Suleiman the Magnificent, Exhibition in Croatia. Kartografija i geoinformacije (Cartography and Geoinformation), 12(20), 88-91.

Kobrin, S. (1979). Political risk: A review and reconsideration. *Journal of International Business Studies*, *10*(1), 67–80.

Kobrin, S. J. (2009). Private political authority and public responsibility: Transnational politics, transnational firms, and human rights. *Business Ethics Quarterly*, *19*(3), 349–374.

Kotcharin, S., & Maneenop, S. (2020). Geopolitical risk and corporate cash holdings in the shipping industry. *Transportation Research Part E, Logistics and Transportation Review*, *136*, 101862. DOI: 10.1016/j.tre.2020.101862

Kotcharin, S., & Maneenop, S. (2020). Geopolitical risk and shipping firms' capital structure decisions in Belt and Road Initiative countries. *International Journal of Logistics Research and Applications*, *23*(6), 544–560. DOI: 10.1080/13675567.2020.1766003

Krastev, I., & Leonard, M. (2014). *The New European Disorder*. European Council on Foreign Relations.

Krauss, C. (2017). Russian uses its oil giant, Rosneft, as a foreign policy tool. The New York Times. October 29, 2017. https://www.nytimes.com/2017/10/29/business/energy-environment/russia-venezula-oil-rosneft.html. Accessed September 12, 2021

Kren, J., & Lawless, M. (2024). How Has Brexit Changed EU–UK Trade Flows? *European Economic Review*, *161*, 104634. DOI: 10.1016/j.euroecorev.2023.104634

Kuame, C. (2022). Cross border trade in Northeast India: Critical analysis. *International Journal of Research in Engineering, Science and Management*, 5(4), 232–236. https://journal.ijresm.com/index.php/ijresm/article/download/1945/1885

Kubas, S. (2022). Suspension, Withdrawal and Expulsion of a Member State from the Council of Europe. *Biuletyn Stowarzyszenia Absolwentów i Przyjaciół Wydziału Prawa Katolickiego Uniwersytetu Lubelskiego*, *17*(19 (1)), 171–179.

Kumar, D. (2016). A Study of Economic Growth and Foreign Direct Investment: An Econometric Approach in SAARC Region. *International Journal of Economics and Management Studies*, *3*(12), 18–22. DOI: 10.14445/23939125/IJEMS-V3I6P117

Kumar, P., & Singh, V. K. (2022). Does Crude Oil Fire the Emerging Markets Currencies Contagion Spillover? A Systemic Perspective. *Energy Economics*, *110*, 106384. DOI: 10.1016/j.eneco.2022.106384

Kumar, S., Khalfaoui, R., & Tiwari, A. K. (2021). Does Geopolitical Risk Improve the Directional Predictability from Oil to Stock Returns? Evidence from Oil-exporting and Oil-importing Countries. *Resources Policy*, *74*, 102253. DOI: 10.1016/j.resourpol.2021.102253

Kutaula, S., Gillani, A., Gregory-Smith, D., & Bartikowski, B. (2024). Ethical consumerism in emerging markets: Opportunities and challenges. *Journal of Business Ethics*, *191*(4), 651–673. DOI: 10.1007/s10551-024-05657-4

Lai, K. (2021). National security and FDI policy ambiguity: A commentary. *Journal of International Business Policy*, *4*(4), 496–505.

Lai, K., & Fortwengel, J. (2025). Constructing an organizational identity with political ideology: The case of Huawei, 1987-2020. *Strategic Organization*. Advance online publication. DOI: 10.1177/14761270251327988

Lawson, C. (1994). The theory of state-owned enterprises in market economies. *Journal of Economic Surveys*, *8*(3), 283–309.

Leckie, S. (1988). The inter-state complaint procedure in international human rights law: Hopeful prospects or wishful thinking? *Hum. Rts. Q.*, *10*, 249.

Lee, C.-C., Tang, H., & Li, D. (2022). The roles of oil shocks and geopolitical uncertainties on China's green bond returns. *Economic Analysis and Policy*, *74*, 494–505. DOI: 10.1016/j.eap.2022.03.008

Lekakis, E. J. (2017). Economic nationalism and the cultural politics of consumption under austerity: The rise of ethnocentric consumption in Greece. *Journal of Consumer Culture*, *17*(2), 286–302. DOI: 10.1177/1469540515586872

Lenihan, A. T. (2018). *Balancing Power without Weapons: State Intervention into Cross-Border Mergers and Acquisitions*. Cambridge University Press.

Lestari, P., & Jazil, T. (2024). The role of religiosity, consumer animosity, and ethnocentrism in explaining the boycott motivation. *Journal of Islamic Economics and Finance Studies*, *5*(1), 134–152. DOI: 10.47700/jiefes.v5i1.7755

Le, T. P. T. D., & Tran, H. L. M. (2021). The contagion effect from U.S. stock market to the Vietnamese and the Philippine stock markets: The evidence of DCC–GARCH model. *The Journal of Asian Finance, Economics and Business*, *8*(2), 759–770. DOI: 10.13106/jafeb.2021.vol8.no2.0759

Leutert, W. (2018). Firm control: governing the state-owned economy under Xi Jinping. *China Perspectives*. June 1, 2018. 27-36. https://journals.openedition.org/chinaperspectives/7605

Levin, A., Lin, C. F., & Chu, C. S. J. (2002). Unit root tests in panel data: Asymptotic and finite-sample properties. *Journal of Econometrics*, *108*(1), 1–24. DOI: 10.1016/S0304-4076(01)00098-7

Levy, B. (1987). A theory of public enterprise behavior. *Journal of Economic Behavior & Organization*, *8*(1), 75–96.

Liechtenstein, A., Luxembourg, A., Macedonia, C. N., & Serbia, F. (2024). Council of Europe. *Organization*.

Li, J., Shapiro, D. M., Ufimtseva, A., & Zhang, P. (2024). Techno-nationalism and cross-border acquisitions in an age of geopolitical rivalry. *Journal of International Business Studies*, *55*, 1190–1203.

Li, J., Shapiro, D., Peng, M. W., & Ufimtseva, A. (2022). Corporate diplomacy in the age of US–China rivalry. *The Academy of Management Perspectives*, *36*(4), 1007–1032. DOI: 10.5465/amp.2021.0076

Lindsay, C. M. (1976). A theory of government enterprise. *Journal of Political Economy*, *84*(5), 1061–1077.

Lin, F., & Meng, X. (2024). Stuck between the great powers: Secondary countries' responses to soft power competition between the US and China during the COVID-19 pandemic. *Journal of Chinese Political Science*, *29*(2), 233–256. DOI: 10.1007/s11366-023-09862-2

Li, Y., Huang, J., & Chen, J. (2021). Dynamic Spillovers of Geopolitical Risks and Gold Prices: New Evidence from 18 Emerging Economies. *Resources Policy*, *71*, 101938. DOI: 10.1016/j.resourpol.2020.101938

Lok Sabha. (1997). *The Constitution (Scheduled Tribes) Order (Amendment) Bill, 1996: Report of the Select Committee*. Government of India. https://eparlib.nic.in/bitstream/123456789/757628/1/jcb_11_1997_scheduled_tribes.pdf

Long, T. Q., Nguyen, L. H., & Morgan, P. J. (2021). Dynamic Connectedness of Financial Stress Across Advanced and Emerging Economies: Evidence from Time and Frequency Domains. *International Journal of Economics and Financial Issues*, *11*(6), 1–15. DOI: 10.1142/S0217590821410125

Lu, B., & Liu, W. (2024). Does Comprehensive Geopolitical Risk Deter FDI Outflows: Evidence from China. *Defence and Peace Economics*, *35*(3), 383–399. DOI: 10.1080/10242694.2022.2160140

Lumineau, F., & Keller, A. (2025). War as a phenomenon of inquiry in management studies. *Journal of Management Studies*. Advance online publication. DOI: 10.1111/joms.13213

Luo, Y. (2021). Illusions of techno-nationalism. *Journal of International Business Studies*, *53*(3), 550. PMID: 34511654

Luo, Y. (2024). Paradigm shift and theoretical implications for the era of global disorder. *Journal of International Business Studies*, *55*(2), 127–135.

Luo, Y., & Van Assche, A. (2023). The rise of techno-geopolitical uncertainty: Implications of the United States CHIPS and Science Act. *Journal of International Business Studies*, *54*(8), 1423–1440. DOI: 10.1057/s41267-023-00620-3 PMID: 37359753

Lütkepohl, H., & Xu, F. (2012). The role of the log transformation in forecasting economic variables. *Empirical Economics*, *42*, 619–638. DOI: 10.1007/s00181-010-0440-1

Lux, S., Crook, T. R., & Woehr, D. J. (2011). Mixing business with politics: A meta-analysis of the antecedents and outcomes of corporate political activity. *Journal of Management*, *37*(1), 223–247.

Mackinder, H. J. (1904). The Geographical Pivot of History. *The Geographical Journal*, *23*(4), 421–437.

Maddala, G. S., & Wu, S. (1999). A comparative study of unit root tests with panel data and a new simple test. *Oxford Bulletin of Economics and Statistics*, *61*(S1), 631–652. DOI: 10.1111/1468-0084.0610s1631

Maharmah, M. H. (2023). Does The Foreign Direct Investment Affect Economic Growth in Jordan in Light of Commercial Openness. *International Journal of Professional Business Review*, *8*(5), e02088. DOI: 10.26668/businessreview/2023.v8i5.2088

Mahjoubi, M., & Henchiri, J. E. (2024). The effect of policy uncertainty on the volatility of bitcoin. *Journal of Financial Economic Policy*, *16*(4), 429–441. DOI: 10.1108/JFEP-08-2023-0222

Mamman, S. O., Wang, Z., & Iliyasu, J. (2023). Commonality in BRICS Stock Markets' Reaction to Global Economic Policy Uncertainty: Evidence from a Panel GARCH Model with Cross-Sectional Dependence. *Finance Research Letters*, *50*, 103877. DOI: 10.1016/j.frl.2023.103877

Marcén, A. G. (2021). The Platform for the Protection of Journalists: A Mechanism for Cooperation between Non-Governmental Organisations and the Council of Europe. *Utrecht Law Review*, *17*(2).

Marchewka, A. (2023). Application of multi-criteria Vector Measure Construction Method (VMCM) to assess importance of foreign direct investment (FDI) to host country's regional economy. *Procedia Computer Science*, *225*, 2497–2506. DOI: 10.1016/j.procs.2023.10.241

Mariotti, S., & Marzano, R. (2019). Varieties of capitalism and the internationalization of state-owned enterprises. *Journal of International Business Studies*, *50*(5), 669–691.

Mark, J., & Roberts, D. T. (2023). United States–China Semiconductor Standoff: A Supply Chain under Stress. *Atlantic Council, 23.* https://www.atlanticcouncil.org/wp-content/uploads/2023/03/US-China-Semiconductor-Standoff.pdf

Marschlich, S. (2022). *Corporate diplomacy: How multinational corporations gain organizational legitimacy: A neo-institutional public relations perspective.* Springer Nature.

Martin, B., Baldwin, L. H., DeLuca, P., Henriquez Sanchez, N., Hvizda, M., Smith, C. D., & Whitehead, N. P. (2023). *Supply Chain Interdependence and Geopolitical Vulnerability: The Case of Taiwan and High-End Semiconductors.* RAND Corporation. https://www.rand.org/pubs/research_reports/RRA2354-1.html

Mazal, J. (2024). *The Dual Use of Civilian and Military Technologies in the Battlefield of the Future.* https://real.mtak.hu/210721/

McCabe, D. (2020). F.C.C. designates Huawei and ZTE as national security threats. *The New York Times*. June 20, 2020. https://www.nytimes.com/2020/06/30/technology/fcc-huawei-zte-national-security.html. Access September 10, 2021.

Mende, J. (2023). Business authority in global governance: Companies beyond public and private roles. *Journal of International Political Theory*, *19*(2), 200–220. DOI: 10.1177/17550882221116924

Menyah, K., Nazlıoğlu, S., & Wolde-Rufael, Y. (2014). Financial development, trade openness and economic growth in African countries: New insights from a panel causality approach. *Economic Modelling*, *37*, 386–394.

Meyer, J. W., & Rowan, B. (1977). Institutionalized organizations: Formal structure as myth and ceremony. *American Journal of Sociology*, *83*(2), 340–363.

Meyer, K. E., Ding, Y., Li, J., & Zhang, H. (2014). Overcoming distrust: How state-owned enterprises adapt their foreign entries to institutional pressures abroad. *Journal of International Business Studies*, *45*(8), 1005–1028.

Meyer, K. E., Li, C., & Schotter, A. P. (2020). Managing the MNE subsidiary: Advancing a multi-level and dynamic research agenda. *Journal of International Business Studies*, *51*, 538–576.

Michelson, E. (2007). Lawyers, political embeddedness, and institutional continuity in China's transition from socialism. *American Journal of Sociology*, *113*, 352–414.

Mignon, V., & Saadaoui, J. (2024). How do political tensions and geopolitical risks impact oil prices? *Energy Economics*, *129*, 107219. DOI: 10.1016/j.eneco.2023.107219

Miles, L., & Kapos, V. (2008). Reducing greenhouse gas emissions from deforestation and forest degradation: Global land-use implications. *Science*, *320*(5882), 1454–1455. DOI: 10.1126/science.1155358 PMID: 18556549

Miller, C. (2022). *Chip war: The fight for the world's most critical technology*. Simon and Schuster.

Milner, H. (1997). *Interests, Institutions, and Information: Domestic Politics and International Relations*. Princeton University Press.

Ministry of External Affairs. (2023). *Question No-1456: India's Act East Policy*. Government of India. https://www.mea.gov.in/lok-sabha.htm?dtl/36927/QUESTION+NO1456+INDIAS+ACTEAST+POLICY Ministry of Tribal Affairs. *Scheduled Tribes Profile*. https://tribal.nic.in/Statistics.aspx

Misangyi, V. F., Greckhamer, T., Furnari, S., Fiss, P. C., Crilly, D., & Aguilera, R. (2017). Embracing causal complexity: The emergence of a neo-configurational perspective. *Journal of Management*, *43*(1), 255–282.

Misiewicz, C., & Stepaniuk, K. (2024). CONSUMER ACTIVISM ON SOCIAL MEDIA DURING GEOPOLITICAL CONFLICT. *Scientific Papers of Silesian University of Technology. Organization & Management / Zeszyty Naukowe Politechniki Slaskiej. Seria Organizacji i Zarzadzanie*, (208). Advance online publication. DOI: 10.29119/1641-3466.2024.208.19

Misra, U. (2000). *The Periphery Strikes Back: Challenges to the Nation-State in Assam and Nagaland*. Indian Institute of Advanced Study. http://14.139.58.199:8080/jspui/handle/123456789/449

Mizrak, K. C. (2024). Crisis management and risk mitigation: Strategies for effective response and resilience. *Trends, Challenges, and Practices in Contemporary Strategic Management*, 254–278.

Mo, B., Zeng, H., Meng, J., & Ding, S. (2024). The Connectedness Between Uncertainty and Exchange Rates of Oil Import Countries: New Evidence from Time and Frequency Perspective. *Resources Policy*, *79*, 104398. DOI: 10.1016/j.resourpol.2023.104398

Mo, H. (2024). A Critical Analysis of Economic, Political, and Financial Determinants Influencing Location Choices of Foreign Direct Investments. *Financial Economics Research*, *1*(1), 83–89. DOI: 10.70267/pnbt8t44

Molinar, C. M. A., & Carrillo, I. M. (2024). Crime and Insecurity as Factors of Uncertainty and Erosion of the Tourist Image of Mexico. In *Tourism in a VUCA World: Managing the Future of Tourism* (pp. 187-201). Emerald Publishing Limited. DOI: 10.1108/978-1-83753-674-020241013

Moltz, J. C. (2019). *The politics of space security: Strategic restraint and the pursuit of national interests*. Stanford University Press.

Monge, M., Rojo, M. F. R., & Gil-Alana, L. A. (2023). The impact of geopolitical risk on the behavior of oil prices and freight rates. *Energy, 269*, 126779. DOI: 10.1016/j.energy.2023.126779

Moore, M., & Tambini, D. (Eds.). (2018). *Digital dominance: the power of Google, Amazon, Facebook, and Apple*. Oxford University Press.

Morales, J. (2024). Semiconductor analyst theorizes that China might want to destroy TSMC instead of capturing it, Chinese invasion of Taiwan would destroy supply chains, cripple South Korean chipmakers. *Tom's Hardware*. https://www.tomshardware.com/pc-components/cpus/semiconductor-analyst-theorizes-that-china-wants-to-destroy-tsmc-instead-of-capturing-it-a-chinese-invasion-of-taiwan-would-also-roil-supply-chains-removing-south-korean-chipmakers-from-contention

Moran, T. (2017). *CFIUS and National Security: Challenges for the United States, Opportunities for the European Union*. https://www.piie.com/commentary/speeches-papers/cfius-and-national-security-challenges-united-states-opportunities

Moran, T. H. (2009). *Three threats: An analytical framework for the CFIUS process*. Peterson Institute.

Morgenthau, H. J. (1948). *Politics among nations: The struggle for power and peace*. Alfred A. Knopf.

Morin, J.-F., & Tepper, E. (2023). The empire strikes back: Comparing US and China's structural power in outer space. *Global Studies Quarterly, 3*(4).

Mulyono, H., & Rolando, B. (2025). Consumer boycott movements: Impact on brand reputation and business performance in the digital age. *Multidisciplinary Reviews, 8*, e2025291. DOI: 10.31893/multirev.2025291

Muñoz, H. E., & Gálvez-Gamboa, F. (2022). Efecto de la incertidumbre de la política económica internacional sobre los mercados financieros latinoamericanos. *Estudios Gerenciales, 38*(165), 519–528. DOI: 10.18046/j.estger.2022.165.5383

Nag, S. N. (2015). *Kamtapur movement in North Bengal: Geo-ethno-environmental and historical perspective* (Doctoral dissertation, University of North Bengal). Shodhganga. http://hdl.handle.net/10603/174126

Nagy, S. G., & Navarro, M. (2025). North American Economic Integration (NAFTA7USMCA). In *The Economics of Regional Integration* (1st ed., pp. 169-194). Routledge.

Naifar, N., & Aljarba, S. (2023). Does Geopolitical Risk Matter for Sovereign Credit Risk? Fresh Evidence from Nonlinear Analysis. *Journal of Risk and Financial Management, 16*(3), 148. DOI: 10.3390/jrfm16030148

Nandi, R. (2014). Spectacles of Ethnographic and Historical Imaginations: Kamatapur Movement and the Rajbanshi Quest to Rediscover their Past and Selves. *History and Anthropology, 25*(5), 571–591. DOI: 10.1080/02757206.2014.928776

Narin, M., & Kutluay, D. (2013). *Değişen Küresel Ekonomik Düzen: BRIC, 3G & N-11 Ülkeleri*. Ankara Sanayi Odası Yayın Organı.

NASA. (2024). *NASA FY24 AI inventory*. Retrieved December 17, 2024, from https://www.nasa.gov/ai-inventory/

National Institute of Standards and Technology. (2023). Preventing the improper use of CHIPS Act funding (Final rule), 88 Fed. Reg. 65600–65620. https://www.govinfo.gov/content/pkg/FR-2023-09-25/pdf/2023-20471.pdf

National Intelligence Council. (2021). *Global trends 2040: A more contested world*. https://www.dni.gov/files/ODNI/documents/assessments/GlobalTrends_2040.pdf

Nazahra, G. N. (2024). Analysis of public responses to political controversies in the beauty industry: A case study of Rose All Day and Esqa Brand owners in support of Israel. *Gema Wiralodra, 15*(1), 350–354. DOI: 10.31943/gw.v15i1.630

Nazir, S., Sohag, K., & Mariev, O. (2025). Geopolitical Risk and Trade Reorientation Dynamics: A Comparative Study. *Emerging Markets Finance & Trade, 61*(8), 2338–2359. DOI: 10.1080/1540496X.2025.2451188

Nedumpara, J. J. (2024). Editorial: Friendshoring, Nearshoring, Greenshoring and Resshoring: Changing Faces of Global Supply Chains and its Impact on International Economic Law - Introduction to the Special Issue. *Global Trade and Customs Journal, 19*(3), 125–128. DOI: 10.54648/GTCJ2024035

Neill, A. (2023). Doubts grow over Taiwan's Silicon Shield. *GIS Reports*. Retrieved from https://www.gisreportsonline.com/r/china-taiwan-silicon-shield/

Newnham, R. (2011). Oil, carrots, and sticks: Russia's energy resources as a foreign policy tool. *Journal of Eurasian Studies*, *2*(2), 134–143.

Nguyen, C. Q., & Le, T.-H. (2021). The Nexus Between Trade Openness and Foreign Direct Investment Amid Structural Economic Vulnerability in Developing Countries. In *Globalization, Deglobalization, and New Paradigms in Business* (pp. 61-86). Palgrave Macmillan. DOI: 10.1007/978-3-030-81584-4_4

Nguyen, T. T. T., Pham, B. T., & Sala, H. (2022). Being an Emerging Economy: To What Extent Do Geopolitical Risks Hamper Technology and FDI Inflows? *Economic Analysis and Policy*, *74*, 123–134. DOI: 10.1016/j.eap.2022.04.005

Nienaber, M. (2020). Germany blocks Chinese takeover of satellite firm on security concerns. *Reuters*. December 8, 2020. https://www.reuters.com/article/uk-germany-china-m-a-idUKKBN28I1U0. Accessed September 10, 2021

Nilsson, M., Chisholm, E., Griggs, D., Howden-Chapman, P., McCollum, D., Messerli, P., & Stafford-Smith, M. (2018). Mapping interactions between the sustainable development goals: Lessons learned and ways forward. *Sustainability Science*, *13*, 1489–1503. DOI: 10.1007/s11625-018-0604-z PMID: 30546483

Ó Tuathail, G. (1996). *Critical geopolitics: The Politics of Writing Global Space*. University of Minnesota Press.

O'Donnell, C., Baker, L., & Wang, E. (2019). Exclusive: Told U.S. security at risk, Chinese firm seeks to sell Grindr dating app. *Reuters*. March 27, 2019. https://www.reuters.com/article/us-grindr-m-a-exclusive/exclusive-u-s-pushes-chinese-owner-of-grindr-to-divest-the-dating-app-sources-idUSKCN1R809L. Accessed September 10, 2021

Oanh, H. K., & Hoang, K. (2021). The bright side of geopolitical risk: Evidence from Chinese firms. *Journal of Financial Economic Policy*, *13*(3), 353–370. DOI: 10.1108/JFEP-04-2020-0076

Obuobi, N. K., Gatsi, J. G., Appiah, M. O., Kawor, S., Amoah, E. K., & Abeka, M. J. (2021). Trade liberalization policies and foreign direct investment inflows in Africa: Evidence from new measures of trade liberalization. *The Journal of International Trade & Economic Development*, *31*(3), 394–409. DOI: 10.1080/09638199.2021.1983009

OECD. (2019). *Policy coherence for sustainable development 2019: Empowering people and ensuring inclusiveness and equality*. OECD Publishing., DOI: 10.1787/a90f851f-

OECD. (2023). *Financing climate action: Progress and challenges.* Organisation for Economic Co-operation and Development. https://www.oecd.org/environment/cc/climate-finance.htm

OECD. (2024). *Policy coherence for sustainable development: Aligning policies in the decade of action.* OECD Publishing. [Pre-publication reference]

Office of the President Republic of China. (2020). *President Tsai designates TSMC founder Morris Chang as Leader's Representative at APEC Economic Leaders' Week* https://english.president.gov.tw/NEWS/6068

Okara, A. (2023). Does foreign direct investment promote political stability? Evidence from developing economies. *Economic Modelling, 123*, 106249. DOI: 10.1016/j.econmod.2023.106249

Okhmatovskiy, I. (2010). Performance implications of ties to the government and SOEs: A political embeddedness perspective. *Journal of Management Studies, 47*(6), 1020–1047.

Okur, M. A. (2015). The American geopolitical interests and turkey on the eve of the september 12, 1980 coup. *Journal of Modern Turkish History, 11*(21), 199–222.

Olanipekun, I. O., & Olasehinde-Williams, G. (2022). Unveiling the causal interactions among the US monetary policy uncertainty, exchange market pressure, and FDI-flows in large emerging market economies. *Journal of Public Affairs, 22*(4), e2684. DOI: 10.1002/pa.2684

Olson, M. (1982). *The Rise and Decline of Nations: Economic Growth, Stagflation and Social Rigidities. New Heaven.* Yale University Press.

Özçeli̇, K. O. (2023). Effects of Geopolitical Risks on Countries' Trade Flows: A Nonlinear ARDL Analysis. [Ege Academic Review]. *Ege Academic Review, 23*(3), 519–530. DOI: 10.21121/eab.1065493

Pace, R. (1999). Malta's Foreign Policy in the 1990s. In *The Foreign Policies of the European Union's Mediterranean States and Applicant Countries in the 1990s* (pp. 195–249). Palgrave Macmillan UK.

Padmapati, R. K. (2022). *General Chilarai.* The Sentinel. https://www.sentinelassam.com/more-news/editorial/general-chilarai-578610

Paikowsky, D. (2017). *The power of the space club.* Cambridge University Press.

Paolino, P. (2009). La posición del PRI en la política mexicana. *Política y Gobierno, 16*(2), 321–348. https://www.scielo.org.mx/scielo.php?script=sci_arttext&pid=S1665-20372009000200003&lng=es&tlng=es

Papaoikonomou, E., Valverde, M., & Ryan, G. (2012). Articulating the Meanings of Collective Experiences of Ethical Consumption. *Journal of Business Ethics, 110*, 15–32. DOI: 10.1007/s10551-011-1144-y

Pekkanen, S. M., Aoki, S., & Mittleman, J. (2022). Small satellites, big data: Uncovering the invisible in maritime security. *International Security*, *47*(2), 177–216.

Pekkanen, S. M., Aoki, S., & Takatori, Y. (2024). Japan in the new lunar space race. *Space Policy*, *69*, 101577.

Peng, H., Wang, M., & An, C. (2024). Implied threats of the Red Sea crisis to global maritime transport: Amplified carbon emissions and possible carbon pricing dysfunction. *Environmental Research Letters*, *19*(7), 074053. DOI: 10.1088/1748-9326/ad59b7

Pesaran, M. H. (2004a). General diagnostic tests for cross-section dependence in panels. *CESifo Working Paper Series No. 1229; IZA Discussion Paper No. 1240.* https://doi.org/DOI: 10.2139/ssrn.572504

Pesaran, M. H. (2004b). A simple panel unit root test in the presence of cross-section dependence. *Journal of Applied Econometrics*, *22*(2), 265–312. DOI: 10.1002/jae.951

Pesaran, M. H., Ullah, A., & Yamagata, T. (2008). A bias-adjusted LM test of error cross-section independence. *The Econometrics Journal*, *11*(1), 105–127. DOI: 10.1111/j.1368-423X.2007.00227.x

Pesaran, M. H., & Yamagata, T. (2008). Testing slope homogeneity in large panels. *Journal of Econometrics*, *142*(1), 50–93. DOI: 10.1016/j.jeconom.2007.05.010

Phillips, K. R., & Slijk, C. (2015). Border Economic Recovery Lags Rest of State. In *Ten-Gallon Economy* (1st ed., pp. 199-212). Palgrave Macmillan, New York. DOI: 10.1057/9781137530172_13

Phillips, T., Allen, K., & Macalister, T. (2015). Kinkley Point: Osborne seeks to ease doubts with £2bn guarantee. *The Guardian*. September 21, 2015. https://www.theguardian.com/business/2015/sep/21/nuclear-plant-project-osbornes-commits-2bn-guarantee. Accessed September 12, 2021

Pickard, J., Thomas, D., Massoudi, A., & Mitchell, T. (2020). UK takes aim at China with revamp of takeover rules, *Financial Times*, November 11, 2020. https://www.ft.com/content/55f848d8-92f8-4c42-9775-dd9d6c55ee91. Accessed September 10, 2021

Pickard, L., & Thomas, D. (2021). UK looks to remove China's CGN from nuclear power projects. *Financial Times*. July 25, 2021. https://www.ft.com/content/c4a3fe02-8535-45a4-aacf-0c4fbce8409d. Accessed September 12, 2021

Pietrobelli, C., & Seri, C. (2023). Reshoring, nearshoring and development. Readiness and implications for Latin America and the Caribbean. *Transnational Corporations*, *30*(2), 37–70. DOI: 10.18356/2076099x-30-2-2

Piña-Barcenas, J., Cedillo-Campos, M. G., Moreno-Quintero, E., & Covarrubias, D. (2024). Graph Theory to Achieve the Digital Transformation in Managing Freight Transportation Corridors. *Mobile Networks and Applications*, *29*, 201–210. DOI: 10.1007/s11036-023-02283-8

Pinterest. (n.d.). *Map of Kamata Kamarupa* [Image]. Pinterest. https://in.pinterest.com/pin/map-of-kamata-kamarupa--531424824773446898/ *(Accessed on June 5, 2025)*

PolicyUncertainty. (2024). *Geopolitical risk index*. https://www.policyuncertainty.com/gpr.html

Porter, T., Spirlet, T., & Epstein, J. (2025). Musk said he wouldn't withdraw Starlink for Ukraine. Europe is looking for alternatives, but would struggle to replace it. *Business Insider*. https://www.businessinsider.com/musk-starlink-threats-europe-faces-obstacles-replace-eutelsat-ukraine-trump-2025-3

Prastiwi, A., & Harsoyo, T. D. (2025). Analysis of the Influence of Consumer Animosity, Religiusity, and Social Media Sentiment on Product Boycott Decisions. *East Asian Journal of Multidisciplinary Research*, *4*(1), 255–270. DOI: 10.55927/eajmr.v4i1.12980

Pseftogkas, A., Stavrakou, T., Müller, J. F., Koukouli, M. E., Balis, D., & Meleti, C. (2024). Shifts in maritime trade routes as a result of Red Sea shipping crisis detected in TROPOMI NO2 data. *Geophysical Research Letters. ESS Open Archive*. https://doi.org/DOI: 10.22541/au.171893482.21861538/v1

Pultarova, T. (2025). Starlink satellites: Facts, tracking and impact on astronomy. *Space.com*. https://www.space.com/spacex-starlink-satellites.html

Qin, Y., Hong, K., Chen, J., & Zhang, Z. (2020). Asymmetric effects of geopolitical risks on energy returns and volatility under different market conditions. *Energy Economics*, *90*, 104851. DOI: 10.1016/j.eneco.2020.104851

Quintana, L., & Salgado, U. (2016). Internal migration in Mexico from 1990-2010: A new economic geography approach. *Problemas del Desarrollo*, *47*(184), 137–162. DOI: 10.1016/j.rpd.2016.01.007

Rajagopal. (2007). *Dynamics of international trade and economy: An inquiry into emerging markets.* Nova Science Publishers Inc. ISBN 1-60021-171-9

Ramonet, I. (1999). *Géopolitique du chaos* [**The geopolitics of chaos**] (translation by the author). Paris: Éditions Gallimard. ISBN 978-2-07-041113-9

Rana, W. (2015). Theory of complex interdependence: A comparative analysis of realist and neoliberal thoughts. *International Journal of Business and Social Science, 6*(2), 290–297.

Rao, A., Lucey, B., & Kumar, S. (2023). Climate Risk and Carbon Emissions: Examining Their Impact on Key Energy Markets Through Asymmetric Spillovers. *Energy Economics, 107*, 106970. DOI: 10.1016/j.eneco.2023.106970

Raswant, A., Nielsen, B. B., & Buckley, P. J. (2025). Space: A new frontier for international business. *Journal of International Business Studies.* Advance online publication. DOI: 10.1057/s41267-025-00783-1

Raustiala, K., & Victor, D. G. (2004). The regime complex for plant genetic resources. *International Organization, 58*(2), 277–309. DOI: 10.1017/S0020818304582036

Ray, S. (2023). Koch Rajbanshis and the Kamatapur Movement: Azadi in Eastern India? In Ranjan, A., & Chattoraj, D. (Eds.), *Migration, Regional Autonomy, and Conflicts in Eastern South Asia*. Palgrave Macmillan., DOI: 10.1007/978-3-031-28764-0_10

Republic of China Ministry of National Defense. (2023). *ROC National Defense Report 2023.* https://www.mnd.gov.tw/newupload/ndr/112/112ndreng.pdf

Reyad, H. M., Ayesha, M., Iqbal, M. M., & Zariyawati, M. A. (2024). The role of ESG in enhancing firm resilience to geopolitical risks: An eastern European perspective. *Business Strategy & Development, 7*(4), e70027. DOI: 10.1002/bsd2.70027

Reynolds, C. (2019). A United States View. In *Industrial Strategy and Planning in Mexico and The United States* (1st ed., pp. 231–243). Routledge., DOI: 10.4324/9780429041129

Rindell, A., Strandvik, T., & Wilén, K. (2014). Ethical consumers' brand avoidance. *Journal of Product and Brand Management, 23*(2), 114–120. DOI: 10.1108/JPBM-09-2013-0391

Rindova, V., & Fombrun, C. (2001). Entrepreneurial action in the creation of the specialty coffee niche. In S. CB & R. E (Eds.), *The Entrepreneurship Dynamic: Origins of Entrepreneurship and the Evolution of Industries* (pp. 236–26). Stanford University Press.

Roberts, T. G., & Kaplan, S. (2022). *Space launch to low Earth orbit: How much does it cost. Center for Strategic and International Studies*. Retrieved from https://aerospace.csis.org/data/space-launch-to-low-earth-orbit-how-much-does-it-cost/

Robertson, A. H. (1954). The Council of Europe, 1949–1953—I. *The International and Comparative Law Quarterly*, *3*(2), 235–255.

Rodríguez, S. A. (2019). Mexico's National Security Paradoxes and Threats in a Geopolitical Context. *Politics & Policy*, *47*(1), 207–232. DOI: 10.1111/polp.12287

Rodrik, D. (1991). Policy uncertainty and private investment in developing countries. *Journal of Development Economics*, *36*(2), 229–242. DOI: 10.1016/0304-3878(91)90034-S

Rogerson, K. S. (2000). Information Interdependence: Keohane and Nye's complex interdependence in the information age. *Information Communication and Society*, *3*(3), 415–436. DOI: 10.1080/13691180051033379

Romero, A. J. R. (2024). El nearshoring en México y su relación con China, Corea del Sur y Japón. *PORTES, Revista Mexicana de Estudios sobre la Cuenca del Pacífico, 2*, 31-54. DOI: 10.53897/RevPortes.2024.02.02

Roy, A. (2014). *Koch Rajbongshi and the Politics of Belonging*. Eastern Book House.

Roychowdhury, A. (2024). *The Rajbanshis and the history of their statehood demand*. The Indian Express. https://indianexpress.com/article/research/the-rajbanshis-and-the-history-of-their-statehood-demand-9263934/

Roy, H. (2014). Politics of Janajatikaran: Koch Rajbanshis of Assam. *Economic and Political Weekly*, *49*(47). https://www.epw.in/journal/2014/47/reports-states-web-exclusives/politics-janajatikaran.html

Ruggie, J. G. (1982). International regimes, transactions, and change: Embedded liberalism in the postwar economic order. *International Organization*, *36*(2), 379–415.

Ruggie, J. G. (1998). *Constructing the world polity: Essays on international institutionalization*. Routledge.

S&P Global. (2024). *Top geopolitical risks of 2024*. S&P Global, Research and Insights. https://www.spglobal.com/en/research-insights/market-insights/geopolitical-risk

Saâdaoui, F., Jabeur, S. B., & Goodell, J. W. (2022). Causality of geopolitical risk on food prices: Considering the Russo–Ukrainian conflict. *Finance Research Letters*, *49*, 103103. DOI: 10.1016/j.frl.2022.103103

Sahm, A. (2010, March). Belarus at the Crossroads? Prospects for Co-operation with the EU, Council of Europe, and OSCE. In OSCE Yearbook 2009 (pp. 123-137). Nomos Verlagsgesellschaft mbH & Co. KG.

Saikia, G., & Senapoti, I. (2019). Autonomy movements in North East India: A study of Koch Rajbongshi autonomy movement (Kamatapur movement) in Assam. *IOSR Journal of Humanities and Social Science (IOSR-JHSS), 24*(3), 10–14. https://www.iosrjournals.org/iosr-jhss/papers/Vol.%2024%20Issue3/Series-8/C2403081014.pdf

Salisu, A. A., Ogbonna, A. E., Lasisi, L., & Olaniran, A. (2022). Geopolitical Risk and Stock Market Volatility in Emerging Markets: A GARCH-MIDAS Approach. *The North American Journal of Economics and Finance, 59*, 101755. DOI: 10.1016/j.najef.2022.101755

Sánchez, T. M. (2024). Old and New Polarization: Democracy, Elections and Conflict in Mexico. *Foro Internacional, 64*(2), 183–187. DOI: 10.24201/fi.v64i2.3099

Sanderson, M. R. (2014). Free trade, food-processing, and migration: An analysis of Mexican immigration in the U.S. Great Plains Region. *The Social Science Journal, 51*(3), 474–482. DOI: 10.1016/j.soscij.2013.11.001

Saner, R., Yiu, L., & Sondergaard, M. (2000). Business diplomacy management: A core competency for global companies. *The Academy of Management Perspectives, 14*(1), 80–92.

Şanlısoy, S. & Kök, R. (2010). Politik istikrarsızlık-ekonomik büyüme ilişkisi: Türkiye örneği (1987–2006). Dokuz Eylül Üniversitesi İktisadi İdari Bilimler Fakültesi Dergisi, 25(1).

Santillán, L. I., Ceja, P. J. J., & Pineda, D. D. (2024). Practical Strategies for The Economic Development of Mexico: Nearshoring Trend. *Mercados y Negocios, 52*(25), 105–126. DOI: 10.32870/myn.vi52.7727

Sarjono, H., Khairunnisa, A. S., Sandy, C. A. N., Leono, M., Melisa, & Soeratin, B. S. (2024). The effect of the Israeli and Palestinian war boycott on Starbucks finances. *Jurnal Ekonomi dan Statistik Indonesia, 4*(1), 13–22. https://doi.org/DOI: 10.11594/jesi.04.01.02

Saxenian, A. L. (2006). *The New Argonauts: Regional Advantage in a Global Economy*. Harvard University Press.

Schelling, T. C. (1966). *Arms and influence*. Yale University Press.

Scherer, A. G., & Palazzo, G. (2007). Toward a political conception of corporate responsibility: Business and society seen from a Habermasian perspective. *Academy of Management Review*, *32*(4), 1096–1120.

Scherer, A. G., & Palazzo, G. (2011). The new political role of business in a globalized world: A review of a new perspective on CSR and its implications for the firm, governance, and democracy. *Journal of Management Studies*, *48*(4), 899–931.

Schultz, K. (2012). Domestic politics and international relations. In Carlsnaes, W., Risse, T., & Simmons, B. A. (Eds.), *Handbook of International Relations* (pp. 478–502). SAGE.

Scott, W. R. (2001). Institutions and Organizations. *Sage (Atlanta, Ga.)*.

Seawright, J., & Gerring, J. (2008). Case Selection Techniques in Case Study Research: A Menu of Qualitative and Quantitative Options. *Political Research Quarterly*, *61*(2), 294–308. DOI: 10.1177/1065912907313077

Secretaría de Economía. (2024a). *Comisión Nacional de Inversiones Extranjeras: Cuarto Trimestre 2024* (No. 2024 enero-diciembre; p. 22). Gobierno de México. https://www.gob.mx/se/acciones-y-programas/competitividad-y-normatividad-inversion-extranjera-directa?state=published

Secretaría de Economía. (2024b). *Inversión Extranjera Directa. Gobierno de México*. https://www.gob.mx/se/acciones-y-programas/competitividad-y-normatividad-inversion-extranjera-directa?state=published

Seker, O. (2023). The contagious effect of economic policy uncertainty in the post-crisis period. *Economía*, *24*(2), 205–218. DOI: 10.1108/ECON-06-2022-0046

Sen, S., Gürhan-Canli, Z., & Morwitz, V. (2001). Withholding consumption: A social dilemma perspective on consumer boycotts. *The Journal of Consumer Research*, *28*(3), 399–417. DOI: 10.1086/323729

Shah, A. A., Paul, M., Bhanja, N., & Dar, A. B. (2021). Dynamics of connectedness across crude oil, precious metals and exchange rate: Evidence from time and frequency domains. *Resources Policy*, *73*, 102154. DOI: 10.1016/j.resourpol.2021.102154

Shahbaz, M., Sharif, A., Soliman, A. M., Jiao, Z., & Hammoudeh, S. (2024). Oil prices and geopolitical risk: Fresh insights based on Granger-causality in quantiles analysis. *International Journal of Finance & Economics*, *29*(3), 2865–2881. DOI: 10.1002/ijfe.2806

Shalal, A., & Roulette, J. (2025). US could cut Ukraine's access to Starlink internet services over minerals, say sources. *Reuters*. https://www.reuters.com/business/us-could-cut-ukraines-access-starlink-internet-services-over-minerals-say-2025-02-22/

Sharma, S., Shimp, T. A., & Shin, J. (1994). Consumer ethnocentrism: A test of antecedents and moderators. *Journal of the Academy of Marketing Science*, *23*(1), 26–37. DOI: 10.1177/0092070395231004

Shattuck, T. J. (2021). Stuck in the Middle: Taiwan's Semiconductor Industry, the US-China Tech Fight, and Cross-Strait Stability. *Orbis*, *65*(1), 101–117.

Shen, M., & Yang, M. (2024). Are Geopolitical Risks Fuelling Trade Protectionism? *Defence and Peace Economics*, *35*(8), 1120–1140. DOI: 10.1080/10242694.2024.2364320

Shugan, S. M. (2007). Editorial-Causality, Unintended Consequences and Deducing Shared Causes. *Marketing Science*, *26*(6), 731–741. DOI: 10.1287/mksc.1070.0338

Shullman, D. (2019). Protect the Party: China's growing influence in the developing world. January 22, 2019. https://www.brookings.edu/articles/protect-the-party-chinas-growing-influence-in-the-developing-world/. Access September 12, 2021.

Simelyte, A., & Antanaviciene, J. (2014). Formation of Foreign Direct Investment Policy: Case of Estonia. *The Engineering Economist*, *25*(2), 177–185. DOI: 10.5755/j01.ee.25.2.4263

Simma, B., Khan, D. E., Nolte, G., & Paulus, A. (2024). *The Charter of the United Nations: a commentary*. Oxford University Press.

Simon, J. (1984). A Theoretical Perspective on Political Risk. *Journal of International Business Studies*, *15*(3), 123–143.

Simpson, A., & Dervin, F. (2019). The Council of Europe Reference Framework of competences for democratic culture: Ideological refractions, othering and obedient politics. *Intercultural Communication Education*, *2*(3), 102–119.

Singh, K. S. (2010). *People of India: An Introduction*. Anthropological Survey of India. https://archive.org/details/people-of-india-intro

Singh, M. P. (2025). *Siliguri Corridor: India's strategic lifeline and a growing concern*. The Times of India. https://timesofindia.indiatimes.com/blogs/voices/siliguri-corridor-indias-strategic-lifeline-and-a-growing-concern

Singha, S. (2018). *Koch or Koch Rajbongshi: Tribal by birth*. The Native Tribe. https://www.thenativetribe.org/blog/koch-or-koch-rajbongshi-tribal-by-birth

Singha, R., & Singha, S. (2025). The Case for Granting Scheduled Tribe Status to the Koch Rajbongshi Community. *SSRN*. https://ssrn.com/abstract=5236639

Singh, V., Correa da Cunha, H., & Mangal, S. (2024). Do Geopolitical Risks Impact Trade Patterns in Latin America? *Defence and Peace Economics*, *35*(8), 1102–1119. DOI: 10.1080/10242694.2023.2299072

Sinha, A., & Ghosh, T. (2021). Impact of Economic Policy Uncertainty on FDI Inflows: Evidence from India. In *Recent Developments in Asian Economics International Symposia in Economic Theory and Econometrics* (Vol. 28, pp. 157–167). Emerald Publishing Limited., DOI: 10.1108/S1571-038620210000028009

Sivaprasad, S., Adami, R., Malki, I., Ibragimova, D., & Yodgorova, F. (2025). Spillover effects of geopolitical risk on the banking sectors of post-Soviet countries. *Review of Behavioral Finance*, *17*(3), 544–562. DOI: 10.1108/RBF-01-2025-0026

Sohag, K., Islam, M. M., Žiković, I. T., & Mansour, H. (2023). Food inflation and geopolitical risks: Analyzing European regions amid the Russia-Ukraine war. *British Food Journal*, *125*(7), 2368–2391. DOI: 10.1108/BFJ-09-2022-0793

Solon, O. (2017). US government bans agencies from using Kaspersky software over spying fears. *The Guardian.* September 13, 2017. https://www.theguardian.com/technology/2017/sep/13/us-government-bans-kaspersky-lab-russian-spying. Accessed September 13, 2021.

Sommerville, M., Essex, J., & Le Billon, P. (2014). The 'global food crisis' and the geopolitics of food security. *Geopolitics*, *19*(2), 239–265. DOI: 10.1080/14650045.2013.811641

Song, E. (2020). South Korean Consumers' Attitudes toward Small Business Owners Participating in the 2019 Anti-Japan Boycott. *Social Sciences*, *9*(5), 74. DOI: 10.3390/socsci9050074

Soriano, V. F. (2019). Facing the Greek junta: the European Community, the Council of Europe and the rise of human-rights politics in Europe. In *Multiple Connections in European Cooperation* (pp. 22–40). Routledge.

Sosa, C. M. M., Ortiz, E., & Cabello-Rosales, A. (2023). Economic Policy Uncertainty Impact on Mexican Economic Activity and Stock and Currency Markets: A DCC Approach. *Lecturas de Economía*, *98*, 39–65. DOI: 10.17533/udea.le.n98a349886

Soussane, J. A., Fakhouri, M. Y., & Mansouri, Z. (2023). The effect of geopolitical risks on TNC location decision from antagonizing countries in the Russian Federation in light of the Ukrainian crisis. *Transnational Corporations Review*, *15*(4), 90–99. DOI: 10.1016/j.tncr.2023.01.002

Soyaltin-Colella, D. (2021). (Un) Democratic change and use of social sanctions for domestic politics: Council of Europe monitoring in Turkey. *International Political Science Review*, *42*(4), 484–500.

SPSS Statistics (Versión 29.0.0.0). (2022). [Software]. IBM.

Srisangnam, P., & Devendrakumar, A. (2018). Unlocking the Northeast Region of India: An ASEAN Connectivity Perspective. In Sarma, A., & Choudhury, S. (Eds.), *Mainstreaming the Northeast in India's Look and Act East Policy.*, DOI: 10.1007/978-981-10-5320-7_5

Stivachtis, Y. A., & Habegger, M. (2017). The Council of Europe: the institutional limits of contemporary European International Society? In Europe After Enlargement (pp. 59-77). Routledge.

Strange, S. (2015). States and markets. *States and Markets*, 1-304.

Suárez-de Vivero, J. L., & Mateos, J. C. R. (2017). Forecasting geopolitical risks: Oceans as source of instability. *Marine Policy*, *75*, 19–28. DOI: 10.1016/j.marpol.2016.10.009

Su, C.-W., Khan, K., Umar, M., & Zhang, W. (2021). Does renewable energy redefine geopolitical risks? *Energy Policy*, *158*, 112566. DOI: 10.1016/j.enpol.2021.112566

Su, C.-W., Umar, M., & Chang, H.-L. (2022). Nonlinear Dependence between Economic Policy Uncertainty and FDI Inflows in China. *Economic Computation and Economic Cybernetics Studies and Research*, *56*(3), 153–168. DOI: 10.24818/18423264/56.3.22.10

Sun, T.-T., & Su, C. W. (2024). How is geopolitical risk associated with food prices? *International Journal of Emerging Markets, ahead-of-print*(ahead-of-print). DOI: 10.1108/IJOEM-01-2023-0004

Sun, P., Doh, J. P., Rajwani, T., & Siegel, D. (2021). Navigating cross-border institutional complexity: A review and assessment of multinational nonmarket strategy research. *Journal of International Business Studies*, *52*(9), 1818–1853. DOI: 10.1057/s41267-021-00438-x PMID: 34176993

Suraji, R., Haque, M., Yasir, M., & Istianingsih, I. (2023). Dynamics of consumer boycotts: Exploring the interplay of expressive and instrumental factors. *Dinasti International Journal of Digital Business Management*, *1*(2), 50–57. DOI: 10.38035/dit.v1i2.309

Sweidan, O. D. (2021). The geopolitical risk effect on the US renewable energy deployment. *Journal of Cleaner Production, 293*, 126189. DOI: 10.1016/j.jclepro.2021.126189

Sweidan, O. D. (2023). The effect of the US macroeconomic indicators on the international geopolitical risk. *Defence and Peace Economics*, *34*(4), 495–511. DOI: 10.1080/10242694.2022.2034103

Swimberghe, K., Flurry, L. A., & Parker, J. M. (2011). Consumer Religiosity: Consequences for Consumer Activism in the United States. *Journal of Business Ethics*, *103*, 453–467. DOI: 10.1007/s10551-011-0873-2

Tabash, M. I., Farooq, U., & Issa, S. S. (2024). BRIC in flux: Understanding the influence of energy policy uncertainty on foreign direct investment flows. *OPEC Energy Review*, *48*(4), 246–260. DOI: 10.1111/opec.12311

Taiwan Ministry of Foreign Affairs. (2025) *SCIENCE AND TECHNOLOGY.* Government Portal of the Republic of China (Taiwan). Retrieved February 4, 2025, from https://www.taiwan.gov.tw/content_8.php

Tajfel, H., & Turner, J. C. (1986). The social identity theory of intergroup behavior. In Worchel, S., & Austin, W. G. (Eds.), *Psychology of intergroup relations* (pp. 7–24). Nelson-Hall.

Tamilselvan, M., Halder, A., & Kannadhasan, M. (2024). Exploring the Ingredients, Mixtures, and Inclinations of Geopolitical Risk. *International Review of Economics & Finance*, *80*, 1–13. DOI: 10.1016/j.iref.2023.11.009

Tanyeri, B., Savaser, T., & Usul, N. (2022). The stock and CDS market consequences of political uncertainty: The Arab Spring. *Emerging Markets Finance & Trade*, *58*(7), 1821–1837. DOI: 10.1080/1540496X.2021.1937116

Teece, D. (2020). Fundamental issues in strategy: Time to reassess? *Strategic Management Review*, *1*, 103–144.

Thakur, R., Malik, S. C., & Nandal, N. (2023). Normality Testing under Neutrosophic Statistics. *Neutrosophic Sets and Systems*, *58*, 149–158. DOI: 10.5281/zenodo.10070527

The BBC News. (2014). Guantanamo prisoner al-Darbi admits MV Limburg attack. *BBC*. https://www.bbc.com/news/world-us-canada-26277556

The Business Times. (2023). US-China tensions are top geopolitical risk, BlackRock says. *The Business Times*. https://www.businesstimes.com.sg/international/us-china-tensions-are-top-geopolitical-risk-blackrock-says

The Economic Times. (2024). How is Starlink Ukraine's strategic tool in the face of Russian invasion [Defence]. *The Economic Times (Online)*. https://economictimes.indiatimes.com/news/defence/how-is-starlink-ukraines-strategic-tool-in-the-face-of-russian-invasion/articleshow/107710900.cms

The Strategist. (2017). The coming of China's space silk road. Link: https://www.aspistrategist.org.au/coming-chinas-space-silk-road/ accessed on 2025-Jan-17.

Times of India. (2014). *Clarify stand on ST tag to Koch Rajbongshis: HC*. The Times of India. https://timesofindia.indiatimes.com/city/guwahati/clarify-stand-on-st-tag-to-koch-rajbongshis-hc/articleshow/29293726.cms

Timmers, P. (2024). Sovereignty in the digital age. In Werthner, H., Ghezzi, C., Kramer, J., Nida-Rümelin, J., Nuseibeh, B., & Prem, E. (Eds.), *Perspectives on digital humanism* (pp. 571–580). Springer.

Timothy, N. (2015). Nick Timothy: The Government is selling our national security to China. October 20, 2015. *Conservativehome*. https://www.conservativehome.com/thecolumnists/2015/10/nick-timothy-the-government-is-selling-our-national-security-to-china.html. Accessed September 12, 2021.

Tiwari, A. K., Mishra, B. R., & Solarin, S. A. (2021). Analysing the spillovers between crude oil prices, stock prices and metal prices: The importance of frequency domain in USA. *Energy*, *220*, 119732. DOI: 10.1016/j.energy.2020.119732

Tomlin, K. M. (2019). Assessing the Efficacy of Consumer Boycotts of U.S. Target Firms: A Shareholder Wealth Analysis. *Southern Economic Journal*, *86*(2), 503–529. DOI: 10.1002/soej.12389

Tran, M. P.-B., & Vo, D. H. (2023). Market Return Spillover from the US to the Asia-Pacific Countries: The Role of Geopolitical Risk and the Information & Communication Technologies. *PLoS One*, *18*(12), e0290680. DOI: 10.1371/journal.pone.0290680

Trommer, S. M., & Chari, R. S. (2006). The council of Europe: Interest groups and ideological missions? *West European Politics*, *29*(4), 665–686.

Truong, L. D., Friday, H. S., & Pham, T. D. (2024). The Effects of Geopolitical Risk on Foreign Direct Investment in a Transition Economy: Evidence from Vietnam. *Journal of Risk and Financial Management*, *17*(3), 101. DOI: 10.3390/jrfm17030101

TSMC. (2025) *Annual Reports*. Taiwan Semiconductor Manufacturing Company Limited. Retrieved February 4, 2025, from https://investor.tsmc.com/english/annual-reports

Tsougkou, E., Sykora, M., Elayan, S., Ifie, K., & Oliveira, J. S. (2025). Peace brand activism: Global brand responses to the war in Ukraine. *Journal of Public Policy & Marketing*, *44*(1), 100–121. DOI: 10.1177/07439156241289079

Tuna, F., & Çalışkan, H. (2022). Jeopolitik risklerin makroekonomik göstergeler üzerindeki etkisi: Türkiye örneği. *Gaziantep University Journal of Social Sciences*, *21*(4), 1989–2003. DOI: 10.21547/jss.1151714

Tupy, M. L. (2005). Trade liberalization and Poverty Reduction in Sub-Saharan Africa, CATO Analysis No.557.

Turhan, R. (2018). The Effect of Dependency Theory on Discussions of 'Underdevelopment' in Turkey. In Roldán, C., Brauer, D., & Rohbeck, J. (Eds.), *Philosophy of Globalization* (pp. 269–286). De Gruyter., DOI: 10.1515/9783110492415-020

U.S. Census Bureau. (2024). *U.S. Trade in Goods by Country* [Dataset]. https://www.census.gov/foreign-trade/balance/index.html#C

U.S. Department of Commerce. (2024). Biden-Harris administration announces preliminary terms with TSMC, expanded investment from company to bring world's most advanced leading-edge technology to the U.S. U.S. Department of Commerce. https://www.commerce.gov/news/press-releases/2024/04/biden-harris-administration-announces-preliminary-terms-tsmc-expanded

U.S. Department of Defense. (2022). *National defense strategy of the United States of America.* https://media.defense.gov/2022/Oct/27/2003103845/-1/-1/1/2022-NATIONAL-DEFENSE-STRATEGY-NPR-MDR.PDF

U.S. Department of State. (2023). *Integrated Country Strategy: Ukraine.* https://www.state.gov/wp-content/uploads/2023/09/ICS_EUR_Ukraine_29AUG2023_PUBLIC.pdf

U.S. Government Accountability Office. (2020). *Defense acquisitions annual assessment: Drive to deliver capabilities faster increases importance of program knowledge and consistent oversight.* https://www.gao.gov/products/gao-20-439

Üçler, G., & Özşahin, Ş. (2020). Jeopolitik risk ve borsa endeksinin nedensellik analizi: Gelişmekte olan ülkeler üzerine bootstrap panel nedensellik testi. *Muhasebe ve Finansman Dergisi*, (87), 167–180. DOI: 10.25095/mufad.756266

UCS. (2022). UCS satellite database. https://www.ucsusa.org/resources/satellite-database

Uddin, M. A., Ali, M. H., & Masih, M. (2017). Political Stability and Growth: An Application of Dynamic GMM and Quantile Regression. *Economic Modelling, 64*, 610–625.

UN ECLAC. (2018). *Regional agreement on access to information, public participation and justice in environmental matters in Latin America and the Caribbean (Escazú Agreement)*. United Nations Economic Commission for Latin America and the Caribbean. https://www.cepal.org/en/escazuagreement

UNCCD. (2024a). Report of the Conference of the Parties on its sixteenth session, held in Riyadh from 2 to 13 December 2024. ICCD/COP(16)/23/Add.1. https://www.unccd.int

UNCCD. (2024b). Annex to the Proposal on the Institutionalization of an Integrated Cycle of Environmental Summits. ICCD/COP(16)/21. https://www.unccd.int

UNCTAD. (2024). *Container port throughput, annual*. https://unctadstat.unctad.org/datacentre/dataviewer/US.ContPortThroughput

UNDP. (2023). *Harnessing digital solutions for climate action*. United Nations Development Programme. https://www.undp.org/publications/digital-climate-solutions

UNEP. (2019). *Global environment outlook 6: Healthy planet, healthy people*. Cambridge University Press. https://www.unep.org/resources/global-environment-outlook-6

UNEP. (2023). *Emissions gap report 2023*. United Nations Environment Programme. https://www.unep.org/resources/emissions-gap-report-2023

UNFCCC. (2015). *The Paris Agreement*. United Nations Framework Convention on Climate Change. https://unfccc.int/process-and-meetings/the-paris-agreement/the-paris-agreement

UNFCCC. (2020). *Report of the Green Climate Fund to the Conference of the Parties and guidance to the Green Climate Fund (FCCC/CP/2020/5)*. https://unfccc.int/sites/default/files/resource/cp2020_05E.pdf

UNFCCC. (2023). *Global stocktake synthesis report*. United Nations Framework Convention on Climate Change. https://unfccc.int/topics/global-stocktake

United Nations. (2021). Our Common Agenda – Report of the Secretary-General. United Nations. https://www.un.org/en/common-agenda

United Nations. (2022). *Treaty on Principles Governing the Activities of States in the Exploration and Use of Outer Space, including the Moon and Other Celestial*

Vargas, M. J. (2024). Paquete económico* 2024 del gobierno de López Obrador en el marco de la incertidumbre económica mundial. *Economía Informa, 446*, 4-25. http://www.libros.unam.mx/economia-informa-446-mayo-junio-2024-6560000002184-libro.html

Veninga, W., & Ihle, R. (2018). Import vulnerability in the Middle East: Effects of the Arab Spring on Egyptian wheat trade. *Food Security*, *10*, 183–194. DOI: 10.1007/s12571-017-0755-2

Villarreal, M. A. (2020). U.S.-Mexico Economic Relations: Trends, Issues, and Implications. *Congressional Research Service,* CRS Report RL32934, 1-28. https://sgp.fas.org/crs/row/RL32934.pdf

VS&B Containers Group. (2024). The impact of geopolitical tensions and conflicts on container shipping and shipping rates. *VS&B.* https://www.vsnb.com/impact-geopolitical-tensions-and-conflicts-container-shipping-and-shipping-rates

Wæver, O. (1995). Securitization and Desecuritization. In Lipschitz, R. D. (Ed.), *On Security*. Columbia University Press.

Wallerstein, I. (1974). Dependence in an interdependent world: The limited possibilities of transformation within the capitalist world economy. *African Studies Review*, *17*(1), 1–26.

Waltz, K. N. (1979). *Theory of international politics, communication*. Addison-Wesley.

Waltz, K. N. (1979). *Theory of International Politics*. McGraw Hill.

Wang, C., Yao, X., & Kim, C. Y. (2025). Is a friend in need a friend indeed? Geopolitical risk, international trade of China, and Belt & Road Initiative. *Applied Economics Letters*, *32*(7), 1021–1028. DOI: 10.1080/13504851.2023.2299275

Wang, D., & Luo, X. R. (2019). Retire in peace: Officials' political incentives and corporate diversification in China. *Administrative Science Quarterly*, *77*(3), 773–809.

Wang, G., Gu, X., Shen, X., Uktamov, K. F., & Ageli, M. M. (2023). A dual risk perspective of China's resources market: Geopolitical risk and political risk. *Resources Policy*, *82*, 103528. DOI: 10.1016/j.resourpol.2023.103528

Wang, L., Ma, F., Niu, T., & Liang, C. (2021). The importance of extreme shock: Examining the effect of investor sentiment on the crude oil futures market. *Energy Economics*, *99*, 105319. DOI: 10.1016/j.eneco.2021.105319

Wang, M., Amiri-Aref, M., Klibi, W., & Babai, M. Z. (2024). Global multi-sourcing network design with inventory planning under uncertainty. *International Journal of Production Research, 62*(21), 7660–7686. DOI: 10.1080/00207543.2024.2323068

Wang, X., Wu, Y., & Xu, W. (2023). Geopolitical risk and investment. *Journal of Money, Credit and Banking*. Advance online publication. DOI: 10.1111/jmcb.13110

Wang, Y. (2012). The interaction between foreign direct Investment and Trade in China's agro-food sector. *2012 International Conference on Information Management, Innovation Management and Industrial Engineering*, Sanya, 179-183. DOI: 10.1109/ICIII.2012.6339627

Warrell, H. (2020). Kaspersky diversifies from cyber security after spying allegations. *Financial Times*. December 5, 2020. https://www.ft.com/content/d8f27227-bdc4-4b8d-a361-345d3de0738a. Accessed September 12, 2021.

Weeden, B. (2020). The United States is losing its leadership role in the fight against orbital debris. *The Space Review*. Retrieved from https://www.thespacereview.com/article/3889/1

WEF. (2024). *The global risks report 2024*. World Economic Forum. https://www.weforum.org/reports/global-risks-report-2024

Wendt, A. (1992). Anarchy is what states make of it: The social construction of power politics. *International Organization, 46*(2), 391–425.

Westermann-Behaylo, M. K., Rehbein, K., & Fort, T. (2015). Enhancing the Concept of Corporate Diplomacy: Encompassing Political Corporate Social Responsibility, International Relations, and Peace Through Commerce. *The Academy of Management Perspectives, 29*(4), 387–404. DOI: 10.5465/amp.2013.0133

Wilkinson, R., & Weiss, T. G. (Eds.). (2013). *International organization and global governance*. Routledge., DOI: 10.4324/9780203795972

Willems, W. J. (2007). The work of making Malta: The Council of Europe's archaeology and planning committee 1988–1996. *European Journal of Archaeology, 10*(1), 57–71.

Williams, M. C. (2003). Words, images, enemies: Securitization and international politics. *International Studies Quarterly, 47*(4), 511–531.

Winter, J. C. F., Gosling, S. D., & Potter, J. (2016). Comparing the Pearson and Spearman correlation coefficients across distributions and sample sizes: A tutorial using simulations and empirical data. *Psychological Methods, 21*(3), 273–290. DOI: 10.1037/met0000079

Witt, M. A. (2019). China's challenge: Geopolitics, de-globalization, and the future of Chinese business. *Management and Organization Review, 15*(4), 687–704.

Witt, M. A., Lewin, A. Y., Li, P. P., & Gaur, A. (2023). Decoupling in international business: Evidence, drivers, impact, and implications for IB research. *Journal of World Business, 58*(1), 101399.

Witt, M. A., Li, P. P., Välikangas, L., & Lewin, A. Y. (2021). De-globalization and decoupling: Game changing consequences? *Management and Organization Review, 17*(1), 6–15.

Wong, C. Y., Yeung, H. W. C., Huang, S., Song, J., & Lee, K. (2024). Geopolitics and the changing landscape of global value chains and competition in the global semiconductor industry: Rivalry and catch-up in chip manufacturing in East Asia. *Technological Forecasting and Social Change, 209*, 123749.

Woo, S., & McMillan, R. (2018). Kaspersky to relocate some operations out of RUssia amid tampering suspicions. *The Wall Street Journal.* May 15, 2018. https://www.wsj.com/articles/kaspersky-to-relocate-some-operations-out-of-russia-amid-tampering-suspicions-1526367600. Accessed Septemner 12, 2021.

Woo-Mora, L. G. (2025). Populism's original sin: Short-term populist penalties and uncertainty traps. *European Economic Review, 172*, 104917. DOI: 10.1016/j.euroecorev.2024.104917

Wooten, M., & Hoffman, A. J. (2008). Organizational Fields: Past, Present and Future. In *The Sage Handbook of Organizational institutionalism* (pp. 55–74).

World Bank Group. (2025, junio 9). *Worldwide Governance Indicators.* Interactive Data Access. https://www.worldbank.org/content/publication/worldwide-governance-indicators/en/interactive-data-access.html

World Bank. (2022). *The Impact of the War in Ukraine on Global Trade and Investment.*

World Bank. (2024). (Forthcoming). Sustainable development outlook 2024: Charting resilient pathways. *World Bank Group.*

World Bank. (2024). *Container port traffic (TEU: 20-foot equivalent units).* https://data.worldbank.org/indicator/IS.SHP.GOOD.TU

WTO. (2023). *Global Value Chain Development Report 2023: Resilient and Sustainable Global Value Chains in Turbulent Times.* World Trade Organization., DOI: 10.30875/9789287075673

Wu, J.-m. (2024a). *Silicon Shield 2.0: A Taiwan perspective*. The Diplomat. https://thediplomat.com/2024/09/silicon-shield-2-0-a-taiwan-perspective/

Wu, R. (2024b). TSMC's role in the chip ecosystem. *Taipei Times*. Retrieved from https://www.taipeitimes.com/News/editorials/archives/2024/11/19/2003827117

Xhauflair, V., Huybrechts, B., & Pichault, F. (2018). How Can New Players Establish Themselves in Highly Institutionalized Labour Markets? A Belgian Case Study in the Area of Project-Based Work. *British Journal of Industrial Relations*, *56*(2), 370–394.

Xiao, C., Ye, J., Esteves, R. M., & Rong, C. (2016). Using Spearman's correlation coefficients for exploratory data analysis on big dataset. *Concurrency and Computation*, *28*(14), 3866–3878. DOI: 10.1002/cpe.3745

Xiong, W., Wu, D. D., & Yeung, J. H. Y. (2024). Semiconductor supply chain resilience and disruption: Insights, mitigation, and future directions. *International Journal of Production Research*, •••, 1–24. DOI: 10.1080/00207543.2024.2387074

Yang, C., Niu, Z., & Gao, W. (2022). The time-varying effects of trade policy uncertainty and geopolitical risks shocks on the commodity market prices: Evidence from the TVP-VAR-SV approach. *Resources Policy*, *76*, 102600. DOI: 10.1016/j.resourpol.2022.102600

Yang, J., & Yang, C. (2021). The impact of mixed-frequency geopolitical risk on stock market returns. *Economic Analysis and Policy*, *72*, 226–240. DOI: 10.1016/j.eap.2021.08.008

Yang, M., Zhang, Q., Yi, A., & Peng, P. (2021). Geopolitical Risk and Stock Market Volatility in Emerging Economies: Evidence from GARCH-MIDAS Model. *Journal of Applied Econometrics*, *24*(3), 357–370. DOI: 10.1155/2021/1159358

Yay, M. (2022). Relationship between right atrial pressure and the Model For End-Stage Liver Disease (MELD) score in patients with advanced heart failure: Correlation analysis and ROC curve method. *Turkish Journal of Thoracic and Cardiovascular Surgery*, *30*(1), 8–10. DOI: 10.5606/tgkdc.dergisi.2022.40073

Yeo, M. (2019). ADF to acquire next generation satellite technology. Asia-Pacific Defence Reporter, 45(6), 12. Retrieved from https://asiapacificdefencereporter.com/jp-9102-adf-to-acquire-next-generation-satellite-technology/

Yiğit, S. (2022). Swiss-EU Relations: The Cold War Years, El Ruha 10th International Conference "Social Sciences & Humanities", Eds: Mercimek & Tan, Iksad Publications November 27-28, 2022, ISBN: 978-625-6380-76-9, pp.476-499.

Yiğit, S. (2022a). Switzerland and the European Union: No Union, Only Close Relations, I. International Anglo-American Cultural and Literary Studies Symposium Proceedings Book, Eds: Tanritanir & Aykac, Iksad Publications, 15.12.2022, ISBN: 978-625-6380-74-5, pp.215-232.

Yiğit, S. (2023). 2022: Unipolar Delusion, Bipolar Illusion and Multipolar Aspiration. Diplomacy and Security, Volume VI, Number 1/2023. Page: 79-99.

Yiğit, S. (2023). Power, Polarity and the Present. The Zambakari Advisory Special Issue: Spring 2023 The Great Power Competition in Eurasia, 146-159.

Yigit, S. (2024). Miscalculated Cause-and-Effect: The Russian Invasion of Ukraine and Finland's Accession to NATO. In Analyzing Global Responses to Contemporary Regional Conflicts (pp. 39-51). IGI Global.

Yigit, S. (2024a). The Vulnerability of Small States in Europe, International Scientific Conference "European Studies: Past-Present-Future" 13 December 2024, Proceedings of the conference #5, ISSN 2960-9976, p.206-215.

Yigit, S. (1996). From here to eternity—Turkey, the European Union and the Customs Union. *Cambridge Review of International Affairs*, *10*(1), 51–60.

Yigit, S. (2022b). Russia's Invasion of Ukraine: The First Seven Months. in Aydın, M., Şiriner, İ., & Koç, Ş. A. *Global Agenda in Social Sciences: Global Studies*, *9*, 417.

Yilanci, V., Hopoğlu, S., & Eryüzlü, H. (2023). The impact of the economic policy uncertainty and geopolitical risks on tourism demand of Mexico. *Theoretical & Applied Economics, 30*(3), 147-164. https://www.ectap.ro/the-impact-of-the-economic-policy-uncertaintyand-geopolitical-risks-on-tourism-demand-of-mexico-veli-yilanci_serta-hopolu_hakan-eryuzlu/a1682/

Yildirim, Z. (2016). Global financial conditions and asset markets: Evidence from fragile emerging economies. *Economic Modelling*, *57*, 208–220. DOI: 10.1016/j.econmod.2016.04.018

Yin, R. K. (2009). *Case study research: Design and methods* (Vol. 5). sage.

Yin, S., Xing, L., Zhang, P., & Duan, Y. (2023). Stability analysis of production networks in the ASIA-pacific region based on nested structure theory. *Xitong Gongcheng Lilun Yu Shijian*, *43*(11), 3214–3229. DOI: 10.12011/SETP2022-2758

Yüksel, Ü., Thai, N. T., & Lee, M. S. W. (2019). Boycott them! No, boycott this! Do choice overload and small-agent rationalization inhibit the signing of anti-consumption petitions? *Psychology and Marketing*, *36*(9), 1–15. DOI: 10.1002/mar.21293

Yu, M., & Wang, N. (2023). The Influence of Geopolitical Risk on International Direct Investment and Its Countermeasures. *Sustainability*, *15*(3), 2522. DOI: 10.3390/su15032522

Zhang, J. Z. (2025). TSMC's market share reaches 64% in Q3 2024; 3nm process gains prominence. *United Daily News*. https://money.udn.com/money/story/5612/8486483

Zhang, S., Shinwari, R., Zhao, S., & Dagestani, A. A. (2023). Energy transition, geopolitical risk, and natural resources extraction: A novel perspective of energy transition and resources extraction. *Resources Policy*, *83*, 103608. DOI: 10.1016/j.resourpol.2023.103608

Zhang, Y., & Hamori, S. (2022). A Connectedness Analysis among BRICS's Geopolitical Risks and the US Macroeconomy. *Economic Analysis and Policy*, *74*, 115–130. DOI: 10.1016/j.eap.2022.08.004

Zhang, Z., He, M., Zhang, Y., & Wang, Y. (2022). Geopolitical risk trends and crude oil price predictability. *Energy*, *258*, 124824. DOI: 10.1016/j.energy.2022.124824

Zhao, S. (2022). The US–China rivalry in the emerging bipolar world: Hostility, alignment, and power balance. *Journal of Contemporary China*, *31*(134), 169–185. DOI: 10.1080/10670564.2021.1945733

Zhao, Y., Chen, L., & Zhang, Y. (2024). Spillover Effects of Geopolitical Risks on Global Energy Markets: Evidence from CoVaR and CAViaR-EGARCH Model. *Energy*, *289*, 119743. DOI: 10.1177/01445987231196617

Zhao, Z., Gozgor, G., Lau, M. C. K., Mahalik, M. K., Patel, G., & Khalfaoui, R. (2023). The impact of geopolitical risks on renewable energy demand in OECD countries. *Energy Economics*, *122*, 106700. DOI: 10.1016/j.eneco.2023.106700

Zheng, Y. (2020). Non-organized boycott: Alliance advantage and free riding incentives in uneven wars of attrition. *Eurasian Econ Rev*, *10*, 123–141. DOI: 10.1007/s40822-019-00138-w

Zhou, H., & Liang, C. (2025). Geopolitical risk and gold price bubbles. *Review of Accounting and Finance*, *24*(3), 353–374. DOI: 10.1108/RAF-09-2024-0369

Zietsma, C., Groenewegen, P., Logue, D. M., & Hinings, C. R. (2017). Field or fields? Building the scaffolding for cumulation of research on institutional fields. *The Academy of Management Annals*, *11*(1), 391–450.

Zimmerman, E. J. (2019). The Foreign Investment Risk Review Modernization Act: How CFIUS Became a Tech Office. *Berkeley Technology Law Journal*, *34*, 1267–1303.

About the Contributors

Bryan Christiansen is an Adjunct Business Professor at Southern New Hampshire University and the Chief Executive Officer of the management consultancy, Soluvex, LLC in New Mexico, USA. He is currently Editor-in-Chief of the IGI Global Book Series, "Advances in Digital Crime, Forensics, and Cyber Terrorism" as well as "Advances in Psychology, Mental Health, and Behavioral Studies". Christiansen is fluent in Chinese, Japanese, and Spanish, and is currently learning Russian. He has presented at several universities in other countries including Oxford University in the United Kingdom. He earned an MBA from Capella University and a BS in Marketing from the University of the State of New York. Christiansen's extensive travels around the world since 1973 have enabled him to produce 50 Reference books on a variety of subjects ranging from cultural studies to organizational sociology. Over 70 percent of these publications have become Scopus- and/or Web of Science-indexed.

John Branch currently teaches a variety of marketing and international business courses at the undergraduate, MBA, and executive levels at the Stephen M Ross School of Business at the University of Michigan (USA), and serves as Co-Director of the Yaffe Digital Media Initiative. Previously, he was the Academic Director of the School's weekend and evening MBA programs as well as the Director of Educational Outreach at the University's William Davidson Institute. John also holds an appointment at the University's Center for Russian, East European, & Eurasian Studies, and maintains a Research Fellowship at the William Davidson Institute. John holds a Bachelor of Engineering Science in electronics from the University of Western Ontario (Canada), a Master of Business Administration from the University of New Brunswick (Canada), a Master of Arts in education from Washington University in Saint Louis (USA), a Doctor of Philosophy in marketing from the University of Cambridge (England), a Doctor of Education from the University of

Michigan (USA), and a Doctor of Professional Studies from Middlesex University (England).

***

Abdullah Açık received his Bachelor's degree in Maritime Business Administration from Dokuz Eylül University, Maritime Faculty in 2013. He continued his postgraduate studies in the same department, earning his Master's degree in 2016 and completing his Ph.D. in Maritime Business Administration in 2020. In 2021, he was awarded the title of Associate Professor in the field of International Trade. His primary research interests include the freight market, dry bulk and tanker shipping, maritime economics, and the application of econometric methods in maritime transport studies.

Jingning Ao, Ph.D., is an assistant professor of business administration at Morgan State University in Baltimore, Maryland. She holds two doctoral degrees: her second Ph.D., from the University of Pittsburgh, where her research focused on SpaceX's self-celebrating strategies on YouTube; and her first Ph.D. from Middle Tennessee State University, where she examined the leisure behaviors of astronauts aboard the International Space Station. Her research lies at the intersection of language, innovation and strategy, with a particular emphasis on entrepreneurial activities within the commercial space sector. Recently, she successfully led an undergraduate research team to NASA's Johnson Space Center, where they earned a finalist position in the NASA MUREP Innovation and Tech Transfer Idea Competition in Fall 2024.

Valeria Caro holds a double major in Business Administration and Marketing & Digital Business from Universidad del Rosario (Colombia), with a minor in Financial Investment Management. Her research examines the interplay between geopolitical risk, financial markets, and international trade, particularly in emerging economies. She has held leadership roles such as President of the School of Business Council and represented her institution in global forums including the Harvard National Model United Nations. A Gorom Association scholar, she has contributed to cross-cultural projects promoting sustainable entrepreneurship and international collaboration. Valeria has worked across public and private sectors in Colombia, the U.S., and Japan, and currently combines her academic research with professional experience in the consumer goods sector at a leading multinational company.

Gianni De Bruyn is an assistant professor of strategic management at San Diego State University's Fowler College of Business. He obtained his Ph.D. in

Business Administration (Strategy and International Business) from the University of South Carolina's Darla Moore School of Business and a Master's in Finance from Peking University's HSBC Business School. His research lies at the intersection of geopolitical tensions and firms' global strategy, with a second research stream examining the role of geography and industry agglomeration in shaping corporate strategy. He has published in Research Policy and presented his work at leading conferences, including the Academy of Management (AOM), the Strategic Management Society (SMS), and the Academy of International Business (AIB). He is a recipient of the Will Mitchell SRF Dissertation Scholar Award and the Best Ph.D. Paper Award at SMS. Prior to embarking on his academic journey, he had professional experience in investor relations and financial engineering.

Juan C. Espinosa is a highly experienced professor who has worked in both undergraduate and graduate settings, with a background in research, teaching, and consulting in the field of organisational behaviour, focusing specifically on leadership, personality, workplace environment, psychosocial hazards, work-related quality of life, employee recruitment, and performance assessment. He has strengths in research methodology, applied statistics within the social sciences - this includes management and psychology - and is an expert in the design, construction, and validation of psychological tests.

Keyan Lai is a Lecturer in International Human Resource Management at the University of Edinburgh. His research focuses on the impact of geopolitics on international business. His research has appeared in leading academic journals, such as Organization Studies, Journal of International Business Policy, and Strategic Organization.

Suphan Nasir received her BS degree in Sociology from Bogaziçi University and her PhDdegree in Marketing from Istanbul University, Turkey. She is currently Professor at Istanbul University and she has been the Chair of Marketing since 2009. She was the chief editor of the International Journal of E-Entrepreneurship and Innovation between 2010 and 2014, and also she was the editor of the International Journal of Higher Education between 2010-2023. Her articles have been published in reputable books and international academic journals. Customer relationship management as well as consumer behavior, sustainability, voter behavior, and higher education issues are the scope of her interest area. She attended some major international conferences as keynote speaker. Dr. Nasir received several scientific publications and best presenter awards. She worked as a mentor, evaluator and team leader at institutional external evaluation and institutional accreditation programs for the Higher Education Quality Board between 2016 and 2021; and also served as a member of the Advisory Board for TÜBİTAK Scientist Support Program between 2019-2022.

Marc Oberhauser is an Associate Professor in the Department of Management at ESCP Business School, Madrid. He is also affiliated as a postdoctoral researcher with the Department of International Management at Friedrich-Alexander University Erlangen-Nürnberg, Germany. Marc is an active member of the Academy of International Business (AIB) and currently serves as Vice President of the AIB Sustainability Shared Interest Group. Marc's research spans two core pillars. The first focuses on integrating sustainability into the international business domain, with particular emphasis on social and environmental issues in global value chains, including human rights violations. The second addresses global challenges such as geopolitical tensions, violent conflicts, and sanction regimes, and their influence on multinational enterprises. He has published in outlets such as International Business Review, European Management Journal, Journal of Business Ethics, Corporate Social Responsibility and Environmental Management, and International Journal of Development Issues. At ESCP Business School, Marc teaches courses on Global Challenges, Intercultural Management, and Sustainability Management across various programmes, including the PhD programme and Executive Education. Marc holds a doctoral degree in Business Administration and Management from Friedrich-Alexander University Erlangen-Nürnberg, Germany.

Nergis Özispa is an Assistant Professor in the Department of Maritime Business Administration at Mersin University, Türkiye. Her research focuses on maritime sustainability, port management, logistics, and the application of digital technologies in maritime operations. Her work often employs quantitative methods such as AHP and ARIMA modeling to address challenges in maritime logistics and sustainability.

Ranjit Singha is a dedicated Ph.D. Scholar in the Department of Psychology at Christ (Deemed to be University), specializing in addiction research. As the developer of the Multidimensional Addiction Behaviour Scale (MABS), his research unravels the complexities of addiction to inform effective prevention, intervention, and education strategies. With over 10 years of experience as a facilitator, Editor and Reviewer, he has conducted workshops and talks that empower individuals with knowledge and tools for healthier decision-making and addiction awareness programs. Additionally, he has led Art of Writing Skills workshops, helping participants enhance their academic and professional communication. With a solid academic record, he has published 195+ scholarly works, including 81+ Scopus-indexed publications, reflecting his commitment to impactful research and dissemination of knowledge.

Surjit Singha is an academician with a broad spectrum of interests, including UN Sustainable Development Goals, Organizational Climate, Workforce Diversity, Organizational Culture, HRM, Marketing, Finance, IB, Global Business, Business, AI, K12 & Higher Education, Gender and Cultural Studies. Currently a faculty member at Kristu Jayanti University, Dr. Surjit also serves as an Editor, reviewer, and author for prominent global publications and journals, including being on the Editorial review board of Information Resources Management Journal and contributor to various publications. With over 15 years of experience in Administration, Teaching, and Research, Dr. Surjit is dedicated to imparting knowledge and guiding students in their research pursuits. As a research mentor, Dr. Surjit has nurtured young minds and fostered academic growth. Dr. Surjit has an impressive track record of over 150+ publications (SCOPUS Indexed 91+), including articles, book chapters, and textbooks, holds two US Copyrights, one patent granted, and has successfully completed and published two fully funded minor research projects from Kristu Jayanti University.

Ziqiao (Vincent) Wang is a doctoral researcher at ESCP Business School, whose research contribution centers on the strategic influence and evolving role of multinational corporations in contemporary geopolitics and global governance. His work examines how major international corporations leverage technological assets and strategic positioning to shape global power dynamics, offering distinct theoretical perspectives and actionable insights across academic, policy-making, and business domains. Vincent served as the Business Engagement Lead for the World Economic Forum, facilitating high-level dialogues among multinational corporations and governmental entities on a global and intercontinental scale. His professional experience includes strategic roles at leading global technology companies such as Apple Inc. and Latch Inc., deepening his expertise in international market strategy, technology-driven innovation, and public-private cooperation. He holds advanced postgraduate qualifications from prestigious institutions across the American, British, and French academic traditions, significantly enriching the interdisciplinary and cross-cultural foundation of his research. His research distinctly highlights broad practical relevance and theoretical significance.

Index

A

B

C

D

E

F

G

T

www.ingramcontent.com/pod-product-compliance
Lightning Source LLC
LaVergne TN
LVHW062327300926
849161LV00007B/1603